D1179517

THE OXFORD HISTORY OF
ENGLISH LITERATURE

VI

THE OXFORD HISTORY OF
ENGLISH LITERATURE

Certain volumes originally appeared under different titles (see title-page versos).
Their original volume-numbers are given below.

ENGLISH DRAMA
1586–1642
THE AGE OF SHAKESPEARE

G. K. HUNTER

CLARENDON PRESS · OXFORD

*This book has been printed digitally and produced in a standard specification
in order to ensure its continuing availability*

OXFORD
UNIVERSITY PRESS

Great Clarendon Street, Oxford OX2 6DP

Oxford University Press is a department of the University of Oxford.
It furthers the University's objective of excellence in research, scholarship,
and education by publishing worldwide in

Oxford New York

Auckland Cape Town Dar es Salaam Hong Kong Karachi
Kuala Lumpur Madrid Melbourne Mexico City Nairobi
New Delhi Shanghai Taipei Toronto
With offices in
Argentina Austria Brazil Chile Czech Republic France Greece
Guatemala Hungary Italy Japan South Korea Poland Portugal
Singapore Switzerland Thailand Turkey Ukraine Vietnam

ISBN 978-0-19-812213-5

TO

SHELAGH

LEWIS. I'm working on 'English Literature in the Sixteenth Century, Excluding Drama', for OHEL.
JOY.   Oh hell?
LEWIS. The Oxford History of English Literature.
JOY.   Sixteenth century. You got the easy one.
LEWIS. You think so?

William Nicholson, *Shadowlands* (1989) Act I, pp. 32–3

Of the difficulties that lie in the way of an editor [of Elizabethan dramatic records]—at least if he regards his work as historical rather than romantic —not the least is to avoid writing a general history of the Elizabethan stage. There is no such thing as a clearly defined historical field; facts are linked to other facts in all directions, and investigation merely leads to further and further questions. Every custom and every institution at once raises the problem of its own origin; every corporation and every social fact is influenced by other corporations or reacts on other social facts. Thus to treat intelligibly any of the several dramatic companies at the end of the [sixteenth] century, or any series of events in the dramatic history of the time demands a knowledge of the constitution of other companies and of the sequence of other events such as at present can hardly be said to exist.

W. W. Greg, Preface to *Henslowe's Diary*, Part II (1908)

Preface

THIS present volume completes the Oxford History of English Literature Series, the earliest volumes of which were published in 1945. The space of time between the first volume and the last has seen a revolution (or even a series of revolutions) in the notion of what literary history is or should be about (if it is allowed that it should exist at all), so that it may be in order (without engaging in a retrospective survey) to give some explanation how the present volume relates to a context that could not have been envisaged by the originators.

The first author designated for this volume was Professor F. P. Wilson. When Wilson died in 1963, I was asked if I would see through the press the interconnected chapters he had written (which I did) and then if I would consider carrying on the project from 1586 to 1642. The latter I declined to do. Some twenty years later the Press asked me to reconsider my decision, and this led me to wonder if the contradictions between history and literature (as I had seen it) could be understood as a challenge rather than an impasse. I believed that, sheltering under the aegis of Tolstoy rather than Ranke, I could use a plurality of historical perspectives to fit together the plays I had to consider, without glossing over their particular and diverse functions as art and entertainment.

Wishing to give proper space to these functions, I have used terms that allow for continuity in aesthetic interest between that time and this. I have allowed anachronistic words like 'theatre' and 'author' to intermingle with the more accurate 'playhouse' and 'poet'. I have used the word 'Elizabethan' to refer to the whole period from 1584 to 1642. Dates are regularized from 'Old Style' to 'New Style'. Quotations are everywhere modernized. The presence of Shakespeare in the company I have to deal with has, of course, threatened to unbalance the whole enterprise. I have therefore assumed a general knowledge of his *œuvre* and used his plays as a means of delineating what he shared with the whole movement to which he belonged rather than as philosophical or political statements to be elucidated out of the historical context.

G. K. H.

Acknowledgements

In the long history of this book I have incurred many debts. It could not have existed without continual access to the resources of the Sterling and Beineke Libraries of Yale and the Bodleian Library in Oxford. In 1978 the Guggenheim Foundation financed a year without teaching, in which I was to think about Elizabethan dramaturgy. I did so, in ways that were not immediately productive but eventually basic to the present enterprise. In 1984–5, the ideal conditions at the Center for Advanced Study in the Behavioural Sciences in Palo Alto allowed me space to consider the proposal of the Oxford University Press that I write this book. There I constructed a first version of Chapter 3 and a general outline of the whole project. I am indebted to many persons who have read portions of work-in-progress and brought light to dark places—Jonas Barish, David Bevington, Mary Bly, Julia Boss Knapp, Paul Leopold, Jenny Morrison, Leo Salingar, Hilary Walford—and especially to three colleagues, Eugene Waith, Lawrence Manley, and Murray Biggs, who have over the years uncomplainingly given their attention to the recurrent avalanches of confused typescript. At a personal as well as an academic level I am indebted to the support of Mary Hunter, Andrew Hunter, and Ruth Hunter.

In this book, as in everything else, I owe most to the dedicatee, who has incessantly read, commented, argued, improved, and so allowed me to know the pains of authorship only as one of the pleasures of a shared life.

I thank the Cambridge University Press for permission to reprint some material first used in an article published in *Shakespeare Survey 42* (1990).

G. K. H.

Contents

Abbreviations

Bentley, *Dramatist*	G. E. Bentley, *The Profession of Dramatist in Shakespeare's Time* (Princeton, 1971)
Bentley, *JCS*	G. E. Bentley, *The Jacobean and Caroline Stage* (7 vols.; Oxford, 1941–68)
Bentley, *Player*	G. E. Bentley, *The Profession of Player in Shakespeare's Time* (Princeton, 1984)
Bullough	G. Bullough, Narrative and Dramatic Sources of Shakespeare (8 vols.; London, 1957–75)
Chambers	E. K. Chambers, *The Elizabethan Stage* (4 vols.; Oxford, 1923)
Grosart	*The Complete Works of Robert Greene*, ed. A. B. Grosart (15 vols.; London, 1881–6)
Harbage–Schoenbaum	*Annals of English Drama 974–1700*, ed. A. Harbage, rev. S. Schoenbaum (London, 1964); rev. S. S. Wagonheim (London, 1989)
Henslowe's Diary	*Henslowe's Diary*, ed. W. W. Greg (2 vols.; London, 1904–8)
Henslowe Papers	*Henslowe Papers*, ed. W. W. Greg (London, 1907)
Herford and Simpson	*Ben Jonson*, ed. C. H. Herford and P. and E. Simpson (11 vols.; Oxford, 1925–52)
Hillebrand	H. N. Hillebrand, *The Child Actors* (University of Illinois Studies in Language and Literature, 11; Urbana, Ill., 1926)
Holinshed	*The Third Volume of Chronicles*, compiled by Raphael Holinshed (London, 1587)
McKerrow	*The Works of Thomas Nashe*, ed. R. B. McKerrow (5 vols.; Oxford, 1904–10; rev. 1966
MLN	*Modern Language Notes*
MLR	*Modern Language Review*
MP	*Modern Philology*
MSC	Malone Society Collections
MSR	Malone Society Reprint
NLH	*New Literary History*
PQ	*Philological Quarterly*
RES	*The Review of English Studies*
RORD	*Research Opportunities in Renaissance Drama*
SEL	*Studies in English literature 1500–1900*
Sh. Q.	*Shakespeare Quarterly*
Sh. S.	*Shakespeare Survey*

Note on the Text

PUNCTUATION and lineation in the references to Shakespeare come from the Riverside edition, ed. G. Blakemore Evans (Boston, 1974), but I have held myself free to accept alternative readings where that seems necessary. Ben Jonson is quoted from the edition of Herford and Simpson (11 vols.; Oxford, 1925–52). The texts used throughout are quoted from those starred in the bibliography. The dates given to plays in the text and the chronology are taken from the 'limits' column in Alfred Harbage's *Annals of English Drama*: the revision by Samuel Schoenbaum (1964) is the basis of the dating, but this has been checked against the latest revision by S. S. Wagonheim (1989); her changes of date have been accepted only where I can perceive a good reason to do so. The earlier and later limits in such dating have been expressed by a multiplication sign standing between 'not before' and 'not after' dates. Asterisks set in the text against an author's name indicate that a biographical note is to be found in the appendix of brief lives. Asterisks are used also in the Chronology, to mark plays known to have been shown at court. Date of publication is given in the text only in cases where the date may be taken to imply something of the play's history (a gap in time can indicate a play too profitable to the company to be sold to a printer, or else a play thought not worth printing).

'Long' titles of plays (e.g. *The Troublesome Reign and Lamentable Death of Edward the Second* or *The Fountain of Self-Love or Cynthia's Revels*) have normally been reduced in the text to conventionally used short forms, except in cases where some generic point is being made. In the Index and Chronology I have included as much of the longer forms as seems practicable. The end-matter is designed so that individual plays can be accessed by date (in the Chronology), by title (in the Bibliography) or by author (in the Index).

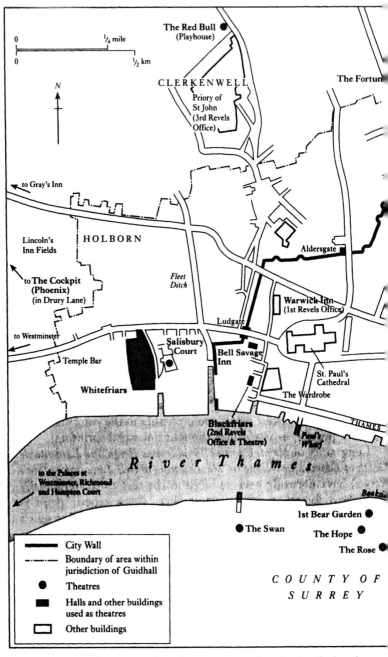

The Red Bull ●
(Playhouse)

The Fortun[e]

CLERKENWELL

Priory of
St John
(3rd Revels
Office)

N

0   1/4 mile
0   1/2 km

to Gray's Inn

Lincoln's
Inn Fields

HOLBORN

Aldersgate

to The Cockpit
(Phoenix)
(in Drury Lane)

Fleet
Ditch

Warwick Inn
(1st Revels Office)

Ludgate

to Westminster

Salisbury
Court

Temple Bar

Bell Savage
Inn

St. Paul's
Cathedral

Whitefriars

The Wardrobe

Blackfriars
(2nd Revels
Office & Theatre)

Paul's
Wharf

THAMES

River Thames

to the Palaces at
Westminster, Richmond
and Hampton Court

Banks[i]

1st Bear Garden ●

● The Swan

The Hope ●

The Rose ●

City Wall

Boundary of area within
jurisdiction of Guidhall

●   Theatres

■   Halls and other buildings
used as theatres

▢   Other buildings

COUNTY OF
SURREY

Map of the City of London and its environs *c.*1575–*c.*1630, showing the location of the main playhouses and other buildings important in the theatrical life of the time. Based on Glynne Wickham's *Early English Stages 1300–1660*, vol. 2: 1576–1660, Part I (London, 1963).

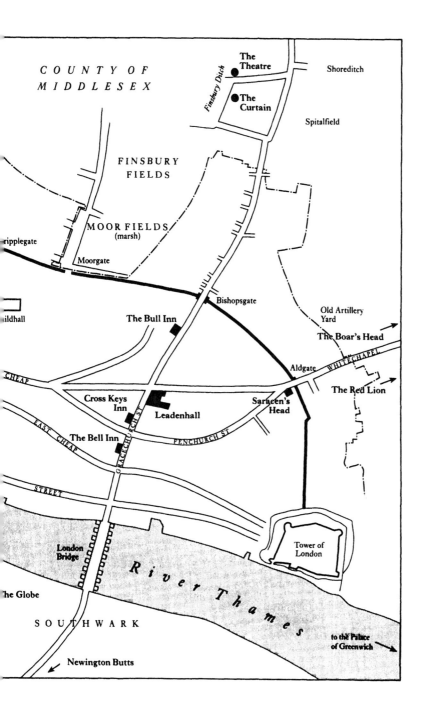

1. Introduction

THIS is a book not about Shakespeare the solitary genius but rather about the world that constituted his life as a writer—the world of the public dramatists, actors, audiences, playhouses, impresarios, who provided him with the basic definition of his *métier*. It was from these that he learnt how to encode his own daily experience and that of his audience inside available forms of expression; they presented examples of what to follow and what to avoid, defined the rivals he had to outshine if his company (and his income) were to survive. A comprehensive explanation of what was involved in living in that situation is, of course, inaccessible to us; historians like to invoke the great events of the time in terms of their now-perceived consequences, but at the actual time these could not be given any generalized or objective meaning outside the local languages that were being invented (*currente calamo*) and communicated inside the communities that the writer drew on and served. So it can be no part of a literary investigation to 'explain' the life of the past, but only to propose an unstable dialectic between our own inescapable modernity and the languages of the locally experienced and documented past—one in which Shakespeare was known in the terms of 'our fellow',[1] with his 'right happy and copious industry',[2] as a working dramatist among working dramatists, though endowed with a marvellous vein of 'honey-tongued' eloquence.[3]

The substance of this book is, therefore, concerned to trace upon an Elizabethan map the web of connections that hold Shakespeare and his fellows in the historical place their language describes and so to define the most obvious connections between them, without assuming that those which bypass Shakespeare need to be devalued. We must also notice, since 'the age of Shakespeare' (which also means 'the age of Elizabethan drama') did not die on the death-bed of its greatest poet, how the circumambient tradition ignored,

---

[1] *The Second Part of the Return from Parnassus* (1601–3), in *The Three Parnassus Plays*, ed. J. B. Leishman (London, 1949), l. 1769; the epistle dedicatory to the First Folio (1623).
[2] Webster, Epistle to *The White Devil* (1609–12).
[3] Francis Meres, *Palladis Tamia* (1598).

absorbed, and modified his achievement, and continued to flourish in happy differentiation until cut down by fiat in 1642. My general aim is, above all, to trace the history of a movement.

I assume that great literature cannot simply transcend its origins but is always, in some way or another, respondent to the conditions under which it was formed. Ben Jonson defined Shakespeare as 'not of an age, but for all time'; but this requires the addendum that he could only be 'for all time' because he was so deeply embedded in the language and so the assumptions of his own age that its experiences became capable of serving as archetypes. As we read or see his plays, we become convinced, as were his contemporaries, by the coherence of his characters. We can easily give reasons for our conviction, and so could they (and no doubt he). The reasons change according to cultural contexts—think of the variousness of Falstaff criticism—but the coherence is not an illusion.

It is convenient to begin this introduction by invoking Shakespeare, as a touchstone generally recognized, even if he is being called up only to be denied his usual significance. The modern understanding is that Shakespeare was a literary man (and so indeed we must see him if we are to fit him into the modern world). But a history which pays attention to the materialist or theatrical elements of his career—the means that join him to his culture and his colleagues rather than separating him from them—must be conducted in terms that challenge the modern viewpoint. This raises issues that derive in part from the belated nature of the present volume (see the prefatory note) and partly from the limitations of the evidence available. The belatedness in fact only reinforces what would always have been the case, given the nature of the evidence; for it would always have been difficult to treat Elizabethan drama by the methods of the two contiguous volumes in the series, by Professors Bush (1945) and Lewis (1954). Organization by historical sequence or by author is hardly a possible way of handling the material of this volume (I speak only of historical limitations, having no wish to assert 'the death of the author' as a philosophic position). As noted in Chapter 2, for most of the period, plays were defined not as 'written by——' but 'as performed by——'; to look at the records of a working theatre of the time (as in Henslowe's Diary) is to see how regularly the authorial role is vested in two or three collaborators—and those subject to the control of the actors—rather than one individual.[4] The case is less extreme when we come to printed texts, but author's name is by no means a regular feature even there. Fair coverage of the works treated in this volume requires us to make allowance for the representative nature of the many anonymous and collaborative plays. And to escape from this problem by making publication, not performance, the centre of the treatment is to take flight from one of the few features of historical record that is clear.

Moreover, most plays of the Elizabethan theatre can be given only hypothetical dates (and the hypothesis nearly always turns on the critic's conception of evidence rather than the play's possession of it), so that developmental sequence can never be more than a sporadic possibility (dates being the nails that hold historical sequences together).[5] Lastly, and most importantly, the play-texts that survive are only a fraction of those that were performed.[6] We have no reason to think this a representative fraction; so no generalization based on it can claim authority.

There are, of course, well-established ways in which these disadvantages can be evaded. Wilhelm Creizenach's magisterial *The English Drama in the Age of Shakespeare*[7] provides a comprehensive survey of the Elizabethan theatrical techniques that can be derived from contemporary comments and surviving texts, but it pays little or no attention to the artistic content or sequence of the plays cited. More obviously in tune with modern interests is the method adopted (for example) in Felix Schelling's *Elizabethan Drama: 1558–1642*[8] where the drama of the time is presented as a developmental order imposed by major authors, so that 'the period of Marlowe' begets 'the period of Shakespeare', 'the period of Jonson',

[4] Henslowe, in the period 1598–1602, makes seven joint payments (at a rough count) for every five singular ones. But sometimes he made his payment to only one member of a syndicate, so the proportion of joint authorship may be much higher.

[5] This is not to say that the careers of some authors are not distinctive enough in literary terms to sustain treatment as separate entities (Marlowe and Jonson provide the obvious examples). But the painstaking sewing together of events that biographers have to indulge in, together with the gaps that remain between the lives and the works, make such biographies feats of art rather than expressions of nature. From a seat in the stalls it is difficult to know why we should think *The New Inn* is by the same author as *The Alchemist*, why the Heywood who wrote *A Woman Killed with Kindness* is the same Heywood who wrote *The Golden Age*, why the author of *The Merry Wives of Windsor* is also the author of *The Tempest*.

[6] *Henslowe's Diary* (ii. 146), guesses that between 2,000 and 3,000 plays were written in the period 1558–1642, of which number 650 survive. Of 282 plays named in Henslowe's Diary, only twenty-nine are extant. See below, pp. 362–3.

[7] (1916); translated from his *Geschichte des Neueren Dramas* (1909).   [8] (1908).

and (eventually) the periods of Fletcher and Shirley. This is a
highly convenient method, easily accommodated to general literary
assumptions, but I have avoided it, not only because it bases on
authorial individuality the choices conditioned by the system at
large, but also because in its stress on 'development' it downplays
the homogeneity of values and techniques that link the earliest
plays to the latest.[9] It is a method which cannot, by its nature,
correct the usual illusion that Shakespeare's art is not only a supreme artistic achievement but also a supreme historical cause,
so that characteristics can only be valued, or devalued, as leading
towards him or away from him. More recent volumes such as *The
Revels History of Drama in English*, volumes iii and iv,[10] and *The
Cambridge Companion to English Renaissance Drama*[11] follow the old
Cambridge History of English Literature[12] and turn history towards
encyclopaedia: they allow their separate critics to pursue separate
aspects inside separated aesthetics,[13] a system made more acceptable in the latter case by removing Shakespeare from the list.

As far as this book is concerned, given the sparseness and
unreliability of the usual 'objective' markers of history—chronology, sure attribution of responsibility for what happens, clear choice
of representative events—it has seemed proper to give primary
attention to what can be investigated directly, the body of play-
texts that has come down to us, however subject these may be to
the vagaries of modern literary understanding. Detailed knowledge
of this corpus at least gives us some room to find the points at

[9] This is not to say that I deny what may be called development, or at least 'chronological drift'. I have separated out the years (from the mid-1580s to the mid-1590s) in which the
basic theatrical structures were being set up (Chs. 3, 4, 5) from those in which the forms so
set up were being exploited and modified. A pattern of growth, flourishing, and decline—
crude energy, vigorous control, empty sophistication (with Shakespeare standing in the
middle)—can indeed be asserted. But when we enlarge the focus to include a representative
number of plays, the pattern blurs: Lyly is never crude; Davenant usually is. We can notice,
especially in comedy, the increasing sophistication of the society depicted, and also the
apparent weariness of a movement whose major triumphs belong to the past. But it is
merely a historical accident that the innovations of Shirley or Brome are cut off in 1642.
Because we cannot tell what would have come next, we tend to suppose that they stand at
an artistic dead end. But if the theatres had stayed open for the next fifteen years, we might
well think of them primarily as 'innovators' or 'precursors'.

[10] *The Revels History of Drama in English*, iii. *1576–1613*, ed. Clifford Leech and T. W.
Craik (London, 1975); iv. *1613–1660*, ed. Lois Potter (London, 1981).

[11] Ed. A. R. Braunmuller and M. Hattaway (Cambridge, 1990).

[12] Ed. A. W. Ward and A. R. Waller (15 vols.; Cambridge, 1907–27).

[13] Sometimes with the effect of moving attention from the past and locating it in a survey
of what has been said in the most recent criticism.

which literary quality intersects with popular status (and so historical meaning).[14] By a survey of fashions and practices I hope to have provided a context in which individual plays, of varying merits, can be meaningfully situated, so that the taste of contemporaries can be seen to face the preferences of moderns. In these terms, *Measure for Measure*, for example, can be seen to be not only a rich and powerful play but as representative of a widespread taste popular with certain groups in a limited period of time.

The question that is central to my discussion is therefore less 'what is this play about?' than 'what is this play like?', supposing that the most historically defensible approach to individual plays is one which draws on the 'schemata'[15] that a competent audience would have learnt from the culture in general and especially from regular theatre attendance. A consequence of this approach is that the plays that get most space are not those that are literary favourites but those whose innovations and conduct connect most richly with the practices found in other plays, these being the only factors that allow us to make generalizations. I give more space to *Tamburlaine* than to *Doctor Faustus* or *Hamlet*, more to *Pericles* than to *The Tempest*, not to make space an index to quality but so as to pursue the filiations that turn the whole web of material into a structure of perception.

Genre provides the framework that seems most useful in connecting like with like, supposing that, even if no consistent definitions can be found, the presence of Comedy, History, and Tragedy as Elizabethan stage conventions shows the relevance for an audience not only of formal distinctions but also of the different qualities of vision they promote. The late-arriving genre of Tragicomedy (drawing on both satire and pastoral), which has its own chapter, points up the danger of too absolute a distinction; and I emphasize the point that Elizabethan plays are continually pushing against the limits of genre, not ignoring them but treating them with familiar

---

[14] I have assumed without argument in several places that plays become effective in both production and reading by their capacity to hold together divergent or even incompatible readings of the same material, so that alternative simplifications become available to audiences and critics in both space and time. I have preferred this way of putting the point to that embodied in the 'New Historicist' language of 'subversion and containment', since it attaches the phenomenon to the medium (which by nature raises dilemmas and then seems to solve them) rather than to the supposed quality of the society.

[15] See E. H. Gombrich, *Art and Illusion* (London, 1960); *The Sense of Order* (Ithaca, NY, 1979).

easiness, playing them against one another as plot and subplot, beginning and ending.

Shakespeare was a 'company man'. His life was devoted to the service of one organization, as actor, writer, and shareholder, and the First Folio appears as a company tribute to his loyalty.[16] It would be convenient to be able to argue that this symbiosis between writer and company makes 'company style' into a principle of organization in our treatment of plays. To some extent it does. No doubt the different qualities of the actors who made up the companies affected the writers; but the evidence left in texts is much too sporadic for the point to be developed—with one exception: the boys' companies projected perforce a distinct range of effects for a distinct audience. But it is easy to overestimate even this. My chapter on the boys seeks to allow for both the difference and the contiguity of the two repertories.

---

[16] We should remember that no other professional dramatist of the time can be so clearly and continuously identified with one company.

2. Preconditions of Elizabethan Drama

Finance for Playhouses

THE key figures in establishing a sophisticated popular drama in sixteenth-century London were not, as we tend to think, the actors or playwrights, for actors and authors and actor-authors had flourished in the period of strolling players, without producing work of literary significance, as the strolling player told Robert Greene* (see Chapter 3). The key figures were the entrepreneurs who used the semi-criminal methods of early capitalism (raising loans and then using the law's confusions to avoid repayment) to finance specific theatre buildings, so constructed that the audience would be required to pay for admission and thus generate profit. And profit was essential if plays of sufficient length and complexity were to be developed. Such an entrepreneur was James Burbage, actor and joiner, who in 1576 (with the aid of his brother-in-law John Brayne) leased a plot of land in Shoreditch, just outside the city walls,[1] and on it raised the first purpose-built playhouse in London (the Theatre),[2] an enterprise so obviously profitable that it spawned an imitation (the Curtain), built on a neighbouring lot almost immediately after. Burbage did not long remain content simply to accumulate profits, however, but with typical entrepreneurial restlessness, invested them in new enterprises: in 1596 he bought and converted a hall in the former monastery of the Blackfriars; and in 1599, the Theatre's lease running into difficulties, his heirs shipped its timbers across the river and built on the Bankside the most famous of all these structures, the Globe.

[1] The location was chosen because it was easily accessible to the London population but outside the moralistic and repressive administration of the city. All the early theatres were placed so as to secure this double benefit.

[2] The name was no doubt designed to associate the structure with classical buildings like the Theatrum Marcelli in Rome. De Witt in his sketch of the Swan (the only picture of the interior of an Elizabethan theatre available to us) is equally persuaded of the appropriateness of the vocabulary of a Roman theatre to describe what he saw. Cf. Heywood, *Apology for Actors*, sig. D2 (cited in M. C. Bradbrook, *The Rise of the Common Player* (Cambridge, Mass., 1962), 91).

The South Bank of the Thames was already a 'playing place',[3] a site of brothels and arenas for bear-baiting and bull-baiting. There Philip Henslowe, pawnbroker, brothel-owner, and general financier, had built the Rose in 1587, and in 1595 Francis Langley, expert money manipulator, built the Swan. At Newington Butts, a mile or so from the river, a playhouse was built in the middle 1570s, probably by Jerome Savage of Worcester's Men,[4] and we hear of performances there in the early 1590s. The careers of most of these men have had to be excavated from the legal records of their financial malpractices,[5] but Henslowe is the only one to leave us a detailed record of the financial underpinning of Elizabethan theatrical enterprise. His 'Diary', the account book of his receipts and expenditures for the companies he financed, mainly the Admiral's Men and Worcester's Men, running from 1592 to 1602, provides us with our only clear shaft of light into the day-to-day methods of Elizabethan theatre ownership. Like the Burbages, Henslowe managed to combine financial acumen with an intimate knowledge of the theatre; his son-in-law was Edward Alleyn, the great tragic actor. These two pooled their resources to outflank the Burbages when the newer and larger Globe began to overshadow the older and smaller Rose;[6] and in 1600 they moved their enterprise to the north-west suburbs, where they built the Fortune, explicitly designed to rival the Globe in size and splendour.[7]

All these were purpose-built playhouses. But before they existed strolling players were performing in London inn-yards (the Bull, the Cross Keys, the Bell, the Bel Savage are all mentioned). The inns not only provided occasional playing places but were structures that could easily be converted into permanent theatres. What looks like the first of these conversions, predating Burbage's 1576 Theatre by nine years but only recently given full documentation,[8]

---

[3] See Steven Mullaney, *The Place of the Stage: License, Play and Power in Renaissance England* (Chicago, 1988).

[4] See William Ingram, *The Business of Playing* (Ithaca, NY, 1992).

[5] See ibid.; also William Ingram, *A London Life in the Brazen Age* (Cambridge, Mass., 1978), on Langley; also Herbert Berry, *The Boar's Head Playhouse* (London, 1986).

[6] As we now know in some detail from the recent excavations. See R. A. Foakes, 'The Discovery of the Rose Theatre', *Sh. S.* 43 (1990), 141–8; John Orrell and Andrew Gurr, *What the Rose Can Tell Us* (London, 1989); Christine Eccles, *The Rose Theatre* (London, 1990).

[7] They employed the same builder and gave him specific instructions to imitate the Globe. See Chambers, ii. 436–9.

[8] See Janet Loengard, 'An Elizabethan Lawsuit: John Brayne, his Carpenter, and the Building of the Red Lion Theatre', *Sh. Q.* 34 (1983), 298–310.

was the Red Lion in Whitechapel.[9] There, John Brayne, Burbage's financier in the Theatre project, arranged to have built 'a scaffold or stage for interludes or plays . . . in height from the ground five foot . . . in length . . . forty foot, and breadth . . . thirty foot' (with a trapdoor).[10] In 1580 Brayne seems to have repeated his plan, this time seeking to convert the George, another Whitechapel inn. We know from the records that the plan foundered almost as soon as it was launched.[11] A more hopeful enterprise was the Boar's Head (also a Whitechapel inn).[12] At the end of a series of complex financial manœuvres this property was leased in 1599 by Robert Browne, the leading actor of Worcester's Men,[13] and by 1604 it was designated 'the especially used and best liked' house for that company.[14] But its importance for the London theatrical scene did not last. Disputes among the various investors who had hoped to corner its profits for themselves culminated in 'assaults and piratical incursions' by Francis Langley. In 1605 the company moved to Henslowe's Rose, and thence (in 1606) to the newly converted Red Bull, the last of the big auditoriums, apart from the dual-purpose Hope, reconstructed in 1614 from the old Bear Garden and used both for plays and for bear-baiting.

The internal arrangements of these buildings show recurrent features. The centre of the structure was the 'yard', to which the entrance doors gave admission. Here the 'groundlings' or 'understanders' stood around the large jutting-out stage. For further payments the public could have access via the internal stairs to the three tiers of galleries that lined the inside walls. Here one could sit on a bench protected from the rain. In the most expensive (topmost) tier the benches were cushioned. The stage itself was also protected by a canopy supported by two massive pillars ('painted to resemble marble', we are told). There was a gallery at the back of the stage (used as an 'upper stage', as 'a lords' room', or as a

[9] Ingram (*Business*, 108) points out that the Red Lion Inn was earlier called the Red Lion farm. So perhaps it was not a converted inn. The site of the playhouse was, however, a 'courtyard'; the carpenter built 'scaffolds', but it is not clear if these refer to stage structure or seating.

[10] He also ordered 'one convenient turret of timber and boards . . . in height . . . thirty foot of assize with a convenient floor . . . seven foot under the top'. So far no one has provided a convincing explanation of the turret.

[11] See C. J. Sisson, *The Boar's Head Theatre*, ed. Stanley Wells (London, 1972).

[12] See ibid. and Berry, *Boar's Head*. Plays had been performed at the Boar's Head, presumably on temporary scaffolds, as early as 1557.

[13] Berry (ibid.) argues for Derby's Men.   [14] Chambers, iv. 335.

'music room'). Underneath the gallery there were two or three doors giving passage onto the stage from the 'tiring house'—dressing room and prop store. Also beneath the gallery was a curtained area where actors could be 'discovered' when the curtains were drawn back.[15] In the middle of the stage was a trapdoor.

By the end of the sixteenth century, however, it was becoming obvious that the real money was not to be found in these large-scale,[16] low-price[17] popular houses but in smaller 'private' theatres, where a higher price (sixpence) could be charged for seats in an enclosed (stone-built) hall, requiring less upkeep than an open wooden one, and lit by candles.[18] There was already a model available for such an enterprise in the playhouses for the boy actors (who provided another field of entrepreneurial clover), the first Blackfriars and the playhouse in St Paul's. This, however, was an example that could not easily be followed. Burbage's original plan for the second Blackfriars playhouse was stopped when the aristocratic residents of the area protested against the inconvenience caused by having a 'common' (that is, adult) playhouse in their midst.[19] And so the Burbages were obliged to lease their property to the Children of the Chapel. But only eight years later the Burbage company (now taken over by James I as the King's Men) was able to buy back the lease, and by 1610 the definitions that excluded them seem to have been altered.[20] This came to be the most fashionable venue in London, used by the King's Men as a winter theatre in alternation with the Globe, which showed plays in the summer, when the court, the lawyers, and the *haut monde* were out of town. The finances of the company show us that the take from the Blackfriars regularly doubled that from the Globe, even though its capacity was less than half.[21]

[15] Denied, of course, by proponents of theatre-in-the-round, in Leslie Hotson's *Shakespeare's Wooden O* (London, 1959), for example.

[16] De Witt spoke of 3,000 spectators in the Swan. Modern scholars are inclined to pitch the number nearer to 2,000.

[17] One penny was the standard price of admission to the yard and did not rise above twopence before 1642. Translations of money are notoriously hard to manage. Andrew Gurr (*The Shakespearian Stage, 1574–1642* (2nd edn., Cambridge, 1980), 12–13) estimates one penny as a sixth of a soldier's daily food ration, 1/72 of an artisan's weekly wage.

[18] For a more elaborated view, see R. B. Graves, 'Daylight in the Elizabethan Private Theatres', *Sh. Q.* 33 (1982), 80–92.

[19] See Hillebrand, 155–7; W. A. Armstrong, *Elizabethan Private Theatres, Facts and Problems* (London, 1958), 2–3.

[20] But see the protest of 1618–19, printed in Bentley, *JCS* vi. 18, alleging that 'under the name of a private house' the players 'convert the said house to a public playhouse'.

[21] See Gurr, *Shakespearian Stage*, 196.

The financial lesson of the Blackfriars was not lost on other theatre entrepreneurs. The only playhouses built in London after this time were 'private houses': the Phoenix, the Salisbury Court playhouse, and the Cockpit-in-Court. The Phoenix is the most interesting of these.[22] Queen Anne's Men, having moved from the Boar's Head (as noted above) to the Red Bull, fell under the control of one of their number, Christopher Beeston, who proved himself to be a manager of remarkable ingenuity, securing his position not by manipulating money sources but by using the playhouse itself as a focus of courtly interest and so a source of social power. In 1617 he converted a cockpit in Drury Lane, in the newly fashionable West End, into a small 'private' playhouse and moved the company there from the Red Bull. Though Beeston had perpetual difficulties with his actors, the location of his new playhouse, its reputation, and the literary quality of its repertory made the Phoenix rival the Blackfriars as a venue for the fashionable audiences of the town.

The Companies

Beeston's troubles with Queen Anne's Men in the Phoenix point to a basic contradiction in the position of acting companies attached to permanent theatres. The situation of strolling players and of London companies forced by plague or other misfortune to tour the provinces represents (one might say) the primitive state of acting freedom, where the actors control their own precarious destinies, colonizing the halls of one town after another and turning them into playhouses by their mere power of representation. The basic form of company structure we find in London still reflects these conditions—organizations defined by a patent to perform and run by actor-shareholders who assumed joint responsibility for the provision of plays, costumes, and the wages of hired men and in the early days moved easily from one playing area to another. Under such conditions these 'sharers' retained something of the freedom of crafts masters in the guilds, in a system divided between sharers (masters), hired men (journeymen), and apprentices attached to individual masters. This was a freedom they could claim as necessary to their 'mystery', a space they needed if they were to

---

[22] Some drawings by Inigo Jones have been thought to give us an internal plan of this building. See John Orrell, 'Inigo Jones at the Cockpit', *Sh. S.* 30 (1977), 157–68.

exercise their creative talents. But the nature of the 'mystery' of acting was very different from that of pewterers or grocers or tailors; the actor's skill depended on a capacity for self-transformation and change, for the exploration of difference, heterodoxy, conflict, rather than a stable and repetitive expertise. Their 'product' lacked substantial definition. Thus a claim that they should have the same status as the London trade guilds would have been received with scorn if it had been made. The enmity of the city authorities, the preachers and the learned, the interruptions imposed by the plague,[23] by Lent, by Sabbath observance, by periods of national mourning, by the undependability and ambiguity of audience response, combining excited approval with supercilious disdain[24]—all these pointed to careers of uncertain coherence, to lives dependent on self-definition and free sale of labour, running completely contrary to everything that the organized world of the City (and the State) thought proper. Actors did indeed move easily from company to company, from one playhouse to another, from London to the provinces. In this sense their careers tended naturally towards that most abhorred of Elizabethan conditions—that of 'masterless men'. The Elizabethan players were saved from that status only by the largely fictional argument that they were 'servants' to a noble lord, a fiction that suited both parties, for it not only allowed the players to impose themselves on reluctant licensing authorities but also gave the lord a free retinue and an opportunity to outshine his peers in cultural display and courtly status.[25] For the Queen, finding 'solace' in plays, but reluctant to pay for them, was bound to appear indebted to the nobleman whose company provided her court with entertainment.

Far more dangerous to the freedom of the acting company than the patron (whose usefulness was in direct proportion to his remoteness) was the forced cohabitation in London of the company 'sharers' with the theatre owner and the 'housekeepers' to whom he had sold shares in the playhouse fabric. These were men well placed to interfere with the details of company life. In theory the

---

[23] For lists of theatre closings because of plague, see Chambers, iv. 345–51, and Bentley, *JCS* ii. 652–72.

[24] See Meredith Skura, *Shakespeare the Actor and the Purposes of Playing* (Chicago, 1993).

[25] It was no doubt the dangers of this competitiveness that persuaded James I to nationalize the London companies by restricting patronage to members of the royal family. See Ch. 8 n. 6 on an earlier attempt to secure the same effect.

relation was governed by mutual interest: the players attracted paying customers by the quality of their 'product'; the customers paid the company, and the company then reimbursed the house-keepers for the use of the building; the actors' freedom led to the entrepreneur's profit. This symbiosis is illustrated at large in the history of the Chamberlain's/King's Men, the best-known organ-ization ('Shakespeare's Company') and the only one to have a con-tinuous existence from 1594 to 1642. The arrangements that secured this stability are sometimes taken to provide a norm, but this is the opposite of the truth. Indeed, even this arrangement seems to have been arrived at by accident more than design. When the Burbages, having bought the Blackfriars playhouse, then had to raise money to build the Globe, they offered shares in the new building to the 'sharers' in the company. Thus a wealthy cadre of actor–owners was created, with terms of association which made it desirable to join the company and improvident to leave it—hence their seventeenth-century ability to attract and retain the best actors and writers in the market.

Elsewhere we find very different conditions.[26] Henslowe's early entries show him content with the status of landlord and financier, leaving company decisions to company members. But the evidence suggests that he soon developed an appetite for more power. In 1597 we find Francis Langley, in competition with Henslowe, binding players as indentured servants to the theatre rather than the company.[27] In the following year we find Henslowe doing the same thing.[28] But there is little evidence that he was able to invade the company solidarity of the Admiral's Men very far. He seems to have fared better when, in 1611, he took charge of the newly formed Lady Elizabeth's Men. In articles of complaint dated 1615[29] the company accused Henslowe of appropriating their goods, re-serving the playbooks on which they depended, keeping actors in financial subjection by charging extortionate interest for loans, so that 'within three years he hath broken and dismembered five

---

[26] Alleyn and Henslowe did in fact think in 1608 of selling shares in the Fortune to the company shareholders, and in 1618 Alleyn leased the building to the company for an annual rent (see Chambers, ii. 442); but this arrangement seems to have collapsed when the theatre burnt down in 1621, an event from which the company never really recovered. See also Bentley, *JCS* vi. 149 ff.   [27] Chambers, ii. 131.

[28] See Bernard Beckerman, 'Philip Henslowe', in Joseph Donohue (ed.), *The Theatrical Manager in England and America* (Princeton, 1971), 37 n. 26.

[29] See Chambers, ii. 248 ff.

companies'.[30] The end towards which all this pointed is not fully documented, however, in Henslowe's lifetime. It is only when we reach the private theatres of the 1610s and 1620s that the dazzle of proximity to court favour seems to have encouraged theatre owners into a sustained bid for absolute control. This returns us to the case of Beeston, who evidently regarded the arrival of Queen Anne's Men in his new theatre, the Phoenix, in 1617, as an occasion to combine the two areas of authority and to seize control of the plays, costumes, and personnel as his own possessions. When the company resisted his claims, he excluded them from the building—they had to go back to the Red Bull—and hired another troupe, hoping no doubt to find them more amenable to his command.[31] But it seems that they were not: in 1622 he repeated the manœuvre, and in 1625 (after the great plague had destroyed most of the organizations) he set up his own group and acquired the patronage of the new queen, Henrietta Maria. But by 1636–7 even that arrangement had collapsed. Queen Henrietta's Men were ousted from the Phoenix and in their place Beeston installed a company of boys called officially 'the King and Queen's young company' but more usually known as 'Beeston's Boys'.[32] This was done, we are told, 'to the end that he might have a company that would take what he would be willing to give them', not as a manager but (as with earlier boys' companies) as 'governor and instructor'.[33]

The discarded companies (apart from Queen Henrietta's Men, who had the Earl of Dorset to look after them) either disintegrated or found themselves back in the open arenas, as popular entertainers on the wrong side of an increasingly wide social divide. The Red Bull, the Fortune, and the Curtain were stigmatized by the *bien pensants* of the time as the homes of vulgar performances and rowdy audiences, and we have paid for this reputation by the almost complete disappearance of their repertory.[34] Even the Globe, if we are to believe the Prologue to Shirley's *The Doubtful Heir* of 1640, could not be allowed to overcome the taint of its public playhouse status:

[30] See *Henslowe Papers*, 86–90.   [31] See Bentley, *JCS* vi. 66–77.
[32] The company seems to have included some adult actors as well.
[33] See Bentley, *JCS* vi. 66–70. Richard Heton, manager of the Salisbury Court theatre, seems to have taken Beeston as a model, setting up a boys' company and seeking a patent that would allow him to 'order, direct, set up and govern' the company. Those that 'will not be ordered and governed by me as of their governor . . . I may have power to discharge from the company'.
[34] See Bentley's essay on 'The Reputation of the Red Bull Theatre', in *JCS* vi. 238–47.

A Prologue at the Globe to his comedy called *The Doubtful Heir*,
which should have been presented at the Blackfriars

Gentlemen, I am only sent to say
Our author did not calculate this play
For this meridian; the Bankside he knows
Is far more skilful at the ebbs and flows
Of water than of wit . . .
No shows, no frisk, and what you most delight in
(Grave understanders) here's no target fighting
Upon the stage . . .
No bawdry, nor no ballads. This goes hard.
The wit is clean, and (what affects you [most])
Without impossibilities the plot;
No clown, no squibs, no devil in't; O now
You squirrels that want nuts, what will ye do?

.   .   .   .

But you that can contract yourselves, and sit
As you were now in the Blackfriar's pit,
And will not deaf us with loud noise or tongues,
Because we have no heart to break our lungs
Will pardon our vast scene.[35]

The Repertory

Henslowe's Diary spells out the method by which an independent
adult company conducted its business, and in particular shows us
how the actors acquired the plays they performed (there is no
reason to suppose that other companies of the time operated dif-
ferently). The playwrights made proposals to the company (the
shareholding actors) in the form of 'some sheets' or 'a plot' (a
scene-by-scene synopsis), or else the company (or its representative) suggested some currently popular theme or scandal (see
Chapter 7 n. 81 on Chapman's *The Old Joiner of Aldgate*) which
one or more writers could develop in their own terms, using their
knowledge of the strengths and weaknesses of the company they
were writing for. The company's approval of the draft loosened
Henslowe's purse strings; he made partial payments in advance
(like modern publishers' advances on royalties) and gave full payment—usually £6—on completion. But before this, the poet read

---

[35] *Shirley's Poems* (1646), cited in Bentley, *JCS* vi. 193–4.

his script to the company (Henslowe sometimes advanced money for wine to lubricate these occasions) and no doubt changes were proposed and accepted. Henslowe's payments were, of course, debited to the company and recovered from their share of the gate receipts (the entry fees to the yard and half the gallery receipts). Thereafter the book belonged to the company; it would be modified by the book-keeper or prompter and revised (if still in the repertory) when the passage of time had tarnished the immediacy of its appeal.

The Authors

Even though, once he had been paid, the playwright lost all control over his work, he had, however, been very well paid. Bentley has compared the fees for playwriting with the emoluments of the learned professions, schoolmasters, curates, and college Fellows, and noted the superior reward that came from playwriting. Of course authors did not do as well as playhouse housekeepers or even actor–sharers, but the risk was less. For writers in pursuit of literary glory, however, the system was unrewarding. The names associated with performances were those of the actors and of the playhouse. It seems likely that hardly anyone attending a performance heard of the author. Dryden, in a letter of 4 March 1699, says that 'the printing of an author's name in a playbill is a new manner of proceeding, at least in England'. The playwright intent on fame could only (if he stayed inside his contract) wait until the company no longer wanted the play; but even then publication in a despised genre was unlikely to attract the attention of the kind of people who mattered. Things were changing, of course, throughout the period. Ben Jonson could hardly have published his 1616 Folio a decade earlier. Even in 1616 the use of the classical 'Works' in the title elicited much scorn; and we should notice the care he took to strike all the right notes, with his allegorical engraved title-page stressing the antiquity of theatrical performance, his table of contents, and his strategy of presenting plays cheek-by-jowl with regular poems, many of them addressed to distinguished members of the social hierarchy.

Jonson also sought to ensure that the texts in his Folio were carefully printed from authorially authenticated copies. Few of his colleagues took such care. When the printed version of a play was not pirated or stolen from its 'grand possessors' in the company, it was still commonly released in the form of a hard-to-read working manuscript and in this form left to the tender mercies of printers unconcerned with literary authenticity. As the status of plays as literature rose through the first half of the seventeenth century, however, the perceived value of the author's name rose with it. Dedications, commendatory poems, epistles to the reader marked the new cachet. It is a strange coincidence that, as the fever of new playwriting subsided (see Chapter 8 n. 15) the reputation of the authors increased.

The evidence that certain playwrights were retained by the companies as poets-in-ordinary may point in the same direction,[36] though it is hard to know when the practice began.[37] The only contract we know about is that set up between Richard *Brome and the manager of the Salisbury Court theatre in 1635. This specifies that Brome will write three plays a year for his employers, will write for no other company, will not sell his plays to a publisher, will undertake revisions of company plays, and will write prologues and epilogues and songs as required. For these services Brome was to be paid fifteen shillings a week for his first contract and then twenty shillings a week from 1639 to 1645. Bentley notes that the pattern of plays written for one company and then released for publication when the contract ends suggests the same pattern of employment as for *Shirley (writing for the King's Men), and before Shirley for *Massinger, and before Massinger for *Fletcher.[38] *Shakespeare preceded Fletcher as a writer for the King's Men; but of course Shakespeare was part-owner of the company he wrote for. If he was employed as dramatist, he was in this sense self-employed.

Acting

I have suggested that the guild structure of the companies must have pulled against the individualism of the actors. The ensemble acting required by most plays must have had the same effect. Given the conditions of performance—a different play every day

[36] See Bentley, *Dramatist*, ch. 6.
[37] The Henslowe papers show Henslowe binding Heywood to the Rose for two years, 1598, 1599. The document makes no mention of play-writing, but Bentley speculates that the form implies duties outside ordinary acting. See Bentley, *Dramatist*, 118–19.
[38] Bentley, *Dramatist*, 111–28.

of the week and a new play (when prices were doubled) every other week—play production could have been managed only by acceptance of a common code of conventions. Rehearsals must have taken place.[39] The German physician Johannes Rhenanus reports that in 1613 the actors were 'daily instructed, as it were in a school, where even the actors of most repute in the place must allow themselves to be taught by the poets'.[40] But even if we take this as a literal truth (Creizenach does not), devising new production methods for new plays cannot have been an option; learning all the lines must have taken all the time available.

T. W. Baldwin has argued that plays were constructed as a system of 'lines', the parts being written with specialized actors in mind.[41] It is an argument that has few supporters. Yet some such system, allowing the actor of the young lover, the smooth schemer, the bluff soldier, the dignified old man (and so on) to have a pre-packaged repertoire of movements and actions, would be appropriate to the crowded schedules of the playhouse, and serve not only as a crutch for memory but allow 'blocking' to be handled as a set of preordained conventions. It is clear that the average Elizabethan actor could not have carried his 'interpretation' so far beyond convention that his fellows could not anticipate what he was going to do next. To handle the incessant re-entries and the regular doubling, which allowed companies of fifteen or sixteen[42] to enact plays with cast lists of forty to fifty characters,[43] must have required a 'professionalism' (involving skill in singing, dancing, fencing, and acrobatics as well as acting) achieved more by the unstated conventions of cooperative group existence than by rules learnt for specific occasions.[44]

No doubt, when other devices failed, the actors knew how to

[39] See *Henslowe Papers*, 124, for proof.
[40] Wilhelm Creizenach, *The English Drama in the Age of Shakespeare* (1916), 395. See also David Klein, 'Did Shakespeare Produce His Own Plays?', *MLR* 57 (1962), 556–60.
[41] T. W. Baldwin, *The Organization and Personnel of the Shakespearean Company* (Princeton, 1927). Cf. Skiles Howard,'A Re-examination of Baldwin's theory of Acting Lines', *Theatre Survey*, 26 (1985), 1–20.
[42] See David Bradley, *From Text to Performance* (Cambridge, 1992), for a detailed analysis.
[43] See William Ringler Jr., 'The Number of Actors in Shakespeare's Early Plays', in G. E. Bentley (ed.), *The Seventeenth-Century Stage* (Chicago, 1968), 110–34; T. J. King, *Casting Shakespeare's Plays* (Cambridge, 1992).
[44] See William B. Long, 'John a Kent and John a Cumber; An Elizabethan Playbook and its Implications', in William Elton and William B. Long (eds.), *Shakespeare and Dramatic Tradition* (Newark, Del., 1989).

make the noises appropriate to the standard situations in which they found themselves.[45] Hamlet tells the visiting players that the clown should not be allowed to extemporize, and this has allowed critics to understand that extemporization was the clown's prerogative. And certainly we know that it was by improvisation in repartee with the audience that famous clowns like Tarlton and Kemp made themselves into stars, outside as well as inside the theatre. But, given the conditions of performance, extemporization must have been a stand-by technique for all actors. If the so-called 'bad quartos' represent the actor's memories of plays they had acted in, then we learn that the power of improvisation they possessed was good enough to persuade some modern critics that such plays provide alternative versions by Shakespeare and others.

These questions about acting have usually been articulated in terms of 'formal' versus 'naturalistic'.[46] This has proved an indecisive debate, in part at least because the terms cannot be given fixed meanings. Contemporary witnesses are agreed that the purpose of acting is to represent nature. But what the actor represents by art can never be the same as the nature that exists 'naturally'. An actor brings to life a stock character by finding a naturalistic means to flesh out a role that is 'formal'; his air of spontaneity is a consequence of his painstaking preparation. In Ben Jonson's *The Devil is an Ass* we are told of an intention to hire a boy actor to impersonate a great Spanish lady; he is praised for the force of his representation:

> To see him behave it,
> And lay the law, and carve and drink unto 'hem
> And then talk bawdy, and send frolics. O,
> It would have burst your buttons . . .
> [He] dresses himself the best, beyond
> Forty o' your very ladies.
>
> (II. viii. 71–4)

---

[45] Peter Thomson (*Shakespeare's Professional Career* (Cambridge, 1992)) quotes (pp. 89–91) an interesting eighteenth-century example of extemporization carrying a leading actor through a text he had not had time to learn. He knew the general contours of the emotions he had to display from performing similar parts in other plays. The other actors seem to have been able to match their responses so that the public remained ignorant of the situation.

[46] See B. L. Joseph, *Elizabethan Acting* (Oxford, 1951; rev. 1964); John R. Brown, 'On the Acting of Shakespeare's Plays', *Quarterly Journal of Speech*, 34 (1953), 477–84; Bernard Beckerman, *Shakespeare at the Globe* (New York, 1962), ch. 4.

The boy actor is praised for representing, like the Japanese *Onnagata*, a femaleness that goes *beyond* the mixed qualities of real life. His 'naturalness' creates the pleasure of art because it is keyed to a coherence that puts to shame the haphazardness of nature as actually experienced.

The Audience

The audience[47] that responded most fully to these signals from the stage was inevitably one that had acquired familiarity with a stage language composed of such signals. And the range of meanings available was, equally inevitably, apprehended as a subset of the language (physical as well as verbal) that could be met outside, in the street, the tavern, the church, or the court. But who were the persons who possessed this familiarity? We have clearer evidence about who did *not* go to the playhouse than about those who did: the professionally pious, the ethically severe, and the socially timid stayed away, or wished it to be thought that they stayed away. And that was a constant factor until the theatres were closed down by just such people in 1642. But the nature of the enterprise and of the people who were caught up in it was by then no longer what it had been sixty years before. The earliest references (such as that from Nashe cited below (p. 23)) define playgoers as a group deliberately nonconformist, drawn from those sections of the population naturally resentful of established and repressive virtue and anxious to subject it to the cut and thrust of theatrical redefinitions: apprentices, students, soldiers, the proletariat (when they could afford it)—those who might equally well be found in the neighbouring taverns and brothels. This is not, of course, a simple class distinction (Nashe includes 'gentlemen of the court [and of] the Inns of Court' in his list of theatregoers), and those who have tried to define the audience on a simple class basis have tended to reveal their own class perspectives more clearly than the facts of the case.

All such attempts are bedevilled not only by the variousness of the audience but by the rapidity with which it changed. As the culture of 1960–90 has shown, the marginal can quickly turn into the received, the fringe take over the centre. Similarly, the London

[47] See Alfred Harbage, *Shakespeare's Audience* (New York, 1941); Ann J. Cook, *The Privileged Playgoers of Shakespeare's London* (Princeton, 1981); Andrew Gurr, *Playgoing in Shakespeare's London* (Cambridge, 1987).

drama of 1580–1642 moved from a despised fringe status, first of all to the centre of an intellectual counter-culture, dominated by the lawyers from the Inns of Court (in the children's theatres of 1600–8), and finally to the élite status of private theatres patronized by the court. We see the court itself becoming hospitable to arts that Elizabeth had kept firmly subordinated to the ceremonies of power. Elizabeth's court appreciated energy above all other talents, whether shown in physical power, as in bear- and bull-baiting, 'tumbling', wrestling, tilts and tourneys, rope-walking, fencing and dancing (admired for its acrobatic skills), or in mental agility, as in enigmas, emblems, wit-contests, cruel jokes, or the exploitation of folly. These were tastes that did not separate the court from the common people; and the chivalric and classical adventure stories that form the staple of the known court plays from Elizabeth's reign seem to have been predicated on the same consensus view of what aspects of human behaviour were most enlivening. But by the time of Charles and Henrietta Maria the *nouvelle vague* in court culture was predicated on states of mind rather than appetite for action. 'Court plays' like Walter *Montagu's *The Shepherd's Paradise*, Thomas *Heywood's *Love's Mistress, or The Queen's Masque*, Lodowick *Carlell's *Arviragus and Philicia*, and Thomas *Goffe's *The Careless Shepherdess* centre on questions of 'purity' in love that could not easily be shared by the population at large. It was a taste that had manifested itself as early as *Fletcher's *The Faithful Shepherdess* of 1608–9, rejected by its original audience at the boys' Blackfriars. However, the later 'private' play-houses, the second Blackfriars, the Phoenix, the Salisbury Court, and their dramatists were bound to acknowledge the new taste when the court espoused it, or else face the charge of uncouth old-fashionedness. That had become the perquisite of the remaining open amphitheatres, the much despised Red Bull and Fortune, where entrance still cost one or two pennies and where action and adventure continued to make their appeal. It was a separation of audiences that marked in its own way a breakdown in the capacity to maintain unity in difference such as had sustained the glory days of the English drama.

3. The Emergence of the University Wits: Early Tragedy

THE possibilities made available to the playwrights who, in the 1580s, transformed English popular drama from a crude folk art to a sophisticated literary system can be seen as the product of economic, social, and cultural factors which had appeared (for the first time in English history) in the preceding decades. The so-called 'University Wits'—*Lyly, *Greene, *Peele, *Lodge, *Marlowe, *Nashe (and perhaps we should give the non-university *Kyd and Shakespeare at least associate memberships)—belonged to a new breed of secular intellectuals. As such they were able, drawing on their Humanistic education, to create a complex commercial drama, using the nationalization of religious sentiment (banned in any explicit presentation) to reach out to a population similarly caught in the contradictions and liberations that history had imposed—drama being the genre most responsive to the tastes and demands of society. Yet the 'Wits' were seldom content to allow that their art was dependent on the public or to agree with Dr Johnson that in the theatre

> The drama's laws the drama's patrons give;
> For we that live to please must please to live.[1]

The grammar school and university education available to these dramatists gave them great rhetorical facility, which they drew on in all their writings (and none of them wrote only plays); but the Humanist bias of university life gave them other gifts, less compatible with life as a popular dramatist. The situation is one that is easy but misleading to describe in modern terms. These were 'scholarship boys', 'outsiders', 'social misfits', 'marginal members'.[2] But they were more likely to see themselves in the image of Cicero, as 'new men' for whom eloquence was only the external sign of

[1] Prologue spoken at the opening of the theatre in Drury Lane, 1747, ll. 53–4, in *The Poems of Samuel Johnson*, ed. D. Nichol Smith and E. L. McAdam (Oxford, 1941), 53.
[2] Cf. Mark H. Curtis, 'The Alienated Intellectuals of Early Stuart England', *Past and Present*, 23 (1962), 25–43.

their political potential, yet who found themselves obliged to endure an iron age short on the specific crises that would justify a high-pitched rhetoric of public warning (ideally combining Cicero with Jeremiah). For men with such ambitions, the status of what Sir Thomas Bodley stigmatized as 'riff-raffs . . . baggage books' and excluded from his library must have seemed a sad disappointment. Their Humanist ideas of service to the State could not but lead them to despise the postures they found themselves adopting—not as the populace's leaders but as its commercial entertainers. However ironically he phrases it, Nashe is pointing to a sad truth in his 'realist' defence of plays:

men that are their own masters (as Gentlemen of the court, the Inns of the Court, and the numbers of captains and soldiers about London) do wholly bestow themselves upon pleasure, and that pleasure they divide (how virtuously it skills not) either into gaming, following of harlots, drinking, or seeing a play. Is it not better (since of four extremes all the world cannot keep them but they will choose one) that they should betake them to the least, which is plays? (McKerrow, i. 212)[3]

We know little about these men outside the works they wrote. Fortunately our concern here is with plays rather than lives. The purpose of this chapter is to deal with characteristic plays of a generation in terms of the techniques which allowed their shared social preoccupations to produce something like a dramatic movement. We do not possess enough knowledge to make clear judgements about authorship and date, but it seems possible to describe in general terms the means by which these men found viable expression for their social attitudes, and to note the variant possibilities that lie behind their separate 'raids on the inarticulate', so that the period from the mid-1580s to the early 1590s appears as an area of open alternatives rather than fixed development.

In mere biographical terms there is much that links the members of this group. All were born in the thirteen-year span between Lyly (1554) and Nashe (1567) and all (apart from Kyd and Shakespeare) graduated from Oxford or Cambridge in regular succession and then came to London to seek their literary fortunes. All came from families in the middle range of society. In London, it is clear, they became aware of one another as involved in common purposes

---

[3] Cf. Sir John Davies' 'In Fuscum' (Epigram 39) and Piermaria Ceccini (cited in Jonas A. Barish, *The Antitheatrical Prejudice* (Berkeley and Los Angeles, 1981), 81).

and ideals; we have evidence that occasionally they wrote together, collaborated in work offered for sale, shared enemies as well as friends, resented imputations of excessive dependence on one another. By the middle 1590s most of them were either dead or withdrawn from authorship.

The transition from humble background to learned status was by no means unknown before this time—Wolsey, the 'butcher's brat' from Ipswich, provides a startling example. But these graduates of the 1570s and 1580s did not look to the Church as a safe basis for a career that began with learning and ended with power. The new classical learning, to which all of them were obviously attracted, pointed to careers in the mode of the Florentine Chancellors, Coluccio Salutati and Leonardo Bruni (where the study of Roman civility provided a model for modern state-building). But in England, self-defining social views, however exciting, provided little ground for economic self-support. Understandably enough, as provident careerists as well as self-conscious intellectuals, these men were unwilling to leave their *alma maters*, staying on in college after the BA even when (as in Marlowe's case) the terms of scholarship support for the MA committed the student to Holy Orders. A clerical living often provided the basis for a literary career in the following two centuries, but in this period of violent and dangerous controversy it offered no refuge. This was not the opening the University Wits were seeking.

What these men say about themselves and about one another, long after graduation, indicates the hold that university values continued to exercise over them. In their writings and reported sayings they certainly continued to exhibit a great deal of contempt for those who were not university men. Nashe, in a survey of contemporary breakdowns in the intellectual hierarchy, describes a modern world in which the properly educated man is continuously threatened by the uneducated pretender to knowledge (who has never moved beyond grammar school) sarcastically referring to such as

deep read school-men or grammarians who, having no more learning in their skull than will serve to take up a commodity, nor art in their brain than was nourished in a serving man's idleness, will take upon them to be the ironical censors of all, when God and Poetry doth know they are the simplest of all. [I] leave these to the mercy of their mother tongue that feed on nought but the crums that fall from the translator's trencher.

(McKerrow, iii. 312)

Mastery of Latin, the language of learning, had given these graduates the sense of having joined a European élite of power and
privilege, a world of shared modes of speech, jokes, and expectations that must have made the actual differences of power or status
seem provisional and adventitious. But these towering ambitions
stood on a very narrow base; in the real world of power in Elizabethan England there was no social scope for such assumptions; in
these terms the University Wits were all doomed to failure.

I have suggested that these university men tended to stick with
student life as long as they could. The next step, a move to London, was taken, as we happen to know in the case of Lyly, only
after failure to obtain a university appointment. But the cold realities of London life must have quickly disabused all the graduates
of any impression that their talents had more than a knock-down
sale value. The basic social networks of local, family, or client
relationships might help a little, but not for long, it would seem,
and certainly not in a way that would give reality to inflated self-
valuation.

Robert Greene may have been the member of this group with
the fewest useful connections; he certainly appears in print as the
most desperate to assert his status and the most driven to actions
that made him despise himself. What Greene's actions were in real
life is quite hard to tell, for he learnt to exploit a journalistic vein
of self-advertisement through overblown repentance rhetoric similar to that used by Snobby Price in Shaw's *Major Barbara*, designed both to fluster and reassure his potential benefactors. What
is probably more revealing than Greene's possibly fictional sins is
his attitude to the actors who were prepared to hire his literary
talent and who, indeed, offered all the Wits the chance to earn
incomes well above the Elizabethan average.[4] Financial recompense of this kind was not, however, what Greene was really aiming to achieve. His *alter ego*, Roberto in *Greene's Groatsworth of Wit*
(1590), becomes 'now famoused for an arch-playmaking poet, his
purse like the sea sometimes swelled . . . seldom he wanted, his
labours were so well esteemed' (Grosart, xii. 134). But this shameful mode of making money soon drives him into a moral decline:
'his company were lightly the lewdest people in the land . . . so
cunning was he in all crafts as nothing rested in him almost but

---

[4] See Bentley, *Dramatist*, Ch. 5.

craftiness' (ibid.). As one would expect in a hierarchical society, money without status comes to represent unnaturalness. And attempts to enforce status only make matters worse. Greene secured the right to call himself *Academiae Utriusque Magister in Artibus*, but what was the profit for him in so proclaiming himself if the only customers for his products turned out to be ignorant and venal tradespeople, 'uncertain, variable time-pleasers, men that measured honesty by profit, and that regarded their authors not by desert but by necessity of time'. Greene's picture of the theatre author may remind us of the complaints of writers in the Hollywood studios of the 1930s and 1940s, but the intellectual context of Humanism gave an extra twist to the knife of commercialism (and we should not forget that Elizabethan authors went to debtors' prisons and actually starved). In a period when ability to recite the opening of the fifty-first psalm (in Latin, of course) could spare a man a hanging—Ben Jonson escaped through this loophole in 1598—and when the possession of an MA entitled one to the legally important status of 'gentleman', it must have been exceptionally difficult to formulate the separation of literary and social rank, eloquence and importance.

When Greene formed his well-publicized attitudes, there was no hint of any other possible system. The only model he could set before himself was that of John Lyly. Lyly's *Euphues, the Anatomy of Wit*, first published in 1578, had gone through four editions by 1580 and seems to have become the most talked-about literary work of its generation. Greene's first prose work, *Mamillia* (1580), is patently parasitic on *Euphues*, just as his later *Menaphon* (1589) is a pendant to Sir Philip Sidney's *Arcadia*. Sidney's career was out of reach, of course. But Lyly, whose background and prospects were more comparable to Greene's, had forged for himself a literary career that proved equally hard to follow, not primarily for literary reasons but rather because Lyly had family connections (however remote) that gave him a toehold in the social system. By 1580 he had acquired the Earl of Oxford as a patron, and in 1584 this connection allowed him to appear as a dramatist. But the move to drama was made under circumstances that Greene could not hope to match. Lyly did not need to venture into the murky world of commercial playwriting. He did not have to offer his wares to the adult acting companies that Greene was to characterize as those 'puppets . . . that speak from our mouths, those antics garnished in our colours' (Grosart, xii. 144) and that Nashe (never one to be outmatched in rhetoric) was to designate 'taffeta fools . . . a rabble of counterfeits' (McKerrow, iii. 324).[5] Lyly's connection with the theatre began, it would seem, when, some time in 1583 most probably, Oxford bought up the lease of the first Blackfriars theatre and 'gave his interest to Lyly', as a legal document of the time tells us. This seems to have provided Lyly with control, or partial control, over a troupe of acting boys from the choirs of the Chapel Royal and perhaps also of St Paul's Cathedral. These, under the title of Oxford's Servants, he took to court in 1584, where they performed his first two plays, *Campaspe* and *Sappho and Phao*. And before the court performances he had already exhibited his plays before small paying audiences, ostensibly to give his boys an opportunity to prepare for the court, but designed also no doubt to secure profit in a more material sense. It is clear that Greene could not follow along the same path, for he had no earl to smooth his way. The favour of such a patron was like Divine Grace: it could not be worked for or deserved; it could only descend, unbidden, from the heaven of hereditary power.

In these early years there was not, as there was to be later, any middle ground between the heaven of patronage and the hell of commercial exploitation. But a gradual process of accommodation and compromise between literary talent and social distinction can be seen growing throughout the period. And so later generations could take over the social advances achieved by earlier writers. By the early years of the seventeenth century acting and playwriting had become occupations of some substance, though still subject to explosions of social as well as moral scorn. The dog-eat-dog world of Elizabethan theatrical capitalism, marvellously documented in William Ingram's life of Francis Langley, *A London Life in the Brazen Age*,[6] complemented by the ambiguous legal status of the actor, alternately vagabond and retainer, moral outcast and royal entertainer, gradually developed into a more stable compromise. Under James I only members of the royal family were allowed to assume patronage of acting companies in London; court performances became a more important economic and cultural element in

---

[5] The survival of these attitudes can be seen in John Cock's character of a 'common player' of 1615 (Chambers, iv. 255–7) and *The Second Part of The Return from Parnassus*, in *The Three Parnassus Plays*, ed. J. B. Leishman (London, 1949), IV. iii, and IV. iv.

[6] (Cambridge, Mass., 1978).

the lives of the companies. These were restraining privileges, of course, and were meant to be so; but they were restraints primarily on those who sought to *use* the theatre for short-term political advantage. Under the new aegis, acting and theatrical management could be viewed as something much more like a 'middle-class' activity. G. E. Bentley has warned us that we should not take the careers of the shareholders in the Chamberlain's/King's company (such as Shakespeare) to be typical of the opportunities open to actors (*Player*, 63). Yet these must have served as models to show many others what kind of status could be achieved following the carefully circumscribed life of an allowed actor or playwright, outwardly deferential to the social establishment and circumspect in statement (if not always in opinion).

In the 1580s and early 1590s there seems to have been no space for such well-integrated cultural positions in the theatre. Consciousness of intellectual superiority coupled to a deracinated existence among marginal members of society could only drive Greene, Marlowe, Nashe, it would seem, towards their different versions of *la vie de Bohème*.[7] In Greene's case at least, this seems to have meant a life that never managed to rise far above desperation, squalor, dreams of escape, and a recurrent tendency to bite the hand that fed him. In a later age Greene and Nashe might well have found comfortable niches in society as 'muckrakers' or 'investigative journalists'; even as early as the times of L'Estrange or Defoe, society had made considerable space for the exercise of such literary talents. Yet as literary historians we should probably praise the cruel restrictiveness of the Elizabethan world that directed the energy and inventiveness of such authors into channels of a literary rather than a merely journalistic kind, into genres, that is, which make a self-consciously formal claim on our attention outside the merely historical circumstances in which they were employed.

In his semi-autobiographical writings Greene several times refers to his relations to the players. The picture he paints is one of the university man wonderingly admired by the uneducated and

---

[7] The description of nineteenth-century Parisian 'Bohemia' in Jerrold Seigel's *Bohemian Paris* (New York, 1986) throws up some unexpected symmetries. Seigel speaks of the Bohemians' 'appropriation of marginal life-styles . . . for the dramatization of ambivalence towards their own social identities and destinies' (p. 11) and comments on 'the basic change . . . for artists and writers coming when 'patronage gave way to the market' (p. 13).

low-class actors, and willing to write his immensely successful plays only because he desperately needs the money to continue his dissolute life. In *Francesco's Fortune* (1590) Francesco (the Greene alternate) 'fell in amongst a company of players, who persuaded him to try his wit in writing of comedies, tragedies, or pastorals, and if he could perform anything worthy of the stage, then they would largely reward him for his pains'. And so Francesco 'writ a comedy which so generally pleased all the audience that happy were those actors in short time that could get any of his works, he grew so exquisite in that faculty' (Grosart, viii. 129). In *Greene's Groatsworth of Wit* the story has become even more pointed. Roberto is rendered penniless and outsmarted by the prostitute he thought to control. He is thrust out of doors, and, sitting against a hedge, he vents his wrath in English and Latin verses. On the other side of the hedge there happens to be a player, who now approaches Roberto:

Gentleman, quoth he (for so you seem) I have by chance heard you discourse some part of your grief . . . if you vouchsafe such simple comforts as my ability will yield, assure yourself that I will endeavour to do the best that either may procure your profit or bring you pleasure; the rather for that I suppose you are a scholar, and pity it is men of learning should live in lack.

Roberto, wondering to hear such good words . . . uttered his present grief, beseeching his advice how he might be employed. Why easily, quoth he, and greatly to your benefit; for men of my profession get by scholars their whole living. What is your profession, said Roberto. Truly sir, said he, I am a player. A player, quoth Roberto, I took you rather for a gentleman of great living, for if by outward habit men should be censured, I tell you you would be taken for a substantial man. So am I where I dwell (quoth the player) reputed able at my proper cost to build a windmill. (Grosart, xii. 130–1)

The player goes on to indicate that he has greatly prospered not only by acting but by writing: 'I was a country author passing at a moral, for it was I that penned the moral of man's wit, the Dialogue of Dives, and for seven years space was absolute interpreter of the puppets. But now my almanac is out of date'. Times and tastes having changed, he now needs a graduate, like Roberto, who is willing to use his sophisticated expertise 'in making plays . . . for which you shall be well paid if you will take the pains': 'Roberto, perceiving no remedy, thought best to respect of his present necessity to try his wit and went with him willingly; who lodged him at the town's end in a house of retail [that is, a brothel]' (Grosart, xii. 132). His new profession earns him the much-needed money, but, as noted above, money earned under these circumstances is seen to be incapable of securing socio-moral status. Roberto so despises those from whom he earns his money that he can define his difference from them only by cheating them: 'It becomes me, saith he, to be contrary to the world, for commonly when vulgar men receive earnest they do perform; when I am paid anything aforehand I break my promise' (ibid. 134). His money is spent among criminals and debauchees and produces execution for some and repentance before death for Roberto. It is at this point that Greene can proceed to warn 'those gentlemen his quondam acquaintance that spent their wit in making plays'—Marlowe, Peele, ?Lodge/Nashe, and 'two more that both have writ against these buckram gentlemen' (ibid. 144)—never more to 'acquaint them [the players] with your admired inventions'.[8]

The story as thus told is a powerful one. But, as far as the history of Elizabethan drama is concerned, the details leave much to be desired. There is no evidence that Greene's dramatic talents had the electrifying effect he describes. And we should note that he tells much the same story about his prose romances of love. In *The Repentance of Robert Greene* (1592) we hear not only that the 'penning of plays' turned him into a swearer and blasphemer, but that

These vanities [plays] and other trifling pamphlets I penned of love and vain fantasies was my chiefest stay of living, and for those my vain discourses I was beloved of the more vainer sort of people who, being my continual companions, came still to my lodging, and there would continue quaffing, carousing and surfeiting with me all the day long.

(Grosart, xii. 178)

Greene's literary career did not, in apparent fact, turn towards drama until the last four or five years of his life, when he had already published some fifteen to twenty books (mostly in only one

---

[8] That the same attitudes persisted even when the social circumstances of the author were quite different can be seen from Marston's *Histriomastix* (1589–99). There the scholar Chrisoganus tries to sell a play to Sir Oliver Howlet's Men for ten pounds. They are content to use the work of Posthaste (sometimes supposed to be Anthony Munday). Chrisoganus rails against their poor taste and their 'thickskinned auditors'. Time will come 'when sweet smooth lines are held for precious', and then these players will starve.

edition in his lifetime, though often popular at a later point). There was a considerable technical gap to be crossed before the stage could be made a vehicle for such talents, and neither the assumptions of the University Wits, nor Greene's imitative talent were of the kind to achieve the first crossing. It was not until Marlowe's *1 Tamburlaine* had transformed the idea of a successful popular play that Greene saw how he too could earn the good money (much better than could be earned by dedicating pamphlets to patrons) that came from writing stage poetry.

It seems likely that, if Greene had followed his own bent, he would have moved in a direction opposite to play-writing. One recurrent feature in the literary lives of the University Wits (and of the whole Renaissance as, following Burckhardt, it is conventionally understood) is an increasing effort to explain the world in terms of individual perception. Certainly Greene, Nashe, Lyly, and Lodge (in their prose writings) show a common interest in literary modes that allow an individual narrator's voice (closely linked to the author's own) to become the principal means of unifying the experiences narrated. And this is not at all surprising, given their own careers (as I have spelt them out above). Deprived of their hopes of public importance, they were reduced to paid employment as entertainers, producing eloquence on order as the price of survival. But the Humanist dream did not go away, and it emerges in the controlling voices they give to prodigals, outcasts, individualists, inevitably opposed to the current social order.

In making their move towards individualism, the Wits were, we might say, establishing the necessary precondition of a sophisticated drama in which the individual voice can be made to represent the struggle for freedom to defy the system: but the road from precondition to achievement was to prove both tortuous and unpredictable. Advance in one genre does not provide a formula for advance in another, even when the aims seem close.

Towards the end of his life Greene abandoned his more distanced way of telling complex stories dominated by chance rather than design and began to invite his readers to take a personal interest in the life of R.G. the great sinner, now patently exposed as both author and protagonist. These 'confessional' pamphlets tell potentially tragic stories of wilful self-destruction. They end, however, with a backward glance from a consensual position: a virtuous and forgiving wife, an influential pastor, a warning dream restores the criminal to the congregation of Christians. In these terms they declare their derivation from the prodigal-son plays of the earlier Tudor period; but they do not fulfil the theatrical purpose of those plays. There, the career of the prodigal was taken to represent the communal life cycle of the Christian individual, and so in that drama figures like Nice Wanton, Hickscorner, or Lusty Juventus appeared as typical rather than specific. Greene is unwilling to allow the flauntingly wicked and flauntingly repentant individual who is telling his story to disappear thus far into the typifying situation. We see everything through his eyes, and it is only through his personality that we can reconcile the implicit claim that we admire the expression of anti-social freedom at the same time as we condemn it. These pamphlets of his are effective precisely because they personalize the experience so powerfully. But the centripetal power of the telling is precisely what separates it from the generalizing capacity of drama.

Nashe's *The Unfortunate Traveller* of 1594 probably provides, in its stylistic brilliance and general accessibility, the best example of what this personalizing mode could achieve. *The Unfortunate Traveller* is, as the title tells us, a tale of misfortunes, but this tale of misfortune is kept everywhere remote from a tragic vision of life. Nashe imposes on his book a central personality, or rather a socially defined voice, that presents the misfortunes in such a way that they seem to be adventures enjoyed by the protagonist as narrator at the same time as they are mishaps endured by the narrator as protagonist, the power of the former creating a proper detachment from the horrors of the latter. The power is largely exercised through control of a dazzling alternation of styles—the Petrarchan style of Henry Howard, the Earl of Surrey, the oratorical style of the Teutonic Vanderhulke, the preacherly style given to the Anabaptists of Munster, the fulfilled revenger's style of Cutwolfe; but behind all these lies the stylistic agnosticism of Jack Wilton himself, the 'hero' of the story, for whom, as we see clearly in the opening section, control of style is control over the accidents of fortune. The narrative, which takes Jack on an unguided tour through the cultural monuments of Western Europe, describes a number of highly 'dramatic' moments; but they are completely untheatrical, for the quality of the experiences is entirely dependent on the agnostic and deflating interventions of the narrator. The exemplary and generalized nature of a journey through the Renaissance is undercut by the deliberately oblique viewpoint of a narrator who is English, juvenile, and irresponsible, an outsider—and yet at the same time an insider who is completely at home in the language and values he derides. And the personality that is foregrounded in this way is one that bears an obvious relation to the social status of the University Wits themselves—perilously self-confident and self-projecting, yet continuously aware of the unbridgeable gap between self-valuation and the values of the world. Jack Wilton's relation to the poetic Earl of Surrey offers a case in point. Their explicit relationship is everywhere presented in a language of social deference and literary admiration. Yet the intense idealism of the Earl's Petrarchan descriptions of his beloved Geraldine is made to seem eccentric by everything else in the story. When the two men are in prison with Diamante, the jealous Venetian's wife, the Earl sighs and makes sonnets: 'He praised, he prayed, he desired and besought her to pity him that perished for her' (McKerrow, ii. 262). The Earl gets the poem, but Jack Wilton gets the girl (and the readers are clearly meant to think that the better alternative). In this period there was, of course, no objective way of validating such subversive attitudes; the pressure of the individual speaker's fantasy can secure a positive response in a controlled narrative; but shift the same material to the stage, and we meet a context in which the individual must not only survive, but persuade us to approve of his 'success' (even if that means only failing splendidly); there one would find the evasiveness and nihilism of Jack Wilton to betray the moral coherence of the plot.

The contrast between the surviving serious drama of the early 1580s and the mode of the University Wits is made easy to see by the overlap in subject matter between the popular Estates Morality plays and the social-survey narrative we find not only in *The Unfortunate Traveller* but in Greene's *Quip for an Upstart Courtier* (1592), and the allegedly anti-Greene *The Defence of Coney Catching* (1592). The Estates Morality is concerned, above all, with the condition of the commonwealth, seen as an organism of well-fitting parts—the lawyer, the soldier, the courtier, the labourer, the clergyman, the merchant—designed by God to fulfil complementary duties in the community. The plays show us this ideal threatened for a time by the unwillingness of the Estates to perform as required. But eventually the balance is restored by supernatural intervention. The Wits impose a subversively personal point of view on this picture of group existence. *The Unfortunate Traveller* simply dissolves the form in parody: it brings Jack Wilton into contact with a large number of 'representative' figures—a Jewish doctor, a German orator, a Pope, his mistress, an Italian revenger, anabaptist tradesmen—each decorously fulfilling the function that convention (or prejudice) had assigned. But there is, in fact, no 'natural' unification to hold these 'representatives' together, apart from the impression they make on the person who meets them all. The end of the 'Moral' play, according to Thomas Heywood's *An Apology for Actors* (1612), is 'to persuade men to humanity and good life, to instruct them in civility and good manners, showing them the fruits of honesty and the end of villainy'.[9]

Heywood, like most Elizabethan 'defenders' of literature, pushes straight moralism further than most surviving examples justify. But it is true that the plays of this early period tend to end with terminally authoritative judgements, so that the enlightened characters, the choric or authorial voice, and an implied audience consensus are moved into a stable alignment. The University Wits, on the other hand, tended to offer an oblique and unsettling point of view, often identified with some more specialist or self-consciously heterodox fraction of the reading public, as in Nashe's 'Induction to the dapper monsieur pages of the court' (McKerrow, ii. 207) or Lyly's statement that '*Euphues* had rather lie shut in a lady's casket than open in a scholar's study'.[10] Hence the problem of finding a way to reproduce on stage the effects they had achieved in narrative.

The preconditions of Estates Satire, the dominant popular theatrical mode in this period, are well exemplified in Robert *Wilson's *The Three Ladies of London* (*c*.1581)—called on its title-page 'A Perfect Pattern for All Estates to Look Unto'.[11] Wilson was a well-known actor, one of the 'twelve of the best' chosen in 1583 to be players for the Queen, and noted in the account of this formation in Stowe's *Annals* (1615 edition) 'for a quick, delicate, refined, extemporal wit'. Wilson's role as a professional player puts him on the other side of the social divide from Greene and Nashe and sets him against the general attitudes of the University Wits; and the

---

[9] Shakespeare Society Reprint (1841), 53.

[10] Lyly, *Euphues and his England*, ed. R. Warwick Bond (3 vols.; Oxford, 1902), ii. 9.

[11] Stephen Gosson (in *Plays Confuted in Five Actions* (1582) sig. D2v) tells us that the author of a reply, *London against the Three Ladies* (1581–2), only wrote the play out of envy that men were commending Wilson's work.

play itself strongly confirms this, especially if one assumes that Wilson not only wrote it, but wrote it for himself to act in, and wrote the part of the clown Simplicity for his own performance. The function of Simplicity in Wilson's play could not be much less like that of Jack Wilton, though he, too, is an outsider. Simplicity does not focus attention on himself as an observer; he simply tells the truth about what is around him. He is the rude but innocent countryman who reaches London without having any grasp of the nature of capitalism, continually exploited by the followers of Lady Lucre, whose corruptions he can perceive but whose dominance he is powerless to affect. Alone among characters in the play, Simplicity is never absorbed into the system ruled by Lucre; but this intransigence does not give him the status of a hero or even the kind of self-sufficiency enjoyed by Jack Wilton. We learn how easy it is to read Simplicity's innocence as ignorance, his naïvety as simple-mindedness, his failure as his own fault. We may accept the doctrinal truth of what Simplicity says about the world, but we cannot identify with him (any more than we can identify with the Fool in *King Lear*). Like the Fool's, his career is a record of failure. We leave him, towards the end of the action, being whipped for crimes he did not commit, while the well-placed criminals he has sought to expose look on and urge the need for exemplary punishment so that society can be properly protected. The eventual reform of society from the vices of capitalism cannot come from inside the action. In the last scene a characterless 'Judge Nemo' descends from heaven (as it were) and condemns everyone in sight. Simplicity's point of view is justified, but Simplicity is not around any more to enjoy the justification. This is, of course, a secular variant of the story of Christ's career in the world; but nothing specific is made of this. It is the social implication that the play spells out: reform, it is implied, cannot derive from any effort by an individual but will emerge from the operation of larger forces far outside human reach. Author and audience can end the play in moral unison, but this is a unison in submission which flattens all the individual characters in the action.

    The relation of this popular author to his popular audience is nicely caught in the Prologue Wilson wrote for *The Three Ladies of London*. Humble and undogmatic, Wilson leaves the decision about what kind of play this is to his listeners. Like the later (and very different) Prologue to *Tamburlaine*, Wilson begins by saying what his play is not; this is not a mythological play, it does not deal with the gods or with war, it is not a pastoral; it is only in fact (he tells us) a trader's stall:

To sit on honour's seat it is a lofty reach:
To seek for praise by making brags ofttimes doth get a breach.
We list not ride the rolling racks that dims the crystal skies,
We mean to set no glimmering glance before your courteous eyes:
We search not Pluto's pensive pit, nor taste of Limbo lake;
We do not show of warlike fight, as sword and shield to shake:
We speak not of the powers divine, ne yet of furious sprites;
We do not seek high hills to climb, nor talk of love's delights.
We do not here present to you the thresher with his flail,
We do we here present to you the milkmaid with her pail:
We show not you of country toil, as hedger with his bill;
We do not bring the husbandman to lop and top with skill:
We play not here the gardener's part, to plant, to set and sow:
You marvel, then, what stuff we have to furnish out our show.
Your patience yet we crave a while, till we have trimm'd our stall;
Then, young and old, come and behold our wares, and buy them all.
Then, if our wares shall seem to you well-woven, good and fine,
We hope we shall your custom have again another time.

Greene, Nashe, Marlowe, cannot be supposed to have been capable of this simultaneous presentation of self and abasement of self. Greene, as the dreamer of *his* Estates Satire, *A Quip for an Upstart Courtier*, just disappears into his dream. Nashe insists on intervening at every part in his Estates Satire, telling us how to react. And both end their actions, untheatrically, without offering us any consensual meaning. Greene just wakes up; Nashe allows Jack Wilton to evaporate in the real daylight of history: 'as my story began with the king at *Turnay* and *Turwin*, I think meet here to end it with the king at *Ardes* and *Guines*' (McKerrow, ii. 328).

Robert Wilson's *The Cobbler's Prophecy* of *c*.1589×1593 was probably performed at court; but it has few characteristics that mark it as exclusively courtly; and we may assume that it was performed also in the public theatre. It offers an interesting companion piece to *The Three Ladies of London*, especially if we allow the figure of Raph Cobbler to be another persona designed by Wilson for himself. The Cobbler is another bewildered prole, this time caught up by fiat of the Olympian gods into a prophetic eloquence which he pours out on rulers and wrongdoers alike. But, like Simplicity,

Raph Cobbler remains very much a marginal figure as far as effective action is concerned. The effective movement to rescue society from the dalliance of Venus and Contempt (two versions of effeminacy) is supplied by Sateros, the soldier, who drives the whole action towards a morally rejuvenating war. The Cobbler, it seems, is going to end up punished (like Simplicity) for his violent and opinionated opposition to his social superiors, but he is pardoned at the last minute, and the gods restore him to proper humility as a working cobbler. Once again the author identifies himself with a truth-teller; but a truth-teller (even one with supernatural eloquence) is necessarily a marginal social figure in terms of social restoration, constantly endangered, and protected only by the jokes and ambiguities he shares with the audience (again like the Fool in *Lear*). The vices of society may be exposed in such ways, but social reform must come about by other means. The community established between Raph Cobbler and his audience is, like that of Simplicity, a community of powerlessness, cemented by their joking together while they wait for the powers that be to make their unforecastable appearance. They secure their permissible comic consensus only by presenting social vice from the essentially ineffective viewpoint of its victims. They show clowns to be better moralists than lords, but their subversions are comic and collusive, easily accommodated inside the existing social hierarchy. There is nothing here that corresponds to the strongly personal comic voice of Jack Wilton, equally powerless, but offering his readers, as it were, a way out of their subjection, the way of a self-sufficient cynicism. Such quirky individualism in the *raisonneur* cannot be used to generate the comforts of comic consensus in the theatre; there the dramatic clarity of a generalized ending requires us to see round the individual and register the complex community that gives him his meaning in the action.

The relationship between the theatrical effects generated by Morality plays and the focus proper to an individual named as a unique individual is shown with great clarity in Nathaniel Woodes's *The Conflict of Conscience* (1570×1581). Woodes's play tells us the story of Francis Spira, an Italian lawyer who had been persuaded to abandon the truth of Protestantism and accept Roman Catholic doctrine; then, faced by the horror of the offence he had given to God, he fell into despair and eventually killed himself. Woodes's first version of the play indicates Spira's real personal name and by

use of a Nuntius at the end of the play describes the logical consequence of his despair in suicide. But the printing of the play
apparently led Woodes to revise his sense of how the material
should be presented. He rewrote the title-page, the Prologue and
the conclusion of the play. At the end of the action, 'Oh doleful
news' is changed to 'Oh joyful news': the protagonist 'that would
have hanged himself with cord | Is now converted unto God', and
dies in a manner that gives God, not his own wilfulness, the
responsibility for his death.

The reasons for this change are spelt out in the play's prelimin-
aries. The name of Francis Spira is suppressed and the type name
of *Philologus* is now presented in title-page and Prologue (as it
always had been in the text itself). Indeed, Woodes seems always
to have been in two minds about the matter. In the first version of
the Prologue he tells us that

> . . . SPERAES name for causes just our Author doth omit,
> And at this time imagine him PHILOLOGUS to be,
> First, for because a Comedy will hardly him permit
> The vices of one private man to touch particularly;
> Again, now shall it stir him more, who shall it hear or see,
> For if that SPERA had been one, we would straight deem in mind
> That all by SPERA spoken were, our selves we would not find.
> But sith PHILOLOGUS is nought else but one that loves to talk,
> And common of the word of God, but hath no further care,
> According as it teacheth them, in God's fear for to walk,
> If that we practise this indeed, PHILOLOGI we are;
> And so by his deserved fault we may in time beware.

In the second version of the Prologue, however, the gambit of
telling and not telling is declined: 'Francis Spera's history' is changed
to 'a history strange and true'; the first line quoted becomes 'And
here our author thought it meet the true name to omit'. What the
Estates Moralities merely assume is now stated explicitly: the
career of an individual must be suppressed if the audience is to be
given a sense of shared experience which true 'comedy' should
convey; the particular significance of Spira's life can be realized in
the playhouse only when his character is generalized; his life can
have meaning only if presented in terms of the shared hope of a
Christian society.[12]

---

[12] There is a strange confluence between this view and the opinion of Aristotle in the
Poetics (1451 b 8 ff.) that poetry describes the general and not the particular.

In these terms it is clear why Woodes calls his play 'a new comedy . . . containing the most lamentable history of the desperation of Francis Spera'. The career of Spera is tragic; but, looked at from a community viewpoint, all must be seen to work out for the best, and so to be part of a larger 'comedy'. This balance of judgement can be set in stark contrast to what we find in the similar story of *Doctor Faustus*. What Woodes cannot achieve (cannot even imagine, I suppose) is a treatment like Marlowe's in which the personally named individual possesses, consistently and simultaneously, as much attachment to and detachment from the social norms as does Nashe's Jack Wilton (and as did the University Wits in their real-life relation to society), yet achieves his status not by the interventions of his author but by a free-standing capacity to act out of his own self-consciousness, so that we can accept the transforming process of the individual experience by which he is carried, willingly and unwillingly, towards his final separation from society in death.

We have then a situation in which the existing theatrical forms, dedicated to communal values, cannot accept a protagonist who negotiates his own status in relation to these values; and, simultaneously, we have a situation in which narrative forms, dedicated to giving voice to the aberrant individual, can confront the community only in the accents of their creators. In Greene, as in Nashe, we see their moves towards a fully realized dramatic form as a kind of dance in blindfold; they know the steps but cannot see the generic space to which they belong. And the blindfolds cannot be removed until Marlowe writes *Tamburlaine*.

Tamburlaine

It was only with the first part of *Tamburlaine* (1587×1588) that the insider–outsider role of the University Wits found a method of imposing its serious potential on the teeming life of the popular stage, without sacrificing the variety and spontaneity of popular plotting. *Tamburlaine*[13] tells the story of an anti-social career which, in its rejection of commonplace morality, offers a distant parallel to Greene's stories of underworld nonconformists such as Ned Browne. Greene's *The Black Book's Messenger, Laying Open the Life*

[13] I use the title *Tamburlaine* to refer to the whole two-part play. When I wish to particularize one part or the other, I describe the parts as *1 Tamburlaine* or *2 Tamburlaine*.

and Death of Ned Browne (1592) shows, as Walter Davis has indi-cated,[14] Greene's admiration for the criminal's commitment to 'pure action' and his pleasure in the superiority he achieves by the exer-cise of technical and manipulative skills. But Browne is still a figure set in a conventional landscape of criminality: 'imagine you now see him in his own person, standing in a great bay window with a halter about his neck ready to be hanged, desperately pro-nouncing this his whole course of life and confesseth as followeth' (Grosart, xi. 6). The desperation, however, belongs more to the narrator than to the racy narrative. Tamburlaine, of course, will have nothing to do with such imposed and self-negating moralism. He is presented as an outsider, but no opportunity is given to exclude him by invoking normative judgements; he simply takes over the norms.

The self-willed tyrant had graced the stage often enough before this time (*Cambyses, Apius and Virginia, Damon and Pithias, Jocasta*), while in the universities the imitation, adaptation, and perform-ance of Latin and Italian tragedies had made the tyrant a primary tragic exemplar. But these tyrants are merely negative instances —men long exercised in the cruelty of power. Tamburlaine is a peasant outsider and usurper determined to seize power and whose dynamism is allowed to justify his innovation. As a true Machi-avellian, Marlowe shifts the balance between the *virtù* of the indi-vidual and the *fortuna* of external circumstances, and so reverses the mode of earlier vernacular tragedy in which the tyrant's brief spasm of success is displayed (like Ned Browne at the window) against the circumambient fact of human incapacity to defy for-tune. Where the predominant rhetoric of the earlier plays was a rhetoric of Complaint,[15] the new mode found its characteristic expression in hyperbole, aspiration, and overreaching. The gap be-tween powerlessness and total power is thus made to seem a gap in talent rather than position. In this sense the play reads like the answer to a University Wit's prayer.

The Prologue to the play demands that we attend to the experi-ence of *Tamburlaine* as to a thunderclap of novelty; here there is no sign of the insinuated humility that had been (and was to be again) the standard formula for pleasing an audience:

---

[14] *Idea and Act in Elizabethan Fiction* (Princeton, 1969), 186.
[15] See John Peter, *Complaint and Satire* (Oxford, 1956), Wolfgang Clemen, *English Trag-edy before Shakespeare* (London, 1955).

From jigging veins of rhyming mother wits,
And such conceits as clownage keeps in pay,
We'll lead you to the stately tent of war,
Where you shall hear the Scythian Tamburlaine
Threatening the world with high astounding terms
And scourging kingdoms with his conquering sword.

We are presented with consciousness of power and confidence in energy as self-evident goods. The past has been abolished, we are told, and a new dramaturgy is proclaimed, which will empower its public by exalting individual achievement, centring on *virtù* not virtue, on power rather than patience. The audience is to be given a new relation to the material presented, to be terrified, horrified, stimulated but not at all reassured that the world can be understood eventually because it is governed wisely (however mysteriously). The cast of *Tamburlaine* is composed almost entirely of emperors, kings, soldans, bashaws, generals, who occupy, however, a world of perpetual and irremediable instability, where energy points not towards satisfaction but only towards further reaches of desire. *Tamburlaine* does not encourage the audience to inject their own experience into the play. The relationships it establishes between its characters are handled with a dehumanizing ceremoniousness. Even the 'love' between Tamburlaine and Zenocrate is presented with something of the glittering coldness of interstellar space. The emotion of wonder or *admiratio* seems to be what is principally aimed at, coupled with Aristotle's 'terror' rather than his 'pity'.

The Prologue draws particular attention to *Tamburlaine*'s poetic style, the 'high astounding terms' which are the first mark of the hero's nature, the verbal 'threatening' and the physical 'scourging', words and deeds being seen as cognate activities. In the play, the capacity to speak the sonorous paragraphs of long-breathed verse is presented as a direct manifestation of greatness.[16] Mycetes, the legitimate and (perhaps consequently) insufficient King of Persia, signals his weakness by not being able to make 'a great and thundering speech'. By the glamour of words Tamburlaine fires the Persian general Theridamas to follow him, and he holds the tributary

---

[16] For all this, it is not easy to think of *Tamburlaine* as an excessively 'wordy' play. As Wolfgang Clemen points out, 'for Tamburlaine the set speech is a necessary and constant condition of his existence; it is the very stuff and substance of his role' (*English Tragedy*, 114).

kings in awe and obedience throughout the play by the charisma of his style. The claim, as a claim by Marlowe no less than by Tamburlaine, was immediately noticed by contemporaries. Greene speaks of Marlowe as a 'prophetical full-mouth', punning presumably on Marlowe/Merlin (Grosart, vii. 8) and characterizes him as one who has set 'the end of scholarism in an English blank verse' (ibid.). There is, presumably, a double charge in this: the end of scholarism ought to be in Latin, not English, and should be concerned with substantive issues not with prosody. Marlowe is seen as too confidently putting his mouth where his scholarship ought to be. Greene evidently had a personal axe to grind. His own plays, he tells us, were 'had in derision for that I could not make my verses jet upon the stage in tragical buskins, every word filling the mouth like the faburden of Bow bell, daring God out of his heaven with that atheist Tamburlaine' (Grosart, vii. 7–8). The language used is instructive: verses strut (*jet*) not only on the feet of prosody but also on the jack-booted feet of God-defying conquerors. Such verse is appropriate only for such immoralists. Greene's incapacity to manage this medium can therefore be taken as a sign of his own proper Christianity. In the next year (1589) Nashe makes much the same point, speaking of 'the alchemists of eloquence who (mounted on the stage of arrogance) think to outbrave better pens with the swelling bombast of a bragging blank verse' (McKerrow, iii. 311). Nashe is perturbed by the connection between bombast and the self-importance of the 'vainglorious tragedians who contend not so seriously to excel in action as to embowel the clouds in a speech of comparison' (ibid.).[17] Joseph Hall (later Bishop of Norwich) addresses the same issue in the third satire of his *Virgidemiarum* (1598). He presents first the social impropriety of a tavern haunter[18] being fired by poetry to imitate the shepherd–emperor—an 'upreared high-aspiring swain, | As it might be the Turkish Tamburlaine . . . Now swooping inside robes of royalty | That erst did scrub in lousy brokery'. There is also the indecorum of the 'poor

---

[17] Cf. the response to a piece of deliberate bombast in the induction to Marston's *Antonio and Mellida*: 'Rampum, scrampum, mount tufty Tamburlaine! What rattling thunderclap breaks from his lips!' (ll. 86–7).

[18] The obvious analogous figure is Shakespeare's Ancient Pistol. 'His gift is a daemon possessing him with the conviction that he is essentially a . . . Tamburlaine', says Leslie Hotson (*Shakespeare's Sonnets Dated* (London, 1949), 61). Cf. Anne Barton, 'The King Disguised: Shakespeare's *Henry V* and the Comical History', in *The Triple Bond* (University Park, Pa., 1975), 100.

hearers . . . gazing scaffolders' whose 'hair quite upright sets' when they see 'the stalking steps of his great personage | Graced with huff-cap terms and thundering threats . . . big-sounding sentences and words of state':

> Then weeneth he his base drink-drowned spright
> Rapt to the threefold loft of heaven's height,
> When he conceives upon his feigned stage
> The stalking steps of his great personage.
>
> · · · · · · · ·
>
> He vaunts his voice upon a hired stage
> With high-set steps and princely carriage,
>
> · · · · · · · ·
>
> Then certes was the famous Cordoban
> Never but half so high tragedian
> There if he can with terms Italianate,
> Big-sounding sentences and words of state,
> Fair patch me up his pure iambic verse,
> He ravishes the gazing scaffolders.

The reaction of contemporaries that it was the style not the action that gave *Tamburlaine* its power,[19] and of later critics[20] that Marlowe's works are poems not plays, might seem to be justified by the language of the Prologue. When Marlowe tells his audience that he will lead them from jigging vein to stately militarism, he is, however, speaking as a dramatist, using poetry to make a social as well as a stylistic point (these two are regularly quite difficult to disentangle). Jigging verse and paid-for clownage belong together as lower-class amusements. 'Stately' is obviously a keyword in this distinction; it reappears in the printer's preface to *Tamburlaine*, called 'so honourable and stately a history', and Kyd in *The Spanish Tragedy* expands our sense of the usage:

> Fie! comedies are fit for common wits;
> But to present a kingly troop withal,
> Give me a stately-written tragedy;

---

[19] We should remember that 'poet' was the only word available to describe dramatic authorship (the word 'playwright' was not in use). Ben Jonson saw the vocal and physical aspects as two sides to one coin. He said that 'the Tamerlanes and Tamer-Chams of the late age . . . had nothing in them but the scenical strutting and furious vociferation to warrant them to the ignorant gapers' (*Discoveries*, Herford and Simpson, viii, § 777).

[20] See George Saintsbury, *History of Elizabethan Literature* (London, 1891), 78: 'It is impossible to call Marlowe a great dramatist . . . Marlowe was one of the greatest poets of the world whose work was cast by accident and caprice into the imperfect mould of drama.'

> Tragoedia cothurnata, fitting kings,
> Containing matter and not common things.
>
> (IV. i. 157–61)

Words like 'honourable', 'stately', 'kingly' all point in the same direction; such plays are not lower class; they keep at bay the reductive popularity of 'clownage' and 'common things'; they deal with what Kyd calls 'matter'—the serious affairs of the great world—in ways that are appropriate to an audience of kings, not one of 'common wits'.[21]

The alignment of Marlowe and Kyd with Sidney's *Apology* on this issue argues that we should see the Prologue to *Tamburlaine* as a self-conscious defence of 'right tragedy', even when the play involved lacks the formal characteristics of the classical models (the chorus, the unities, limitation on the number of actors, deaths off-stage, and so on).[22] Words like 'stately', 'kingly', 'astounding' refer primarily to a quality of tragic grandeur in the life projected (a quality that will elicit the favourite Renaissance idea of *admiratio*). In this sense we must allow that the rhetorical tone of *Tamburlaine* may dominate the structure but cannot be separated from it, the two aspects of the play cohering inside a single vision.

The claim to have moved away from popular taste towards something more noble (supposing that to be the claim made in the Prologue to *Tamburlaine*) looks distinctly curious in the context of the comments quoted above from contemporaries. A writer like Joseph Hall sees *Tamburlaine* as popular fustian, as a peasant's idea of dignity, not the thing itself. But in other, more strictly develop-mental, terms one can see that Marlowe has made a case. In the particular matter of 'clownage', which had seemed such an issue to Sidney and *Whetstone,[23] Marlowe could claim to have rectified what was wrong with his predecessors. The story of *Tamburlaine* is told from a remarkably consistent point of view, inside a unified

---

[21] This view should probably be associated with the doctrine that tragedy 'maketh kings fear to be tyrants' found in Sidney's *An Apology for Poetry* (ed. G. Shepherd (Manchester, 1965), 117), Sir Thomas Elyot's *The Book of the Governor* (ed. Ernest Rhys (London, 1907) 41), and Heywood's *Apology for Actors* (1612), sig. B2.

[22] Part I also lacks the usual tragic marker of the death of the hero—though Aristotle does not require this. The Prologue ends by asserting that we are looking in a 'tragic glass'; but we cannot be sure that the Prologue is not referring to the full two-part structure, ending in Tamburlaine's death.

[23] See the dedication of *Promos and Cassandra* (1578).

set of values, dignified as well as monomaniac. The printer of the first edition (1590) tells us that the play was originally performed with 'some fond and frivolous gestures' which 'haply . . . have been of some vain-conceited groundlings greatly gaped at'. It is not clear whether the 'gestures' were theatrical or textual elements. That Marlowe himself was reluctant to have them included (though he could not, of course, have prevented their publication) is strongly suggested by the uniform contempt for aesthetic impurities that links the Prologue and the printer's preface 'To the gentleman readers: and others that take pleasure in reading histories'. There is a clear pitch here for the educated reader: the 'fond and frivolous gestures', though 'they were shewed upon the stage in their graced deformities', would now 'seem more tedious unto the wise than any way else to be regarded . . . now to be mixtured in print with such matter of worth, it would prove a great disgrace to so honourable and stately a history'.

What Marlowe has achieved in *Tamburlaine*—an achievement especially obvious in Part I, but pervading the whole two-part structure—is poetic unity in a text whose 'dignity' is not stiff and formal (as in the preceding tragedies of the Inns of Court, such as *Jocasta*, *Gismond of Salerne*, *The Misfortunes of Arthur*) but 'spacious' enough (as Nashe says) to be perfectly capable of accommodating a variety of linguistic, social and generic effects inside a single dominant tonality.[24] Tamburlaine himself is by no means without humour—of his own grisly kind. His sardonic treatment of his victims, such as Mycetes, Bajazeth, and the virgins of Damascus, gives us something of the same sense of cruel randomness that we find in lower-class as well as tyrannical figures of earlier tragedy (Ruff, Huff, and Snuff in *Cambyses*, for example), but comic violence has now been made entirely consistent with the grandeur of power that this particular peasant (or shepherd) has obtained. Marlowe's really transforming innovation is an impersonal view of history which allows some to win while others lose, but avoids moral valuation of any individual's rulership. This allows his hero to appear both as a 'Scourge of God', a divinely programmed instrument of God's wrath against the corrupt world, and also as a self-pleasing Nietzschean superman who uses the

[24] Clemen (*English Tragedy*) makes the important point that Marlowe's poetry allows us to understand the loosely articulated and repetitive syntax as an occasion for spontaneous not preconditioned thought, enlarging itself by the process of being spoken.

sense of apocalypse surrounding him to degrade the defenceless and make games out of weakness. The gap that appeared in earlier tragedies between the high-life plot of princely fall from power and justification and the low-life plot of short-term comic inefficiency— comically inefficient even in cruelty and exploitation—had set the top-side view of violence and control against the bottom-side ('theirs' against 'ours' in popular audience terms), and this was proper enough, as a wholly believable image of 'how things are'. *Tamburlaine* takes this 'mongrel' form and assimilates destructiveness and magnificence, randomness and destiny, cruelty and control, inside a single style and a single character, simultaneously glamorous and repulsive, politically realist but also fantasy-ridden and self-indulgent.

Tamburlaine's own speeches everywhere juxtapose terror and beauty, pairing blood and guts with poetic contemplation. We may observe the characteristic mixture in lines such as

> Whose shattered limbs, being tossed as high as heaven,
> Hang in the air as thick as sunny motes
>
> (Part 2, III. ii. 100–1)

or

> Our conquering swords shall marshal us the way
> We use to march upon the slaughtered foe,
> Trampling their bowels with our horses' hooves—
> Brave horses, bred on the white Tartarian hills:
> .   .   .   .
> Legions of spirits fleeting in the air
> Direct our bullets and our weapons' points
> And make our strokes to wound the senseless air,
> And when she sees our bloody colours spread,
> Then victory begins to take her flight
> Resting herself upon my milk-white tent.
>
> (Part I, III. iii. 148–61)

The same effect is procured in such episodes as the paean to beauty and poetry in Act V, Scene ii, of Part I (set between the murder of the virgins of Damascus and the tormenting of Bajazeth), the burning of towns in Part II to signify undying love for Zenocrate ('the houses burnt will look as if they mourned'), the speeches 'all air and fire' spoken from a chariot pulled by captive kings.

Part I ends when Tamburlaine 'takes truce with all the world'.
But the 'truce' has little power in plot terms. Tamburlaine's discovery that

> Every warrior that is rapt with love
> Of fame, of valour, and of victory,
> Must needs have beauty beat on his conceits
>
> (v. i. 180–2)

allows us to hear the claim that militarism and love are now in
balance. And certainly by that point we are willing to admit the
need for a rest. But, like a rest in music, this is only a breath before
the completion of the phrase: the war breaks out again at the very
beginning of Part II. The emphasis on aspiration, striving, upward
mobility, and consequently on the instability of the great world,
has been too continuous to allow us to believe in oaths and treaties.
This is a royal world, but not seen as a heaven of magnanimity and
justice; only as an unceasing struggle between different levels of
energy, whose consequence is the plot, and whose expression is the
verse.

Tamburlaine is a play written not only in a particular kind of
verse but in verse written for a particular kind of acting. The voice
of the actor must impose on the audience the same mixture of
admiration and alienation that fictional characters respond to inside the play. Edward Alleyn, who played Tamburlaine and Faustus
and the Jew of Malta, and probably Kyd's Hieronimo as well, has
acquired a reputation as something of an Elizabethan barnstormer,
loud of voice, commanding of presence, athletic in movement.
Certainly these qualities cannot be considered a disadvantage for
the performer of Tamburlaine; but the list by no means exhausts
the capacities that the part of Tamburlaine demands, or that Alleyn
possessed (after all, he played Dr Faustus). Shewring and Barker
have shown how far the verse-speaking of Tamburlaine requires an
extraordinary combination of force and control, more in the mode
of opera than of the modern stage, if the combination of line and
paragraph rhythms is to be mastered.[25] Let us take a comparatively
low-level piece of functional verse—Tamburlaine's threats against
the conquered Turkish kings in Part II:

[25] M. Shewring and C. Barker, 'The Theatre Poetry of Christopher Marlowe, with
specific reference to *Tamburlaine*, Part I and Part II', an unpublished presentation to the
Shakespeare Institute of the University of Birmingham, 28 May 1981.

> I will, with engines never exercised,
> Conquer, sack, and utterly consume
> Your cities and your golden palaces,
> And with the flames that beat against the clouds
> Incense the heavens and make the stars to melt,
> As if they were the tears of Mahomet
> For hot consumption of his country's pride;
> And till by vision or by speech I hear
> Immortal Jove say 'Cease, my Tamburlaine',
> I will persist a terror to the world,
> Making the meteors that, like armèd men,
> Are seen to march upon the towers of heaven,
> Run tilting round about the firmament
> And break their burning lances in the air
> For honour of my wondrous victories.
>
> (Part II, IV. i. 191–205)

The quality that makes such lines as these new and exciting in the history of Elizabethan dramatic language is not, in spite of what is often said, the fact that they are iambic pentameters unrhymed (*Gorboduc* had offered that unexciting metric twenty five years earlier). It is rather the power they offer the actor to combine a rhythmic forward drive with a repetitive affirmation, projecting individual claim to power, on the one hand, and a ceremonial endorsement of it, on the other. The fifteen-line passage quoted above forms a single sentence (as in Fredson Bowers's punctuation), demanding sustained vocal control. Yet the lines accumulate as separate powerful hammer-blows with an obvious recurrent pattern, see-sawing very often in a double hemistich structure based on two cognate nouns (cities . . . palaces, vision . . . speech, flames . . . clouds, heavens . . . stars, consumption . . . pride, meteors . . . men, honour . . . victories) often emphasizing the see-saw by alliteration (conquer . . . consume, consumption . . . country, meteors . . . men) and cadenced with the characteristic Marlovian dactylic rhythm (exercise, palaces, armèd men, firmament, victories), most characteristically an exotic personal name (Màhomet, Tamburlaine). But it is not only the rhythm of the 'mighty lines' that shows this instinct for the balance of forward drive with repetitive stasis. The structure of the whole passage is balanced between two sections, one of seven lines, one of six lines, each beginning 'I will' and each magnifying earthly terror by moving quickly to apocalyptic images of the heavens consumed by flames. The two sections hinge, it will be noticed, on the single limitation on total power and total terror that is allowed, the concessive couplet:

> And till by vision or by speech I hear
> Immortal Jove say 'Cease, my Tamburlaine'.

The destructive advance of this terror among men is at the same time an integrated part of the divine plan and the divine stasis. Tamburlaine's rage among men seems to be forever advancing, and yet does not move at all.

The Sons of Tamburlaine

It can hardly surprise us that this powerfully alienating and yet totally self-assured vision acted with a force of revelation on Marlowe's contemporaries. The attempts to imitate *Tamburlaine* indicate both the immediate urge to repeat the success and the difficulty of replicating a model in which all aspects of the dramaturgy reflect one another. The point may be made in personal no less than literary terms, for Marlowe is one of the few Elizabethan dramatists whose work seems understandable as a personal vision no less than as a contribution to the repertory. As I have already noted (pp. 22–8), the raffish and 'bohemian' lives of Greene and Nashe reflect their marginal social status as educated outsiders; Greene and Nashe, however, both send out clear signals that they accept the underlying assumptions of the status quo which excludes them. But Marlowe's commitment to the 'outside', all the evidence suggests, was unrelenting. His relationship to his contemporaries seems to have been as much an alienated cat-and-mouse game as his relationship with his dramatic characters. As Thomas Kyd reports in the second confession he supplied to Lord Keeper Puckering: 'all which [blasphemies] he would so suddenly take slight occasion to slip out, as I and many others, in regard of his other sudden rashness in attempting sudden privy injuries to men, did overslip.'[26] In other words, Marlowe delighted to trap his companions into agreeing with or assenting to the blasphemies he proposed to them, which they tended to allow because of their fear that he might stab them if they disagreed with him. Such

---

[26] See F. S. Boas, *Christopher Marlowe* (Oxford, 1940), 243.

characteri\stics are well suited to the work he probably undertook
as a spy in the Jesuit seminary at Rheims—work which must again
have drav n on cold-hearted ability to play games with the lives of
his companions, taking on the role of a disaffected English Catholic,
wheedling confidences from Jesuit aspirants, and reporting all to
his spymasters in London. Such a diamond-hard temperament,
taste for extremity, obsessive contempt for human weakness, cynical
detachment from ends but fascination with the technical means by
which moral preference is expressed—all this is well suited to the
construction of a particular kind of drama, of great power and great
inner consistency, demanding imitation but almost inimitable.

I have argued that *Tamburlaine* was a model that showed how
Humanist learning could be employed in popular entertainment,
redefining dramatic possibility by redefining the audience's capacity for empathy. But many plays had to be written before the
example could be reconciled with the more usual definition of
theatrical consensus. Not only the narrow intensity of the model
but the innate conservatism of the theatre, the desire to stay with
the known and the safe, to offer the audience a little bit of everything (including bits of *Tamburlaine*), all counted against any whole-
sale change. When the great plague of 1593–4 destroyed much of
the theatrical life of the capital (see pp. 359–60) a great number of
plays that broken-up companies could no longer perform were
released for publication; and the repertory that is thus revealed
provides an interesting picture of the diversity of the fare that was
presumably on offer in the period preceding 1593. One particular
set of texts has been associated with the Queen's Men, once the
premier company in town but by this point at the end of their
metropolitan life.[27] The plays in this list—the unassigned *King
Leir, Selimus, Clyomon and Clamydes, The Famous Victories of Henry
V, The True Tragedy of Richard III, The Lamentable Tragedy of
Locrine* ('By W.S.'), Peele's *The Old Wife's Tale*, Greene's *Friar
Bacon and Friar Bungay* and *James IV*, Wilson's *The Cobbler's
Prophecy, A Looking Glass for London and England* by Greene and
Lodge—give us a revealing picture of the range of tastes being
catered for: some plays by the University Wits, some by profes-
sional players, some showing the influence of *Tamburlaine*, some

[27] See G. M. Pinciss, 'Thomas Creede and the Repertory of the Queen's Men, 1583–
1592', *MP* 67 (1970), 321–30.

quite innocent of it. A historian of drama would naturally wish to put these plays in some kind of developmental sequence, but there is no evidence that the public or the companies wished to see the new drama drive out the old. The evidence of the repertories in Henslowe's Diary suggests that the post-1594 companies were entirely pragmatic; no doubt they assumed that a variety of fare (old and new) was likely to tempt a variety of appetites.[28] In these terms it should not surprise us that the drama after *Tamburlaine* offers us a spectrum rather than a history. This is not to say that there was no change or development. There was; and *Tamburlaine* was a principal element in it. But the central effort, it would seem, was to articulate novelty inside familiar perspectives, mixing old saws with 'modern' instances.

Of the tragedies that were released in 1594, the most obviously 'old fashioned' is *The Lamentable Tragedy of Locrine* (1591×1595).[29] Its poetic mode derives from Spenser's *Complaints* (printed 1591) and *The Mirror for Magistrates* (first printed 1559), and the dramatic structure goes back to such earlier academic tragedies as *Gorboduc* of 1562 and *The Misfortunes of Arthur* of 1588. Like these, *Locrine* is (as is its contemporary, *King Leir*) a fable of national unity, of order and disorder, of the internecine quarrels that nearly destroy the royal family, and so the nation. Brutus, who brought the Trojan dynasty to Troynovant or London, dies in Act I, exacting from his son Locrine a promise to preserve family cohesion. The cohesion works well enough to defeat the invading Scythians (also called Huns and Troglodytes)—whose Emperor 'leads Fortune tied in a chain of gold'—but it breaks down when Locrine abandons the wife prescribed by his father, preferring the Hunnish princess, Elstrid. One disloyalty leads to another until the whole royal line is decimated.

The effect of *Tamburlaine* on this antique structure is linguistic and incidental, heavily dependent on strings of geographical and mythological names:

> I'll pass the Alps to wat'ry Meroe,
> Where fiery Phoebus in his chariot,

---

[28] The lists of unprinted plays 'reserved' by the Master of the Revels for the King's Men and Beeston's Boys in 1641 and 1639 (see Bentley, *JCS* i. 65–6, 330–1) show that the mixture of old and new remained a feature of the repertory up to the closing of the theatres.

[29] We know the play was still on the boards in 1595, since the epilogue prays for the Queen in the thirty-eighth year of her reign.

> The wheels whereof are decked with emeralds,
> Cast such a heat, yea such a scorching heat,
> And spoileth Flora of her chequered grass;
> I'll overrun the mountain Caucasus,
> Where fell Chimaera
>
> .   .   .   .
>
> I'll pass the frozen zone, where icy flakes
> Stopping the passage of the fleeting ships,
> Do lie like mountains in the congealed sea.
>
> (ll. 856–67)

These gaudy trappings are not, however, allowed to interfere with the play's older system of dramatic organization, based on the string of peripeteias that fortune imposes on the action, as pride and vaunt, leading to battle, lead on to complaint and suicide by the vanquished and new hubris by the victors (thus setting the wheel turning for the next peripeteia). Tamburlainian hubris is thus released in speech only to be cut down in actions which, in their formal and repetitive nature, describe a world of Complaint, of continual mutability. The extraordinarily formal dramatic structure suggests indeed that the action exists only for the sake of the situations it can generate. Each of the five acts marks a specific stage in the story and also displays one particular moral exemplum, set out at the beginnings of the acts in moralizing dumbshows explicated by Ate, the goddess of discord, who here (as in *Jocasta*, *The Arraignment of Paris*, *Caesar and Pompey*) represents the general threat that the energies of life cannot be reduced to order or system.

Robert Greene's *The Comical History of Alphonsus, King of Aragon* (1587×1588; printed 1599) shows the example of *Tamburlaine* having a much more invasive and destructive effect, in a work that is nearer to a repeat than an imitation. Greene's play was no doubt designed to catch the same wave as Marlowe's ('if you liked *Tamburlaine* you will like this'). But it is soon apparent that Greene's talents will not support the role of a duplicate Marlowe. It is presumably to *Alphonsus* that he refers when he tells us that he has been thought incapable of making his 'verses jet upon the stage in tragical buskins'; but if he lacks resonant poetry, he loses the justification for Tamburlaine-like actions, and so can only show a trail of events without motives. Alphonsus begins, like his model, as an outsider with everything to win. But Greene has not the daring to make him a real outsider. His hero turns out to be that good old romance standby, the legitimate heir unjustly exiled (as in *Common Conditions*, for example) and seeking only to reinstate his father. He is employed (like Tamburlaine) by a Cosroe figure who hopes to defeat a Mycetes lookalike, and, once again, with a victorious army under his command, he can seize the crown. Again, as in *Tamburlaine*, the transfer of power is achieved by the hero's ability to persuade various generals to abandon their former employer. But here the persuasion derives not from an eloquent new vision of *virtù* but from old loyalties to the former ruling house. Greene's transfer of the weight of the plot from intensity of self-projection to continuity of conventional action means that the *Tamburlaine* narrative is soon exhausted.[30] Alphonsus crowns his tributary kings in the Marlovian manner; but then the defeated Cosroe figure flies to Turkey and becomes a client to Amurack, the Great Turk, and the conflict can start over again. *Tamburlaine*'s plot is no less repetitive, but the brilliance of response its protagonist brings to one challenge after another makes each event seem new.

Greene's subordination of the force of individual *virtù* to the explanatory framework fits his play neatly into an older theatrical mode. As in *The Rare Triumphs of Love and Fortune*, *The Cobbler's Prophecy*, and *A Looking Glass for London and England*, the action of *Alphonsus* is bound together by a framing device of supernatural manipulators who tell us what will happen and moralize the consequence. The play opens with the descent of the goddess Venus: 'After you have sounded thrice, let Venus be let down from the top of the stage, and when she is down, say . . .', and it ends with her ascent: 'Exit Venus; or if you can conveniently, let a chair come down from the top of the stage and draw her up.' At crucial points Venus is joined by the nine Muses, who, in an induction, debate with her the fate of heroic poetry in an age of cultural decline. Calliope is an outcast member of the sorority until Venus, with the unsung virtue of Alphonsus on her mind, acts as her sponsor. The goddesses then retreat to Parnassus, where they will witness/write the play that follows. Clearly Greene wishes to present his hero's *virtù* as guaranteed not by the quality of his utterance but under the aegis of an heroic poetry tradition which can be evoked even if it cannot be exemplified.

---

[30] In spite of this it appears that Greene contemplated a second part. In the Epilogue Venus promises to return 'to finish up his [Alphonsus's] life'.

Greene's second attempt in the Marlovian mode, *The History of Orlando Furioso* (1588–92), is available to us only in a form so obviously garbled that it would be foolish to say anything too categorical about it. But the very choice of Ariosto's epic (and of these elements out of Ariosto's epic) implies fairly clearly that Greene's attitude to the 'epic' world of *Tamburlaine* has been revised. The mad Orlando is a figure who, in a recurrently Ariostan fashion, straddles the borderline between the heroic and the comic. The effect of this deflating mode on the epic rhetoric of Tamburlaine thus comes to look appropriate to a self-conscious enjoyment of the heroic absurd. Una Ellis-Fermor, in her enlightening discussion of Marlowe and Greene,[31] makes the point that Greene's parodic versions of Marlovian rhetoric are closer to the original than his 'straight' imitations. By means of parody Greene has given himself the space to acknowledge the resistance his own style creates, so allowing him to develop his own style by a process of assimilation. Greene's *Orlando Furioso* is at its most Tamburlainian in the speeches of Sacrepant, the self-glorifying villain of the piece. But Sacrepant's villainy owes more to comedy than to tragedy: his exchanges with servants and messengers show him as a *miles gloriosus* rather than a tyrant, and signal to us that we are free to enjoy the excesses of his melodrama without fear of what it will lead to. This is shown clearly in his self-conscious run through the standard topics of ambition:

> Sweet are the thoughts that smother from conceit:
> For when I come and set me down to rest
> My chair presents a throne of majesty;
> And when I set my bonnet on my head
> Methinks I fit my forehead for a crown;
> And when I take my truncheon in my fist
> A sceptre then comes tumbling in my thoughts.
> My dreams are princely, all of diadems.
> Honour: methinks the title is too base—
> Mighty, glorious, and excellent—
> Ay, these my glorious Genius sound within my mouth;
> These please the ear and with a sweet applause
> Makes me in terms co-equal with the gods.
>
> (ll. 257–69)

---

[31] Una Ellis-Fermor, 'Marlowe and Greene', in D. C. Allen (ed.), *Studies in Honor of T. W. Baldwin* (Urbana, Ill., 1958), 136–49.

The evil deeds that mark the progress of Sacrepant's ambition—centrally tale-telling that Angelica loves Medor, so causing the excessively heroic Orlando to lose his wits—are more comic than fearful. Greene has caught from Ariosto something of the nursery charm of giants and ogres whose frightening qualities are half-reality and half-self-indulgence, the mind being invited to amusement at its own capacity for empathy. The positive power that Greene preserved from Marlowe into the writing of his best plays, the comedy *Friar Bacon and Friar Bungay* and the romantic history *James IV*, gave him just this ability to find the rhetoric of passion both impressive and amusing, to invite our enjoyment of human capacity to fall into eloquence without requiring us either to scoff or to be swept off our feet.

1 Tamburlaine presents itself self-consciously as a challenge to the tradition of earlier public drama. It was a challenge that made a great impact; but (as so often in revolutionary manifestos) the real changes were effected by subsequent compromise rather than initial statement. The play remained a towering monument of theatrical potential, but the mixed modes it denounced were never really exiled from the stage; and Tamburlaine's heroic rhetoric, in so far as it survived, survived as only one mode among many. Thus the opening of *A Looking Glass for London and England* (1587×1591), written by Greene and Lodge, strikes an immediately familiar note:

Enter RASNI, *King of Nineveh, with the three* KINGS OF CILICIA, CRETE, *and* PAPHLAGONIA, *from the overthrow of Jeroboam, King of Jerusalem.*

> RASNI. So pace ye on, triumphant warriors;
> Make Venus' leman, arm'd in all his pomp,
> Bash at the brightness of your hardy looks,
> For you the viceroys are the cavaliers,
> That wait on Rasni's royal mightiness:
> Boast, petty kings, and glory in your fates,
> That stars have made your fortunes climb so high,
> To give attent on Rasni's excellence.
>
> · · · · · · · ·
>
> Great Jewry's God, that foil'd stout Benhadab,
> Could not rebate the strength that Rasni brought;
> For be he God in heaven, yet, viceroys, know,
> Rasni is god on earth, and none but he.
>
> (ll. 1–30)

The pomp of Rasni is, however, only one facet of *A Looking Glass for London and England*, and by no means the dominant one. As the title tells us, the play is designed as a moral mirror which will show its audience the deformities of the contemporary London and England. Its purpose, that is, is identical with that of the Estates Morality form spoken of above, and one strand of the action at least shows life in terms very similar to *The Three Ladies of London*—the usurer despoils both the clown and the gentleman; the lawyer and the judge are venal; the life of the tavern turns on boasting and lechery and eventually murder. The court of Rasni, King of Nineveh, is, of course, very remote from anything found in *The Three Ladies of London*, but the biblical context of Jewish history gives the tyrant's grandeur an explicit moral meaning that links it with both its own low-life scenes and the modern counterparts in London and England. Hosea, set above the stage by an angel, is tireless in his prophetic denunciations of sin and its consequence; and Jonah, arriving by whale, preaches repentance with such force that sinners no sooner hear his words than they resolve to change their ways. The scenic splendours of the play (characters struck by lightning, swallowed by subterranean fire, arbours raised by magic, a hand carrying the sword of vengeance suddenly manifested in the air) are not, as in *Tamburlaine*, the consequence of human achievement but are the signs of God's presence and pressure on the world. Rasni may accept his priests' explanations that these are the phenomena of Nature, but we are meant to know better and to anticipate the final supernatural intervention. The glory of Rasni, when seen in the biblical context, is mainly handled as a moral exemplum, not as a challenge to moral standards (as in *David and Bethsabe*, discussed pp. 60–3). His actions are compromised by their dependence on the flattering parasite, Radagon, and his wives. The Marlovian rhetorical pigment is one touch here, placed peripherally not centrally, in a structure that returns us to the diffuse mode of pre-*Tamburlaine* dramaturgy—the mode that the Prologue to *Tamburlaine* claimed to be superseding.

Thomas Lodge's *The Wounds of Civil War* (1587×1592) is one of the best of these post-*Tamburlaine* tragedies, drawing on the resonance of Marlowe's hyperbole, but placing it once again in a framework which 'explains' the individual drive as only one part of a balanced system.[32] What is especially effective in Lodge's play is

---

[32] Cf. Clemen, *English Tragedy*, 134–40.

the structure of the system, supplied on this occasion by the Roman state at the time of the civil war between Marius and Sulla. The presence of *Tamburlaine* is particularly obvious in the presentation of Sulla ['Scilla']. He appears in 'his chair triumphant of gold, drawn by four Moors', and his stated intention to harness the captured client kings of Mithridates 'to draw like oxen in a plough' seems to be repeating Marlowe, even though Sulla changes his mind and has the princelings put to death instead.[33] Less precisely imitative, but perhaps more telling, is his rhetoric of self-glorification:

> You Roman soldiers, fellow mates in arms,
> The blindfold mistress of incertain chance
> Hath turn'd these traitorous climbers from the top
> And seated Scilla in the chieftest place,
> The place beseeming Scilla and his mind.
> For were the throne where matchless glory sits
> Impal'd with furies threat'ning blood and death,
> Begirt with famine and those fatal fears
> That dwell below amidst the dreadful vast,
> Tut, Scilla's sparkling eyes should dim with clear
> The burning brands of their consuming light,
> And master fancy with a forward mind,
> And mask repining fear with awful power.
> For men of baser metal and conceit
> Cannot conceive the beauty of my thought.
> I, crowned with a wreath of warlike state,
> Imagine thoughts more greater than a crown,
> And yet befitting well a Roman mind.
>
> (II. i. 1–18)

Even here, however, as the last line indicates, Lodge is reading *Tamburlaine* in an unMarlovian focus: fortune rather than *virtù* is the decisive agent; and as in later Roman plays (see Chapter 9), personal power appears as a political phenomenon, and this leads us to judge success from a distanced and generalized point of view. Lodge sees Sulla's dictatorship as one kind of political achievement; but he also indicates that politics will not yield more than temporarily to any one mode of control. He is returning to the old pattern of Fortune's wheel, as now Marius succeeds and now

---

[33] The chariot pulled by kings appears, before *Tamburlaine*, in Gascoigne's *Jocasta* (1566), where it is said to derive from the practice of Sesostris, king of Egypt. So Lodge's usage cannot be definitively associated with Marlowe. See E. M. Waith, 'Marlowe and the Jades of Asia', *SEL* 5 (1965), 229–45; R. Cockcroft, 'Emblematic Irony: Some Possible Significances of Tamburlaine's Chariot', *Renaissance and Modern Studies*, 12 (1968), 33–55.

Sulla, but with the Tamburlainian difference that fortune is now being seized, not imposed (as in *Locrine*). What holds both sides together is the complexity of the Roman system, whose checks and balances ensure that change is always more likely than conquest. Lodge offers us something like a political version of the Estates Morality, showing successively the time-serving or compromising activities of some politicians, the severe or idealistic intransigence of others, the bullying of generals, the timorous pliability of one ally (Minturnum), the resoluteness of another (Praeneste), the fate of eloquence in Mark Anthony (the elder), and of female *Romanitas* in Sulla's wife and daughter. And these alternatives are never fixed in any evaluative hierarchy. All we are given is the traditional moralism that society cannot be relied on and that greatness has no stability. Marius and Sulla are both allowed some degree of super-natural congratulation, but there is no sense that their acts are being endorsed. Both leave the world at the moment of their su-preme achievement, visited by messengers from 'heaven' who tell them it is time to quit. Clearly Lodge sought to highlight these moments and compressed his sources to achieve the effect. Marius, now elected consul for the seventh time, is seated in a pleasant grove surrounded by 'frolic citizens'. Seven eagles suddenly ap-pear; with 'reverent smile' he acknowledges the portent and feels 'the deadly pangs approach'. One act later Sulla finally achieves election as perpetual dictator; but almost immediately he notices that his dead enemies are now secure from 'Fortune's laughs or lours' while he is not. He plans to retire from the instability of success to a 'country cave'. But before he can do so, Genius ap-pears and pronounces Latin palindromes, telling him that what grew up must run down; he makes testamentary arrangements, dies and is celebrated. If Lodge is imitating *Tamburlaine*, he must be allowed not only to have politicized but also to have remoralized the story of success. Marlowe certainly allows for the instability of greatness, seeing power as less a state than a process that 'Wills us to wear ourselves and never rest'. But, where Tamburlaine finds this marvellously exhilarating, Lodge notes the weariness it pro-duces. In that strangely Büchner-like scene in Act V where Sulla, now withdrawn from the dictatorship, has to deal with the 'two burghers', Poppey and Curtall, and the case of the daughter im-pregnated by 'a soldier of yours', Lodge shows how illusory is even the hope to retire. The only stability he shows lies in the grave.

The Wounds of Civil War presents individual aspiration as a glamorous human characteristic but treats it as only one among the several possibilities that politics must allow for. Roman history provides a framework that encourages but also defuses the self-assertion of the heroic individual. *The First Part of the Tragical Reign of Selimus, Emperor of the Turks* (1591×1594), often ascribed to Greene, can also be called a political play.[34] But the conditions that allow Lodge to show Sulla's drive towards tyranny inside a political order that can contain it are very different from those of a play about near-contemporary politics, in which the title-page draws our attention to the fact that the Selimus we see on the stage was 'grandfather to him that now reigneth'.[35]

The invitation to the audience is to beware. Tamburlaine's career could have been presented as another oriental horror story of uncheckable power, but the dazzling language of the play as written keeps our attention focused on the conqueror, not on his victims. Tamburlaine's rise is presented as a non-political phenomenon; he moves through the world like a force of nature, a hurricane or a pestilence; and this tends to disable moral judgement. But the space in the audience's sympathy for anti-social aspiration can hardly be sustained in situations defined as clear and present danger. The story of *1 Selimus* is predicated entirely on the premiss that what is set before us is the real politics of a real political Hell of Muhammadism, violence and treachery, designed, as Painter tells us in his parallel treatment, 'to renew the ancient detestation which we have, and which our progenitors had, against that horrible Termagant and persecutor of Christians'.[36] And so this is a scene in which the audience is bound to identify with the victims, for it is they who reflect the position of the contemporary European powers, watching the inexorable and inexplicable Turkish advance and seeing it as fuelled by a system in which political and military efficiency must be judged the product of devil-worship.

At the end of the play (and of his life), Corcut, the retired and scholarly brother to Selimus, reveals that he has become a Christian

---

[34] *Selimus* and *Locrine* share a number of lines, and both plays draw poetry from Spenser's *The Faerie Queene* and *Complaints*. See *Locrine*, ed. Jane L. Gooch (New York, 1981), app. C.

[35] The 100th novel of William Painter's augmented *Palace of Pleasure* (1580), in its title calls its tragical tyrant 'Sultan Solyman, late the emperor of the Turks and father of Selym that now reigneth'. (see *The Palace of Pleasure* (4 vols.; London, 1929), iv. 200).

[36] Ibid.

convert, and from this advantageous standpoint he prophesies doom.[37] Even without his confirmation, it would be clear that *1 Selimus* offers us a looking-glass for London and England designed not to convert but to appal. The escape hatch left to the audience is, of course, the memory that Providence is on Our Side. Yet the image of dynastic history as a hell of ambition, betrayal, and murder which we find in *1 Selimus* is interestingly close (even when moderated to a domestic tone of voice) to the image of English history which Shakespeare was elaborating in these same years in the three parts of *Henry VI*.

If George Peele's *The Love of King David and Fair Bethsabe. With the Tragedy of Absolon* (c.1581×1594) had been first performed, as the Harbage–Schoenbaum *Annals'* composite date suggests, in the same year as *1 Tamburlaine* and *The Spanish Tragedy*—1587—this must have been a year of multiple innovation. Some of the rhetoric of the play suggests that Peele may have had *Tamburlaine* in mind; if so, we may argue that he has deliberately constructed an anti-*Tamburlaine* play, the story of a king whose strength must be seen not as the imposition of individual vision on the world around him but rather as a capacity to accept and even rejoice in the vicissitudes imposed upon him, caught as he is between individual desire and the requirements of a God-given office, in the Christian cycle, that is, of temptation, fall, repentance, and forgiveness. Peele gives us a somewhat disjointed account of the well-known events of David's life as found in the second book of Samuel, events that had been handled in diverse ways by many Humanist authors.[38] But Peele seems not to be following any of these previous treatments. His concern is less with the king than with the psalmist, 'Israel's sweetest singer', concentrating on his 'holy style' rather than his 'happy victories', and drawing his theme principally from the penitential psalms, traditionally understood as meditations on David's relations with Bethsabe and the consequences thereof. David's willingness to sin in order to possess Bethsabe is explicated by Peele as part of the paradox that the beauty the poet responds to is both holy and sinful, desired and forbidden. The pursuit of this point brings Peele close to Marlowe. In Act V of *1 Tamburlaine* we hear that Zenocrate's sorrows

---

[37] The Epilogue also promises that a Part II 'shall greater murders tell'.
[38] See I.-S. Ewbank, 'The House of David in Renaissance Drama', *Renaissance Drama*, 8 (1965), 3–40.

lay more siege unto my soul
Than all my army to Damascus walls.

(v. i. 155–6)

and this reminds Tamburlaine of the power of poetry to carry
feeling beyond the point of rational control. But to feel this, he
says, is to sin against his nature:

> But how unseemly is it for my sex
>
> .   .   .   .
>
> To harbour thoughts effeminate and faint,
> Save only that in beauty's just applause,
> With whose instinct the soul of man is touched
> And every warrior that is rapt with love
> Of fame, of valour and of victory
> Must needs have beauty beat on his conceits . . .

(v. i. 174–82)

In *Tamburlaine*, this is only a moment. Having raised the point, the
hero immediately assumes power to close it down: he can deal with
both impulses, because he himself is both accuser and defender.
But Peele has chosen to write a play in which God is the accuser;
man may rebel, but rebellion can hardly be presented in such a
context as other than a prelude to repentance. David's rapture at
the beauty of Bethsabe and the poetry in which he expresses it must
be modulated into the joy of accepting and praising whatever God
decrees. And the pattern is endemic: it repeats itself in the story of
Absolon, David's 'beauteous son'. Refusal to exact full punishment
for Absolon's murder of Ammon leads directly to David's loss of
the throne that God has entrusted to him. Solomon, the chosen
of the Lord, must take over the power, but 'Absolon, the beauty of
my bones, | Fair Absolon, the counterfeit of Love, | Sweet Absolon,
the image of content' (ll. 1683–5) continues to be the emotional
focus of David's life. David, the chosen of God, and David, driven
by the force of individual choice, poetic and passionate, are inseparable and yet are continually at odds with one another.

The poetry of the Bible and particularly that of the Song of
Songs provided Peele with a model of languorous and exotic sen-
suality quite opposite to the activist energy of Marlowe's verse.
Even when the two poets are at their closest, as in the praises of
Bethsabe and Zenocrate, it is easy to see how the poetry points in
opposite directions. Here is Tamburlaine's first praise of Zenocrate:

> Zenocrate, lovelier than the love of Jove,
> Brighter than is the silver Rhodope,
> Fairer than whitest snow of Scythian hills,
> Thy person is more worth to Tamburlaine
> Than the possession of the Persian crown,
> Which gracious stars have promised at my birth.
> A hundred Tartars shall attend on thee,
> Mounted on steeds swifter than Pegasus.
> Thy garments shall be made of Median silk,
> Enchased with precious jewels of mine own,
> More rich and valurous than Zenocrate's.
> With milk-white harts upon an ivory sled
> Thou shalt be drawn amidst the frozen pools
> And scale the icy mountains' lofty tops,
> Which with thy beauty will be soon resolved.

(I. ii. 87–101)

And here is David's praise of Bethsabe:

> Now comes my lover tripping like the roe,
> And brings my longings tangled in her hair.
> To joy her love I'll build a kingly bower
> Seated in hearing of a hundred streams
> That for their homage to her sovereign joys
> Shall as the serpents fold into their nests
> In oblique turnings wind their nimble waves
> About the circles of her curious walks,
> And with their murmur summon easeful sleep
> To lay his golden sceptre on her brows.
> Open the doors and entertain my love;
> Open I say, and as you open, sing:
> 'Welcome, fair Bethsabe, King David's darling'.

(ll. 115–27)

Marlowe's frozen splendours carry Zenocrate out of the possibility of human contact, out into a glittering and bleached landscape glimpsed as in silent flight through icy mountains and ecstatic isolating transformations. We are given the impression that the stronger the poetic pressure the more depersonalized is the individual's hold on its reality. Peele, on the other hand, presents love as a process of enclosure, and slowing down. The movement is centripetal, into the bower, the nest, the marriage space inside the doors. And nature joins human desire in this movement: hair entangles, the streams infold the walks, the snakes knot into smaller space; at the centre is the immobile warmth of oneness.

We may see the contrast between the two protagonists as a version of a further contrast between the creative power of the artist who seeks to give local habitation and familiar shape to remote experience and that of another kind of creator whose energy defamiliarizes the expectable. The king–poet, directed towards God but dependent on the sensory stimulus of beauty, mirrors, though in extreme form, the natural dilemma of fallen human nature, drawn forward to the beauty that seems to speak of God but is forbidden by God. Yet at the same time he mirrors human capacity for salvation (in contrast to Tamburlaine's self-sufficiency and 'hardness of heart'). In the play, as in the Psalms, David's sins are part of the immediacy of his relation to the divine. And it is thus that he can survive to the end and hand on his inheritance to Solomon (though the child of sin) and so eventually to the 'man of sorrows', Jesus Christ.

David and Bethsabe marks what may be regarded as a limit of university wit. And it is presumably significant that the limit is created not by secular power but by religious assumption. The poet is the servant of God and his assertion of individual vision is at its frailest when it encounters the framework of divine command. It is equally significant that the power of Marlowe's assertion is equated by contemporaries with his 'atheism'. The personality to which his coevals responded in this way has, however, seemed to critics of later ages to be merely representative and to embody all those aspects of the Renaissance that made it opposite to the supposed consensus of the Middle Ages—individualist, self-glorifying, scornful of convention. But when we move from our sense of the man to an examination of the plays, the clear-cut image begins to fade. Earlier Elizabethan drama was marked, as I have already noted, by the diffuseness of its organization, not simply in the mixture of tragedy and comedy, kings and clowns, as often remarked, but also in the complex alternation between innumerable characters of varied geographical and social backgrounds, historical and modern, symbolic and realistic. *1 Tamburlaine* offers the popular theatre a challengingly new pattern in which the whole action is dominated by a single character whose defiance of Fortune is never countermanded. But judged by the subsequent history of Elizabethan tragedy, the new hero did not create a dynasty. Certainly even Marlowe's own career shows continuous compromise with the forms and expectations of the drama which preceded him.

Of course it is not hard to find the *Tamburlaine* vision repeated in *Doctor Faustus*, *The Jew of Malta*, and *The Massacre at Paris*, and perhaps anticipated in *Dido, Queen of Carthage*. All show the same fascination with power, not with power derived from legitimate institutions but with the power of individual will to transform society into a mere externalization of personal vision. They all show situations where the corrupt and decadent possessors of power are ripe for replacement by new sources of individual energy. Overweening and overreaching self-confidence give to Barabas, Faustus, and the Guise a heroic flamboyance that allows them to dominate their plays and their audiences with a hubristic rhetoric of self-justifying demand and promise.

Yet these revolutionary bearers of *virtù* are all (except in the case of *1 Tamburlaine*) diverted from purity of will by having to acknowledge the conditions within which success alone is possible. They are differentiated from one another mainly by their different compromises between the basic Marlovian model and the 'mongrel' tendencies that still dominated the theatre. 'Fond and frivolous gestures' may have been expunged from the printed text of *Tamburlaine*, but they reappear in the clown scenes of *Doctor Faustus* (even in the less clownish, and often preferred, 1604 text), and are completely integrated into the career of the Jew of Malta. Modern readers are particularly troubled that the 'noble', 'humanistic', or 'scientific' aspirations of Faustus (the easiest character for an academic readership to find sympathetic) are so soon ensnared in the tedious triviality of Rafe and Robin and reduced to tricks and games, even if played with popes and emperors. But it is clear from all these plays that the poetic intensity of Marlowe's atheistic and anti-establishment vision was by no means incompatible with 'such conceits as clownage keeps in pay'. It is possible, of course, that these aspects of the plays were forced on a shrinking and disdainful Marlowe by the players. This would fit with the Greene/Nashe idea of the relationship between poet and the playhouse. But it is hard to imagine why Marlowe should have even begun to write *The Jew of Malta*, that 'farce of the old English humour' as T. S. Eliot calls it, showing 'the terribly serious, even savage comic humour, the humour which spent its last breath in the decadent

genius of Dickens',[39] if he was not relying on his capacity to fuse
the tragic vision of an articulate individualist *contra mundum* with
the bitter farce of a criminal underworld (prostitute and pick-
pocket) no less *contra mundum*. It is surely significant that the
modern theatrical success of *The Jew of Malta* (first restaged 1964),
The Revenger's Tragedy (1966), Marston's *The Malcontent* (1973),
and Kyd's *The Spanish Tragedy* (1982) has been facilitated by
finding in such plays qualities that appear also in Brechtian drama
and the theatre of the absurd. And such qualities, decentring the
tragic hero and his psychological motivation, taking an ironic attitude to success, understanding generic collisions (between the high
and the low, the tragic and the comic, the symbolic and the realistic) as indicators of mode rather than errors of judgement, are
precisely those that draw on the 'mongrel' aspect of Elizabethan
drama. The modern discovery that these are highly theatrical qualities indicates mainly a breakdown in the late Victorian valuation of
psychological unity[40] in responsible public figures, but the discovery is not simply an illusion of the modernist imagination; it picks
up elements actually there, in Marlowe among others, alongside
the heroic will's determination to control its environment.

In *2 Tamburlaine* (1587×1588) the hero faces a series of military
enemies, and defeats them, one after the other, much as in Part I.
But this series of successes is set in a context that makes its meaning very different. George Ian Duthie has pointed up the parallelism of the two parts of *Tamburlaine* by noting that 'In Part I the
most dangerous foe that Tamburlaine had to face was Zenocrate
. . . In Part II Marlowe confronts him with an even more dangerous foe—Death himself.'[41] The parallelism points up the difference: Zenocrate's beauty is a challenge to Tamburlaine, but it is a
challenge he can overcome; death, on the other hand, is not
defeasible. Tamburlaine displays his ethos, wounds the earth, challenges the gods, burns the town where Zenocrate died, carries her
hearse always with him; but none of this is more than show; he
now lives in a world in which prisoners escape, sons rebel, wives
sicken, and where even 'Tamburlaine, the Scourge of God, must

---

[39] *Selected Essays* (London, 1932), 123.

[40] The decline in the reputation of *Hamlet* as the world's greatest play can probably be
attributed to the same causes. See R. A. Foakes, *Hamlet versus Lear* (Cambridge, 1993).

[41] 'The Dramatic Structure of Marlowe's "Tamburlaine the Great", Parts I and II',
English Studies 1948 (London, 1948), 118.

die'. The joy in the exercise of irrepressible will-power which informs Part I is largely gone; the only direction forwards is now downwards; and, while he weakens, the complex world, which had gone quiet while he raged, reasserts itself in all the bewildering variety of its disorder. Tamburlaine is too grand to negotiate, let alone intrigue, but clearly enough the space for intrigue is opening up in front of Marlowe. *Doctor Faustus*, *The Jew of Malta*, *The Massacre at Paris*, all bring the tragic farce of the overreacher's ambition nearer to home than *Tamburlaine* ever does. All likewise take place in a period of time that the original audience could accept as, roughly speaking, 'the present'. The events dramatized in *The Massacre at Paris* belong to 1572×1589 and the other two, though they cannot have dates affixed to their action, are treated less as 'history' than as 'contemporary life'. The expansive poetic vision that allowed Marlowe to draw a whole landscape of remote geographical romance into the quasi-historical chronicle of Tamburlaine must shrink into a scene we ourselves can judge, as a picture of the way life is.

Doctor Faustus (1588×1592), *The Jew of Malta* (1589×1590), and *The Massacre at Paris* (1593) all deal with megalomaniac heroes hemmed in by contracts and expectations, which they evade rather than conquer, and which return at the end to destroy them. Of the three, *Doctor Faustus* is the least concerned with intrigue: the nature of the contract and of the evasion is made clear at the beginning and a simple logical progression is thus set up: (1) Faustus is dissatisfied with the limits to knowledge; he makes a pact with the Devil. (2) He uses the magic skills he has obtained, finds that the aspiration to know and enjoy leads only back to himself, thinks of repentance, but is bullied back into compliance. (3) He has left repentance too late; he is paralysed by terror and despair and cannot escape the contract. Into this simple but terrifying progression, given a marvellously eloquent expression in terms of both hope and fear, Marlowe has woven a series of loosely articulated 'shows', which may or may not involve Faustus's presence, but which act as an external commentary on the choice he has made, seen mainly not from an intellectual's personal viewpoint but from the rough and ready perspective of a confused, greedy, and cowardly world of physical rewards and physical punishments, which the Doctor may despise but to which he irremediably belongs (as the final shrieks of pain indicate). The comedy of *Doctor Faustus* is thus integral to the situation of a superman who is also a fool, but the actual deployment of the comic dimension is left remarkably open. The documentary evidence of early theatrical adaptation and the textual evidence of early revision indicate the extent to which *Doctor Faustus*, although it joins comedy and tragedy, high life and low life, as necessary bedfellows, yet leaves the precise relationship between them as an issue of editorial or theatrical interpretation.

The *Jew of Malta*, on the other hand, is through-composed and dominated by intrigue, so that insertion or addition would be very difficult. Barabas's clownage is a symptom (as is Faustus's) of the restriction in his direct power, and its exercise is a mark of his ironic alienation from the political world in which he is embedded. Even in his buffoonery, however, Faustus remains the grave scholar, aware of the terrifying context which gives him his fun, so that the collision of tragedy and comedy belongs to psychology rather than situation. But Barabas displays no concern for Last Things. No stratagem is too 'low' for his participation and enjoyment if it offers an opportunity to expose and defeat those who believe they are secure in power or righteousness. Thus when Barabas comes in disguised as a French musician, bringing his poisoned posy for Ithimore, Pilia-Borza, and Courtesan, his fury at being outwitted and his total commitment to the comic role that will secure his revenge are presented without differentiation. One need only compare Barabas's treatment of his role with the comparable performance of Jonson's Volpone as Scoto of Mantua (*Volpone*, II. ii) to see how quickly Barabas loses his 'character' in the part he is playing. If it is just to see *Doctor Faustus* as given its full dimension by a series of 'shows' (as suggested above), then it is equally worth noting that The *Jew of Malta* is also strung together on a series of 'shows'; but this time they are shows by Barabas himself, as he responds to disaster after disaster in a series of more and more imaginative self-transformations. One can see why The *Jew of Malta* remained for as long as the record stretches one of the most popular pieces in Henslowe's repertory; it gives a model of 'villain tragedy' to the next age, offering its audience both the excitement of a dominant personality powerfully projected and the plot fascination of a role that is always unstable, having only cleverness of intrigue to justify its power.

Edward II (1591×1593) and *The Massacre at Paris* deal with explicit political history, and they treat history as a framework that defies attempts to assert control by intrigue. *Edward II* is the most easily differentiated of Marlowe's plays, and it seems proper to deal with it in the company of other plays about English history. *The Massacre at Paris*, on the other hand, even though we have only a sadly mutilated text, clearly belongs in the line discussed in the preceding pages. The play—more properly described by Henslowe's name for it—*The Guise*—presents Edward Alleyn with yet another opportunity to enact the self-projection of one who believes

> That peril is the chiefest way to happiness,
> And resolution honour's fairest aim.
>
> (ii. 95–6)

But the recent and local Duke of Guise (killed 1588) does not have the wide spaces of Asia to gather his assault on 'the sweet fruition of an earthly crown'. Tamburlaine's sense of his own inevitable freedom from moral restraint has now become the self-conscious nonconformity of an amoral villain trapped in a moral (and moralizing) world. And, so far as one can tell, the play itself does not seek to escape from the crude moralizing that sees the Guise, Catherine de' Medici, Philip of Spain, and the Pope as unrelievedly black, and Henry of Navarre, the Huguenots, and Queen Elizabeth as completely white. Guise is given little space to create a free field of personal assertion; he must channel his aggression through a thousand petty conduits, a pair of poisoned gloves here, an assassin's bullet there, without even conveying Barabas's comic enjoyment of his own ingenuity. The domestic detail of the Guise's downfall, caught in the palace intrigues of Henri III's *mignons*, indicates how far we have moved away from Tamburlaine's conception of *virtù*. The Guise's death makes no crack in this world; the Queen Mother grieves that the political manœuvres she was planning now have to be revised; Guise's brother, the Duc du Maine, allows a friar to suggest that Henri III ought to be killed, but the fulfilment of that purpose is shown, as is much else in the play, as part of the web of politics, not as a consequence of individual motivation. We are here much closer to the world of Kyd's *The Spanish Tragedy* than to that of *Tamburlaine*, to a world where the effort of the individual to escape from the net that holds him cannot be a grand gesture but must be a series of small, carefully planned, movements, coordinated not only by resolution and ruthlessness but also by secrecy and deception.

Victim Tragedy

If *Tamburlaine* taught this generation the excitement of an individualism that dominates the world, Kyd's *The Spanish Tragedy* (1585×1589) offered a complementary and opposite definition, showing individuality as created by carrying the sufferings of the world in a mode not only sanctified by Christianity, but also exemplified in all those branded as outsiders. As noted above (pp. 22–3), Kyd* can be called a 'University Wit' only by grace and favour, for there is no evidence that he (or Shakespeare for that matter) attended university. Indeed, the attacks on these two dramatists in the pamphlets of 1589–92 tell us very clearly that they were regarded, by some of the inner group at least, as unqualified interlopers, incapable of genuine scholarship, pilfering employment from better men, and acquiring reputations for work they could only have stolen from the university-trained writers around them.

The attack on Shakespeare I shall discuss below (pp. 85–6). The attack on Kyd (or, less probably, on some other, unidentified, playwright) appears in Nashe's preface 'To the Gentlemen Students of Both Universities' set before Greene's *Menaphon* (1589); it is, characteristically, both personal and obscure. But the contempt of the recent graduate (Nashe was 20 or 21) for the ageing hack (as Nashe presents him) is entirely clear:

> It is a common practice nowadays amongst a sort of shifting companions that run through every art and thrive by none, to leave the trade of Noverint whereto they were born and busy themselves with the endeavours of art, that could scarcely Latinise their neck verse if they should have need. (McKerrow, iii. 315)

Kyd's father was a 'noverint' or a scrivener and it is commonly supposed that Kyd himself worked at the same trade—the trade whereto he was born. And the identification seems to be rendered even stronger a few lines later where Nashe speaks of 'English Seneca's . . . famished followers' coming to

> imitate the Kid in Aesop who, enamoured with the fox's newfangles, forsook all hopes of life to leap into a new occupation; and these men, renouncing all possibilities of credit or estimation, to intermeddle with Italian translations; wherein how poorly they have plodded . . . let all indifferent gentlemen that have travelled in that tongue discern by their twopenny pamphlets. (ibid. 315–16)

This contemptible playwright knows hardly any Latin; authorship is just another workaday job for him; he is attracted by the glamour of being a writer but unaware of the ridicule his ineptitude must create; all he can do is follow the line of least resistance: dramatize English translations of Latin authors, confuse ancient and modern worlds ('thrust Elysium into Hell'), and versify in the most rudimentary form of versification ('bodge up a blank verse with ifs and ands').

It is hard to see the author of *The Spanish Tragedy* in this diatribe, in spite of the references to *kid*, to *noverint*, and to *translations*, all of which point in that direction. Here is a play unusually full of Latin, some of it apparently of Kyd's own composition; and if the play within the play was really performed in 'sundry languages' (as the text tells us), it was written with dialogue in Greek, French, and Italian as well. It contains no quotations from the English versions of Seneca's tragedies, first published in the 1560s, and collected in a composite volume in 1581. Its blank verse seems to contain no more *ifs and ands* than do the plays of other men. Perhaps we should allow that Nashe's 'Kid in Aesop' is a composite figure made out of all the traits of ignorant pretenders to education he could imagine. Even less than in Pope's *Dunciad* is there need here to tailor the type figure of the Grub Street hack to the actualities of real writers. But the idea of Kyd seems to have contributed to the picture.

The Spanish Tragedy does not in fact cling to the periphery of drama dominated by the university Wits, but is rather in itself a central artefact that alters now (and altered then) the whole conception of that tradition. It became, indeed, a main supporting pillar of that idea of tragedy that the generation of the Wits handed down to subsequent writers. When Ben Jonson comes to write his prefatory poem for Shakespeare's First Folio (1623), he looks back to the beginnings of Shakespeare's long career and praises him for having surpassed the work of those writers who dominated the stage when he first made his debut ('thy peers'). Jonson will

> Tell how far thou didst our Lyly outshine,
> Or sporting Kyd or Marlowe's mighty line.

The three authors named are well chosen: these are the three great pioneers. Lyly's court comedies are the earliest domestication into English of the stylistic control, conceptual sophistication, and inner coherence of classical and Italian comedy. Marlowe is seen as the inventor of a tragic rhetoric powerful enough to impose a single and obsessive vision on its audience. Kyd, no less, is the innovative master of his own field,[42] the creator of a tragic form capable of giving sufficiently complex stage meaning to the mystery of human suffering. Jonson had thought, we know, that Kyd's methods (and some of Shakespeare's) were intolerably old-fashioned, too much larger than life to be lifelike. Yet the Shakespeare elegy shows the other side to this—a compensating awareness that *The Spanish Tragedy* is of central *historical* importance as a foundation document for mature Elizabethan tragedy.

The standard dating for *The Spanish Tragedy* overlaps with that for *1 and 2 Tamburlaine*. There is no evidence that one play is indebted to the other; but between them they mark out a range of mature options that define the space to be occupied by Elizabethan tragedy for the next fifty years. The arrival of *Tamburlaine* made the bigger noise; but *The Spanish Tragedy*, less self-consciously innovative, may well have carved the deeper impression, for it served to show how the traditional multi-level plot could be adapted to satisfy the expectations of more classically-minded authors and more sophisticated London audiences. In number the allusions and references generated by *The Spanish Tragedy* at least equal those to *Tamburlaine*, but the references are of a very different kind and they stretch over a longer period. They are not references to the author or his vision. Indeed it is by the merest chance that one reference includes the information that the author was called Kyd.[43] The reputation of *The Spanish Tragedy* depended above all on theatrical reminiscence. The play seems to have continued for a long time as one of the great showpieces of the public stage, passed from company to company, patched and 'augmented' by other writers, supplied with a forepiece or 'Part I' (*The First Part of Jeronimo, with the wars in Portugal* (1600×1605), with a comic counterpart, *Don Horatio; or The Spanish Comedy* (c.1584×1592), with the story of its Act V masque represented as a full-length play—*Soliman and Perseda* (c.1589×1592)—carried to Germany by

---

[42] In 'Tyrant and Martyr in M. Mack and G. de F. Lord (eds.), *Poetic Traditions of the English Renaissance* (New Haven, 1982), 85–102, I have argued for the symmetry between the two authors as one between the tyrant figure and the martyr. The basic contrast of types is touched on in Walter Benjamin, *The Origin of the German Tragic Drama* (London, 1977), 69.   [43] Heywood, *Apology for Actors*, cited in Chambers, iv. 253.

the English players, adapted and translated to fit these altered circumstances. Even the boy players 'borrowed' it for their own theatre.[44]

Of course, a flood of reminiscence is by no means the same as a surge of praise. Among the Jacobean satirists, the memory of *The Spanish Tragedy*'s highly theatrical emotions is evoked only to be scorned for unnaturalness and excess. Kyd's versification and rhetoric are indeed old-fashioned, even when set against Marlowe's— inevitably so, since they are largely derived from the practices of the preceding generation of poets. But his means are perfectly adapted to the uses they serve. Tamburlaine's long-breathed paragraphs project a joyous control of life's possibilities. For all the power it gives to individual passion, Kyd's poetry aims rather to articulate an entangling web of relations, and its force depends on the preserved tension between urgency of individual feeling and the necessity, imposed by the social structure of the represented world, to postpone, double back, 'go by' (as Hieronimo famously described it) in rhetoric as in action. Even in the most famous soliloquies we are made aware of this limiting pressure from outside no less than the emotional pressure from inside:

> HIERONIMO. O eyes! no eyes, but fountains fraught with tears;
> O life! no life, but lively form of death;
> O world! no world, but mass of public wrongs,
> Confused and filled with murder and misdeeds.
> O sacred heavens! if this unhallowed deed,
> If this inhuman and barbarous attempt,
> If this incomparable murder thus
> Of mine, but now no more my son,
> Shall unrevealed and unrevengèd pass,
> How should we term your dealings to be just,
> If you unjustly deal with those that in your justice trust?
>
> (III. ii. 1–11)

In its fusion of poetry and drama this passage allows us to see in miniature something of the quality that gave *The Spanish Tragedy* its hold on the Elizabethan imagination. The opening gambit comes from the sonnets of Petrarch and Sidney, but the general effect is not one of distanced poetic artifice but of a desperate search for an appropriate language. It is not a Tamburlainian rhetoric, however,

---

[44] See Ch. 7 n. 100 for a caveat.

where the onward rush marks power by its capacity to turn to its purposes all the impediments that syntax puts in its way. Kyd's is a rhetoric based above all on iteration and revision, on iteration that constantly doubles back in denial of its premisses (so that *life* becomes *lively death*, *sacred* turns into *unhallowed*, *mine* into *no more my*, *just* into *unjustly*). The echoic effects of the last two (rhyming) lines and the stretching-out of the final line to fourteen syllables complete the impression we are given of a speaker desperate to speak out but unable to extricate himself from the enclosing artfulness of a language that insists on its own connections, going round and round the same circuit of *just, unjustly, justice, trust*. Nor are we dealing here with a poetry based on natural speech rhythms like that of Shakespeare, using images and tropes to suggest depths of interconnection and so of thought, but rather with a poetry of surfaces, of patently artificial verbal patterns brought to attention by the 'figures of words' that rhetoricians set against 'figures of thought'.

This is not to say that there is no forward movement in this speech. As the anaphora on *O* modulates into the anaphora on *If this*, the speaker is carried without pause from the internal to the external, from the denial of self to interrogation of the universe, reformulating the particular as a general condition ('how shall *we* trust'). But for all this he ends up where he began. The refusal of the experience of death to reveal meaning is reflected in the refusal of the arbitrary patterns of syntax to become merely expressive in response to intention or purpose. The self-conscious and deliberately paced rhetoric, the figures of words that control the syntax— these insist on the presence of basic interconnections standing outside human purposes. And against these Kyd sets disruptive personal passion, denial of pattern, rejection of the hierarchical ordering of experience, madness (which none the less must express itself through the systems of order and art). We see Hieronimo desperately trying to control himself, to believe in system, but continually broken up by emotion that denies such system, and indeed by the discovery that the only accessible system is that which his speech is constructing for him. Act III, Scene xiii, for example, opens (in the unaugmented text) with a careful scholastic review of the alternatives available to the speaker, deduced from a series of Latin *sententiae*, and then laying out their practical consequences (a mode of exposition not dissimilar to that found in the opening soliloquy of *Doctor Faustus*). By this method Hieronimo comes to the apparently necessary conclusion that he is required to work towards a 'secret yet a certain' revenge. And in these terms he achieves something like control and patience:

> No, no, Hieronimo, thou must enjoin
> Thine eyes to observation, and thy tongue
> To milder speeches than thy spirit affords,
> Thy heart to patience, and thy hands to rest,
> Thy cap to courtesy, and thy knee to bow,
> Till to revenge thou know When, Where, and How.

(III. xiii. 39–44)

The weight of the last three words (following the false rhyme on *know*) gives the actor a marvellous chance to indicate how paper-thin is the control achieved. Citizens enter to ask Hieronimo (in his function as 'Knight Marshall') to deal with their legal petitions, and he responds to them at first as the complete master of system. But then the old man, one of the petitioners, tells him of his mur-dered son. The parallel to Hieronimo's own case cracks the retain-ing walls of sanity a little. Again Hieronimo tries to control himself. But by accident he pulls out the handkerchief soaked in Horatio's blood which he always carries with him. The whole rational con-struct of distinction between inside and outside, past and present, one person and another, is engulfed by the 'raging sea' of passion. The sight of the handkerchief—a wonderful prop for the actor, pointing forward not only to Rutland's bloody handkerchief in *3 Henry VI* but also to Desdemona's handkerchief—signals a take-over of rational discourse by the revenge phantasmagoria of hellish sprites and tormenting hags that Kyd may be remembering from the Inns of Court tragedians or the Seneca translators of the 1560s. In moving into this mode Kyd takes enormous risks, and it is part of his greatness that he is willing to take them. Hieronimo's mad assumption that the old man is in fact his 'sweet boy', Horatio, returned from Hades, may remind us of the comic moment in *The Taming of the Shrew* when Petruchio and Kate meet the old father and pretend to think him a 'young budding virgin, fair and fresh and sweet'. Placing madness at the centre of tragedy must always carry the danger of moving through the grotesque into the comic. But Kyd handles the grotesque with the assurance of a master. Hieronimo stands at the head of a great line of Elizabethan tragic madmen; his creator must be credited with the perception that passionate derangement gave the poet access to a rhetorical landscape of bizarre juxtapositions and metamorphoses of more than Ovidian force, all the more powerful for being set inside a world striving for rational meanings.

The continuity/discontinuity tension in *The Spanish Tragedy* has its largest expression in the continuity/discontinuity contrast between the natural and supernatural worlds depicted. Like many other plays of the period, *The Spanish Tragedy* is introduced, commented on, and concluded by supernatural characters who stand between the spectators and the action and show us the contradictory orders of the two worlds. Kyd is subtle and ironic in the relationship he establishes between the natural plot and the supernatural overplot, where Greene, in *Alphonsus*, for example, is crude and mechanical. Kyd's supernatural beings do not live on a wholly separated plane from that of the human beings. Andrea is newly dead and his much imitated initial speech, which describes his Virgilian descent into Hell, spells out in terms of human motivation the impulse that drives the ghosts of the killed to return to the scene of their sorrows. In the London production of 1982 the movement of the chalk-faced Andrea in and out of the social games of his erstwhile companions reinforced continuously the bewilderment of his simultaneous presence and absence. But his choric companion, 'Revenge', is not at all bewildered. Like Hamlet's father, in this if in no other respect, he sees straight through the indirections and convolutions of human behaviour to the final 'reward' such actions require. But Shakespeare, of course, everywhere humanizes and ironizes the rigid pattern of human incapacity he inherited from Kyd and other University Wit forebears, and this allows space for the supernatural pressure on the human scene to be judged in merely human terms (just as he contains their schematic rhetoric inside naturalistic phrasing). We would be affronted in Shakespeare's play if the ghost reappeared at the end of the action (after the death of Claudius at any rate) and pronounced the malediction given to Kyd's Revenge:

> Then haste we down to meet thy friends and foes:
> To place thy friends in ease, the rest in woes;
> For here though death hath end their misery,
> I'll there begin their endless tragedy.

(IV. v. 45–8)

Shakespeare privileges a final perception of human asymmetry and uncertainty; Kyd brings his action to rest on news of a punishing supernatural order. And this seems a just difference of ending; for Kyd reminds us continually (as Shakespeare does not) that the supernatural is an essential part of the human scene, counterpointing the petty plots of individuals against the Grand Plot, already completed.

From many points of view *The Spanish Tragedy* looks like another answer to *Tamburlaine*. Here the most thrusting, the most ambitious, the most self-confident persons (Lorenzo and Viluppo in particular) turn out in the end to be practical failures, while the emotional, the vague, the uncertain of purpose, the slow-moving (Hieronimo, Bel-Imperia, Alexandro) eventually have their values vindicated. The hard-edged 'man of action' (like Marlowe's Barabas or Guise) sees life as infinitely manipulable, and concentrates his energy on immediate advantage, but these strengths become his limitations when they close consciousness to the implications of what is happening around him: Balthazar's interest in Bel-Imperia is seen by Lorenzo as a path for his own ambition, but he fails to consider the effect on Bel-Imperia. At a lower level but on the same track, we see Pedringano, 'most ignorant of what he's most assured', shutting his eyes to the reality of the gallows in front of him because he believes (falsely) that he is in command while his executioner is not. Marlowe's *Tamburlaine* associates poetic and emotional power with political success. Kyd associates these powers with political helplessness. Hieronimo's most famous speeches are rhapsodies of grief, discoveries that the terrifying irrationality of nightmare does not disappear when one wakes up:

> [*Enter HIERONIMO in his shirt &c.*]
> HIERONIMO. What outcries pluck me from my naked bed,
> And chill my throbbing heart with trembling fear,
> Which never danger yet could daunt before?
> Who calls Hieronimo? Speak, here I am.
> I did not slumber, therefore 'twas no dream.
> No, no, it was some woman cried for help,
> And here within this garden did she cry,
> And in this garden must I rescue her.
> But stay, what murd'rous spectacle is this?
> A man hanged up and all the murderers gone,
> And in my bower, to lay the guilt on me.

This place was made for pleasure, not for death.
[*He cuts him down.*]
Those garments that he wears I oft have seen—
Alas, it is Horatio, my sweet son!
O no, but he that whilom was my son!
O was it thou that call'dst me from my bed?
O speak, if any spark of life remain!
I am thy father. Who hath slain my son?
What savage monster, not of human kind,
Hath here been glutted with thy harmless blood,
And left thy bloody corpse dishonored here,
For me, amidst these dark and deathful shades,
To drown thee with an ocean of my tears?
O heavens, why made you night to cover sin?
By day this deed of darkness had not been.
O earth, why didst thou not in time devour
The vild profaner of this sacred bower?
O poor Horatio, what hadst thou misdone,
To lose thy life ere life was new begun?
O wicked butcher, whatsoe'er thou wert,
How could thou strangle virtue and desert?
Ay me, most wretched, that have lost my joy,
In losing my Horatio, my sweet boy!

(II. v. 1–33)

The brilliantly realized effect of this speech is largely achieved by the collision it sets up between the uncertainty of an intimate and unprotected personal life (marked visually by the nightshirt) and the public outcry that heaven acknowledge sin. Hieronimo begins by responding to his night fears as if they were only irrational lacunae in a naturally benevolent world. But the focus quickly changes, and again with a completely naturalistic justification ('I wasn't asleep; that was no dream; it was real; it came from a particular place, a particular source; I must find that place, person, reality'). The ways in which the mind seeks to naturalize aberrant experience, the steps it takes to bring it under control—these are exactly mimicked. The issue narrows down; and we wait for the anagnorisis we can foresee, while in line after line Hieronimo lists the facts and refuses to name the meaning. Even after the outcry of recognition comes in line 14, Hieronimo's gift for rationalizing reasserts itself in the *correctio* of line 15 and in the apostrophes of 16 and 17. It is only when the focus changes to the question of responsibility that a formal rhetoric to connect the grieving father to the indifferent world takes over. Having eventually defined himself in his basic role ('I am thy father'), Hieronimo is positioned (as in the moment between recitative and aria) to begin his interrogation of the universe (Who . . . why . . . why . . . what . . .) and incessant apostrophe ('O heavens . . . O earth . . . O poor Horatio . . . O wicked butcher'), so returning again, as in a circle, to the pathos of the speaker ('Ay me, most wretched') and the informal intimacy of 'Horatio, my sweet boy'.

This power of Kyd's to evoke the collision between the uncertainties of individual identity and the artful formulations of role (which alone gives access to power in action) has its clearest expression in the final bloodbath, which transforms play into ritual, action into pure meaning. This is the first of the many Elizabethan denouements achieved by a play within a play (as in Tourneur's *The Revenger's Tragedy*, Marston's *Antonio's Revenge* and *The Malcontent*, Middleton's *Women Beware Women*, and Massinger's *The Roman Actor*). The playlet of 'Soliman and Perseda' reduces to their simplest forms the roles that Lorenzo, Balthazar, Bel-Imperia, and Hieronimo have played throughout the main action. But now they act mere actors, puppet stereotypes, condemned (as if already in Dante's Inferno or Sartre's *Huis clos*) to repeat forever the same limited routines of tyrant, lover, fair captive, and schemer. They have already joined the world of Andrea and Revenge, and this, Hieronimo insists in his afterword to the playlet, is the only real world:

> Haply you think, but bootless are your thoughts,
> That this is fabulously counterfeit,
> And that we do as all tragedians do:
> To die today for fashioning our scene,
> The death of Ajax or some Roman peer,
> And in a minute, starting up again,
> Revive to please tomorrow's audience.
> No, princes: know I am Hieronimo,
> The hopeless father of a hapless son,
> Whose tongue is tuned to tell his latest tale,
> Not to excuse gross errors in the play.
>
> (IV. iv. 76–86)

And so saying, Hieronimo reveals the body of the dead Horatio behind the arras. This, he insists, is the reality that has turned appearance inside out; this is the touchstone of loss, devaluation, and despair that has revealed to him the truth about the world— the 'truth' that success can be achieved only by submitting to the rules of an inexorable and freedom-destroying system, a system certainly non-human and probably anti-human as well.

As co-sponsors of mature Elizabethan tragedy, *Tamburlaine* and *The Spanish Tragedy* offer contradictory yet complementary visions of life. *Tamburlaine* sponsors all the lives of the great criminals or would-be great criminals, the self-conscious social exceptions (Damville, Bussy D'Ambois, Byron, Volpone, Giles Overreach, Hoffman, Coriolanus, numerous Turkish sultans). *The Spanish Tragedy* sponsors rather the heroes who must endure, who must enter into the destructive element before they can deal with it, who must destroy themselves in order to succeed (Tourneur's Vindice, Hamlet, Othello, Ford's Giovanni, Heywood's Frankford). A strongly imagined social or political network usually draws characters into this second category, where evil is understood to exist less in the motives of individuals than in the consequences of the social structure. *The Spanish Tragedy* can hardly be called a political play; its political establishment is more ignorant than malign. But its central perception that political confusion is a natural breeding ground for vendetta and injustice proved highly appropriate to plays dealing with recent politics (and it is entirely possible that it was meant to draw on current English concern with political issues in Spain and Portugal).

Peele's *The Battle of Alcazar* (1588×1589; printed 1594), like Marlowe's *The Massacre at Paris*, dramatizes recent true events (the actual battle took place in 1578). The Presenter tells us at the beginning of the play (unfortunately, he is referring to a fictional item), 'Say not these things are feigned, for true they are.' Peele makes strenuous efforts to explain the genealogical intricacies of the Barbary kingship and to clear up the tangle of political aims that link King Sebastian of Portugal, Philip II of Spain, Tom Stukeley (the Pope's candidate for 'King of Ireland'), the Turkish Emperor, and Queen Elizabeth herself. What his realistic aims achieve is in fact a picture of the tangled web of *Realpolitik* in which all the characters are enmeshed. And so we are brought to see with ironic pity those characters who believe most strongly that they are acting freely (King Sebastian of Portugal and Tom Stukeley, the English adventurer), for they too 'march in a net' as Hieronimo puts it, are bought and sold before ever they set foot in Barbary. Stukeley's bemused career ends with a reminiscence of Tamburlaine-like glory:

> There did Tom Stukeley glitter all in gold,
> Mounted upon his jennet white as snow
> Shining as Phoebus in King Philip's court.
>
> (ll. 1470–2)

But, as the last line indicates, the reality is that this Tamburlaine lives on a leash. The only freedom available belongs to Philip II (whom we never see), the hidden spider at the centre of the web, and *per contra* to Muly Mahamet, 'the Moor', whose freedom is that of the total immoralist, weighed down by none of the clogs of honour or integrity, and liberated by defeat into a heaven of rhetoric. It was this total freedom in villainy that gave Peele's image of Muly Mahamet its contemporary reputation, particularly in the episode of his exile in the wild mountains of Barbary (an episode that Ben Jonson parodied in *Poetaster*). Here, exempted from the pressures of political action, 'the Moor' can revel in the free physical aggression of a king among beasts (though elsewhere a beast among kings). He feeds his starving Queen, Calipolis, with the meat of a lioness he has just killed:

> Hold thee, Calipolis, feed and faint no more.
> This flesh I forced from a lioness,
> Meat of a princess, for a princess meet.
>
> (ll. 584–6)

Jonson's parody hardly needs to exaggerate, for it is clear that Peele is aiming less to secure pity and terror than on 'going over the top'. The play's political realism demands that the excesses of rhetoric be seen, as if not quite comic, at least inside an ironic and self-conscious mode.

If the Prologue to *Tamburlaine* is a defence of generic purity in tragedy and a proposal to free popular tragedy from what Sidney called its 'mongrel' status, then we may see *The Spanish Tragedy* as a restoration of the *status quo ante*. Alfred Harbage has argued that *The Spanish Tragedy* was innovative and remained a powerful factor in the tradition of Elizabethan tragedy because it showed how comic methods could be used to create tragic effects, 'thus producing a species of comitragedy':

When Kyd's Lorenzo maneuvers Pedringano into slaying Serberine, the authorities into arresting Pedringano, and the latter into remaining silent until the moment of his execution because of the hope of a pardon, he is behaving not like Atreus or Clytemnestra but like Matthew Merrygreek or Diccon of Bedlam. Not only is the effect of the action sometimes comic, as when Pedringano stands with a rope about his neck while Lorenzo's Page comforts him with an empty box supposedly containing his pardon, but the very methods used are the traditional ones of comic intrigue . . . [In comedy] the resulting quarrels are trivial, hence in harmony with the trivial means used to foment them; but after Lorenzo's maneuvers with deceptive appointments and an empty box, Serberine and Pedringano are dead.[45]

The mixture of knockabout comedy and serious tragedy that Sidney objected to (as found in such plays as Preston's *Cambyses* (*c.*1558× 1569) or R.B.'s *Appius and Virginia* (1559×1567)) sets its opposites in crude juxtaposition. Kyd offered juxtapositions held together by irony; and it was irony that allowed the dramatists of the popular stage to unify their extraordinary range of subject matters, finding the same bitter mixture of comic potential and tragic consequence in domestic imbroglios as in the massacres of tyrants.

The anonymous *Lamentable and True Tragedy of Master Arden of Faversham in Kent, who was most wickedly murdered by the means of his disloyal and wanton wife* (1585×1592)—sometimes attributed to Shakespeare, sometimes to Kyd or Marlowe—shows the powerful appropriateness of the mixed mode to a small-town scandal that today would be confined to the local press. But the interest in factual authenticity, which keeps irony well beneath the surface, is liberated from mere reportage in this case by the variety of rhetorics it inherits from the drama of self-projection. Recent 'historical' tragedies like *The Massacre at Paris* or *The Battle of Alcazar* had already presented the victims of intrigue as less the passionate rhetoricians of undeserved injustice than as persons caught by their own implication in the wrongs they suffer, unable to disentangle the strings that bind them to the wrongdoers. The strings are drawn even more tightly in the circumscribed bourgeois world of Faversham in Kent, where everyone acknowledges the universality of justice, but no one can articulate it except as a rhetoric of self-defence. The Painter defends his part in the murder plot by

[45] 'Intrigue in Elizabethan Tragedy', in Richard Hosley (ed.), *Essays on Shakespeare and Elizabethan Drama* (Columbia, Mo., 1962), 37–44.

citing the 'sharp-witted poets whose sweet verse | Makes heavenly
gods break off their nectar draughts' as the justification why 'we
that are the poet's favourites | Must have a love' (Sc. i, ll. 251–6);
Alice Arden, that 'bourgeois Clytemnestra', as J. A. Symonds calls
her, is (unlike her Aeschylean counterpart) desperately anxious
to maintain appearances, intensely conscious of caste, presenting
herself alternately as doting on and contemptuous of Mosbie, her
lover; Mosbie takes up the pose of a rhetorical villain, assuring us
(and himself) that he will get rid of Alice as soon as he has secured
her fortune. But none of these rhetorics points outwards to action;
the general impression made is of evasion rather than purpose.

These are people whose 'Renaissance Individualism' and break
with convention can be sustained only by avoiding self-scrutiny,
who dare not lift their eyes lest they see (and be seen) in too long
a perspective. Master Arden is obviously a purposeful capitalist, en-
closer, profiteer, but these sucesses give him no language to justify
his moral status. Given his power over money, is it possible he is
a cuckold? When he tries to articulate his grievance, his self-image
as loving husband, the language of revenge tragedy and the issue of
class distinction merge together in a self-contradictory mixture:

> I am by birth a gentleman of blood,
> And that injurious ribald that attempts
> To violate my dear wife's chastity
> (For dear I hold her love, as dear as heaven)
> Shall on the bed which he thinks to defile
> See his dissevered joints and sinews torn.
>
> (i. 36–41)

This makes it sound as if Mosbie would be more welcome in
Arden's bed if he had been better born. And indeed the role of
status in this small commercial community provides the central
means by which the grand patterns of good and evil, wrongdoing
and revenge, can be expressed (and concealed). The attachment to
petty detail renders both criminal and victim incapable of carrying
through the grand gestures that theatrical self-dramatization demands. Instead of a chain of consequences, the plot turns out to be
a paratactic sequence of failures and 'improvisations', as Martin
Wine's edition calls them. Mosbie's and Alice's increasingly desperate efforts to get rid of Arden lurch uncontrollably towards
farce. In the end, abandoning subtlety, they simply slaughter him
in his own house and are quickly apprehended and executed.

As many modern examples show ('Ealing comedies', for example), there is much drollery in the collision of middle-class complacence and criminal behaviour. But the intrusion of comic-grotesque figures from the old moral and religious drama into the bourgeois world of *Arden* gives the play a darker resonance. The flamboyant acting parts in *Arden of Faversham* are provided not by Arden, or Alice or Mosbie (the story's principals), but by Shakebag and Black Will, the two professional ruffians or 'heavies' who are hired to commit the murder the amateurs cannot achieve. These two dramatize themselves as superior to the petty considerations that bind the townsfolk, but their self-importance, their menacing assurance that to them murder is an easy and everyday activity, their contempt for the conscience-stricken and timorous amateurs, throw into definition the thin crust that divides Faversham from Hell, reducing plot and consequence to a haphazard blow in the dark, struck without anxiety and with a chillingly genial assurance that this is the way the world has to be. Greene, who subcontracts his promise to murder Arden to these two, wishes to plan the action; but Black Will will have nothing to do with such intellectuality:

> GREENE.   Here's the angels down
> And I will lay the platform of his death.
> WILL. Plat me no platforms! Give me the money,
>   and I'll stab him as he stands pissing against a wall.
>
> (II. 95–8)

What we see here is the tragedy of intrigue being broken down again into a more primitive Elizabethan mode, but in a structure which does not keep intention and fate apart (as in *Cambyses*, for example), but shows how one is forced to become the other.

Arden of Faversham gives the impression of a deliberate experiment in unheroic tragedy by a dramatist well acquainted with the heroic repertory. The self-consciousness of the author is well illustrated in the Epilogue:

> Gentlemen, we hope you'll pardon this naked tragedy
> Wherein no filed points are foisted in
> To make it gracious to the ear or eye;
> For simple truth is gracious enough
> And needs no other points of glozing stuff.
>
> (Epilogue, ll. 14–18)

'Simple truth' is, of course, a complex notion and one that the author seems to be invoking to give a particular focus to his work. If the plain style is to be validated, it is not as a guarantor of truth, but only as a particular mode of telling. *Arden of Faversham* is most often placed by critics in a genre called 'domestic tragedy' (see pp. 479–87), but the homilies (which abound) do not add up to an explanation. The title-page's description of Alice as a 'disloyal and wanton wife' is endorsed. But when the Epilogue looks back over the play it sees a different moral, derived from a supernatural source:

> But this above the rest is to be noted:
> Arden lay murdered in that plot of ground
> Which he by force and violence held from Reed;
> And in the grass his body's print was seen
> Two years and more after the deed was done.
>
> (Epilogue, ll. 9–13)

The play ends with the law acting with its usual brutal generalization, so that the innocent bystanders are hanged along with the responsible agents. Others escape the law:

> As for the ruffians, Shakebag and Black Will,
> The one took sanctuary and, being sent for out,
> Was murdered in Southwark as he passed
> To Greenwich, where the Lord Protector lay.
> Black Will was burnt in Flushing on a stage;
> Greene was hanged at Osbridge in Kent;
> The painter fled, and how he died we know not.
>
> (Epilogue, ll. 2–8)

This invites the auditor to look back on events of some forty years earlier (Arden was murdered in 1551). Are we to suppose that justice was finally fulfilled? Is the painter assumed to be frying in Hell for his crime, as Alice fried on earth? Was Black Will burnt by accident or as part of the divine plan, which will not permit murder to go unpunished? The play seems to endorse the latter idea as its explicit ideology, yet it undercuts that by the fidelity with which it shows ordinary life progressing in terms that are much more random—however ill-adapted to randomness are the expectations of those who live ordinarily. The particular tragedy of Arden is absorbed into the larger obscurity of everyday behaviour, which it illuminates but cannot explain.

I have spoken of *The Spanish Tragedy* as an attempt to absorb the variousness of Elizabethan popular drama into a unified structure focused by the protagonist's agonizing search for meaning. This process of search and discovery is manifestly less exciting than Tamburlaine's takeover by the rhetoric of assertion. Perhaps it is only to be expected that the university man should make the big statement of principle while the 'unqualified' workman produced the more finely articulated structure. Shakespeare shared with Kyd the difficult role of a peripheral membership in the University Wits generation. Like Kyd, he drew on himself the charge that his plays showed him to be an ignorant imitator of other men with better trained minds. Indeed, to the offence of being without a university degree Shakespeare had added the further offence that he was a player. If the players were no longer obliged to ask university authors to write plays for them but could delegate the task to one of their own (inevitably ignorant) mates, then the financial basis of University Wit playwriting disappeared. And so Greene in his *Groatsworth of Wit* moves speedily from a general attack on the players, to a concentration on the player-writer:

Yes, trust them [the players] not: for there is an upstart crow, beautified with our feathers, that with his *Tiger's heart wrapt in a player's hide* supposes he is as well able to bombast out a blank verse as the best of you, and being an absolute Johannes fac totum is in his own conceit the only Shake-scene in a country.   (Grosart, xii. 144)

Shakespeare was not, of course, the only player–writer in London. Robert Wilson and Richard *Tarlton must have been known to Greene; but these men seem to have been players first and authors only second. Their plays were not directly competing specimens in the University Wit mode. Shakespeare's were, as the reference to 'bombast out a blank verse as the best of you' seems to indicate. The Cambridge University play, *The Second Part of The Return from Parnassus* (1601), shows the Cambridge graduates, who are the central figures, seeking employment from Kemp and Burbage, the principal actors of the Chamberlain's Men. The exchange at this point suggests that Shakespeare's talents may have been flaunted by the players. Kemp tells the graduates: 'Few of the university pen plays well; they smell too much of that writer Ovid and that writer Metamorphoses and talk too much of Proserpina and Jupiter.

Why here's our fellow Shakespeare puts them all down.' (ll. 1766–9). This is close to the issue raised by Greene, even though the particular 'university man' Kemp has in mind is Ben Jonson ('O that Ben Jonson is a pestilent fellow . . . but our fellow Shakespeare hath given him a purge that made him beray his credit' (ll. 1770–3). By 1603 the generation of the University Wits had disappeared; but the issue, and Shakespeare's relation to it, seems to go on unchanged.

Shakespeare's marginal status created social and personal difficulties for him. But in literary and dramaturgic terms the presence or absence of a degree is not an issue. If *The Spanish Tragedy* is thought of as belonging to the group of experimental tragedies produced in this period—plays drawing on Humanist education and modifying popular expectations by the light of classical traditions—then Shakespeare's first tragedy, *Titus Andronicus* (1594), can hardly be excluded. It is undoubtedly a belated contribution to the mode, whether it is dated 1589×1592 or 1594, but this does not much affect its status as a member of the group of radical and experimental tragedies written under the shadow of *Tamburlaine* and *The Spanish Tragedy*.

Titus Andronicus repeats the central situation of *The Spanish Tragedy*. Like Kyd's play it responds to Tamburlaine's example by showing self-projection as free only when the projector is separated from society by madness; and, like Kyd, Shakespeare finds the exemplum of that madness in the inability of a father to find legal redress for the secret murder (or, in this case, rape) of his child. His frustration makes him grasp at the fantasy of total individual justice, and it is by enacting that fantasy that he is able to bring his life to rest on the idea of a perfect retribution. Titus, like Hieronimo, achieves this in a theatrical celebration which satiates the hunger (ours as well as his) to see absolute and unimpeded justice taking over from the imperfect world, joining victims to victimizers in a strict-time dance of death. But the complex design of *The Spanish Tragedy* has been greatly simplified in the imitation. Shakespeare strips away the supernatural level of causality that Kyd provided, and at the same time he declines to employ anything like Kyd's parallel plot, where the Portuguese Viceroy mourns for the supposed death of his son, Balthazar, and so prepares us for Hieronimo's mourning for the death of *his* son, killed to advantage Balthazar. The plot that Shakespeare retains is thus, in comparison to Kyd's, unilinear and direct. This simplification does not, however, make its movement any less demanding of attention, for we can understand the direction it takes only when we understand action in terms of character—the particular kind of person Titus Andronicus happens to be. Hieronimo begins *The Spanish Tragedy* as a nondescript bystander, a minor functionary in the Spanish court. In the whole of the first act he is given only twelve (wholly conventional) lines, allowing him to show his pleasure in his son Horatio's military success, and then another twenty impersonal lines are allotted to him as descriptions of the courtly show being staged. It is not, in fact, until the last scene of the second act, with the plot developed and Horatio dead, that Hieronimo emerges as a person with any character at all, though then, with the thunderclap 'What outcries pluck me from my naked bed', he instantly sets the tone that will dominate the rest of the play, the tone that gave *The Spanish Tragedy* its fame and status. Titus Andronicus, on the other hand, dominates his play from the beginning. By line 20 we hear that he has been chosen for the 'Roman empery'; his biography follows; use of his name calms a political dispute, a captain announces his near arrival, *drums and trumpets* sound, a procession enters with others, *as many as can be*, and finally Titus speaks. If Hieronimo comes up into visibility by reason of his loss and grief, Titus rather descends into personal life. When this happens (climactically in Act III, Scene i), Titus is already established as a person whose reactions are known and whose responsibility for his own mode of behaving is clear to us.

Titus's military achievements, his family history, his social prominence, the reverence with which the Roman public treats his name —all these establish him as a prototypical Roman soldier of the old school, inflexible, self-punishing, intensely focused on a narrow band of values, modelled perhaps on the description Horace gives to Achilles (*impiger, iracundus, inexorabilis, acer*). His reaction to deprivation and sorrow thus loses something of the universality of fatherhood that Hieronimo displays. What Shakespeare offers us instead is a meditation on the political issues involved, issues that seem to arise naturally in Elizabethan drama wherever there is any strong engagement with the Roman world (see Chapter 9): should Titus have accepted the crown? should he have treated his prisoners by less rigid standards? should he have favoured Bassianus? Questions of this kind mark out a range of political possibilities open to Titus but not relevant to Hieronimo, who presents a much purer image of undeserved suffering and mere martyrdom. If Titus' suffering is universal, it is rather because it expresses the destruction of a whole culture, a total value-system that belongs not simply to Titus himself but to Roman history in general. There is here a sense of blankness, a disappearance of the sources of meaning that misses the personal poignance of Hieronimo in the search for something larger. This 'heroic' quality in *Titus Andronicus* goes beyond what Kyd seems to have aimed at when he made his hero a person without ambition for political power and fixed him in a timescale approximately modern.

The 'heroic' mode was, of course, the forte of *Tamburlaine*, and *Titus Andronicus* shows the influence of *Tamburlaine*, not only in the concentration of its energies in a simple progressive plot, but in some of the versification also. Thus Saturninus's love-speech to Tamora:

> And therefore, lovely Tamora, Queen of Goths,
> That like the stately Phoebe 'mongst her nymphs
> Dost overshine the gallant'st dames of Rome,
> If thou be pleased with this my sudden choice,
> Behold, I choose thee, Tamora, for my bride,
> And will create thee Emperess of Rome.
>
> (I. i. 315–20)

But when it comes to the central matter of the madding passion raised by total loss, the music of the verse has a very different resonance.

> MARCUS. But yet let reason govern thy lament.
> TITUS. If there were reason for these miseries,
> Then into limits could I bind my woes:
> When heaven doth weep, doth not the earth o'erflow?
> If the winds rage, doth not the sea wax mad,
> Threat'ning the welkin with his big-swoll'n face?
> And wilt thou have a reason for this coil?
> I am the sea; hark how her sighs doth blow!
> She is the weeping welkin, I the earth:
> Then must my sea be moved with her sighs;
> Then must my earth with her continual tears
> Become a deluge, overflow'd and drown'd:
> For why my bowels cannot hide her woes,
> But like a drunkard must I vomit them.
>
> (III. i. 218–31)

This passage is not written without recourse to the Kyddian figures
of words: the anaphoras on *If. . . When . . . If,* combined with the
series of rhetorical questions culminating in line 224, control the
structure of the first half of the passage; and the anaphora on
'Then must my . . .' in lines 227–8 points up the repetitive nature
of the rhetoric in the second half also. But even at this early stage
in his career Shakespeare's rhetoric is dominated not so much by
the figures of words as by the extraordinary fluency of his tropes
(metaphor, simile, metonymy). Here, as elsewhere in the play, the
power of the writing derives largely from its capacity to transform
our sense of the suffering individuals by assimilating them into the
processes of the external world. It is no doubt a sign of Titus'
incipient madness that the assimilation is so complete, as in the
extraordinary catachresis of the last two lines. But once again (as
in Kyd) madness is a means of telling the terrible truth about the
world. When Marcus describes the raped and mutilated Lavinia,
who has just stumbled out of the forest, still bleeding, her beauty
and her violation are presented in direct relation to one another as
interconnected aspects of a single (Ovidian) vision in which individual refinement and the civilization which surrounds it are seen
to exist in a symbiotic relationship with counterbalancing barbarism and destruction. The greater the horror of the event, the
greater the delicacy evoked in its handling. The loving arms and
the bloody axe, the aspen fingers and the pruning knife, the tongue
singing and the tongue torn out, the slavering Cerberus and the
Thracian poet (also mutilated, it should be remembered), the
monster and the maiden—these complementary pictures of doing
and done-to, of action and emotion, of outer world and inner, are
used as the essential tropes for our understanding of the meaning
of life as depicted:

> MARCUS. Speak, gentle niece, what stern ungentle hands
> Hath lopped and hewed and made thy body bare
> Of her two branches, those sweet ornaments,
> Whose circling shadows kings have sought to sleep in,
> And might not gain so great a happiness
> As half thy love? Why dost not speak to me?
> Alas, a crimson river of warm blood,
> Like to a bubbling fountain stirred with wind,
> Doth rise and fall between thy rosed lips,
> Coming and going with thy honey breath

·   ·   ·   ·   ·   ·   ·   ·

O, had the monster seen those lily hands
Tremble, like aspen leaves, upon a lute,
And make the silken strings delight to kiss them,
He would not then have touched them for his life.
Or, had he heard the heavenly harmony
Which that sweet tongue hath made,
He would have dropped his knife and fell asleep,
As Cerberus at the Thracian poet's feet.

(II. iv. 16–51)

To say that the characters in *Titus Andronicus* are presented as
emblems, or turn themselves into emblems as we hear them talking, is to make an obvious point. But the use of terms like 'emblems' in this context deserves further explication. The emblematic
quality of Tamora, Chiron, and Demetrius is made quite explicit
in the final act when they present themselves to Titus as Revenge,
Rapine, and Murder; but this does not turn their relationship with
others in the play into anything like allegory. It does, however,
point to a less explicit but more pervasive mode throughout the
play which renders actions less as enactments than as ritualized
commentaries on the meaning of what is happening. There is a
strange procession at the end of Act III, Scene i, where, having
circled Titus while he 'pledges' them and swears to 'right your
wrongs', the characters present then proceed to pick up the sev-
ered parts of their relatives and make a slow exit:

> The vow is made. Come brother, take a head,
> And in this hand the other will I bear;
> And, Lavinia, thou shalt be employed;
> Bear thou my hand, sweet wench, between thy teeth.
> [*To Lucius*] As for thee, boy, go get thee from my sight.
>
> (III. i. 278–82)

It might be argued that these actions are 'about' family severance;
but such an argument leaves wholly untouched the larger question
why Shakespeare chose so grotesque a method of conveying this
(or any other) meaning. The scene seems to require (as in the Peter
Brook production of 1955) a deliberate ritualization in which the
action is slowed down, bracketed off by all the bizarrerie that modern production methods allow—and even then Vivien Leigh had to
be spared the hand-carrying. In 1955, the shrilling *musique concrète*,

the wildly unnaturalistic costuming, the slow and reverential movements by which the mutilated limbs were raised aloft in their
reliquaries—these effects made the scene a high point of 'cruel'
theatre *à la Artaud*. We knew we were watching a religious activity,
even though we were given no idea what religion this was. Here, as
elsewhere in the play, the characters seem to be absorbed into a
rule-ordered mode of behaviour; but the nature of the rule is never
exposed. Hieronimo discovered that the wicked world offers effective action only to those who accept a nightmare logic from which
it is impossible to awake. *Titus Andronicus* shows us the same
nightmare, though in less personal terms. A 'secondary world' of
the appalled imagination is here added to the historical facts of
Roman politics. The co-existence of the Gothic and the Roman,
the actions in the forest and the actions in the city—such facts
allow us to see the double vision of nightmare and 'reality' as not
simply a matter of internal against external perception (madness
against sense) but as a coherent response to the facts of individual
experience inside a history which does not disappear even when
one is awake. When Marcus sees Lavinia stumbling out of the
forest he asks for death rather than this *post-mortem* nightmare:

> If I do dream, would all my wealth would wake me!
> If I do wake, some planet strike me down,
> That I may slumber an eternal sleep!

> (II. iv. 13–15)

As in *The Spanish Tragedy*, what is left for these characters (the
Andronici) is not the possibility of change or a new life but only
the completion and externalization of the pattern which gives their
existence its primary meaning. But Shakespeare, unlike Kyd, has
somewhat hedged his bets. In Kyd's play the protagonist's dedication to revenge is underwritten by the supernatural figures who (at
the end) take over the completion of the pattern, so that there is no
possibility of freedom. Shakespeare does not offer his protagonist
an exit from the nightmare any more than Kyd does, but he gives
emphasis also to the continuing existence of a political world in
which there is some possibility of progress. And so Shakespeare
can end his play, after the ritual bloodbath has washed away the
past, with the reasserted possibility of free political compromise.
The Ovidian picture of torture, exploitation, and destruction as
basic characteristics of the world, of human freedom as necessarily

an illusion for existences dominated by arbitrary inhuman forces—
this picture is not denied by Shakespeare; but it is complemented
by another in which the surface facts of life are also allowed to exist
in all the richness of their ordinary meanings. In this taste for a
double vision of life in which the facts of history are allowed to be
a necessity, and yet never taken to be a sufficient explanation, even
Titus Andronicus can be seen as a portent of a Shakespearian future
for Elizabethan drama.

4. Early Comedy

Generic Self-Consciousness

THE preceding chapter argues that Elizabethan drama was directed away from shapeless 'mongrel' mixtures of rustic humour and tyrannical violence by the revolutionary examples of *Tamburlaine* and *The Spanish Tragedy* with their 'stately' modes of poetry, coherent structures, and 'astonishing' emotions, but that the natural mongrelism of a popular theatre gradually absorbed the innovations. It would be wrong, however, to think of this absorption as simply a relapse; self-consciousness about the genres being drawn on provided some degree of control over the mixture, so that the mixing became in the end the measure of a sophisticated and novel art form in which comedy and tragedy not only contrasted with one another but collaborated as variant aspects of a unified and realistic vision. This was not (as in Italy) a matter of theoretical debate but of practical necessity. The generic demands of tragedy and comedy had no simple or necessary affinity to the kinds of stories that audiences liked to hear and dramatists therefore had to tell. No such symmetry was available as appears, for example, between the forms and the restricted subject matter of Aeschylus and Sophocles. The popular 'romantic' stories of love and fortune cut completely across the boundaries of genre as traditionally conceived (tragedy as 'the falls of princes', for example) and were thus equally open to comic, tragic, or historical treatment. Nearly all the authors we have to deal with wrote in more than one genre.

This does not mean that authors were constantly having to move between one constricting choice and another. The conflict between the supply side and the demand side of the entertainment industry tended to turn the concept of genre from a set of rules into a technique of multi-layering. The oppositions were most easily resolved (as is usual in practical affairs) by compromise, by providing something for everybody, so that the different languages and viewpoints appropriate to different genres could become part of the drama, as is obvious (among the plays already dealt with) in the case of *Arden of Faversham*, where the play both promotes and subverts its title-page generic definition. And if this can happen in tragedy, with its historical prestige and its clearly defined formal indicators, how much easier is the process in comedy, with its weaker (non-Aristotelian) theoretical base.

Early signs of this capacity to incorporate generic contradiction can be seen in a number of the Inductions to early plays, which dramatize the problem of genre I have been speaking about.[1] One of these Inductions—that to Greene's *The Comical History of Alphonsus, King of Aragon*—has already been mentioned: there we meet the Muses in disarray, with Calliope, the Muse of heroic poetry, as a particularly depressed victim of modern unheroic values. Calliope is rescued by Venus, however, and these two then retire together to Parnassus to write *Alphonsus, King of Aragon*. The combination of these improbable co-sponsors may be taken as a sign of Greene's self-consciousness about the heroical comical enterprise he was engaged in. But the point cannot be taken very far in this play. In *Alphonsus*, Greene seems to be more interested in the degeneracy of the age that prevented him from writing classical tragedy than in the problems of cross-generic composition.

To see the issue in these latter terms, it is convenient to begin by looking at two later exercises in the Elizabethan tragic mode, the anonymous *Soliman and Perseda* (*c*.1589×1592), often attributed to Kyd, and the equally anonymous *A Warning for Fair Women* (*c*.1598×1599). In both these plays disputatious Inductions and Choruses raise the generic question quite specifically. Both plays are, it should be noticed, tragedies of love and therefore perhaps essentially unclassical. In *Soliman and Perseda* the disputants are Love, Fortune, and Death, in *A Warning for Fair Women* they are Comedy, History, and Tragedy, but neither the distinction of names employed nor the gap in time of composition marks any real difference in the nature of the dispute being conducted: the basic issue in both cases is between Tragedy and Comedy. In *Soliman and Perseda* Death immediately announces himself as servant to Melpomene (the Muse of Tragedy) and as 'wholly bent to tragedy's discourse', for 'what are tragedies but acts of death?' (Induction, ll. 6–7). In other words, final unification of the play's structure by acts of death defines its generic status. And so at the end of the

---

[1] An Italian example of the same device appears in the introductory debate between *commedia* and *tragedia* in Alessandro Piccolomini's *L'Ortensio*.

action Death takes possession of the stage, declares it his realm by
an enumeration of the corpses, and banishes his competitors:

> Pack, Love and Fortune, play in comedies,
> For powerful Death best fitteth tragedies.
>
> (V. v. 28-9)

But Love and Fortune are not silenced by this; they look to the
continuous instability of the action as proof of their powers, Love
pointing to the veering emotions of the lovers, Fortune to the
external operations of chance and war. As act succeeds act the
audience's expectations are shunted from hope to fear as failure
follows success and then vice versa. Even at the end of the action
Love and Fortune refuse to accept Death's valuation of his 'deeds
. . . of consequence' as against their 'trifles'. Passion and Chance,
they tell us, will continue to be aspects of life that demand our
commitment, however summarily excluded from the organization
of life that art has imposed on this particular action.

A Warning for Fair Women presents a more purely literary version of the same basic dispute. The Induction discovers Tragedy
and History in their standard allegorical gear, Tragedy with a whip
in one hand, a knife in the other, History with a drum and an
ensign (marking his concentration on war). The representation of
Comedy as a fiddle player is more unusual. As in Soliman and
Perseda, the main dispute turns on the right of Tragedy to dominate a stage where (we learn) different kinds of plays are shown on
different days. Once again Tragedy argues that Comedy (and History) are only concerned with 'slight and childish' matters, designed 'to tickle shallow unjudicial ears'. Tragedy sees his role as
defined by the quality of the emotional response he can elicit:

> I must have passions that must move the soul,
> Make the heart heave and throb within the bosom,
> Extorting tears out of the strictest eyes,
> To rack a thought and strain it to his form
> Until I rap the senses from their course.
> This is my office.
>
> (ll. 44-9)

For Comedy, however, the proper definition of tragedy is more a
matter of the lurid externals:

How some damned tyrant, to obtain a crown,
Stabs, hangs, impoisons, smothers, cutteth throats;
And then a Chorus too comes howling in
And tells us of the worrying of a cat;
Then of a filthy whining ghost,
Lapp'd in some foul sheet or a leather pilch,
Comes screaming like a pig half sticked
And cries *Vindicta*, revenge, revenge.
With that a little rosen flasheth forth
Like smoke out of a tobacco pipe or a boy's squib.
Then comes in two or three like to drovers
With tailors' bodkins stabbing one another.
Is not this trim? Is not here goodly things
That you should be so much accounted of?

                                                    (ll. 50–63)

Both these views of tragedy are in fact fulfilled in the course of
the play. In a series of choruses Tragedy introduces spectacular
dumb-shows in which bowls of blood, 'ebon tapers', and 'mazers
made of dead men's skulls' are deployed. We hear that

The ugly screech-owl and the night raven
With flaggy wings and hideous croaking noise
Do beat the casements of this fatal house.

                                                    (ll. 783–5)

Allegorical figures of Lust and Chastity walk among the London
citizens who make up the cast list.

A Warning for Fair Women is a play which is close to *Arden of
Faversham* in both subject matter and treatment. This play, like that,
highlights the contradiction between the received idea of 'stately'
tragedy and the 'naked' facts of the case. In both plays the rhetoric
of generic self-consciousness is humble and apologetic, but the
point that traditional tragic art cannot deal with these modern lives
remains firm. Even more obviously than in *Arden*, *A Warning for
Fair Women* provides us with a contradiction so balanced that we
cannot tell what guideline to follow. In the course of the plot we
see the drift to murder emerging imperceptibly out of the random
processes of neighbourhood life. But at the same time the choruses
and dumb-shows tell us that lust and sin are being imposed on the
characters by an infection coming straight out of Hell. The play
ends with what at first glance looks like an apology. But is it one?

Perhaps it may seem strange unto you all
That one hath not revenged another's death
After the observation of such course.
The reason is that now of truth I sing,
And should I add or else diminish aught
Many of these spectators then could say
I have committed error in my play.
Bear with this true and home-born tragedy,
Yielding so slender argument and scope
To build a matter of importance on,
And in such form as haply you expected.
What now hath failed, tomorrow you shall see
Performed by *History* or *Comedy*.

(ll. 2722–35)

'Truth' and 'art' are here set against one another as inescapably connected but also incompatible values. 'Perhaps you expected this to be another standard revenge play', he seems to be saying, 'but if I gave you that then those among you who know the facts'—and the end of the Induction seems to imply that there are many of these—'will reject the play as trivial fictionizing'. In these terms Truth seems to be endorsed above Art. But the very fact that the play exists seems to deny the preference (the problems of 'docu-drama' are obviously not confined to the twentieth century). This play (and *Soliman and Perseda* to a lesser extent) shows genre less as a compact with an audience to indicate how life can be made explicable by a particular organization than as a self-consciously artificial structure to be understood in terms of the difficulty of representing truth and fact. The audience is invited to enjoy the cultural allusions and the theatrical conventions—the stage is hung with black for the performance of a tragedy, we learn from the Induction. These conventions have to be seen as generic comments on the life depicted, not as forms necessary to the expression of it.

Soliman and Perseda and *A Warning for Fair Women* are plays that turn out to be tragedies; and it has been convenient to start with them; tragedy, being the most clear-cut of dramatic genres, makes the argument for self-conscious manipulation most easy to justify. Comedy, as a more evasive genre, easily sliding into tragi-comedy and romance, allows a mixed focus to appear entirely 'natural', especially for dramatists seeking the approval of non-specialist audiences.[2] Yet quite early in the period we can observe the same process of generic self-consciousness operating here also. The anonymous play *The Rare Triumphs of Love and Fortune* was probably presented at court in 1582. In terms of subject matter, what we find in it is the traditional romantic farrago of love, royalty, disguise, exile, and restoration that the even earlier *Clyomon and Clamydes* (1570×1583) and *Common Conditions* (1576) had shown in possession of the popular stage. But in *The Rare Triumphs of Love and Fortune* the farrago is no less placed by judgement than indulged by performance. And once again the judgement is indicated by a frame-plot.

The opening scene of *Love and Fortune* is placed on Olympus. From that point of view the nether world of man is seen as an indeterminate realm contested between the Olympian powers 'whereby all things in perfect course abide', and the infernal powers, Pluto and Tisiphone. Fortune, here the daughter of Pluto (not of Jupiter, as was traditional[3]), appears as the activist proponent of infernal discord, separation, and mutability. Venus (or 'Love') is chosen to be the supernal representative of human cohesiveness and unification—perhaps because of some memory of her role as Juno's antagonist in the *Aeneid*. But Love and Fortune are not only the antagonists of the dramatized narrative; they are also (in some degree) equivalent to Comedy and Tragedy, as these appear in the other Inductions discussed.[4] In the opening act both goddesses are allowed to display their powers over human life in a series of mythological 'shows' before Jupiter. But claims for superiority on this basis prove insubstantial and the gods decide that they must allow further testing, this time on human specimens whose natural liability to love, jealousy, resentment, and self-sacrifice will give the goddesses ample opportunity for creative interference. The alternation which follows, between Venus' control and Fortune's

[2] In the period 1576 to 1593 there are twice as many plays with happy as with unhappy endings.

[3] See Howard R. Patch, *The Goddess Fortuna in Medieval Literature* (Cambridge, Mass., 1927), 133.

[4] Fortune is the Muse of tragedy (in the older sense of that word) as the contriver of the falls of princes: 'Lo, such am I that overthrows the highest reared tower | That changeth and supporteth realms in twinkling of an hour' (ll. 169–70). She despises Venus because 'What be the tragedies, the terrors that she makes? | Let's see the mighty monarchs, the kingdoms that she shakes' (ll. 157–8). Venus, as Comedy elsewhere, is said to deal only with 'wanton sugared joys' and 'foolish toys' (ll. 159–60).

(with 'trumpets, drums, cornets, and guns') adds even further to the bewildering complexity of a romance plot already more convoluted than that of *Cymbeline*—which it resembles in a number of respects. Under such circumstances human powers prove incapable of untying the knots that gods have put together. Jupiter intervenes finally and requires the contestant goddesses to cooperate in procuring a happy ending. Only then can the madman be cured, the dumb made to speak, children restored to their parents, the criminals forgiven, the exiles returned to their homes, and the lovers secured to one another.

What *The Rare Triumphs of Love and Fortune* shows us is the appropriateness of romance narrative to the generic alternations I have been discussing, alternations structured here as conflict between supernatural powers (as also in Lyly's *The Woman in the Moon* (1590×1595)). The author has not sought to remove the absurdities of romance; but he has imposed on the tortuosities of romance narrative an external order making for comedy, so that we may understand 'All discord, harmony not understood; | All partial evil, universal good'. It is just this capacity to link contradictory elements by a self-conscious play between generic possibilities that makes *The Rare Triumphs of Love and Fortune* so interesting a precursor of the greater comedies to follow.

A Most Pleasant Comedy of Mucedorus the King's Son of Valencia and Amadine the King's Daughter of Aragon (1588×1598) has little claim to belong among 'greater comedies', but it does have a claim to be the most popular play of the period, having been reprinted thirteen times before 1639. The story it tells is not unlike that of *Love and Fortune*, involving once again a princess and her (apparently) lower-class beloved, exile from court to a savage forest, mistaken trysts, abductions, confused and confusing servants. And once again the complex romantic tale is framed by a generic disputation in Induction and Epilogue—this time between Comedy and Envy (the latter another obvious *alter ego* for Tragedy). As in *A Warning for Fair Women*, each of these figures appears on the stage in the traditional habiliments of the function. Comedy is an ingratiating maiden, 'joyful, with a garland of bays on her head'; Envy appears with 'his arms naked, besmeared with blood' and is supplied with 'drums within' and cries of 'stab, stab'. Comedy defines her role by her desire to please: 'Comedy, play thy part and please, | Make merry them that comes to joy with thee' (Induction,

ll. 3–4), and again 'Comedy is mild, gentle, willing for to please |
And seeks to gain the love of all estates' (ll. 37–8). Envy, on the
other hand, aims to 'thunder music . . . shall appall the nymphs'
(l. 21). Eventually their dispute leads to a compromise which, like
that of *Love and Fortune*, allows them to exercise power one after
the other. But in this case the alternation is not set up to indicate
the caprice that is part of supernatural power, but rather to test
Comedy's ability to repair the damage that Envy can create. As
Comedy puts it:

> Then, ugly monster, do thy worst;
> I will defend them in despite of thee;
> And though thou thinkst with tragic fumes
> To brave my play unto my deep disgrace,
> I force it not; I scorn what thou canst do.
> I'll grace it so thyself shall it confess
> From tragic stuff to be a pleasant comedy.
>
> (Induction, ll. 64–70)

And so Envy must be given the first move in the game to follow.
In the original version, the play proper opens with Amadine and
her cowardly betrothed, Segesto, attacked by a bear. Segesto runs
away, but Mucedorus, apparent shepherd but true prince (as in
Sidney's *Arcadia*), appears and quickly disposes of Envy's ursine
champion 'which hath bereaved thousands of their lives' and
presents its head to the princess. Envy's powers are in fact at a
continuous disadvantage in this play. In spite of the Induction's
tragical talk of 'arms and legs quite shivered off . . . the cries of
many thousands slain . . . turning thy mirth into a deadly dole', the
play itself never converts death into horror. As Comedy tells Envy
in the Epilogue:

> Thy threats were vain, thou couldst do me no hurt.
> Although thou seemdst to cross me with despite
> I overwhelmed and turned upside down thy block
> And made thyself to stumble at the same.
>
> (Epilogue, ll. 4–7)

Comedy, like Venus in *The Rare Triumphs of Love and Fortune*, is
explicitly characterized as carrying a reparative female function
that holds society in concord in spite of the incursions of martial
destructiveness. In the same passage from the Epilogue she twits
Envy with his masculine defeat:

How now, Envy? What, blushest thou already?
Peep forth; hide not thy head with shame,
But with a courage praise a woman's deeds.

(Epilogue, ll. 1–3)

And in both plays this idea of the function of the female comic
Muse leads author and audience towards a final invocation of Queen
Elizabeth, the ultimate protectress of concord and stability.[5]
Comedy may fail to achieve more than a temporary victory over
Envy, but the sight of the Queen at the end of the play forces the
antagonist into total prostration:

My power has lost her might. Envy's date's expired
Yon splendant Majesty hath felled my sting
And I amazed am. [*Fall down and quake*][6]

(Epilogue, ll. 65–7)

Greenian Comedy

The Inductions of this early period give us interesting reasons why
such comedies do not split apart under their alternation of moods,
mingling of kings and clowns, their conviction of overlap between
national destinies and the intimacies of love. Their success is a
tribute, I take it, to a widely diffused skill in self-conscious juxta-
posing and balancing of genres. A group of interrelated comedies
of the crucial late 1580s and early 1590s shows us these same skills
operating in slightly less self-conscious terms, and allowing a degree of unimpeded naturalism to carry the meaning. These are
plays traditionally associated with the name of Robert Greene:
Friar Bacon and Friar Bungay (*c*.1589×1592), *The Scottish History
of James IV* (*c*.1590×1591; printed 1598), *George a Green, the Pinner*

---

[5] The revised version of *Mucedorus* (first printed in 1610 and ending with praise of James
rather than Elizabeth) gives Envy a further final argument. He tells us that he is going to
devise a new kind of comedy, founded on envy ('I'll overthrow thee in thine own intent'
(Epilogue, l. 30)). This new comedy will 'cast native monsters in the moulds of men, | Case
vicious devils under sainted rochets' (ll. 20–1). A new kind of comic writer, seemingly based
on Ben Jonson ('This scambling raven with his needy beard' (l. 40)), will embody envy
inside comedy. And this will produce general theatrical destruction, for the authorities will
be forced to act against the adult actors no less than the principal malefactors, the boys. The
defence of romantic comedy's ability to balance and eventually to defuse the destructiveness
of male aggression will be weakened under these circumstances, which call out for social
reformation rather than the manipulations of genre seen in these earlier plays.

[6] Cf. Jonson's *Cynthia's Revels*, discussed in Ch. 7, pp. 296–9.

of Wakefield (1587×1593; printed 1599), *Fair Em, the Miller's Daughter of Manchester* (*c.*1589×1591), and the manuscript play that editors have named *John of Bordeaux* (or, more tendentiously, *The Second Part of Friar Bacon*) (1590×1594; MS). As the overlap in the possible dates indicates, these public theatre comedies can be considered as contemporaries. They also share a number of more integral features: they are all exercises in romantic history (or historical romance): they present the romantic association of royal persons with idealized figures of a lower social order—figures whose moral integrity and national loyalty serve to counteract the temptations of greatness and help to restore national unity. The historical period which provides the setting is neither close enough nor realistic enough to raise any particular political issues for the Elizabethan audience. Real historical names are used in fact only to give fictional constructs some claim on latter-day nostalgia.

Of these five plays only one offers an external generic commentary at all comparable to those discussed above—*The Scottish History of James IV slain at Flodden. Entermixed with a Pleasant Comedy Presented by Oberon, King of the Fairies.* The title-page gives us a good foretaste of the kind of mixture one can expect, a mixture that may seem already familiar to most readers from (for example) the 1598 title of Shakespeare's *The History of Henry IV . . . with the Humorous Conceits of Sir John Falstaff.* But the similarity is deceiving. Shakespeare's play is a historical chronicle that integrates into its dynastic story a sense of the realm at large where individual 'conceits' create an alternative reality. Greene's play can exercise no such claim; its history is only a piece of pasteboard fiction; the mention of Flodden Field in the title is the merest window dressing (it is never mentioned in the play). The story comes, in fact, out of Giraldi Cinthio (*Hecatommithi*, III. i) and 'James IV' is any prince indulging in adultery (a spacious list), having a powerful neighbour addicted to the preservation of virtue: it is not clear if Henry VII or Henry VIII is intended. The point is crisply made in Sir George Buc's manuscript note on the title-page of the quarto (now in the British Library), which states under the *Scottish History* label 'rather fiction of English and Scottish matters comical'.

The generic conflict that the double title of Greene's play seems to promise ('*History . . . Comedy . . .*') does not work out in practice in quite those terms. The conflict is rather between the cool assurance of comedy and the anguished uncertainty of romance. Oberon, King of the Fairies, is an extraterritorial being whose amused knowledge that all will be well draws on his detachment from all human sorrow and worldly accident (more like Shakespeare's Puck than his Oberon). Bohan, the misanthrope who tells Oberon the story of James IV, stands opposite to this: he has found the world to be deceptive and treacherous and has sought his own kind of detachment by living in a tomb. But being no fairy he cannot detach himself from the ups and downs of the tale (or 'jig', as he scornfully calls it) that he must recount if he is to justify his attitude. The narrative is thus seen from two incompatible points of view, and each commentator finds confirmation of his own perspective in what the play enacts. Bohan can point moralistically to the wickedness of the king, but Oberon can reply with evidence of the virtue of the ladies:

> BOHAN. Judge, fairy king, hast heard a greater ill?
> OBERON. Nor seen more virtue in a country maid.
>
> (Act II, Chorus, 8–9)

The magic Oberon is justified by his foreseen ending, when the invading army forces James back into the path of English virtue. But Bohan is no less justified in misanthropy. Virtue achieved only under threat does not supply much of a basis for belief in human goodness.

The other comedy in my list generally allowed to come from the pen of Robert Greene (and not simply out of his 'school') is *The Honourable History of Friar Bacon and Friar Bungay*. Here too we may see a pattern of royal wilfulness in love, abetted by the complacency of his subjects, but eventually proving nobility by self-correction, leading to an appropriate royal marriage. Edward, the Prince of Wales, must marry Elinor of Castile, for dynastic reasons. But he is obsessed by the rustic beauty of Margaret, the fair maid of Fressingfield. A romantic contradiction is thus opened up between social duty and personal passion—though the individual, of course, hopes to secure both advantages. In the subplot the same pattern shows itself. Friar Bacon's magic is analogous to the prince's love: it offers the romantic dream of unrestricted fulfilment. But romance must be cut down to comedy. Bacon is no Oberon; his magic, like Edward's love, must act through human intermediaries. Edward instructs Lacy that his function is to be a proxy for the prince, preparing Margaret for the coming royal seduction; Bacon must entrust care of the Brazen Head to his servant Miles. Both intermediaries fail: Lacy falls in love with Margaret, Miles falls asleep at the crucial moment, and both principals have to accept that in dangerous matters beyond human control (passion and magic) repentance is what is required and an understanding that power is available only inside the strictest limits. As the proverb told Elizabethans: 'That which is above us pertains nothing to us.'

The generic balance in this play lies between the tragic violence that power encourages—Edward will stab Lacy; Bacon's perspective glass encourages the sons of Lambert and Serlsby to kill one another—and the countering need to live inside the norms of social order. As in *The Rare Triumphs of Love and Fortune* and *Mucedorus*, a final reconciliation between power and love is guaranteed by an invocation to Queen Elizabeth, in whose reign loving power holds together the nation and the whole hierarchical system.

The manuscript play now usually called *John of Bordeaux*[7] was evidently written (by Greene or another) as a sequel to *Friar Bacon and Friar Bungay*; it is one of the least effective plays in the group, lacking the generic balance that characterizes the others. It is tempting to link this to the foreign setting, national sentiment being one of the coordinating factors that most easily leads to a happy ending. The presiding monarch of *John of Bordeaux*, the Emperor Frederick, is taken from the cast list of *Friar Bacon*, where he appears, being Henry III's brother-in-law, among the distinguished guests at the royal wedding. But now he is in his own realm, in 'Hosburg' (probably *Hapsburg*—see *Friar Bacon*, Sc. iv, l. 45), while his armies, led by John of Bordeaux,[8] are fighting the Turks under Amurath for control of Ravenna; it can be seen from this that even by Greene's standards the 'history' in this play is a jumble, without any settled influence over the romantic and melodramatic events that appear and disappear in a random succession. Friar Bacon is visiting Frederick's court by invitation, and once again we see him in competition with the German magician,

---

[7] For a full description, see the MSR edition by Renwick (1936). He describes the MS as a draft 'reconstructed by at least five' writers, 'a shortened version of a longer text . . . made for a company already familiar with the play', in which the clown's part has been fully preserved and the serious elements greatly curtailed (pp. vi–viii).

[8] The name seems to be derived from Lodge's *Rosalynde* (1590), where it comes from the Tale of Gamelyn. In Lodge's version we learn that 'John of Bordeaux . . . passed the prime of his youth in sundry battles against the Turks'.

Vandermast. Needless to say, he wins all the contests. The narrative of princely passion is recognizably the same as in *Friar Bacon and Friar Bungay*: the heir apparent (now Ferdinand, as formerly Edward) is in love with another resistant beauty, and again (like Edward) he seeks help from the court magician (Vandermast). But this beauty is already married and indeed is wife to the absent general, John of Bordeaux; and the methods taken to secure her consent—deprivation of home, husband, and honour, beggary, imprisonment, condemnation to death—require a melodramatic treatment instead of the idyllic compromises of *Friar Bacon*. Only Friar Bacon's good old English magic can prevent impending catastrophe; for here there is no historical or pseudo-historical consensus such as identification with national virtue will provide. The final pages of the manuscript are fragmentary, but it is fairly clear from the fragments that Bacon engineers the happy ending that the structure of the play demands—exposure and forgiveness of Ferdinand and restoration to honour of John of Bordeaux and his family. What Bacon cannot achieve in this play (it would seem) is an effective balance between the accumulation of wickedness and the sense of a simultaneous gaiety and comic confidence that cornucopian poetry and nationalism provide.[9]

The Pleasant Conceited Comedy of George a Green, the Pinner of Wakefield errs, if at all, on the other side of this precarious balance between comic confidence and romantic threat. The good-natured jingoism of the central character so dominates the action that the historical disasters that threaten—invasion by a Scottish king 'James' and baronial rebellion against an English sovereign 'Edward'—are never given any hold on our imagination. The virtuous world of independent yeomen in a historically distanced time is, as in other plays, set against the corruptions of the court and the aristocracy, only the sovereign himself being exempted from criticism. But here the representative of rustic virtue is not a blushing milkmaid but a hearty 'pinner' (keeper of the local pound or pinfold), the hero of his provincial community and already by the time of the

---

[9] It must be allowed that the poetic power of *John of Bordeaux* is particularly hard to evaluate. The manuscript, faithfully reproduced in the Malone Society type-facsimile, saves paper by filling out its pages with fifteen-syllable lines (one line approximately for every line and a half of the versification). To read the play in this format is to learn the extent to which readers are dependent on the coincidence between the visual pattern on the page and the aural effects.

play the subject of popular folk-tale.[10] The journey, in disguise, of
the two kings, Edward and James, from the court to the north
country where they will meet this paragon, is presented as a learning experience. What is learned in this case is the explicitly political lesson that nationalist loyalty arises out of the soldierly
self-respect that is generated by local independence. As in more
modern exposures of superior persons to a 'frontier ethic', the
kings learn this by joining in perforce, subjecting themselves to the
hearty rough and tumble of northern manners, especially in Bradford, 'where all the merry shoemakers dwell'. By giving as good as
he gets, Edward proves himself worthy to receive loyalty, to act as
guarantor for traditional privileges, to be their king. This stress
on a natural bond between the sovereign and his humble subjects—as between a leader and the soldiers of his army (compare
comments on *The Famous Victories of Henry V* in Chapter 5 and on
The Shoemakers' Holiday in Chapter 8)—was designed, no doubt,
to exclude a corrupt court aristocracy and was for this reason, no
doubt, a good selling point to popular audiences. The image was,
of course, already embodied in the figure of Robin Hood; and
George a Green is presented in the play as a second Robin Hood
(without needing to acquire the status of a fallen nobleman); the
two men meet, challenge one another, fight at quarter staves, admire one another's prowess, and join forces. The nostalgic creation
of this idyllic man's world in the north where

> Though we Yorkshire men be blunt of speech,
> And little skilled in court or such quaint fashions,
> Yet nature teacheth us duty to our king,
>
> (ll. 1198–200)

and where social habits that would be incompatible in the south
can coexist in balanced harmony, shows itself in love no less than
politics. George's wooing of Bettris Grimes presents the same
emotional pattern as appears in his relation to the king, mutual
loyalty preserved through thick and thin, strict respect for traditional values and for patriarchal rights, contentment with things as
they have always been, and an extreme reluctance to allow any

---

[10] The romance of George a Green (*The Pindar of Wakefield*) is printed by W. J. Thoms,
Collection of Early Prose Romances (London, 1828). There is a ballad (entered in the Stationers' Register in 1557–8) in F. J. Child's *English and Scottish Ballads* (Boston, 1885–6), iii.
204–7. The pamphlet of 1632 is ed. E. A. Horsman (Liverpool, 1956).

change. By excluding the dangers of sexual passion from the comic structure, *George a Green* loses much of the tension that elsewhere gives a sharp edge to the interrelationship of pretentious high life and merry humble life, corruption and innocence. The consensus that in other comedies has had to be sought for with difficulty is always readily available in this play; the denouement only confirms what is never seriously in doubt.

Fair Em, the Miller's Daughter of Manchester, with the Love of William the Conqueror can hardly be by Robert Greene, since he ridicules its author in the preface to *A Farewell to Folly* (1591), but clearly it belongs with the other 'School of Greene' comedies. As the extended title indicates, *Fair Em* is yet another historical romance, the 'historical' elements being taken, once again, from a romantic novella, this time novel 4 in Wotton's *Courtly Cautels* (1587). The plot is polarized between an impatient English sovereign (here called 'the Saxon Duke' and 'William of Saxony') and a virtuous country maiden. The polarization between these stereotypes belongs in this case, however, only to the structure, not to the plot, for here there are two separate plots (an 'Em plot' and a 'William plot') and the two never meet until the last scene. At that point William, having re-ennobled Em's unjustly banished father, makes the right choice between her various suitors. Elsewhere the royal lover and the country maiden appear in alternating, thematically parallel scenes throughout the play, each displaying inside a separate context the appropriate polarizing characteristics. But there is no tension, no conflict, for there is no meeting; Em stays in rustic Manchester; William pursues his infatuations mostly in Denmark. He sets out for that country at the beginning of the play, having fallen in love with Blanch's picture; but when he sees the real Blanch he hates her and loves Mariana instead. He plans to steal Mariana away to England, but only succeeds in stealing the disguised Blanch; discovering this, he hates all womankind. Back in Manchester Em is being pursued by three suitors (and the clown). She puts off two of the suitors, hoping to secure the third. But when the three of them meet together they decide that she hates mankind, and her preferred suitor therefore takes his love elsewhere. Appealing against this before William, Em makes him realize that there are indeed virtuous women in the world. The self-awareness that this revelation produces leads to his staying with Blanch, and reconciling himself to his exiled subjects. He selects as a husband for Em the only lover who has remained faithful to her.

We are given to understand in *Fair Em* that constancy is the prime virtue in love, whether in the cottage or the palace. But what William learns from Em's example relates not only to love but also to politics: the reconciliation between England and Denmark as between William and his displaced subjects grows from the same principle, the principle we have already seen exemplified in Venus, in the allegorical figure of Comedy, in Ida (in *James IV*), in Rossaline (in *John of Bordeaux*), in Margaret, the fair maid of Fressingfield. The spirit of these early romantic comedies, one might say, is most effectively represented by the forgiving and reconciling figure of womankind, constant in affection, patient in affliction, resistant to improper pressure, and capable, in nostalgically viewed historical time, of direct and exemplary political effects. It is she who, like the honest yeoman, best manages to combine the demands of particular relationships with the sense of a community of shared values and beliefs. She is without ambition for herself and so provides the ballast that ties overweening princely ambition to reality and continuity, and so to a sustainable happy ending.

Classical Comic Forms

A traditional view of the development of English comedy presents the story as a straight-line movement through classically inspired 'regular' forms to a technical fulfilment in the well-made play. But a look at the detail of Elizabethan drama does nothing to support this. We have already seen in the comedies discussed an impulse to accommodate opposites rather than seek clear generic definition. *Ralph Roister Doister* (1545×1552) and *Gammer Gurton's Needle* (*c*.1552×1563) may be the treasures of progressivistic history, but there is no evidence that they provided models of comedy for the Elizabethan public stage. The popular success of the received comic form and the need for comedy to be 'pleasing' (as noted above) both discouraged a search for generic purity; and purism in comedy could never offer the cachet of 'tragoedia cothurnata, fitting kings'.

The *rules* of comedy, derived in grammar schools from the practice of Terence,[11] would have driven a wedge between theatrical

---

[11] See T. W. Baldwin, *Shakspere's Five Act Structure* (Urbana, Ill., 1947).

practice and public taste, if they had been strictly followed. Instead of the romantic licence to develop the plot over a long stretch of time and space, the rules demanded that the action be concentrated. Instead of princes and noblewomen (mixed with clowns and citizens), the rules required the characters to be persons of middle or low social status and their concerns were to be limited to the petty issues of domestic life. The 'correct' comedy should be written in the language of everyday existence, purified from grossness, but not aspiring to the *meraviglia* or *admiratio* which creates indecorous terror by suggesting that human passion can break down the protective walls of social existence.

For all the theoretical contempt they generated, the old mongrel forms did not necessarily produce incompetent theatre pieces. And indeed the prejudice against them did not aim to produce better-liked plays, but only more easily defended ones. Then, as now, it was a critical snobbism, as much social as literary, that lay behind the objections to popular forms. This did not mean, of course, that such objections were without effect on theatrical practice. But it was an effect registered in the public theatre's own terms, never so strong that it could keep at bay the traditional folk elements, as in the Renaissance drama of France or Italy.

The neoclassical precept that exerted most pressure was that which demanded unity of action secured by a single controlling intrigue. It was a demand that fitted neatly into the whole Humanist enterprise to replace Gothic multiplicity by clarity of line and harmony of parts, as seen, for example, in such models as the Pazzi chapel, the Queen's House at Greenwich, or Raphael's 'The School of Athens'. But just as classicism in Tudor/Stuart architecture seldom achieved a status beyond that of one system among many (as in Inigo Jones's portico for Old St Paul's), so in Elizabethan drama it operates as an impulse rather than an achievement.

Progressivistic literary history[12] has tended to look on 'plot unity' in drama as a Good Thing that earlier periods must have been struggling to achieve. And it is true that the models provided by Seneca and Terence seem to have been appreciated; but the lessons they offered were only randomly embodied. Even in comedy, where classical influence on plot structure is least open to controversy,[13]

[12] As, for example, in George Pierce Baker's widely influential *The Development of Shakespeare as a Dramatist* (New York, 1907).
[13] See T. W. Baldwin, *Shakspere's Five-Act Structure*.

there is no evidence of a regular advance towards the plot-directed play. The drama up to 1642 represents a struggle, not between progress and retreat (meaning good and bad) but between alternative ideas of excellence, hardly compatible but equally justified in practice. I have called the virtues of the Greenian comedies 'cornucopian', and in pages to come I will praise Lyly's *Mother Bombie* and *Gascoigne's *Supposes* as comedies characterized by neatness, logic, and self-conscious restraint. These different vocabularies do not require us, however, to assume that one set of praise words excludes the other, even if, considered separately, they do tend to pull in opposite directions, towards fantasy or realism, the notional past or the equally notional present, poetry or prose, large and various casts or small and interrelated ones. For all the theoretical tension between them, these opposites are often found together, or occupying adjacent places in a large and hospitable terrain.

The ideal of unity as a desirable feature in a good play can of course be shared by playwrights who have completely different definitions of unity. But criticism, which can hardly evade the duty to make definitions, has tended to suppose that difference requires defence or attack. The earlier critical position—that Elizabethan drama was lamentably slow to join the movement out of Gothic barbarism into classically inspired plot unity—has in this century been countered by a contrary view, that Elizabethan drama was mercifully spared the tyranny of the rules and owes its greatness not to plot unity but (as in *The Waste Land* or the *Cantos*) to the non-sequential force of parallelism, irony, and analogy. But these new insights, like the insights of the positivist historians, have been bought at the price of downgrading plays that operate on different principles—Jonson's tightly plotted tragedies, Middleton's intrigues, and the elegant social comedies of Fletcher or Shirley.

It is convenient to begin discussion of comedy obviously responsive to the demands of the neoclassical canons (without, however, ceasing to be 'Gothic') with consideration of a play obviously carrying the marks of 'the school of Greene'. The manuscript play of *John a Kent and John a Cumber* (1587×1590), probably by Anthony *Munday, is parallel[14] to *Friar Bacon and Friar Bungay* not only

[14] I. A. Shapiro, in 'The Significance of a Date', *Sh. S.* 8 (1955), dates *John a Kent* in 1589, probably before Greene's play. If this is allowed, then we must allow that Munday was the innovator, Greene the imitator. Munday's magicians deserve the double billing, but the title of Greene's play is entirely misleading. Friar Bungay is a very minor character, Bacon's rival in only one scene.

in title but also in subject matter, both dramatists using a rivalry between medieval magicians to affect the progress of a rivalry in love. These similarities belong, however, mainly to the surface. Munday constructs the imbroglio of magicians and lovers in terms of the five-act structure of a 'regular' New Comedy plot. In *Friar Bacon* the magicians involved (Bacon, Bungay, Vandermast) are relevant to the action most obviously by their power to organize side 'shows' and entertainments for their courtly audience. These activities offer episodic intensifications around a love plot that would probably reach the same conclusion even without their presence. Their strands of action are interwoven with sundry other strands to create a dazzling heterogeneity, a cornucopian fullness. Inside such a structure it is difficult, and would be pointless, to pull out particular filaments so as to describe their individual plot functions. Munday's play, however, uses its magicians not simply as intensifying elements but as the controlling intelligences whose rival deceptions create the structure of the play. A. E. Pennell in his edition of *John a Kent and John a Cumber* (1980) has shown how easy it is to set out this alternation of control in schematic form: Kent controls the first three scenes, Cumber the next three, Kent controls five, and then Cumber and Kent alternate, scene by scene, until Kent scores his decisive victory in the final episode. The virtues that Munday is aiming for are not those associated with variety and passionate change of mind but rather consistency and an ingenious but logical movement forward.[15] To achieve this effect, the lovers have, of course, to be changed from individuals to mere pawns in the 'game' played between the two monkish manipulators. Indeed we are told explicitly by John a Kent that he is postponing the happiness of the 'proper' pair (which he could secure straightaway if he chose) so that he can 'sport himself a while' with an adequate rival player, and this the undesirable lovers immediately provide by importing John a Cumber from Scotland.

Munday's allegiance to the plot ideals of New Comedy does not mean that his play is entirely without episodic intensifications: a group of mechanicals prepare an entertainment; a boy plays on a tabor to mislead travellers; an aubade is organized; there are threats of battle and historical reminiscences. The location, somewhere around Chester and the Welsh Marches, is kept indefinite. The characters are noblemen and landowners; they seem to belong to a

---

[15] Francis Meres in his *Palladis Tamia* (1598) called Munday 'our best plotter'.

distant past.[16] But none of this begins to match Greene's *Bacon and Bungay* in energy and inventiveness. We may judge that the mixture of classical order and freewheeling romance attempted here has overstrained Munday's capacities.

The neoclassical elements that Munday tried to combine with Greenian romance in *John a Kent and John a Cumber* were not, of course, novelties in 1589 (or even 1584). They had by this time a considerable history in the drama even of England; but their influence always tended to show itself at the academic margin rather than the commercial centre. The originals (Plautus and Terence) were performed recurrently in the universities, but the reputation they carried in the culture at large was at some remove from their actual plays. For these reflected (robustly in Plautus, pallidly in Terence) the manners of a world that had disappeared, one which could be supposed to have deserved its oblivion, given its antipathy to a truly Christian civilization. On the other hand, the *form* of classical (especially Terentian) comedy could be judged, in terms of the logical organization of its elements, to reflect a Humanist intuition about life's capacity for order. If tragic action reveals the world in terms of anti-social, anti-rational drives that can be contained only by a ritualizing remoteness in presentation (choruses, high poetry, scenic splendour, estranging attitudes), comedy, on the other hand, can reassure audiences by showing how the pattern of correct relationships emerges 'naturally' from a progression of events. By concentrating on the appetites of those in the lower segments of society, classical comedy reassured its audiences that the forces making for reconciliation can always be made to triumph.

By the 1580s the divorce of classical form from the mimesis of classical life had already been completed (even in England), partly by the formalistic commentary on Terence as taught in schools, which dissolved the texture of the drama into a maze of literary rules, and even more effectively by the diffusion of the school drama or 'Christian Terence' that Humanist schoolmasters wrote for their pupils—such as the *Acolastus* (1529) of Gnaephius (or Fullonius), Stymmelius' *Studentes* (1549), Macropedius' *Asotus* (1510), and their English imitations.[17] These took the standard

---

[16] The names seem designed to recall the early thirteenth century: the famous Ranulph, Earl of Chester, d. 1232; the famous Llywellan ('the Great'), d. 1240; the famous Earl of Pembroke (William Marshall), d. 1219.

[17] See F. P. Wilson, *English Drama 1485–1585* (Oxford, 1968), 96 ff.

New Comedy plot of the son outwitting the father and reworked it from the point of view of the father (and the Father in Heaven) so that the witty slave became the diabolical tempter (or Vice) and the neatness of the plot a tribute to the ingenuity of Providence. Both these school processes inevitably affected all literate persons in the age. At the same time a stream of neoclassical influence was coming from another (and complementary) direction, from the *commedia erudita* of the cinquecento Italian dramatists, who had no brief to reproduce the heavy moralism of the schoolmasters and so were able to fit into the given form an image of life that was recognizably modern, though inevitably (to English eyes) daringly exotic. It is this latter channel that leads the neoclassical form of comedy as close to the popular London stage as the English situation allowed.

The university drama of this period was, inevitably, in Latin, and this by itself made a barrier between the two stages; but it was not an impermeable barrier. Most of the university plays have perished, but three Cambridge comedies of the period when commercial comedy was making its first moves—*Hymenaeus* of 1579, *Pedantius* of 1581, and *Victoria* of 1580×1583 (surviving in manuscript)—reveal the extent to which Italian versions of the classical form had become the accepted mode in élite circles. Italian *commedia erudita*, in its developed and more influential form (that reached English university performance through imitation of later playwrights such as Pasqualigo, Grazzini, and Della Porta) varied from the Graeco-Roman model most pervasively, and most influentially, by making the young girl sought by suitors the active centre of the intrigue. In that great model play, Terence's *Eunuchus*, the object of the intrigue, the enslaved Pamphila, never speaks and is seen only once, probably veiled, at line 232. She is raped (as a slave) and betrothed (as a citizen) without, so far as we know, expressing any wish or intention whatsoever. The only female figure given power of choice or intrigue in classical comedy is the independent courtesan who can use her witty capacity to play her lovers against one another to secure a means of financial survival. Italian comedy extended this freedom even further, giving to the bourgeois daughter (or wife) besieged by lovers a capacity (like that of the *adolescens*) to delay or avoid the preferred choice of the father and eventually to secure the man she wants. *Hymenaeus* (1579), perhaps written by Abraham *Fraunce (who certainly acted in it), is an adaptation of the tenth novel of the fourth day in Boccaccio's *Decameron*. It is instructive to notice how far the adaptation moves the story towards the dramatic stereotype: the girl (Julia) is no longer a wife; she has become a daughter; and she is no longer enjoying an intrigue with a lover. She is now, in the standard mode, the object of three suitors, one (acceptable) already in place, and two grotesques, a pedantic doctor and a drunken German. The play ends (as recurrently) with the arrival of the lover's father and his financial endorsement of Julia as an acceptable wife. But Julia herself is the main actor in this intrigue, negotiating between her father and her lovers and disposing of the apparent corpse of her true lover not only with aplomb but with the appropriate rhetoric:

> Paulisper vale, ego te brevi sequar.
> Sed in longum vale, mora brevis longa mihi
> Imo aeternum vale, nunquam te rursus videro.
>
> (IV. i. 74–6)

Julia does not have the resource that was made available to so many later Italianate heroines—that of leaving home and following her lover in disguise—which appears in the Cambridge *Silvanus* (acted in January 1597) and in the immensely popular *Gl'ingannati*, acted in Siena in 1531, given in Cambridge in a Latin version (*Laelia*) in 1594, and finding its modern point of fame in Shakespeare's *Twelfth Night*. Yet Julia's adventures are sufficient by themselves to show how far university comedy in Latin provided a conduit through which the Italian taste in comedy could reach towards the girl-centred romantic comedies of Shakespeare.

The most interesting of these early university comedies,[18] for the purposes of this history, is Abraham Fraunce's *Victoria*, derived from Luigi Pasqualigo's *Il fedele* (1576) and performed at St John's College, Cambridge, some time between 1580 and 1583 (most probably in 1582). This translation from Italian into Latin is of particular historical interest because only a few years later the same Italian play was translated into English (probably by Munday) —apparently without reference to the Latin—under the title of *Fedele and Fortunio. The Deceits in Love: Excellently Discoursed in a Very Pleasant and Fine Conceited Comedy of Two Italian Gentlemen.*

---

[18] *Pedantius*, the third Cambridge comedy I have mentioned, is usually discussed as a satire on Gabriel Harvey (drawn on for the portrait of the pedant lover); but in formal terms he is simply another grotesque *innamorato* competing unsuccessfully for the hand of the much besought maiden.

Translated out of the Italian and Set Down According as it Hath Been Presented before the Queen's Most Excellent Majesty (1579×1584).[19] Pasqualigo's original play provides us with a complex picture of an idle and (from a modern perspective) an unpleasant society. It is not entirely clear if the author wrote it to expose viciousness to scorn or simply to show life as he expected his audience to understand it. Certainly the title and the name of the principal male character suggest some degree of satire: the 'faithfulness' of Fedele himself is shown only in terms of the violence with which he plans revenge against Vittoria, the mistress who has dared to forget him while he was absent. To express this 'faithfulness' he informs her husband of her current, but not her past, infidelities, suggesting that he poison her slowly, and so escape detection, instead of stabbing her at once (as was the first plan). This gives him time and leverage to enforce Vittoria's return to his bed, threatening to withhold the information that will clear her name and save her life. Vittoria, for her part, only fails in her counter-plot to kill Fedele by choosing the wrong lover to undertake the deed. The 'closing' (*clauduntur*) of what the Latin version calls its 'happy ending' (*exitu foelici*) is thus happier in plot than in human terms. The whole play, of which the Fedele and Vittoria plot is only one strand, is a labyrinth of sexual intrigues principally carried out through the agency of the servants (there are eight personal servants out of a cast of eighteen). But here there is little of the difference in standards of behaviour that in English comedy differentiate masters and servants: they chase the same women and employ the same methods to secure them. Munday's notions that these are 'Italian Gentlemen' begins itself to look satiric (or else xenophobic).

Abraham Fraunce's Latin version, probably written when he was a Fellow of St John's College, Cambridge, is presented to his patron, Sir Philip Sidney, as a diversion from the 'tragical evils of the time'. He follows Pasqualigo fairly faithfully, but shows his academic background by enlarging the pedantry of Onofrio, Fortunio's tutor, who is pursuing Vittoria for himself. He thus changes the play by bringing it closer to the model represented best at Cambridge by *Pedantius*—the girl being pursued by a trio

---

[19] See the edition by Richard Hosley (New York, 1981). For Hosley's plausible conjecture that the play was performed at court in 1584 by Oxford's boys, see pp. 144–5, where the bearing of this idea on the plays of John Lyly is explored.

of suitors, a Pedant, a Miles Gloriosus, and an Innamorato (Fedele). Clearly Fraunce saw little need, either for the entertainment of Sidney or for the sake of the Cambridge students (if the play was actually performed), to modify the image of the world that Pasqualigo presents. The real changes occur, significantly enough, when the play comes to the point of performance in English, and then the Italian text is radically changed to what seemed acceptable, though Italianate, from an English point of view. The key change (here as in the *Hymenaeus* version of Boccaccio) is that Victoria ceases to be a randy wife and becomes a virginal daughter, the object of rival suitors—the 'two Italian gentlemen' and the braggart Crackstone (who combines the roles of three of the original servants).[20] Most of the servants' intrigues either disappear or are represented as crude efforts to overcome their masters' scruples. Thus Virginia no longer participates in the plan to secure Fedele for herself, and Fortunio's design to compromise Virginia is turned from a sexual to a social adventure. The three versions of this play (Italian, Latin, English) allow one to observe the penetration of English theatrical life by the Italian taste and understand the modifications that were required as the action moved closer to the London stage. Munday's version reached the court, performed by boys one may assume, and was probably performed also in the boys' own 'private' playhouse in the Blackfriars. Here at last we are within hailing distance of the public stage. But if the play had really been written for that milieu, one must conjecture that Vittoria would have suffered still further Anglicization, perhaps bringing her closer to the reparative feminine role we have seen at large in Greenian comedy.

The comic repertory of the universities, with specific debts to Roman plays and Italian imitations, represents tastes that come as close to those of continental Humanism as the English theatre ever came. The Inns of Court in London no doubt shared many of these tastes. But the London milieu inevitably brought its student audience closer to court drama and the professional theatre than the universities were allowed to be. What is even more important for our purpose is that the plays at the Inns were mainly in English, and on some occasions written by professional dramatists. These

---

[20] The half-title to *Fedele and Fortunio* reads 'with the Merry conceits of Captain Crackstone'.

factors allowed cross-fertilization to a degree not possible in Oxford or Cambridge. Two excellent comedies performed at the Inns of Court survive from the early years of the Elizabethan drama— Gascoigne's *Supposes*, performed at Gray's Inn in 1566, and Shakespeare's *The Comedy of Errors*, probably performed at Gray's Inn in 1594. Taken together these two plays provide an interesting further commentary on the dilemmas and opportunities that classical and neoclassical models provided, inside general expectation of a romantic concern with individual states of mind.

Gascoigne's *Supposes* (1566) is a translation of the prose version of Ariosto's *I suppositi*, first performed in Ferrara in 1509. The mode to which this plot (together with its imitations in French and Spanish) belongs is best indicated by the language of some popular titles: *Supposes* (*Suppositi*); *Errors*, 'Deceptions' (*Inganni*), 'The Deceived' (*Gl'ingannati*). These attach to a class of comedies in which we watch citizens who think they know who they are, and think they know how to deceive others without being deceived themselves, who trust they understand what is going on around them, what happened in the past, and what seems to be happening before their eyes. The plots are, of course, set up so that none of these presuppositions is justified. We in the audience are given a position of superior outlook so that we can watch the bewilderment and anxiety of the characters with the secure delight of a god's-eye view. What this mode of comedy offers, which the straight intrigue of a manipulator against a simpleton (as in Machiavelli's *Mandragola* and in so many of the stories in *The Decameron*) does not, is some sense of social life as a multidimensional structure stressed between the contrary pressures of the many different members of a complex but unified society: fathers want daughters to marry rich pantaloons, while daughters hope to marry virile youths; the youths' fathers in their turn try to force them to marry convenient heiresses; servants complicate the relationships at every point, quarrelling among themselves, offering help while seeking self-advantage; courtesans temporize to attract additional gifts; parasites construe all relationships in terms of the next meal. We can see that the shared situation of these people is essentially static, any movement forwards at any point in the system being inevitably compensated for by an answering movement backwards at another point; we can see this, but the characters (thus inferior) can not. The characteristics of this world, though transformed into patterns of incredible neatness, are in fact made out of recurrent aspects of the entirely familiar world everywhere around us. Ariosto presents to the Ferrarese of his original audience an authenticated series of genuinely Ferrarese situations. And the style (at least in the prose version) allows us to believe that we are hearing the kinds of things that people actually say. Gascoigne cannot repeat Ariosto's evocation of the original audience's actual city; but his prose style gives us much the same sense of an ordered transcription of speech unselfconsciously used as direct communication.

If we say that the worlds depicted in these plays are 'essentially static', this does not mean that their materials cannot be turned around, and around. This is indeed their principal comic resource. Gascoigne tells us in the Prologue that 'you shall see the master supposed for the servant, the servant for the master, the freeman for a slave and the bondslave for a freeman, the stranger for a well known friend, and the familiar for a stranger'. Characters in these 'Error' plays continually suppose they see the person because they see the social role; but there is no suggestion that the role (master, servant, familiar, stranger, and so on) loses thereby any of the significance that society expects it to have. Ariosto adds to the point that Gascoigne translates here a rider that Gascoigne omits: 'E vi confessa l'autore avere in questo e Plauto e Terenzio seguitato' (he is thinking of the *Eunuchus* and the *Captivi*). This slightly overstates the dependence: the imitation does not produce a duplicate; the density of the 'supposing' in Ariosto (as of the 'errors' in *The Comedy of Errors*, seen in relation to those in Plautus' *Menaechmi*) really transforms the effect from anything found in Plautus and Terence. Terence's Phaedria in the *Eunuchus* disguises himself in order to gain access to his beloved, as do Ariosto's Erostrato and Shakespeare's Lucentio in *The Taming of the Shrew*. But where the Roman author shows us disguise and error as part of a personal history, Ariosto/Gascoigne and Shakespeare treat them rather as aspects of the human condition, pointing us more towards the instability of human identity than towards the impulse of the plotter. We are required to respond to the comic double pressure of society's need for a set structure of roles, while at the same time we see the individual's discomfort with whatever roles are marked out for him.

The gap between the Inns of Court production of *Supposes* and that of *The Comedy of Errors* (*c*.1590×1594; printed 1623) measures the whole story of the establishment of Elizabethan commercial drama. By the time of Shakespeare's play there was a well-founded professional theatre in London with a considerable repertory and a sophisticated technique to express the nuance of individual experience. And Shakespeare draws directly on this inheritance in handling his story of old Aegeon, the despairing father of a disintegrated family who is brought into *The Comedy of Errors* to confront the hard-headed world of Plautine farce. Plautus' *Menaechmi* is written to give priority to such a world, where the tension between the various characters is already at snapping point when the play opens. It gives the citizen Menaechmus the control of our attention. We see his social entanglements, understand his relationships to the Matrona, his wife, to Erotium, the courtesan, and to Peniculus the parasite, so that, when the action begins and Menaechmus the traveller arrives, he joins a society whose reactions we can anticipate—a society of cheating and exploitation, of looking after number one. And so we quickly discover that the traveller is a man well adapted to flourish in such a society. In *The Comedy of Errors*, however, we begin not with the society but with the intruder and victim, old Aegeon, and in the light of his experience we see the traveller less in terms of his adaptability than his disorientation, his loneliness, his despair of ever finding his family.

In the *Menaechmi*, Act II, Scene i, the servant, Messenio, who is in many ways the presenter of the action, complains that there is no point of continuing to search for the lost brother: 'Let's go home.' But Menaechmus [Sosicles] is held on course by his personal emotions:

> ego illum scio quam carus sit cordi meo.
>
> (l. 246)

The servant cannot understand this:

> quin nos hinc domum
> redimus nisi si historiam scripturi sumus.
>
> (ll. 247–8)

From his point of view the only reason for not returning home is if they are going to be making up a story. The clear opposition here between fact and fiction, sense and sensibility, seems to be one that Shakespeare is not anxious to preserve. Messenio perceives

that the emotional story of the lost twin brother is too like romantic fiction to be tolerable as a guide to action. But Shakespeare
apparently is happy to suggest that the factual details of our experience cannot be extricated from the explanatory matrix of our romantic fictions. *The Comedy of Errors* derives the 'true' story of old
Aegeon—the first history we hear in the play—from the 'mouldy
tale' of Pericles, Prince of Tyre, or rather from *Pericles'* source, the
late classical romance of Apollonius of Tyre, a tissue of improb-
abilities vouched for as true by Gower in the *Pericles* play and
strongly recommended in *Errors* by the reluctance to tell it manifested by Aegeon. As told by him, it also recommends itself as an
expression of that romantic longing for fulfilment which can give
a whole life articulated meaning. Greek Romance narrative and
New Comedy plot structure are not, in fact, as incompatible (at
least in technique) as Messenio suggests:[21] they share the use of
anagnorisis or recognition as a device which can move the confusions of life into a final celebration of recovered relationships
and so of individual identity. Between the two genres there is,
however, a marked difference of atmosphere: in New Comedy the
recognition comes like a cutting of the Gordian knot—as the unexpected solution to an impossible tangle;[22] in romance it is part of
an expectable system. The *commedia erudita* shows a tendency to
compromise. Thus in *Suppositi/Supposes* we learn at the end of the
play that Dulippo, the servant who pretends to be his master
(Tranio in *The Taming of the Shrew*) is the son of the pantaloon
wooer, Cleandro. So the competition for the girl is removed—
Cleandro had hoped to have another son by her—and Dulippo is
spared the need to return to his status as a servant (he was really
of the master class all along). Ariosto and Gascoigne show their
period by the unRoman use they make of the long lost father's
feelings: 'this is my son out of doubt whom I lost eighteen years
since, and a thousand times have I lamented for him . . . O fortune,
how much am I bound to thee if I find my son!' (Bullough, i. 153).
But the emotional highlighting is only a passing moment in Ariosto:
elsewhere Cleandro is 'Doctor Dottipole . . . the old dotard'; longing
for meaning in his life is the least of his characteristics; recognition
is still handled mainly as a plot issue. Such longing is, however,

---

[21] See Madeleine Doran, *Endeavors of Art* (Madison, 1954), 171–82.
[22] The modern equivalent is the discovery of who-done-it in detective fiction.

characteristic of Greek Romance and it is the very *raison d'être* of
Aegeon's existence. 'Hopeless and helpless' in his search for his
family, his condemnation to death in the opening lines of the play
only gives legal expression to the suicidal despair of a life that has
exhausted itself in fruitless longing.

Yet Shakespeare is careful to ensure that Aegeon's crossings of
the Mediterranean have not been merely romantic but also as
practical as even Messenio could wish. The presence of romantic
individualism as well as self-interest in the procedures of the merchant–adventurer allows Shakespeare to show the world of errors,
deceptions, and supposes to be one in which loss and gain can be
construed in terms both of money and of emotion. The life depicted in New Comedy provides a natural basis for this double
take. The *Menaechmi* views social life as a petty competition for
goods, for status, and for freedom to impose oneself on other
people, so as to escape their imposition. Shakespeare by no means
denies this image, but he is careful to represent the acquisitive life
as more specialized and regulated than it seems to be in Plautus.
Thus Antipholus' relationship with the courtesan and with his
wife is not shown as quite the opportunistic struggle for advantage
that we find in the *Menaechmi*. Erich Segal has argued that the
Menaechmi is built on a contrast between *voluptas* and *industria*, the
former embodied most clearly in the courtesan (*Erotium*), the latter
in the *matrona*.[23] If this is what Shakespeare saw in the play, it is
clear that he rewove these opposites into a different pattern, not
allowing emotion and profit, though sometimes pulling in opposite
directions, to be construed as inevitable opposites.

In the opening exchange of the play the Duke of Ephesus establishes his position as primarily the guarantor of laws, 'which princes,
would they, may not disannul'—laws that protect trade for 'merchants our well-dealing countrymen' (where 'well-dealing' carries
the sense of both 'good commercial practice' and 'moral behaviour'). Death is defined in these speeches as the necessary consequence of 'wanting guilders'—the coinage chosen suggests that
Ephesus is conceived of as an antique Antwerp—and so by fair
exchange this present Syracusan merchant must now pay a thousand marks or die.

But the opening scene is by no means a one-way commercial

[23] 'The Menaechmi: Roman Comedy of Errors', *Yale Classical Studies*, 21 (1968), 77–93.

street. As elsewhere in this chapter, the impulses to romantic identification and to hard-headed exploitation are required to interrogate one another, both speakers espousing self-deceiving and
incompatible values. The Duke speaks half for mercantilism, half
for feudal authority, the merchant half for family solidarity and
half for entrepreneurial action. Neither seems to notice his divided
duty. And these confusions go back a long way. In his tale Aegeon
has to confess that his sorrows began when 'the great care of goods
at random left | Drew me from kind embracements of my spouse'
(I. i. 42–3). The 'kind embracements' have already, however, yielded
profit in the 'pleasing burden' of twin sons.[24] And when the pregnant wife follows her husband to Epidamnum and there bears her
family's increase, it looks as if both worlds can be satisfied at once.
But what Aegeon feels to be retribution for preferring profit to
family is not avoided, only postponed. The proud mother wishes
to return from commerce to home (other twins are bought as
servants, so as to complete the symmetry). The fatal journey home,
designed to secure the profits of the past rather than to claim the
future, none the less blows away all the good fortune that has so
far attended them. The family is split; and mercantile Aegeon,
gambling on the possibility of recovering what he had lost, goes
on searching and so loses almost everything else. This now seems
to be the final stage: death is the natural and logical end of this
history of successive wrong choices and deprivations.

Even in the following scene, when the content signals that we
have moved from *Pericles* to Plautus, the same paradoxical union of
nature and commerce continues to appear. The merchant we meet
here (in fact Aegeon's wandering son) has taken good commercial
steps to avoid a fate like that we have just witnessed in his father's
case: he has banked his money with another (Ephesian) merchant
and has a false identity prepared in case trouble arises. Sociability
is not the source of the compact with his Ephesian contact. Business comes first; the Ephesian must leave in order to take up an
invitation 'to certain merchants | Of whom I hope to make much
benefit' (I. ii. 24–5). He is soon away, with 'Sir, I commend you to
your own content'. 'Own content' is, however, a phrase that trig-
gers in Antipholus' mind powerful memories of a different value

---

[24] The double meaning was particularly apt to the classically minded since the Greek
tokos means both 'parturition, offspring' and 'interest'; the Latin *fructus* straddles the same
gap.

system in which content cannot belong to the individual but only to the family group:

> He that commends me to mine own content
> Commends me to the thing I cannot get.
> I to the world am like a drop of water
> That in the ocean seeks another drop,
> Who, falling there to find his fellow forth,
> (Unseen, inquisitive), confounds himself.
> So I, to find a mother and a brother,
> In quest of them (unhappy) lose myself.
>
> (I. ii. 33–40)

What the world of Ephesus seems to offer to both Aegeon and Antipholus (and what the art world of New Comedy offers to Shakespeare) is an orderly system of time (fixed inside an orderly social and commercial system)—time to be used to collect ransom for Aegeon, time to undertake the tasks Antipholus must perform in Ephesus; but this is time that these isolated individuals can apprehend only as meaningless vacancy, and that the society can define only as madness. For the despairing father it exists only 'to procrastinate his timeless end'; for the son it soon becomes so confused that he completely loses his temporal bearings. The latter point is driven home immediately after the 'content' speech quoted above. The servant has been sent to lodge the security money in a safe place. He re-enters, or so it seems, and is greeted as one who can banish dark musings about identity, restore the order of the day: 'Here comes the almanac of my true date.' But this is the other Antipholus' servant, and the engagement diary of the businessman will not be restored to him until the end of the action when 'the calendars of . . . nativity' have returned 'true date' to the whole family.

What Shakespeare has done is to take the ordering system of New Comedy and place it in an estranging perspective, which shows its assumptions to be not the 'natural' but only the learned routines of particular social groups. These are, of course, the groups that farce tends to fasten on—those who live too securely inside predetermined social systems, those we might call, briefly and anachronistically, the bourgeoisie. But, unlike nineteenth-century farce, *The Comedy of Errors*, though it redefines private 'content' as madness, has a larger purpose than *épater les bourgeois*.

The end of the play is very different from that of the *Menaechmi*. In the Roman play the main joy that we are asked to rest on is the joy of having got away with it. The two brothers will return *in patriam*, but not before an essential commercial precondition— an auction of Epidamnan goods, including Menaechmus' wife, 'si quis emptor venerit' (l. 1160). *The Comedy of Errors* ends, however, not with a business deal but with a miracle. The play comes back to the romance story of old Aegeon. The time of his reprieve is up, but time is no longer a merely sequential medium. The solemn procession to the place of execution has hardly entered before it is overwhelmed by farcical confusions as various petitioners demand contrary assurances about what happened when. We are given unmistakable signals that anagnorisis is upon us; but before that true cadence can sound we must hear once again the contrary music of Aegeon's frustrated longing and despair:

> O time's extremity,
> Hast thou so cracked and splitted my poor tongue
> In seven short years, that here my only son
> Knows not my feeble key of untuned cares?
> Though now this grained face of mine be hid
> In sap-consuming winter's drizzled snow,
> And all the conduits of my blood froze up,
> Yet hath my night of life some memory,
> My wasting lamps some fading glimmer left,
> My dull deaf ears a little use to hear;
> All these old witnesses—I cannot err—
> Tell me thou art my son Antipholus.
>
> (v. i. 308–19)

Shakespeare has reserved the play's most powerful poetry for a special effect—to show us the tragic abyss of estrangement at the very moment of its comic release. For now romance finally absorbs error in a characteristic expression of the comic-miraculous. One by one the errors are unpicked and repositioned as truths. But they are not, we should notice, discounted: the dinner, the chain, the purse of ducats, the diamond, are presented as the factual markers by which any society (not just a bourgeois one) comes to know itself. Yet at the same time as these stubborn and irreducible facts are asserted, identity is celebrated in terms of a different set of values. At a new gossips' feast the Duke will act as godfather for the rechristening of the members of the family miraculously reconstituted. Their names, the signs of their belonging together, integrate them not only inside the family but also inside the state. A sub-plot coda replays in a final vaudeville exit the comfort of established relations:

> DROMIO E. Methinks you are my glass and not my brother.
> I see by you I am a sweet-faced youth.
> Will you walk in to see their gossiping?
> DROMIO S. Not I, sir. You are my elder.
> DROMIO E. That's a question; how shall we try it?
> DROMIO S. We'll draw cuts for the senior; till then, lead thou first.
> DROMIO E. Nay, then thus: [*clasps his brother's hand*]
> We came into the world like brother and brother,
> And now let's go hand in hand, not one before another.
>
> (v. i. 418–26)

The simultaneity of a jostling exit makes a good theatrical joke;[25] it also raises, one last time, the basic question of the competitive ethic, and it offers once again the play's response, which is not to deny it or preach against it, but to set it side by side with the incommensurate ethic of brotherhood and family solidarity, and to leave it there without further comment.

The Comedy of Errors places the opposing energies of New Comedy and romantic agony inside a coherent system which lays before us the double desire of men to profit and exploit, and at the same time to pity and belong. *The Taming of the Shrew* (*c.*1594✕*c.*1598), drawing not on Roman Comedy directly but on Renaissance adaptation of its form (and so already subject to romantic influence), offers a much less stark opposition. Instead of the *Comedy of Errors* frame plot/main-plot structure, which allowed Plautus' story to be judged from a viewpoint that contradicted its assumptions, *The Taming of the Shrew* works mainly by placing similar stories side by side so that each not only reflects the other but reflects it in a distorting mirror. The inherited story is (once again) the one told in

---

[25] There may be, in addition, a reference to the Show of Amity in the *Gesta Grayorum* of 1594✕1595 (ed. W. W. Greg (MSR; 1915), 25), where the representatives of Gray's Inn and the Inner Temple enter arm in arm to show that their quarrel over precedence has come to an end. It is probable that *The Comedy of Errors* was performed as part of the *Gesta Grayorum*.

Ariosto's *I suppositi* and repeated in Gascoigne's *Supposes.*[26] A gentleman student (Lucentio) has been sent to Padua to complete his
education; he sees Bianca as he arrives, and that puts paid to the
idea of study. He plans to gain access to her house and at the same
time evade parental scrutiny by switching names with his servant
(Tranio); the servant will seem to study while the master takes
service in the household of his beloved. But instead of the access
leading to rape (as in the *Eunuchus*) or to cohabitation (as in the
Suppositi), English decorum demanded that Lucentio's gentlemanly
love should lead to honourable courtship and so to honourable marriage. The natural movement of the structure allows us to anticipate
the way in which individual desire and social requirements will
reach their common vanishing point in matrimony. It does so effortlessly, because we see this story not as free-standing but as a variant
of the other stories that are being told at the same time. In itself it
offers us no more than one plausible pattern of relationship.

As recurrently in Elizabethan Comedy, this pluralistic view of
the world that requires each plot to keep company with other
plots, stresses the double-sidedness (even if not the equality) of
social relations—relations between siblings, between fathers and
children, superiors and inferiors, in male rivalry as well as between
men and women. The play is a tangle of attempts at dominance,
as Baptista the father tries to dominate his daughters, Bianca and
Kate, Kate to dominate Bianca, Petruchio to dominate Kate,
Vincentio to dominate Lucentio, and Tranio, the 'Lord', to dominate Sly, the tinker. But few of these dominances can be exerted
directly. Pretence and play-acting can set up situations in which
one character is disadvantaged by being absorbed into another's
'game' or 'play'; but where, in *Supposes*, such games are mainly used
to tie the gamesters to fear that they will be discovered, Shakespeare adds to this a recurrent sense of triumph that an oppressive
system is yielding to individual desire. Even in the Induction,
where Sly is being set up to believe he is a lord watching 'his'

---

[26] The connection between *The Taming of the Shrew* and Ariosto/Gascoigne is complicated by the existence of another play, *The Taming of a Shrew* (*c.*1592–4), with virtually the
same plot as Shakespeare's but very little verbal connection (being written in a high Marlovian
style). Is this a source play for Shakespeare or a 'bad quarto' or does it bear some other,
undecidable, relation to Shakespeare's play (like that of *The Troublesome Reign of John* to
King John (see p. 223))? Brains have been dashed against walls from various angles in the
hope of securing an answer to these questions, but in vain. For a nicely balanced scepticism
on the question, see Bullough, *Sources*, i. 57 ff.

players perform *The Taming of the Shrew*, we have to allow that Sly is no mere victim: he has at least as much fun watching the play as the Lord has in watching Sly (and as much power in persuading the audience to accept his view of the action); furthermore he is given the capacity (if we accept the final scene of *The Taming of a Shrew* as part of the story) to understand how he can refashion reality in the light of his 'dream' of the shrew plot. The game of the lovers to outwit the fathers (Baptista and Vincentio) succeeds only because the fathers see economic sense in their proposals and choose to agree.

In Ariosto/Gascoigne the 'supposes' are means by which individual intentions eventually overcome social impediments. In Shakespeare they are rather the means by which relationships are freed from preconditions, made open and responsive to change of circumstance. Kate as shrew is shown imprisoned inside her own anger, capable of only one mode of response. Petruchio's answering game of violent concern for her welfare obliges her to shift gear from life to game, which she then plays with characteristic verve and enjoyment. Their final joint triumph over the other husbands and wives should not be noticed without recording the pleasure *both* take in it. The educational process has turned the social outcast into a dominant insider.

The Taming of a Shrew gives the Baptista figure three daughters. Shakespeare detaches Hortensio from the family and attaches him to an otherwise unknown 'widow', and so produces a bipolar structure which balances the Petrarchan against the realistic, the woman's power against the man's, the Italian story against English folk-tale, romance against farce. It seems that a set of equivalences is being offered, an equivalence which the vocabulary of main plot and sub-plot does much to conceal. Modern discussion has tended to treat the Petruchio–Kate plot as if it existed in isolation and should be thought 'real', where the Bianca–Lucentio one is 'conventional' or 'fictional'. But it is the two plots taken together that define the outlook of the play. They set against one another the fictional possibilities of a time of life (adolescence) when the alternatives have not moved out of reach of one another[27] (as even Sly

[27] Cf. *As You Like It*, III. ii. 409–15: 'I, being but a moonish youth, [would] grieve, be effeminate, changeable, longing and liking, proud, fantastical, apish, shallow, inconstant, full of tears, full of smiles; for every passion something, and for no passion truly anything, as boys and women are for the most part cattle of this colour.'

believes they have not). At such a time they can be understood as modes of involuntary play-acting that stable society both inside the play and in the audience can both deprecate and enjoy.

If we see *The Comedy of Errors* as a direct confrontation with Plautus, and *The Taming of the Shrew* as an absorption of Renaissance versions of Roman Comedy into a pluralistic structure, we may look at *Two Gentlemen of Verona* (1590×1598) as a third stage (without drawing any chronological conclusions) in the adaptation of continental models. The main outline of *Two Gentlemen* comes eventually from the immensely popular play *Gl'ingannati* (1531), but only as it was rehandled in Montemayor's pastoral romance, *Diana* (translated 1598). Shakespeare can now achieve balance not by introducing romance elements into a classical form but by moving chronologically from a neoclassic situation to a romantic conclusion. He begins his play with a typical New Comedy situation, with a milieu not unlike that of Munday's 'Very Pleasant and Fine Conceited Comedy of Two Italian Gentlemen' (*Fedele and Fortunio*). The opening scenes introduce us to the *adolescentes*, Proteus and Valentine, burdened by neither work nor responsibility, and with wealthy and indulgent parents, to the witty servant, Speed, and the rustic servant, Launce, to the father, Antonio and his trusty servant, Pathino—in short to the usual kind of neoclassic cast. Love for Julia totally controls Proteus' mind and separates him from his companion, Valentine. There is, of course, an impediment to this love's fulfilment, not on this occasion the opposition of a parent, nor the absence of money to buy the girl, but a more internalized sense of gentlemanly tentativeness on Proteus' part, and on Julia's side a ladylike respectability that prevents her from even allowing it to be known that she will read his love-letter. The social structures within which the play organizes its characters are both formal and repetitive, thus creating the recurrent neoclassical effect of a world whose limited range of possibilities allows us to anticipate the logic of events. The central pattern of connection and differentiation is again one which is standard in neoclassic comedy: a father, his young adult son, and a conflict of loyalties imposed on the son and concealed from the father. In the first place we have the 'home-keeping' diagram of Verona, in which Antonio is the father, Proteus is the son, while Julia and Valentine represent the alternative claims on Proteus' future. At this point in the play the pattern is largely static; but at the end of Act I the calm is broken by the

father's command that Proteus follow Valentine to Milan and so
(consequently) abandon Julia. The expectable pattern breaks up as
the unities of time and space are shattered. In Milan there exists,
however, an identical situation. Here the Duke is the Father, Silvia
is the child, and the alternative suitors are Valentine and Thurio.
The arrival of Proteus in Milan begins the complications; for here
there is no place for him in the diagram. For a moment there is a
hint of the Italian three-suitor situation: Thurio the Pantaloon,
Valentine the *innamorato*, Proteus the braggart. But Proteus soon
turns into a different kind of rival and pushes the play into a more
tragic mode. Moreover, Julia's arrival, disguised as 'Sebastian',
introduces a more romantic form of lover's yearning and frustration in which Julia loves Proteus, Proteus loves Silvia, Silvia loves
Valentine—a form which, here as in *Twelfth Night*, encourages
expressions of frustrated emotion rather than ingenuity of intrigue.

Two Gentlemen of Verona uses the standard patterns of Italianate
comedy in a way which ignores the sense of life which they were
designed to produce. There is little trace of intrigue, meaning a
plot to secure a desired end, which faces difficulties and opposition
and eventually overcomes them. Proteus plots to disadvantage
Valentine, but the plot succeeds too easily to be impressive. Much
more impressive is the psychological turmoil imposed on Proteus
when he finds that a change of place becomes a change of mind.
The audience is not caught up and is not meant to be caught up in
linear expectations about what will happen next. We cannot be
certain in what kind of world the characters will next appear. All
we learn is that patterns of relationship that give stability in one
situation destroy it in another. *Two Gentlemen of Verona* begins
with the problems of family life in Verona, but the solution to
these problems can be found only in a forest outside Milan, with
a duke and a band of outlaws. It is a common response to say that
Shakespeare has confused his generic categories. But the 'confusion' is precisely what we have noticed as the recurrent system of
Elizabethan comedy.

One factor that is obviously crucial is the progressive change of
place. In the Italianate comedy of courtship there is no escape from
'home', from the given context of the street and the houses and
the families, the limitations and the obsessions of a small cast of
characters fixed inside their social roles. The energy of competition
between persons in such a situation naturally expresses itself in a

web of trickeries, *inganni*, deceptions, supposes. But the static
nature of each separate neoclassical pattern in *Two Gentlemen of
Verona* is subverted after every few scenes by a departure. The
play begins with Valentine's farewell to Proteus when he leaves
Verona for Milan. In Act II, Scene ii, Proteus says farewell to Julia
and also leaves for Milan. In Act II, Scene vii, Julia will follow
Proteus. In Act III, Scene i, Valentine is banished from the court
in Milan. In Act V, Scene i, Silvia and Eglamour leave the court
to join Valentine in the forest. In Act V, Scene ii, Thurio, Proteus,
and the Duke make the same journey to the forest. The ideal of
constancy is thus played inside a world of continual change. In
such a world, stability cannot be derived from the unchanging
nature of the relations in which all are enmeshed; stability becomes
a psychological rather than a social characteristic, and the reward
of happiness when it comes at the end of the action seems to be
justified (if at all) by the fact of being a person who 'deserves'
happiness, not by the chance of having a servant who can out-trick
everyone else in town. The famous difficulty of the end of the play
when Valentine simply hands over his beloved Silvia to her would-
be rapist, Proteus, is obviously connected with this collision of
genres. The medieval ideal of friendship between men as the supreme good in human relations has no place in an urban society. It
belongs to an ethic of honour, basically military honour, and to the
religious implications of that ethic. The 'clever' lover cannot be
rewarded for his trickery in the context of such an ethic, for in
the language of romance such activity is called 'betrayal' and 'sin'.
In Italianate comedy the rejected lover is likely to be foolish, even
grotesque, a pedant or a braggart, but it would be a category error
to think of him as 'sinful'. In his handling of Proteus Shakespeare
seems to be rejecting the whole world of manipulative comedy.
Forced into a situation in which cleverness is of no avail, he is
faced in the forest by the truths of betrayal and sin. And in a
sudden volte-face he is restored to the ethical stability which he
jettisoned when he first saw Silvia. Shakespeare leaves no doubt
that this 'conversion experience' is being construed in specifically
religious terms:

> Forgive me, Valentine; if hearty sorrow
> Be a sufficient ransom for offence,
> I tender't here: I do as truly suffer
> As e'er I did commit.

Valentine certainly understands it in these religious terms:

> Then I am paid;
> And once again I do receive thee honest.
> Who by repentance is not satisfied
> Is nor of heaven nor earth, for these are pleased;
> By penitence th'Eternal's wrath's appeased.

(v. iv. 74–81)

The happiness with which the play ends is thus not simply the plot happiness of boy gets girl but rather the discovery of a psychological cleansing, which can justify plot happiness, though with an edge of dubiety which we will come to recognize as characteristically Shakespearian.

Comedy at Court

In the previous pages I have distinguished two strains in Elizabethan comedy, one deriving from classical example and one from the native tradition of romantic extravagance, of medleys and gallimaufries.[28] It remains to consider how this distinction relates to the social difference between a courtly and a public audience. It is a common modern assumption that classic forms and logical structures are characteristic of works designed for well-trained audiences, while the rough and ready plotting and generic mixing of the popular playhouses call naturally on the emotions of the undifferentiated public.

These are indeed assumptions that seem appropriate to·the end of the period this book is concerned with, when the gulf between private and public theatres, the Phoenix and the Red Bull, marks a clear social divide, but they are by no means justified at the beginning of this history. In the reign of Elizabeth the idea that a

---

[28] How far these could go may be seen from the report of Lupold von Wedel, who visited Southwark in 1584: 'dogs were made to fight singly with three bears . . . after this a horse was brought in and chased by the dogs, and at last a bull, who defended himself bravely. The next was that a number of men and women came forward from a separate compartment, dancing, conversing and fighting with each other; also a man who threw some white bread among the crowd, that scrambled for it. Right over the middle of the place a rose was fixed, this rose being set on fire by a rocket: suddenly lots of apples and pears fell out of it down upon the people standing below. Whilst the people were scrambling for the apples, some rockets were made to fall down upon them out of the rose, which caused a great fright but amused the spectators. After this, rockets and other fireworks came flying out of all corners, and that was the end of the play' (Chambers, ii. 455).

'court taste' equals a taste for classical decorum can be argued only in special cases. In this area we may have to think of John Lyly as the Marlowe of court comedy—the man who found a form which allowed two divergent aesthetics to coexist in harmony.

In the seventeenth century the distinction between classic and native comes to be associated with another distinction—that between the boy actors who performed in 'private' playhouses and the adult actors who performed on 'public' stages. But this again is a distinction that is not documented before the time of Lyly. It is true that the records of the court in the 1570s and 1580s show a clear bifurcation in the repertory, the boys performing plays unremittedly classical in subject matter: *Ajax and Ulysses* (1572), *Narcissus* (1573), *Alcmaeon* (1573), *Quintus Fabius* (1575), *Timoclea at the Siege of Thebes* (1574/5), *Mutius Scevola* (1577), *Alucius* (1579), *Scipio Africanus* (1580), *Agamemnon and Ulysses* (1584). At the same time we find the men performing plays predominantly post-classical: *Chloridon and Radiamanta* (1572), *Herpetulus the Blue Knight and Perobia* (1574)—perhaps two plays—*The Solitary Knight* (1577), *Three Sisters of Mantua* (1578), *The Duke of Milan and the Marquess of Mantua* (1579), *The Knight [of] the Burning Rock* (1579), *The Soldan and the Duke of——* (1579), *Felix and Philiomena* (1585).

The distinction may, however, be more one of title than of treatment. Classical titles do not require classic (as against romantic) dramaturgy. Stephen *Gosson (playwright turned play-scourge) tells us in his diatribe against acting, *Plays Confuted in Five Actions* (1582), that '*The Palace of Pleasure*, *The Golden Ass*, *The Aethiopian History*, *Amadis of France*, *The Round Table*, bawdy comedies in Latin, French, Italian and Spanish have been thoroughly ransacked to furnish the playhouses in London' (cited in Chambers, iv. 216)—pointing, presumably, at the public playhouses. Gosson has compiled his list with the explicit purpose of denigrating the public playwrights by revealing the unsavoury nature of their sources (modern bawdry and medieval romances being seen here, as in Ascham's *The Schoolmaster*, as joint portents of corruption). He includes such classical texts as *The Golden Ass* and *The Aethiopian History* because their immoral content cancels their classic status.[29]

---

[29] The index of stories in Painter's *Palace of Pleasure* (1580) should remind us that such romantic compilations were drawn quite indifferently from 'romantic' and 'classical' sources.

In the preceding paragraph Gosson tells us of two plays with classical titles which, if we met them in a list of payments, we might expect to represent classic drama. But Gosson's comments show how mistaken we would be. He tells us of

the history of Caesar and Pompey and the play of the Fabii at the Theatre, both amplified there where the drums might walk or the pen ruffle; when the history swelled and ran too high for the number of the persons that should play it, the poet with Proteus [?Procrustes] cut the same fit to his own measure; when it afforded no pomp at all he brought it to the rack to make it serve. (Chambers, iv. 216)

Gosson's scorn of spectacle and exaggeration is consistent with Beaumont's attitude to the Grocer and his Wife in *The Knight of the Burning Pestle* of 1607 or so (see Chapter 7, pp. 336–8). But the fifteen-year gap between the two statements has produced a change in the underlying assumptions. Gosson's attitude derives from his understanding that *all* drama is bound to betray the sober truth; the necessarily wayward narratives of plays are simply the formal expression of their total failure to hold on to any moral centre. Beaumont, on the other hand, scorns the lower-class tastes of the Grocer and his Wife not from a moral position but from the point of view of aesthetic snobbism. A 'correct' taste is one which defines not only an aesthetic preference but also a class position. The 'gentlemen' in the private playhouse have come to see the boys perform a play of neatly plotted social discriminations. Their space and their taste are invaded when the Grocer and his Wife climb onto the stage and demand that the plot be disrupted to make room for a string of chivalric adventures, to be enacted by Rafe, their apprentice.

The citizen's wife tells the gentlemen that Rafe has played Mucedorus before the Wardens of the Grocers' Company. In terms of the sharp distinctions that Beaumont's play deploys, this marks *Mucedorus* of 1588×1598 as a piece of popular theatre (by 1607×1610). But the Epilogue to *Mucedorus* tells us that the Master of the Revels thought it suitable for the sovereign's viewing in 1610. It is clear that the 'classic' taste of the universities and the Inns of Court was not yet (even by that date) in control of the court.

It is clear that the distinctions that come easiest to us cannot be relied on to describe courtly comedy. Yet some distinctions can be

made. Two plays written specially for courtly performance—Peele's
The Arraignment of Paris of *c*.1581×1584 and Nashe's *Summer's
Last Will and Testament* (1592)—and perhaps we ought to add
Peele's *The Old Wife's Tale* (*c*.1588×1594) to the list—show how,
in a courtly milieu, the boys can divert the variousness of a medley
plot into something of delicacy and charm, held together by poetic
skill rather than plot. We must suppose that the boys' great strength
lay not in physical activity but in their voices, shown in singing no
less than speaking and so in their capacity to make style project
meaning; and this is precisely what we find in these plays.

The Arraignment of Paris seems to have been performed at court
at some date fairly close to that of *The Rare Triumphs of Love and
Fortune*, played (see pp. 98–9) by the men of the Earl of Derby's
company; and in structure the two plays are very similar (as is
Wilson's *The Cobbler's Prophecy*, also presumed to have been played
at court[30]). All these begin by showing us the intrusion of disorder
into an Olympian system designed to preserve a precarious balance. In Peele's play, Ate, the goddess of discord, appears as prologue and tells of her plan to lob a bombshell disguised as a golden
apple into the arena of vanity and jealousy occupied by Juno,
Pallas, and Venus, the *grandes dames* of Olympus. On the other
side of the same system are the humble and uncompetitive sylvan
gods, and the shepherds and shepherdesses, presided over by Flora
and Diana. Above all stands Jupiter (as in *The Rare Triumphs of
Love and Fortune*), his legal deputy being Diana, and then (moving
upwards again) *her* ideal, Queen Elizabeth, the final, stabilizing,
non-competitive recipient of the golden apple. The obvious difference in organization between this play and *The Rare Triumphs of
Love and Fortune* is that *The Arraignment of Paris* offers a narrower
and more abstracted image of social existence. The mortal lovers
here are themselves part of the divine scheme; they do not represent the gross and recalcitrant material the gods are obliged to
work on in the other play. Peele shows us no blundering servants
like Lentulo, the hungry and rough-mannered rustic, or Penulo,

---

[30] The presence of *The Cobbler's Prophecy* among court plays (the stage directions imply
this) requires us to include moral plays of advice among those that the Queen could enjoy.
It is interesting that in this play (unlike the others discussed here) the recovery of order
depends on human action more than divine fiat. Only under these conditions can the soldier
be properly honoured, the scholar converted from courtly fripperies to heroic praise, the
duke redeemed from his over-merciful rule.

the court parasite determined to rise in society by betrayal and tattle. The characters of *The Arraignment of Paris* seem, in fact, not only in a comparison with *The Rare Triumphs of Love and Fortune* but seen against the general norms of Elizabethan drama, to be extraordinarily homogeneous. In large part this is due to the dominance of the poetry. Peele, like the author of *The Rare Triumphs of Love and Fortune*, employs an ingeniously varied metrical palette: blank verse, poulter's measure, heroic couplets, hexameters, songs in sundry languages, are skilfully deployed to express different human and divine responses. The metrical systems of the two plays do not, however, secure the same range of effects: *The Rare Triumphs of Love and Fortune* includes prose and unscannable tumbling verse inside its spectrum; *The Arraignment of Paris*, on the other hand, extends its range into a variety of lyric measures. Between these two plays we have crossed, it would seem, the boundary which separates the poetic modes C. S. Lewis called 'Drab' and 'Golden'; and it can be argued that this 'golden' quality when it appears in drama emerges first in association with the special capacities and limitations of the boy actors—verbal capacities compensating for mimetic limitations.

The controlling poetic quality of *The Arraignment of Paris* brings it close to the non-dramatic poetry of the time—especially Spenser's *The Shepherd's Calendar*, published in 1579 as the work of 'the new poet', and therefore presenting a model of 'the new poetry'. Spenser himself, in his poetic persona as Colin Clout, appears in Peele's play, as in his own poem, as a paradigm of constancy in love in a world where the principle of constancy is everywhere praised, though inevitably plea-bargained away between the power-brokers of Olympus. Peele's play accommodates Colin inside an antithetical structure more appropriate to a play than to a set of eclogues, providing him with an *alter ego* in the visiting shepherd Paris, who abandons Oenone as soon as Venus becomes his patroness. The fate of Paris and his family in the Trojan War is recurrently evoked, in the grand rhetorical manner that is appropriate to it, as a counterweight to Colin's quiet death, just as the humble exercises in the pastoral genre, where gods and men, in what Empson calls a 'beautiful relationship',[31] are set against the battles of gods and men that characterize epic. The one figure who can cross this line is 'Eliza,

---

[31] *Some Versions of Pastoral* (London, 1950), 11.

queen of shepherds all', in whose praise shepherds and Olympians are at one. *The Arraignment of Paris* is one of the few Elizabethan texts that seems by its form to be impossible to place outside a specific court occasion, since Elizabeth's actual presence is demanded for the final scene when she is given the golden apple. It may indeed be that there was another final scene written for performance in the Chapel Boys' private theatre in the Blackfriars. But in terms of the text we have, the play must be allowed to reflect the social condition (even if not the form) of the masque rather than the independent drama.

Nashe's *Summer's Last Will and Testament* can be seen as a masque disabled by its own antimasque, allowed therefore to be a piece of social unreality. It is generally assumed that it was written to be played before the Archbishop of Canterbury at his palace in Croyden. References in the text strongly suggest that it was performed by boys (though Will Summers himself may well have been played by a man).[32] It seems unlikely that this text was ever performed for the public. It is a work of extraordinary literary fluency and 'golden' eloquence in speech and song. All these characteristics link *Summer's Last Will and Testament* to *The Arraignment of Paris* and set it against the adult actors' early comedies for the court, *The Rare Triumphs of Love and Fortune* and *The Cobbler's Prophecy*. Such distinctions should not, however, conceal the real continuities between all these plays. *Summer's Last Will and Testament* is predicated once again on an explicit struggle between Order and Disorder, though it ends without any positive affirmation. Order is here represented by the natural sequence of the seasons, by the analogous human and social ordering of an individual life from youth to age, together with the moral structure of potential, achievement, excess, and restriction (as in Marston's *Histriomastix*). Against this Nashe sets his awareness that the poetic vision of order is not fulfilled in human practice. Drawing on the widely diffused Renaissance taste for rebuses, puns, and perspectives, Nashe matches Summer the season against his antitype, Will Summers, Henry VIII's celebrated jester.[33] The central point that Will

---

[32] Will Summers calls them 'pretty boys, if they would wash their faces and were well breached an hour or two' (ll. 117–18).

[33] The title as it appears in the entry in the Stationers' Register (28 Oct. 1600) sharpens the joke still further: 'A book called Summer's Last Will and Testament presented by Will Summers'. That is, Summer's last will by Will Summers.

Summers exists to make is that the play being performed is only a play, its order a piece of artifice imposed on the audience by a professional writer—that is, by a person shielded through formal education from ordinary folks' experience and their spontaneous or 'extemporary' reactions (and shielded also by self-importance from the true conditions of entertainment). So he derides the author as a fool like himself—not, however, a fool 'by nature and by art' like himself but a plain 'Idiot' (that is, one without control of his art) who is 'making himself a public laughing stock' (ll. 20–4). Summers will demonstrate how much has been lost by the courtly move to entertainment based on literature; he will sit on the stage 'as a chorus and flout the actors and the author at the end of every scene' (ll. 91–3). So at the end of the first episode he complains that the audience must be thirsty after 'listening to this dry sport' (l. 424) and longs for an old-fashioned play of the Prodigal Son, which would allow the actor to indulge himself in the pleasures of disorder and opting-out: 'let the prodigal child come out in his doublet and hose all greasy, his shirt hanging forth and ne'er a penny in his purse and talk what a fine thing it is to walk summerly or sit whistling under a hedge and keep hogs' (ll. 435–9). And again, hearing Winter speak of the incommodity of the arts, he congratulates himself that 'when I should have been at school construing *Batte, mi fili, mi fili, mi Batte* I was close under a hedge or under a barn wall playing at span-counter or jack in a box' (ll. 1465–8).

Will Summers's prose opposition to the versified masque-like celebration of order in the rest of the play aligns him in many ways with such characters as Wilson's Raph Cobbler or Simplicity (in *The Three Ladies of London*). But these characters clearly belong to a moralizing tradition that stretches back to *Piers Plowman*; they look up at the pretensions of the powerful from a common-sense but also a Christian perspective, which is allowed to be just even when it is not effective in the world. But Nashe's sophisticated irony puts his raisonneur at a much greater distance than are Wilson's, placed as he is by the self-conscious rhetoric of his role. His going-over-the-top linguistic exuberance, characteristic of Nashe, turns his complaint into fun. His praise of disorder and the spontaneous good life is without coercive edge. He bewails the loss of Christmas hospitality, but does so ironically, in a self-consciously 'medieval' folk prophecy:

Ah, *Benedicite*
Well is he hath no necessity
of gold, ne of sustenance;
Slow good hap comes by chance;
Flattery best fares;
Arts are but idle wares;
Fair words want giving hands;
The *Lento* begs that has no lands.
Fie on thee, thou scurvy knave,
That hast nought and yet goest brave:
A prison be thy death bed,
Or be hanged, all save the head.

(ll. 1738–49)

If I am right in surmising that Toy, who played Will Summers, was an adult actor accompanying a performance by boys, one can see how Summers's jokey presentation of the action as poetic unreality would fit the theatrical conditions. Summers invites the (adult) audience to share with him something like the Vice's traditional fun-loving complicity in the sins of the real world. 'We know what's what; they don't' is the basis of his claim to intimacy: 'we know meanings; they know only words.' Order, decorum, artistry, are presented as admirable ideals, and emerge as such— the songs in *Summer's Last Will and Testament* are high points in Elizabethan lyricism—but they are also matters outside the reality of daily life that adults ('like us') know about.

John Lyly is never mentioned in *Summer's Last Will and Testament*, but an invocation of his invisible presence gives us an easy way to bring into focus the polemical relation to current fashion that Nashe's courtly method involves. Lyly seems to be present in Nashe's play as the representative of just that hidebound and formalistic kind of drama that Will Summers (in this, Nashe's mouthpiece) disdains and disrupts. Nashe was, of course, more fired as an author by opposition than by collegiality, and by 1592 Lyly's reputation was sufficiently declined to make him easy game. But there is more than chronology or personal rivalry involved; *Summer's Last Will and Testament* shows us that there is a genuine opposition of literary ideals between the two authors as well as a considerable overlap. Lyly's inflexible method of writing (Euphuism) is, it is implied, incapable of personal expressiveness: he is 'one of those hieroglyphical writers that by the figures of beasts, planets, and of stones, express the mind as we do in A, B, C' (ll. 591–3). Lyly's method provides Nashe, indeed, with a springboard for his whole play, for the Prologue to *Summer's Last Will and Testament*, read out in mockery by Will Summers as a 'scurvy Prologue . . . made in an old vein of similitudes' (ll. 26–7), begins with a parody of the opening passage in Lyly's Blackfriars Prologue to *Campaspe* (1580×1584).[34] Lyly's Prologue begins:

They that fear the stinging of wasps make fans of peacocks' tails, whose spots are like eyes. And Lepidus which could not sleep for the chatting of birds set up a beast whose head was like a dragon: and we which stand in awe of report are compelled to set before our owl Pallas's shield, thinking by her virtue to cover the others' deformity.

As always in Lyly, the only subtext that can be discovered in the somewhat impersonal and oracular mode of his writing lies buried in the space between the detached members of the paragraph. The Prologue is, of course, an apology; it also, however, sets up a somewhat adversary relation between the players and the audience: the players expect 'stinging', but their 'spots' or imperfections are also the 'eyes' which allow them to see what is going on in the auditorium. 'And Lepidus', as the second sentence rather mysteriously begins, found a way of dealing with the 'chatting' (which surely glances at the noise of the audience before the play begins) by setting up a dragon to frighten them; the dragon then reappears as 'Pallas's shield' (carrying the Gorgon's head), a defensive cover for her favourite animal, the owl. It is hard not to believe that there is some reference here to that living Pallas, Queen Elizabeth, who is protectress of the owlish Lyly and will defend him from stinging. Nashe begins his Prologue to *Summer's Last Will and Testament* with the same story about Lepidus:

At a solemn feast of the Triumviri in Rome it was seen and observed that the birds ceased to sing and sat solitary on the housetops, by reason of the sight of a painted serpent set openly to view. So fares it with us novices that here betray our imperfections; we, afraid to look on the imaginary serpent of Envy painted in men's affections, have ceased to tune any music of mirth to your ears this twelvemonth, thinking . . . it is the nature of the serpent to hiss . . .

---

[34] Compare M. R. Best, 'Nashe, Lyly, and *Summer's Last Will and Testament*', *PQ* 48 (1969), 1–11.

The class cal story serves in both cases to express the mixture of apology and aggression in the boys' relation to their audiences. But Nashe has a further point to make: the serious mode of the boys as set up by Lyly is also the object of Will Summers's scorn:

> How say you my masters, do you not laugh at him for a coxcomb? Why, he hath made a Prologue longer than his play. Nay, 'tis no play neither, but a show. I'll be sworn the jig of Rowland's godson is a giant in comparison of it. What can be made of 'Summer's last will and testament'? Such another thing as Gillian of Brainford's will, where she bequeathed a score of farts amongst her friends.   (ll. 73–80)

The ambiguity that Nashe's play leaves us with allows us to respond to the charm and fragility of the world the boys represent but conveys also a robust enthusiasm for the real world's teeming vulgarity and variousness, which plays acted only by boys or written by Lyly cannot hope to represent.

The poised deference and the tact that Lyly shows in his presentation of the central monarchical characters of his plays—Alexander, Sappho, Ceres, Cynthia—has suggested to many readers later than Nashe the latent political point that his dramatic worlds simply exclude the popular voice represented by Will Summers and show to Elizabeth a simple mirror image of her absolutism. But in fact the disenchanted voice is by no means kept silent in Lyly (or in Elizabethan England). The obvious play to cite here is indeed the one that Nashe quotes in *Summer's Last Will and Testament*—the *Most Excellent Comedy of Alexander, Campaspe and Diogenes*—in which we see Diogenes (important enough to get his name on the original title-page) completely unimpressed by the *hegemon*, Alexander the Great; comic and civic harmony is achieved only because Alexander accepts Diogenes' right to highly vocal individual intransigence (as he also appreciates Apelles' professional right to understand beauty better than a king can). It must be allowed of course that this 'defence' of civil resistance is weaker in Lyly's subsequent comedies, which show a retreat from history into mythology and present the engagement of power with its limitations in terms which permit a more *de haut en bas* form of resolution. The opposition moves, as it were, inside the orbit of power as a merely formal expression of antithesis. Thus, in *Sappho and Phao* (1582×1584), Sappho the royal figure and Sappho the woman betrayed by love for a humble ferryman are opposed only in the passive and psychological terms of withdrawal and pain, not in the active terms of alternative politics. In *Midas* (1589×1590), Midas's power and his folly are likewise opposed in terms of individual choice and error, not those of personal confrontation. Midas is forced into compromise not by a human opponent but by a god (Apollo). Elsewhere, as in *Gallathea* (?1585), the opposition is active enough but is expressed entirely as existing between gods. The human characters, at a natural disadvantage, have to accept manipulations from above, which, being favourable, they are given no reason to oppose. *Endymion* (1588) presents a scene in which the mythological and the human are confusingly mixed. But the central conflict between Cynthia and Tellus (the former, representing Queen Elizabeth, the latter, any number of antithetical possibilities) is handled in an abstracted fashion appropriate to gods, and once again the human lovers have no option but to accept what is offered from above and be grateful for it.

These plays do not present political engagement between hierarchy and subversion. The principal effect made is of distance, separation, and disengagement. A resolute aestheticism justifies the fiction as a thing complete in itself, teases somewhat with suggestions of *drame à clef*, but resolves all the issues without reference to anything outside its own seamless self-sufficiency. The court prologue to *Sappho and Phao* asks the Queen to imagine that the whole action has been a dream. Similarly the (court) prologue to *Endymion* says: 'We present neither comedy nor tragedy nor story nor anything but that whosoever heareth may say this, "Why here is a tale of the Man in the Moon."' The play disables itself by declaring that it is only a plaything, an unreality, which is, of course, what Will Summers said about it in Nashe's play. The disabling, however, is now to be seen from an angle opposite to that of Will Summers, from above and not from below. The highly polished surface of poetic boys' theatre reflects only the decorum of the courtier, deferential but disengaged; too well balanced either to support or to subvert the world around it.

We have noticed recurrently the double pressure on playwrights from the alternative ideals of variety and unity, and we have considered the different ways in which socio-literary opposites and incompatibles were put together, so that they could meet not only the popular demand for change of focus and shift of emotion but also that other (Humanist) demand that a single vision should control all the phenomena; for had not Horace demanded

> denique sit quidvis simplex dumtaxat et unum.
>
> (*Ars poetica*, l. 23)

It is one of the secrets of the great success of the Elizabethan dramatic movement that these opposites are able to coexist so fruitfully in most of the drama of the time. Thus it is no accident that the opposition that Nashe sets up between his play and Lyly's *Campaspe* is set between two plays so competitively close to one another—both courtly plays, both plays for boys, both well formed, yet open in construction, both dependent on the liberating effect of song. If we compare Lyly's plays to Roman comedy or *commedia erudita*, we can see that he is no less wedded to variety than Nashe. After all, the most memorable expression of the principle comes in Paul's prologue to Lyly's *Midas*:

> Gentlemen, so nice is the world that for apparel there is no fashion, for music no instrument, for diet no delicate, for plays no invention but breedeth satiety before noon and contempt before night. . . . At our exercises soldiers call for tragedies—their object is blood; courtiers for comedies—their subject is love; countrymen for pastorals—shepherds are their saints. Traffic and travel hath woven the nature of all nations into ours and made this land like arras, full of device, which was broadcloth, full of workmanship. Time hath confounded our minds, our minds the matter; but all cometh to this pass: that what heretofore hath been served in several dishes for a feast is now minced in a charger for a gallimaufrey. If we present a mingle-mangle our fault is to be excused because the whole world is become an hodge-podge.

Lyly presents an enigmatic perspective which allows him both to mourn the passing of a supposed former unity (in which intention and expression bore a direct relation to one another) and at the same time to rejoice in a modern sophistication where opposites can coexist without being required to contradict one another.[35]

In this we can see both the continuity as well as the opposition that attaches Lyly to Nashe, and the balancing act Lyly brings to the traditions of English comedy. Diogenes and Will Summers

---

[35] Robert Weimann ('History and the Issue of Authority in Representation', *NLH* 17 (1986), 449–76) argues that this Prologue shows Lyly accepting the political heterogeneity of the audience as an authorization of his work. But the imputed heterogeneity seems more like an excuse for dramaturgy that *evades* political choice than, in itself, a political statement.

both exist to contradict the ethos of the play and to subvert its closure by a series of *ad hoc* improvisations. But Will Summers belongs to the true tradition of the moral medley, in which his opposition, like that of Bohan or Simplicity or Raph Cobbler, stands outside the system and cannot be resolved (indeed Summers has to cling to the audience to protect him from the play). The comic conclusion must face down the implacable nay-sayer; and in many cases the opposition continues to resonate in the memory in something of the same way as does (to take the most famous example) Malvolio's 'I'll be revenged on the whole pack of you'.

Neoclassical comedy, on the other hand, usually creates its alternative points of view through the continuous presence of the family servants, following their own agenda. Their down-to-earth appetites (gastric and sexual) are set against the more anxious emotions of the young masters and mistresses and the long-term financial anxiety of the merchant-fathers. But there is much collusion and overlap. The servants belong to the family: they can set up parodies; but they are always parodies dancing attendance on a power structure to which they are entirely subordinate.

Lyly's plays live somewhere in between these two models. They do not (outside the anomalous *Mother Bombie* of 1587×1590) offer anything like the neoclassical unity of a modern urban setting where different points of view are held together by continuous cross-intrigue. His understair world of cheeky boy servants draws on many of the characteristics of Roman slaves and Italian servants; but he seldom allows them to interfere in the main action: their struggles with the world are conducted in their own separate terms, and most often in their own separate plots. They do not subvert; but neither do they accept or join. And in the main plots Lyly's figures are too disengaged from one another, too free of social positioning, to allow the plausible exchanges of intrigue. His characters appear rather as if standing in their own space, using others only as instances of the wonderful paradox of their coexistence. Diogenes is an opposition figure; but he is also an Athenian and a theorist. He can tune his discords to the competing parts, so that the audience hear not a jarring conflict but a dangerous harmony.

Lyly's control of the heterogeneity he creates is derived in part from the constructional neatness of the neo-Terentian dramaturgy taught in schools; but even more tellingly it is secured by the

distinctive uniformity of the famous euphuistic style. Lyly does
not hold his action together by showing us a social unity in the
world depicted. But his style makes everyone, whether princes,
pages, gods, nymphs, foresters, or students, sound much the same:
self-conscious and self-controlled, dry, witty, analytic, in a mode
designed 'to move inward delight, not outward lightness, and to
breed (if it might be) soft smiling, not loud laughing; knowing it to
the wise to be as great pleasure to hear counsel mixed with wit as
to the foolish to have sport mingled with rudeness' (Blackfriars'
prologue to *Sappho and Phao*). The argument continues here with
a more specific glance at the kind of play he has chosen not to
write: 'They were banished the theatre at Athens and from Rome
hissed that brought parasites on the stage with apish actions or
fools with uncivil habits or courtesans with immodest words.' As
history this is rather odd, as anybody's quick reading of Plautus
will indicate. But the polemical point is clear enough. The objection to 'sport mingled with rudeness' takes us back to Sidney once
again, and Lyly may well have the *Apology for Poetry* in mind here,
the ideal of 'soft smiling' looking like a restatement of Sidney's
'comedy . . . of delight', which he, like Lyly, opposes to the 'loud
laughter' that arises from 'scurrility'.[36] Lyly is not, however, repeating Sidney's views in order to follow him into an attack on the
tragicomedy of the popular stage; he seems to be aiming at competition nearer home, at the comedy of modern Terentian imitation,
with which his structural methods align him but from which he
clearly wishes to differentiate his version of learned comedy.
Pasqualigo's *Il fedele*, translated (perhaps by Anthony Munday) as
Fedele and Fortunio, discussed already (see pp. 114–15), and possibly brought to court about the same time as *Sappho and Phao*,
and performed by the same troupe of Oxford's boys, gives us a
good, and possibly a pertinent, example of the kind of play Lyly
seems to have in mind. Pasqualigo's text gives us a cast list of old
lechers, bawds, live-in lovers, pedants, *braggart soldiers*—modern city
people, freed from hierarchy, 'each character more repellant than
the other' as the usually even-tempered F. S. Boas puts it.[37] Lyly
aims to replace this with a comedy in which a courtly audience will
take delight 'in things that have a conveniency to [them]selves'
instead of laughing at 'things most disproportioned to [them]selves'

---

[36] *Apology*, 136.   [37] *University Drama in the Tudor Age* (Oxford, 1914), 141.

(to borrow from the same passage in Sidney once again). One basis for this transmutation of neoclassical structure into a vision of delight is a removal of the scene of action from the city into a self-consciously fanciful and remote region of classical myth or allegory, where a nobler version of love can be explored in freedom from the constraints of real life. The combination of the classic and the romantic in these plays is important to their control of focus: the sobriety of one acts as a brake on the free fantasy of the other. And in terms of sobriety of language Lyly and [Munday] are at one. In presenting *Fedele and Fortunio* to the Queen, the translator speaks of the style of a comedy

> In which he used no thundering words of state
> But clipped his wings and kept a meaner gate.
>
> (Prologue before the Queen, ll. 5–6)

Avoidance of stridency marks the decorum which enables the author not only to escape the impropriety of 'words of state' but also to concentrate on a limited range of interconnections so that the play, being complete in itself, avoids dangerous reference to any specifics outside its own range. In his very different way we can see Lyly pursuing the same limited interconnections which, as in the contrapuntal music the children were trained in, evoked discord only as a function of harmony. Both playwrights are aiming at tightly controlled structures in which emotions are strictly patterned inside the social and conceptual framework.

Lyly's capacity to combine control and variety is evident in his first play, *Campaspe*; and his method changed very little from that time forward. The play is composed of a series of distinct units, each one used to convey a different response to the situation they all share—the arrival of Alexander the Great in Athens. Apelles the painter, Diogenes the Cynic, Plato, Aristotle and other philosophers, the generals Hephestion and Clitus, Campaspe the Theban captive—each of these has a different relation to Alexander; and yet, taken together, they make up a unified picture of the *polis*. The scenes are short and disjunct; each one focuses on one aspect; and then the play moves on to another grouping and another exploration. By and large, individuals are not changed by their interactions; they exist to present specific (even if complex) points of view: Alexander is powerful and magnanimous; the generals love war, fear love; Diogenes is scornful of complaisance and compromise;

Apelles is humble, but emboldened by awareness of his own worth; Campaspe is humble and tremulous. The brilliantly sharpened dialogue stays close to intellectual debate, focusing on such themes as civil versus military values, the relationship between power and independence. Love in this context is less an emotion to be expressed than a subject to be debated, or passed from voice to voice in the manner of a madrigal.

Like other court plays, *Campaspe* seems to have been written for 'Terentian' or 'simultaneous' staging, with specific locations set out as booths, capable of opening and revealing an interior space, the rest of the stage being unlocalized and providing room for movement between one booth and another. This obviously meshes with the play structure set out above. We see groupings or characters established in specific places which then serve to define their place in society. On one side of the stage in *Campaspe* is the tub of Diogenes; on the other side is the workshop of Apelles. The physical reality of these objects serves to make them the fixed points from which our imaginations can build up the whole network of social relations. This is an anti-romantic daylight world; nothing that is started is allowed to disappear into shadow, and nothing that is individual is allowed to escape scrutiny or challenge by other members of the cast with clearly defined alternative attitudes.

This inquisitorial if not polemical relationship between characters points to an ending that satisfies by separation rather than union (thus allowing individual difference to survive). Alexander decides to leave Athens and conquer Persia; war, not love, is to be his proper *métier*. Athens (like Apelles and Campaspe) is pardoned and dismissed; the bourgeois comforts of the painter and his model can be allowed to continue in the diminished world that remains. This military apotheosis of Alexander at the end of the action reflects neatly the conditions of court drama. As Alexander moves beyond the Athenian imbroglio and looks down on it from above, so Lyly's Athenian play sinks down before its queenly spectator and acknowledges that her *métier* lies far beyond the play situation she has condescended to adorn by her presence.

The implied reference to the court context of his plays is handled by Lyly with a deft lightness of touch which politicizing critics have been anxious to load down by the discovery of specific political allegories. Alexander—like Sappho, Ceres, and Cynthia—is in some sense, of course, a mirroring of Queen Elizabeth. But the image created reflects her in terms of queenly quality rather than individual behaviour. The plots Lyly uses, narrating the threats to hierarchical coherence, whether internal or external, and ending with the recovery of balance or control, can be made to refer to particular political occasions only because these tend to follow recurrent general formulae. When Lyly turns to indubitable political allegory, as in *Midas* (Midas is Philip II, whose possessions in the Indies turn everything to gold), the effect is in fact a loss of sharpness rather than a gain—a loss we may seem determined to create elsewhere.

After *Campaspe* Lyly never again found so coherent a social milieu for his dramatized actions. At the same time, and not uncoincidentally, he chose to transform his admired rulers from male to female. In his second play (*Sappho and Phao*) he concentrated attention on the idea of female heroism he derived from Ovid's *Heroides*, where the heroic shows itself as a struggle against overmastering passion and a return to duty, rather than (as with Alexander) an escape from personal entanglement into the noble simplicity of war. Imitating the *Heroides* allowed Lyly to give his antithetical mode of writing a more intense inner dimension than would have been appropriate to Alexander. The rhetoric of the divided mind, where reason battles against emotion, was used by Ovid to catch the pathos of his abandoned and soliloquizing heroines (Sappho, Medea, Ariadne, Dido, and so on) in the medium of a wit which is both intensifying and distancing. Ovid's heroines are tragic figures—reason can have little function in the violent tenor of their lives—but Lyly's comic mode requires that the demeaning passion be resolved not by suicide but by a recuperative rationality that enforces the return of social order. His heroines are thus heroic both in the Ovidian sense (high-born, famous, mythological, powerfully emotional) and in the moral sense of being controlled, responsible, benevolent. That they have the additional advantage of reflecting the image of Queen Elizabeth cannot have been irrelevant. But the principal dramatic advantage comes from the opportunity given to represent a piquantly expressed refusal to understand what love is, an indirection in erotic conversation, entirely appropriate to children acting adult roles. *Campaspe* shows this in the dialogue of the 'two loving worms' Apelles and Campaspe, loving, but unwilling to admit to a love that might enrage their master, Alexander. In *Sappho and Phao* and *Gallathea* this emotional tone is made central to the whole play.

Human vulnerability and immersion in the tidal to and fro of personal relations are everywhere in Lyly brought to bear witness against the desire for constancy, in Alexander, in Sappho, in Phillida and Gallathea, in Ceres' nymphs, in Pandora; but these psychological conditions are always presented inside worlds where they can be referred to a static order ('things as they ought to be').[38] The creation of a space to allow this can come into existence through a ruler's self-control or by the fiat of magnanimous supernatural powers who are able to transform whatever is amiss, and at the same time secure the unstinting praise and loyalty of those who have been transformed, whether the change be one of sex, as in *Gallathea*, or of self-perception, as in *Midas*, or of understanding of the world, as in *Endymion*. In setting up situations in which gods or godlike humans have to intervene to restore an order that the passionate tendency to self-will in human agents threatens to destroy, Lyly is following (as the previous pages will have indicated) a well-beaten track in courtly drama. Yet the manner in which he follows the track is entirely his own. In plays like *The Arraignment of Paris*, *The Rare Triumphs of Love and Fortune*, *The Cobbler's Prophecy*, the overarching apparatus of divine control appears as something like a court of last resort. The gods set up, or allow, a human experiment; and then the human actors have to try to manage as best they can with what the gods have left them. But in Lyly's plays, characteristically, the representatives of system, fate, necessity, are integrated into the diversified pattern of action. Gods and humans make up together rather than separately what Lyly's societies aspire to—a world unified in the general aims and attitudes available to it. The plays end typically with compromise achievements rather than *diktat*. In *Gallathea*, it is true, Venus solves the love problem of Phillida and Gallathea by using her power to transform one of them (characteristically it doesn't matter which) into a man. But this is not simply a fiat from above; it facilitates only what the humans desire and ask for. In *Endymion* the command that Endymion's love should not express itself as other than adoration simply places the hero at his appropriate point on the scale which leads down through the less noble love of Eumenides and Semele to the mere carnality of Sir Tophas. It is the best fate

[38] The delicate comedy of maidenly love inside a paternalistic order continues to fascinate audiences at least as late as the story of Natalya Petrovna in Turgenev's *A Month in the Country*.

available to him (as to the others), given the limiting conditions both inside and outside their selves. *Love's Metamorphosis* (1588× 1590) ends with a compromise between Cupid and Ceres: the acceptance of love demanded by Cupid and the foresters must coexist with the faithfulness demanded by Ceres and the nymphs. The concordat is worked out on high, but it fulfils the necessities of the human relationships below, and so gives us a complex mixture of assent and resistance that recalls Shakespeare, in the structuring of emotions, if not in the rhetorical mode.

CERES. Well, my good nymphs, yield. Let Ceres intreat you yield.
NISA. I am content, so as Ramis, when he finds me cold in love or hard in belief, he attribute it to his own folly, in that I retain some nature of the rock he changed me into.
RAMIS. O my sweety Nisa! Be what thou wilt, and let all thy imperfections be excused by me, so thou but say thou lovest me.
NISA. I do.
RAMIS. Happy Ramis!

(v. iv. 131–9)

The Woman in the Moon (1590×1595) has been thought to represent Lyly's one attempt to break out of the conventions of tightly controlled witty prose comedy for the boys to act at court (it is his one play in verse). It may be significant that this change takes us back to something more like *The Rare Triumphs of Love and Fortune*—to a plot, that is, where an Olympian arrangement drives humans towards chaos, finally requiring a second Olympian conference to correct what has gone wrong. Yet even here Lyly shows us human capacity for free choice. At the end of the play Pandora is allowed to choose her own astral destiny and elects to live, not with Saturn, Jupiter, Mars, Sol, Venus, or Mercury, but with Cynthia, the Moon:

> For know that change is my felicity
> And fickleness Pandora's proper form.

(v. i. 301–2)

As at the end of most of these plays, human need for inconclusiveness is an inevitable element inside the totalizing pattern.

Mother Bombie shows Lyly at his closest to the Roman and Italian mode of a modern urban intrigue managed by witty servants in order to secure their own pleasure and freedom. Here we are no longer in a remote or symbolic setting but in Rochester in Kent where 'Mother Bungay . . . the great witch of Rochester' (as Reginald Scott calls her[39]) lived as a matter of fact—in the very region where Lyly spent his own early life. As if to compensate for this degree of realism, *Mother Bombie* is of Lyly's plays the most obviously artificial in construction, its symmetries delightfully exposed in every scene. Four fathers with four children (two male, two female) seek, as is usual, the most profitable possible matches. Two of the fathers are wealthy, two of only moderate estate. But the children of the wealthy fathers are idiots (though this is not known abroad), while the children of modest households are highly accomplished. Wealth and desire are thus, as usual, at odds. The four servants of the four fathers form a conspiracy to right the potential wrongs: they will fulfil the love of the accomplished children and marry off the fools to one another. But there are two more children in the play, the poor children of an old woman. Their problem, deriving from their incestuous love for one another, cannot be solved by the servants' manipulations. Here Lyly has to draw on a more mysterious power, whose local representative is the oracular Mother Bombie. Her prescience leads to the discovery that the incestuous pair are not in fact brother and sister but the heirs to the two rich fathers. So the rich children turn out to be entirely suited (they are already in love) as are the children of the two middling fathers, and the two idiots, now known to be brother and sister, can be properly looked after in the rich households where they have grown up. The servants, whose manipulations have led to symmetries beyond anticipation, are forgiven the lies they have told to achieve these ends.

Nearly every plot device in *Mother Bombie* can be paralleled in Roman comedy and its Renaissance imitations. What is less easily parallelled is the method by which they are accumulated and organized. Lyly is not interested, it would appear, in the element of comic panic by which cross-intrigues usually aim to hold their audience's attention nor in the sense of bitterness which the grotesque passions of Plautus' Euclio or Pyrgopolynices evoke (comedy as a Hell that can be laughed at). There is only one major intrigue. Once the four servants have promised to effect what the four fathers desire, they have almost total control of the action. The

[39] *The Discovery of Witchcraft* (1584), bk. XVI, ch. iii.

fathers feel a certain unease at what is happening, but there is no counter-intrigue and none of those recurrent paroxysms of extempore invention that we meet, for example, in *I suppositi*. The tone of *Mother Bombie* is sweet and self-congratulatory. In a world so totally symmetrical, where speech, like action, moves in prose stanzas of double or triple repetition, the emphasis falls inevitably on fulfilment rather than surprise. We watch the servants move the other characters as if they were chess pieces being used to illustrate checkmate in seventeen scenes. And, as in chess, our enjoyment of the spectacle derives from our sense of the ways in which cleverness turns into inevitability. The effect is to congratulate society (represented by an audience of the powerful) on the mathematical confirmation of a basic order that can be discovered under surface anarchy.

Peele's *The Old Wife's Tale: A Pleasant Conceited Comedy*[40] is said on the title-page to have been *Played by the Queen's Majesty's Players*; that could mean either the Queen's Men or the Children of her Majesty's Chapel. There is no external evidence that it was a court play, but if we ask what plays it is most like, then a family resemblance begins to appear, that requires us to think of *Summer's Last Will and Testament, The Arraignment of Paris*, even of *The Cobbler's Prophecy* and *The Rare Triumphs of Love and Fortune*— rather than of Greenian historical romance or Italianate bourgeois comedy.[41] The motivation is arbitrary in the extreme: we never know where we are or what will happen next. Yet this arbitrariness is entirely to the point in the evocation of romantic charm and absurdity that Peele so skilfully and so economically organizes. *The Old Wife's Tale* offers us a final variation on the alternation of romance and realism discussed so many times above.

As in *The Rare Triumphs of Love and Fortune* and in Induction plays like *Mucedorus*, the romance story is presented self-consciously as a *tale*, told or organized by a figure whose mode of telling frames and explains the action as a generically controlled fiction. But in

---

[40] The form *wife's* is not standard; but it is made necessary by the fact that there is only one *old wife* and that the substance of the play is the *tale* she tells.

[41] Chambers (iii. 48) says that it 'was evidently staged in a way exactly analogous to that adopted by Lyly'. Pinciss ('Thomas Creede and the Repertory of the Queen's Men, 1583–1592', *MP* 67 (1970), 323) notes that 'the frequent songs, the lack of physical activity are all elements of the productions of the Children of Paul's or the Chapel'. F. S. Hook, in the C. T. Prouty edition of Peele (iii. 372), says the play 'finds its proper place in the tradition of court comedy and entertainment'.

this case the occasion of the telling is not a debate in Olympus but a night without a bed in the cottage of Clunch the blacksmith; his wife, Madge, is the old wife whose 'tale' is the play's story. The social status of the cottager who tells the story thus determines the genre of the tale. In *The Rare Triumphs of Love and Fortune* the dispute between Venus and Fortune gives an appropriate setting to the passionate complexities of chivalric romance. In *The Old Wife's Tale* the cottage romance that Madge tells is, equally appropriately, a tissue of folk-tale motifs—the wicked magician, the abducted maiden, the brothers in search of their sister (hence the early interest in the play as an analogue or source to *Comus*), the man changed into a bear, the true lover, or 'wandering knight', who learns the spell that will destroy the magician and release the maiden, the 'grateful dead' living corpse who serves as an agent for the lover and secures his victory, the Abraham-and-Isaac test of true faith in love.

Yet to think of Madge's story as only a dramatized folk-tale underprivileges the complexity of Peele's dramaturgy. The social ambience of the story draws on the status of the audience in the cottage as well as the narrator. Madge tells her story to no village gossips but to the courtly pages Frolic and Fantastic, who have lost their way after accompanying their master on an amorous adventure. Their opening exchange, with its singing, its Latin tags, its snip-snap repartee, is strongly reminiscent of scenes of boy pages in Lyly; and their initial conversation with Clunch the smith suggests at first that he has been introduced into the play to perform like Motto the barber in Lyly's *Midas* or like Grim the collier of Croyden in *Edwards's *Damon and Pythias*—as a slow-witted butt for their fast-paced jokes. But once we reach the cottage and Madge takes over, the manners of simple folk are given a power to neutralize courtiers' superiority without, however, requiring us to forget their sophistication. The first suggestion of 'an old wife's winter tale' as a way of passing the night-time is slightly condescending. Frolic asks for 'a tale of the Giant and the King's Daughter and I know not what. I have seen the day, when I was a little one, you might have drawn me a mile after you with such a discourse' (ll. 87–90). But even so mild an effort to take on the role of a supercilious auditor draws down Madge's rebuke: 'Nay, either hear my tale or kiss my tail.' 'Well said', replies Fantastic, 'on with your tale, Gammer' (l. 118). And from that moment there is no breach of understanding between the smith's wife and the courtly pages. This is not to say that they all retreat together into a state of nursery innocence. The play is a tissue of sophisticated linguistic cross-references. Huanebango may not be a portrait of Gabriel Harvey, but the hexameters he delivers (ll. 646–55) are clearly aimed at one or another of the clumsy hexametrists of the age. The lover's name is that of the constant though earthly lover in Lyly's *Endymion*. The name of Sacrapant, the magician, comes from Ariosto, probably via Greene's *Orlando furioso*, a play Peele quotes directly in the lover's presentation of himself to the rescued maiden (ll. 853–6). The rhetorics of incantation (ll. 653–9), of the hostess as saleswoman (ll. 735–65), of village chat (ll. 454 ff.), of Erastus' folk-prophecies (ll. 157 ff., 439 ff.), of Booby's clownery—all these are presented with sophisticated consciousness of difference; but they are pieced together without any one of them being used to claim centrality. They all exist at the same distance from us, as if they were all equally natural elements in an abstracted system.

The Old Wife's Tale succeeds in making the great diversity of its materials extraordinarily coherent by avoiding issues of character or narrative probability, by allowing the generic frame to control our perceptions of the play to a degree not found in other works we have discussed. As a narrative exhibiting the evasive logic of a dream with greater thoroughness than either *Endymion* or *A Mid-summer Night's Dream*, as a play of enacted as well as described enchantment, *The Old Wife's Tale* might have been expected to end by returning its audience to the real world, explaining away its dream fiction with a Lylyan gesture of disengagement. But Peele does not choose to 'place' his fiction in these terms. When the old wife's tale ends, light is perceived to be coming through the shutters. The realistic lineaments of the cottage appear again. The insouciance of the characters in the play, who show little or no sense of the gaping holes in the coherence of the world they inhabit, fades before the daylight need for explanation. But all the old wife offers, out of one world and into the other, is a moral paradigm. Jack, she tells the pages, 'was the ghost of the poor man that they kept such a coil to bury, and that makes him help the wandering knight so much'. The simplest of moral relationships ('one good deed deserved another') is presented as the explanatory cause of the chivalric romance. One begins to wonder if the whole play, frame plot as well as inner plot, is not set up to illustrate this lesson. How real is the old wife? In her final statement she speaks as if she herself had been inside the story: 'When this [final reconciliation of Delia and the wandering knight] was done, I took a piece of bread and cheese and came my way.' In the context it sounds as if the bread and cheese are a charm to disenchant. The pages too must pass through the same process. 'And so shall you have too before you go', the old wife continues. The play ends with evasion rather than the usual resolution and self-definition. Perhaps (who knows?) this reflects the uncertainty of genre noted at the beginning of this discussion. The court and the popular theatre undoubtedly put different pressures on the playwright, but the tastes of queen and folk were by no means incompatible. The convenience of boundaries in literary history should not blind us to the ease with which any culture can move across them.

5. Early History Plays

A Historical Genre?

HISTORY plays are clearly different from comedies and tragedies in ways which do not resemble those that separate comedy from tragedy. Our understanding of this latter separation begins at the formal level: happy endings are set against sad endings, social integration and the future against social isolation and no [earthly] future, low life versus high life, reality versus mythology, collo- quial immediacy against distancing rhetorical splendour. Of course, to rest on these formal points is not to assume that we cannot extra- polate larger distinction from such bases and invoke God, Time, and the seasons. But history plays can make little claim to partici- pate in any of these grand binary schemes. It can easily be argued that this genre has a tendency to collapse like an unstable isotope into the more stable condition of either comedy or tragedy. Cer- tainly the word 'history' as it appears in Elizabethan play titles shows us that the age had no clear generic definition in mind. We hear of (for example) *The History of Troilus and Cressida*, *The True Chronicle History of King Leir*, *A Pleasant Conceited History Called The Taming of a Shrew*. In such titles 'history' has collapsed into its basic synonymy with 'story'.

The great event in the history of the history play is the designa- tion of ten plays (out of thirty-six) in the Shakespeare First Folio as 'histories'—for these ten plays are sufficiently like one another to provide a pragmatic definition of the genre. In these terms a history play is a play about English dynastic politics of the feudal and immediately post-feudal period—usually about tensions be- tween central government and the barons. There can be no doubt that Heminge and Condell had (as theatre men) noticed an even more relevant factor: that a theatrical audience has a relationship with stories about its own intelligible past which is different from the relationship to other kinds of stories.[1] Several much quoted

---

[1] Cf. Coleridge: 'In order that a drama may be properly historical it is necessary that it should be the history of the people to whom it is addressed' (*Shakespearean Criticism: Samuel Taylor Coleridge*, ed. T. M. Raysor (London, 1960), i. 138).

testimonies of the Elizabethan period confirm this view of the role of the history play in the patriotic culture of the time.[2] But a wave of national self-confidence, following the defeat of the Armada in 1588, cannot be asserted as the whole explanation. The earliest and standard-setting history plays are not simply celebrations of national greatness, but indeed put the incompetencies and malignities of English governments at the centre of the picture (as in *Henry VI*, *Edward II*, *Richard III*). The identification with a glorious English past appears only as a military identification; the 10,000 spectators who embalmed the bones of Talbot with their tears[3] wept because the government was too inept to give him support.

But there is an even more important factor: patriotism will not be reinforced for long if the story told comes to be known as mere fiction. Historical narratives can impose identification with the past only if they are accepted as (in some sense) true. And this provides another difference from Comedy and Tragedy, which can be properly enjoyed as feigned or fictive. History appears in the Induction to the anonymous *A Warning for Fair Women* (see Chapter 4) as a guarantor of factual accuracy, but in the quarrel of the genres its unfortunate role is that of a neutral in a family quarrel; between the alternative trajectories of death and happiness no third possibility is allowed. The Induction to the anonymous *True Tragedy of Richard III* (1588×1594) gives the history play a more interesting role, making it the client of truth:

POETRY. Truth, well met!
TRUTH. Thanks, Poetry. What makes thou upon a stage?
POETRY. Shadows.

---

[2] Nashe praises subject matter 'wherein our forefathers' valiant acts . . . are revived, and they themselves raised from the grave of oblivion and brought to plead their aged honours in open presence: than which, what can be a sharper reproof to those degenerate days of ours?' (McKerrow, i. 212). Heywood in his Apology for Actors (1612) says: 'What English blood, seeing the person of any bold Englishman presented, and doth not hug his fame and honey at his valour . . . as if the personator were the man personated? . . . What coward, to see his countryman valiant would not be ashamed of his own cowardice? What English prince, should he behold the true portraiture of that famous king Edward the Third . . . would not be suddenly inflamed with so royal a spectacle, being made apt and fit for the like achievement?' (sig. B4). He also tells us that 'plays have . . . taught the unlearned the knowledge of many famous histories, instructed such as cannot read in the discovery of our English Chronicles, and what man have you now that cannot discourse of any notable thing recorded, even from William the Conqueror' (sig. F3).

[3] Nashe (McKerrow, i. 212).

TRUTH. Then will I add bodies to the shadows.
Therefore depart and give Truth leave
To show her pageant.
POETRY. Why, will Truth be a player?
TRUTH. No, but Tragedia-like for to present
A tragedy in England done but late
That will revive the hearts of drooping minds.

(ll. 7–16)

The claim is that the historical material of Richard's reign, 'being done in England but of late', is 'true', and can be verified by the audience. Poetry can only (as in Plato) offer 'shadows', but Truth can give substance to poetic shadows by showing things that actually happened, what 'the Chronicles make manifest' (l. 21). Truth has to allow herself to appear 'Tragedia-like' in order to secure the effects described, but the recentness of the events and faithfulness to the chronicles can counteract the danger that poetry must mean lies.

The sense that truth has to be invoked to justify history plays is a recurrent feature of the word in Elizabethan play titles. I have discovered thirteen uses of the word 'true' among titles of plays published between 1573 and 1616, four times attached to plays about English history, four times to plays about Ancient British history (always as 'true chronicle history'), three times to plays about Roman history, and twice to plays about recent notorious murders (both called 'lamentable and true').[4] Of course the word *true* found in such contexts is, like other words in title-pages, a piece of advertising copy not a scientific description; what I take to be significant is therefore only the fact that *this* was the word found recurrently appropriate to advertise plays about history. The word is significant only because it designates a set of claims against a set of received expectations. 'Truth' in these terms may be said to be a word that indicates the precondition of a history play.

The statement in the induction to *The True Tragedy of Richard III* that Truth will have to appear 'Tragedia-like' in order to present the tragic truth she has to tell points to the difficult relation between ends and means. The end (truth) can hardly be achieved without a shaping process which disengages it from the particulars it contains. Without some such process the history play could not be expected to survive outside its original occasion.

[4] See G. K. Hunter, 'Truth and Art in History Plays', *Sh. S.* 42 (1990), 17.

Much twentieth-century criticism has sought to deal with such questions by allegorizing both history and the mimetic process. The Tudor understanding of history, we are often told, turned individual reigns and individual successes and failures into exemplary instances of the intervention of God (or, as many moderns prefer, of the Historical Process). In particular, the eight plays of Shakespeare that run a continuous course from *Richard II* to *Richard III* are said to present a pattern of divine punishment for national apostasy through which the Tudor audience could identify itself as the final inheritor of God's forgiveness once the crime had been expiated. Inside the plays of the sequence, consequently, we must look *through* individual lives and personal relations so that we may understand their places on the giant wheel of historical necessity (Jan Kott's 'Grand Mechanism'[5]). 'Truth' in these terms is identified as the shape of an overarching purpose. That there is something of this in the plays need not be denied; but the experience of seeing or reading Shakespeare's history plays, or (more pertinently) of being deeply moved by them, owes very little to this type of conceptual organization. And this is not, incidentally, what Elizabethan title-pages mean when they use the word 'true', which refers there rather to the truth of factual detail, authenticated by the witness of historians.

In a similar vein we are recurrently told that the chronicles (particularly Edward Hall's) are marked by an overall design that controls their presentation of detail. But to read continuously in the Chronicles is to discover that they exemplify less the grand historical design than the complexity, dispersal, randomness, even incomprehensibility of actual happenings.[6] In his dedication to

---

[5] In *Shakespeare our Contemporary* (Garden City, NY, 1964).

[6] Abraham Fleming, in his Epistle 'To the Readers Studious in Histories' set before the 'First Part of the History of England' in the 1587 edition of Holinshed's Chronicles, says that it would be a wonderful work if historians were able 'to correct the accounts of former ages so many hundred years received, out of uncertainties raise certainties, and to reconcile writers dissenting in opinion and report. But as this is unpossible, so is no more to be looked for than may be performed: and further to inquire as it is against reason, so to undertake more than may commendably be achieved, were foul folly'. Cf. Montaigne, *Des Livres*, on Froissart: 'Froisard . . . representeth unto us the diversity of the news then current [*la diversité mesme des bruits qui couroyant*], and the different reports that were made unto him. The subject of a history should be naked, bare, and formless; each man according to his capacity or understanding may reap commodity out of it. . . . Let them [the historians] boldly enstall [*Qu'ils estalent hardiment*] their eloquence and discourse; let them censure at their pleasure, but let them also give us leave to judge after them. And let them neither alter

Burghley, Holinshed says that the reading of his volume will 'daunt the vicious' and 'encourage worthy citizens'. But in the actual telling of his story Holinshed fails to show that history points a moral in either direction. And when he does risk causal moralization, that too appears random and particular rather than explanatory. Thus, when Edward IV arrives at York and swears on the sacrament that he has invaded England only to claim his rightful dukedom of York, Holinshed comments as follows:

For this wilful perjury (as hath been thought) the issue of this king suffered (for the father's offence) . . . And it may well be. For it is not likely that God, in whose hands is the bestowing of all sovereignty, will suffer such an indignity to be done to his sacred majesty and will suffer the same to pass with impunity.[7]

The tentativeness of the explanation here, the limitation imposed on the connection made, is entirely characteristic of the author. What was published under Holinshed's name was, in his own phrase, a 'collection of histories'; the pluralism attaches both to the variety of sources drawn on and to the collaborative effort that went into the production, and both these point away from explanatory clarity. The *wie es eigentlich gewesen* view of truth[8] may be in Holinshed's mind, but is nowhere invoked as a unifying perspective. Indeed, one might say that the closer the chroniclers bring us to the documentation of the past the more obscured becomes the overview.

The chroniclers show themselves well aware of this. Holinshed offers us the guidance of 'some say', 'others allege', 'it is reported that', but makes little or no sustained effort to assess accuracy or probability. And, when the absence of explanatory connection is particularly blatant, he throws up his hands in a gesture that might be despair or might be piety, as when he says of the usurpation of Bolingbroke that he cannot make sense of it: 'But . . . the providence of God is to be respected and his secret will to be wondered at. For as in his hands standeth the donation of kingdoms, so

nor dispense by their abridgements and choice anything belonging to the substance of the matter; but let them rather send it pure and entire with all her dimensions unto us. (Florio's translation (Everyman edn.; London, 1910), ii. 103–4).

[7] *Holinshed*, 680a. 65 ff.
[8] See Stephen Bann (*The Clothing of Clio* (Cambridge, 1984), 8–14) on the ambiguity of this phrase.

likewise the disposing of them consisteth in his pleasure.[9] In such cases a providential pattern emerges, but less as an overall explanation than as a justification for the humanly inexplicable,[10] and as a way of suggesting belief that *somehow* the narrative must hold together.[11] A dramatist who makes his way through such actual chronicles—and we should remember that Shakespeare could not lay his hands on a copy of *Shakespeare's Holinshed*—has to achieve his design by means of rigorous exclusion and reshaping. But, if I am right in assuming that the ideal of truth to the experience of life in the past remains a defining quality of the Elizabethan history play, then the process of streamlining history into a watertight cause-and-effect kind of structure can easily carry the history play beyond its *telos*; for the demonstration of Art inevitably diminishes our acceptance of Truth.[12]

This takes us back to the comparison between Comedy, History, and Tragedy. Tragedies and Comedies operate inside efficient and well-tested modes for the artful unification of experience, and it has sometimes seemed as if the history play could not achieve such unity unless it fell into the artful method of one or the other of its siblings. This was an agreed and probably an inevitable view among neoclassical critics, whose respect for Art allowed variations from the canon of Tragedy and Comedy only as consequences of ignorance or boorishness: history plays were 'common . . . among our rude ancestors', Dr Johnson averred.[13] He calls the history plays

a series of actions with no other than chronological succession, independent on each other, and without any tendency to introduce or regulate the conclusion . . . a history might be continued through many plays; as it had no plan it had no limits. . . . Nothing more is necessary . . . than that the changes of action be so prepared as to be understood . . . no other unity is intended, and therefore none is to be sought.[14]

[9] Holinshed, 499b. 64 ff.

[10] See Abraham Fleming's epistle 'To the reader studious in histories' in the 1587 Holinshed: '[This] is not a work for every common capacity; nay, it is a toil without head or tail, even for extraordinary wits.'

[11] See Frank Kermode (*The Sense of an Ending* (New York, 1967)) for a masterly account of the human necessities in such a belief.

[12] Sidney's *Apology for Poetry* tells us that 'the historian in his bare *was* hath many times that which we call fortune to overrule the best wisdom. Many times he must tell events whereof he can yield no cause: or, if he do, it must be poetical' (ed. G. Shepherd (Manchester, 1965), 110). For a general discussion of the issue of art and truth, see Philip Edwards, *Shakespeare and the Confines of Art* (London, 1968).

[13] *Selections from Johnson on Shakespeare*, ed. Bertram H. Bronson and Jean M. O'Meara (New Haven, 1986), 226.   [14] Ibid. 16, 22.

In the jargon of the Russian Formalists and their followers, such plays exhibit *fabula* but no *sjužet*: they are mere transcripts of chronology, and chronology provides the only articulation they possess.

It takes very little reading in Shakespeare's historical sources to learn what nonsense this is. But the general issue is not so easily disposed of. History plays are not controlled by the formal closures of death or marriage; they allow the open-endedness of history itself to appear—when one king dies another king emerges; time and politics grind on with a degree of indifference to the life-cycles of individuals. But to say that *Richard II*, *Richard III*, and *King John* are simply tragedies that are poorly unified because open-ended is clearly inadequate as a description. The dialectical relation between Art and Truth seems central enough to require a further effort to define the dramaturgy of history plays, preferably in their simplest and most unsophisticated forms, whether as Shakespeare employed them or as Shakespeare inherited them.

F. P. Wilson has famously remarked that 'there is no certain evidence that any popular dramatist before Shakespeare wrote a play based on English history'.[15] If that is to be believed, then *Henry VI* is, however sophisticated in itself, the great originating event in the history of the history play. But should one believe it? A glance at the history of the Tudor history play suggests that, of course, Shakespeare's practice radically altered the nature of history play-writing and historical fiction in general; but Shakespeare could not, any more than God, invent *ex nihilo*. The material on which he laid his seal manual had been evolving throughout the preceding fifty years. He inherited a complex of attitudes and assumptions that both limited and liberated his capacity to articulate a vision of politics that still gives its stop-and-start process an acceptable structure. The Reformation no doubt created a general awareness that there were different ways of conceptualizing the past. The self-consciousness of the Tudor princes about differences between current governments and their predecessors inevitably showed up change as a political process and so as a set of alternatives: 'how if . . .', 'let us imagine that . . .', 'did things need to happen that way?', and, above all, 'what made things happen that way?' The standard and safe answer, that God was responsible, no doubt came easily to minds used to the perspective of Final Causes;

---

[15] *Marlowe and the Early Shakespeare* (Oxford, 1953), 106.

but even the most ardent supporters of the Tudors must have noticed that they were not living day to day in a theoretical kingdom of Ends, but in a contingent world—in one where proximate causes ruled all perceivable existence—governed by the incoherences of human nature, including royal human nature. Thus providence could be (and was) both celebrated in theory and contradicted in practice.

Such a sense of the role of chance (or Fortune) in human affairs no doubt pushed thinkers and writers in a direction where there was already a literary and philosophic tradition well able to support them. And so the governmental demand for an accepting and passive outlook could easily be married to a traditional pleasure in the falls of the rich and the famous, providing a simultaneous admiration for greatness and celebration of fortunate distance from it. Such an attitude is perhaps most easily seen in *The Mirror for Magistrates* ([1555]; 1559; 1563; 1578; 1587), whose authors found in the chronicles of the preceding century a Tussaud gallery of victims 'hanged, slain, murdered, banished, starved, drowned, surfeited' (as the 1559 Index tells us), who not only exemplified the triumphs of Fortune but also, in terms of the recurrent political situation in which all the victims were trapped, defined the route to the much celebrated present as a *via dolorosa* of kill or be killed; and so the rhetoric of Complaint lay easily to hand to describe the truth about the current world. By its presentation of all the actors in this bloody progression as victims, by its capacity to give tongue and so human feeling to all the different sides in the political struggle, *The Mirror for Magistrates* can be read, in its vision of the ineluctable gap between the civilized present[16] and the unendurable past, as a disarticulated version of Shakespeare's first tetralogy.

Held together only by its damnable iteration of viewpoint, its powerful men brought low in death and finding recompense only in the chance to tell their repetitive individual histories, *The Mirror for Magistrates* cannot give us the openness of conflict that drama exposes in history. Controlled as they are by uniform tragic retrospection, these moralized autobiographies necessarily lack any sense of history actually being made before our eyes, of the future being created as we participate in the action. Here as elsewhere in the

---

[16] Well represented by the antiquarian gentlemen who discuss the historical and literary issues that their ghostly informants describe.

literature of the so-called 'late-medieval' (early Tudor) period, the
basic Christian question 'How can a good God permit these terrible
things to happen?' is given the basic but stifling Christian answer,
'Do not look for recompense or justice in a fallen world which
exists only as a preparative for the true life elsewhere'. This allows
the narrators to stand safely inside the circle of their own piety
while the ghosts around them demonstrate that Hell is here on
earth. The history play proper, running from *Henry VI* through
the lifetime of Shakespeare, lacks the comfort of this protective
screen. To read or see these plays is to participate directly in the
dangerous instability of the political world without the safety net
of the narrator's separated self-definition; also without the exclu-
sionary focus that Comedy and Tragedy provide. These genres
present us with worlds in which politics are carefully tailored to
the characters who live there. Hamlet's Denmark, Berowne's
Navarre, Leontes' Sicily, all present us with acute images of political
worlds, but the developments in these plays achieve their political
consequence as by-products of personal and emotional relationships.
And it is this latter focus that gives us our sense of encompassing
reality in such genres, allowing us space to register the political
instabilities of the worlds depicted (Denmark, Navarre, Sicily) only
as convenient fictional contexts for truly personal lives. But history
plays do not show us worlds that can be so conveniently subordinated. There we identify as easily with a historical truth as with the
reality of the persons trying to cope with it, and so find it easier to
accept its relevance to our own situation.

The danger of this elision between past and present is that it can
lead to a simplified and vulgarized sense of the persons shown, as
if they existed only to face *our* political problems;[17] and one may
argue that the fear of such vulgarism is a factor in several of the
scholarly modes of the twentieth century. The movement represented by L. L. Schucking, E. E. Stoll, and Lily B. Campbell
(among others) should perhaps be referred to now as 'old' historicism, to distinguish it from the post-1960s 'new' variety. It was a
historicism that can be seen as the natural culmination of more
than a century of preceding investigations of Elizabethan meanings
and attitudes, seeking positivist truth about the past. The result of

---

[17] The great modern exemplar of this use of the history play is the 1945 Laurence Olivier
film of *Henry V*, produced in wartime to reinforce patriotism and responded to by millions
as a glorification of 'us' as we had been and presumably could be again.

all this work was to make it clear that 'we' are not like 'them', so that if we wish to understand their writings we must try to understand the terms in which they actually meant them. This has led (as with other historicisms) to the privileging of Tudor political events, thus finding the stable truth of the play in an area beyond anything easily available to a modern theatrical audience. We are told, for example, that King John's fight against the Pope was a powerful subject for Elizabethans because it was taken to refer to the Tudor struggle against the same authority. Likewise the issue of Bolingbroke's usurpation (or change of dynasty) should be understood, we are told, as a reflection of contemporary anxiety about the Elizabethan succession. Another aspect of the same scholarly desire to stabilize the meanings of history plays in an understanding free of modern political indeterminacy appears in Dr Tillyard's celebrated work on the intellectual world of the Tudors,[18] in which the metaphysical idea of Order is used to explain Elizabethan politics in terms that cut it off from modern political conflict.

Another part of the same effort to rescue the history play from political and generic instability appears in the construction of a genetic sequence that leads us back to the guild cycles and the morality plays, most particularly to *Skelton's *Magnificence* (1515) and *Bale's *King Johan* (?1534, 1538, 1561). Bale's play seems particularly apt for this purpose, given its overlap in subject with Shakespeare's *King John*, and the anonymous *Troublesome Reign of John, King of England*, as also in the ambiguous status of its cast list, in which allegorical names double with historical ones—Sedition with Stephen Langton, Dissimulation with Simon of Swinsett, Usurped Power with Pope Innocent III, Private Wealth with Cardinal Pandulph. Such characteristics lead Irving Ribner, for example, to tell us that in *King Johan* 'we can see the history play emerging from the morality'.[19] The argument makes much sense if one chooses to define genres by the presence or absence of genetic traces. If, however, one is looking for central effects that, having survived through time, continue to explain our interest, then Bale's play looks less like a direct ancestor. Bale offers us a total coincidence between political position and moral meaning: the king is defined

---

[18] See especially his *The Elizabethan World Picture* (London, 1943) and *Shakespeare's History Plays* (London, 1944).

[19] *The English History Play in the Age of Shakespeare* (Princeton, 1957; repr. New York, 1965), 34.

wholly by his role as God's repesentative on earth; political life is not an art of survival but a vehicle for timeless moral patterns appearing in history because they exist always, in heaven. In these terms the analogues between the past and the present are not analogues at all but straight identities. The Pope, Antichrist, and Pharaoh are not simply like one another; they are different names for the same thing, as are Joshua, King John, and Henry VIII.[20]

The argument of this chapter runs against this line of explanation, and seeks to derive definition of the history play not from origins but from consequences. I argue that we today still respond to Shakespeare's (and other) history plays because we accept as true to our experience the balance between an acceptance of general explanations and a rejection of their particular meanings. Compared to the chronicles, the plays are liberal with explanations, but only so that they can be confronted by the randomness of historical truth; thus political duties are set against personal behaviour, national unity against individual self-realization, completion against openness, art against chronology.[21]

These contradictions appear regularly in a form that must have had a particularly powerful resonance for Elizabethan ears: as an opposition between the power of the monarch and that of the great magnates, often the current king's father's brothers. These feudal lords, with their quasi-independent provincial power, their liveried armies, their contempt for bureaucracy, for 'bed-work, mappery, closet war'[22] point back to what David Riggs has identified as the dominant heritage of the early history play, the heroic heritage of *Tamburlaine*.[23] The peers' self-image, their power over an audience's imagination (as shown in Nashe's response to Talbot, cited above), depends primarily on the claim of the great soldier to represent the national ethos, combining his own honour with that of

[20] I am not saying, of course, that Bale was incapable of recognizing the difference between King John and King Henry. But what he regarded as significant in history was not the difference but the identity, an identity evident in so far as each in turn embodied the same position in the same struggle—a struggle which never ceases and never changes.

[21] The dichotomy has a natural critical corollary. It means that the plays are neither sealed inside the presuppositions of their own time, so that we today can give only passive assent to their strangeness, nor yet wholly manipulable into modern meanings. The facts are separated out, made free, as it were, so that they may belong to different patterns of perception; but the characters in the play must be understood to be creating meanings that we could not choose. [22] *Troilus and Cressida*, I. iii. 205.

[23] David Riggs, *Shakespeare's Heroical Histories: 'HENRY VI' and its Literary Tradition* (Cambridge, Mass., 1971).

the country as he fights hand to hand against a hated enemy. But the history play does not simply validate the excitement of identifying with a charismatic soldier; it also allows that in the political terms such power is likely to drive the country towards anarchy— a threat never far below the surface of Elizabethan England and demanding the continual (and proper) vigilance of the central government. And of course the model is not simply an Elizabethan one. Its political truth and power over the mind does not depend on a local threat widely known, for the failure of social and individual values to match one another is understood in all ages. We all respond to the charm and power of the anarchic individual (the two qualities sometimes combined, as in Hotspur, sometimes separated, as in Falstaff and Tamburlaine). Yet we equally well understand the need for national and social order, the justification for *raison d'état*, for necessary and even virtuous Machiavellianism.

The Elizabethan writers of history plays advanced these opposed pieces into action through a variety of gambits. Frequently the king, hemmed in by his militaristic peers, can realize himself only by a non-political retreat into his own private sphere. This is the pattern in *Henry VI* and *Edward II*. Or his retreat may be given the further dimension of a quasi-political court party, as in *Woodstock* and (to a lesser degree) *Richard II*. Henry IV, to look a little further ahead, suppresses the personal in the interest of the statesmanlike: his desire for personal fulfilment is presented, but perpetually postponed till the time when he can lead his army to Jerusalem, when his son will inherit an unflawed title to England (and France). And meanwhile (in his 'unquiet time' or holding operation) the richness of the national life must be expressed through other men. In the *Richard III* plays, on the other hand, the centralizing power of the king controls political anarchy on the periphery by creating moral anarchy at the centre. This shifts the weight of the balancing factors. The anarchic force of the peerage is played down, and interest is focused rather on its capacity to create the conditions for change, to redeem the country from a tyrant—a redemption in which, in providential consequence, Henry VII does not have to play Bolingbroke. The most successful kings, Henry V (in *The Famous Victories* as also in Shakespeare's play), Edward I, and Edward III, possess a combination of Tamburlainian military glamour and careful political control. The power of these history plays to outlive Elizabethan patriotism rests, it would seem, on their capacity to escape from merely celebratory presentation, on their power to show us the natural tension between personal and public, and on the possibility that the 'personal' may be no more than a mode of political rhetoric.

The two broad categories of English royal power that this survey indicates, show up, in plays that survive, in sequences that are more than merely random. Interconnections between the reigns of Edward I and Edward II, Edward III and Richard II, Richard I and John, Henry IV and Henry V—even, in more circumscribed terms, Richard III and Henry VII—suggest a generative pattern of strong kings and weak kings[24] (or at least aggressive kings and defensive kings) in a natural alternation by which the first necessarily produces the second: the ghost of the predecessor haunts the successor reigns we see. I shall, therefore, discuss the individual plays in an order that highlights this sequential relationship.

Preconditions of Maturity

The two earliest Elizabethan works that can be categorized as history plays offer us previews of the techniques I have spoken about: one, the anonymous *Famous Victories of Henry V*, celebrates the charismatic moment when king and commons, centre and periphery, come together; the other, the *Richardus Tertius* of Thomas *Legge, Master of Caius College and sometime Vice-Chancellor of Cambridge University, analyses the necessary tension between these social levels as a source of historical movement. Legge's Latin play, acted in 1579, and the anonymous *Famous Victories*, most probably acted before 1588, both precede Shakespeare's earliest known work, and therefore give us an interesting sense of the genre Shakespeare inherited. Though separated from one another by the great gulf that lay between the academic and the popular stages, they show also the common features that the disposition of the time imposed on the Vice-Chancellor no less than the hack, and indicate the possibility of a future confluence in mature Elizabethan drama.

Reasons for Dr Legge's choice of the reign of Richard III are not hard to imagine. The Tudor dynasty had very early in its life set up the figure of Richard III as a *monstrum horrendum* whose

---

[24] For another handling of this topic, see Michael Manheim, *The Weak King Dilemma in the Shakespearean History Play* (Syracuse, 1973).

political existence could be wholly explained by his moral status (not to mention his physical condition), so identifying by opposition the moral status of his successors. The reign was thus politically safe (all its political possibilities could be reduced to moral meanings), as were few other reigns in relevant English history. What is more, its events had already acquired, in Sir Thomas More's Suetonian (though incomplete) *History of King Richard III* (probably written in the 1530s), an aesthetic structure of beginning, middle, and end, showing Richard's early political success, his inability to check his murderous tendencies, and so the consequences leading up to Bosworth.[25] Legge's sense of history in many respects conforms to the sprawling mode of chronicle truth in its episodic progression, its large cast of characters, its geographical diversity, and its interest in spectacular occasions (the penitential procession of Shore's wife, the coronation of Richard). But at the same time it is clear that Legge, as a Humanist scholar writing for the approbation of other Humanist scholars, wishes to emphasize the classical form of tragedy implicit in the life of Richard. This is evident not only in the form but also in the language used. He seems to have written his play with his Seneca open in front of him.[26] Tyrant tragedy was, of course, well established as the tragic form *par excellence* in continental Humanist no less than Senecan repertory. And indeed two prime examples, pseudo-Seneca's *Octavia praetexta* (then accepted as genuine) and Albertino Mussato's *Ecerinis* of 1312–15 (usually called 'the first modern tragedy'), had already shown how apt the form was to the careers of recently dead tyrants (Nero and Ezzelino da Romano) seen from the angle of the next administration as monstrous intrusions into the world of the normal. Legge shows no awareness of Mussato, and he would have had little sympathy with the Paduan's medieval diabolism—Satan as Ezzelino's physical progenitor—had he chanced to read him. For all that, the two plays show equally the pervading neoclassical tendency to explain a historical sequence in terms of the hellish wickedness of an individual.

---

[25] Willard Farnham—who has written the best critical remarks on Legge's play—refers this structure to the form of *De Casibus* tragedy with its 'ascent, apex, descent', its 'aspirans', 'triumphans', 'moriens' form (*The Medieval Heritage of Elizabethan Tragedy* (Oxford, 1956), 366).

[26] See the elaborate treatment of this topic in G. B. Churchill, *'Richard the Third' up to Shakespeare* (*Palaestra*, 10; Berlin, 1900).

The *Octavia praetexta* (which Legge had certainly read) offered him the much-admired classical characteristics of restriction on time, place, number of actors on stage, a tight-lipped limitation on what might be shown—formal qualities that made it virtually impossible to represent the complexities of modern politics. In the Senecan play Nero is seen at that crucial moment in his career (AD 62) when he escaped from the tutelage of Burrhus and Seneca, displaced Octavia, the virtuous wife chosen to give him his best claim to the throne, and embraced instead the charms of Poppaea and the stimulus of total crime. In handling the material in this way, pseudo-Seneca does not distort history. In the Budé edition, Leon Herrmann remarks 'L'auteur ne semble avoir pris avec l'histoire que le minimum de liberté indispensable.'[27] But the historical moment is being used less to explain the sequence of events than to provide occasion for political debates between norms of virtuous rule and the desire to define oneself by going beyond the norm. The play can thus be seen as not only a story about Nero but also as a generalizing didactic treatise about personal power, and so an appropriate model for both Mussato and Legge. Classical tragedy concentrates our attention on a small family group of characters, a group whose shared memories stretch back through time and concentrate psychic pressure by retrospection of crimes and betrayals, accumulators of resentment that now explode in the present. But a historical sequence that leads up to the arrival of the Tudors must be prospective, even if only in the sense that the crimes of the past cancel each other and so create space for the renewal of virtue. What interests the Roman author is not the political conflict but the effect of political events on Nero's paranoia, and so the chance to delineate *furor*. Legge's Richard can certainly be interpreted as a paranoiac, but that is not the focus the history requires: Richard's wickednesses are shown as more political than psychological; it is the quality of his interactions with other political figures, not his megalomania, that determines his moral status. Before his palace intrigues can be effective, he must plan how to justify himself before the people.

Legge was without doubt an admirer of the intense effects procured by Seneca's concentration on criminal impulses; but the sources and his audience's knowledge of the history depicted gave

[27] (1926), ii. 213–14.

him a story that could have meaning only as a process winding forwards towards the present, through plots, intrigues, deceptions, laundering of evidence, and improvisation in the face of unexpected developments. For one thing, the Richard III story concerns the acquisition of power, where the Nero story deals with power already acquired; the latter provides occasions for moral commentary, the former for political performance. Richard cannot be represented as, like Nero, a vehicle for malignities that operate through him to the undoing of an existing stability. Legge must deal with the realities of the reign, and so Richard must be shown as a Machiavellian rather than a Senecan villain, as a manipulator of the moral world rather than a denier of it, switching masks as he uses one lie, one 'friend', to replace another. He belongs to a specific society, fashioned by the presences around him and so surviving in its terms rather than any of his own. The difference can be pinpointed by the different uses of the classical chorus. For an academic tragedian, Legge is very sparing in the use of a chorus, and when he does use one, as in the *chorus procerum tumultuarum* in Act III, Scene iii, of Part I and the *chorus civium* in Act III, Scene iii, of Part II, he uses them for political rather than moral commentary—to represent the pressure of mass politics on the action: panic over the civil disorder that Richard has organized, reluctant endorsement of his claim to the throne (followed by impotent disgust that consent has been secured by self-evident chicanery and double-talk).

The main interest of Legge's *Richardus Tertius* for readers today lies in its relationship with the later popular plays on Plantagenet history. To see him as a morning star of that repertory is to concentrate on the aspects of his dramaturgy that could not be assimilated to the Senecan model. But, when we look at him from the other end of the same relationship, we can see how short a distance he has travelled from classical exemplar towards the norms of the popular stage. His Richard is indeed no mere vehicle for abstract or supernatural forces and *is* responsive to the political forces around him; but if we compare him to the protagonists of the anonymous *True Tragedy of Richard III* and of Shakespeare's *Richard III*, we must allow that he is, as against their active heroes, an essentially *passive* figure, caught between his need for accommodation and his taste for blood. Such a sense of him could, of course, be understood as a mere fact of psychology, but Legge's interest in the divided mind is essentially that of a political analyst who sees such character traits as embodied in the country no less than the prince (the tyrant creating a kingdom in his own image and himself in the mirror of the divided and disordered kingdom). Thus we see Brackenbury fluctuating between fear of Richard and his desire to save the young princes and see the citizens assenting to Dr Shaw's sermon but withholding belief from his argument. Richard is in this play, as in the others, the dominant political presence, but he is not the commander of the stage. He is allowed little space to establish himself by soliloquy; other characters—Catesby, Buckingham, Brackenbury, Tyrrell, Queen Elizabeth, Queen Anne, Henry of Richmond—are given an equal if not greater opportunity to place themselves in relation to the frightening and disorienting world in which they all live. The realization of a political world is, of course, a major move towards the creation of the Elizabethan history play. As a replacement for the malevolent metaphysical world of Seneca, it opens up a flexible range of possible actions, including (as here) the possibility of a religiously sanctioned happy ending. The parts are placed in an ironic relationship to one another: outside the Machiavellianism of the powerful monarch there is a kingdom of values, alternative to his kingdom. Yet the nature of the relation between virtue and power remains obscure. The history play comes of age in precisely this moment of ambiguity; but it must remain doubtful whether Legge himself knew he was caught in an ambiguity. His aim was, I presume, to write a play which would not only be politically correct but would bring the received annals of his own country inside the structures of classical art.

The other early play that is generally allowed to have preceded Shakespeare's debut is the anonymous *The Famous Victories of Henry V* (1583×1588). The play seems to have belonged to the Queen's Men, but it survives only in an imperfect text, cut for provincial touring. Like *Richardus Tertius*, this is a story of strong kingship, but this time it is the strength of comic self assurance that we see, playing the merry games that strength loves to impose on weakness. Henry as prince and king embodies political success not only as a power that comes from above but (more obviously) as a natural extension of bully-boy dominance. In both phases of his life he provides a populist role model for genial chauvinism, fulfilling for an unanalytical audience the patriotic self-reinforcement that Heywood celebrated as the function of history plays (see above, n. 2). As prince he endears himself to such an audience by appearing himself to be one of the dispossessed, an enemy to rule and respectability. As king and military commander he provides the same chauvinist reinforcement, uniting commons and baronage into a homogeneous national body.

In the first half of the play the exploitable Other is defined by class rather than nationality. Here the enemy is bureaucracy, respectability, the money ethic—eventually the King himself and his business machinery, especially his tax-gatherers (recurrent objects of assault throughout the popular drama) and his enforcers of legal restriction, the Watch and the Lord Chief Justice. Hal and his crew of knights—Tom, Ned, and Jocky Oldcastle—are young, mischief-loving, aggressive; their victims are old, fearful, staid, withdrawn. The play asks its audience to identify with the former and despise the latter. There is, of course, a possibility that a popular audience will see these pranks as only wild-oats sowing by upper-class hooligans, playing defiance of the Establishment as a prelude to joining it. But the play takes steps to avoid this, aligning the Prince and his gang with a genuine proletariat, one group being as marked by taste for spontaneous and comic aggression as the other. The 'knights' rob the exchequer (which is only 'a trick of youth' (l. 11)), while Cuthbert Cutter ('The Thief') robs a poor carrier (Dericke—played apparently by the famous clown, Richard Tarlton). But the Prince's understanding of what unites the two actions as well as what differentiates them, his resolute defence of 'his man', the Thief, indicates that the difference is only one between the top and the bottom of a homogeneous community ('we are all fellows . . . and the king my father were dead we would be all kings' (ll. 93–4)). The connection is further reinforced by Dericke's impersonation of the Prince (ll. 386 ff.) and by Dericke's and the Cobbler's rerun of his climactic anti-establishment action (boxing the Lord Chief Justice's ears) as a fun scenario. When the clowns take the heir-apparent to be one of their own, the relation of the social orders becomes a complex issue.

Yet the Prince, unlike Dericke or Thief, is destined to inherit the bureaucratic power he despises and exploits; and here the author has to evade another misreading—that the popular prince is simply another populist rhetorician (a possibility that Shakespeare incorporates into his version as a genuine uncertainty). The text of

The Famous Victories of Henry V is marked, of course, by extreme compression of the matter it enacts, and indeed the Prince's transition from outsider to insider is over before we have had time to register it. We are quickly moved from England to the war in France, and there the earlier pattern soon re-establishes itself. The change in the target of the Prince's aggression, from the bureaucracy to the French, has been indicated even before Henry IV dies. And as soon as that happens the new king dismisses his gang of knights, and within seventy lines he has rehearsed his genealogy, defied the French ambassador, returned the Dauphin's tennis balls, established the Lord Chief Justice as protector of the realm, and left for his fleet at Southampton. When we next meet Dericke and John Cobbler again, they are being pressed to rejoin the Prince's entourage, this time as common soldiers. In the new situation we find the French nobility characterized by very much the same qualities as those formerly attributed to the English hierarchy, by their sense of superiority and self-satisfaction; and the pleasure of seeing them brought down to comic incoherence is shared by king and commons alike. Dericke and the Cobbler end their war by telling us about their Schweik-like capacity to maximize booty while minimizing fighting. The Cobbler asks Dericke how he survived. 'Why, I will tell thee, John', answers Dericke:

> Every day when I went into the field
> I would take a straw and thrust it into my nose
> And make my nose bleed; and then I would go into the field,
> And when the captain saw me, he would say,
> 'Peace! a bloody soldier' and bid me stand aside.
> Whereof I was glad.

(ll. 1426–31)

They share with us their ingenious plan to use the funeral entourage of the heroic Duke of York to smuggle their stolen goods back home. And when they get home, they tell us, they will show what they have learnt in France by burning down Dericke's house, preferably with his wife inside it. At the same time and in a not altogether different vein we see a ferociously genial king impose his comic energy on the cowed French royal family. The formal rhetoric of 'good brother of England' and 'good brother of France' provides only a comically inadequate cover for the peremptory relations of victor and victim, master and servant, allowing the English to combine the pleasures of magnanimity with those of conquest. The same self-pleasing combination appears in Henry's relation to Katherine of France. As early as the first interview with the French ambassador Henry has roundly declared that he will dispossess the French king, 'and perchance hereafter I will have his daughter' (l. 826). Now he joins marriage to submission and disinheritance, his other war aims. And he completes his triumph in this field with the same blunt directness he has employed in all his other dealings:

> Tush, Kate, but tell me in plain terms,
> Canst thou love the King of England?
> I cannot do as these countries do,
> That spend half their time in wooing.
> Tush, wench, I am none such.
> But wilt thou go over to England?
>
> (ll. 1373–8)

And of course he gets his way.

The play ends with arrangements for the wedding. No hint is given that Henry had little time left to live and that the fruit of this marriage was the disastrous Henry VI.

Strong and Weak Kings

In response to F. P. Wilson's view that 'there is no certain evidence that any popular dramatist before Shakespeare wrote a play based on English history', I have argued that *Richardus Tertius* and *The Famous Victories of Henry V* are not only pre-Shakespearian history plays but indicators of the problems that the later history plays (including Shakespeare's) would have to absorb. *The Famous Victories* offers the enjoyment of personal and so national power as a flattering mirror for a nationalist audience. In *Richardus Tertius* we see the instinct for power devalued as the national destiny becomes a moral touchstone. In *Henry VI* these two versions of history are allowed to stand in balanced competition with one another, without any intention to promote judgement between heroic anarchy as a natural expression of human nature and the idea of politics as a negotiation between wickedness and salvation. By bringing all this together, Shakespeare's three parts of *Henry VI* can be seen to carry all the burden that Wilson placed upon it; it certainly seems that it did in fact provide an innovative example, using not kingly strength (as in the preceding plays) but kingly weakness to bring to a common focus both the heroic and the moral view of national history, so that other historical dramatists of the 1590s were able to learn from his example.[28]

Modern studies of the three *Henry VI* plays (Part I, ?1590; Part II, c.1590; Part III, c.1591; printed 1623[29]) have been dominated by anxieties about authorship, order of composition, and dating. These anxieties do not, however, seem to have inhibited the contemporary playwrights who responded to their powerfully dramatized episodes. And this may well offer a focus for the present enterprise. It does not seem to matter for present purposes whether *1 Henry VI* was written first or devised subsequently to look like the first part. Adaptations and modern productions have proved that each play in the *Henry VI* sequence is capable of standing alone. But there are some cross-references and ironies that will be registered only by those who attend to the sequential order.[30] The epic scope of the work[31] and the ambition of the fledgling playwright demand

[28] Henry VI had in fact appeared on the Elizabethan stage slightly earlier than this. The 'platt' or plot summary of a play called *The Second Part of the Seven Deadly Sins* (surviving among Edward Alleyn's papers from Dulwich College) is generally believed to have been written by Richard Tarlton (d. 1588) (see Chambers, iii. 497). The play starts with Henry in 'a tent . . . placed on the stage', but actually, it would appear, imprisoned in the Tower. He dreams, or has presented to him by the poet Lydgate, three playlets, the first of Envy (dealing with Ferrex and Porrex), the second of Sloth (Sardanapalus), the third of Lechery (Tereus and Philomela). At the end of these spectacles 'Henry speaks. To him Lieutenant [of the Tower], Pursevant and Warders . . . to them [the Earl of] Warwick. Lydgate speaks to the audience and exit' (the text is reproduced in W. W. Greg, *Dramatic Documents from the Elizabethan Playhouses* (Oxford, 1969)). Henry seems to have been chosen as the passive spectator of these sins because in English history he was the helpless spectator of the worst of times. One might guess that in his final words he warned the audience to beware of a repetition. The historical moment of the action seems to be 1470, when Warwick (or his colleagues) released Henry from the Tower.

[29] Henslowe speaks of a 'Harey the vj' as new on 3 March 1592, but it is not clear that this refers to any part of Shakespeare's play.

[30] At one point at least we seem to see Shakespeare assuming that the audience will enjoy coming to the playhouse with a piece of information that the characters on the stage do not possess. In *2 Henry VI*, I. iv, the spirit-raisers prophesy to the Duchess of Gloucester that certain events will occur in the future. The spirit tells the Duchess that 'the duke yet lives that Henry shall depose'. The Duchess supposes that the duke is her husband; but those who know the story can relish the irony that the duke will turn out to be the Duke of York.

[31] The years to which the *Henry VI* plays are assigned were years of great theatrical turmoil, with companies appearing and disappearing at bewildering speed. The situation may have had some effect on Shakespeare's conception of these plays. It seems that some plays of this date were performed by two companies in temporary amalgamation. This might help to explain the epic effects evidently aimed at. For recent treatments, see Stanley

attention of a *Festspielhaus* intensity, but the texture of the writing opens itself to a wide range of popular interests. The first words of the first part of *Henry VI* certainly strike a note worthy of the opening of a pre-planned trilogy (or tetralogy). This may be the first performance poetry that Shakespeare ever wrote, but it gives no evidence of either poetic or dramatic uncertainty. The verse is certainly stiff and ritualistic, but so it must be if it is to carry a ritual lament for the good times dead and a prophecy of the bad times to come:

> Hung be the heavens with black, yield day to night!
> Comets, importing change of times and states,
> Brandish your crystal tresses in the sky,
> And with them scourge the bad revolting stars
> That have consented unto Henry's death—
> Henry the Fifth, too famous to live long!

The verse is Tamburlainian in its sweep and certainty, but its power is carried not by the assurance of an outsized ego but rather by a vision of national destiny outside the range of any individual. David Riggs has properly suggested that

> Shakespeare's [*Henry VI*] plays embody a kind of sequel to Marlowe's, an assessment of the chaos that ensues when the weakling son succeeds the all-conquering father. The earlier ideal is glimpsed only through its disintegration, a process that begins with the demise of Henry's great lieutenants, Bedford, Salisbury, and Talbot.[32]

One can see this disintegration enacted in poetic terms in the opening scene, as the epic ritual moves hierarchically from the single voice of the eldest surviving brother (Bedford) through antiphonic repetition by the younger brother (Humphrey of Gloucester) and so by way of the bar sinister uncles (Exeter and Winchester) to a conflict of voices that Bedford cannot control (ll. 44–56). The problem is reinforced by the external witness of the three messengers, whose stories of territorial losses confirm the new weakness and provide the fuel for its continuance.

This extraordinary scene, in which ritual and symmetry create

---

Wells and Gary Taylor, *William Shakespeare: A Textual Companion* (Oxford, 1987), 95, and Scott McMillin, in 'The Book of Sir Thomas More: Dates and Acting Companies', in T. H. Howard-Hill (ed.), *Shakespeare and Sir Thomas More* (Cambridge, 1989), 57–76.

[32] David Riggs, *Shakespeare's Heroical Histories* (Cambridge, Mass., 1971), 98.

historical meaning, ends with an attempted reformulation of the traditional pattern, as Bedford, Gloucester, and Exeter number down the line in a repetitive assurance that they will make both military and governmental preparations to recover Henry V's empire. But Winchester, the churchman uncle who has no part to play in all this secular bustle, ends the sequence with subversion rather than confirmation. His role cannot be contained inside constraints inherited from Henry V. His professionally appropriate statement that Henry's success was due to the prayers of Holy Church had sparked the first flare-up; now he makes plans for a slower burning fire that will eventually destroy the whole Valhalla:

> Each hath his place and function to attend:
> I am left out; for me nothing remains;
> But long I will not be Jack out of office.
> The King from Eltam I intend to [steal],
> And sit at chiefest stern of public weal
>
> (I. i. 173–7)

The following scene is in France—the play proceeds in large measure by switching from one realm to the other—and looks at the same situation from an alternative point of view. The death of Henry V is now simply one of the vicissitudes of history, lying outside recovery by any individual. Bedford in Act I, Scene i, sees the heavens as not only interpretable but even as speaking clearly to men; but now we hear that, just as astronomers cannot calculate the orbit of Mars, so princes cannot foretell the movements of the historical process. In England we saw the royal brotherhood aiming to remedy loss by heroic action; now in France, at the siege of Orleans, English heroism is shown as heroic precisely because it is 'mad-brained' (I. ii. 15), against all the odds. But history throws up mad-brained heroism indifferently, on either side; the coming of La Pucelle gives the French an equally irrational (or miraculous) power, which the resolutely practical and anti-prelatical English cannot hope to match.

The thesis and antithesis of these opening scenes in *1 Henry VI* indicate well the process by which Shakespeare's ironic control of his historical vision is achieved. He celebrates heroic determination in the face of loss, the bravery of hopeless resistance, and makes a national emblem out of the careers of the Talbots, father and son. But at the same time he shows history as an indeterminable process

that creates different heroisms where they can least be expected—
for example, in a shepherd maid, a girlish Tamburlaine—and invokes the countervalue of political effectiveness as an alternative
justification for success. We are offered two sets of assumptions
that coexist without capacity to compromise. The supernatural is
constantly invoked, and it may actually be involved, or it may be
only a turn of speech. The power that animates the Maid may be
of the Devil; or is her function as 'scourge' (I. ii. 129) like that of
Tamburlaine, the 'Scourge of God'—to be used by God for His
mysterious purposes (to free France) and then be put in the fire?
The presence of God's will in history is not denied in these plays;
but those who proclaim it are usually suspect characters—Saunder
Simcox and Margery Jourdain in Part II, for example, but above
all King Henry himself. He sees God's hand everywhere and is
thereby rendered incapable of knowing what is happening around
him, let alone controlling it. The death of Winchester in 2 Henry
VI is the great exemplum of what looks like divine vengeance on
the evil doer, and his death pangs exhibit the standard rhetoric
of guilty conscience and despair—all the more obviously because
of contrast to the calm acceptance and clear conscience of 'good'
Duke Humphrey when he is ensnared (and eventually murdered)
by his enemies, Winchester and Suffolk. But the apparent operation of the moral law in the case of Winchester, and in the death
of Suffolk (when public conscience requires the king to banish him
and so expose him to public revenge), is contradicted by the case
of York, who lies, intrigues, and betrays, and yet succeeds in his
dynastic aims and dies heroically, outfacing enemies more cruel
and merciless than himself. And when characters like Margaret,
Warwick, Clifford, and Somerset fall, their falls are attributed to
unforeseen political rather than moral causes, or else to chance.
God's intervention, if we are to believe in it, has to await the
Second Coming of the Lancastrians in the unpredictable epiphany
of Henry Tudor.

It is characteristic of the ambiguous status of the separate Henry
VI plays, both when interconnected and when considered free-
standing, that they present historical development in distinct and
separated stages, each picking up a different aspect of the overall
decline from dynastic unity to national chaos. Part I concentrates
on the loss of the empire in France. The alternation of its scenes
between England and France allows us to contrast the rudderless
yawing of the English ship of state with the empty-headed but

successful French, animated by the witch or prophetess Joan. Her anti-English magic is neutralized at the end of the first part, but this is no sooner done than its power is reinserted into the heart of English civil existence in the shape of Margaret of Anjou, the she-wolf of France. Part II thus picks up the French threat but translates it into the domestic politics we have already seen at work in Part I. There the home-bred quarrels prevented appropriate action in the foreign war; here the quarrels have become the appropriate action, all other aspects of political life having vanished. Thus the civil disasters latent in Part I now assume their malignant form and destroy everyone in sight. The factious uncles (Gloucester and Winchester) are both dead by the middle of Part II; but we can see that their inability to make common (Lancastrian) cause has created space for a new faction, that of York, whose rivalry is no longer aimed at another peer but at the king himself, with the whole house of Lancaster attached to him. After the murder of Duke Humphrey, the principal defender of unity, we may well feel that the revulsion against his murderers is morally appropriate, but even when a killing is undertaken for such a reason (as in the lynching of the Duke of Suffolk), it must also be allowed to be a further step towards social collapse. Episodic development ingeniously postpones the inevitable in the entertaining scenes of Cade's diversionary anarchy and in Cade's death in the garden of the paradigmatically English Alexander Iden ('Eden' in Holinshed, 'Eyden' in the Quarto). The natural tensions of the society can still be dealt with by invocation of traditional values. None the less the inevitable end cannot be long lost sight of; and it soon finds its most powerful expression in Young Clifford's magnificent lament over his dead father's body—a speech which, in the closing moments of Part II, previews the apocalyptic world of Part III.

> O, let the vile world end!
> And the premised flames of the last day
> Knit earth and heaven together!
> Now let the general trumpet blow his blast,
> Particularities and petty sounds
> To cease! . . .
>
> .   .   .   .
>
>   Even at this sight
> My heart is turned to stone: and while 'tis mine
> It shall be stony.
>
>   (v. ii. 40–51)

Part II ends with the first battle of the Wars of the Roses, seen as a mêlée of scarcely distinguishable barons, King Henry in flight, and Somerset, the other survivor of 'all the line of John of Gaunt' (Part III, I. i. 19), dead at the precocious hands of the future Richard III.

The variety of intriguing social episodes in *2 Henry VI*—Peter and the Armourer, Humphrey's detection of the 'miracle' of Saunder Simcox, the conjuring and condemnation of Eleanor Cobham, Suffolk's capture, Iden's loyalty, and above all Cade's revolt—all these make this the most accessible of the three *Henry VI* plays. The development of the dramas is, as I have indicated, a process of elimination, but the pretenders to power, as they 'shine, evaporate, and fall', exhibit an extraordinary vivacity. The sombre historical movement can be seen as a framework holding together a magnificent series of genre episodes whose exhibition of momentary human freedom defies the inevitabilities of history, and provides a preview of *Henry IV*.

3 Henry VI has little space for such humanity, as the action reels from St Albans to Wakefield, to Towton, to Barnet, to Tewkesbury, each a staging-post in slaughter as fathers lose sons and sons lose fathers to those they in turn will have to kill. This is a world dehumanized by war; and there is little space in such a world for what we call 'character' (exercised through options, as Aristotle tells us). The pressure of events forces the figures to fulfil the roles predetermined by preceding history: violence and nihilism in the Queen and Clifford and Richard of Gloucester, ambitious self-interest in Warwick and Clarence, domestic pieties only among those who are helpless—King Henry, and York when he is tied to the stake. The most powerful scenes in this play—King Henry on the molehill after Towton, the tormenting of York on *his* mole-hill—use their energy to deny rather than assert freedom of choice (and so 'character'). Margaret's staging of the taunting, the crowning with a paper crown, and the killing of York stands apart from the history in which it is embedded as a masque of horror, symbolic of the state of the world we have before us, immobilized (like an episode from *The Inferno*) in the monstrosity of its attitudes. To exhibit a capacity for mixed feelings (as Northumberland does here) is to be excluded as an alien.

The scene of Henry on *his* molehill is very similar in its construction, though completely antithetical in its valuations. This is staged as an interlude in the middle of the battle of Towton, with Clifford's very different vision of battle placed on either side of it. Its role as an emblematic commentary on the war is thus timed precisely for us in a real historical moment. But it is also placed out of time. King Henry is both himself ('chid from the battle') and also the performer of a smoothly impersonal and unexpressive poetry whose balanced formalities are as far as possible from the gestural intensities all around it—as far as is the shepherd's life from the warrior's. Here, in this imaginary space between the battle lines, life is precisely measured out by God and nature:

> O God! methinks it were a happy life
> To be no better than a homely swain;
> To sit upon a hill, as I do now,
> To carve out dials quaintly, point by point,
> Thereby to see the minutes how they run:
> How many makes the hour full complete,
> How many hours brings about the day,
> How many days will finish up the year,
> How many years a mortal man may live.
> When this is known, then to divide the times:
> So many hours must I tend my flock,
> So many hours must I take my rest,
> So many hours must I contemplate,
> So many hours must I sport myself,
> So many days my ewes have been with young,
> So many weeks ere the poor fools will ean,
> So many years ere I shall shear the fleece:
> So minutes, hours, days, months, and years,
> Passed over to the end they were created,
> Would bring white hairs unto a quiet grave.
>
> (II. V. 21–40)

This evokes a world in which men die in their beds; but all around the molehill is the struggle of men who will never see their beds again. When figures from the battle enter this mystically regulated dimension (the son who has killed his father and the father who has killed his son) they too must partake in a formality which renders their passion as if seen from a great distance, as if frozen by their contact with the ritual of apocalypse which enclose king and subjects, passive sufferers joined inside an endless patience.

The political innocence and ineffectiveness of King Henry,

when seen in a primarily political context in the earlier parts of the trilogy, make him a frustrating and even irritating character. But the same qualities allow him to appear at the end of the sequence as an effective remembrancer of all the qualities that have vanished from the war-torn landscape. In this role we might even find in him an anticipation of King Lear when he too comes to see prison as the best part of his kingdom—though Henry is, of course, without the freedom of fiction-making imagination that attaches to the sufferings of Lear. In the final scene of his life, when, as the last victim of his house, he comes face to face with his polarizing opposite, Richard of Gloucester, we are given another of these static historical tableaux that enact meaning rather than action, and here we are allowed to see reduced to basic form the conflict of passivity and activity[33] that underlies so much in the three plays, representing ideal and real inside historical time. Here Henry is released from any of the pressures to compromise that accompany him while there is a future or a dynasty to safeguard. Now stripped of any future, he has the strength both to name the straight moral meaning of what is in front of him and to prophesy the political consequences of Richard's isolating singularity (at once his strength and his nemesis). Henry has never been concerned with what works; that is all that concerns Richard; Richard is at his best in battle; Henry can only run away. Yet, in terms of the see-saw of history, one can see that each has made the space for definition of the other. Now, at this crossroad, they move in clearly defined opposite directions. For Henry, as 'royal saint', martyrdom is the natural route out of time. Richard's embodied evil moves forward easily and inevitably into politics as its natural environment.

Henry VI offers us a closely linked sequence, defined by the death of Henry V at the beginning of the sequence and by the death of Henry VI at the end. Since these are history plays, we cannot, however, say that the end of a reign is the end of the story: the death of Henry VI means the extinction of the direct Lancastrian line. The final episode of *3 Henry VI* describes the consolidation of the new dynasty: Edward has 'made a footstool of security' (v. vii. 14) and has a son to succeed him; all will now be 'stately triumphs, mirthful comic shows | Such as befits the pleasure of

---

[33] Edward comments when Richard takes off from the battlefield to perform the murder: 'He's sudden if a thing come in his head' (v. v. 84).

the court' (v. vii. 43–4). But Shakespeare deliberately undercuts this idea of a conclusion. We are not allowed to hear these lines without irony, for we have already heard Richard of Gloucester announce that he has alternative plans for the future—and Richard is beginning to emerge here as the figure with the greatest theatrical force.

As in the previous plays of this sequence, so here between the end of *3 Henry VI* and the beginning of *Richard III* we are given a natural bridge to carry us across the gap—a connection indeed more prominent here than between the other parts.[34] The famous first speech of *Richard III* is a direct and immediate reply to the last speech of *3 Henry VI*, and indeed the later play has often been performed with the ending of the earlier one as its opening, most continuously in Cibber's version and most prominently in Olivier's film. Edward plans 'courtly shows'; Richard replies (to us) that he is 'not shaped for sportive tricks' and so 'hates the idle pleasures of these days'. He has his own style of pleasures he tells us, centred on the elimination of all the members of the royal family that stand between him and the crown; and Clarence will be the first. This is going to be our actual entertainment.

In spite of these links, *Richard III* (1591×1592) is usually performed as a wholly independent work; it has more obvious self-sufficiency than any part of *Henry VI*, and, as a free-standing play, it has a history of continuous theatrical success. Even if the first scene begins with a kind of reply to the last words of *3 Henry VI*, the first force felt from the stage comes from the isolation of the speaker. The pressures of the past are picked up and transformed into the psychological quality of an actor whose actions are immediately intelligible to us, not as conditioned by a historical determinism but as manifestations of a particular cast of moral being. The Wars of the Roses are over, Richard tells us; peace has returned; history as change has ground to a halt. 'That's what you might think,' he assures us; 'watch me and you will see how I can start things again.' But now time moves to a different music,

---

[34] We should notice that the technique is present in all eight of the plays dealing with Lancaster and York. *Richard II* ends with Henry IV's plan to make a voyage to the Holy Land; *1 Henry IV* begins with Henry reiterating this same plan. *2 Henry IV* ends with Lancaster's prophecy of wars in France, and *Henry V* begins with the Chorus's evocation of such a war. *Henry V* itself ends with a forecast of the unquiet reign of Henry VI, 'which oft our stage hath shown'.

controlled by a single powerful will that manipulates everything that happens—that writes the play, one might say. A comparison of Richard with his father, Richard, Duke of York, sets out a model of this change. York is known to us by his political activity; we understand what he does by its particular consequences rather than its general motivations, and the process of his life has to be followed through the warp and woof of alternative aims and cross alliances. In its complexity this process mirrors the truth of history as experienced and as described in the chronicles. But *Richard III* presents history, though we see the protagonist having to luff and tack through the political shallows of his time, as the artful plot of its central character (who speaks one-third of all the lines, more than any other Shakespearian character apart from Hamlet). And, if we compare the 'wrangling pirates' of this play—Richard, Margaret, the Queen and her relatives, Hastings, Buckingham—with the quarrelling magnates of *2 Henry VI*—Gloucester, Winchester, Suffolk, York, the Queen—we can see the same basic difference. In *2 Henry VI* power is indeterminate, and the catch-as-catch-can methods of grappling for it can make sense only when time has eliminated half the contestants. In *Richard III*, however, power is no longer a fumbled ball that everyone can chase but is rather the social expression of a psychological and theatrical dominance already achieved. In this the play resembles *Tamburlaine*; but Tamburlaine is not given the psychological complexity that in *Richard III* is used to create an ironic disparity between what the mind knows of itself and what it knows of the world it can control. We have already looked at Shakespeare's ironic detachment from the ambitions, aims, rhetorical excitements, of the historical contestants he deals with. In the *Henry VI* plays this shows itself chiefly through the unmediated juxtaposition of alternative angers, ambitions, and wills, so that, though it is easy to see what people do, it is hard to grasp the function of 'doing' in a meaningless world. Clearly some characters are good and others are bad, but our desire to see these distinctions exposed in terms of plot, success, and succession is continually postponed by an author who may (or may not) be invoking Providence. In *Richard III*, where the coming of the Providential Tudors presses more heavily on the story, and threatens to turn the protagonist into a moralized monster from the apocalyptic Last Days, the countervailing pressure of irony is moved to a more central position, out of plot and into character. With some debt, no doubt, to Marlowe (as if *Tamburlaine* was being rewritten from the perspective of *The Jew of Malta*), Shakespeare shows his successful man of action as self-aware, sardonic, risk-enjoying, a natural actor, wonderfully at home in the make-believe of the theatre. The historical complexity of the plot is made easy for us to follow by the continual reports on progress that Richard shares with us; but at the same time we are given a sense of mystery, an illusion of third dimension, by our uncertainty what this confidence man means by all these confidences. To end the play, Shakespeare has finally to subordinate the natural theatrical enjoyment of successful duplicity to the moral simplifications of good and bad, and to bring the whole material of York and Lancaster to rest in a Tudor dynastic heaven in which change cannot be contemplated any more. He does so with masterly brevity and in terms more powerfully realized as psychological self-defeat than as interpersonal conflict. By counterpointing a psychological pattern of intention against a historical pattern of events, Shakespeare has been able to hold our attention not only to the willed process of an individual career but also to the constraints that both ensure its success and require its downfall.

Richard III is often compared to Senecan tragedy (which had already provided the format for Legge's play on the same subject). As a self-described villain Richard certainly bears some relation to Lycus, Atreus, Nero, Agamemnon. But even in Legge's academic Latin exercise in classical reconstruction there is (as I have noted) an obvious contradiction between Senecan form and modern world—a world in which political villainy must operate in the context of Tudor ideas of shared responsibilities, especially those embodied in the legal system. Shakespeare is unSenecan in a very different way from Legge, and yet his Richard too seems to be required to make an equally strong acknowledgement of the world of duties and obligations around him. Shakespeare's Richard is, among other things, a great comic creation, and his power over us is derived in large part from the comic delight he gives us as we share in his unorthodoxies, his playful exploitation of received ideas. There is an exhilarating sense of release for us in the extraordinary victories he is able to pull off against all the odds, in his easy colloquial style with its quicksilver shifts of focus and change of address, in his comic disbelief that he can be getting away with it, not (as with Vice figures) in isolated moments of subversive triumph, but as a continuous and coherent quality of political activity. And all this, we should note, is parasitic on the continuing existence of a world of duties and responsibilities which is present, in place, waiting to be subverted (and is guaranteed to return again, after subversion).

The first three acts of the play show Richard's positive powers in full operation. He is able to use the English nobility's obsession with the past to entrap them while he himself plays free. The fact that these obsessions are never explained to us—we are never told why Hastings hates the Queen's family—gives them exactly the right status. Richard's manipulations in this period achieve a run of uninterrupted success. By the beginning of Act IV he has won it all: between Scenes i and ii he is crowned and acclaimed as king. What next? What scope remains for such psychological qualities? This is the hinge of the play, the point at which the action begins to reverse itself or at least to go round the same course for a second time, like a programmed toy rather than a free individual. Fulfilling the stereotype of the tyrant, he now reveals himself as obsessed by fears—fears which, as in the traditional Senecan tyrant, can be assuaged only by further crimes. At this point Shakespeare marks what is happening by the insertion of an extraordinary scene taken from the tragic repertory of Complaint—Act IV, Scene iv, the scene of the wailing queens. Shakespeare's most blatant defiance of chronology in this play is his revivification of Margaret of Anjou, already dead in exile for many a year. But it is not difficult to see why she is essential to his plan. In general one can say that Shakespeare needs Margaret to supply an opposition voice as powerful as Richard's own. She is proof against his blandishments, for she has already lost everything; she is without hope and therefore without illusions. The scene of the wailing queens marks the triumph of Margaret's viewpoint. The old Duchess of York (Richard's mother), Elizabeth (queen to Edward IV), and Anne Neville (queen to Richard III) join her in evoking a War of the Roses perpetually present, in which one Edward is always destroying another Edward, one Richard always attaining power by the death of another Richard. The retrospect of history that the mothers and wives of its victims and victors give us is one seen as outside time, unchanging in essence though always different in its accidents (in this like Henry VI's molehill). And Richard too is part of this pattern; for all his self-proclaimed power to act only in accordance with his own wishes,

and for all his success in achieving his desires, his career is preordained. Margaret's opening words in the scene:

> So now prosperity begins to mellow
> And drop into the rotten mouth of death
>
> (IV. iv. 1–2)

pick up Richard's initial words in the play:

> Now is the winter of our discontent
> Made glorious summer by this sun of York
> And all the clouds that loured upon our house
> In the deep bosom the ocean buried.
>
> (I. i. 1–4)

Summer has given way to autumn, and the drive to fruition has
met its natural cyclical conclusion in the ripe fruit rotting where it
falls. The invocation of the cycle of the seasons marks the historical time of the play as equally cyclical. The 'son' of York (Edward
IV) can do no more than the sun does, rise and fall, ripen and rot;
its achievement has been only an expression of its rotation. The
second half of Act IV, Scene iv, shows this rotation exemplified in
Richard's wooing of the Mother Queen for the hand of her daughter Elizabeth, so picking up and repeating his wooing of the Lady
Anne in Act I, Scene ii. Richard plans this as a pre-emptive strike
against Richmond. But his jumping through the same hoops on a
second occasion suggests rather the limitation of his mind and his
history. Margaret's passive acceptance of her own pastness, her
confinement to reiteration, thus becomes a model for Richard himself. Two characters who seemed to be opposites when we first met
them are now revealed as occupying the same historical slot.
Margaret is not among the ghosts who throng to Richard's tent in
Act V, Scene iii, but the masque of murders past all ritually reanimated in the present is one that reproduces her choric function.

*The True Tragedy of Richard III: wherein is shown the death of
Edward the fourth, with the smothering of the two young princes in the
Tower; with a lamentable end of Shore's wife, an example for all
wicked women. And lastly the conjunction and joining of the two noble
houses, Lancaster and York* (?1591×1594) is difficult to place in any
developmental relation to either Legge's *Richardus Tertius* or Shakespeare's *Richard III* (the range of possible dates for it would allow

it to appear on either side of Shakespeare's play). A discussion of it has to allow what is recurrently obvious—that plays of this period exist in relation to one another less as sequences than as sets of parallel attempts to achieve aesthetic control over similar material. Though acted by the Queen's Men and therefore part of the popular repertory, *The True Tragedy* is quite academic in its rhetoric and its structure. Its interest in Richard's reign is not analytic in Legge's mode; yet its protagonist is still very much the same quasi-Senecan victim of forces outside himself. What *The True Tragedy* manages to give us, with extraordinary facility, is a sense of the historical process itself rushing past us as well as its victims and of Richard carried by the storm rather than controlling it, conscious that he is the recipient of Fortune's fickle favours but determined to grasp whatever is placed before him.[35] The play's few extended exercises in eye-level history seem designed to show us human beings seeking shelter from this onrush (in vain): Mistress Shore, Queen Elizabeth, Gray, Rivers, the princes in the tower, even Edward IV himself (seen on his death-bed). I have already mentioned (pp. 156–7) the opening conversation between Truth and Poetry. Truth, whose business it is to present the substance ('body') of the play, gives us a Lancastrian report on York's rebellion against Henry VI ('claiming the crown by wars, not by descent' . . . 'by outrage suppressed that virtuous king' (Scene i, ll. 20, 29)). The matter of the *Henry VI* plays having been delivered in the classical manner, *ab extra*, we are then shown what is in some degree equivalent to a classical prologue: the ghost of Clarence passes across the stage, leaving behind him a shield with an obscure (presumably garbled) Latin motto, certainly promising horror of one kind or another. The idea of using Clarence as a Senecan *protatica persona* from the underworld is, one must suppose, what lies behind this appearance; but if that is so, it is an idea that has no effect on the rest of the text.[36] The motivation of the action in this play does not come from supernatural soliciting out of the underworld but (as in Legge and Shakespeare) from the interaction of historical events and a particular personality. When the play proper opens, thus introduced *in medias res*, we find ourselves in a domestic scene, essentially hushed and insecure, grouped around Edward IV's death-bed.

---

[35] Cf. Farnham, *Medieval Heritage, passim.*

[36] Churchill (*'Richard the Third'*) argues that the whole play shows an attempt to create a genre half-way between revenge tragedy and chronicle history (pp. 400 ff.).

The first two scenes of *The True Tragedy* make their effect without the presence of Richard on the stage, and both seem designed to set up before our eyes a world subject ineluctably to the swing of Fortune. The dying Edward IV and his daughter Elizabeth—a girl of 16 or 17 at the time, who seems to be given prominence here only because she was the grandmother of Queen Elizabeth—struggle to reconcile the warring factions represented by Hastings and 'Lord Marcus' (the Lord Marquess Dorset). When the King asks them (and us)

> Ah Gods, sith at my death you jar
> What will you do to the young Prince after my decease?
>
> (ll. 130–1)

we already know the answer. Eventually, after 140 lines, the two enemies agree to shake hands and swear amity. But a concord achieved so shakily after so much effort can give little confidence to either audience or king:

> to thee, Elizabeth, my daughter:
> I leave thee in a world of trouble . . .
>
> . . . .
>
> As thyself art virtuous, let thy prayers be modest;
> Still be bountiful in devotion.
>
> (ll. 177–83)

It is obvious that the good Christian end, domestic pieties, and irenic hopes of a king whose power is all behind him fail to match the intentions of those who have the prospect of power still before them. The second scene reinforces the point from a completely different angle. Here we witness the political ineffectuality of Christian goodness in the career of Jane Shore, Edward's mistress. When word of Edward's death is brought to her, she responds at once with knowledge that the glory has departed, that the wheel is now spinning her down to misery. In spite of her incessant works of charity, she must not look for any recompense or gratitude. The citizens around her look up fearfully at the storm brewing and try to run for cover.

The world of Fortune thus sketched out, we are in a position to meet Richard and to discover that he too sees a world subject to the power of Fortune:

Why so, now Fortune make me a king, Fortune give me a kingdom; let the world report the Duke of Gloucester was a king, therefore Fortune

make me king. If I be but king for a year, nay, but half a year, nay, a
month, a week, three days, one day, or half a day, nay, an hour, swouns,
half an hour, nay, sweet Fortune clap but the crown on my head that
the vassals may but once say 'God save King Richard's life', it is enough.

(ll. 443–9)

Accepting the role of Fortune to this degree means escaping
from the restrictions of morality. The aspiring Richard, being carried upwards on the wheel, need only remember that it was the
sword that brought him fame and that secured his brother on the
throne. Richard's clear sense here of 'the sweet fruition of an
earthly crown' reminds us inevitably of Tamburlaine; but he is a
Tamburlaine confined to a *political* context. The possibilities open
to him are defined in terms of the values he intends to negate—
true inheritance, a king under God, renown, 'the honour of . . .
father' (in this respect he is closer to Shakespeare's Edmund than
to his Richard). His accusations against Earl Rivers, his stage man-
aging of the quarrel with Grey, his operation through the council
to dispose of Hastings and to get both the princes into his power,
his employment of Dr Shaw and Buckingham to clear his path to
the throne—all these political triumphs are achieved by manipulating accepted legalities. This Richard is indeed only irregularly
present on the stage (in seven scenes out of twenty) and is witnessed more clearly by the way people respond to his pressures
than by his presented actions.

The most interesting fictional character created in this play
(created, it would seem, out of a single sentence in More[37]) is the
'Page' who accompanies Richard, imitates him, and undertakes to
fulfil all his wishes; he also retails to 'Report' the final description
of his master's heroical actions at Bosworth. 'Page' is only one of
several low-life characters who comment on the treachery and violence of those above them and yet conform to their requirements—
the innkeeper at Northampton, Lodowick, those implicated in the
murder of the princes. But, whereas these appear and disappear in
response to particular actions, the Page acts continuously as a
mirror of power as seen from a low perspective, aware of what is
happening to himself but unable to escape from it:

---

[37] St Thomas More, *The History of King Richard III*, ed. Richard Sylvester (New Haven,
1976), 36.

why thus by keeping company am I become like unto those with whom
I keep company. As my Lord hopes to wear the crown, so I hope by that
means to have preferment, but instead of the crown the blood of the
headless light upon his head . . . for blood is a threatener and will have
revenge.   (ll. 896–901)

Being shown Richard recurrently in the mirror of such popular
moralizing (even though it is a moralizing incapable of creating
political effects), we are well prepared for the shift of perspective
created (here as in Shakespeare) when the wheel reaches the top
and he achieves the crown:

> The goal is got and golden crown is won,
> And well deservest thou to wear the same
> That ventured hast thy body and thy soul.
> But what boots Richard, now the diadem
> Of kingdom got by murder of his friends?
> My fearful shadow that still follows me
> Hath summoned me before the severe judge.
> My conscience, witness of the blood I spilt,
> Accuseth me as guilty of the fact,
> The fact a damned judgment craves,
> Whereas impartial justice hath condemned.
>
> (ll. 1398–408)

The sense of increasing derangement in this scene (Scene xiv) is
brilliantly managed to show Richard facing the facts of desertion
with hysterical busyness and random accusation against everyone
around him, set in strong contrast to Richmond's calmly controlled
verse in the scene that follows. Richard's tremendous final soliloquy, with its thirteen epistrophes on 'revenge' (ll. 1874–96)—a
speech which gives Hamlet his call-signal for violent and horrific
rhetoric in his Mousetrap (see *Hamlet*, III. ii. 254)—is a *tour de
force* of rhetorical self-projection and deserves a round of applause
for its own sake. But, considered from a plot point of view, it is
characterized as *merely* verbal; it is the outcry of a Richard being
carried down the stream of history in the wrong direction, in a
'commonwealth which now flows faster than the furious tide that
overflows beyond the banks of the Nile' (ll. 2099–100), and will not
stop until the peers have elected Richmond 'first in regard they
account thee virtuous, next for that they hope all foreign broils shall

cease and thou wilt guide and govern them in peace' (ll. 2088–91). The final section gives us a 'Messenger', whose function picks up that of 'Report' at ll. 2002 ff. and of 'Truth' in the Induction, and allows us to sail away from Richard to the golden land of the Tudor establishment. Queen Elizabeth, the 'Mother Queen' of the text, recites the glories of the Queen Elizabeth to come and prays for her continuance:

> For if her Grace's days be brought to end
> Your hope is gone, on whom did peace depend
>
> (ll. 2222–3)

The Richard of *The True Tragedy* is willingly swept along by the tide of Fortune. In the terms of this metaphor we must say that Shakespeare's Richard is the better oarsman, seizing and creating his fortune rather than merely accepting it. Of course we all know that Shakespeare was the better psychologist; but the reasons why he can be made to seem so are more interesting than the mere assertion. In part Shakespeare can create this impression because he can give Richard and his victims a much richer range of contacts, memories, and exploitabilities. The great theatrical success of *Richard III*[38] has been as a free-standing play, but one may guess that it was written as part of a continuous creative vision encompassing the three *Henry VI* plays as well. The accumulated weight of sixty-one inglorious years of political chaos—from 1422 when Henry VI inherited the throne until 1483 when Edward IV died (Shakespeare conceals Edward's twelve years of peaceful reign)—presses heavily on Richard's world as not so much the past as a continuing present, and gives Shakespeare a freedom from chronology that Legge and the author of *The True Tragedy* do not possess. By misdating the death of Clarence by five years and the burial of Henry VI by twelve years and by reanimating Margaret, Shakespeare replays the issues of the Wars of the Roses as if they were still current. His fictional control thus allows him to use the great political events as if they were demonstrations of temperament, absorbing the experience of the past into psychology of the

---

[38] *Richard III* (mainly in Cibber's version) was certainly one of the most popular Shakespeare plays throughout the nineteenth century, perhaps the most popular. Arthur Colby Sprague has described the version as 'cunning, prosaic, vulgar', but did not point out that only the 'vulgar' can make a work 'popular' (*Shakespeare's Histories* (London, 1964), 124).

present.[39] And it is this presentness that gives the play its hold on the imagination. Thus the famous scene of the wooing of the Lady Anne (I. ii) deals with a genuinely important issue in the reign; but the fame and power of the scene do not lie here. It is the impudently comic capacity to transform history into personal experience (but without sacrificing political reality, in the romantic manner) that gives it its memorability—precisely the gift that Shakespeare had on offer to his contemporaries—a gift they were not all anxious to accept.

George Peele's *The Famous Chronicle History of Edward the First, surnamed Edward Longshanks, with his return from the Holy Land. Also the Life of Llewellen, rebel in Wales. Lastly, the sinking of Queen Elinor, who sunk at Charing Cross and rose again at Potter's Hithe, now named Queenhithe* (1590×1593), belongs to the same years as Shakespeare's *Henry VI* plays; but it is hard to believe that Peele saw in Shakespeare's mode of writing history anything that required his imitation. Peele's play stands slightly to one side of the whole tradition discussed in this chapter. Of course the kind of historical matter he was dealing with made some overlap inevitable, but his dramatic method and the general effect of his play seem to point us to the author rather than the problems of historical writing we find elsewhere, and to require comparison with *The Old Wife's Tale, The Battle of Alcazar, The Arraignment of Paris, David and Bethsabe*—with plays that all stand on one side of the surviving popular repertory. The documentary evidence suggests that *Edward I* was performed by the Admiral's Men;[40] but there is nothing in its mode that would make it unsuitable for the child actors. The performance is carried by stately eloquence, golden poetry, spectacular and processional staging.[41] As in Peele's patriotic poems of

---

[39] Thus Clarence's Dream (I. iv. 9 ff.) is a vision of Hell as the place where the crimes of the Wars of the Roses can no longer be consigned to the historical past but belong to a perpetual and inescapable present. The procession of victim-ghosts who appear in Richard's tent before the Battle of Bosworth can be taken to repeat the same point.

[40] See F. S. Hook's edition in C. T. Prouty (ed.), *The Life and Works of George Peele* (3 vols.; New Haven, 1952–70), ii. 7.

[41] Thus 'Enter the nine lords of Scotland with their nine pages' etc. (ll. 632 ff.); 'The trumpets sound. Queen Elinor in her litter borne by four negro moors, Joan of Acon attended on by the Earl of Gloucester and her four footmen. One having set a ladder on the side of the litter she descendeth and her daughter followeth.' (ll. 1015 ff.); 'After the christening and marriage done, the heralds having attended, the bride is led by two noblemen', etc. (ll. 1927 ff.).

chivalry, *The Honour of the Garter* (1593) or *Polyhymnia* (1590), the high celebratory tone of the presentation turns historical events into masque-like occasions, strung along a rather thin and improbable narrative line.[42]

We first meet the major characters of this play in a processional entry from the Crusades. Edward shows his dignity of character in his response to news of the deaths of his father, his son, and his uncle (the King of the Romans), leaves them to 'heavenly blessedness', and turns to the glories of the present, his peers, his soldiers, and (especially) his wife, Elinor of Castile. Elinor's desire for glory matches Edward's, but is expressed in terms of self-will, expensive clothes and other manifestations of what Peele and his contemporaries regarded as 'Spanish pride'.

To call *Edward I* 'celebratory' or 'masque-like' is not to deny it a complex or effective structure. The similarity as well as the distinction betweeen Edward's military glory (his conquest of Wales and Scotland) and Elinor's self-glorification as a power in her own right builds up a mutually supportive emotional life—a royal love-story in fact. It is this which connects the historical and unhistorical events and leads to their eventual breakdown. Elinor's climactic action, her murder of the Lady Mayoress of London because she had seemed to rival her in splendour and self-confidence, is not basically different from Edward's destruction of Llewellen of Wales and his humiliation of John de Balliol, King of Scotland; but his military self-assertion is approved on nationalistic grounds, while her Spanish pride is eventually seen as only the outer expression of a lifetime of crime and deception, marked by God for eventual destruction. When Elinor invokes Him to justify her innocence, He responds, in the most spectacular episode even in this play, by causing her to sink into the ground at Charing Cross and not emerge again until she reaches Potter's Hithe (to the consternation

---

[42] F. S. Hook conjectures that some at least of its incoherences can be accounted for if we suppose that the scenes of Elinor's pride (which come from ballad sources) were interpolated into a more purely political version (derived from the Chronicles), the coherence of the original having been sacrificed to accommodate the ballad interest. The argument for interpolation is a strong one, but, as Professor Hook indicates, gives us absolutely no hold on any supposed ur-text. Most troubling is, I think, the question raised against the extant ending of the play (which depends on ballad sources). It is impossible to imagine what the play could be like outside the present combination of love and imperiousness in Elinor, royalty and uxoriousness in Edward; and the present ending is entirely appropriate to that explosive mixture. Certainly the play as printed must reflect some Elizabethan's view of a possible structure, and there appears to be no alternative but to deal with the text as it is.

of the potters living there); and she emerges as one fit only for confession and death. Allowing for the differences that history imposes, one can see here the same pattern as noted in Chapter 3 in *David and Bethsabe*: sexual fascination and national glory appear as both complementary and incompatible. Each can be given endorsement by spectacle and poetry. But in religious and ethical terms they coexist only to destroy one another.

The play ends (or seems to end, for textual disturbance makes the placing of the final speeches quite uncertain) with Edward's nationalist glory fatally compromised by his beloved Elinor's life of sin. Yet his love cannot be forgotten:

> You peers of England see in royal pomp
> These breathless bodies be entombed straight
> With tried colours covered all in black
>
> .   .   .   .
>
> And in remembrance of her royalty
> Erect a rich and stately carved cross
> Whereon her statue shall with glory shine,
> And henceforth see you call it Charing Cross;
> For why, the chariest and the choicest queen
> That ever did delight my royal eyes,
> There dwells in darkness whilst I die in grief.
>
> (ll. 2630–47)

Meanwhile the political world has proved equally unmanageable. The Scots are in arms again; and, though Mortimer presents Llewellen's head, there seems to be yet another revolt in Wales. The only legitimate child left to the king is Edward of Caernarvon, the first Prince of Wales. There is no suggestion in the play of what the future holds for this inheritor of glory; but an audience or readership may well have found it difficult to exclude from consciousness the story that Marlowe was dramatizing in these very years.

The provincial sub-plot of fleeting the time in Wales not only acts as a foil to the nation-building history of the main plot but replays the pattern of the Edward and Elinor story in its attempt (and failure) to hold together the idyllic life of the greenwood and the political activities designed to secure Welsh independence. The 'game' of Robin Hood is not allowed here to have its usual function of reinforcing virtuous royal power, nor is it simply condemned as treason. The values of traditional Welsh life and the popular comedy that attaches to them are played against both national requirements and courtly pride. Both sets of values seem to be undercut, but a political understanding that might explain this is not supplied. *Edward I* shows us in a series of tableaux the surfaces of various styles of life, but each of these is to be enjoyed for itself, not for the light it throws on other aspects.

Marlowe's *The Troublesome Reign and Lamentable Death of Edward the Second, King of England: with the tragical fall of proud Mortimer. And also the life and death of Piers Gaveston, the great Earl of Cornwall and mighty favourite of King Edward the Second* (1591×1593) treats (like *Edward I*) the contradictions between the private and public life of the sovereign. But whereas in Peele's play these are handled in terms of well-digested and stable antinomies—male versus female, power versus powerlessness, public versus private— in *Edward II* the whole action turns on the collapsing of such accepted boundaries. As is usual in 'strong-king' plays, *Edward I* is thin on irony; it is only in the weak king's reign that the present can be given double focus by the memory and consequences of the father's militaristic and successful reign. The quarrel between the peers and the king thus replays that between the king and his father, so that the attempt to make him into the man his father was turns into the attempt to judge his private life by the standards of his public role. *Edward I* appears, as noted above, as a rather isolated play among those discussed in this chapter. *Edward II*, on the other hand, stands in the middle of a developing series of 'weak-king' plays, obviously connected with one another and offering variations on a recurrent mode of understanding history.

Edward II has clearly been affected by *Henry VI* (and probably owes something to *Richard III* as well). The longing of the weak king (Henry/Edward) for privacy and peace, the Machiavellian energy of his supplanter (York/Mortimer), the estrangement of his queen (Margaret/Isabel), the separation from his son (Edward/ Edward) are marks of a shared structure, but sharpened by Marlowe into a more tautly organized plot recording the collision of private fault and public retribution. It is hard to speak of Henry VI having a private life. His friends, like his enemies, are all political figures. He can escape into the margin of the scene, into isolated tableau-like moments where his wholly admirable but wholly inappropriate sentiments mark the discontinuity between 'the royal saint' and the 'wrangling pirates'; but he cannot find another world out there. Edward, on the other hand, is given a specific grasp on another way of life which is not simply separate from politics but opposite to it, depending not on power but on love, not on the general but on the particular. Henry seeks consensus and compromise; Edward scorns the compromises offered by Isabel the Queen and Mortimer Senior ('The mightiest kings have had their minions'); he treats his private preferences with the absoluteness of a sovereign but his public duties as entirely contingent.

Marlowe's play begins with 'the sly inveigling Frenchman', Piers of Gaveston, returning from his continental exile and determined never to go on his travels again. He will live in amorous delight with the king, whatever the opposition of the church, the 'lordly peers', and the death-bed instructions of Edward I—all the standard sources of political value. It means nothing to Gaveston that even 'the multitude, that are but sparks | Raked up in embers of their poverty' (I. i. 20–1) are against him. He declines to reward the veteran soldiers who appeal to him, referring them to a 'hospital' (a fatal word in this period); he will pay only for 'wanton poets, pleasant wits | Musicians that with the touching of a string | May draw the pliant king which way I please' (I. i. 51–3). This power will grow out of the feminine art of pleasing not from the masculine art of conquering. The court will be the scene not of military displays but of 'Italian masques . . . sweet speeches, comedies, and pleasing shows' (ll. 55–6), the haunt of lovely boys dressed as nymphs, the loveliest of them in mythological nudity. Death and the hunt will be reduced to the poetic unreality of Ovidian metamorphosis, for 'such things best please his majesty'.

We do not in fact see any of this continental decadence in the evocation of Edward's life that follows,[43] which is too taken up with struggle, to leave space for enjoyment of anything that might go into the space. But the powerful presentation of decadence at the beginning of the play acts as a guiding image of what Edward would achieve, did the plot allow it—a feudal warriors' hall turned into a Renaissance pleasure dome. What we are shown is the effect of Gaveston's presence on Edward himself. There is no need to show

---

[43] We hear later, however, that 'idle triumphs, masques, lascivious shows . . . Have drawn thy treasury dry' (II. ii. 157–9).

him as a tempter who will 'draw the pliant king'; Edward rushes
towards his doom with an erotic appetite for self-destruction that
blanks out the whole world else, turning every other relationship
(most damagingly that with Isabel, Princess of France and Queen
of England) into a tiresome impediment. The cult of an isolating
aesthetic sensibility, when found at the centre of national life, must,
of course, be judged politically as a vice rather than a folly, as an
incapacity to face the reality that cannot be removed, only postponed, and where every postponement magnifies the destructive
element.

   The king's first move shows the gap between royal will and political reality with particular clarity. It is a move against the Church,
the institution most difficult to coerce. The Bishop of Coventry
had used his political power to have Gaveston exiled. Now, Edward
orders, Gaveston should become the new bishop and Walter de
Langton (bishop and Lord Treasurer) can serve as his chaplain.
But the power of the Church remains undiminished by such non-
performative (and therefore unkingly) utterances. The Archbishop
threatens to release the nobles from their oath of allegiance (as does
the Pope in *King John*) and then Edward (like John) has to obey,
even though (like John) he rails against the Pope at the same time
as he submits to him. It is commonly said[44] that his diatribes against
'Proud Rome' with its 'superstitious taper-lights | Wherewith thy
antichristian churches blaze' (I. iv. 97–9) must have been approved
(and have been meant to be approved) by the Elizabethan audience. Certainly the involvement of the Church with the barons in
the process of 'wresting [the King] too much', as Holinshed puts
it,[45] cannot have strengthened their cause in Elizabethan eyes. Yet,
as so often in Marlowe (and recurrently in the best drama), the
choice is not between good and bad, right and wrong, but between
capacity and incapacity for action. When we watch the 'presump-
tious' actions of the Church and the barons (the word is Holinshed's
again) and the incapacity of the autointoxicated Edward, who loves
Gaveston more than England because Gaveston 'loves me more
than all the world' (I. iv. 77), now kissing his crown and now
railing against Mortimer rather than the Pope, what concerns us
mainly is consequence for the future.

---

[44] See Roma Gill's note on I. iv. 96 in her edition of the play (London, 1967).
[45] Holinshed, 321b.

Edward II is one of the few Elizabethan history plays (*Richard III* is another) that avoids the integrative function of low life's mimicry of high-life behaviour. The only incursion of low life occurs at the beginning, when the three discharged soldiers ask Gaveston for alms. But they are more symbolic in function (like the mower in Act IV, Scene iv) than in any way representative of a different level of national existence. It is not hard to imagine why this recurrent aspect of the genre is absent from the play. In fact we can see Marlowe distorting the chronicles to achieve a different kind of effect. He allows Gaveston to be spoken of (without contradiction) as a 'peasant', a 'lown', 'hardly a gentleman', 'basely born'. Holinshed, on the other hand, shows that the conflict between the minions and the barons is not a class issue at all. Gaveston is 'a goodly gentleman and a stout'; the principal objection to him stems from his refusal to allow the precedence of the old baronage. The same point can be made even more strongly about the Spencers (in fact a powerful noble family). Their quarrel with the Mortimers is over the disposal of Edward de Bruce's land (what Holinshed calls in a sidenote 'the chief cause of the variance between the Spencers and the Lords'[46]); and the parliamentary writ of banishment against them was in fact repealed by the bishops and the major earls.[47] Marlowe is not interested in this kind of authenticity. Clearly what he sees in the reign of Edward II is a pattern which replicates that found in other Marlovian plays. As in *Tamburlaine* and *The Jew of Malta*, so in *Edward II*, the image of the outsider who attains to power by unorthodox means defines a central focus in Marlowe's vision of life. The dramatic structure that will support such a vision is not one dependent on parallelisms between a predatory baronage and a population made desperate to escape subservience (as between Jack Cade and the Duke of York) but rather one focused on the conflict between the old possessors and unorthodox newcomers who assault the citadels of privilege. One can also say, however, that Marlowe's vision, as it moved from romance towards political realism—from *Tamburlaine* to *The Jew of Malta* to *The Massacre at Paris* to *Edward II*[48]—showed the charisma of the outsider figure and the acceptability of his methods growing steadily more suspect, while compensatingly the seriousness, or at least the

---

[46] Ibid. 325b.   [47] Ibid. 328a.
[48] I am assuming a chronology that is commonly allowed but cannot be proved.

inevitability, of the old possessors became more allowable. Had he gone on, one feels, he could have become a crusty conservative. The dramatic pattern, in *Edward II* as elsewhere in Marlowe, is one of incremental repetition. As by the irresistible drive of Tamburlaine, the unquenchable resourcefulness of Barabas, so in a negative form, by virtue of the vacuum left at the centre by Edward II, one substitute is sucked in after another: Gaveston, the Spencers, and, eventually, Mortimer Junior. The complexity of the power structure here means that none of these offers exact repetition, as the play moves from an action fuelled by personal emotion to one that derives from political intrigue. Gaveston at one end and Mortimer at the other end do not look at all like one another, but their structural relation to Edward turns out to be surprisingly similar, as one, like the other, tries to deal with the problem of living the impossible role of Edward's *alter ego*. 'I am thyself . . . another Gaveston', says Edward to his minion at the beginning of the play. By the end it is Mortimer who is the second Edward:

> The prince I rule, the queen do I command;
> And with a lowly congé to the ground
> The proudest lords salute me as I pass.
> I seal, I cancel, I do what I will.
>
> (v. iv. 48–51)

He has now replaced Edward on his throne, his bed, and even in his fatherhood.

Finally there is Lightborn, Edward's murderer. The murderers of princes in most history plays are brutish and ignorant men, ground down by hardship into an acceptance of murder as manual labour, highly profitable (if one can survive). Powerful dramatic effects can be made by the discovery of conscience in such hardened hearts. Such is the treatment of Jack Denton and Black Will in *The True Tragedy*, the murderers of Clarence in *Richard III*, and the murderers of Woodstock. Lightborn is different from all these: he is an exotic professional, an artist in extermination:

> I learned in Naples how to poison flowers;
> To strangle with a lawn thrust through the throat;
> To pierce the windpipe with a needle's point;
> Or whilst one is asleep, to take a quill
> And blow a little powder in his ears,
> Or open his mouth and pour quicksilver down.
>
> (v. iv. 31–6)

Lightborn is the second importer of Italian delicacies we have met in the play. Gaveston at the opening of the action planned to impose himself on the king by offerings of Italian culture. At the end of the play the king will be imposed upon by another side of what the age thought of as 'Italianism'—heartless aestheticism bred in a society without traditional loyalties. It would be easy to make the actor who plays Gaveston play Lightborn as well. Unfortunately there is no evidence that the Elizabethan theatre used doubling as an interpretive as well as a practical resource. But for a modern audience such a doubling would bring home what is undoubtedly a feature of the play: Marlowe's imposition on the historical sequence of a powerful pattern of action and reaction, an irony of steps seeming to move in one direction while in fact going the opposite way. I call this 'action and reaction', not 'crime and punishment' because the play does not offer us space for the definition of 'crime': 'How have I transgressed, | Unless it be with too much clemency?' asks Edward after his capture (v. i. 122–3). In spite of the self-indulgence, one can see that there is a genuine question here. Edward wishes to be alone with his Italianate friend, and his wish is fulfilled with horrible exactitude by one who will 'draw the pliant king which way' he pleases, in a physical if not in an emotional sense. But is his passivity, his weakness, his clemency, a *crime*, deserving of this vile symmetry?

Marlowe's sense of history is, among all the dramatists we are considering in this chapter, the least able to allow the openness of the genre. History is for him a trap which springs shut on human nature, whatever that nature may be. Of course he closes, as do other history play-writers, with the evasive presence of a boy king who can both act decisively to close the issues of the previous reign and yet avoid any indication of his own programme. He places Edward III's revenge against Mortimer (dated 1330) immediately after the murder of Edward II (in 1327), so that it can be seen as a simple act of filial piety. Mortimer's head has to be brought in and placed on Edward's coffin as a mark of closure. With this emblem in front of us on the stage we are given little encouragement to ask what solution to the political problems thus exposed can be hoped for.

The anonymous *The Reign of King Edward III* (c.1590×1595) is a highly sophisticated history play in a romantic mode quite opposite to Marlowe's. It begins, as do *King John*, *The Troublesome Reign of John, Henry V* (and also the second half of *The Famous Victories*), with an ambassadorial challenge from France, a challenge which in all five plays serves to elicit a powerful nationalistic response from the English monarch. In all these plays the challenge involves the dynastic issue of proper inheritance; in three of them (*Famous Victories, Henry V, Edward III*) the particular issue is the Salic Law used to reject Plantagenet claims to the French crown.

It is not hard to understand the popularity of this mode of opening a history play. A powerful occasion for antagonistic rhetoric is provided, leading to orders for immediate action, and so an expectation of trumpets and drums, the thrill of battle and the gratification of English victories. It also provides, of course, in the interstices of the intention so forcefully presented, occasions for delay and for counter-currents to show themselves, and for a more complex evaluation of the heroic English leader. Of the three kings we meet in these plays, John turns out to be the least assured, foiled by the counter-currents most integral to his dynastic claim. Henry V (in both *The Famous Victories* and *Henry V*) is suspect (though falsely) because of his wild youth. More significantly, in *Henry V* the conspiracy of Cambridge, Scroop, and Grey reminds us of the unfinished business of the Lancastrian usurpation. In *Edward III*, no less than in these plays, the expedition to punish French pretensions can be undertaken only when local and personal affairs have been disposed of.

It is in the handling of this episode before the invasion can begin that *Edward III* most obviously marks out its difference from other plays. The first moves are indeed the usual ones: the Scots must be dealt with before the French can be tackled (compare *Famous Victories*, ll. 770 ff.). But it is not contumacious barons who provide the opposition in *Edward III*; in his advance north to chastise the Scottish king, Edward runs into a still more formidable foe— the beautiful Countess of Salisbury—for whom he conceives an ungovernable passion. King Edward's passionate debate with the Countess, with Warwick her father, with Lodowick his poet, and above all with himself (derived from Bandello via Painter's *Palace of Pleasure*), is in fact a debate between kingship and tyranny. He can legitimately bind his subjects by oath to do whatever he commands; but is it proper for an English king to command everything he desires? The answer comes with the Countess's offer to divorce her husband, but only by stabbing the image of him lodged in her heart. The conflict between the anointed king and the loyal subject is exposed as an impasse that cannot be resolved except by self-destruction. It is only when this lesson has been learnt that Edward's heart is sufficiently purged of tyrannical self-interest to justify his conquest of France and his fatherhood of Edward the Black Prince (the unstained moral hero of the piece). The romantic assurance of these scenes of passion, and the quality of the verse that sustains them, have persuaded many to think this part of the play written by Shakespeare. It is certainly hard to imagine Shakespeare, at this point in his career, writing anything else in the play.

The last three acts, showing the conquest of France (and envisaging the subsequent conquest of all other contumacious countries), return again and again to the potential conflict between integrity and power, particularly in the matter of fulfilling oaths, an issue considered at great length in Act IV. In the final episode, at the siege of Calais, Edward honours the letter of his promise to spare the town but refuses to show mercy to the six citizens whose lives are the price of his forgiveness. There seems to be a reminiscence here of Tamburlaine's action against the virgins of Damascus; but again the distinction between an English sovereign and an oriental tyrant makes its appearance. Edward's intention to drag the burghers around the walls of Calais 'and after feel the stroke of quartering steel' reflects the proper implacability of the military commander and of the father who will not move to rescue his son from the enemy. But this Tamburlaine is also part of a domestic world in which women have power to fulfil their different but equally relevant social perceptions. Tamburlaine's Zenocrate can only weep and wring her hands; Queen Philippa bears a much more complex relation to the world of power. She has been 'grievously displeased' that Copeland would not give up to her his prisoner, the King of Scots. At Calais Copeland defends his refusal as required by the 'public law at arms'; he surrenders his prisoner to the king and expects to receive the reputation and reward that only the king can give. And Edward assents to the propriety of such an arrangement, knights and pensions Copeland. But in the matter of justice or mercy for the burghers of Calais the Queen has a different role to play, a duty to remind her husband of his obligations to God and to humanity, to forgive the suppliant burghers, especially if he hopes to be *king* of France and not simply its conqueror. The moral structure of the play demands that, being English, he must do so. And so he does.

The successful 'strong king', *Edward III* suggests, must inevitably struggle for a point of balance between the norms of military power and those of just behaviour. In part the play conveys this by the conversation it sets up between the king and alternative centres of virtue—the Countess, the Queen, the Black Prince. In part also the effect is obtained by the implicit contrast with the manners of the tyrant, most obviously Tamburlaine. When it is feared that the Black Prince has been slain, Edward with Tamburlaine-like rhetoric promises that in his obsequies 'in the stead of tapers on his tomb | An hundred fifty towers shall burning blaze' (v. i. 173–4). But the conqueror's rhodomontade is immediately undercut by the homely domestic pride with which the father and mother welcome home their victorious son, who now completes their national as well as domestic triumph by bringing in the French royal family as his captives.

The success of the reign of Edward III, not only in his conquest of France, but also in his fertility in producing 'seven sons . . . as seven vials of his sacred blood' (*Richard II*, I. ii. 11–12), sounds like a reproachful knell in the plays of discord that follow in the chronology, when neither conquest nor inheritance can any longer be assured. The paradox of the success that breeds failure, the strength that begets weakness, seems to have made the reign of Richard II particularly interesting to playwrights, as the point at which the constituent parts of monarchical success most obviously came to pieces, the point at which weakness and strength, we might say, had their most interesting conjuncture.

The chronological relation of the play of *Woodstock*—or *The First Part of Richard II* as it is sometimes called—(1591×1595; MS) to *Edward II* and to *Henry VI*—most relevantly to *2 Henry VI*—is quite uncertain, but it is clear enough that the three plays are tied together somehow. A. P. Rossiter in his edition has presented an elaborate argument for a *2 Henry VI*—*Woodstock*—*Edward II* chronology by which Marlowe was enabled to 'turn his hand to a study of petulant weakness' when he took up the suggestions that *Woodstock* offered.[49] That *Woodstock* (like *Edward II*) is indebted

---

[49] *Woodstock: A Moral History*, ed. A. P. Rossiter (London, 1946), 63.

to 2 *Henry VI* is probable enough; but priority between the two debtors seems impossible to determine. Fortunately the interesting issue is not who followed whom but rather to note the different effects that different dramatists made out of roughly similar situations: a young king, 'protected' by uncles (here York, Lancaster, and Thomas of Woodstock, Duke of Gloucester) and other associated barons, seeks to realize himself by listening to the advice and comfort of flatterers and so sets up personal rule at the head of a court party in opposition to the traditional king-and-peers alliance. 'True Englishness' is aligned in *Woodstock* with the uncles and earls who fought alongside the late king in his foreign wars. But the new king's party does not know how to keep foreign ways under English control. This leads to lavish expenditure on imported gew-gaws, disengagement from the traditional life of the country, and a careless imposition of unfair taxes to pay for courtly self-indulgence. This, in turn, leads to general unrest and the danger of riot and rebellion. The uncles' efforts to preserve or restore the great days of the late king, produce, however, only civil strife. Unlike *Henry VI* and *Edward II*, *Woodstock* does not carry this chain of events to its logical conclusion, but stops at a point of truce: Richard, having accepted the advice that Thomas of Woodstock should be murdered, is suddenly repentant and may now (as far as this play is concerned) have become a reformed character; the barons capture and execute the flatterers (Bagot, Greene, Tresilian, Bushy, Scroope) and restore the traditional order. As we are told in conclusion:

> Thus princely Edward's sons, in tender care
> Of wanton Richard and their father's realm,
> Have toiled to purge fair England's pleasant field
> Of all those rancorous weeds that choked the grounds
> And left her pleasant meads like barren hills.
>
> (v. vi. 1–5)

It is easy, under these circumstances, to see why we might think of this play as a forepiece to Shakespeare's *Richard II*, which, after all, begins with a veiled reference to the murder of Woodstock— the historical matter at issue between Mowbray and Bolingbroke. It cannot, however, have been Shakespeare's aim to continue the story as told—if we suppose that he was following it; rather he has chosen to repeat its basic pattern, resurrecting the cast of flatterers anachronistically disposed of in *Woodstock*, uncovering in the process a depth and complexity of motive in Richard himself (who is in *Woodstock* a rather rudimentary character).

As depicted there, Richard displays neither the resolute otherworldliness of Henry VI nor the emotional fixation of Edward II. His character is defined mainly by the company he keeps: the young men who form his council are more interested in fashion than statecraft and what they need is money rather than power. As in *Richard II*, Richard is willing to become landlord of England, not king, if that will mean a steady supply of spending money. The money can then be screwed out of the peasantry by those who have no aristocratic scruples about the methods necessary. The collapse of class ethics in the pursuit of money is nicely illustrated in Tresillian's rise from petty clerk to Lord Chief Justice. As himself a figure without objective claims to power, whimsically appointed and treating his appointment whimsically, he reveals, in comic–horrific caricature, the process of corruption that the weak king creates, and in these characteristics he is hardly distinguishable from the vice–clown figure of Nimble, his assistant. It is a neat piece of moral pattern-making that he is betrayed at the end by this same servant, who takes literally the lesson of 'every man for himself' that he has learnt from his master.

Against this well-defined group the author has built up a set of antithetical values centred on the historically revalued 'Protector', Thomas of Woodstock. In truth, Woodstock was a factious troublemaker and a continual threat to the stability of the realm, but here (partly, it seems, drawing on the model of Shakespeare's Humphrey of Gloucester) he is

> Plain Thomas, for by th' rood so all men call him
> For his plain dealing, and his simple clothing:
> Let others jet in silk and gold, says he
> A coat of English frieze best pleaseth me.
>
> (I. i. 99–102)

These sartorial choices are, of course, only the outsides of moral distinctions. Woodstock is especially associated with domestic order, his loyal wife, his loyal servants, and his home at Plashy, seen as a model of old-fashioned country housekeeping, which he leaves, to undertake national duties, only unwillingly. When the court popinjay comes to Plashy to deliver Richard's message, he has to bring his horse into the courtyard for fear of muddying his fashion boots, and then he mistakes the duke for a groom; but the 'plain' nobleman can still run rhetorical rings round the London exotic when he chooses to do so. Woodstock's attachment to the locality, to the nation and its traditions, keeps him gruffly responsive to the popular temper, concerned about the sufferings of the commons, whose love protects him from direct assault. It is entirely in keeping with this system of significances that he is arrested under the cover of a neoclassical masque, bundled away in masked finery, and shipped out of the country to Calais, where he is murdered.

On the key political question of the age, raised by all these weak-king historical plays—how far can rebellion against an inefficient and corrupt king be justified or even palliated—*Woodstock* is evasive, drawing on the usual escape clause that the king has been misled by flattering and self-interested counsellors, quite different from the true peers, who are represented (in spite of history) as loyal and disinterested. Richard's youth can be brought in (and is) to further this defence. The second half of the play seems to show the author trying to distance the king from his wicked counsellors. Immediately after the kidnapping of Woodstock, the virtuous queen dies. We hear of how Richard

> rends his princely hair,
> Beats his sad breast, falls grovelling on the earth
> All careless of his state, wishing to die.
>
> (IV. iii. 113–15)

And when his aunt of Gloucester shares his sorrow

> He takes her in his arms, weeps on her breast,
> And would have there revealed her husband's fall
> Amidst his passions, had not Scroope and Greene
> By violence borne him to an inward room;
> Where still he cries to get a messenger
> To send to Calais to reprieve his uncle.
>
> (IV. iii. 124–9)

These are the last sentiments we hear from Richard in the play (unless, of course, he turned up on the missing last page of the manuscript). And they are sentiments only. The countermand sent to Calais never gets there, whether by natural delay or by the intervention of the flatterers we are not told. It is not entirely clear that

Richard will be able to sustain the moral perception he has suddenly achieved. Nothing in the character he has so far displayed suggests it; but the movement of the play supports the idea of some such compromise between external force (the removal of the flatterers) and internal recuperation. *Woodstock* would then come to rest on a political idyll which neither the chronicle story nor any observation of political reality could support. It was left for Shakespeare to point out that such convergence between emotionalism and political weakness is essentially unstable, that it can produce a truce of convenience but not a happy ending.

The Life and Death of Jack Straw, a notable rebel in England. Who was killed in Smithfield by the Lord Mayor of London (1590×1593) is, among the plays considered in this chapter, not only the shortest (1,210 lines in the Malone Society Reprint) but also the most rudimentary in dramatic organization. It consists of little more than alternating scenes, in which (A) the rebel leaders exchange doggerel hopes of enjoying a communitarian future (where, none the less, Parson Ball would be Archbishop of Canterbury), while in (B) the government notables utter establishment pieties against rebellion. The rebels (as in the Jack Cade scenes in *2 Henry VI*) are comically confused and illogical, burning records and making dynastic claims, alternately utopian and realistic (foreseeing the gallows as the inevitable end of the affair and acknowledging that 'we owe God a death'). The court notables rehearse, in their stiff blank verse, what must seem to the modern reader to be the equally utopian vision of a corporate state in which soil, mankind, and God are integrated into a totally fulfilling hierarchy. Between these two extreme positions the play fails to imagine any interaction. It offers us only a straight narrative, carrying us along the rebels' advance from Kent and Essex into London, including the failed interview with the king (the young Richard II[50]), and then we have the climactic confrontation in Smithfield when the Essex contingent agreed to go home and the obstreperous Jack Straw was stabbed by William Walworth, Lord Mayor of London.

It has been suggested that the play's stress on the mayoralty of William Walworth (beyond what the chronicles require) may be

---

[50] As F. P. Wilson has pointed out (in Helen Gardner (ed.), *Shakespearian and Other Studies* (Oxford, 1969), 14), we are never told which king this is.

associated with celebration of the mayoralty of John Allot, a member of the Fishmonger's Company, in 1591 (Walworth had belonged to the Fishmongers).[51] This is an attractive conjecture. It is hard to believe in *Jack Straw* as a vital part of the history-play tradition in the popular theatre. Though it begins with a wonderfully sharp vignette of the complex interaction between the governors and the governed (the tax collector insists on searching Jack Straw's daughter to find if her pubic hair proves her to be of taxable age), the complexity quickly resolves itself into separated stereotypes. On the other hand, if the play was written for a celebration of London government, then its development towards specific praise of Londoners' loyalty and mayoral courage (compared to Roman virtue) is explained, as also the display of originating myths for extant civic traditions—the knighting of every Lord Mayor and the placing of the bloody dagger on the city's coat of arms.

It is a convenience to group Shakespeare's early history plays as the interlinked parts of a tetralogy. It would be a similar convenience to set up Shakespeare's 'second tetralogy' (*Richard II, 1 Henry IV, 2 Henry IV, Henry V*) inside a similarly organized later chapter. But other considerations suggest that convenience can be bought too dear. *The Tragedy of King Richard II* (1594×1595), is stylistically attached to a later phase of Shakespeare's writing, and it bears an obvious relationship to the dramatized reigns of Henry IV and Henry V.[52] It is not the purpose of this chapter, however, to write a history of Shakespeare's career; it aims to group together, within limited chronological spans, plays that make interrelated points about historical material. *Richard II* clearly owes certain fictional perspectives to *Woodstock*[53] and a considerable debt to *Edward II*'s demonstration how to interweave history and tragedy.

---

[51] Chambers, iv. 22. Thomas Nelson's pageant of 1590 'set forth by the worshipful Company of the Fishmongers', placed Walworth and Jack Cade in a context of allegorical figures representing ideal government. See R. Withington, 'The Lord Mayor's Show for 1590', *MLN* 33 (1918), 8.

[52] See Tillyard, *Shakespeare's History Plays*, 244, where it is argued that such virtues as *Richard II* possesses derive from its function 'as part of a great structure'. The play is too simple, except as 'befits an exordium' (like Wagner's *Rheingold*, no doubt).

[53] Most obviously at II. i. 128, where Thomas of Woodstock is represented by Gaunt as a 'plain, well-meaning soul' (as in *Woodstock* but not elsewhere). It is a clear convenience for Shakespeare to use Thomas as a reinforcement for the characteristics that appear here in Gaunt and elsewhere in Edmund of Langley—all relics of a time before the advent of individualism and sophistication.

It has seemed more important to emphasize these compositional relations rather than the continuity of subject matter in the comical histories of Henry IV and Henry V.

Even if Shakespeare's *Richard II* had perished, it would be clear from *Woodstock* that the reign of Richard offered a dramatic pattern close to that of *Edward II*. There is, of course, a general interconnection between Shakespeare's and Marlowe's plays. I have noted above the debt that Marlowe owed to *Henry VI*. *Richard II* in turn shows us what Shakespeare learnt from Marlowe's history play, so that he was enabled to carry the 'weak-king' formula to its final degree of finish. Marlowe developed the unworldly passivity of Henry VI—equally the puppet of the good Duke Humphrey as of the malignant others—into a role of extraordinary emotional pathos, developing passivity into a passionate and petulant quality of self-assertion that cries out to be satisfied but cannot be answered inside the conditions of feudal history, so that personal and public worlds (equally vivid) are in tragic collision. Edward has personal *needs*, but no understanding of a public policy that could ensure their satisfaction: to give priority to the defeat of the barons he would have to be able to turn himself into a baron. Shakespeare, on the other hand, creates a Richard who is highly conscious of his public role and shows no inclination whatsoever to escape from it in order to secure his private tastes. It is inconceivable that this play could have begun, like *Edward II*, with some flatterer telling us how he will exploit the king's power. Richard's obsession is with his own image, and his friends are entirely subservient to that. The role he sets for himself is entirely appropriate to the political world he lives in. Only he fatally misconstrues the conditions within which such an image can be sustained.

From the point of view of the barons, Richard appears to be very much the same kind of king as we find in *Woodstock*—immature, prey to flatterers, spendthrift, excessively taken with 'lascivious meters' and Italian innovations (see II. i. 17 ff.), yet assumed to be capable of coming to his senses when experience and good advice from uncles have taken effect. When he himself speaks, however, we hear a different music, impressive, effectively regal, winning, above all (and saying it all) powerfully poetic. It is in this that one can see Shakespeare moving outside the range of his contemporaries, in his use of the resources of his medium to create an effect not simply of poetic virtuosity (as appears in his narrative poems) but of virtuosity as the defining language of a particular temperament playing a particular role inside a particular situation. For this is not simply a matter of character. To call Richard a poet, as Pater and others have done, is, of course, to substitute created for creator. None the less we should not suppress the true observation that Richard's identity is made most convincing by his power to turn his sense of himself into poetry. The protagonist of this play provides a charismatic role for a great *jeune premier* actor (a great lyric tenor perhaps) in a mode of charaterization that has, so far as we know, no precedent (unless it be Romeo).[54] It is a method of characterization that is liable to sentimentality, in actor or critic, but we should notice that it is placed (as explicit poetry usually is in Shakespeare) in a context that is soberly unindulgent. We are not expected to withhold pity; but there is no doubt that reponsibility for the pitiable state attaches to the victim.

The opening scenes of the play, the challenge and counter-challenge of Bolingbroke and Mowbray, play history as a series of heraldic vignettes in which the king's performative utterances (saying as doing) are entirely appropriate to his role at the centre of a ritual handed down to him from the past, a ritual in which he has, like a priest, a purely impersonal function to perform. The very opening words:

> Old John of Gaunt, time-honoured Lancaster,
> Hast thou according to thy oath and band
> Brought hither Henry Herford, thy bold son,
> Here to make good the boisterous late appeal . . .

conjure the present out of a past in which legendary figures like John of Gaunt[55] render 'oath and band' to confirm our sense of a world operating by unquestioned and immemorial rules (the opening of *King Lear* comes to mind as a parallel effect). In this opening

[54] There is one speech in *Edward II* that seems to sound this note, though with a brevity that makes any general statement about it hard to sustain. It comes at the end of Edward's life when he pathetically confides to his murderer the torments he has endured: 'Tell Isabel the Queen, I looked not thus | When for her sake I ran at tilt in France, | And there unhorsed the Duke of Cleremont' (v. v. 68–70). The violence of the contrast here between sweetness and horror makes it hard to assess it against the slower-paced effects in *Richard II*.

[55] He appears as the hero of one of Hieronimo's entertainments (*The Spanish Tragedy*, I. vi), as the subject of what may be a play, entered in the Stationers' Register in 1594, and in a projected play, *The Conquest of Spain by John of Gaunt*, by Hathway and Rankins, entered in Henslowe's Diary for 1601.

everyone present fulfils the functions expected: the contestants orate their decorously passionate speeches, the heralds trumpet their conditions, gages are thrown down and picked up, the king arranges a second performance on St Lambert's Day, and the cast disappears, to take off their greasepaint, as it were.

If this is a picture of royal weakness, it is a very different kind of weakness from any that we have seen in preceding plays. If this is only shallow play pretending to be deep reality, then the whole state apparatus is involved in the weakness and raises for us the difficult (perhaps impossible) question, 'What then *is* political reality?'[56] In Act I, Scene ii, set between the two heraldic scenes, we learn (what we already know from *Woodstock*) that the crucial issue between Mowbray and Bolingbroke, the murder of Woodstock, is in fact the responsibility of Richard himself. But there seems to be no way in which this charge can be incorporated into the public rhetoric available to this society; to attack the agent (Mowbray) while exonerating the principal (Richard) keeps the fabric of the state intact as everyone involved wishes it to be. The sonorous music of courtly self-satisfaction can then roll splendidly past us like an ornamental chariot; the protest placard raised by the bitter Duchess of Gloucester must be stowed away for the time being.

The question this splendid music poses for its audience is the question that any show too perfectly achieved, too unaware of its own provisional status, creates for its theatre public: 'How long before something different happens?' Reality thus becomes conceived of as a trap dug in the path of the procession, and the process of the play's action is seen as the prepared expectation of unforeseen change. Richard's weakness, we may say, lies in his assumption that, if the surface stays the same, the process also stays the same. But the process of history is perpetual movement; and here, for the first time in our discussion, we find set out the implications of the obvious truth that a history play must be a play about Time, a perception that will point towards tragedy to the precise extent that time's movement is resisted, most especially when that resistance comes from a definition of self as unique and unchanging. Richard's feudal inheritance, his imagination of the

---

[56] This is a question that nineteenth-century critics thought it easy to answer, assuming that political strength could be defined in terms of such values as 'manliness' and 'action', leading to freedom: see Coleridge and Dowden, for example. It is not evident that Shakespeare shared these assumptions.

magical world of Edward III, faces here the reality that these ritual splendours have to be paid for (as in *Woodstock*), and cannot be paid for from the traditional sources that the ritual celebrates. In *Woodstock* an easy ending is provided by Richard's belated revulsion against the crimes of his immaturity. But Shakespeare's play is made of sterner stuff, and provides no point of re-entry into the glamorous past. When time-honoured John of Gaunt dies, that past dies with him. His celebrated praise of England is a farewell to the possibility of such sentiments, and the speech itself, as we do not always remember, does not culminate in praise but in condemnation of an economic present in which 'this precious stone set in a silver sea' is only a pawnbroker's pledge, unredeemable except for hard cash. The generation of Edward III cannot, in any case, be continued in the reign of Richard, for he has 'tapped out and drunkenly caroused' the blood of Edward's son, Thomas of Woodstock.

But blood is not the most important loss to be considered—though blood is in many senses what the old system lived on. More significant is the fact that he 'taps out' Gaunt's rents and revenues as soon as the old man is dead. It is this sacrifice of honour to economics that shakes the ground beneath the throne. The Queen first senses the tremor in Act II, Scene ii, as a quality of feeling; and her sense of it is not to be stilled by Bushy's assurance that it is only imagination. She is right to resist his reductive comment; for in such a play the shaking of the state must also be registered as a shift in the structure of imagination, a slippage in the system of emotions that holds it together. The Queen's sudden perception, not of a realignment in the political forces but of an abyss of meaninglessness opening at her feet, serves as a preparation for Richard's much more elaborate and self-destructive oscillation between confidence and despair in the following act—a swing of perceptions that provides the hinge of the play.

Richard's weakness in the face of Bolingbroke's apparently reasonable initial demands, his evident inability to find any sticking point between *all* and *nothing*, has puzzled commentators, for neither psychological nor political probabilities seem to require it. One can, of course, produce specially tailored explanations to fit the case: Shakespeare is representing the March of History, the inevitable decline of feudalism in the face of bourgeois values; or the play is a study of a particular kind of temperament. What seems to be unnoticed in such explanations is the degree to which external political events and internal interpretation of life are fused in this play, so that the loss of imaginative coherence and the loss of political control are thought of as two versions of the same thing.

The dream of poetry is of an organic utterance that will represent mind and action, the internal and the external worlds, as mutually interdependent, so that every expression of the self will define the vision within which action can be made objectively meaningful. It is within some such ideal that Richard dreams his life. Given his inheritance, nothing more conceptually novel has been demanded of him ('We were not born to sue, but to command'). And so when power ceases to flow from him as naturally as poetry, no modification of the system seems possible, except by a transfer of the totalizing method from total power to total impotence, to 'worms, graves, and epitaphs' (what Donne calls 'absence, darkness, death, things that are not'[57]), to a political vision which sees England as 'the field of Golgotha and dead men's skulls' and to the rhetoric of *contemptus mundi*, which preserves the unity of his inner life by allowing him to construct those elaborate arias of renunciation and farewell that Lamb famously compared to Edward II's 'reluctant pangs of abdicating royalty'.[58] There is, in fact, as much of welcome as of reluctance in Richard's version; by such means his power over his audience becomes greater than ever, and he indulges himself to the hilt. In prison in Pomfret, we hear not only his dismissive impatience with the kind of world in which success is possible but also his pleasure in the creative power over experience that great poetry can convey:

> I have been studying how I may compare
> This prison where I live unto the world:
> And for because the world is populous,
> And here is not a creature but myself,
> I cannot do it. Yet I'll hammer it out:
> My brain I'll prove the female to my soul,
> My soul the father, and these two beget
> A generation of still-breeding thoughts.
>
> (v. v. 1–8)

---

[57] 'A Nocturnal upon St. Lucy's Day'. The witty validation of nothingness in Donne's poem provides a useful comment on Richard's rhetoric of privation.

[58] *The Works of Charles and Mary Lamb*, ed. E. V. Lucas (7 vols.; London, 1903–5), iv. 24.

Thus the inner world creates an outer one, as control in one sphere recreates control in the other.[59]

Edward II shows the tragedy of the king as an inevitable consequence in a world of power struggles where villainy is (as in *Henry VI* and *Richard III*) the natural means through which power achieves its victories. *Richard II* is less ruthless in its connections; it is a play in which moral evil is not invoked as the natural explanation why politics works as it does. And to that extent (opening up its processes to the mysterious movements of history) it is that much more a model history play. Edward is, like Richard, the author of his own tragedy; but he shows little sense of the world that is taking shape around him, or of the ways that political history and personal tragedy interact. Richard, on the other hand, is given the joy of creativity as well as the pain of having to act out the role he has created. He achieves this creative freedom by making a radical distinction between *his* trajectory and that of the state. History is left in the possession of the pragmatic and withdrawn Bolingbroke, who shows little interest in the question 'Who am I?' As a practised politician, he reacts (and will react) to every political twist and turn with renewed diligence and an appropriate reconstitution of the self. As Henry IV, he has been seen as a characterless functionary. Inside *Richard II* it might be more appropriate to see him as occupying the space left vacant by Richard, the deglamourized space of a business king who knows how to rule but not why he should do so, and is therefore prey to a guilt that cannot be assuaged by the histrionic self-assurance that marks out Richard's power in the theatre of kingship.

It is hard to write a history play that is not also a *political* play. Yet the history plays considered in this chapter do not seem to have raised issues of censorship. Plays that do so[60] in this period seem to have been those dealing with reigning monarchs or with issues of public order among groups found in the theatre (the rioting apprentices in *Sir Thomas More* might be cited). The one

---

[59] Richard, it is interesting to note, is allowed a degree of explicit religious confidence in his destiny that Shakespeare denies to his tragic heroes proper. In the case of Lear or Othello, for example, such confidence would overbalance the positive as against the negative side of the catharsis. In a history play, where the cards are so much more heavily stacked against individual success, a confidence in heavenly compensation has less chance of cancelling out the certainty of earthly loss.

[60] I am thinking of such texts as Chapman's *Byron* plays, Massinger's *Believe as you List*, the multi-authored *Book of Sir Thomas More*, Middleton's *A Game at Chess*.

exception is *Richard II*. It is clear that this play was given a fair bit of political attention from early in its career. Its subject, the deposition and murder of an anointed sovereign, in breach of God's alleged contract with the world, is certainly designed to arouse strong political emotions; and the fact that the deposition scene was not printed in Elizabeth's reign shows that these emotions were assumed to be dangerous. We know that a special performance of a play on this subject was bespoke by the supporters of the Earl of Essex on the eve of his unsuccessful rebellion against Elizabeth (8 February 1601), and this tells us that the government judgement was right: the pleasure of seeing a successful rebellion of the past can encourage those who are contemplating a contemporary *coup*. The same general point may be made about revivals (and suppressions) of *Richard II* in 1678–82, in the period of the Titus Oates plot and the demand for an Exclusion Bill to secure the 'pre-abdication' (as it were) of the heir apparent, the future James II. That the play allows parallels between one monarch and another and one usurper and another is not in question. Queen Elizabeth saw the connection as clearly as the Essex conspirators. In August 1601 (six months after Essex's execution), when William Lambarde was showing her the muniments in the Tower, she remarked to him, 'I am Richard the Second: know ye not that?'; and in response to his words about Essex she added, 'This tragedy was played forty times in open streets and houses.'[61] That Elizabeth's 'this tragedy' refers to Shakespeare's play is by no means certain; if the play offended her, she could easily have plucked it out. But even if that was her meaning, her reaction tells us very little about the political meaning of *Richard II* for those who are not sovereigns fearing usurpation.

Of course elements in this play or any other may be seized on by an audience with a local political situation in mind, and made to refer to that excitement. And indeed for that moment the play becomes a part of general politics. But these are ephemeral situations arising from largely accidental connections between a generalizing vision and current live events. Such appropriations are an inevitable part of our responsiveness,[62] but are merely tangential to any fiction

---

[61] E. K. Chambers, *William Shakespeare: A Study of Facts and Problems* (2 vols.; Oxford, 1930), ii. 326–7.

[62] I am thinking here of such inflammatory events as the famous productions of Addison's *Cato*, Hugo's *Ernani*, Synge's *Playboy of the Western World*, Ibsen's *Enemy of the People* (as performed by Stanislavski in Petrograd in 1905—see Michael Meyer, *Ibsen: A Biography* (Harmondsworth, 1971), 529–30).

that is capable of being revisited and found meaningful in one situation after another. It is only because the politics of the play carry this complex interpretability that we continue to attend to them. Shakespeare's *The Life and Death of King John* (1591×1598) is the third play about this reign that has survived from the Tudor period. In Shakespeare's *œuvre* it stands out as isolated from the historical continuum of all the other history plays. It has, of course, several features that link it to the standard issues: it deals with a conflict between the centralizing royal power and the feudal baronage; it concerns dynastic war between England and France, ending with English victory (or at least survival); it shows us a weak king standing in the shadow of a glamorous predecessor (Richard Cœur de Lion) and unable to impose himself on the warrior society that he has inherited. Less usual is the concern of the play with the religious aspect of these standard issues. It is commonly argued that it was this religious aspect that endeared the subject to the Elizabethan dramatists and their public. Clearly it was anti-papal fervour that drove Bishop Bale to produce his *King Johan* (1538). The anonymous *The Troublesome Reign of John, King of England, with the discovery of King Richard's base son (vulgarly named the Bastard Faulconbridge); also the death of King John at Swinstead Abbey* (1587×1591) also gives the religious issue great prominence. Shakespeare has much less of this; the historicist explanation of Shakespeare's play—that it is meant to be understood as a contribution to anti-papal sentiment—seems not to be sufficient to account for the emphasis that he has chosen.[63] It may be indeed that we need no more justification for Shakespeare's play than the existence in *The Troublesome Reign* of a model play that possessed sufficient strength to stimulate and justify rewriting. This would give *The Troublesome Reign* something of the same role in relation to *King John* as *The Famous Victories* bears to *Henry IV* and *Henry V*.[64] The prologue to Part I of *The Troublesome Reign* begins by invoking *Tamburlaine*—a comparison that gives us our first fix on its intentions:

---

[63] See E. M. Waith, *Patterns and Perspectives in English Renaissance Drama* (Newark, Del., 1988), 252–88, for a cogent argument against the merely historicist explanation.

[64] One way of cutting the Gordian Knot that ties the two texts together has been chosen by Professors Peter Alexander (*Shakespeare's Life and Art* (London, 1939), 85) and Ernst Honigmann (in his Arden edition of the play (London, 1954)), who argue that *The Troublesome Reign* is a reported or pirated text of Shakespeare's play. This is an attractive view, since it gives the great merits of *The Troublesome Reign* a simple explanation. The consequence, that *King John* must be dated before 1591, has, however, dissuaded most scholars.

You that with friendly grace of smoothed brow
Have entertained the Scythian Tamburlaine,
And given applause unto an Infidel,
Vouchsafe to welcome (with like courtesy)
A warlike Christian and your countryman.

The reference to *Tamburlaine* may help to explain why this play is presented in two parts ('quite unnecessarily', says Bullough[65]). Certainly some sense of a symmetrical pattern of rise and fall in John's career may be aligned (very roughly) with the two-part pattern in *Tamburlaine*. The first part of *The Troublesome Reign* begins with what may be a reminiscence of *1 Henry VI*, opening with a ritualistic praise of the late famous warrior monarch—Richard, Cœur de Lion, 'Scourge of Infidels'—whose untimely end has 'clad this land in stole of dismal hue'. Elinor, the Queen Mother, who speaks the epitaph, has, however, a plausible second son to bring forward: 'A King that may in rule and virtue both | Succeed his brother in his empery' (Part I, ll. 7–8). John, however, has no sooner claimed the throne than the usual challenge arrives from France; Arthur, as the heir of Geoffrey, Elinor's elder son, is John's superior in the line of succession. On the other hand, John's claim has legitimacy, for Richard's will had debarred Arthur and named John the heir (though this fact is never made explicit in the play).[66] John is not a usurper, like Henry IV; yet his strongest claim is like that of the Lancastrians: he comes to rescue the land from incompetence and anarchy. Arthur is not only a child (his juniority is much exaggerated in the plays), but a child backed by the French.

The challenge from France will be answered by war only incidentally in this play, and the hint that the definition of legitimacy itself will be the central issue is soon reinforced by a second episode in the first scene. In this, Faulconbridge chooses to acknowledge illegitimacy (and so loss of his inherited lands) so that he can claim genetic inheritance from Richard Cœur de Lion and enter into the exciting world of national aggression and self-justifying martial endeavour.

The Prologue suggests that John is to be the Christian

---

[65] Bullough, iv. 4.

[66] This was an issue that had considerable local resonance in the sixteenth century when the contested wills of Henry VIII and Edward VI were central to the debate about the succession to the crown. The possibility that it is part of the subtext of the *John* plays does not, of course, entitle us to suppose that these plays are *about* the Tudor succession.

Tamburlaine of this story. In terms of plot, character, or rhetoric, nothing can seem less likely. The Dauphin strikes more rhetorical poses, though only in order to deceive; but at the level at which policy operates, English and French methods are indistinguishable. Indeed self-consciousness about the gap between fact and rhetoric is one of the characteristic devices of this play. The Prologue tells us that John's heroic qualities show themselves in his challenge to 'the man of Rome'; but the promise is not borne out by action: what we actually see is total submission to the Pope, and abject prayer for permission to wear the crown on his terms.

In plot terms, however, it is possible to suppose that by the end of Part I John has achieved by his shuffling a political security comparable to what Tamburlaine achieved by conquest. The question of legitimacy, however, is still a worry, and must continue to be so while Arthur is alive; but to kill Arthur is to define oneself as a 'tragic tyrant stern and pitiless' (l. 1702). It is this political conundrum that gives *The Troublesome Reign* its coherence. John cannot be a Tamburlaine; he is nervous, unstable, dependent on others; and in any case he does not operate in a never-never land in central Asia. His progress has to be realistically political, not a matter of relentless advance, but one of tacking and turning to avoid the shallows, the surprises, the becalmings of a journey without a satisfactory chart.

Part I begins with a death (Richard I's) that changes the political landscape. Part II begins with a similar catastrophe—Arthur's accidental death. This is an event that throws a strong ironic light on all the patchings that led to 'bliss' at the end of Part I. Now the barons will ally themselves with the Dauphin, who (Arthur being dead) can claim to be the true heir. The Legate Pandulph's Machiavellian plan for the destruction of English sovereignty (Part I, ll. 1170 ff.) is fulfilling itself before our eyes. John's inattentive self-congratulation ('Now John thy fears are vanished into smoke' (Part II, l. 155)) marks him out, retrospectively, as incapable of understanding what the Holy Father had foreseen long before. The cost of his ignorance is abasement: he must abandon his high ambitions, crawl before his enemy, accepting his own failure. As he tells himself:

> Thy sins are far too great to be the man
> T'abolish Pope and Popery from thy realm.
>
> (Part II, ll. 278–9)

His only recompense is that history will eventually do for him what he cannot do for himself. In the future 'A king shall reign' who will dismantle all the Papacy's claims against England. Unlike Tamburlaine's, John's career is given a historical perspective which allows us to see his struggles and his failures as part of a process through time, and still at the time of writing (say 1588) a major issue. As a historical figure of this kind, he can hardly sustain the pose of a military hero.

The second part of *The Troublesome Reign* is not (as in 2 *Tamburlaine*) a downward drift punctuated by brilliant episodes of self-assertion, but a hapless confusion of accidental murders, true prophecies disbelieved, oaths sworn without intention to fulfil them, armies losing their way, supply ships stranded on sandbanks, treasure swallowed by the Wash. Finally a sick and hopeless John, worn out by history's inconsequence, is poisoned by a comic monk and dies describing himself in the rhetoric of a desperate villain (close to that of Aaron in *Titus Andronicus* (v. i. 125 ff.)), a vision of Hell opening in front of him:

> How have I lived, but by another's loss?
> What have I loved, but wrack of other's weal?
> When have I vowed, and not infringed mine oath?
> Where have I done a deed deserving well?
> How, what, when, and where have I bestowed a day
> That tended not to some notorious ill?
> My life, replete with rage and tyranny,
> Craves little pity for so strange a death.
>
> (Part II, ll. 1056–63)

Yet, though he cannot call on Christ himself, John is granted a last-minute vision of his successor-king (Henry VIII) eventually achieving by virtue what he has failed to attain by crime, as the sinful King David could not be the builder of the temple but was granted a vision of its completion.[67]

King John's unsatisfactoriness as a free-standing tragic hero is a measure of the attention the author of *The Troublesome Reign* gave to the inconclusiveness of true history. The play can end satisfactorily only by transferring the weight of continuity to another level and using an innovative feature that marks the nameless author's

---

[67] See Peele's *David and Bethsabe*, discussed in Ch. 3.

genius and his theatrical importance. I refer to the use of comic fiction to catalyse tragic history, allowing us to see the whole process from an ironic viewpoint. The background of *Tamburlaine* has some bearing on this second strand also. The Bastard Faulconbridge is not simply a comic double; like Tamburlaine, he is an illegitimate outsider who must make his way by self-confident energy and freedom from received opinions. Unlike Tamburlaine, however, he knows that the disbelief in conventions that social marginality allows can turn one's own life as well as that of others into a comic scenario. Faulconbridge's function in the play is to show us politics as a rhetorical game covering the reality of self-interest. In this he has much that he shares temperamentally with Shakespeare's Richard of Gloucester, but unlike Richard (or Tamburlaine), though he is an outsider, he believes in national virtue and is without ambition for himself (after an opening flutter with Blanche). His initial choice, to be Richard Plantagenet rather than Philip Faulconbridge, is a choice made with a high degree of comic self parody that engages the identification of audiences:

> JOHN. Young man, how now, what, art thou in a trance?
> ELINOR. Philip, awake! The man is in a trance.
> PHILIP. *Phillipus atavis aedite Regibus.*
> What saiest thou, Philip—'sprung of ancient kings'?
> *Quo me rapit tempestas?*
> What wind of honour blows this fury forth?
> Or whence proceed these fumes of majesty?
>
> .   .   .   .
>
> Why how now? Knowest thou where thou art?
> And knowest thou who expects thine answer here?
> Wilt thou upon a frantic madding vein
> Go lose thy land and say thyself base born?
>
> (Part I, ll. 239–66)

John, as the possessor of power, has to temporize and collaborate with his enemies, to accept that the English king's authority is insufficient to cope with the Papacy and its continental supporters. But the Bastard, detached from the responsibilities of power, can take up the more populist, consistently anti-papal, anti-monastic viewpoint. In the one scene in *The Troublesome Reign* for which there is no counterpart in Shakespeare's play, we see the Bastard carrying out John's order to 'ransack the abbeys, cloisters, priories,

| Convert their coin unto my soldiers' use' (Part I, ll. 1107–8). Written in fluent fourteeners (for the Bastard) and macaronic Leonines (for the friars), the scene is, both in the tone that the versification provides and in its structure, a classic farce in which every chest and cupboard that should contain stashed-away gold reveals only evidence of lechery among nuns and friars—yet always with the promise of a further hiding-place that will be consecrated, this time surely, to Mammon and not to Venus. But Faulconbridge's hearty anticlericalism is not only a knockabout negative. He has a positive theology as well: he alone in the play enunciates the standard Tudor doctrine of obedience, telling the revolting peers that only God can dispossess a king (Part II, l. 464), and that the issue of kingship cannot be settled by the Pope, but only by God-given strength of arms. The proud tradition of English martial prowess (represented by Richard Cœur de Lion) is the one thing that will ensure the survival of national independence. And so he tells John:

> Comfort, my Lord, and curse the Cardinal.
> Betake yourself to arms, my troops are pressed
> To answer Lewis with a lusty shock.
> The English archers have their quivers full,
> Their bows are bent; the pikes are pressed to push.
>
> (Part II, ll. 710–14)

But John can only answer 'Philip, I know not how to answer thee'. Between the populist Faulconbridge and the troubled politician whose 'heart is mazed, my senses all fordone' (Part II, l. 223), who can only act opportunistically, the gap in resolution grows wider and wider. As the play develops, John sinks into political doubletalk, self-accusation, lethargy; Faulconbridge becomes the undeviating voice of popular Englishness and national pride. The claims of politics and of patriotic self-assertion never actually separate John from the Bastard, but as political action reveals itself as a more treacherous quicksand than the Wash itself, the sense of national survival in the play comes to be embodied in the Bastard, the only character who can support the upbeat final speech.

The end of the reign, as the chronicles retail it, is entirely apt to this purpose. The abbot and monk plot to poison the king as he rests in their abbey. Clerical resentment at nationalization is given here its full expression; and so the political and the religious—

patriotic come together once again for a grand finale. Faulconbridge acts in his characteristic way by killing the abbot: 'There lie the abbot, abbey-lubber, devil. | March with the monk unto the gates of Hell' (Part II, ll. 1030–1). The final patriotic speech, in which the Elizabethan current enemy, Spain, is joined to those actually dramatized, dismisses Popery as simply another continental intrusion into English self-sufficiency: for the moment one Henry (III) will take over the unified state. Another Henry (VIII) and his successors will put an end to papal and continental interference, once and for all.

The Troublesome Reign can be thought of as something like a pattern-maker's template for King John, for the structure, not only of the action in general but even of the progression of events inside each scene, is reproduced with remarkable fidelity (though the language is completely different. In Part I of The Troublesome Reign—that is, up to Act IV, Scene iii, in King John—only one scene fails to generate a corresponding scene in King John. Yet, for all the closeness of the two plots, there are very notable differences of emphasis, which I believe can be shown to be interestingly representative of Shakespearian dramaturgy in general. The most obvious distinction between the two versions concerns the Bastard, the most triumphantly innovative feature of the anonymous play, and yet, looking back at him from Shakespeare's point of view, a feature not fully exploited.

In the opening scene, The Troublesome Reign introduces not only Philip, but his brother Robert, and his mother, as three participants in a case of legitimacy to be decided by the king. The argument is conducted in terms of the plaintiff, Robert, who introduces and describes the issue, Philip declining to 'open my mouth to unrip the shameful slander of my parents' (Part I, ll. 87–8). Shakespeare changes the relationship between the characters; he gives Philip greater prominence[68] and can be seen to be using his new Philip for a typical Shakespearian purpose: to turn argument into ethos. The comic presentation of legitimate Robert's physical disadvantages, his 'three farthings face', his 'eel-skin legs', translates The Troublesome Reign's legalistic rhetoric of

[68] One may describe the difference here in purely numerical terms: in The Troublesome Reign Robert has 72 lines in the episode (up to Philip's soliloquy), Philip has only 20. In King John the situation is inverted: there Philip has 62 lines, Robert has only 22.

> his external graces that you view
> (Though I report it) counterpoise not mine:
> His constitution's plain debility
> Requires the chair, and mine the seat of steel
>
> (Part I, ll. 361–4)

into a physical immediacy that prompts the actor and sharpens our sense of the kind of person we have in front of us. The same point can be made in terms of Philip's (new) sneaking admiration for whoever it was that got him and gave him his heroic frame and temperament (not Robert's father, surely). In *The Troublesome Reign* the issue is handled less as choice than as confession. The rhetoric of self-discovery in Philip's long speech (quoted in part above, p. 221) uses Kyddian direct statement of antithetical feelings as an explanation (rather than an expression) of the emerging self. And there it is only after this *altercatio* that Elinor offers her patronage and John ennobles his new kinsman. Shakespeare at this point invents a new soliloquy by means of which Philip can share with the audience the delights of ethos—what Robert Smallwood has called his 'self-commitment to the present . . . his confident sense of his own identity',[69] descanting on his change of name in such a way as to distance himself from what has happened to him, assuring us that he still has the same point of view, whatever he is called, and finding his own life strangely comic, as if he was a detached commentator, a member of the audience at his own performance:

> Well, now can I make any Joan a lady.
> 'Good den, Sir Richard!'—'God-a-mercy, fellow!'—
> And if his name be George, I'll call him Peter;
> For new-made honour doth forget men's names.
> 'Tis too respective and too sociable
> For your conversion.
>
> (I. i. 184–9)

The same pursuit of ethos shows itself in the great enlargement and intensification of Constance's role and in the development of Arthur from a political pawn to a private individual. The personal rhetoric of these two, mother and son, has provided actors and actresses (commonly actresses for both roles) with famous occasions to sweep audiences off their seats in great waves of sentiment

---

[69] Shakespeare, *King John*, ed. R. L. Smallwood (London, 1974), 21.

and sympathy. It is particularly interesting in terms of this change to see what Shakespeare has done in the most celebrated theatrical episode of the play—the scene of the blinding of Arthur. The Arthur of *The Troublesome Reign* is, of course, in the identical situation, and his rhetoric is designed no less clearly to persuade his kindly keeper. But the mode of rhetoric is entirely different. The Arthur of *The Troublesome Reign* bases his appeal on religious arguments. John is 'Satan': 'Subscribe not, Hubert, give not God's part away' (Part I, l. 1383). Stichomythia emphasizes the formality of the debate on a standard Tudor question: 'Can a subject invoke God's ordinance to disobey a command by God's anointed?' The formal method being employed here is powerfully effective, giving a sharp edge to the tense situation. But Shakespeare does not present Arthur as a debater. He is a terrified child whose arguments derive from a specifically childish perspective (as that is understood by adults):

> When your head did but ache,
> I knit my handkercher about your brows
> (The best I had, a princess wrought it me)
> And I did never ask it you again.

> (IV. i. 41–4)

The nineteenth-century habit of playing Arthur as an *ingénue* female role may push Shakespeare's dramaturgy here even further than he intended (and certainly further than twentieth-century taste allows), but it catches something that is genuinely present and certainly altered from what is there in *The Troublesome Reign*.

The emphasis on ethos and the reduction in direct self-explanation exposes Shakespeare's dramatic technique here, as elsewhere, as an art of indirection. We may compare *King John*, Act IV, Scene ii, with *The Troublesome Reign*, Part I, Scene xiii, to illustrate this point. In the anonymous play we are shown a complex diagram of specific political forces, each in contradiction to the other, and in combination pointing to political anarchy: to be secure John needs a second coronation; but he is already secure and needs no such ceremony. The confiscated wealth will strengthen the crown, weaken the Church; but the prophet reports that John will surrender his crown before Ascension Day. Arthur will be given freedom and the peers will confirm their loyalty; but Arthur is dead and the peers will revolt. No, Arthur is still alive. What we are shown is a series of veering and unstable attempts at control what with each move sinks further into a chaos of lies, anger, dissimulation—short-term answers to a long-term problem.

Shakespeare makes the same point, but lights it from a different angle. What we are shown in clear statement in *The Troublesome Reign* happens off-stage, or is noted by implication. Shakespeare does not allow John his sixty-one-line tirade when the peers abandon him; he cuts him short after only three lines. A Messenger from France brings news of a likely French invasion and tells of the deaths of Elinor and (possibly) of Constance. The Bastard then adds a more general sketch of a diffused atmosphere of foreboding:

> as I travelled hither through the land,
> I find the people strangely fantasied,
> Possessed with rumours, full of idle dreams,
> Not knowing what they fear, but full of fear.

(IV. ii. 143–6)

Specific news is turned into atmospherics; the world is full of apocalyptic portents: 'Old men and beldams in the streets | Do prophecy upon it dangerously' (IV. ii. 185–6):

> I saw a smith stand with his hammer, thus,
> The whilst his iron did on the anvil cool,
> With open mouth swallowing a tailor's news,
> Who, with his shears and measure in his hand,
> Standing on slippers, which his nimble haste
> Had falsely thrust upon contrary feet,
> Told of a many thousand warlike French
> That were embattailed and ranked in Kent.
> Another lean unwashed artificer
> Cuts off his tale and talks of Arthur's death.

(IV. ii. 193–202)

Both these handlings of this crucial scene in the history of King John's reign display sophisticated control of a complexly organized situation. But Shakespeare's differences from *The Troublesome Reign* are fascinating not only as a window into his workshop; they also offer us an insight into the whole development of Elizabethan dramaturgy. What Shakespeare exemplifies, and what *The Troublesome Reign* is quite innocent of, is the development of what we may call a third dimension, the sense given of a further world out there, out of sight, where other possibilities are pursued, where smiths and tailors stare at events and make no sense of them, all the time resonating against the world we *do* see. On one plane we are given the circumstances of the reign, on the other we glimpse the discontinuous inner lives of characters, each plane tilted to reflect something of the shape of the other, so that history can be read both as a narrative of interlinked events that happened in the past and as an image of personal experiences which are complex, indeterminate, and understood in the present tense.

The Troublesome Reign used the Bastard as a reanimation of the warrior (Henry V-like) qualities of Richard Cœur de Lion, now found in the context of a politically ambiguous and so militarily unsuccessful reign. Shakespeare has kept the rough soldiership that defines the Bastard in *The Troublesome Reign*, but has extended his anti-political stance beyond the contempt for monkish laziness and slyness which marked him in the other play. Now he stands out against the whole political world of compromise and deceit. He thus acquires a position that makes him the obvious counterweight to John himself. John's career as a failed national hero can be reanimated on the modern stage, it seems, as a species of comedy (so played in the brilliant production by Deborah Warner in 1988), defining comedy by its concern for the present and its vagueness about the future. In this, as in so many respects, Faulconbridge is a preview of Falstaff. This is not how he appears at the end of the action, but it is certainly how he begins, and it is the quality in him which makes the strongest impression today.

The dates of *Richard II* and *King John* are uncertain enough to give critics freedom to arrange them in either order as signposts of progression in one direction or another. I have noted above the convention of aligning *Richard II* with the plays of the following reigns (*Henry IV*, *Henry V*). In that case *King John* is most conveniently thought of as (being a generally unpopular play) as the earlier. A reverse chronology is, however, equally possible, and it may be worth while considering its implications. *Richard II* is a tragical 'weak-king' history play which links back to *Henry VI* and *Edward II* and concentrates historical meaning (with unique force) in its portrait of the suffering king. King John comes to an equally unfortunate end; but his career is not focused for us in the mirror of self regard. He is one figure among many; his misfortunes and incompetencies, seen from outside, reflect the (frequently comic) inconsistencies of political existence—of a world in which the complexity of aims and intentions continually undermines individual plans for the future. In this respect it is *King John* rather than *Richard II* that provides the precondition for the *Henry IV* plays, as a first draft of the history play seen as a group portrait of the national life, combining engagement and disengagement, comic and grave, in high life as in low life, and presided over by the debunking imagination of an anti-politician, Faulconbridge or Falstaff.

6. Later History Plays

THE *Famous Victories of Henry V* appears in Chapter 5 as an isolated representative of the genre of comical history—a genre one would expect to find popular among audiences and therefore often written and frequently printed. But in the period 1588–96 the history play (as represented by the surviving texts and by what one can deduce from surviving titles) appears to be a rather serious matter. Among the history plays so far considered, only *Edward III* and *Jack Straw* end with anything like happiness, and in *Jack Straw* the escape of the king and the city from mob violence is a hairsbreadth's chance; in *Edward III* likewise, the happy survival of the Black Prince is represented as a miraculous chance. The image of political life that these plays contain makes a tragic end more probable than a comic one; success is a temporary effect in worlds dominated by political contingency.

I have noted that Shakespeare's *Henry VI* established in 1590 or so the dominance of this history–tragedy pattern in the popular theatre. In 1597–8 we find Shakespeare once again an innovator in history play-writing. In the two parts of *Henry IV*, he turned his back on tragic history, and resuscitated not only the story of *The Famous Victories*, but also the mode of history it exemplified, and in so doing he created a model which shaped history play-writing for many years ahead.

It would be easy to argue that the turn I have described was caused by external events in the declining years of Elizabeth. But the description of such relationships as cause and effect is as un-provable as seductive, and narrowly dependent on the prejudge-ments of the asserter. All a literary history is competent to offer is literary evidence. What we know is that Shakespeare in 1597 turned back to material previously dramatized in *The Famous Victories*. One need not argue that the earlier play had a specific effect on the infinitely more sophisticated works he now wrote; yet the story of the prodigal prince with the common touch who becomes a na-tional hero-king does seem to have offered a pattern that allowed Shakespeare to describe concord between individuals of different classes as a basic value in national history; and of course it *may* be

the case that the world (and the techniques) of 1597 made it possible and desirable to assert that value where the world of 1590 did
not. Or it may simply be that the subject matter of the next part of
the historical sequence made it inevitable.

The nature of *Henry IV* is most usually described in terms of its
position in the sequence. The turn from *Richard II* to *1 Henry IV*
can be described as a turn from ritual to realism, expressing a shift
in the reigns from sacramental monarchy in undisputed lineage
to what I have called a business monarchy—sovereignty justified
by the organizational efficiency of the Lancastrian kings Henry IV
and Henry V. The connection between the historical material and
the formal means used to express or explain it poses another of those
chicken-and-egg conundrums in which phenomena belong together
but do not demand cause-and-effect representation.

Comical History

Whatever the particular cause that can be held responsible for the
expressive form of *Henry IV*, there can be no doubt that the pattern once created was seen immediately to be applicable to reigns
other than those that linked Shakespeare and *The Famous Victories*.
The history plays of the earlier period show us kings who seek to
realize their individualities inside worlds shaped by the pressures
of baronial and political contest and who are likely to be destroyed
by the contradiction between the personal and the political. For
them, every personal decision turns out to have an inescapable and
frustrating political dimension. Henry VI, Edward II, Richard II,
King John, all long for a world in which politics can be a fulfilling
process of externalizing preferences. Edward III has to abandon
the Countess of Salisbury. Edward I has to face the gap between
his love for Elinor and the political liability she creates. King John
sighs for independence he cannot achieve. The basic conflict lies
between personal will and a social requirement that reality be
defined in political or anti-personal terms. Prince Hal, however, is
given the space to turn personal choice into political profit.

It may be said that Henry IV, no less than these earlier monarchs, is caught in desires (for family concord and dynastic legitimacy) that he cannot achieve. But in his case these ends are no less
politically than personally desirable, and this gives Henry a strength
against which those with a less balanced sense of reality (Glendower,

Hotspur, Mortimer, Falstaff) throw themselves in vain. He, and the dramatized kings who follow him, are individuals caught in history, without being victimized by it. The political problems they face magnify the scope of their personal problems but do not render them insoluble. Henry IV expresses sorrow that his son is dissolute and wishes that Harry Percy could be proved to be his heir; and of course the succession to the throne is an important political issue. But the wish and the sorrow do not set king and country at odds. If we compare with this the relationship between Edward III and the Black Prince in the play of *Edward III*, we can see how Shakespeare's command of poetic nuance has allowed him to incorporate political implications inside the direct language of personal experience. In *Edward III*, the Prince serves his father as a reminder of the claims of legitimate wedlock (II. ii. 88 ff.); his dangers provoke thoughts of revenge and his military prowess joys his father's heart. But the emotion is expressed entirely inside the language of formal and political relations. When the Prince escapes from encirclement, his father's first response is:

> Well thou hast deserved a knighthood, Ned!
> And therefore with thy sword, yet reeking warm
> With blood of those that fought to be thy bane,
> Arise, Prince Edward, trusty knight at arms.

> (III. v. 89–92)

The new stress on the king as simultaneously a public and a private person shows itself in the increasing popularity of the topos of the king in disguise (as seen in *Henry V*, *Edward IV*, *Sir John Oldcastle*, *When You See Me, You Know Me*).[1] This may be described as an invasion of the history play by the mode of romance, and certainly the later history plays are increasingly focused on romantic issues. But in the plays dealt with early in this chapter, the shift should not be described as simply the absorption of one genre by another. It involves a positive revaluation of history itself and in particular it requires us to reconsider the role of humble or non-courtly life in relation to the great world of political or military activity. In earlier history plays (leaving *The Famous Victories* to one side) the humbler members of the community are trapped

---

[1] See Anne Barton, 'The King Disguised: Shakespeare's *Henry V* and the Comical History', in *The Triple Bond* (University Park, Pa., 1975), 92–117.

under the deindividualizing pressure of the political world. The peasant revolts of *Henry VI* and *Jack Straw* show us the lives of humble persons caught, no less than their superiors, in relationships of power, of organization, system, strength, and weakness. They show us the great world played out in a parodic version by those who have political instincts and desires but lack political status, and who therefore fit inside the traditional and 'natural' discipline of coercive feudal leadership. It is this high–low symmetry of violent male competitiveness that accounts for the coherence of *The Famous Victories*. But symmetry in these terms is limiting not only in the conception of the king but also in the range of possibilities opened up for his subjects. The comic–horrific roles available for them allow their knockabout violence to be openly enjoyable; but it also excludes them from history as the record of national development.

What Shakespeare has achieved in his preservation and revision of the mode of *The Famous Victories* becomes obvious if we compare these figures of appetite and social anarchy with their great inheritor, Falstaff. Falstaff is created to walk along the fault line where the personal and political join, showing off his terrifying agility and comic brio, prescient of the pressures on either side of him and knowing well how to keep the ambiguity of his position— aristocratic and populist, cowardly and self-confident, old and young, ponderous and agile, committed and detached—not only unresolved but also unresolvable. Falstaff cannot be described simply as a commentator on Lancastrian kingship. Yet his integral presence in the Henry IV plays and his ghostly shadow in *Henry V*, the degree to which he can make a home for himself in these plays, argues a natural connection. For all his chameleon powers of self-transformation, it is impossible to imagine a role for Falstaff in *Richard II* or *Richard III* (*King John* seems just about possible, for after all the Bastard Faulconbridge flourishes there). An imaginative world in which the idea of centralism dominates our sense of political possibility is unlikely to provide space for Falstaff. He needs a world of dispersal and disorder, of failures in communication, the indeterminacy of transitions long drawn out. The 'unquiet time' of Henry IV provides exactly the context Falstaff needs—a period of unremitting crisis, continually threatening, never resolved. In *Richard II* the process of transition is presented with startling brevity (one minute all-powerful, the next minute a cypher); in the

Henry IV plays there is no catastrophic climax, no great spiritual good, such as annointed royalty, to be treasured, then, paralysingly, known as already lost. The idea of national order in the Lancastrian plays is a *political* ideal and endures threat and survival without any need for the passionate invocation of extraterrestrial forces; it survives by resourceful attention to detail, and patient manipulation of the territory. And these are the terms that supply a common language for Falstaff as for the Henrys.

A reduction of the claims of national history on God's concern for anointed monarchy not only makes the scene suitable for Falstaff; it also allows individual character to be observed everywhere, achieving historical effects through domestic emotions. The political adeptness that allows Prince Hal to become England's hero is achieved at a purely personal level. *Richard II* begins with the brilliantly rhetorical king commanding, and apparently in command. *Henry IV* begins with a 'shaken and wan' king hoping to escape out of the muddied morality and the temporizing that is his political *métier* and into the certainties of a religious crusade. But there is to be no escape from this divided and unsatisfactory world, to which Henry's talents are so well adapted. Politics, as it appears here, is not a matter of the grand and once-and-for-all gesture, but grows out of the minutiae of local situations and personal disputes. The baronage does not appear (as in *King John* or *Edward II*) as a social force with its own vision of the desirable society, but as a collection of resty individuals of uncertain loyalty, military men irritable without a foreign war and venting their proud spirits in domestic assertion and challenge. No doubt this is an accurate enough image of a feudal society; and Henry is perfectly capable of dealing with it.

To call *Henry IV* (*1 and 2*) plays about a baronial conspiracy to dethrone Henry and replace him by Edmund Mortimer, Richard's nominee, is fair enough in terms of the history it contains, but totally misrepresents the dramatic effects actually created. The possibility of Henry's dethronement is never a live issue dramaturgically imagined. The 'foolish Mortimer' (as Henry calls him) makes no impact, and it would be difficult to envisage him as the destined usurper. Of course, the Percys *could* have been treated in the traditional image of the baronial opposition, but instead they are exposed less as a threat to the regime than as specimens of anachronistic feudal monomania, understandable of course in terms of the mindset their geographical position on the Scottish border requires. The structural basis of *Part I*, set up in the parallel between the two sons and the two fathers, Henry and Northumberland, points our attention away from any likelihood of political change and towards the perpetually recurring situation of intergenerational conflict. Ethos, not plot, provides the key to this situation, and the conspiracy against Henry gives us a gallery of types rather than an organization of power. The famous and marvellous scene where the would-be triumvirs, Hotspur, Glendower, and Mortimer, meet together (Act III, Scene i) is no sinister cabal but an occasion for high comedy, the comedy of natures that will never be able to understand one another, that coexist without natural coherence, having no common discourse except what expresses their shared discontent with the current situation. If this is a picture of anarchy, it is one in which political anarchy (as seen in the dividing up of the map) is the subordinate consequence of a preceding psychological anarchy. Revolt is attractive to Hotspur and Glendower largely as an excuse for games of psychological dominance. Hotspur does not really care about the land as long as he can be seen to have won the debate. As soon as Glendower gives in, Hotspur loses interest:

> I do not care. I'll give thrice so much land
> To any well-deserving friend;
> But in the way of bargain, mark ye me,
> I'll cavil on the ninth part of a hair.
>
> (Part I, III. i. 135–8)

Ethos likewise dominates in a place less obviously set up for its triumph, in the climactic contest between Hal and Hotspur at the Battle of Shrewsbury. What we are shown here is a chivalric contest for honour rather than a struggle for political success. By this point in the play the Prince has put behind him his anti-parental *déclassé* games and is now as perfect a knight as his father could desire. And that makes him into the virtual double of Harry Hotspur. Their contest has all the glamour of a championship bout between two well-matched ethical contenders—the political issues are the least of it. Of course politics can hardly be indifferent to glamour, but it must stay in control. And this is the relation we see established in Shrewsbury: while the glittering son swoops across the scene 'like feathered Mercury', the prudential father is hiding behind his array of lookalikes, diverting the enemy's chivalric energies into fruitless slaughter. No suggestion of blame attaches to Henry's stratagem, for the leader's survival is the overriding political necessity. And we should note that the distinction between politics and charisma is not allowed to be exact; when need arises, the king is yet bold enough to fight the Douglas on his own account; and yet he has to be rescued from death by his brilliant warrior son.

The complexity of attitudes that informs the scene at Shrewsbury, the interaction of the personal and the political that the battle displays, makes this episode a paradigm of the new kind of history play in which personal qualities interpenetrate the impersonal forces of historical change. And the complexity thus achieved is what separates the young Hal from the young Hotspur (in Shakespeare's specially designed version of their ages). For Hotspur, honour is the motive force that gives life its joy and meaning. For Hal, honour is one calculated joy among others, one that on this occasion assumes priority, but whose employment always needs to be measured and manipulated. And in this context Falstaff's stratagems, first pretending to be dead (the virtue of prudence) and then stabbing the dead Hotspur (to cash in the reputation for honour), show how well he fits in.

Shakespeare's Hal is obviously drawn from the model of the prince that appears in *The Famous Victories*. The relationship between the two figures may give us our best evidence to explain the meaning of this enigmatic creation, showing us also how the potential power of the early history play was turned into an actual achievement. The Prince in *The Famous Victories* shows the lineaments of a folk hero. While he is leading his gang of outlaw knights, he shows no sign of a divided mind. He is determined, it would seem, to assert his commitment to the underworld milieu and to dismay those who (like his father and the Lord Chief Justice) expect him to show himself what he calls 'a well toward young man'. To such hopes his answer is 'I had as leif they would break my head with a pot as to say any such thing' (ll. 493–4). It is only when he sees his dying father weeping for his sins that he decides to be 'born new again' and acquires political responsibility for the kingdom. In this structure Henry IV is merely a lay figure, present in the action only because of his relationship to his son. We meet him in only three scenes in *The Famous Victories*: once to be told that the Prince has been committed to jail, once to confront Hal when he comes to court with his cloak full of needles and decides to repent, and once again (in a continuation of the preceding interview) when he awakes to find that Hal has taken the crown (as in *2 Henry IV*, IV. v). In all these cases King Henry represents the forces of social respectability that the folk hero must both reject and appropriate (usually by marrying the king's daughter).

It is easy to see the aspects of Shakespeare's version that repeat this pattern. But Shakespeare's prince must not only face the social and familial expectations of the king; he must also fit in with the political system that his father has set up. And at the same time he must be seen to have changed it. The double duty of the folk hero, to emerge with difficulty from a position outside the system of power and respectability but to end up at its centre (as in *Jack and the Beanstock*), is thus reworked as a self-conscious political programme. One way of talking about this is to see *Henry IV* as a *Bildungsroman*, focused on 'the education of the prince'. But Hal seems less engaged in discovering himself than in discovering the opportunities for control that are available. In *The Famous Victories* we easily understand the Prince's slumming as a spirited and rebellious refusal to grow up as his father's boy. But in *Henry IV* this psychological plausibility has gone: there is now no box on the ear for the Lord Chief Justice, no committal to prison, no tattered cloak covered with needles, no demand that his gang must be given privilege at court. Instead, we have a self-conscious, carefully controlled (and explicitly confessed) game of separation from the courtly Establishment, a teasing ambiguity imposed on the meaning of what he is doing. Of course he tells us, and his companions also, that he will reject them when it is to his advantage to do so. All the same it is entirely clear that his experience of the common people is enormously enjoyable. If this is an education, it is an education through enjoyment, a sowing of wild oats so as to learn how to live without oats.

We may invoke here C. L. Barber's persuasive distinction between 'holidays' and 'workdays'.[2] Beginning with Hal's own 'If all the year were playing holidays | To sport would be as tedious as to work' (Part I, I. ii. 204–5), Barber points to the combination of 'playing' and 'tedious' as the dialectic the play uses to move forward:

---

[2] *Shakespeare's Festive Comedy* (Princeton, 1959).

'Shakespeare dramatizes not only holiday but also the need for holiday and the need to limit holiday.'[3] Comedy, with its blithe assumption that personal desire can expect to find fulfilment in social fact, depends for its attractiveness on its interim quality, its lack of consequence, and, as interrogated by history, belongs to the world of 'sport', not that of truth. Certainly Falstaff's attractiveness depends on his holiday status, his power to divert us temporarily from the serious, the real, the consequential. But we are allowed to see clearly how uncomic it would be to live with Falstaff inside history, that is, for more than a holiday, to cope with his self-centredness, his unreliability, as if that were the only framework for life. And yet the play itself, by the limitation it imposes on our relation to its presence, privileges 'sport' as the mode of our attention in a playhouse. Our response to these comic histories, it might be said, depends on our ability to construe them as play no less than as politics, and to allow at the same time that play is part of historical reality, pointing up its dependence on ephemeral and spontaneous human behaviour.

As I have noted above (p. 229), the collision of comedy with history raises more difficult issues than appear in the combination of history with tragedy. The image of the king as a tragic hero (even if only in the *de casibus* sense[4]) expresses the nature of the world in terms we immediately recognize as politically as well as personally true. The inadequacy of Richard II's glamour in the context of historical reality can be effectively drawn on to account for our sense of his tragic destiny, so reinforcing what we already believe about personal existence in a political world. C. L. Barber would wish to mend the comic 'unsatisfactoriness' of the end of 2 *Henry IV* by inserting some such recognition of the balance sheet of success: 'Shakespeare might have let the play end with this ["way of the world"] attitude dominant, a harsh recognition that life is a nasty business . . . with the single redeeming consideration that that political order is better than anarchy.'[5] Barber seems to be arguing that the interpenetration of workday and holiday, state ritual and personal fulfilment, reality and dream, public and private, would only thus come to be recognized. But the Brechtian mix of realist politics and broad comedy that Barber seems to be

[3] Ibid. 192.
[4] See W. Farnham, *The Medieval Heritage of Elizabethan Tragedy* (Oxford, 1956).
[5] Barber, Shakespeare's *Festive Comedy*, p. 217.

asking for takes us far from the Shakespearian mode in history. Shakespeare, more even-handedly than Brecht, allows that the glamour and excitement of power displayed, no less than comic deflation of the mechanisms needed to produce it, are integral to a true image of power. To demystify its existence, by giving private values the capacity to define it, denatures political truth, and also takes away the focus that allows political history to be effectively theatrical. Falstaff's relation to the Lord Chief Justice may well remind us of Adzak's relation to justice in *The Caucasian Chalk Circle*. Adzak, like Falstaff, is disorderly, drunken, and lecherous; but his selectively exploitative regime (and he is given a genuine regime) makes room for love and fun and creativity inside a society still smarting under the formalities of protocol, highlighting proletarian values held to have historical meaning. Adzak's holiday regime is offered as an imperfect model derived from true human instincts, with the justifying possibility that these instincts can one day be given a correct political embodiment. But a holiday with Falstaff is not even a potential alternative to the Lancastrian situation; it is merely parasitic upon it. The comedy he offers is antipolitical; we admire him as the Houdini of political life: constantly drawn towards the glamour of political importance and constantly having to perform miracles of escapism from the knowledge of his own political irrelevance. We are invited to enjoy him, not to consider joining him.

Falstaff's relation to Hal (as against Hal's to Falstaff) is often described as 'love'. When the newly crowned Henry rejects him, his heart, we are told, 'is fracted and corroborate'. Perhaps we should remember who tells us this (Pistol) and make appropriate allowance. Certainly the parasitic relation between Falstaff and Hal seems to demand that we see it in less sentimental terms. For the centre of their relationship is not attachment, but competition; not competition for power, for that is pre-empted in the play, but competition for audience response. They live together in a world in which opposite possibilities continually coexist; the play provides no secure spaces in which Hal can ignore comedy or Falstaff escape politics. In the famous episode of the knocking on the door (Part I, II. iv), the inn is invaded by the messengers of the King and appropriate political judgement is passed on its status as a sanctuary for enjoyment. At Shrewsbury Hal is both contemptuous of Falstaff's frivolity and responsive to his jokes. Comedy and history, the low and the high angles of viewpoint, the politically generalized and the comically private—all of these dichotomies belong in a situation that makes their elements both contradictory and inseparable. Each tries to occupy the other's space, the Prince seeking to rewrite the private behaviours of individuals (such as Francis the drawer) as political copy, Falstaff aiming to set up familiarity and charm as values that are vital to the political process. The estrangement or rejection at the end of Part II perhaps ought to be seen as a necessary loss for both parties, in a situation where personal loss is the inevitable price of power. But of course it is hard to take this quite even-handedly when one party can use the estrangement as a gateway to glamour and success, while the other must retreat from it into meaninglessness and death. But in a history play, the situation that *Henry IV* has set up cannot end otherwise.

Though *Henry IV* appears to be exemplary for the later Elizabethan history plays in which a pattern of English history is presented inside a comic plot structure, it does not follow that its complex and subtle form could provide a pattern for successful imitation. It should certainly be seen as part of a broadly based movement. Henslowe's Diary for 1598 and the years following records a continuous production of history plays. In 1598 we have *1 and 2 Earl Godwin and his three sons*, also known as *The Welshman's Prize* (*Drayton, Wilson, *Chettle, *Dekker), *The Famous Wars of Henry I and the Prince of Wales* (Drayton, Chettle, Dekker), *Pierce of Exton* (Drayton, Wilson, Chettle, Dekker), *The Funeral of Richard Cœur de Lion* (Drayton, Chettle, Munday, Wilson), *The Downfall and Death of Robert, Earl of Huntingdon* (Chettle and Munday). In 1599 we have *2 Henry Richmond* (Wilson), *The Spencers* (Chettle and *Porter), *Robert II, King of Scots* (Chettle, Dekker, *Jonson), *1 Sir John Oldcastle* (Drayton, *Hathway, Munday, Wilson), *William Long[sword]* (Drayton). Thereafter the tide begins to recede: in 1600 we hear of *Owen Tudor* (Drayton, Munday, Hathway, Wilson), and *2 Sir John Oldcastle*. In 1601 there is *The Rising of Cardinal Wolsey* (Drayton, Chettle, Munday, Smith), *The Life of Cardinal Wolsey* (Chettle), and *The Conquest of Spain by John of Gaunt* (Hathway, Rankins); in 1602, *1 and 2 Lady Jane* (Chettle, Dekker, Heywood, Smith, *Webster), and *Malcolm, King of Scots* (? Charles Massey). Henslowe's record stops shortly afterwards, but no other source suggests that the tide of history plays ever turned back.

The most interesting text to survive from this group of Henslowe plays is *The First Part of the True and Honourable History of the life of Sir John Oldcastle, the Good Lord Cobham*, for which the authors were paid ten pounds on 16 October 1599, and then another ten shillings ('as a gift') somewhere between 1 and 8 November of the same year. The first payment included an 'earnest on the second part for the use of the company' and between 19 and 26 December a further four pounds was disbursed 'to pay Master Drayton for the second part of Sir John Oldcastle'. Properties were bought for the second part in March 1600, so it seems that the play was performed. Clearly there was also an intention to print it, for the Stationers' Register records on 11 August 1600: 'Thomas Pavier: Entered for his copies . . . the first part of the history of the life of Sir John Oldcastle, Lord Cobham. Item: the second part of the history of Sir John Oldcastle, Lord Cobham, with his martyrdom'. But there is no trace of any such publication.

The auspices of *Oldcastle* are unusually clear and they point to a situation of inter-theatre rivalry and political involvement that might well be present in other cases. But there, lacking evidence, conjecture is liable to be mere self-indulgence. In this case the political motive-force derives from a definable source, from the powerful Brooke family, the Lords Cobham, who counted Oldcastle among their distinguished ancestors. As Chambers says: 'Clearly the play was an answer to *Henry IV*, in which Sir John Falstaff was originally Sir John Oldcastle.'[6] The clarity that is available leaves, of course, a number of further questions in still deeper shadow. Shakespeare, we know, changed the historical Oldcastle into the unhistorical Falstaff. But why did he ever think he would be able to represent this nobly connected Protestant martyr as a 'pampered glutton' and get away with it? E. A. J. Honigmann has suggested that Shakespeare wrote thus because he 'wanted to amuse Essex,

[6] Chambers, iii. 307. David B. McKeen, *The Memory of Honour: The Life of William Brooke, Lord Cobham* (2 vols.; Salzburg, 1968), gives the fullest extant account of Cobham's life; he quotes Richard James's preface to the *Legend and Defence of the Noble Knight and Martyr, Sir John Oldcastle* (1625), where the change in the play is referred to 'offence being worthily taken by personages descended from his [Oldcastle's] title, as peradventure by many others also who ought to have him in honourable memory'. John Weever in his *The Mirror of Martyrs* (1601) makes the production of Shakespeare's play a symptom of modern degeneracy: 'O times untaught, men scorners of sound teaching, | Lovers of plays, and loathers of preaching.'

Southampton, and their friends'.[7] Certainly we know that Cobham and Essex were enemies,[8] but public intervention in such great matters seems an improbable piece of boldness for a mere playwright. Was he then operating under the protection of his own patron, George Carey, the second Baron Hunsdon? The Carey family's hold on the office of Lord Chamberlain had been interrupted by the appointment of Cobham to that office in 1596; and this seems to have made the situation of Shakespeare's company somewhat perilous.[9] And what was the role of the Henslowe company's patron, whose name proudly adorns the title-page of the Oldcastle play: 'the right honourable the Earl of Nottingham, Lord High Admiral of England'? We know that his daughter married Henry, Lord Cobham, in 1599. Were both plays promoted by political faction, or one, or neither? Probably we shall never know. Fortunately, the answers to such questions are likely to be rather marginal to the issues of literary criticism, which must be concerned more with what authors made out of the political potential than with the situation itself.

At least we can say that in the Admiral's play we have the Oldcastle that the Brooke family would like, specifically set against the Oldcastle–Falstaff that Shakespeare had concocted and the Chamberlain's Men performed. The Prologue to *Oldcastle* spells out the contrast:

> The doubtful title (gentlemen) prefixed
> Upon the argument we have in hand
> May breed suspense and wrongfully disturb
> The peaceful quiet of your settled thoughts.
> To stop which scruple let this brief suffice:
> It is no pampered glutton we present,
> Nor aged counsellor to youthful sin,
> But one whose virtue shone above the rest,
> A valiant martyr and a virtuous peer

---

[7] E. A. J. Honigmann, 'Sir John Oldcastle: Shakespeare's Martyr', in J. W. Mahon and T. A. Pendleton (eds.), *Fanned and Winnowed Opinions: Essays Presented to Harold Jenkins* (London, 1987), 127–8. McKeen's discussion, Honigman's principal source, is sceptical of such explanations.

[8] See e.g. J. S. Neale, *The Elizabethan House of Commons* (London, 1949), 214–15; McKeen, *Memory of Honour, passim.*

[9] See the letter from Nashe to William Cotton: 'the players . . . however in their old lord's time they thought their state settled, it is now so uncertain they cannot build upon it' (McKerrow, v. 194).

In whose true faith and loyalty expressed
Unto his sovereign and his country's weal
We strive to pay that tribute of our love
Your favours merit. Let fair truth be graced,
Since forged invention former time defaced.

The opening lines here imply that this matter is dangerous, and that the audience might well be disturbed to find themselves involved in the political issue raised by the name Oldcastle; but on this occasion they can be reassured. This is no 'forged' slander of a nobleman but a 'fair truth' that is safe to behold because it is both 'true and honourable' as the text says, confirming the standard virtue of noble inheritance and also presenting accurate history.[10]

Oldcastle locates its history in a historical moment that would have been very difficult for the creator of Falstaff to deal with—in the period immediately after the accession of Henry V, when the new king is consolidating his disturbed realm in preparation for the expedition to France. This is precisely the moment at which Shakespeare calls time out; 2 Henry IV ends with Henry's repudiation of his riotous followers, but also with his promise to reinstate them if they too can reform and join the new world he is creating. The epilogue tells us that Falstaff will in fact be a part of that new world though not how the necessary transformation will be achieved; but when Henry V starts, all that we hear about him is how he has died. The minor rioters, Pistol and Bardolph, are present in the new play, but only to be swallowed and spewed out by the new morality. And that process would, we must suppose, have faced even greater difficulty with the bulk of Falstaff. The moral stance of The Famous Victories, which Shakespeare has kept somewhere in his sights throughout the Henry IV plays, is specifically repudiated. But, as the Henslowe play tells it, Falstaff was never more than the shadow of a historical ghost anyway. In Act III we hear how the Admiral's Sir John (the thieving priest of Wortham) fell into his evil ways: he was himself set upon and robbed by the wild prince 'when that foul villainous guts that led him to all that roguery was in's company' (III. iv. 103–5). All that belongs to the

---

[10] It is one of the paradoxes of this situation that the play of Oldcastle is most available in the modern world under the rubric of 'written by William Shakespeare'—an attribution added to the second Quarto, dated 1600, but in fact printed in 1619 as part of a scheme to produce a collected Shakespeare out of material already in the publishers' control.

past (Falstaff is now too fat to mount a horse), but it is a past that *Oldcastle*, unlike *Henry V*, need not repudiate. The technique here is rather to develop that history, as if chronologically, into a new key in which religion (a dramaturgical absence in *Henry IV*) has become a central factor. The new 'Sir John' is not simply a priest who has to steal in order to support his wench ('Doll'), his drinking, and his dicing, his clerical activities—'tithes, offerings, christenings, weddings, burials' (IV. i. 70–1)—being insufficient. More integrally, he is seen as representative of the whole popular life 'of the old church . . . swear, drink ale, kiss a wench, go to mass, eat fish all Lent and fast Fridays with cakes and wine, fruit and spicery, shrive me of my old sins afore Easter and begin new afore Whitsuntide' (IV. iii. 139–43). This is a world in which service books are given the same status as 'Bevis of Hampton, Owlglass, The Friar and the Boy, Elinor Rumming, Robin Hood' (IV. iii. 168–70)—works of popular superstition and credulity, regularly thought in Elizabethan times to have been written by 'idle friars and wanton canons'.[11]

In this context the role of Oldcastle as Protestant nobleman and martyr serves as a focus for the intertwined issues of politics and religion.[12] He thus raises a problem that was central to the Tudor state: can one combine loyalty to the sovereign with liberty of conscience? Shakespeare presents the issue in the speech of no less an authority than Henry V himself: 'every subject's duty is the king's', he tells Williams on the night before Agincourt, 'but every subject's soul is his own' (IV. i. 176–7). But Shakespeare makes this as a personal point; he does not develop the paradox in action. *Oldcastle* is less subtle and more dogged (more tied, we might say, to Foxe's *Book of Martyrs*). The inability of the bad old system to allow appeal from the bishops to the king is presented as the basic cause of the loyal but anti-papal Oldcastle's misfortunes. The 'Bishop of Rochester'—historically speaking Thomas Arundel, Archbishop of Canterbury—is a malignant heresy hunter in a mode we can recognize from later portrayals of the sixteenth-century bishops Bonner and Gardner, memorably presented in Foxe as

---

[11] Roger Ascham, *The Scholemaster*, ed. Edward Arber (London, 1927), 80.

[12] The religio-political implications are made evident in Father Parsons's *A Treatise of the Three Conversions of England* (1603–4), pt. iii, where he argues, against Foxe, that Oldcastle was 'a ruffian knight, as all England knoweth, and commonly brought in by comedians on their stages' (see Chambers, *William Shakespeare* (2 vols.; Oxford, 1930), ii. 213).

scapegoats for the religious traumas of the mid-sixteenth century, and therefore as the enemies of God-given royalty.

The *Oldcastle* authors execute a clever balancing act between their two main sources, Foxe and Holinshed. In Foxe, Oldcastle is a proto-martyr of the Tudor religious settlement, and Henry V, by his reluctance to intervene in the religious quarrel, is responsible for his death. In Holinshed, and even more in the play, Henry is cleared of responsibility: plagued by treason, he lacks clear evidence of Oldcastle's innocence in secular matters. Henslowe's authors contrive to set the free-conscienced Oldcastle not only against the bishops but equally against the politically disruptive lollardy of Sir Roger Acton and his heterogeneous crew of rebels. In this middle-class version of a revolution from below and also in its baronial counterpart, the dynastic plot of Cambridge, Scroop, and Grey, it is expected that Oldcastle must move from anti-bishop to anti-king. But in his exemplary role as a loyal Tudor Protestant, he refuses to join the rebels. It is he who reveals the Cambridge plot to the king. But Henry is unable to give full attention to the truth about Oldcastle that is in front of him. Concerned above all with his expedition to France, he leaves the church hierarchy free to exploit its medieval powers. Part I ends with a sixteenth-century equivalent of the modern film's car chase: Oldcastle, his loyal wife, and his resourceful servant escape through a bewildering series of low-life situations and disguises until, at the assizes in Hereford (mirroring the location of the opening scene), they are enabled to plead their case under quasi-Elizabethan secular law. Concealing their names, they avoid the issue of heresy and rest their defence on the factual evidence of their doings as 'John of Lancaster and Joan, his wife'. And the secular law saves them, allowing them to escape into Wales under the protection of Lord Powis (another Lollard peer, whose life had been spared at the instance of Oldcastle). Presumably Part II carried the action from this point through Powis's subsequent betrayal of Oldcastle and so to the martyrdom. It seems like enough therefore that the two-part structure had much the same downfall-and-death shape (in which the hero escapes disaster by extraordinary luck at the end of Part I, only to repeat the trajectory in Part II, this time failing to extricate himself) as in Chettle and Munday's *Huntingdon* plays and Chapman's *Byron*. In this as in so many other matters, Shakespeare's *Henry IV* may be thought to provide the originary impulse. Of course, when the 'hero' is Falstaff, the evasion of disaster at the end of Part I has a very different relation to the final rejection from that found in these other plays.

Sir John Oldcastle is a valuable introduction to Shakespeare's play of *Henry V* (1599), for it allows us to see the ambiguities and pitfalls that appear as soon as one considers its political content with a sophistication beyond that of *The Famous Victories*. Shakespeare's *Henry V* is, in fact, a more radical rewriting of the *Henry IV* story than is the professedly opposition play, for *Oldcastle* takes over the picture of the national life that it finds in *Henry IV* even as it tries to set the record straight. Of course *Henry V* is a continuation, not a rewriting. But it is a continuation that, as it looks back in time, abolishes rather than preserves the comedy of national life enacted in *Henry IV*. Shakespeare takes pains to suggest a seamless continuity, particularly in the final prophecy given to Prince John (the future Duke of Bedford):

> I will lay odds that ere this year expire,
> We bear our civil swords and native fire,
> As far as France.

(V. v. 105–7)

But at a deeper level the continuity is a rejection. The national life of *Henry IV* was represented as, throughout, a struggle to maintain the 'natural' historical system against comic individualistic disorder (whether in Falstaff or Glendower). Suddenly, at the beginning of *Henry V*, we are told that

> Never King of England
> Had nobles richer and more loyal subjects

(I. ii. 126–7)

and that

> those that were your father's enemies
> Have steeped their galls in honey, and do serve you
> With hearts create of duty and of zeal.

(II. ii. 29–31)

It is by no means clear how this national unity has been achieved, unless politics has simply dissolved in personal charisma. Such statements must of course be taken inside context; the afflatus of the

French campaign is such that national cohesion must be supposed to have become (by a parallel to the King's conversion) a new national characteristic. As we have noticed before, the king who leads his army abroad is regularly represented as a king who has no problems at home. Initially there are realistic thoughts of Scottish sneak attacks, but they are irrelevant thoughts: the Scotsman, as well as the Welsh and the Irish, turns up in Henry's army as part of a wholly integrated national force.

Political understanding in *Henry V* demands a very different response from that found in any preceding history play by Shakespeare. In *Henry IV* no less than *Henry VI* the central political problem is to formulate a way of balancing incompatible ambitions. But here, as recurrently in post-1596 history plays, the political issue emerges most forcefully as a personal rather than a national problem, focused on the way politics is perceived rather than the way it exists. Even in a scene that most strongly reminds us of the political issues of these earlier plays, the detection of the conspirators Cambridge, Scroop, and Grey, the matter is so handled that the dynastic elements (that would have been central in an earlier treatment) are subordinated. Cambridge denies that French gold was the cause of his treachery; but we are not told what Holinshed reveals: that Cambridge's plan was to put the legitimate Mortimer on the throne so that his own heir (the future Duke of York) could succeed the childless Mortimer. But this is not the central issue as Shakespeare tells it. The King's characteristically iterative speech allots nine lines to Cambridge and Grey; the next fifty concern the personal relationship between Henry and Scroop and bewail the difficulty of probing beneath the rhetoric of friendship to uncover the reality of personal trust. Even in this centrally political situation the accent is personal.

It may seem strange to speak about *Henry V* as a 'personal' play. The standard opinion is that Henry himself is but thinly endowed with personal feelings and that this play lacks the idiosyncratic richness of the usual Shakespearian experience. Henry is indeed narrowly committed to the task in hand; the personal feelings he expresses are all tied to the national situation. This, however, is only as much as to say that politics here do not define personal life from outside (as in *Richard II* and *Edward II*, for example); instead, political issues are represented as if they belong naturally inside the King's personal and emotional outlook. This change of focus involves a change of rhetoric. The King is given a spectrum of modes of persuasion: peremptory to ambassadors, exhortatory to the army, contemplative in soliloquy, bantering to Katherine, pious when appropriate, earnestly prosaic to the soldiers. The problem for character study is to see how these various address systems belong together, to imagine the person they notionally define. And this does indeed create an interpretative problem. But the difficulty does not infringe the fact that each of these rhetorical modes works as a personal dialect and by this means achieves political power over the person addressed, whether that be Bedford or Gloucester, Fluellen, Katherine, or Scroop, or the Dauphin. The war in France is a political event, but it is handled as if that was the same as a personal quest—to teach the Dauphin a lesson, to show how wrong are those who judge the King by his 'wilder days', to reveal how he embodies the spirit of England. Of Henry IV's advice to his son that he should 'busy giddy minds | With foreign quarrels' *Henry V* reveals no memory. The political interpretation of the war is handed over to the Archbishop of Canterbury, who represents the King himself as naïvely unaware of such a dimension, judging national issues only by the non-political standards of propriety and honour.

Henry V can thus be seen as a history play that sets the directness, the innocent self-expression, the naïvety of 'God's soldier' against the deviousness and sophistication that belongs inescapably to his role as a political figure. Henry is sometimes compared to Tamburlaine, the great original of Elizabethan conqueror-heroes. But Tamburlaine drives politics in front of him; his rhetoric of power cannot be doubled as political calculation; its floodtide simply sweeps away differences of situation. Henry, however, is naturally attuned to each variation in his context, to the English as to the Anglo-French situation and to the demands of a religiosity which justifies his success not by Tamburlainian defiance of God but by equally spectacular humility before Him: *non nobis Domine . . . sed nomini tuo da gloriam.*

The presence of this central dialectic (or contradiction) between personal naïvety (deriving from *The Famous Victories*) and sophisticated political calculation may have provided Shakespeare with the impulse to invent a unique technical characteristic in this play: an epic chorus that not only fills out the narrative detail of a single developing story (whose single-mindedness supports narrative continuity) but interprets the action from a heroic (not to say hero–worshipping) point of view.[13] To imagine a *Henry V* that fulfils everything that the chorus describes, and omits everything that the chorus does not mention, is to imagine a very different play—one in which 'the mirror of all Christian kings' provides the only focus and from which Fluellen and Canterbury (the second and third speaking parts), Ely, Pistol, Nym, the Dauphin, the English as well as the French nobility have all disappeared. What the play as written, complete with chorus, gives us is a continuous dialectic between the king and the nation (his personal 'body' and his national role), epic and history, heroism and fact, interpretation and truth (interpretation telling us that truth is insufficient; truth telling us that interpretation is suspect).

The conflicts that are recurrent in history plays are here represented formally, as elements in structure rather than subject matter. Sometimes the contradiction is obvious and perhaps meant to be so. Thus at the beginning of Act II we are told that

> Now all the youth of England are on fire
>
> .   .   .   .
>
> . . . and honour's thought
> Reigns solely in the breast of every man.
>
> (Act II, Chorus, ll. 1–4)

Straight away we are introduced not to the 'youth of England' but to Nym, Bardolph, Pistol, and the quondam Mrs Quickly, and the fight that results has nothing to do with England's honour but is entirely concerned with the possession of the unsavoury hostess and her tavern revenues. Is this scene designed to suggest that the war in France is *really* the same kind of scramble for possession, however disguised by rhetoric and posturing? Not only the chorus but the play fails to say so.

Shakespeare's method seems designed to point to such questions rather than answer them. The rhetorics employed expose the too easy assumption of a coherent common language which holds a nation together and defines its members in their opposition to foreigners. It is clear that the theatrical aggression of Nym and

---

[13] The Quarto version of *Henry V* (1600; 1602, [1619]), which omits all the choruses, is usually supposed to represent a version of the play shortened and simplified for provincial touring—see Stanley Wells and Gary Taylor, *Modernizing Shakespeare's Spelling: With Three Studies in the Text of 'Henry V'* (Oxford, 1979). One cannot say that the omissions in the Quarto make the story incoherent. Interestingly, however, by removing the dialectic they make it a work much closer to *The Famous Victories of Henry V*.

Pistol inflates them beyond sustainable reality.[14] But is the case of more exalted speech patterns any different? Our response to poetic eloquence suggests that it is; here, we may believe, we find universal values. But the dialectic shows that even the golden poetry of the chorus has its leaden underside; it does not, however, suggest that we can simply reverse the valuations.

The action of Act III, Scene ii, contradicts the chorus from a different perspective. The chorus does speak of the treachery of Cambridge, Scroop, and Grey, but defines their fault as their failure to be 'kind and natural' (that is, to belong to the family of Englishmen). They accepted money from France and thus they are denationalized. But once again the reality of the action is very different and much more complicated. As I have noted above, the central issue addressed in the scene is that in the interactions of life (as against the privileged overview) there is no way of telling what another person's words mean, knowing who is the traitor, who the friend. Or, again, we may take the account of the night before Agincourt as it is presented by the chorus and as it appears in the action. The chorus tells us how

> The royal captain of this ruined band
> Walking from watch to watch, from tent to tent,
>
> . . . .
>
> . . . visits all his host,
> Bids them good morrow with a modest smile
> And calls them brothers, friends, and countrymen.
> Upon his royal face there is no note
> How dread an army hath enrounded him;
> Nor doth he dedicate one jot of colour
> Unto the weary and all-watched night;
> But freshly looks, and overbears attaint
> With cheerful semblance and sweet majesty;
> That every wretch, pining and pale before,
> Beholding him, plucks comfort from his looks.
>
> (Act IV, Chorus, ll. 29–42)

---

[14] That these dialects do not derive from any identified community but are appropriated from self-pleasing stereotypes (play scraps and so on) may provide us with a distinction that allows us to separate Bardolph and company from the regional soldiers in Henry's army, Fluellen, MacMorris, and Jamie. The members of the latter group are able to subdue their individual touchiness about nationality and its accompanying idiolect to the larger purpose of the anti-French campaign, as separate elements in a common enterprise—though MacMorris's splenetic 'What ish my nation' (III. ii. 122) indicates how thin is the surface of commonality.

All the energy in this version comes from the royal 'sun'; no one talks back. How different is the enactment of the scene, showing the difficulty and embarrassment of the deroyalized Henry as he tries to argue down the unbemused understanding of the situation displayed by his common soldiers, finally being obliged to quarrel when he can no longer argue.[15]

To look at *Henry V* in terms of its position in the historical sequence Shakespeare wrote may allow us to see the dilemma of the hero in the history play in a context large enough to explain Shakespeare's move, after *Henry V*, from history to tragedy. The four plays running from *1 Henry VI* to *Richard III* draw on a pattern that is so deeply embedded in Western culture that it can be taken for nature. We know the pattern best in the Christian story of Paradise, Fall, corruption, redemption, new paradise. In the history of Shakespeare's first tetralogy, Paradise is represented by the reign of Henry V, remembered but not recoverable. Inside the sequence we live in the fallen world, which pursues its predetermined course, slaughtering its saints and deepening its corruption, until, in the reign of Antichrist Richard III, signs mark the imminence of the Tudor Apocalypse (initiated but not enacted). The second tetralogy, *Richard II*, *1 Henry IV*, *2 Henry IV*, *Henry V*, follows much the same pattern. The first play in the sequence evokes the paradisal reign of Edward III; the feudal forms of that golden age are still in place at the beginning of Richard's reign, but they cannot be realized by Richard. As the sequence develops we are again traversing divided counsels and uncertain aims, culminating this time in personal betrayals (Prince John's deception of the rebels at Gaultree forest and Falstaff's exploitation of the foolish justice in Gloucestershire) rather than political anarchy—portents seen now in a comic, rather than a tragic, perspective. And so with *Henry V* we come back again to the point represented in the earlier tetralogy by the accession of Henry VII. But with a difference. Henry VII is required only to make a stiff pious speech and gesture forwards to the good times to come and the pattern, in formal

---

[15] Michael Goldman (in *Shakespeare and the Energies of Drama* (Princeton, 1972), 68) has made the very relevant point that the sticking place for the soldiers in this scene is not loyalty to the public role of the king ('I determine to fight lustily for him' (IV. i. 189)), but comes when Henry tries to transfer that loyalty to the personal aspect of his royal body— the area of his private choices (whether or not he is the sort of *man* who will refuse to be ransomed). This seems to the king himself to be an integral part of his royal nature, but the soldiers think of it as quite different.

terms even if not in terms of poetic assent, is fulfilled. But Henry V has to live through his own play at the same time as he completes the larger pattern. He is obliged to display the things that Henry VII can keep in decent obscurity. Apocalypse and reality compete for our attention, and the result is (to say the least) strained and difficult.

This question returns us again to the problem of the chorus. Should we see the chorus as Shakespeare's answer to the divided role that Henry's position in the tetralogy requires him to play? Does its rhetoric enact the mythic pattern while the play proper deals with the contingent world of daily life, the fallen world one might say, which persists at the same time as the Second Coming is proclaimed? Certainly the chorus has the effect of isolating the ideal Henry from the muddying and muddling complexities that attend on any attempt to render general experience in idealizing terms. The final chorus allows that the cycle does not end here. And its next turn will show us not the rule of the saints but the reign of Henry VI,

> Whose state so many had the managing
> That they lost France and made his England bleed:
> Which oft our stage hath shown.
>
> (Epilogue, ll. 11–13)

The chorus, it seems, also knows that the ideal is contingent and that our acceptance of this play must be associated with our knowledge of the one that followed in time.

When Shakespeare gave Henry V his embarrassing experience as a disguised king he was no doubt drawing on the audience's acquaintance with stories like that of George a Green. The disguise topos fits naturally into the idea that history is not simply a series of political manipulations but rather a demonstration of the continuity of basic (male) national character, joining the king to the lowliest of his subjects in the pursuit of their common national enterprise. Hence, of course, its recurrent military flavour. Both Edward I and the kings of *George a Green* have to fight with commoners before they can establish, in terms of their shared humanity, the respect that is due to them as the leaders of a nation in arms. For the soldier, 'jealous of honour, sudden and quick in quarrel, | Seeking the bubble reputation | Even in the cannon's mouth', perpetually violent in defence of his individual as well as his national dignity, is both the most treasured and the most difficult of the king's subjects. The figure of the unbemused and independent commoner in many of these later histories might be thought to be a representation of that natural resistance to imposed order that appears earlier in the political histories of an unruly baronage.[16] As a personal solution to a political issue, the mingling of the disguised king with his independent subjects provides an effective but rather sentimental conclusion, which Shakespeare alone among his contemporaries seems willing to question. Henry hopes to find that the soldiers admire him *as a person*; but 'that is more than [they] know'; when Williams learns that the soldier who challenged him was the king, he does not (as in the earlier romanticized encounters, or like Black Will in *When You See Me, You Know Me*, or Hobs the tanner in *Edward IV*) accept the heartening conclusion that the king is a good fellow, a lusty gentleman. Instead he shows resentment that he was imposed upon by a faked show of equality and spurns Fluellen's financial congratulation. And Shakespeare likewise seems to be questioning the assumption of history-as-comedy that king and commons can really be as one. When Henry V, like his father before him (and his son after him), complains that he cannot enjoy the life or sleep of a commoner, Shakespeare allows us to see the factitiousness as well as the loneliness involved. The comedy that *Henry V* makes possible (and the play does end, very specifically, as a comedy) is the high comedy of political success. When Shakespeare returns to the history-play genre, in *Henry VIII*, he specifically rejects the king-as-commoner possibilities that Samuel *Rowley had exploited in *When You See Me, You Know Me* (see below, pp. 265–7).

Sentimental History

The attractions of the history play did not, of course, simply wither on the tree because Master Shakespeare was already shifting his gaze. I have already spoken of the busy-ness of Henslowe's team. Probably the document that shows us most interestingly which way the wind was blowing is *1 and 2 Edward IV*, usually attributed

---

[16] Cf. Louis B. Wright, *Middle Class Culture in Elizabethan England* (Chapel Hill, NC, 1935), 621–7.

to Heywood (1592×1599).[17] The play was entered and printed in 1599 (five times reprinted), with the title: *The First and Second Parts of King Edward the Fourth. Containing his merry pastime with the tanner of Tamworth, as also his love to fair Mistress Shore, her great promotion, fall and misery, and lastly the lamentable death of both her and her husband. Likewise the besieging of London by the Bastard Falconbridge and the valiant defence of the same by the Lord Mayor and the citizens. As it hath divers times been publicly played by the Right Honourable the Earl of Derby his servants.*

The historical events described here overlap with those found in Shakespeare's *3 Henry VI* and *Richard III*, but the focus (as will be evident from the title-page) is on that slice from the history of those times that Shakespeare chose to ignore[18]—the dozen or so years of Edward's undisturbed power, between the Battle of Tewkesbury in 1470 and his death in 1483. Not that the author is particularly anxious to stress the dynastic issues even of this period; the political events that are referred to are handled casually and out of focus. Thus at one point Edward, while frolicking in the country-side, receives a letter from his brother Richard telling him that old King Henry VI has died in the Tower. It is welcome news, of course; but Edward is more immediately interested in his playful relationship with the tanner of Tamworth. A little later we are told that Edward has altered his decision to stay the night in the tanner's cottage and has ridden back to London:

> The occasion, Henry's death within the Tower,
> Of which the people are in sundry tales,
> Some thinking he was murdered, some again
> Supposing that he died a natural death.

> (p. 56)

But we hear no more of this. As the recipient of news says, 'well . . . that concerns not us'. In *Edward IV*, politics are perceived as a diversion from the real life that takes place in face-to-face contact between individuals. Even the King's power is seen as essentially personal; it is his jovial character rather than his activities that endears him to the nation.

---

[17] The earlier date depends on some perceived relation with *The Tanner of Denmark*, mentioned by Henslowe in 1592. I cannot see anything more than an adventitious connection, and so would prefer to put the play at the later end of the range.

[18] Cf. the case of *Oldcastle* (discussed p. 242).

Thus *Edward IV*, though it deals with materials that appear in Shakespeare's first tetralogy, treats them by methods that seem to have been learnt from the Henry IV and Henry V plays. *1 Edward IV* begins with a revolt against the new king's power, in the name of Henry VI, as *Henry IV* does in the name of Richard II. In reality, the dominating impulse in both cases is less to change the dynasty than to defend baronial power from the centralizing monarchy. In *Edward IV*, however, the revolt (led by Thomas Neville, the Bastard Falconbridge) lacks any believable political impetus. Falconbridge tells us that 'we do not rise like Tyler, Cade, or Straw', but his followers are in fact more like a mob than a faction:

> desperate, idle swaggering mates
> That haunt the suburbs in the time of peace
> And raise up alehouse brawls in the street.

> (i. 18)

Their central motive is to plunder the city, to shoe their horses with silver from Cheapside, to have a gold chain each, and to cut off the heads of all who ask for payment. And so it is fitting that their defeat is less a national event than an exhibition of the military importance of citizen virtue as in *Jack Straw*, treated above. We see order, system, discipline as more effective than swaggering militarism, in warfare as in life. The King arrives only when the London citizens have completed their work. Dynastic history has moved, it would seem, into its bourgeois phase.

If the beginning of *1 Edward IV* reminds us of the events of *1 Henry IV*, the beginning of the second part reminds us even more strongly of *Henry V*. Edward is now leading his army in France, claiming the throne as his dynastic right, prompted to this by Burgundy and the Constable of France. But the point of similarity, once established, is soon taken over by commercial rather than military initiatives. Lewis of France buys peace, Edward forgets his dynastic claim, and Burgundy and the Constable, who are concerned only for their own advantages, are squeezed dry between the two kings. Edward, as in the matter of Henry VI's death, moves quickly back to his personal pleasures, this time to the central issue of the play—the career of his celebrated mistress, Jane Shore. It is Jane Shore who provides the focal point for the divergent interests of this two-part structure. In the opening scenes of Part I she and her husband are leading members of the brave citizen resistance to Falconbridge. Her famous beauty also makes her one of the specific demands of the rebels. Shore is told to 'run, rascal, and fetch thy wife to our general presently'. But family loyalty, like the loyalty of apprentices to their masters, and like civic responsibility, is basic to the strength of the citizen army. Matthew Shore fights, he tells us:

> First to maintain King Edward's royalty,
> Next, to defend the city's liberty,
> But chiefly, Jane, to keep thee from the toil
> Of him that to my face did vow thy spoil.
> Had he prevailed, where then had been our lives?
> Dishonoured our daughters, ravished our fair wives,
> Possessed our goods and set our servants free.
> Yet all this nothing to the loss of thee.
>
> (pp. 23–4)

Even if the worst comes to the worst, Jane tells her husband, she is able to play the part of another Lucrece. As she is made to say, with rather too obvious irony:

> Jane will be thy honest, loyal, wife.
> The greatest prince the sun did ever see
> Shall never make me prove untrue to thee.
>
> (p. 24)

When 'the greatest prince' is the Shores' own prince, however, loyalty is divided, and Jane's promise that 'These hands shall make this body a dead corse | Ere force or flattery shall mine honour stain' gradually weakens into compliance, as Edward's erotic pressure and power of command combine to force her from the shop to the court.

As a history play in praise of the bourgeoisie, *Edward IV* is committed to a difficult ethical balance. Matthew Shore, that model citizen, cannot be represented as a contented cuckold—this is the role of the citizen in the anti-city plays put on by the boys' companies—and so his proper pride in himself makes self-imposed exile the only option available. Jane, too, must be given moral status: she is consistently shown as a fair penitent, as one whose 'success' is made bearable only by the good works she can perform through her influence on the King, sustaining the indigent, and rescuing the unjustly punished. And Edward is no less free from blame. His jolly, extroverted nature, enjoyment of power, appreciation of common physical existence, gives him the status of 'a frank franion, a merry companion and loves a wench well' (p. 44); and this makes him a preferable king to the 'advoutry' Henry VI. The handling of the alternative claims that Henry and Edward can make on the support of their subjects marks the distance of these later kings from the ideal of God's vicegerent upon earth, the consequent turn towards ethos, imperfect humanity, as the link that binds king to subject. When, in *Edward IV*, Richard seizes the throne from Edward's children, the focus is less on the slip from legality to illegality than on the human change from relaxation to fanaticism, as the generosity of outlook that allowed Jane Shore to break through legalism gives way to the narrow self-interest of Dr Shaw, Mrs Blague, Rufford—all taking their cue from Richard himself, but exemplified in this new world in domestic relationships rather than political struggle. The play ends with Jane and her husband composing a final tableau, reconciled in forgiveness at the point of death (as in Heywood's *A Woman Killed with Kindness*), holding hands over the coffin of Master Ayres who has been executed for helping Jane. The central figures being dead, the play can rush its political conclusion by drawing on the audience's knowledge of received history and Shakespeare's *Richard III*. The final speeches show us Buckingham's request for reward, Richard's refusal, and Buckingham's determination to 'fetch thee [Harry Richmond] home and seat thee in his throne' (p. 187). It is assumed that the prophecy requires no enactment. *Edward IV*'s focus on political history as backdrop to personal lives rather than independent subject matter can thus be preserved, without concealing the actual course of political events.

The centring of *Edward IV* on the martyr figure of Jane Shore points to a recurrent characteristic of later history plays. The virtuous female victim of the inhuman workings of the power system is shown in the young Princess Elizabeth in the first part of Heywood's *If You Know Not Me, You Know Nobody* and—with appropriate modifications—in the mature Elizabeth of Dekker's *The Whore of Babylon*, in Lady Jane Gray in Dekker's and Webster's *Sir Thomas Wyatt*, and in Katherine of Aragon in Shakespeare's *Henry VIII*. The complementary figure of the virtuous male martyr may well have appeared in the second part of *Sir John Oldcastle*— though Oldcastle (at least as he appears in the first part) is rather too self-confident and active to fit the stereotype precisely. Jane Gray's husband, Lord Guildford Dudley, youthful, innocent, trusting, is a better paradigm of the ethos given to the politically disadvantaged in these dramatizations of Tudor politics, which we can see further exemplified in the histories of *Thomas, Lord Cromwell*, *Sir Thomas More*, in the episodes of Buckingham and Cranmer in *Henry VIII*, and (by a final flowering) in the richly ambiguous career of Perkin Warbeck.

It is tempting to link the concentration on Tudor history in history plays written at the end of the sixteenth and the beginning of the seventeenth century to some relaxation of the rules forbidding dramatization of current politics. But for this we have no specific evidence. Certainly the dramatists seem to have taken the opportunity (perhaps created by the death of Elizabeth), though with appropriate tentativeness, focusing their material in personal rather than political terms, and everywhere endorsing the standard ideals of the Tudor state—self-sufficient nationalism, the rule of secular law, curtailment of ecclesiastical independence, loyalty to the crown. In these terms the martyr can be presented as an ideal figure of the Elizabethan present, trapped in the struggles of the recent past—particularly that recent struggle in which the current religious settlement was forged.

The famous History of Sir Thomas Wyatt: With the Coronation of Queen Mary and the Coming in of King Philip (1602×1607), said on the title-page to have been written by Dekker and Webster, is usually supposed to be a reported and abbreviated version of *1 and 2 Lady Jane*, for which, on 15 and 21 October 1602 (and again on 27 October—for a second part), Henslowe paid not only Dekker and Webster but also Heywood, Chettle, and Wentworth Smith. Henslowe was commissioning this play for Worcester's Men, performing at the Rose; by the time of the title-page of *Sir Thomas Wyatt* the company had been renamed 'The Queen's Majesty's Servants', and was now performing at the Curtain and the Boar's Head. These changes may have determined a rewrite. For all this confusion, *Sir Thomas Wyatt*, however, offers us a remarkably balanced and unconfused image of Marian politics as seen from an Elizabethan perspective. The structure combines two very different martyr plots: on the one hand, we have the innocent victim (Jane), on the other, the virtuously committed counsellor (Wyatt); on the one side, the passive female, on the other, the active male.

And each protagonist courts a different disaster: the representedly innocent Lady Jane (and the similarly innocent Guildford Dudley, her husband) are easily entrapped in baronial plots against Mary Tudor, the legitimate heir; Sir Thomas Wyatt supports Mary's accession but believes that he can 'rescue' her from her corrupt advisers.

The baronial ambition to turn a debated succession to the crown into a family advantage is handled in this play in very different terms from those we find in earlier histories, such as *Henry VI*, *Richard II*, and *King John*. In such plays legality was a desirable but transparent fiction; military power was the reality. But in this Tudor version, action waits until legality is assured. The limit this imposes on baronial energy can be seen in the dependence of Suffolk and Northumberland (fathers to Jane and Dudley) on the votes cast in the council. They claim that they are justified by an earlier vote; and so, when Sir Thomas Wyatt persuades the next council meeting that Mary Tudor is the legitimate heir, their whole enterprise falls to pieces. The claim that Suffolk and Northumberland thought their initial actions legitimate does not save them from the block, of course. Yet the very fact that it is put forward as a serious defence tells us that we are in a world where legality has become something more than the rhetoric of dynastic aspirants trading genealogies, has become indeed the touchstone of stability in a time when everything else (religion most particularly) is uncertain. Mary Tudor's repudiation of her oath that she will, as sovereign, respect freedom of worship, is presented, both here and in Heywood's *If You Know Not Me, You Know Nobody*, as a key instance of her unsuitability to rule as a legally constituted sovereign, in spite of her dynastic claim.

Wyatt's rebellion against Mary, when the marriage to Philip of Spain puts her beyond the reach of good counsel, seeks to rescue the sovereign from errors made primarily on religious rather than political grounds, and from advisers like Stephen Gardner, Bishop of Winchester, who is seen here, in the image that Foxe drew, as the relentless persecutor of true faith. But for all this religious sanction, Wyatt's rebellion, like Northumberland's, can only be a confused and half-hearted affair, broken by desertions and switches of loyalty; his execution is the logical end to a career in which religious and political ideals can find no constitutional expression; and so one must also regard the executions of Jane and Guildford, whose beauty, youthfulness, and love are qualities that exist only to be exploited by the society they live in. What we seem to have is a just image of a history too close to the lives of audience and author to be absorbed into a grand pattern, yet expressing problems too immediate and too important to be expressed merely as romantic fiction.

The title-page of *Sir Thomas Wyatt* tells its readers that the play will present *The Coronation of Queen Mary and the Coming-in of King Philip*. In fact, the extant text shows us neither of these events, though both are implicit in the dialogue. It may well be that *2 Lady Jane* showed them, and that they were cut out when the two parts were condensed into one, but remembered again when the title-page was devised. Thomas Heywood begins his *If You Know Not Me, You Know Nobody. Or The Troubles of Queen Elizabeth* (1603×1605) as if he was determined to recompense readers for the omission of this material from a play in which (possibly) he had been involved. Though in the main his story is a continuation of the history told in *Sir Thomas Wyatt*, the opening scene is patently devised as a recapitulation of the Lady Jane story. The standard opening gambit of a political discussion among courtiers tells us that 'concerning Wyatt and the Kentish rebels, their overthrow is past; the rebel dukes . . . each one had his merit' (ll. 22–6). Then Mary enters from her coronation; the promise to the Suffolk men that she would (if crowned) respect freedom of religious conscience is rehearsed (and repudiated) once again. We hear that Philip 'has landed at Southampton' (l. 139).

Heywood's theatrical purpose in giving us this information is not, of course, to remind us of *Sir Thomas Wyatt*, but to wind up the tensions that will drive his own story of 'the troubles of Queen Elizabeth'. Wyatt's rebellion is remembered so that Sir Henry Beningfield and Stephen Gardner (the principal villains of the piece) can argue that Elizabeth must have been a confederate in the plot, and therefore must be handled as an enemy. And it is this handling that forms the substance of Heywood's play.

Elizabeth is not (like Jane) a martyr characterized by innocent childishness and loving trust, but a potent political martyr, weakened by illness, fear, and ill-treatment, the object of unceasing plots to defame or murder her, but remaining constantly loyal and obedient to her sister the Queen, as the properly constituted authority. Her disengagement and obedience (here represented as true virtue, not, as among modern historians, as astute calculation) can only enrage Bedingfield and Gardner, who control Queen Mary's point of view; but the old nobility, Sussex and Howard, while they allow the necessity that the Queen should take all precautions, quickly detach themselves from the scenario of persecution and enlist the humanitarian support of King Philip, who is presented as a just and fair ruler. It is the intervention of the King (alerted by the sharp-minded Thomas Gresham) that finally saves Elizabeth's life and permits her to combine the roles of patient sufferer and saviour-in-waiting.

The relation of the two queens is presented as a fact of human nature rather than an issue of policy. Mary is an active figure of power, taking advice, giving orders, determined to defend her prerogative and cut off rebellion by instant punishment. Elizabeth is depicted as one whose values lie within (having no control of anything outside herself). As a symbol for the distressed nation, she is the natural object of identification and support by the humble in history (and the humble in the audience)—by the boy who brings her a nosegay (and is whipped for it) and by the villagers who ring the bells when she passes by (and are beaten).

The first part of *If You Know Not Me, You Know Nobody* was one of the most successful plays of the period, being printed eight times before the closing of the theatres (in 1605, 1606, 1608, 1610, 1613, 1623, 1632, and 1639). It was perhaps some premonitory sense of its power as a get-penny that persuaded Heywood to write and the publisher to register (in September 1605—three months after the entry for the first part) 'a book called the second part of If you know not me you know body [*sic*], with the building of the exchange'. The second part (1605) was printed in 1606 by the same publisher as for Part I: *The Second Part of, If You Know Not Me, You Know No Body. With the Building of the Royal Exchange: And the Famous Victory of Queen Elizabeth in the Year 1588*. The unsatisfactoriness of this as a title seems to be acknowledged by the substitution of a variant one in some copies of the original printing: *The Second Part of Queen Elizabeth's Troubles. Doctor Parry's Treasons: The Building of the Royal Exchange, and the Famous Victory in 1588. With the Humours of Hobson and Tawny-Coat*. This play was reprinted three times (1609, 1623, and 1633), twice with the original title-page and once with the revised one.

It is worthwhile lingering on these titles. Both versions indicate something of the pushed-together heterogeneity of Part II and the adventitious or catchpenny nature of its connection to Part I. The Prologue, first printed in Heywood's 1637 *Pleasant Dialogues and Dramas* and then in the 1639 quarto of Part I, speaks of two views of Elizabeth contained in the plays: 'In the one | A pitied lady: in the regal throne | A potent queen'. But in Part II as we have it Elizabeth has only a walk-on part. Two thousand lines pass before she makes her entrance, to open the Royal Exchange and knight Gresham; then she speaks twenty-eight lines and exits. Two hundred lines later she appears again and in sixty lines we see Dr Parry's attempt on her life. In spite of the calm benevolence with which Elizabeth handles this event, it probably qualifies as a 'trouble'. But it is the only one shown. The play ends with the Queen organizing the defeat of the Armada.[19] These royal events are, moreover, episodes detached from the main movement of the play; nothing in the plot requires their presence, nor does anything derive from them. It seems probable, as has been several times suggested, that the Queen Elizabeth episodes have been inserted into a pre-existing biographical play about Sir Thomas Gresham,[20] so that it could be given a 'Part II' billing and ride to popularity on the coat-tails of the first part.

Whatever the preconditions, there can be no dispute that the substance of the second part of *If You Know Not Me* is provided by the plot of Sir Thomas Gresham, heroic capitalist, and his scapegrace nephew John—for whom, we should note, Gresham is less a hero of commerce than a stereotypical usurer (who has 'cosen[ed] me of my patrimony' (ll. 170–1)). Hobson the haberdasher offers a rougher version of capitalist enterprise; his character seems to be modelled on that of Simon Eyre in Dekker's *The Shoemaker's Holiday*. Tawny-coat the pedlar works at the bottom of the system, but with same entrepreneurial pride and energy as sustains his betters. The interconnection of the comical activities of these characters creates an image of Elizabethan commerce as

[19] The probability that this Armada episode originally appeared at the end of the first part (and was performed in that shape up till 1633) has been argued with typical disengagement by Sir Walter Greg in his Malone Society Reprint of Part Two. A transfer of this kind would help to explain the disparity in the lengths of the two plays: Part One is 1,569 lines, Part Two is 2,925.

[20] Parallel in form to *Cromwell* and *Sir Thomas More* discussed below. A play called *The Life and Death of Sir Thomas Gresham, With the Building of the Royal Exchange* is mentioned in Beaumont's *Knight of the Burning Pestle* (1607×?1610).

the natural expression of English energy, pushing through Europe as far as Barbary. When Gresham's Royal Exchange is opened, the event is seen in an international context: Constantinople, Rome, Antwerp, Emden, Frankfurt, Venice provide the obvious comparisons, and 'a Russian Prince, the Emperor's ambassador' is brought into the picture as a further tribute to London's central position in world commerce. Considered as a history play, the second part of *If You Know Not Me* glorifies, we may say, this new mode of English conquest as an appropriately bourgeois alternative to feudal pride, now exemplified by the Spaniards. Middle-class comedy seems to be taking over from feudal English history as the motive force in national progress—as indeed it should do if history play-writing is itself a part of history.

Dekker's *The Whore of Babylon* (c.1606×1607), performed by 'the Prince's Servants', is a play with a considerable overlap in subject matter with the second part of *If You Know Not Me*: both plays concentrate on the Parry attempt to murder the Queen, and follow this by the speech at Tilbury and the defeat of the Armada. We know that Dekker and Heywood had been collaborating in the writing of history plays, and it has been plausibly conjectured that the shared historiographical work of that time[21] allowed Dekker to take over the 'regal-throne' aspect of Elizabeth's life that Heywood had promised but never produced, concentrating this time on the actual political activity of the Queen rather than her benign over-lordship of social and economic existence in the capital. External conditions may well have caused this change of focus. The Gunpowder Plot of 5 November 1605 catalysed a national mood of alarm and self-justification and that may have encouraged Dekker[22] to show the history of the 1580s from an angle very different from 2 *If You Know Not Me*.

I have noted above on several occasions the strong connection between these later history plays and the description of English national destiny that we find in Foxe's *Acts and Monuments of the English Votaries*. The notion of Truth that we find in Foxe is not that discussed in Chapter 5—a correspondence between the action

---

[21] Marianne G. Riely's elaborately annotated edition (New York, 1980) argues this (pp. 10–12), and points to the well-documented historical expertise of another common collaborator, Michael Drayton.
[22] Riely (ibid. 19–21) points to Dekker's *The Double PP* (1606), clearly a reaction to the Gunpowder Plot and a work with many parallels in *The Whore of Babylon*.

described and the historical evidence provided by witnesses and documentary detail. The truth that is relevant in Foxe is that of direct revelation of divine meaning in history. And so at the beginning of *The Whore of Babylon* 'Truth' is discovered asleep in the reign of Mary Tudor. When Mary dies, Truth removes the blindfolds from the eyes of the English councillors, who receive 'the book'[23] and are now enabled to know the meaning of what is happening to the country. Dekker's play probably marks the fullest dramatic expression of this apocalyptic political vision, not because it borrows most heavily from Foxe's text but because its structure is based most completely on Foxe's sense of English history as a religious unfolding. This basic vision has to be, of course, manifested through a theatrical technique that is uniquely old-fashioned for its period. Where *Sir Thomas Wyatt* and *If You Know Not Me* offer the spectators quasi-realistic representations of the persons and events dealt with, and allow the meanings of these events to emerge indirectly, *The Whore of Babylon* uses the action on the stage as a direct statement of meaning, being 'Truth' in Foxe's rather than the documentary sense.

Spenser's *The Faerie Queene* (especially Book I) provides Dekker with the fundamental metaphors for his play.[24] England is a 'Fairyland' fought over by ideological opponents—on one side the Fairy Queen/Titania/Elizabeth/Una/the Anglican Church, on the other side The Whore of Babylon/'The Empress'/the Pope/Duessa/. In Spenser these grand polarities produce separate chivalric adventures of several different kinds, with no clear chronological connection between them. Dekker's action, however, remains tied to a historical process of plottings, subversions, attack, and defence.[25]

---

[23] Elizabeth showed herself well attuned to these resonances. In her coronation procession she responded to the image of *veritas temporis filia* by herself assuming the role of Truth and announcuing that 'time hath brought me hither'. When the figure of Truth presented her with a bible in English inscribed *verbum veritatis*, she kissed the book and laid it to her heart. See John Nichols, *Progresses of Queen Elizabeth* (3 vols.; London, 1823), i. 48–51.

[24] Behind both Spenser and Dekker lies the Book of Revelation.

[25] He obviously feels the need to justify himself for breaches in chronology of a kind standard in history plays. In the Epistle to the Reader he says: 'I may, by some more curious in censure than sound in judgment, be critically taxed that I falsify the account of time, and set not down occurents according to their true succession.' He replies: 'I write as a poet, not as an historian, and . . . these two do not live under one law' (cf. Marston on *Sophonisba*). Judith Doolin Spikes (in 'The Jacobean History Play', *Renaissance Drama*, NS 8 (1977), 139) speaks of the 1607 Quarto as 'a reading text prepared by Dekker'; his unusual sensitivity to 'truth' may be a mark less of the dramatist than of the historical polemicist.

In Spenser the identification of personae with historical persons is fleeting and marginal to the total effect; meaning is pitched at a level of generality that leaves the contingencies of history far behind. But in Dekker it is the identification with history that gives the generalities their substance. The stories of 'Campeius', 'Ropus', 'Paridel' follow the documented lives of Edmund Campion, Dr Lopez, Dr Parry in close detail and show Dekker as a painstaking collector of historical facts. When Elizabeth's councillors give advice that requires them to be differentiated (as in the preparations for the Armada), the differentiation corresponds to that in the chronicles.

It is inevitable that there is less pressure to identify the separate supporters of the Apocalyptic Empress; and the lack of specificity here fits in with the moral point being made; these are slippery characters, lacking the steadfastness of English virtue (defined, once again, by countrified clown-like 'plain dealing'). The Third King (Spain), left behind in England after Philip II's matrimonial rebuff, can run through a gamut of disguises. These give him access to different levels of society and permit him to subvert native malcontents (like Edmund Campion). Here we are at the Spenserian end of Dekker's range, but even here a scene like that of the temptation of Campion (Act II, Scene ii) has a sharply realistic definition very far from the mode of *The Faerie Queene*.

The history plays discussed in this chapter seem to show a general drift from a political to a personal focus, from concern with kings and nobles as agents of dynastic change to a concern with ethical survival under the pressure of historical instability. *The Whore of Babylon* marks a temporary reversal of this trend—a reversal perhaps produced by the reminder contained in the Gunpowder Plot that historical change is produced by unsubtle and large-scale oppositions. If we choose to say this, we should also note that the reversal did not carry the history play back to the position it had occupied before 1597. International conspiracy is presented, not as a matter of conflict between persons in power, but rather in the manner of modern spy fiction, as an abstracted and all-embracing explanation why events go one way rather than another. It may be significant in this connection that the most human elements in the story concern those who are most puzzled by the contradictions in their political loyalties. Campeius and Paridell are malcontented intellectuals, mini-Faustuses, unable to reconcile with their traditionalist feeling for native virtue their consciousness of superiority, and the large promises of greatness offered by their spymasters. Like later spies, they cannot shake off their emotional origins for all the intellectual excitements of treason and the possibility of a new historical era. The puzzling relation between individual conceptions of virtue and the realities of politics is handled in a unique way in *The Whore of Babylon*, but the puzzle itself is recurrent in the history plays of the early seventeenth century and can be detected inside the great variety of forms that are used.

The presence of Queen Elizabeth in these later history plays obviously requires the dramatists, however personal the focus, to impose a generalizing mode of representation on her portrayal, whether hagiographic as in *If You Know Not Me* or allegorical as in *The Whore of Babylon* or merely prospective as in *Henry VIII* or *The Duchess of Suffolk*. Henry VIII was probably the last sovereign who could be dealt with in the personal, not to say backslapping, terms that allow male sociability to interact with the possession of power—as with Edward I or Edward IV or the 'little touch of Harry in the night'. And this is how Henry VIII appears in Samuel Rowley's *When You See Me, You Know Me: or The Famous Chronicle History of King Henry the Eight, with the Virtuous Birth and Adventurous Life of Edward, Prince of Wales* (1603×1605).[26] Rowley's play (printed 1605, 1613, 1621, 1634) gives us an entirely believable, and apparently accurate, picture of the personal life of Henry— achieved, it must be allowed, by a cavalier attitude to the facts of history. The king is moody, violent, unpredictable, frightening, finding fulfilment in personal relations rather than political action. The latter is delegated to Wolsey, who is exhumed after sixteen years in the grave to carry just this facet of the action.

We meet Henry desperate for an heir. Jane Seymour dies in giving birth to the prince; and Henry's life is then dominated by the purely personal guilt of a husband whose wife has died to fulfil his hopes. Only Will Summers, his *alter ego*, jester, and the spokesman for his anti-political scepticism about power, knows how to break his melancholy,[27] so that the King can return to active life

---

[26] The title is clearly meant to link with that of *If You Know Not Me, You Know Nobody.* Fame and integrity are to be understood as two aspects of the same nexus.

[27] Rowley may be remembering stories of Tarlton, who performed similar offices for Queen Elizabeth. See *The Dictionary of National Biography, s.v.* Tarlton.

and fulfil his political functions. But his choice of action is not to take politics seriously, to control Wolsey and Bonner, who are busy plotting to safeguard their own powers from Protestant interference, but to walk disguised through London so that he can 'see our city's government' (l. 938). Such a retreat from the formalism of government allows a king, even when he is not the leader of a marauding army, yet to appear as one who shares in the individual lives of his subjects. In the streets of London Henry joins up with Black Will, the notorious outlaw, and he is given detailed instructions how the strong can outflank the forces of order; the watch is once again a collection of Dogberrys. Fortunately for the citizens, the bully-boy instincts of these two are essentially competitive; their sword-and-buckler fight cannot be ignored even by *this* Watch, and Henry finds himself in prison (the Counter), where he can learn even more about the society he governs and moralize still further about the inequalities that money enforces.

Here, as elsewhere in the play, Henry is a poor man's hero, an exclaimer against things as they are rather than an inventor of means by which they can be changed. The corrupt servants who have been detected can be punished; Black Will's violence can be given space in a military campaign; but the predominant image is the popular one of a world in which corruption and pain are natural conditions.[28] The passivity that this view implies is very much a characteristic of this Henry in his political role. *When You See Me, You Know Me* is a play of spectacular occasions (an ambassadorial legation, the instalment of a new queen, the state visit of the Emperor Charles V), but these appear as endorsements of events already decided rather than actions leading to results. The Popish Plot of Wolsey, Bonner, Gardner, and Princess Mary to undo the Protestantism of Katherine Parr, Princess Elizabeth, and Cranmer (now tutor to Prince Edward) is likewise seen as a contest for possession of a more or less passive Henry. It takes the intervention of Will Summers to make public the deceits of Wolsey. The denouement, the state visit of Charles V, is made the spectacular

[28] Chettle and Munday's First Part of *The Downfall and Death of Robert, Earl of Huntingdon, Afterward called Robin Hood of Merry Sherwood* (1598) makes the same point. The play is presented as if a play-within-a-play, devised by Skelton to entertain an anonymous king (presumably Henry VIII). The action, which 'expresses noble Robin's wrong' (l. 2226), is thought to be subversive. But the king himself 'surveyed the plat | And bad me boldly write it' (ll. 2219–20). The king is on the side of the outlaw (and the dramatist) but cannot change the power structure.

occasion for Summers's revelation. The King endorses what is revealed ('I did suspect what here the Fool hath found' (l. 2850)—but he has done nothing about it). After Wolsey's expulsion, Will Summers can reoccupy a central position at court as the 'mere English' representative of plain speaking and manly directness, trading bawdy rhymes with king, queen, and emperor. Politics gives way to personal values. If we can hang on to these, the implication runs, we can all be not only happy but successful.

The treatment of Henry VIII in Rowley's play is obviously parallel to that found in Shakespeare's (or Shakespeare's and Fletcher's) *The Famous History of the Life of King Henry the Eighth* (1613). Even though a nine-year gap separates the two plays, the basic strategy of royal representation stays the same. Like Rowley's, Shakespeare's monarch is a largely passive figure, always seeking the good (as the play defines it) but seldom able to enact it, moving uneasily and testily between the bewildering uncertainties of evidence and advice and presiding over the great events of his reign in ceremonial splendour, but not taking responsibility for their meaning.

The Prologue to *Henry VIII* is often understood to be denying the similarity of the two plays. This, it says, is a play 'sad, high, and working [having power to move us], full of state and woe' and will disappoint those

> That come to hear a merry, bawdy play,
> A noise of targets, or to see a fellow
> In a long motley coat guarded with yellow . . .

The references seem to point to the sword-and-buckler fight between Henry and Black Will in *When You See Me*, and to the interventions of Will Summers and Patch (Wolsey's fool). And certainly the emphasis on 'state and woe' in Shakespeare's play makes such interventions improbable. But we should notice that in Rowley they are not present simply as crowd-pleasing merriness or bawdry. Henry's low-life adventures and the licence he gives Will Summers to be a stand-in for his own anti-political attitudes supply human body to the ceremonial political figure; thereby, of course, they decentre political activity and move the play towards norms of comedy that Shakespeare had obviously decided to avoid. Yet the need for such a body cannot be avoided; and Rowley's choice leads our eyes towards a problem in Shakespeare's handling of history in this play.

Shakespeare's story develops from those parts of the reign that Rowley omitted—the fall of Katherine of Aragon and the rise of Anne Boleyn—and so is able to move towards an event that is a genuine political climax: the christening of Elizabeth by Cranmer and so the establishment of a Protestant monarchy. By comparison, the visit of Charles V (Rowley's climax) is a merely theatrical event. Shakespeare's play culminates in Elizabeth's christening; but the connection of her triumph with the rest of the action in *Henry VIII* remains obscure, for the Reformation has not been made a recurrent issue.[29] What we are given is a series of brilliant rhetorical moments linked together without being attached to an overriding purpose.

The role of Wolsey is symptomatic of the technique being employed. The play regularly cites Wolsey as the cause why the great events of the reign occur: the Field of the Cloth of Gold, the fall of Buckingham, the divorce of Katherine are all said to be engineered by him, to secure his own purposes rather than the good of the nation. The play never raises the question what royal purposes are served by Wolsey. He certainly allows the dynasty's centralizing aim and control of the great nobles to be achieved without the King's personal involvement. The court appears as a splendid ceremonial expression of kingly power, presided over by a gracious and generous monarch; the noblemen are courtiers rather than feudal magnates, and this is a matter with genuine political significance; but nothing political is made of it. Politics goes on (rather mysteriously) somewhere behind the scene. That makes it a thoroughly modern situation. But it is a situation which no one in the play can articulate; the universal assumption is that the trappings of power and the reality of power are indivisible, the monarch being defined as the person who both decides the issues and gives the orders. Henry is not portrayed as a weak king; we do not see him (like Edward II or Richard II) desiring ends that he cannot impose. It is rather that the issues of this reign are too frustratingly complex, too ambiguous, to be handled by royal will-power. Henry can terrify his subjects by his rages, but these are expressions of power without political meaning. The divorce is said to proceed from a scruple of conscience which the King himself describes in detail in Act II, Scene iv. But such a scruple cannot be handled in the terms that Henry IV and Henry V use when they consider how

---

[29] See Matthew H. Wikander, *The Play of Truth and State* (Baltimore, Md., 1986), 47.

their dynasty obtained the crown. There the individual conscience raises the question of political means; here the question is one of personal conduct. Henry is torn between love and admiration for Katherine and the evidence of God's displeasure visited on his male children. And of course there is also the sexual glamour of Anne Boleyn, though this is viewed at a very deliberate distance. When Wolsey falls, Henry does not gather the reins of power into his own hands and become the kind of sovereign the play seems to ask for. His intervention in Gardner's conspiracy against Cranmer is hesitant and devious. When he joins the council, his condemnation of its conduct is imperiously eloquent, but it is so to suppress discord rather than assert his own purposes.

Henry VIII is, among the Shakespeare history plays, the one which most faithfully and accurately reports the language of the sources, Holinshed and Foxe. *All is True*, the title that is given us in accounts of the fire that occurred during its performance in June 1613 (destroying the First Globe), may point to the author's awareness of this feature. Yet the truth that is told is a limited one; Sir Henry Wotton, in his account of the fire, refers to the play as 'some principal pieces of the reign of Henry VIII'.[30] The description is a just one: the truth points to the facts of history; but we are not given the understanding that would link the facts into an interpretative sequence. What holds the play together is less the individual's drive towards political success that animates the earlier history plays than a perception of the unreality that links all such ambitions. The central figures of the reign, Buckingham, Katherine, Wolsey, even Anne Boleyn, move effortlessly from self-assertion into the Christian self-denial that produces the best poetry available.[31] Wolsey's sudden discovery of his spiritual vocation and his description to Cromwell of 'a way . . . to rise in' has often been censured for its political evasiveness:

> fling away ambition . . .
> Love thyself last, cherish those hearts that hate thee;
> Corruption wins not more than honesty.
> Still in thy right hand carry gentle peace
> To silence envious tongues.
>
> (III. ii. 440–6)

[30] Chambers, ii. 419.
[31] E. M. Waith cites praise of the *pathetick* powers of this play from Samuel Johnson and Francis Gentleman (*The Arts of Performance in Elizabethan and Early Stuart Drama* (Edinburgh, 1991), 75–8.

But political evasiveness is central to the whole play's pattern. Cranmer's prophecy of the greatness of Elizabeth's reign, when

> every man shall eat in safety
> Under his own vine what he plants, and sing
> The merry songs of peace to all his neighbours.
>
> (v. v. 33–5)

forecasts a world in which the Christian vision ('God shall be truly known') has become the controlling principle of a state which everywhere else has withered away. But, like other political *witherings*, this one has more power when expressed as a dream than as a course of action.

Henry VIII shows a world in which power can express itself in its royal guise only by static pageants; personal eloquence is the privilege of those whose power is under threat or lost. John *Ford's *The Chronicle History of Perkin Warbeck: A Strange Truth* (*c.*1629×1634), the last, and one of the best, of seventeenth-century history plays, takes this perspective a stage further. Henry VII, who occupies the only true centre of political power in this play, has escaped from the myth of kingship into its reality. He requires neither pageantry nor eloquence. Money, he tells us, is the most reliable means by which policy can be turned into authority:

> Money gives soul to action. Our competitor,
> The Flemish counterfeit, with James of Scotland,
> Will prove what courage, need, and want can nourish
> Without the food of fit supplies.
>
> (III. i. 29–32)

And so it proves in the plot. Perkin Warbeck, the pretender to the English throne, claims power on the basis that he is in reality Richard, Duke of York, the baby that Richard III thought he had strangled in the Tower. And the proof that convinces his backers that his claim is true lies in precisely those qualities that Henry VII does without—eloquence, kingly words, and noble bearing. James IV of Scotland is romantic and adventurous, and thus feeds on such a kind of proof. He sees kingship in moral and chivalric terms; he is enraptured by the romance of lost heirs restored to their rightful inheritance through a kingly power that is sanctified by virtuous action. In this he is the natural representative of his court, where (in contrast to Henry's) the rational niceties of love and honour are the grave topics of conversation. But romance does not completely take over James's politics. When Bishop Fox refuses to yield Norham Castle (Act III, Scene iv) and when James's offer of single combat is handled as a matter of policy rather than one of nobility, the Scots turn to rapine (the other side of romance), and James treats with scorn Perkin's protective attitude to his theoretical kingdom. Finally the wily Spanish envoy holds out the prospect of marriage to Margaret Tudor, and James finds that he prefers dynastic profit to ethical posture.

In this Machiavellian world the distinction between the reality of power and the rhetoric of kingship can be more sharply focused than in the notionally idealistic world of *Henry VIII*. The fall of Buckingham in *Henry VIII* is the structural equivalent of the fall of Stanley in *Perkin Warbeck*; and in both cases the justice of the condemnation is highly ambiguous. But in the Buckingham case we face the ambiguity of a right verdict reached for wrong reasons; in *Perkin Warbeck* the ambiguity reflects on the King himself: he both condemns Stanley and refuses to face him; and at the same time he banishes Clifford, the accuser, and curses him. And so he endorses Stanley's description of Clifford as a 'state informer'. How are we to understand Henry's attitude to state information? He despises it but he needs it. He admires qualities of kingliness that he cannot commit himself to if he is to remain king; and these are qualities most fully represented in the play not by Henry the real king, but by Perkin the pretend king.

History tells us that Perkin failed. But are we then to understand that success in action is the only standard by which history can endorse value? Ford was the heir of a modern historiography that was disposed to accept such a valuation.[32] But stage plays need to be more multivalent. We hear that Perkin has bewitched the Scottish king; but when we hear him speak we too are bewitched. If he is a player king, we in the audience are obliged to respond to the theatrical power that constitutes the theatre's representation of kingliness. *Perkin Warbeck* offers us no alternative rhetoric by which we might judge *his* to be mere pretence; his tone is noble, controlled, ceremonious. Moreover, his claim to acceptance is confirmed by the most important personal relationship in the play, that with Katherine Gordon, his wife. When King James insists on the wedding, Katherine is reluctant. But once bound, she embraces her

---

[32]   Francis Bacon's *History of Henry VII* (1622), one of Ford's primary sources, is one of the earliest English examples of 'politique' history in the tradition of Machiavelli and Guicciardini.

fate with a calm dignity that reflects Perkin's own, with a personal nobility that shows up the question of Perkin's royalty or imposture as emotionally irrelevant. By acting like royal persons, by displaying self-control, mutual esteem, superiority to accident, they create a sense (and a good theatrical sense) in which they *are* royal persons. As Perkin says to Katherine, after his capture:

> Spite of tyranny,
> We reign in our affections, blessed woman!
> · · · · · · · ·
> Even when I fell, I stood enthroned a monarch
> Of one chaste wife's troth pure and uncorrupted.
>
> (v. iii. 121–7)

Such 'troth' is indeed a 'strange truth', a truth that, made central to the play, turns *Perkin Warbeck* into what Jonas Barish calls an anti-history.[33] It is no doubt to achieve this focus that Ford distorts his sources, excluding from the story Perkin's miserable end, his confession of imposture (extracted by torture), and allowing Katherine Gordon to end her career with a vow of perpetual widowhood, giving us no hint of her three subsequent husbands. The play can thus conclude with a validating rhetoric of constancy and heroism which even Henry is alleged to admire.

In presenting the historical issue as one between efficient kingship and poetic kingliness, Ford is returning to an issue best known to us from *Richard II*. In both cases the truth that emerges is that in history the poetic and theatrical powers cannot hope to win a contest against prosaic efficiency; but the play that shows us this can still turn the historical loser into the hero of the theatre. What separates *Richard II* from *Perkin Warbeck*, and indicates the shift in historical perspective, is that Richard lives in a world where his personal glamour still has a powerful political meaning. Perkin's glamour exists (like that of the actor) as the mere instrument of his hope for power, in a world that endorses the contradiction between hope and reality. This attenuation in the freedom of political possibility links *Perkin Warbeck* to *Henry VIII* as plays in which the values of private life are the last bastions of personal significance in a political world where effective power depends on bureaucratic impersonality.

---

[33] Jonas Barish, '*Perkin Warbeck* as Anti-History', *Essays in Criticism*, 20 (1970), 151–71.

Biographical History

A very similar point can be made about plays of historical biography, written around the turn of the century, plays in which the private individual comes to power by dint of personal virtue, only to discover that virtue cannot be fulfilled by political success. It is not surprising, given the tendency of later history plays to focus on individual rather than political values, that Tudor political history is sometimes handled in this way. The pseudonymous *True Chronicle History of the Whole Life and Death of Thomas, Lord Cromwell*, 'written by W. S.' (1599×1602), Anthony Munday's *Sir Thomas More*, with its various rewritings and additions (now dated by Scott McMillin as originally written in the early 1590s and revised after 1603[34]), Thomas *Drue's *The Duchess of Suffolk* (1624; printed 1631), all belong to this category. They are all, perhaps inevitably, biographies of a particular kind, in which, as in the later history plays discussed above, the exercise of real political power is kept tantalizingly out of focus. In this respect they may be differentiated from *Oldcastle*, in which the virtuous subject of biography is pursuing an active career in favour of change. They are all placed in that most troublesome period of Tudor rule, when Henry VIII's repudiation of Rome raised to an unprecedented degree the issue between private conscience and public loyalty. This was the period when the Humanist dream of secular virtue leading upwards to state service was taking hold. What, from the point of view of the virtuous scholar, seemed to be on offer was a 'natural' congruity between classical moral assumptions and service to the state. But from the viewpoint of the king, it would seem, the relationship looked more like a temporary expedient to cover the next crisis.

   In the *Cromwell* play we first meet the hero as the studious son of the local Putney blacksmith, learning that he must adapt his scholarly habits to the noise of the forge that defines his economic reality. Wolsey is his model, but the harsh world of nascent capitalism and not the Church is the medium through which this Thomas must make his way. First in the hurly-burly entrepôt of Antwerp and then in Italy he learns that human sympathy and

---

[34] Scott McMillin, *The Elizabethan Theatre and 'The Book of Sir Thomas More'* (Ithaca, NY, 1987). See also *Sir Thomas More*, ed. Vittorio Gabrieli and Giorgio Melchiori (Manchester, 1990), 26–7.

mutual support are the only comforts available to the man exposed
to the winds of fortune:

> We that live under the work of fate
> May hope the best, yet knows not to what state
> Our stars and destinies hath us assigned.
> Fickle is Fortune and her face is blind.

(II. i. 53–6)

To know the world is not, of course, to control it. The wisdom of
experience 'is the jewel of my heart', he tells us (II. i. 6); and it is
for his experience as 'a scholar and . . . a linguist that hath travelled
many parts of Christendom' that Cromwell is prized when he
returns home, selected by Wolsey as his aide and after Wolsey's
fall succeeding to the Secretaryship and then to the position of
Lord Chamberlain, Baron Cromwell and Earl of Essex.

His 'experience' tells him that political power must not blind
him to personal integrity; he remains faithful to his domestic and
commercial origins, kneeling to his father and supporting those
who helped him in the early stages of his ascent. But Power cannot
help breeding envy and competitiveness:

> He that in court secure will keep himself
> Must not be great, for then he is envied at.

(v. iv. 17–18)

Cromwell is too virtuous to know how to escape the net that is
spread for him by the usual demon, Bishop Gardner of Winchester, Foxe's 'arch-persecutor of Christ's church'.[35] Cromwell's friends
try to warn him of the impending doom; but he is too intent on the
King's business to read their letters. If he could see the King, 'no
better trial I desire than that' (v. iii. 36). But the King is inaccessible.
At the end of politics Cromwell must return to his stoical acceptance of Fortune as the real ruler of the world. This is not, of
course, to blame the King. The axe has hardly hit the block before
a messenger brings his majesty's reprieve. The King is good; but
his goodness is powerless to break through the web of political
practice. The complexity of a modern bureaucratic administration,
its corruption and unpredictability, supplies all the characteristics
traditionally associated with Fortuna. The King's servants must

---

[35] *The Acts and Monuments of John Foxe*, ed. Catley and Pratt (8 vols.; 1843–9; repr. New
York, 1965), viii. 628.

not assume that their virtue (or the virtue of their master) exempts them from that condition.[36]

The Book of Sir Thomas More (*c*.1593)—the title is that found on the cover of the manuscript—is a celebrated text, for reasons that have little or nothing to do with its function as a history play. The manuscript (BL Harley 7368) presents us with the remains of an original text (apparently by Anthony Munday) together with objections to that text in the hand of Sir Edmund Tilney, Master of the Revels from 1581 until some time in the first decade of the seventeenth century, revised and supplemented by 'additions' in five different hands, A, B, C, D, E.[37] Some of these hands have been identified with Munday, Chettle, Dekker, and Heywood (a mostly Henslowe crew); but what has made *Sir Thomas More* a centre of scholarly attention is the possibility that 'hand D' might be the hand of William Shakespeare. And this possibility has been so tantalizing that it has all but obliterated the idea that the play might be worth writing about as a theatrical document, capable of effective production on the stage. But *Sir Thomas More* has shown that it can indeed pass this test (at the Nottingham Playhouse in June 1964[38]), and there it emerged as an effective drama, closely related in subject matter and treatment to *Cromwell*.

As in *Cromwell*, the play of *Sir Thomas More* shows us a Humanist scholar, bourgeois in background, rising in state service by giving evidence of eloquence and learning; he becomes Lord Chancellor, but never forgets the domestic pieties of his origins. At the height of his success he suddenly and unexpectedly falls from power, is stripped of his offices, and beheaded. But his dignity remains undisturbed; he shows virtue as an untroubled acceptance of the destructiveness as well as the constructiveness of the system within which he must live. The stories of the two plays are thus basically the same; but in *Sir Thomas More* the story is told with a poise and a sophistication that far exceeds anything in *Cromwell*.

---

[36] An interesting version of the story appears in the third book of Bandello's *Novelle* (novel 34), concentrating on the relation between Cromwell (Cremonello) and the Italian merchant, Francesco Frescobaldi.

[37] See Chambers, iv. 32–4; McMillin, *Elizabethan Theatre*, 94–5; and the Gabrieli and Melchiori edition.

[38] Directed by Frank Dunlop. Ian McKellen played the title role. See the comments in *Plays and Players*, July 1964, pp. 8–12. On a subsequent amateur performance, see Tony Howard in *Research Opportunities in Renaissance Drama*, 26 (1978), 61–2, noting 'the undoubtedly theatrical qualities of the play'.

Cromwell shows us a commercial world of every man for himself and shows us the protagonist rising above that world by a steadfast moral understanding. But natural envy cannot be evaded. Bishop Gardner is the specific cause of Cromwell's fall, but Cromwell is content to remind auditors that figures of his kind are an inevitable part of the political world.

Cromwell could be presented to the play's audience as an ideal Elizabethan statesman caught in a time not yet perfected, in a world exposed to storms that Elizabeth had calmed. Sir Thomas More, Humanist hero and Catholic martyr, had a more ambiguous relationship to the received politics of the Elizabethan age, and this may have reduced the author's reliance on the political simplifications that support the other play. Less time is spent in *More* purveying the romance of a rise from obscurity to power. Sir Thomas is shown as more continuously self-conscious of the contradiction between virtue and politics, between the happy condition of the present moment and the uncertainty of the future. It is this awareness that provides the argument of More's great speech to the Londoners rioting against foreign merchants—the principal *literary* evidence for Shakespeare's authorship:

> You'll put down strangers,
> Kill them, cut their throats, possess their houses
> And lead the majesty of law in lyam,
> To slip him like a hound. . . . Say now the king,
> As he is clement if th'offender mourn,
> Should so much come too short of your great trespass
> As but to banish you, whither would you go?
> What country, by the nature of your error,
> Would give you harbour?
>
> .   .   .   .
>
> Why, you must need be strangers. Would you be pleased
> To find a nation of such barbarous temper
> That, breaking out in hideous violence,
> Would not afford you an abode on earth,
> Whet their detested knives against your throats,
> Spurn you like dogs, and like as if that God
> Owed not nor made not you
>
> .   .   .   .
>
> What would you think,
> To be thus used? This is the strangers' case,
> And this your mountainish inhumanity,
>
> (II. iii. 129–51)

More's well-documented playfulness or 'mirth' is presented as another aspect of this same sense of the world as a set of temporary accommodations and passing shows. He dresses his servant Randall in the robes of the Lord Chancellor and defies Erasmus to tell the inside from the outside. When an actor goes missing in the Interlude of *Wit and Wisdom* he improvises the part of Good Counsel so effectively that he seems to have conflated the roles of actor and councillor. When he says in the interlude, 'Judge not things by the outward show: | The eye oft mistakes right well you do know' (III. ii. 274–5), we understand the relevance of the sentiment to his life as well as the ironic distance created by the context in which he says it. More's central act of discrimination between reality and show is, of course, his refusal to treat his loss of power and condemnation to death as occasions for tragic passion. The King's decision is presented as simply another example of the inexplicable operation of fortune, a proper test for the resolved soul. In fact the play never bothers to tell us what is actually said in the articles Henry requires the Council to sign.

The focus is not on the demand made (or the price to be paid) but on decorum, the proper response—the right answer in the fairy-tale terms that seem to lie behind such plots. The reward for the right answer is not, in either *Cromwell* or *Sir Thomas More*, the hand of the princess, but simply a confirmation of the heroism that entitles them to be protagonists of heroizing plays.

Thomas Drue's *The Duchess of Suffolk* (1624) shows us Foxe's stories continuing to make a popular audience (at the Fortune) thrill at the daring self-definition, outside accepted social limits, that the Reformation allowed. Bishop Bonner, playing here his usual role of Belial to Gardner's Beelzebub, seems to have had a personal vendetta against Katherine Willoughby, widow of Charles Brandon, Duke of Suffolk, and his agents pursued her across Europe; and so she finds a marginal place in *The Book of Martyrs*. Even in Foxe, there is very little evidence that this was a *religious* persecution. But it is easy to assimilate it to Foxe's hagiographical pattern of truth–persecution–justification, and this is the structure that gives Drue's chase-and-escape narrative its claim to appear in the company of these other martyr plays. Drue sharpens this angle by turning Dr Sands (Sandys), whose story appears in Foxe a few pages later than the Duchess's, into a chaplain in her household, so making the narrative of his pursuit and escape a part of hers. He also presents the marriage of the Duchess to her servant, Richard

Bertie, as an analogous proof of her virtue. Bertie's loyalty, care, resourcefulness, and boldness in emergency make him a natural survivor in the world of humiliation, flight, and concealment that occupies so many pages in Foxe, where religious absolutes recurrently depend for their survival on a gift for opportunism and plausible lies. As a popular story of hair's-breadth escapes, providing the pleasure of seeing Bonner's and Gardner's plots frustrated, *The Duchess of Suffolk* gives its audience a stock romantic tale of loss and recovery that can be authenticated as a part of history— a vignette of Latimer and Ridley and Cranmer in Oxford reminds us of the alternatives to flight and evasion. Sir Henry Herbert, the Master of the Revels, found the play as presented to him to be 'full of dangerous matter' and in need of 'reformation'. Presumably a story of religious persecution, however romantically shaped, could not wholly avoid the dangerous suggestion that history reveals patterns not only of what *was* but of what *is*.

The privileging of private lives in these biographical plays marks a retreat from the concept of history as a matter of national success and failure. Urged on, no doubt, by the same current as produced Fletcherian tragicomedy, even the historical plays that put politics at the centre of the action tend to absorb the public focus into the private and require personal relations to be the main sources of value. *Davenport's *King John and Matilda* (*c.*1628×1634), like earlier King John plays, shows John as a brutal, disorganized, spasmodic character, but on this occasion these characteristics are due less to his bad political judgement than to his insane obsession with Matilda. Even his willingness to accept Magna Carta and to give up his crown to the Pope are now understood less as signs of his political desperation than of his erotic dementia.[39] When kings of England are understood mainly as lovers, we know that national history is in the process of transferring its location to Ruritania.

---

[39] The dementia was partly taken from the second of Chettle and Munday's two interlinked plays: *The Downfall of Robert, Earl of Huntingdon, afterward called Robin Hood of Merry Sherwood: with his love to chaste Matilda, the Lord Fitzwater's daughter, afterwards his fair Maid Marian*; and *The Death of Robert, Earl of Huntingdon, Otherwise called Robin Hood of Merry Sherwood: with the lamentable tragedy of chaste Matilda, his fair Maid Marian, poisoned at Dunmow by King John* (1598). It was presumably the general presence of the Robin Hood legend that made it easy, even in Elizabeth's reign, to push to its limit the opposition of innocent country and corrupt court, and to treat a king of England as an unmitigated villain.

7. The Boy Actors and the New Dramaturgy

COMEDY

THE mythological and fantastic comedies of John Lyly (see Chapter 4) were the product not only of a particular talent but of the tradition of using English choirboys as actors. H. N. Hillebrand has traced the history of English drama written to be performed by boys back into the Middle Ages with a marvellous wealth of documentation, but we are left, after all the lawsuits and records of payment are transcribed, only with shadows cast by the events. We know the names of a number of the Tudor choirmaster–authors who were involved in the system—William Cornish, Sebastian Westcott, Richard Edwards, Richard Farrant, William Hunnis— but, with the exception of Edwards's *Damon and Pythias* (?1565), the relationship between the theatre tradition and the individual talent that could exploit it can only be guessed at. The first information that allows us to combine theatrical and literary perspectives comes when we learn in 1584 that John Lyly became the lessee of the indoor theatre in the Blackfriars that Richard Farrant, Master of the children of St George's Chapel in Windsor, had set up in 1576 for the ostensible purpose of 'exercising' his boys in preparation for their court performance. Lyly was paid for taking two plays to court on 1 January (*Campaspe*) and 3 March (*Sappho and Phao*) 1584. From the title-pages we learn that these plays were designed also for the Blackfriars (before a paying audience). The earliest documented commercial activity of the boy players thus remains a consequence of their court function.

It is sadly characteristic that this perspective window is hardly opened before it is shut again. Lyly obtained the lease of the playhouse only as part of a deal designed to keep the Blackfriars landlord at bay. By the middle of 1584 the deal had collapsed and the playhouse was closed. Lyly survived as a playwright by transferring his activities to the theatre in the precinct of St Paul's Cathedral,[1]

---

[1] The exact location of this playhouse is uncertain, though often guessed at. See Chambers, ii. 16. Cf. W. Reavley Gair, *The Children of Paul's* (Cambridge, 1982).

where another set of choirboys acted in plays. But there, of course, he was no longer an author–theatre-lessee.[2] Six years later (or so) the Paul's Boys enterprise was also shut down,[3] and Lyly's playwriting career came to an end.

The special literary and dramatic qualities of Lyly's plays can easily be understood as responses to the theatrical as well as the social conditions in which they were produced. The playhouses of the Paul's Boys and the Blackfriars' Boys charged higher prices, were smaller in size, enclosed; their élite or coterie status,[4] their connection with the court, the rarity of their performances[5]— these conditions all point towards a dramaturgy (see Chapter 4) that distanced Lyly's plays from those designed for the large open-air playhouses of the adult actors.[6]

When, after the 1584 and 1590 closures, the boys started acting again in 1599 or 1600,[7] the purely theatrical conditions were

---

[2] Gabriel Harvey (*Works*, ed. A. B. Grosart (3 vols.; London, 1884–5), ii. 212) calls him 'Vicemaster of Paul's', but this is intended as slander. not as a description of an official position.

[3] The reasons for this inhibition are not entirely clear. It is commonly supposed that involvement in the Martin Marprelate controversy was an important factor. Gabriel Harvey (*Works*, ed. Grosart, ii. 132) tells us that Lyly was 'entertained' by the bishops to write in their defence, as was Nashe (see McKerrow, v. 34–65). Nashe (ibid. i. 92) makes it evident that plays were part of this campaign. Lyly speaks of plays already performed and others that 'are penned' and await licence for the next onslaught (*The Complete Works*, ed. R. Warwick Bond (3 vols.; London, 1902), iii. 408). The description of the knockabout style of these plays (as in their extant pamphlets) suggests that Lyly and Nashe may have gone too far in their translation of the rough-and-tumble Martinist style into gross theatrical action and so brought down on themselves the anger of those they were ostensibly defending. If this is the story, it is one that was to be repeated many times in the history of the relationship between the boys' theatre and the authorities. It is worth noticing that when the Paul's boys were shut down the adult players seem to have survived. Chambers sets out the documents in the controversy, as they affect the theatre, at iv. 229–33.

[4] See the statement about the Paul's playhouse in Marston's *Jack Drum's Entertainment*: 'I like the audience that frequenteth there | With much applause. A man shall not be choked | With the stench of garlic, nor be pasted | To the barmy jacket of a beer-brewer' (ed. H. Harvey Wood, iii. 234).

[5] The evidence, as usual, is conflicting. The most received opinions are that the boys played either one or three days a week for six months in the year. See David Farley-Hills, 'How Often did the Eyases Fly', *Notes and Queries*, 236 (1991), 461–6.

[6] The antithesis is less clear in the case of Peele. Shakespeare's comedies of the mid-1590s show a public-theatre dramatist quickly taking up Lyly's characteristics and adapting them to public-theatre performance. See Ch. 8.

[7] The date for the opening of the Blackfriars is clear enough. On 2 September 1600 Henry Evans obtained a sublease of the theatre building and immediately set about creating a company (see Hillebrand, 151 ff.). The situation at Paul's is less clear. Rowland White wrote to Sir Robert Sidney on 13 November 1599 that 'My Lord of Derby hath put up the plays of the children in Paul's to his great pains and charge', but nothing is known of any

unchanged. It would be natural to suppose that the boys' dramaturgy would also stay the same. In some respects this is true; but
other factors are present:[8] the larger movement of taste which was
taking the 'Elizabethan' towards the 'Jacobean' was already in train,[9]
and the boys' companies were in the vanguard of this change.
Their repertory of 1599–1610 is a repertory of innovation—innovation that was fostered by the overlap between authors and management, by acting methods, audience demands, and a more complex
relation to the court.[10]

But if the boys innovated, the adults were quick to copy; and so
the two systems bore quite a new relationship to one another. The
history of the boy players in this period is in one sense a success
story, but it is a story whose success destroyed the distinctions that
existed at the beginning; it is a story of plays whose new angles
and new attitudes were so well adapted to the expectations of the
developing culture that they were soon in vogue all over town. One
important element in the story is the improved social status of
actors, as writers of acceptable rank became part of the organizations. The children's companies were first in this market, attract-
ing slightly raffish gentlemen authors from the Inns of Court and
eventually even noblemen. Even if 'David Lord Barry' turns out to

---

connections between the Paul's company and the Earl of Derby. Marston's *Antonio and Mellida*, written for the company, is usually dated 1599×1600; but no certain date can be supplied. Certainly the playhouse was in operation by 1600.

[8] One factor that should not be lost sight of, which no doubt affected the relationship between the boys and other actors, was a reduction in the role of choirmasters and so a more direct control by financial entrepreneurs. There was, in consequence, an increasing separa-tion of the acting boys from the choirs in which they nominally served. The choirmasters' right to press-gang boys for singing in the royal chapels had given them access to a free supply of acting fodder. A suit brought against the Chapel managers in 1601 tells us that the boys kidnapped were 'no way able and fit for singing . . . nor taught to sing, but . . . abusively employed . . . only in plays and interludes . . . amongst a company of lewd and dissolute mercenary players' (Hillebrand, 162–3). The crown was characteristically slow to amend the abuse. But in 1606 the Master was forbidden to employ press-ganged boys as actors 'for that it is not fit or decent that such as should sing the praises of God Almighty should be trained up or employed in such lascivious and profane exercises' (Chambers, ii. 52).

[9] See F. P. Wilson, *Elizabethan and Jacobean* (Oxford, 1945) and Hiram Haydn, *The Counter-Renaissance* (New York, 1950). A figure like Thomas Nashe should, however, warn us not to make too much of contrast in the history of drama. If the Nashe and Jonson banned play *The Isle of Dogs* (1597) had survived, our sense of a continuous development between the fantasy of Lyly and the satire of Marston might well be stronger.

[10] It is often thought that the prime cause of such changes ought to be found in history. The social facts may indeed be selected from life, but it is the artful shaping that gives them their meaning and makes straight cross-reference too simplifying.

be mere Lording *Barry, more pirate than peer,[11] there remains the case of William *Percy (third son of the Earl of Northumberland).[12] By the end of the period even the adult companies could call on the services of such oxymoronic gentleman–professionals as *Beaumont and Fletcher (one the son of a bishop, the other of a judge).

The inhibition of the two boys' companies through the 1590s came at a crucial moment in the history of English culture. This decade saw a sudden explosion of literature and drama that has continued to astonish the world. It was a decade of extraordinarily rapid change, the decade in which the anti-establishment attitudes of the Inns of Court were bearing fruit, the years when John Donne, *John Marston, Thomas Campion, John Hoskins, John Davies, Henry Wotton, Edward *Sharpham, George Sandys, Francis Davison, Everard Guilpin were all in residence, the decade of such avant-garde and politically sceptical works as Bacon's Essays, Hayward's Henry IV, Fulke *Greville's Mustapha, and the early 'humours' plays of Jonson and *Chapman. When the boys started up again at the end of the decade, they were in a different intellectual world from that of Lyly, one turned in on the contradictions of social existence, a world which they had to adapt to or perish.

It looks as if the boys' first response to the reopening was, naturally enough, to resurrect some of their earlier successes. Lyly's Love's Metamorphosis (c.1588×1590) was published in 1601 (entered in the Stationers' Register, 25 November 1600) as 'First played by the Children of Paul's and now by the Children of the Chapel' (that is, first at Pauls' before 1590 and now at the Blackfriars in 1600), and about the same time the Paul's Boys seem to have performed the anonymous The Maid's Metamorphosis (1599×1600) and The Wisdom of Doctor Dodypoll (1599×1600), plays presumably included among those that Marston called 'musty fopperies of antiquity' that 'do not suit the humorous age's back | With clothes in fashion' and 'Mouldy fopperies of stale poetry, | Unpossible dry fictions'.[13] Jonson said much the same thing at the Blackfriars in his induction to Cynthia's Revels: 'They say the umbrae or ghosts of some three or four plays, departed a dozen years since, have been seen walking on your stage here: take heed, boy, if your house

[11] See C. L'Estrange Ewen, 'Lording Barry, Dramatist', Notes and Queries, 174 (1938), 111–12.

[12] Author of six comedies apparently intended for the Paul's Boys but not printed and perhaps never performed.

[13] Jack Drum's Entertainment, Prologue/Act V (H. Harvey Wood ed., iii. 179, 234).

be haunted by such hobgoblins 'twill fright away all your spectators quickly' (ll. 194–7).

Marston and Jonson, the founding fathers of the new drama,
are at one in their avant-garde hope to obliterate the past with an
explosion of novelty; and the boys' companies proved to be the
appropriate launching-pad for their ambitions. They came to this
common point, however, from different directions. Marston was
part of that Inns of Court counter-culture I have mentioned. The
heir of a wealthy and distinguished family, he was destined for the
law, like his father, but it was as the author of violently unstable
and bitter satires (1598, 1599) that he made his name in the Middle
Temple.[14] The first play normally attributed to him (whether as
author or reviser), *Histriomastix: or The Player Whipped* (1589×1599;
printed 1610), was written, it would seem, for some private occasion, probably an Inns of Court celebration. It is a curious cross
between a Morality play and a community pageant, with the cycle
of peace–plenty–pride–envy–war–poverty–peace illustrated by the
varying fortunes of different and uncoordinated groups (some ninety
characters in all), gentlemen (and their wives), merchants and lawyers, a company of 'common' players (the object of the title), and
various 'russetings and mechanicals'—all commented on by disillusioned gentlemen observers. Fluent though incoherent, it takes
a sour view of social improvement, even though the Queen is
enthroned as Astraea at the end of the play. Only the isolated neo-
stoic has the capacity to resist (even if not to change) the fluctuations
of fortune.[15]

The boys' companies seem to have offered Marston as a regular
playwright an opportunity to combine the destabilizations of satire
(and the *hauteur* of neo-stoic withdrawal) with the natural appeal

[14] O. J. Campbell (*Comicall Satyre and Shakespeare's 'Troilus and Cressida'* (San Marino,
1938)) has argued that the key date in the new dramaturgy is 1 June 1599, when the
Archbishop of Canterbury and the Bishop of London ordered that the works of Hall,
Marston, and Davies be withdrawn and that the books of Nashe and Harvey be brought in
and burnt. They further decreed that 'No satires or epigrams be printed hereafter' (see
Edward Arber (ed.), *Transcript of the Registers of the Company Stationers of London 1554–
1640* (5 vol.; London, 1875–7), iii. 316). Campbell believes that this act forced the theatre
to become 'the dramatic channel of the satiric spirit' (*Comicall Satyre*, 3). He ignores the
avant-garde plays that precede the ban and errs in saying that non-dramatic satire vanishes
at this point. See the list of 'satires and epigrams' in the *Cambridge Bibliography of English
Literature*, ed. George Watson (Cambridge, 1974–7), 1333–7.

[15] See Jean Jacquot, 'Le Répertoire des compagnies d'enfants à Londres (1600–1610)', in
Jean Jacquot (ed.), *Dramaturgie et société* (Paris, 1968), esp. 731–5, 782. Jacquot prints an
interesting series of plates illustrating the moral schema of *Histriomastix*.

of sympathetic involvement in a developing story—the prerequi-
site of audience interest. His first play for the boys, *Antonio and
Mellida* (1599×1600), is an extraordinary tissue of novelties. It
begins with the young players discussing their parts and comment-
ing on the impossibility of representing the standard roles: tyrant,
lover, fool, parasite, *miles gloriosus*, disguised prince. Their disengagement from the parts they are to play and their suspicion of the
rhetoric in which they are presented show the facts of the plot to
be palpably unreal and the emotions palpably factitious. But, when
the play itself opens, we find ourselves caught up in a high poetic
idiom of undoubted power to command our response to the history of the speaker—a power in no way infringed by the fact that
he is wearing the Amazon disguise he had earlier called absurd:

> ANTONIO. Heart, wilt not break? And thou, abhorred life,
> Wilt thou still breathe in my enraged blood?
> Veins, sinews, arteries, why crack ye not,
> Burst and divulsed with anguish of my grief?
> Can man by no means creep out of himself
> And leave the slough of viperous grief behind?
>
> (I. i. 1–6)

The Prologue tells us that poetry of this kind is part of Marston's
ambition:

> O that our Muse
> Had those abstruse and sinewy faculties
> That, with a strain of fresh invention,
> She might press out the rarity of art.
>
> (ll. 9–12)

What we seem to be offered in this highly self-conscious play is not
the sweet middle style of regular comedy but the lurid image of an
absurd world which is simultaneously ridiculous and tragic (Marston
does not seem to have conceived of *Antonio and Mellida* as separate
from its tragic twin, *Antonio's Revenge*). The boys are both the effective vehicles of a powerful poetry of passion and despair and at the
same time the parodists[16] of human pretension to emotional power.

---

[16] R. A. Foakes ('John Marston's Fantastical Plays', *PQ* 41 (1962), 229–39) argues that
children's parody of adult emotions is the whole purpose of the *Antonio* dilogy. It is true
that the wild and romantic poetry that Marston produces is well over the top, but it is
thereby made entirely appropriate, I would argue, to minds unhinged by the fragmentation
and unintelligibility of the world.

Marston wrote only for the boys. Jonson came to the newly re-established Blackfriars from several years of play-writing in the adult theatre. No doubt both of them relished the opportunity to impose themselves on boy actors trained to subservience[17] (as were all Elizabethan children). I have spoken in Chapter 3 of the clash between Humanist assumptions about literary power and the fact of writing plays to the order of ignorant and consequential actors. The boys' theatre offered more space to realize the Humanist image of an author as the agent of civilization, the conscience of his culture, allowing him to be, in avant-garde plays, the scourge of evasive sentimentalities. Such an image sustained Jonson's career and probably Marston's as well, and no doubt marked the boys' theatre for both of them as an institution where the writer could cut a figure as a person with interesting views. The Inductions of both make much of the backstage existence of the author as one of the factors the élite and literary audience is expected to respond to.[18]

What links Marston and Jonson (though polemically opposed figures) as avant-garde dramatists for the boys' companies? Their insistence on the author's personality as part of the play is only one element in a larger confluence of techniques that exploit the obvious gap between the boy actors and the adult roles they performed. Much has been made in recent years of the theatrical self-consciousness of Shakespeare's plays, of the 'breaks in illusion' that mark his dramaturgy.[19] But when we compare the repertory of the boys with that of Shakespeare's company we can see how 'realistic' the latter is in fact. In Shakespeare the occasional evocation of art or wit as against 'life' only adds piquancy to the main effect—our identification with the quasi-real emotions of the characters. In the boys' drama, on the other hand, play, pretence, affectation, trickery, lie at the centre of the dramatic method. 'Life'

---

[17] See Alfred Harbage, *Shakespeare and the Rival Traditions* (New York, 1952): '[The child actor was] little more than a chattel, divorced from his parents, huddled up in lodgings . . . worked to what must have been the limit of physical endurance, and provided only with his subsistence' (pp. 32–3).

[18] Marston and Jonson did not create this situation. An overt statement of the author's responsibility for the play can be seen in a rudimentary form in Lyly's Prologues and Epilogues.

[19] See (e.g.) S. L. Bethell, *Shakespeare and the Popular Dramatic Tradition* (London, 1944), Anne Righter/Barton, *Shakespeare and the Idea of the Play* (London, 1962), and indeed the whole cult of 'metadrama' as a cure for the incoherence of realism.

here is less a matter of individual morality than a social game in which we watch the players trying to move rapidly and unobserved towards their objective, as strategists intent on avoiding capture and rewarded by a success that the slow and the clumsy cannot hope for. Our identification is with manipulation of the rules of the game, which we allow to be *like* life but by no means a representation of it. Hence, no doubt, the alienating function of the Marston–Jonson Inductions and the recurrence of the rehearsal scene which we find not only in the episode in *Cynthia's Revels* where Amorphus rehearses Asotus in the act he must put on if he is going to shine as a courtier (II. iii. 11–69) but again and again in the boys' (as later in the men's) repertory.[20] In these cases and in all the other examples of deliberate role-playing in boys' plays the world must be seen as a place where speech and identity are counters paid out to society so as to secure a position of advantage, not as expressions of selfhood.

In Jonson's case, this presentation of life as a game leads to plays in which skill is equated with a properly balanced temperament and where social clumsiness becomes a mark of moral deficiency. In Marston, it leads rather to an emphasis on the difficulty, even the pain, of having to play for survival. For to succeed in the terms of such a world is not to be in the clear. As his Malcontent tells us, even as he is achieving his success: 'O God, how loathsome this toying is to me . . . [but] better play the fool lord than be the fool lord' (V. iii. 43–6). In both these authors, passionate desire to succeed coupled to passionate loathing for the folly of the world (especially of the courtly world, the only place where success really counts) imposes on their protagonists and audiences a fierce antinomy between satiric revulsion and the comic closure of what (for lack of a better phrase) one must call romantic hope.

The Two Stages

The role that the children's theatre played as a focus for literary innovation is clear. But, as noted above, the men were quick to respond to the same pressures; and so the situation in 1600 seems

---

[20] Cf. the rehearsal of the false Albano in *What You Will* (III. i. 1 ff.), Monsieur D'Olive being prepared for his role as ambassador (II. ii. 126 ff.), George Pye-Board rehearsing Captain Idle in *The Puritan* (I. iv. 183 ff.), Fromaga instructing the Gentleman Usher, in *The Fleer* (I. ii. 35–85), Witgood instructing the Courtesan how to present herself as a rich heiress (I. i. 47 ff.) in *A Trick to Catch the Old One*, Piero rehearsing Strozzo in fake repentance in *Antonio's Revenge* (II. ii), Anselm rehearsing Fuller how to woo in *How a Man May Choose a Good Wife* (ll. 374–628).

to have been much more fluid than commentators have suggested. In 1596 James Burbage leased certain rooms in the Blackfriars and converted them into a small indoor theatre (66′×46′), where, no doubt, he intended the members of his Chamberlain's company to perform before a more élite and a better-paying audience.[21] As I have noted in Chapter 2, the project proved premature. Burbage's heirs had to lease the property to the revived Chapel Children in 1600, and it took another ten years for the project to be fulfilled and for Shakespeare's company to acquire the élite status of playing in a private house. But we should remember that an awareness of the social possibility was there twelve years earlier. The James Burbage story links to the well-known passage in *Hamlet* in which Rosencrantz tells the prince about the sad fortunes of 'the tragedians of the city', obliged to travel because their customers have been stolen from them by 'an eyrie of children, little eyases' who 'are now the fashion' (II. ii. 339–44). Putting the two things together, it looks as if Burbage's original intention was to make such a thing impossible by moving his adult actors across a public–private boundary that was beginning to look permeable. The *Hamlet* passage suggests, moreover, that something more than financial rivalry was involved, that aesthetic and eventually moral distinctions can be made. The children's theatre has gained its audience, Hamlet tells us, not by the quality of its regular drama but by setting up controversy, making 'the poet and the player [go] to cuffs in the question' (II. ii. 355–6).

Jonson on the other side, urges an equally black-and-white distinction. His serving man's balladeer in *The Case is Altered* (1597× 1598)—presumably a fling at Anthony Munday—tells the other servants:

You shall have some now (as for example, in plays) that will have every day new tricks, and write you nothing but humours; indeed this pleases the gentlemen, but the common sort, they care not for't, they know not what to make on't; they look for good matter, they; and are not edified with such toys . . . Tut, give me the penny, give me the penny, I care not for the gentlemen, I; let me have a good ground, no matter for the pen, the plot shall carry it.   (I. ii. 60–77)

Munday defends a dramaturgy that depends on good stories (as noted above, he is 'our best plotter' in Meres's *Palladis Tamia*)

---

[21] This was a different hall in the Blackfriars from the one where Lyly's plays had been performed.

and on 'matter'—a good positive morality that edifies its hearers. Against this Jonson sets good writing ('the pen') and 'humours', a sceptical look at real contemporary manners. Modern critics, and particularly Alfred Harbage,[22] have energetically supported the hard-and-fast distinctions that Shakespeare and Jonson seem to be making. Harbage writes from the generous perspective of a socially committed critic who cherishes art for its power to unite all classes in a common experience. Understandably, he finds Shakespeare's art to be of this kind. Then he extends the virtue to encompass the whole of what he calls 'Shakespeare's theatre'—that is, the public theatre of the Elizabethans and Jacobeans. Here he finds a life-enhancing drama of broad sympathies catering for a popular taste for exciting action leading eventually to the triumph of goodness. On the other side of the fence he sees a coterie drama of narrow sectional values, characterized by sneering satire, whose standard themes are said to be 'sexual transgression, coupled in tragedy with treachery and murder and in comedy with cupidity and fraud'. 'The public plays emphasize actions, the private ones attitudes; the public plays valiant or villainous deeds, the private ones clever or stupid schemers'. The distinction that Harbage describes is handled in literary terms, but it is basically a moral distinction between the ethical health of the folk and the social sickness of the élite. He sees the takeover of the Blackfriars in 1608 as an action that 'involved some measure of ethical capitulation'.[23]

Harbage paints his picture in effective broad strokes, but a look at detail fails to confirm its truth. The new dramaturgy, in the Counter-Renaissance[24] taste, throws up very similar plays on either side of his boundary. Discrimination between the private *Cynthia's Revels* and its fellow Comicall Satyre, the public theatre's *Every Man Out of his Humour*, between Chapman's *All Fools* and his *A Humorous Day's Mirth*, between *Middleton's *Michaelmas Term* and his *A Chaste Maid in Cheapside*, between his *The Phoenix* and Shakespeare's *Measure for Measure*, does not turn on issues of moral health or sickness.[25] The clearest description of the new taste

---

[22] *Shakespeare and the Rival Traditions* (New York, 1952). Harbage takes for granted the historical truth of the argument mounted in Campbell, *Comicall Satyre*. See p. 283 above.
[23] Ibid. 71, 86, 89.   [24] See Haydn, *The Counter-Renaissance*.
[25] The overlap receives its most precise statement in the Induction to Marston's *The Malcontent*, where the King's Men justify their performance of a play that formerly belonged to the Queen's Revels Company). See further n. 65. Apart from the Induction, the only changes made from the boys' version of *The Malcontent* are some 450 additional lines

appears not in a children's play but in the Epistle 'To the comic play-readers, venery and laughter', set before *The Roaring Girl* (1610) by Middleton and Dekker, written for Prince Henry's Men at the Fortune Playhouse:

> The fashion of play-making I can properly compare to nothing so natur-ally as the alteration in apparel; for in the time of the great crop-doublet your huge bombasted plays, quilted with mighty words to lean purpose was only then in fashion: and as the doublet fell, neater inventions began to set up. Now, in the time of spruceness, our plays follow the niceness of our garments: single plots, quaint conceits, lecherous jests, dressed up in hanging sleeves: and those are fit for the times and termers.

A reading of the fifty-five (or so) surviving plays from the chidren's repertory does not support the idea of their homogeneity.[26] There are, of course, some kinds of plays that do not appear in that reper-tory, but they belong most obviously to genres that were going out of fashion everywhere: there are no chronicle histories, no domestic tragedies, few sword-and-buckler plays, few sentimental comedies. Yet that leaves a considerable variety of effects (often to be found in one play): satire of the court in Jonson and Marston; Italianate urban intrigue in Chapman; citizen frolics by Dekker; realist financial intrigue by Middleton; sophisticated tragicomedy in Fletcher, in *Machin and *Nathan Field; idealizing political tragedy by Chapman; frenzied intrigue tragedy by *Mason; static neo-classical tragedy in *Daniel and Marston.

It is easy to be misled by the statements of the dramatists and publishers in this period if we assume that they are engaged prim-arily in literary criticism. Financial survival was in fact the principal issue, and the literary points being made can usually be seen to relate to commercial or social advantage. But this is handled with an appropriate duplicity. Middleton's Epistle to *The Roaring Girl* offers, in the first half quoted above, the image of liberated life:

---

of text, mostly adding new jokes to existing scenes, many given to the one new character, the clown Passarello. The reason for these additions is said in the Induction to be 'to abridge the non-received custom of music in our theatre' (ll. 83–4). For more details see *The Malcontent*, ed. George K. Hunter (London, 1975), pp. xlvi–liii.

[26] O. J. Campbell, even though he is arguing in general that 'the select audience that gathered at the Blackfriars . . . took a special delight in social and ethical satire', still has to allow, when he comes to particular plays, that their taste was catered for by 'the complica-tions of a romantic tale . . . true lovers', the 'incredible villain', and 'crude melodramatic situations' (*Comicall Satyre*, 155).

'good to keep you in an afternoon from dice at home in your chambers, and for venery, you shall find enough for sixpence'. But then the wind turns and the appeal becomes focused on propriety and safety:

'tis the excellency of a writer to leave things better than he finds 'em; though some obscene fellow . . . would have ripped up the most nasty vice that ever hell belched forth and presented it to a modest assembly, yet we rather wish in such discoveries, where reputation lies bleeding, a slackness of truth than fulness of slander.

The doubleness of Middleton's argument (satiric, but nothing personal) reflects the variety of attitudes we find in his play. The risquée Moll Cutpurse cuts no purses here; she may be a social deviant (she dresses in men's clothes) but in action she is relentlessly moral and an enforcer of moral behaviour in others.

The notion that the boys' plays emphasize is that theirs are the theatres of daring and scandal, telling what no one else is willing to say, but saying it all in the cause of virtue.[27] Their frequent brushes with the law could be taken as guarantees that they were indeed living up to their reputation. It was a risky (if profitable[28]) venture, not entirely safeguarded by all the duplicity the authors could muster. And it was in the nature of such tightrope-walking that it led to a fall. The blizzard of suits that kept the management on edge (and give us most of the information we have today) show how intertwined were profits and the high-risk drama of controversy that *Hamlet* describes. The shareholders of the Paul's Boys seem to have tired of the struggle about 1606; they sold their plays to the stationers and accepted a retainer of £20 per annum from the Blackfriars company to keep their playhouse shut.[29] But the removal of the competition did not save the Blackfriars Boys for long. In 1608 the manager of the 'Children of the Revels' (formerly the Chapel Children), impoverished by plague and closed down

---

[27] The Induction to Day's *The Isle of Gulls* (1606) rehearses the kinds of evaluating questions the gentlemen–auditors might ask: 'are lawyers's fees and citizen's wives laid open?'; 'is there any great man's life characterized?'; 'is there any good bawdry?'; the author denies that he dare indulge in any such possibility: 'Strike at abuse, or ope the vein of sin | He is straight informed against for libelling.'

[28] In the lawsuits which resulted from the transfer of the Blackfriars back to Burbage (printed in *A Chronicle History of the London Stage*, ed. F. G. Fleay (London, 1890)) a moiety of the profits of the theatre (as a boys' theatre) is said to have been 'above the sum of one hundred and fifty pounds per annum, only for the use of the said great hall, without all manner of charges' (p. 249).   [29] See Hillebrand, 215–16; Chambers, ii. 55 f.

for political indiscretion, agreed to surrender his twenty-one-year Blackfriars lease to the King's Men; the company started again in a hall in the Whitefriars, but never regained its éclat; in 1613 they were amalgamated with the Lady Elizabeth's Men and the history of boy playing from this point fades into indistinction.[30]

Comedy as Satire

The part Ben Jonson plays in the establishment of the children's dramaturgy gives us a remarkable insight into the relationship of authorial persona and company style. He wrote only three full plays for the boys—*Cynthia's Revels*, *Poetaster*, and *Epicoene*—but the force and clarity with which he articulates what he expects of his audience and what he takes authorship to mean in such a context give us a powerful sense of a thought-out agendum, one sharply dismissive of alternatives and scornful of the vernacular past. He came to the boys' theatre after experience with both Henslowe and the Chamberlain's Men. His plays for Henslowe have perished in all but name; one may assume that they were of a different character from those he acknowledged. Yet *The Case is Altered*, performed by the boys some time before 1609, but written for an adult company about 1597, already shows Jonson's ambition for classic status (though he did not allow this play into the canon of his *Works*). *The Case is Altered* is classical in the sense that its plot is derived from Plautus' *Captivi* and *Aulularia*, but even Plautus is not classical enough for Jonson's developed taste; the comedy of identity lost and recovered again through love was not to reappear in his plays till the 'dotages' of his last years.

Some time before 1598 Jonson had turned to the Chamberlain's Men. *Every Man in his Humour* (1598)[31] is Jonson's first canonical comedy, and his first based on the explicit idea of humours. It seems to show his hope for a comedy centred on a poetry of rational self-control that the Chamberlain's Men's audience would be happy to identify with. The play is not classical in the sense of having a Roman source, but it displays a strongly 'classical' sense of restriction in the control of form—the whole action takes place

[30] Cf. Ch. 10 n. 7. See also the references to Christopher Beeston and Richard Heton in Ch. 2.

[31] I speak here of the original (Italian) form of the play, as performed in 1598, not about the form revised for inclusion in the 1616 *Works*, where the action is moved to London.

in a limited time (between breakfast and supper in one day) in a sharply circumscribed urban area (designated in the revised version as Hoxton to Cheapside); the characters all relate to one another as members of a natural family grouping (and its hangers-on). Above all, the sense of order is given its pervasive presence by a linguistic decorum that marks the speakers as either inside or outside the circle of social acceptability. The servants of *The Case is Altered* were characterized by ignorance of their own debasement. In *Every Man in his Humour* our condescension is directed more towards pretentiousness than ignorance. The tone is harsher, for pretension is more dangerous in society: many a Stephano passes for a gentleman, Matheo for a poet, Bobadilla for a soldier;[32] and so they must be exhibited here in a peep-show of fools by those insiders who invite us to share their superior laughter. The figure of Lorenzo Junior (Edward Kno'well), who possesses all the qualities that outsiders can only parody, is thus highlighted in his success by their failure. The comedy of these satirized characters in *Every Man in his Humour* is, however, only a sideshow. Satire is not the mode that gives us our focus on such classical types as Lorenzo Senior (Old Kno'well), the angry father, Thorello (Kitely), the jealous husband, or Giuliano (Downright) the quarrelsome brother —persons who live at the centre of the plot. These may well be called 'humorous' characters, but not in the sense of humour as something 'bred . . . by self-love and affectation, and fed by folly' (Q text: III. i. 157–8). Subjected to the discovery that the world is not as they wish it to be, these men lose their natural power to balance self-justifying assertion against civil detachment. Assertion takes over, like a disease. But the memory of their former rationality persists everywhere around them; it is in the interest of the whole society that they should not be excluded but be coaxed back into the honoured place they have left vacant.

By Jonson's own standards, *Every Man in his Humour* must be seen as a play of amiable and even temper (and it became even more so in its revision for the 1616 printing). The classic beauty of its organization gives space to the proliferating energy of folly and allows it, even under the shadow of satire, a free inventiveness to which we can respond with excitement, even with admiration.

---

[32] I give the Italianate names first and add in brackets the corresponding English names of the later version when these are difficult to deduce.

Like Falstaff, Bobadilla captivates our response by his capacity to reinvent his own self-esteem after each humiliation and to use his extraordinary verbal resources to transform every indignity into a self-pleasing triumph. Who could hate him? Satire would tell us that he is a monster, but theatrical experience shows that he is the life and soul of a play which has achieved recurrent success as a comedy not as a satire.

Jonson's next play, *Every Man out of his Humour*, the first clear indication of the social reach of his avant-garde dramaturgy, was also performed by the Chamberlain's Men (1599). The title suggests that it should be read as a sequel to *Every Man In*. However, it is anything but a sequel. It is rather a deliberate rejection of those aspects of *Every Man In* that have allowed it to remain a theatrical success. That play shows us a family group of normal, even if sorely tried, characters, who move purposively through their plot, and in their spare time construct a zoo in which the 'monsters' can be contained, stimulated, observed, and laughed at. In *Every Man Out* the zoo has become the world and there is now no plot to carry people across plot-time, only a recurring set of circulating imbecilities. This is a London populated, evidently exclusively, by obsessives and pretenders, their minds fixed unswervingly on the possibilities of folly in front of them. Occasionally the folly develops a kind of crazy charm, as when we see Puntarvolo organizing his return home from hunting as the adventure of a wandering knight in a romance: as he approaches his 'castle' he spies the waiting gentlewoman:

Stay: mine eye hath, on the instant, through the bounty of the window received the form of a nymph. I will step forward three paces, of the which I will barely retire one; and, after some little flexure of the knee, with an erected grace salute her—one, two, and three—Sweet lady, God save you.   (II. ii. 8–13)

The difficulty in coming to terms with *Every Man Out* lies in fact less with the fools than with the commentators; but, alas, this is a play with more commentary than laughter. Inside a context which moves only by the random and arbitrary influence of 'Lady Chance' or 'Strumpet Fortune', the obsessive commentator is likely to be seen as less the contemner than the object of contempt.

In *Every Man In* there is a weak cohesiveness between the fools, Matheo, Stephano, and Bobadilla, each happy to be associated with the others' gifts. In the darker world of *Every Man Out*, the pretenders can only cling to social status by undercutting one another's claims. This darkness shows also in the way that Asper, the righteously severe scholar of the literary-critical commentary in the play, has to become Macilente, when he joins the action, contemptuous of the world but at the same time twisted by envy of sillier men's worldly success.

Jonson is anxious in his presentation of this play to stress its originality. He invented a new genre for it (and the next two plays); these are not comedies but 'comical satyres'; he cites the traditional Donatus–Cicero definition of comedy but paraphrases it in terms which are designed for his own purposes as 'a thing throughout pleasant and ridiculous, and accommodated to the correction of manners' (III. vi. 207–9). *Every Man Out* is not, he tells us, to be thought of as a play like *Twelfth Night* or any other romantic comedy in which there is 'a duke to be in love with a countess and that countess to be in love with the duke's son and the son to love the lady's waiting maid . . . with a clown to be their serving man' (III. vi. 196–9). In the Induction we hear it is 'strange, and of a particular kind by itself, somewhat like *Vetus Comoedia*' (ll. 231–2). What he seems to mean is that his play resembles the freewheeling satirical drama of Aristophanes.[33] In fact, Jonson's play is only freewheeling in form; in content it is laboriously repetitive and didactic; what he is aiming for, he tells us, is a work in which 'good men and virtuous spirits that loathe their vices | Will cherish my free labours, love my lines' (Induction, ll. 134–5). With such an aim, the most that *Every Man Out* could hope for is a *succès d'estime*. Theatre history suggests that even that may be too ambitious.

In terms of classic theatricality, Jonson's movement from *Every Man In* to *Every Man Out* looks like a total perversity. But as an exploration of contemporary behaviour, recapturing not so much the form as the moral status of classical literature, *Every Man Out* has much interest. By setting the play in contemporary London, presented in great topographical detail (The Palace Stairs, The Mitre Tavern, The Counter, the western end of the aisle of St Paul's), Jonson was making a claim for truth in the sense of fidelity to fact (a claim he repeated in the revised *Every Man In*). His

---

[33] Jonson uses the same term to describe old *English* drama. See the 'Conversations with Drummond' (Herford and Simpson, I. xvii. 410). But that does not seem to be the usage here.

characters are, of course, types rather than individuals, but he could well claim that in such cases the X-ray machine gives a truer picture than the camera, showing the skull beneath the skin, the skeletal dance of death behind the court celebration.

In Brechtian terms one might say that Jonson was offering his audience not the passive pleasures of recognition but the privilege of understanding how reality could be made better. But, unlike Brecht's, Jonson's satire carries no external formula for political or social change. This makes it hard for him to stay inside his play world. In the original version Macilente finished his sojourn at court 'with a purposed resolution (his soul as it were new dressed in Envy) to malign anything that should front him; when suddenly, against expectation and all steel of his Malice' he sees the Queen, and 'the very wonder of her presence strikes him to the earth, dumb and astonished'.[34] His view of the world is immediately transformed:

> Envy is fled my soul at sight of her,
> And she hath chased all black thoughts from my bosom,
> Like as the sun doth darkness from the world.
> My stream of humour is run out of me
>
> . . . .
>
> And I have now a spirit as sweet and clear
> As the most rarified and subtle air.
>
> (Epilogue played before the Queen, ll. 4–15)

This seems to have been an ending designed not only for a court performance but also at the Globe, where an actor represented Queen Elizabeth: 'it had another catastrophe or conclusion in the first playing (*dia to ten Basilissan prosopoesthai*)[35] many seemed not to relish' (appendix X, ll. 1–3), and so the author had to abandon what he had devised. One can see why Jonson was affronted by the need to change. As in the parallel case of the royal letter at the end of Molière's *Tartuffe*, an intervention *ex machina* seems to be the only logical way of transforming a world too corrupt for human intervention. Having set up comical satyre as the form that will use comedy to secure the ends of satire, and having chosen to use the

---

[34] Herford and Simpson, III, app. x, ll. 27–31.
[35] That is, 'because the Queen was being impersonated'. The monarch also appears on the London stage (this time without objection) in Middleton's *The World Tossed at Tennis* (published 1620).

satirist's privilege to depict the real life around him, how could
Jonson bring his bilious survey to a comic ending? Not by plot
means, since there is nothing *inside* his created world that could
effect a change from bad to good, dissent to assent. Only an inexplicable force descending from above can create the *miracle* (Jonson's
own word) that turns Saul into Paul, Macilente into Sir John
Falstaff.[36]

The problem created by making court manners the centre of
action in a comedy for a public playhouse is entirely evident. The
reopening of the boys' playhouses at this point must have seemed
to Jonson to give him just the vehicle he needed to fulfil his
ambition for a comedy that would bring Humanist ideals to bear
on courtly behaviour. In offering his next play, *Cynthia's Revels: or
The Fountain of Self Love* (1600×1601), to the Chapel Children, he
was not only joining a writer-dominated theatre, as noted above,
but allowing himself to imagine that its audience would at last
provide the 'good men and virtuous spirits that loathe their vices'
that he was seeking.

Cynthia's Revels shows Jonson trying to adapt his satiric stance
to the new theatrical conditions. The wide-ranging social scene
and the realistic evocation of daily life in the central aisle of St
Paul's and elsewhere are no longer in evidence. The typified characters move closer to straight allegory and relate to one another in
a masque-like ensemble more suitable for boys' presentation at
court.[37] The play begins with a homage to Lyly as the last important dramatist to write for the Chapel Children. Cupid had been
proscribed for his pursuit of Diana's nymphs in Lyly's *Gallathea*,
where we hear of the nymphs 'using him like a prentice, whipping
him like a slave, scorning him like a beast' (v. iii. 33–4). Now he
intends to use Cynthia's revels to 'redeem the minutes I have lost
by their so long and over-nice proscription of my deity from their
court' and to 'follow some of Diana's maids' (I. i. 110–12, 107–8).
The Induction, in which the boys quarrel over the right to speak
the prologue and then spite the prologue-speaker by telling the
audience the story, makes brilliant use of children's natural detachment from the purposes of adult life and sets the scene for the

---

[36] In this as in other respects Jonson's court masques are the direct heirs to his comical
satires.

[37] Herford and Simpson assume that the Quarto text reflects the performance at court
(IV. 17).

opening of the play proper in the witty dialogue of Mercury and Cupid (soon to appear as pages themselves). Already, even in this episode, however, Jonson shows his unwillingness to stay within the limits that Lyly observed. The reference to the 'black and envious slanders, hourly breathed against [Diana] for her divine justice on Actaeon', points to the execution of Essex with a clarity Lyly sedulously avoided in his evocations of the court; and as soon as Jonson introduces his human characters the Lylian atmosphere dissolves and we are thrown back into a sneering satire on modern manners. I have noted elsewhere that the relation of *Cynthia's Revels* to Lyly's *Endymion* is that of a positive celebration turned into a negative one.[38] And in these terms Jonson's play illustrates the change of emphasis between the boys' theatre of Lyly's day and that of 1601. Jonson celebrates the temperament of scholarship (as does Marston's contemporary *What You Will*[39]) but with strident antithesis rather than the light and shade of Marston's play. *Cynthia's Revels* is an exercise in judgement rather than exploration, and Crites the scholar (who in some sense represents the author) is not simply a marginal commentator, like Marston's Quadratus, but is the inescapable positive figure of the whole action. *Every Man Out* weakened its satiric force by exposing the *raisonneur* Asper as the envious obsessive Macilente (so criticizing the critic). Jonson seems to be determined not to reproduce that problem, and so surrounds Crites with a flattering claque of all the best people, the allegorical virtues, the gods Mercury and Cupid, and Cynthia herself, who screen the commentator from the least breath of criticism. If *Cynthia's Revels* is a compliment to the Queen (who is represented in some sense by Cynthia), then the compliment seems to be conditional on the Queen approving Jonson's Humanist values and their consequence in the understanding of society.

The dramaturgy of *Cynthia's Revels* makes no attempt to follow the Lylyian mode of romance found in the early boys' repertory when their playhouses reopened in 1599/1600. It is against such plays presumably that the Induction warns the audience (see above, pp. 282–3). Jonson's rejection of these *umbrae*, or plays long dead, takes on a somewhat factitious air, however, if we turn to consider another *umbra* from earlier dramaturgy. The play of *The Contention between Liberality and Prodigality* was apparently in existence by

---

[38] *John Lyly: The Humanist as Courtier* (London, 1962), 291.　　[39] See pp. 318–19.

1575,[40] but it seems to have been resurrected for the Chapel Children when they started playing again and was 'played before her Majesty', probably on 22 February 1601.[41] *Liberality and Prodigality* must then have been in the Chapel Children's repertory at the same time as *Cynthia's Revels*, and it is hard to believe that Jonson did not know it. The similarities are remarkable. In both plays the plot sets Money (Jonson's Argurion) against Prodigality (Jonson's Asotus) and the contest is judged by Virtue (Jonson's Arete). In both cases the prodigal fails, in the careless delights of the moment, to notice that his sustaining wealth is being alienated and that economics as well as moral standards must destroy him.[42] But, of course, it is morality and not satire that controls the action in *Liberality and Prodigality*, so that the whole issue is contained inside a clear and familiar pattern. The vices of the earlier play (in characters like Tom Tosspot and Dick Dicer) are vices of conduct not of character, and they can be treated as malfunctions in an otherwise ideal and self-correcting state machine. But the malfunctions of Jonson's characters are temperamental and demand scorn and horror rather than a criminal trial. What was probably of most interest to Jonson was the role given in the earlier play to the Queen or 'Prince', who holds the whole economic system together by her moral authority, with Virtue as her agent, Equity as her judge, and Liberality—a mean between Prodigality and Tenacity (or hoarding)—as the paymaster who dispenses justice by rewarding Captain Well-Done, the wounded veteran, and dismissing mere place-seekers. It is not surprising that Jonson was attracted to the morality form. But he redefines the issues. The appropriate judge is not now the civil magistrate but the scholar-poet who can probe the surface of language and tell what behaviour is false, self-serving, or indecorous; for approval or punishment now depends on a judgement of manners as the signals of morals. Crites (Greek for

---

[40] See Hillebrand, 128 ff.

[41] The text printed in 1602 refers to 'the three and forty year of the prosperous reign of Elizabeth' (that is, to 1601), though otherwise it looks like a model of early Tudor dramaturgy.

[42] Twenty-five years later (in *The Staple of News*, second intermean, ll. 14–19), Jonson still remembers this pattern. Mirth says: 'That was the old way, Gossip, when Iniquity came in . . . but now they are attired like men and women o' the time . . . Prodigality like a young heir and his *Mistress* Money (whose favours he scatters like counters)'. The scattering of counters [coins] may have been part of the original production of *The Contention between Liberality and Prodigality* (see Hillebrand, 130).

judge) is given the power to identify for Cynthia the 'mimics, jesters, panders, parasites, | And other such-like prodigies of men' (III. iv. 20–1) who haunt the court. In this his role is very close to that of the narrator in formal (non-dramatic) satire. As in *Every Man Out*, much of the energy of the play goes into elaborate descriptions of the courtlings' self-love, impudence, foolishness, prodigality, inconstancy, deformation by travel, *nouveau-riche* pretension. These read well as satiric exercises, but lack the impersonal authority that would make them proper for a morality play. The ending (as in *Every Man Out*) cannot come from anything *inside* the play and can only be secured by quasi-divine fiat. In this *Cynthia's Revels* resembles Lyly once again. But in Lyly's plots the fiat opens a way forward into compromise for characters frustrated by the status quo. In Jonson the frustrating pretences of courtliness are exposed and confessed, but there is no way for characters to reach out to new possibilities. The only realistic comment for such people is Elbow's on Pompey in *Measure for Measure*: 'Thou art to continue now, thou varlet, thou art to continue' (II. i. 191).

The angry satire and polemic, not to mention what the Herford and Simpson edition calls 'the immense and undisguised complacency' of *Cynthia's Revels* (i. 396), leads directly to the so-called *poetomachia*[43] between Jonson on one side, represented by *Poetaster: or The Arraignment* (1601) performed at the Blackfriars, and Marston and Dekker on the other side, represented by *Satiromastix: or The Untrussing of the Humorous Poet* (1601), performed at Paul's (and also at the Globe). The occasion of this 'throwing about of brains' as it is called in *Hamlet* (II. ii. 358) is made significant for a history of drama[44] only by the definitions of dramatic quality that

---

[43] The most to-the-point discussion of the issue appears in Cyrus Hoy's introduction to *Satiromastix* in the *Introductions, Notes, and Commentaries to Texts in 'The Dramatic Works of Thomas Dekker'* (Cambridge, 1980), i.

[44] I should mention here the strange addendum to the war of the theatres to be found in the Cambridge academic play *The Second Part of The Return from Parnassus* (Part III of the *Parnassus* sequence, acted ?1601–3). I have already mentioned (pp. 85–6) the scene in which Kemp and Burbage interview the Cambridge graduates who hope to be hired as actors. Among other remarks, Kemp tells them, 'O that Ben Jonson is a pestilent fellow, he brought up Horace giving the poets a pill: but our fellow Shakespeare hath given him a purge that made him beray his credit'. Chambers (iv. 38–40) and J. B. Leishman (in his edition of the play) have supposed that the 'purge' ought to be *Satiromastix* and that the Cambridge authors thought that Shakespeare had written it, because that play was performed by Shakespeare's company at the Globe as well as by the boys in the Paul's playhouse. Kenneth Muir, on the other hand (*Troilus and Cressida* (Oxford, 1982), 6), thinks that it is Kemp's ignorance that is being satirized.

emerge by the way. Cyrus Hoy remarks that 'what at bottom the war of the theatres was about was the moral responsibility of the satirist. How disinterested in fact was Jonson's exposure of folly and vice?'.[45] In *Poetaster* Jonson answers this question by presenting himself in the person of Horace, justified in his scorn for the poetasters by the judgement of Augustus and Maecenas (a safer stay for Jonson than Elizabeth and Burleigh). The 'Rome' represented by such characters provides him with a scene in which he can make bad writing the sign of bad morals,[46] a species of treason, and so he can define literary criticism as a social duty: writing as inflated as Marston's, as opportunistic as Dekker's, or as lascivious as Ovid's, must be judged by the prince himself and subjected to appropriate state punishment—Ovid to banishment, and Crispinus (Marston) to a lexical emetic which makes him throw up all the hard words in his vocabulary. In *Satiromastix* (which answers Hoy's question more directly than does *Poetaster*), Horace (Jonson) is represented as a social hanger-on and toady, desperate to establish himself as an independent moralist but fearful of being held responsible for his judgements. We know his writing is corrupt, not because it is bad writing, but because he himself is dishonest; his verse is concocted to exploit social possibilities, though he presents it as an essential part of a well-regulated state (like Augustan Rome).

It looks as if the *poetomachia* was not much appreciated by the authorities. The passage in *Hamlet* where the matter is mentioned was not printed in the good quarto of 1604 and the 'Apologetical Dialogue' which Jonson added to the text of *Poetaster* was (as he tells us) 'only once spoken upon the stage' and was not printed till 1616. There is no record of official suppression in 1601/2 similar to that of 1599 (see above, n. 14) but the effects seem to argue a similar determination to silence controversy. We know that Jonson, having reached the dead end of *Poetaster*, retired to lick his wounds and think about writing tragedy. We may detect, at the same time I believe, a related though spasmodic retreat from satire in the repertory of the boys and a re-emergence of more civil forms.

[45] *Introductions*, ed. Hoy, i. 194.
[46] Cf. Jonson in *Discoveries* (Herford and Simpson, VIII. 593): 'wheresoever manners and fashions are corrupted, language is. It imitates the public riot. The excess of feasts and apparel are the notes of a sick state; and the wantonness of language of a sick mind'.

Intrigue Comedy

The taste for 'humours' and satiric portraiture did not vanish by fiat, and much of the comedy in the boys' repertory continued to turn on a dialectic between the desire for neat and amusing plotting in the mode of New Comedy and a contrary interest in sharply realistic but inevitably static exposures of human weakness, often conducted from a self-consciously superior viewpoint. Such classicism as is present is, of course, merely English, and this often allows some fusion of the roles of intriguer and satirist-judge. In New Comedy the detail of the intrigue is usually carried out by a slave or servant;[47] but his cleverness is no sign of superiority; the young master for whom he operates shows his class by his inability to imagine what the next sharp move will have to be and what plausible lies will facilitate it. But the slave, freed by his status from the usual proprieties, must attempt both to deceive and be liked by those whose power over him cannot be avoided. He must exploit human weakness by perpetual activity, driven by the hope that all will turn out well and that he can escape the lash and the treadmill. If the young gentleman is to act as intriguer, it must be to secure some way that measures his innocence or at least allows him to be excused by the force of his passions.

George Chapman is the author whose comedies show best the double role of intriguer and commentator in a dramaturgy that aims to reconcile witty exposé and well-plotted comedy. He is obviously drawn to the figure of the scholar commentator, but is evidently unwilling to give him a godlike moral advantage or the Jonsonian rhetoric of outrage that goes with it. His early humours comedy, *A Humorous Day's Mirth*, seems to be the play Henslowe refers to on 11 May 1597 as 'The comedy of umers'; it therefore precedes the ban on satire and the re-establishment of the boys' playhouses. It has every mark of an apprentice effort (though fewer, Parrott soothingly reminds us,[48] than his preceding comedy, *The Blind Beggar of Alexandria* (1596)).[49] Lemot, the French king's witty minion, is the intriguer: he splashes his way through a wash

---

[47] As also (exceptionally) in Jonson's *Every Man in his Humour*, where Musco (Brainworm) performs all the functions of the Roman slave.

[48] *The Plays of George Chapman: The Comedies*, ed. T. M. Parrott (2 vols.; London, 1914), ii. 688.

[49] But remember that this play was one of the great successes of the Admiral's repertory.

of 'humorous' courtiers and ladies, with mischievous intent to reveal to their jealous partners the secrets of one spouse after another. His labyrinthine intrigues amuse the king but do not take us in any particular direction. He is given the power to mislead but not to understand his victims. It is Dowsecer, the melancholy scholar, who is given the complementary superiority of moral judgement. He finds the world hateful, but his eloquent soliloquies point him towards withdrawal rather than satiric involvement; it is his contemplative eloquence that inspires love, and love cures his melancholy and restores him to society. Yet it is not clear how he will fit into the society we are shown.

The anonymous *Sir Giles Goosecap* (1601×1603) is normally assigned to Chapman, and certainly it is in Chapman's style. It may be his first play for the boys. Parrott's edition (ii. 893) reads it as close to *Cynthia's Revels*. For it is a play without an intriguer, a play 'of dialogue instead of action as a means of revealing character'. As in *A Humorous Day's Mirth*, the thinker and the social whirl of fools are shown as radical but only loosely connected opposites. The thinker (Clarence) lives in a separate dimension, screened from the world by his admiring patron, Lord Mumford. But he cannot be screened permanently from life. With much self-chastisement he admits to love for Eugenia, one of the bevy of ladies wooed by Goosecap and his vacuous companions, and this brings him within reach of them; but there is no confrontation. The lady is reluctant to leave the pleasures of society (vacuous or not) for the abstruse speculations of her melancholy admirer. Sir Giles's folly, or rather oddity—his skill in perfumery, embroidery, and woodturning—is a considerable benefit in the social scene she enjoys. And she is not condemned for choosing to stay there. Eventually, however, she suffers some kind of conversion and pledges herself to Clarence in terms that may well be Neoplatonic (and are certainly obscure enough). Goosecap and his companions fare less well. They are put in their places in the witty exchanges of their courtship routines and by the observations of their sharp Lylian pages, but they are not pilloried by scorn or excluded from social life. The poise that allows one to see society as ephemeral, yet know that it forms the scene in which nobility of nature must appear or not be known at all, is adumbrated in *Sir Giles Goosecap*, but in philosophical terms that are mainly mysterious.

A Humorous Day's Mirth and *Sir Giles Goosecap* are both plays in which the retired scholar and the busy socialite draw on alternative and incommensurate (philosophic and dramatic) sources of authority. They are in consequence plays of a somewhat wayward progression, more interesting in detail than in development. Roman and Italian New Comedy offered Chapman a way out of this impasse, but only if he was prepared to reduce the role of the independent thinker. And this, clearly enough, was difficult for him. The remaining Chapman comedies illustrate his struggle to achieve complex unity in the intrigue, and yet not to lose the image of virtuous and effective scholarship.

The plot of *May-Day* (1601×1609) is based squarely on that of Alessandro Piccolomini's *L'Alessandro* of c.1545, a play celebrated for the skill with which it dovetails three separate actions. It is clear that the central aspect of the plot for Piccolomini is that of the two exiles from political turmoil in Palermo: Lucrezia, living in Pisa as Fortunio, and Aloisio, living there as Lampridia. Hence the Italian denouement concentrates on the standard anagnorisis of lost family members and lost sexual identities recovered when the boy reveals himself as a girl and the girl as a boy, and they declare their undiminished love for one another.

Chapman does not excise this story but makes it an accessory to another strand of the plot—the more farcical story of the *vecchio innamorato* who convinces himself (if no one else) that he is now in the full flood of sexual attractiveness and virility, thus placing himself in a position where he can be manipulated into a series of humiliating disguises and embarrassing revelations. Chapman's denouement takes the shape, recurrent in his comedies, of a formal celebration (a 'May-night show') in which all three plots are worked out in a masque, as if in a dream, so that the problems disappear into a game and moral distinctions attenuate into merriment.

This reordering of priorities moves the saturnine scholar Lodovico (Piccolomini's Alessandro) into the position of a dominant intriguer. His pleasure, like Lemot's, lies in exploiting weaknesses rather than condemning them, but his understanding allows us to share his judgements. He provides us with a point of view in terms of which we can relish the moral decorum as well as the exact timing of the juxtapositions and cross-cutting. The stasis of Jonsonian formal satire must accommodate itself to the dynamic effect of change and chance, so that judgement must be incorporated in intrigue before it can reach its conclusion.

Chapman's *All Fools*[50] once again (as in *May-Day*) constructs a comic intrigue out of the situation of two neighbouring fathers: Gostanzo (the name of the *vecchio innamorato* in *L'Alessandro*) is a heavy father, and Marcantonio, an easy-going one. The contrast is derived from Terence's *Adelphoe*, but is worked into an intrigue, derived from the *Heautontimorumenos*, of almost impenetrable complexity. Young A is married to B, and C is in love with D; but the fathers can be manipulated to believe that A is in love with D and C with B, and, being more interested in triumphing over one another than in noticing what is happening under their noses, they allow the real relationships to flourish under the protection of the false ones. Thus is set up a tissue of continuous role-playing and tight-knit cross-intrigues that draws directly on the natural talents of the boy performers.

The central issue of *All Fools* is, inevitably, to secure the socially approved union of the young lovers by manipulating the obsessive folly (or 'humour') of the heavy father. The work of this manipulation, carried out in Terence by the slaves, is here given to Marcantonio's younger son (as in *May-Day* to the victim's nephew). These are both detached scholars and observers of other men's affairs; though they appear now without the earlier *raisonneurs*' philosophic pretensions, they retain something of their predecessors' reluctance to descend into the arena of actual contemporary behaviour. The Prologue shows Chapman quite self-conscious about the difficulty of placing his drama between the dangerous 'personal application' of Jonson and the alternative danger that plays without it will seem but 'toys':

> Who can show cause why th'ancient comic vein
> Of Eupolis and Cratinus (now revived
> Subject to personal application}
> Should be exploded by some bitter spleens,[51]

---

[50] The play is dated both 1599 and 1604 in Harbage–Schoenbaum, on the assumption that the present text is a revision of that for which Henslowe paid Chapman in January and July 1599, under the heading of 'The World Runs on Wheels, and now All Fools but the Fool' (*Henslowe's Diary*, ii. 203). The connection of titles seems tenuous. The play was printed in 1605 as 'presented in the Blackfriars', and it was probably performed at court on New Year's Night 1605. Given the nature of its dramaturgy, it seems best to treat it here as part of the boys' repertory.

[51] That is, 'hissed off the stage by angry persons'.

Yet merely comical and harmless jests
(Though ne'er so witty) be esteemed but toys,
If void of th'other satirism's sauce?

(ll. 13–19)

The immensely complicated twists and turns of the plot collapse
into compromise at the end. Chapman's denouement takes us, as
in *May-Day*, to a specific social celebration where all the characters confront one another and learn to face their follies without
subterfuge. But no hierarchy of understanding is established. One
by one the characters who are exposed are able to turn the tables
on their tormentors. The helter-skelter of reversals allows us to see
that all the anxieties we have shared are only part of a game. *All* are
Fools. And this liberates the young lover to enunciate his mock
encomium on the cuckold's horn (the natural fate of all men): 'Is't
come to this? Then will I make a speech in praise of this reconcile-
ment, including therein the praise and honour of the most fashionable and authentical HORN' (v. ii. 219–21)—and so he does for
the next eighty-nine lines (v. ii. 224–303).

The range of Chapman's comic drama shows, I have suggested,
the effort to achieve a form of comedy in which the judgement of
the scholar and the social whirl, truth and game are set against one
another, but in terms less stark than appear in Jonson's comical
satyres. The *commedia erudita* gave him an image of the unattached
intellectual able to hold the play together by investing his cleverness in the manipulation of unexamined social assumptions. In-
triguers of the type of Machiavelli's Callimaco (in the *Mandragola*)
are brilliantly successful seducers, but their intelligence is aimed at
conquest, not understanding. How to match the comedy of exploitation with the impulse to anatomize and judge is a dilemma that lies
at the centre of these comedies, and it is one that Chapman never
really solved.

The *Gentleman Usher* (*c*.1602×1604) and *Monsieur D'Olive* (1604)
show Chapman in a different mode, dispensing with the manipulator and allowing the philosophic seriousness of the thinker to be
incorporated into the structure of society. These are plays centred
on the formalities and ceremonies by which a noble society regu-
lates itself. Ceremony, one might say, shows here the idea of Game
given its most exalted validity. It embodies the standards of social
decorum against which individuals must be tested. Ceremony does

not need the approval of any ruler; in itself it shows what society is meant to be.[52] In these plays we see it invoked to distinguish those who can read *meanings* as against those who recognize only forms—as do the foolish characters who give the plays their titles, and as do the villains who see its metaphoric structures only as occasions for deception and self-advancement (as masques are used elsewhere as opportunities for murder). The boy players must have been very effective agents of this idea, half-serious, half-playful, drawing on the qualities of elegantly disengaged ceremoniousness they displayed in royal entries and processions.

The Gentleman Usher shows the Duke, the centre and validator of ceremony, as unwilling to understand the restriction that his role demands. Too besotted with desire to notice that others are using ceremonial occasions for nefarious purposes, he becomes a betrayer of his own state. He has to be rescued, not by intrigue but by the suffering and semi-mystical vision of Strozza, his virtuous counsellor. The villainous favourite, Medice, incapable equally of verse scansion or social decorum, is thereby revealed as an impostor to nobility, and obliged to confess that he is not Medice but Mendice, formerly king of the gypsies, and so constitutionally incapable of spiritual understanding.

The other pretender in the play, Bassiolo, is the 'Gentleman Usher' of the title, the organizer of the play's ceremonies, one who knows 'what's fit' (v. iv. 167). But his control of the forms and externals of ceremony deludes him into the comic assumption that he is ennobled by this knowledge, whereas true nobility derives only from perception of the inner meaning. But Bassiolo need not be punished like Medice; he ends in a shower of (ironic) acclamations. His lack of central understanding labels him not as a villain but only as a comic figure, entirely acceptable inside his proper space.

Monsieur D'Olive (1604) offers a variant version of a value system mediated through ceremony, one which relates philosophic understanding to action in the world. The high-minded and noble characters have dealt with their sorrows by turning them into

---

[52] See D. G. Gordon's excursus on the Goddess Ceremony in Stephen Orgel (ed.), *The Renaissance Imagination* (Berkeley and Los Angeles, 1975), 110–16. Chapman's comedy can be seen in these terms to be aspiring to the condition of the court masque, where (see Appendix, pp. 529–30) the distinction between the meaning or 'soul' and the form or 'body' is a central issue.

rituals. St Anne's wife has died; her embalmed body sits in a chair in his study, and there he weeps and mourns her loss. Vaumont and his Countess have lived in a Platonic *ménage à trois* with Vandome, but when Vandome travels abroad, the Countess displays such excessive grief that her husband falls into an unPlatonic jealousy. This so outrages the high-minded Countess that she entombs herself in her own quarters and, like Shakespeare's Romeo, 'shuts fair daylight out | And makes [herself] an artificial night' (i. i. 139–40).

Vandome returns from his travels as a philosopher grown into a man of action, prepared for the intrigues (tricks and illusions) that are required to take both St Anne and the Countess out of their self-enclosing ceremonies, and liberate them into a daylight world of reciprocity and change. To this extent he has become a mildly cynical intriguer. But the transition from knowledge to action is not presented here as a loss. To achieve virtuous ends in society requires not only penetration into human weakness but power to move the characters from solipsism to cure. The cure, of course, can be achieved only because they understand perfectly the moral equations offered. There is no sense in which St Anne and the Countess are being victimized by Vandome's manipulations.

In the sub-plot dealing with Monsieur D'Olive, the intention to ridicule is entirely obvious. But D'Olive's courtly tormentors are not given any advantage over their victim other than sophisticated knowingness. Once again the issue is one of drawing out the self-enclosed and self-admiring individual into the larger and harsher world of give-and-take, where self-indulgent ceremoniousness will be exposed to public scrutiny. The plot to persuade D'Olive that he has been appointed an ambassador and must therefore act with 'stiff-hammed audacity' succeeds up to a point. But his fluent command of the forms of discourse, though not its content, has its charms as well as its absurdities; he is innocent of malice. And the end is not expulsion but compromise. He learns quickly that his 'court honour' is a joke:

MUGERON. My Lord! My Lord Ambassador!
D'OLIVE. My Lord Fool am I not? . . . I'll be no longer a block to whet your dull wits on.

(v. ii. 60–72)

The Duke secures him against his 'ambassadorial expenses', and the final lines 'Be all made happy in the worthy knowledge | Of our worthy friend, Monsieur D'Olive', though spoken with tongue in cheek, is without rancour.

These comedies by Chapman can be seen as a series of experiments in which the hierarchical values of comical satyre are faced by the theatrical truth that comedies move naturally towards dispersed acceptances rather than isolating judgements.[53] But Chapman's is not the only route away from comical satyre. Compromise between the social definition provided by static satire and that emerging from developing intrigue can take many forms. The case of Marston is particularly interesting in this respect. Of all the dramatists for the children's theatre, Marston is the one closest to Jonson in general outlook and most opposite to him in particular techniques. In his *Antonio and Mellida* and *Antonio's Revenge* diptych he found a method of turning the impetus of his formal satires towards a completely different kind of effect. Jonson's satiric energy drove him towards a realism that had to justify itself by naming names, so that *Poetaster* is the Pyrrhic victory of his method. Marston moved satire into a phantasmagoria of grotesquely exaggerated forms, which bore the same relation to reality as nightmare to daylight. He employs a stylistic register that continually defies Jonson's norms of decorum; his words and his plot teeter all the time on a high wire stretched between vision and absurdity. Marston is, it would seem, far more sceptical than either Jonson or Chapman. His focus on the indeterminacy of power is not complemented by any idea of a political or moral system that can guarantee an eventual rapport between upper and lower, inner and outer. The world his thoughtful men are drawn into and must abhor is controlled not by pretenders but by bizarre political villains (surrounded by comic toadies). In *Antonio and Mellida* these sharp antinomies rule· all. Piero the Duke of Venice is in politics a tyrant, in rhetoric a

---

[53] The opposition between action and ethics may be thought to be carried to its logical extreme in Chapman's last (and in some respects best) comedy, *The Widow's Tears* (1603×1609), where the mediating commentator disappears completely and the prevarications of plot are broken down by the brutal energy that in Jacobean drama characterizes younger brothers on the make, jealous husbands, and widow-hunters. Here this quality, isolated in the Graeco-Roman past from the rules and complexities of modern society, allows no barrier to protect idealism from sexual 'reality', female virtue from male will-to-power. This brings *The Widow's Tears* closer to *Bussy D'Ambois* than to any of Chapman's comedies. Tharsalio's determination to overcome fortune by confidence is a comic equivalent to Bussy's dedication to *virtù* and sweeps aside with equal contempt all the impediments that an effete society can propose. Cf. E. M. Waith, *Ideas of Greatness* (London, 1971), 131–2.

madman; his court is a danger-laden circus of swirling affectations where only stoical passivity can offer protection. The only way to outmanœuvre him is by destabilization even more extreme than his own. His daughter's lover, Antonio, the defeated prince of Genoa, having lost all, can use the indeterminacy of his position at the Venetian court (as Amazon, stoic, lover, corpse) to change roles faster than the pursuers can decode them, and so he achieves a comic ending due more to virtuoso acting than any change of heart; and as soon as his performances end, as we learn in Part II, Piero regains the initiative.

Marston's development as a dramatist for the children shows his continued fascination with affectations and inanities, but increasingly he places these inside structures that stress continuity rather than fragmentation. In his London comedy of bourgeois life, *Jack Drum's Entertainment* (1600), he subjects fantastic adventures (like those of the 'musty fopperies') to the domestic authority of a Highgate patriarch, Sir Edward Fortune. His comedy of the Venetian bourgeoisie, *What You Will* (1601), likewise allows loss of identity to appear as a mere inconvenience, covered by the insurance of a stable city environment.[54] When he returns to the Italianate court again in *The Malcontent* (1600×1604), Marston finds a simpler way of putting together the antinomies of tragic exile and a comic court, stoicism and passion, the outrage of the superior mind at actions that are necessary and an acknowledgement of their necessity if one is to survive. The double-sided figure of Altofront–Malevole as Duke–Malcontent and Stoic–Satirist joins these opposites together as alternative vocabularies for the same person, different parts that one mind must play, and play to the top of its bent. We see the legitimate Duke, overthrown by a cabal, returning to his own court in disguise (like other dukes discussed below) to purvey a brilliantly cynical and anti-idealist eloquence that gives him among those who have usurped his dukedom the reputation of being a man who understands the world (not to mention the pleasure that epigrammatic cynicism gives to the audience). His seeming lack of scruple also suggests to the usurpers that he is a handy man to have around for the next *coup*. And so, as *coup* succeeds *coup*, the instability of the dukedom allows him to use his inwardness with the system to engineer his own return. Malevole is balanced on a

[54] The plot is taken from Sforza D'Oddi, *I Morti Vivi* (1576).

narrow ledge between belief and disbelief: he speaks as a *satyr* or wild man who despises all civilized limits but plots as a *satirist* with a specific ethical purpose. In *Antonio and Mellida* there was a real antinomy between desperation and patience, with no sense of how they could coexist, but in *The Malcontent* the satiric vision is controlled as a self-conscious performance, a permission of the will to enlarge and fantasticate, to use human examples to release emotional identification with the worst, while virtue lies beneath as an unspoken (and largely unspeakable) aspiration. The violences of satire are integrated into a structure that moves the whole genre towards tragicomedy,[55] finally revealing its values as located not in the public world of power but in the private love of man and wife.

In the Prologue to *Parasitaster: or The Fawn* (1604×1606) Marston defends his play as one where 'no rude disgraces | Shall taint a public, or a private name'. He offers instead a 'nimble form of comedy | Mere spectacle of life and public manners'. The plot replays that of *The Malcontent*, but without evoking the latter's intensity of revulsion or its political implications. The central issue in the play is not political legitimacy but married procreation, 'you genital | You fruitful, well-mixed heats' (v. i. 5–6). The central Duke figure is not here dispossessed; he is in fear of dynastic dispossession only because his son seems disinclined to marry and provide an heir. And so he sends the son to 'Gonzaga's' court in Urbino, ostensibly to woo the Gonzaga princess for his father. He himself follows him there, disguised as *Faunus*,[56] and acts as promoter of a love match between the son and the princess, as libertine philosopher (out of Montaigne), and as satiric commentator on the alternatives to married procreation as seen in a procession of grotesque courtlings: Nymphadoro, who loves all, Amoroso Debile-Dosso [weak-back], the impotent husband, Herod Frappatore, the incestuous pretender to universal conquest, Don Zuccone, the needlessly jealous husband.

As a scene of courtly folly, *The Fawn* reminds one of *Cynthia's Revels*. But Faunus is no Crites. He tells us at the beginning of the play that he is tired of the ceremonious restraint, the 'repressed

---

[55] See Ch. 10. On tragicomedy and satire, see G. K. Hunter, 'English Folly and Italian Vice', and 'Italian Tragicomedy on the English Stage', both reprinted in *Dramatic Identities and Cultural Tradition* (Liverpool, 1978), and *The Malcontent*, ed. Hunter, pp. lxi ff.

[56] Presumably the name was chosen for its satyric connotations, but it also derives from the English *fawn*—to flatter.

heat', the 'carriage regular | Apted unto my place' that belongs to a duke: 'we must once be wild'; he will take upon himself 'the least of disranked shapes' and taste 'the appetite of blood' (I. i. 41-55). What he discovers as a serving man in Urbino is the extent to which he has been screened by his flattering courtiers from the real truths of an open world. Now he will take revenge[57] by 'fawning' on others (that is by agreeing with whatever they say and encouraging their folly, so that it will sprout and show its head),

> Till, in their own-loved race they fall most lame
> And meet full butt the close of vice's shame.

(I. ii. 349-50)

In spite of this heavily moralistic intention, the ending is completely genial. The folly unravels as it is caught up in a medieval court entertainment.[58] The patent artificiality of this mode of 'cure' is set in contrast to the consummation of the son's and princess's married love, which occurs simultaneously 'above'. Episodic and disconnected, the entertainment serves as antimasque to the hidden mystery of procreation, as surface against centre. The satiric fun here floats easily on the surface of a deeply conservative notion of the good and the true. No doubt that made it all the more acceptable to the élite audience it entertained.

The effectiveness of a mixture of this kind, of large-scale political survey coupled to small-scale personal satire, had been tried out, probably earlier than *The Fawn*, in Middleton's first play, *The Phoenix* (1603×1604).[59] This begins with another Duke of Ferrara, who (like Shakespeare's Vincentio) has ruled his city with too much pity, so that 'complaints . . . seven, nay seventeen years [have been] neglected' (I. i. 105-6). The Duke is now anxious to pass on the cares of office to his son (Phoenix). He is persuaded that he should send him abroad to study 'affections actually presented' before he sits on the throne. But the son understands that more useful experience can be obtained by travelling through 'the bowels of this dukedom'. Accompanied by the faithful Fidelio, he moves

---

[57] Cf. the 'revenge' of Justiniano in *Westward Ho* (see below, p. 322).

[58] Philip Finkelpearl has argued (in *John Marston of the Middle Temple* (Cambridge, Mass., 1969), 227 ff.) that the form came from a source closer to Marston than the Middle Ages—from the Middle Temple's 'Prince d'Amour' revels of 1597-8.

[59] Like most modern commentators, I incline to the view that *Blurt, Master Constable* (1601×1602) is by Dekker rather than Middleton.

through a London-lookalike landscape of varied corruptions and sharp practices (as formerly in Estates Satire). It emerges that the source of Ferrara–London's many-faceted disorder lies in that 'angel sent amongst us, sober law . . . voiced like a virgin, and as chaste from sale' (I. iv. 197–200), still 'sacred' in its institution, but curently 'foul' in its practice. The Justice of the Peace, the attorney, and the scrivener are shown as an unholy trinity of tricksters who betray the wife, protect and profit from the thief, and decline to save the innocent from the powerful. Much of this resembles the experience of the *picaro*: as in the story of the Captain who sells his wife before he goes to sea again; and some of it anticipates 'city comedy': as in the episode of the knight and the jeweller's wife, bound to one another in an erotic-mercantile exchange of 'My Pleasure' and 'My Profit'.

But, unlike the adventures of the *picaro*, these are not treated as random episodes; they are held as evidence of the moral disease that sustains the frame plot of a quest for truth, without anywhere suggesting, as does Faunus, that the commentator has a natural affinity with the world he condemns. The end of the play shows the same soft focus. Treason is finally frustrated, and by melodramatic discovery the dukedom is reanimated; the good and the bad are revealed and distinguished. Tangle, the prime comedian of the play, whose entanglement in law terms has driven him into a madness,[60] is wheeled on to complete the political action. Is legal corruption a serious or a comic matter? Middleton does not seem to have made up his mind.

The difficulty of holding together the comedy and the satire of the ruler-in-disguise play appears even more damagingly in Edward Sharpham's *The Fleer* (1606), another play for the boys written by a literary novice, but not providing this time the prelude to a distinguished career. Sharpham was a young gentleman of Devon who had been in the Middle Temple since 1594 and was obviously modelling himself on that other alumnus of the Middle Temple, John Marston. The title[61] and much else in *The Fleer* is directly cribbed from *The Fawn* and it is elsewhere indebted both to Marston's *The Malcontent* and his *The Dutch Courtesan*. Its central

---

[60] When Middleton repeats these characteristics in Dampit in *A Trick to Catch the Old One*, he does so without any good humour. Dampit cannot (like Tangle) be rescued by a comic cure. What we are shown is the irrecoverable slide of legal corruption into hell.

[61] *OED* defines *fleer* (v. 3) as 'to flatter'.

figure is Antifront (compare Altofront in *The Malcontent*), deposed Duke of Florence who, like other dukes in this grouping, quickly disappears into disguise, reappearing in London as 'Fleer', a witty serving man. Sharpham's play, like Middleton's but unlike Marston's, thus sits on the edge of city comedy. Fleer finds employment in the brothel occupied by his two daughters—a situation which seems to give him neither surprise nor anxiety. There he is able to observe his daughters' relations with various gallants, including Piso, the vacationing heir of the Florentine usurper. Matrimonial intrigue leads somewhat inconsequentially to melodramatic actions and reactions; but all is stilled by the news that Piso Senior has died. Hearing of his accession, Piso Junior wishes the usurpation undone; and so Fleer is able to reveal himself as Antifront and reassume his power.

The Fleer shows little understanding of the underlying Stoic– Calvinist value system that gives substance to Marston's cynical rhetoric. Fleer is an intriguer whose royalty is without aura; his exile exists without reference to past or future, and indeed his main function is to make cynical and witty remarks. To some extent we may guess that Sharpham saw what he was doing. In the most remarkable speech in the play he tells us that

the city is like a comedy, both in parts and in apparel, and your gallants are the actors; for he that yesterday played the gentleman now plays the beggar; she that played the waiting-woman now plays the quean; he that played the married man now plays the cuckold and she that played the lady now plays the painter. Then for their apparel, they change too, for she that wore the petticoat now wears the breech; he that wore the cox-comb now wears the feather; the gentleman that wore the long sword now wears the short hanger . . .   (II. i. 124–33)

What Sharpham has not noticed is that a play cannot present instability effectively without handling it from a stable point of view.

John *Day's *Law Tricks: or Who Would Have Thought It* (1604× 1607) is better organized professionally than Sharpham's play (as befits a busy dramatist of long standing), but it can make no better use of the departed duke plot than to fill the gap in authority with games of deception (as if Lucio had been made deputy in *Measure for Measure*). When Ferneze, the Duke of Genoa, leaves to search for his daughter, his son Polymetes is left in charge of the state.

But the father is scarcely gone before the daughter returns (in disguise, of course) to tease and titillate her sober-sided brother, to such effect that he changes from a scholar to a roysterer and a lover. When he hears his father is dead, he distributes offices and wealth at random. But the news was false; when the father returns, the son has to devise a series of elaborate hoaxes to conceal the truth. The deceptions, of course, become more and more unstable and finally collapse when the daughter chooses to reveal her identity. The pleasure in Day's play is obviously meant to rest on the ingenuity of its plot. In his Epilogue he points to his subtitle and claims that his play justifies it:

> Who would have thought such strange events should fall
> Into a course so smooth and comical?
>
> (ll. 2309–10)

Day's later play, *Humour out of Breath* (1607×1608), shows the facility with which the dramatists of the time could switch the same material from genre to genre. Poetic, delicately fanciful, and Lylian, this play shows the disguised-duke theme at an even further remove from its satiric origins. The plot resembles that of *Antonio and Mellida*: the defeated and exiled Duke of Mantua and his son wander in the territories of the victorious Duke of Venice; the son of Mantua falls in love with the daughter of Venice, who is, however, no helpless Mellida but a high-spirited though coquettish ('humorous') lover. But one disguised duke is not enough for Day's plot. At the same time, the sons of Venice are wandering in search of love, disguised as shepherds, followed and observed by their disguised father. When the sons meet and fall in love with the daughters of Mantua (disguised as fisherwomen), the father tries to intervene, but fails. The symmetry of organization requires every Jack to end up with his Jill. The fact that symmetry is the law of this world is pushed home by the organization of the verse, in stichomythia, in quatrains, anaphora, and epistrophe. Not a breath of realism spoils the exquisite verbal fantasies. It may be worth remembering that *Humour out of Breath* was being played by the boys in the same season as Fletcher's *The Faithful Shepherdess* (1608).[62] We may guess that Day was using an old plot to catch a new taste.

---

[62] See Ch. 10.

The disguised-duke plot could be adapted to answer the various interests and attitudes of the private-theatre audiences, and so of their playwrights. There is, however, one surviving play of this kind that stands outside the boys' repertory. Shakespeare's *Measure for Measure* (*c*.1603×1604) is regularly seen as an exception inside Shakespeare's *œuvre*.[63] But in the children's theatre, as we have seen, the figure of the disguised sovereign who manipulates the lives of his subjects belongs to a considerable tradition. Around just this time we find protagonists serving as virtuous manipulators of one kind or another, in *Westward Ho* (Justiniano), *Northward Ho* (Bellamont), *Monsieur D'Olive* (Vandome), and *The Dutch Courtesan* (Freevil). And around 1604, using the standard chronology, the manipulator appears, as in *Measure for Measure*, as a disguised duke in three children's plays (*The Phoenix*, *The Malcontent*, *Law Tricks*).

It is tempting to follow up the indication in *Hamlet* that the fashionable plays of the boys were cutting into the profits of the Globe, and speculate that Shakespeare wrote *Measure for Measure* in some degree of emulation. The years 1603–4 were years of great theatrical confusion, the years of the Queen's death, of the new sovereign, of the great plague which shut the playhouses from 19 March 1603 to 9 April 1604. The Chapel Children were playing in a theatre (the Blackfriars) that they had leased from the King's Men, and there seems to have been some talk in 1604, when the managers of that playhouse were impoverished by the plague, of returning the lease.[64] It was in this year (presumably) that the King's Men 'stole' Marston's *The Malcontent* from the boys and performed it at the Globe with a Marston–Jonson style of Induction (written by Webster) in which two private-theatre patrons claim the right to sit on the stage of the Globe, complain of the garlic breath of the groundlings, and talk to Condell and Lowin (who justify their 'theft' of the play as only a matter of exchange).[65] Is it conceivable that Shakespeare, acting in *The Malcontent* in the midst of all this to-and-fro, saw a way of handling the current boys' theme that would make it appropriate for the adult players, thus

[63] J. W. Lever in his edition (London, 1965) calls it 'a conscious experiment in the new medium of tragicomedy' (p. lx).   [64] See Chambers, ii. 509.
[65] 'SLY. I wonder you would play it [*The Malcontent*], another company having interest in it. CONDELL. Why not Malevole in folio with us, as Jeronimo in decimo-sexto with them? They taught us a name for our play: we call it *One for Another*' (Induction, ll. 76–80).

bringing into the Globe some of the cachet that attached to the rival playhouses? The plot of *Measure for Measure* owes something to *All's Well that Ends Well*, of course, in its redemption of a brash new world by recovery of the values of an older one, and in its reliance on that romantic plot solvent, the bed trick; but the emphasis on urban disorder and on the role of public law as the corrupt bedfellow of private vice makes *Measure for Measure* quite unlike anything Shakespeare had written so far. It is a strength of the Marston plays we have considered that the absentee dukes are both scornful of the corruption they uncover and (as their language shows) complicit in its excitements. But the end towards which their purposes point is never in doubt. In Shakespeare, political purpose almost disappears into the psychological exploration that the double role permits. We see Angelo's implication in the sin of Claudio as part of the process of discovering himself. The Duke's disguise as a friar serves as a commentary on his own confusion of morals and politics, virtue and power. Where *Measure for Measure* remains closest to the children's plays is in the sub-plot material of Lucio and Pompey, Mrs Overdone, Froth, Elbow, Abhorson, who depict an unchanging underworld incapable of repentance. Against this, Shakespeare sets not the moral superiority of the observers but only the higher vices of the thinking classes, whose thinking makes their lives unstable and whose movement through the plot can hardly be resolved by anagnorisis. Marston's brilliantly inventive language allows him to express in imagery a complexity of attitude that is not mirrored in a depth of character. Shakespeare, on the other hand, uses his poetry to create individual tones of voice, so that we seem to be feeling our way through the labyrinths of self-image and self-deception and sharing the difficulty of knowing which is which. Hence the soliloquies and statements of objective truth in the play ('Be absolute for death . . .', 'Ay, but to die and go we know not where', 'He who the sword of heaven shall bear') cannot ever evade the question, 'Why is he saying this?'

These depths and complexities make difficulties, of course, for the kind of plot that Shakespeare is employing. In *The Comedy of Errors, A Midsummer Night's Dream, As You Like It*,[66] we see rulers who begin in the public world of order; then front stage is taken

---

[66] The pattern can be sustained in *As You Like It* only by splitting the duke into two halves, one good, one wicked.

over by private disorder, which the dukes are unable to engage with because they see it only from the standpoint of public control; at the end they reassume power, having acquired some understanding of private emotions; they put the aberrants in their place, and the public threats from vice and folly are cancelled. *Measure for Measure* offers us this same pattern, but the presence of corruption has emerged so strongly as a facet of personality that it can hardly be disposed of in the denouement. Angelo, who is installed as the problem-solver, has to learn that it is he who is the problem, and so we understand that the problem can hardly be solved. Occupying the position of the 'son' in other disguised-duke plays, he aims to show that vice can be treated as an objective aspect of public order, as a plot issue: Claudio's private sin can be treated as a public crime. But the play gives no support to that idea of a solution. Isabella too, who had hoped to preserve virtue as a private possession, is forced into the arena of confused public values: the persuasive power available to her cannot be secured by principles but only by body language.

The play's title points up its difference from the other examples of the disguised-duke routine. They treat the separation of the orderly from the disorderly as a given fact. Shakespeare sets up the troubling idea of equivalence to counterpoint the distinctions between superior and inferior on which order depends (Marston does something similar in *The Malcontent*, but to very different effect): Angelo is equivalent to Claudio, Ragozine is equivalent to Barnardine, Mariana to Isabella, Angelo is the Duke's 'substitute'. So (in another sense) we may see Isabella's puritanism as equivalent to Angelo's. Behind all this, like an informing shadow, lies the larger and vaguer notion of Christian brotherhood (see the puns on friar and brother, sister and nun). The idea that 'we are all sons of the same Father and brothers in sin' is the heart of Isabella's argument with Angelo; and the power of the poetry tells us that we should take the idea with great seriousness:

> Why, all the souls that were were forfeit once,
> And He that might the vantage best have took
> Found out the remedy. How would you be
> If He, which is the top of judgment, should
> But judge you as you are?

(II. ii. 73–7)

But this disabling of human judgement disables not only Angelo but the Duke himself and renders suspect the notion that there is a natural order there waiting to be restored. In this sense we may understand *Measure for Measure* as not only an imitation of a children's theatre mode but also a critique of it.

What we have seen in the children's plays so far considered is a dramaturgy stretched between the demands of the classical comic tradition of intrigue creating closure and the felt need to present the author's (and presumably the audience's) contempt for social folly. It is the obvious advantage of an intriguer in the classical model that he can manipulate a settled shape out of the disordered world he finds; but in the private theatres this may have seemed too bland an acceptance of things as they are. Protagonists like Crites and Macilente, Malevole and Faunus, show themselves more concerned to define difference than to achieve settled social harmony; the ends they secure come about through change of focus rather than reformation: encouragement to folly or castigation of vice allows the foolish or vicious characters to be seen in a different context; but they cannot be changed. Malevole achieves a return to the throne; but the plot by which he achieves it is absurdly off-hand: he suddenly announces: 'My lady comes to court; there is a whirl of fate comes tumbling on; the castle's captain stands for me, the people pray for me; and the Great Leader of the just stands for me' (v. iv. 89–92). This is the first we hear of these pointers to a conclusion, and all the process we are given. Even when the pressure of a satirist on the stage is not a factor (as in *The Phoenix*, or *Law Tricks*, or *Humour out of Breath*), there seems to be a reluctance to subject the tricks and games to the tight control of an intriguer. None of these plays gives us the pleasure of classical dramaturgy's ordered process, leading us forward sure-footedly through transformations to the desired end.

This seems to be true even among plays obviously in touch with the canons of classical comedy. I have already mentioned Jonson's *The Case is Altered*, where the denouement has the classical precedent of a chance exchange of prisoners (as in Plautus' *Captivi*).[67] One can add Marston's *What You Will*, the story of a Venetian

---

[67]   It seems that the Plautine plays most imitated in this period are those in which (as in the *Menaechmi*) the denouement comes about through coincidence rather than intrigue.

husband supposed lost at sea. His supposed widow is besieged by offers of replacement, and so his brother, anxious to discourage them, dresses up a local perfumer as the lost spouse. The mere rumour of survival will, he hopes, break off the match. But the real husband returns at just that moment, thus creating the situation that has sustained comedy since at least the time of Plautus' *Amphytruo*,[68] as the returned husband tries to assert his identity against that of the more plausible substitute. But Marston is not content to leave this neat plot standing on its own. He requires us to see it from the viewpoint of a set of gentlemen of education and leisure who divert the action from plot progression to a haphazard set of comical games, commented on from a cynical and disillusioned point of view. The satire has no real target, but it still works to deny the sense of progressive purpose that the basic plot possesses.

Marston's *The Dutch Courtesan* (1603×1604) turns these matters around by allowing us to think of the satirist not as a guardian of values but as a self-indulgent verbalizer. Freevil, the central figure, is contemptuous of the idea that we can distance ourselves from corruption by defining it. His aim is to demonstrate to his friend Malheureux (and to the audience) the naturalist (Montaignian) lesson that men belong to nature, and need not verbal formulae but extraordinary Grace to escape the demoralizing pressures of the body (or 'the blood' as Marston calls it). At the beginning of the play we are told that 'the difference betwixt the love of a courtesan and a wife is the full scope of this play, which, intermixed with the deceits of a witty city jester, fills up the comedy'. The difference between the courtesan and the wife is in fact identified as the special case of the distinction between Nature and Grace, body and soul.

Freevil's naturalism allows him to live on both sides of this dichotomy; he is cynically knowing about corruption and prizes the rationality which allows him to accept its inevitability; yet he remains open to the grace which descends on him from his not accidentally named betrothed, Beatrice. His attachment to Franceschina, the 'Dutch courtesan', is severely controlled. Brothels are 'most necessary buildings. Ever since my intention of marriage I

---

[68] See also Stith Thompson, *Motif Index of Folk Literature* (Bloomington, Ind., 1932–6), N. 681.

do pray for their continuance' (I. i. 59–60). But as a married man he will no longer haunt them, though others will (and must). Set against his scorn for rhetorical effusions is the set-piece moralism of Malheureux, vulnerable because he is one of those who have substituted language for experience and (in the words of the Prologue to *Antonio's Revenge*)

> winks and shuts his apprehension up
> From common sense of what men were, and are,
> Who would not know what men must be.

Malheureux has relied on prejudgement and satiric distance to protect him from the harlot's wiles. Evil, seen as naturally resident in Franceschina, a 'creature made of blood and hell' and cut off from normal life by her grotesque foreign lingo, can be dealt with, he thinks, without being faced in physical reality. His mind being a tissue of sentimental assumptions, his body betrays him as soon as he meets his seductress. Freevil's intrigue thus requires that Malheureux be driven from the specious compromise he clings to (that he can commit himself to a passion for Franceschina and yet stay in control of his life); he must be forced to find his identity again in a place so bare of comfort (Tyburn) that his body submits to the direction of his soul.

The 'witty city jester' of the play's argument (Cocledemoy)—a character who continued to amuse audiences into the nineteenth century—replays Freevil in a series of *lazzi* against a profit-shaving vintner. The tone is entirely different from that of the main plot, but the discriminations are closely related. The vintner, like Malheureux, aims to lead a divided moral life, to profess religiosity while at the same time choosing not to think about his own commercial practices. He too ends up in the shadow of the gallows, acknowledging his sin, and so he, like Malheureux, can be saved at the last minute.

City Comedy

The Dutch Courtesan is a play of London life, high bourgeois in the main plot, mercantile in the sub-plot. But it can hardly be called a city comedy. Its philosophical interests, its lack of concern for class distinctions, upward or downward mobility, take it outside the concerns of a genre that is defined for us most usually by the central presence of a young gallant struggling for self-realization against the impersonal requirements of a cash economy. The standard form of this kind of comedy was not realized, of course, by a flash of inspiration but by slow growth and accretion. We can see elements of the fable in many preceding plays—in the episodes of Fallace and Deliro in *Every Man out of his Humour*, in the Rose and Lacy plot in *The Shoemakers' Holiday*, in the relationship between the jeweller's wife and the knight in *The Phoenix*, in the story of the usurer's daughter in Haughton's *Englishmen for my Money* (1598), in the relaxed shopkeepers' romances in *The Fair Maid of the Exchange* (1594×1607)—but Dekker and Webster's play for the Paul's Boys, *Westward Ho* (1604), looks like the best starting-point for an exploration of the genre.

It should not surprise us that this is a genre that came to maturity in the boys' theatres, with their Inns of Court clientele, rather than in the theatres of the men. Young 'gallants', caught inside a city dominated by a puritan business ethic, were likely to be responsive to stories of erotic triumph as compensation for their official juniority and financial disadvantage. Moreover, stories of tricksters were (as I have noted) particularly appropriate to the talents of the boys, and trickiness provides the obvious means by which the young man can take advantage of capitalist enterprise and yet preserve his self-respect. The conflict of 'gentlemanly' values and capitalism was, of course, a fact of London life, and some critics have taken these plays as pictures of true history.[69] But the coherence of the picture belongs to art and not to life.

At the centre of the pattern of London life shown in *Westward Ho* lies the exchange equivalence of sex and money. The rich, busy, self-satisfied merchants have the money; the spendthrift gentlemen need money to maintain their swaggering style; the two are tied together by the bonds of credit and debit.[70] The third term that holds the equation together is supplied by the merchants' wives, competent, independent, somewhat neglected by husbands in search of profit, and dreaming of escapist sexual adventures.

---

[69] See e.g. L. C. Knights, *Drama and Society in the Age of Jonson* (London, 1937).
[70] See *The Dutch Courtesan*: 'The merchant thrives not but by the licentiousness of the giddy and unsettled youth' (I. ii. 43); and the Jonson–Marston–Chapman *Eastward Ho*: 'How would merchants thrive, if gentlemen would not be unthrifts? How could gentlemen be unthrifts if their humours were not fed?' (I. i. 38–40).

These wives bear some resemblance to the modern stereotype of the bored suburban wife, ripe for adultery. And it is adultery (or potential adultery) that completes the comic circle of desire and panic:[71] the gallants desire money; the wives desire the attention of the gallants; the husbands hope to keep the gallants closely tied to their purse strings, and at the same time desire their wives to be chaste.

Dekker and Webster handle the problem of these equations in two different but interrelated plots, first as a melodramatic confrontation in which an earl seduces the wife of an Italian merchant with promises of unimaginable luxury, but then is forced into high-style repentance when the husband appears for the assignation disguised as a succubus, with his wife as a corpse. The 'Italianate' revenge thus shadowed is then translated into a comic vein. The Italian (Justiniano) will have his own (comic) revenge by showing that other men's wives are equally susceptible:

They say for one cuckold to know that his friend is in the like headache ... [is comfort]. Have amongst you city dames! You that are indeed the fittest and most proper persons for a comedy. Nor let the world lay any imputation upon my disguise, for court, city and country are merely as masks, one to the other, envied of some, laughed at of others. And so to my comical business.   (I. i. 221–9)

Justiniano thus carries forward the role of the intellectual provocateur we have met in Chapman and Jonson, though without any pretension to superior status. His role is to encourage the wives to move from sexual imaginings to adulterous reality. And so, under his guidance, they set off, Westward ho, to an assignation in the shady suburb of Brainford [Brentford]. But female wit turns out to be a genuine alternative to sexual melodrama, and everyone ends up with some part of what they want. Once in the inn, the wives devise witty means to frustrate their would-be lovers. The husbands who arrive, puffing with righteous indignation, are confuted with evidence of their own gallantries. And, as the final lines allow, 'these men [the gallants] are civil', that is, are not out of phase with

---

[71] This provides an interesting variant on the romantic circle of love which Jonson satirizes in *Every Man Out* (Herford and Simpson, III. vi. 196–9) and which one finds (for example) in the *Arcadia* and in *Gl'ingannati* (Gherardo loves Lelia loves Flamineo loves Isabella loves Fabio/Lelia). There is a late and highly self-conscious example in Sharpham's *Cupid's Whirligig* (Peg loves Newcome loves Nan loves Slack loves Wife (Lady Troublesome)).

city manners; the merchants will forgive them 'like pitiful fathers'. The Italian reveals his part in the escapade, the sin is unloaded on Mrs Birdlime, the bawd, who is expelled from the company. For the rest 'All is but a merriment, all but a May game' (a phrase which should remind us of Chapman); the carnival ends with restoration of the (somewhat shaky) status quo.

Westward Ho has been much disliked as a disillusioning image of human nature.[72] Most of those who have decried it have seen the Jonson–Chapman–Marston response, *Eastward Ho* (1605)—played at the 'other' boys' playhouse, the Blackfriars—as a deliberate corrective, a 'conscious protest . . . against the new comedy of Middleton and Dekker. . . . this picture is of honesty, industry and sobriety victorious over roguery, idleness and dissipation'.[73] Indeed, with Dekker on one side and Jonson on the other, it is possible to think of the *Eastward Ho/Westward Ho* confrontation as a reprise of the poetomachia. But the terms of opposition as well as the personnel are different. The new play has been written

> Not out of Envy, for there's no effect
> Where there's no cause; nor out of imitation,
> For we have evermore been imitated;
> Nor out of our contention to do better
> Than that which is opposed to ours in title,
> For that was good, and better cannot be.
>
> (Prologue, ll. 1–6)

The fact that the Prologue is good-humoured does not mean, of course, that the difference of viewpoint is without substance, or the values at issue wholly different from those in the poetomachia. The diagrammatic picture of London in *Westward Ho* leaves the individuals a considerable freedom to renegotiate status. The plot is loosely articulated (all the more realistic for that) and regularly sacrifices continuity to local effects. *Eastward Ho*'s plot, on the other hand, braces its picture of London life with the ethical clarity

---

[72] Felix Schelling saw it as marking 'the depth of gross and vicious realism to which the comedy of manners descended' (*Elizabethan Drama* (2 vols.; New York, 1908), i. 502–3); Thomas Marc Parrott found in it only a 'laxness and confusion of morals' (*Chapman: The Comedies*, ii. 840); Louis B. Wright thought it was a play 'which sentimentalized vice and mocked the virtues of respectable citizens' (*Middle Class Culture in Elizabethan England* (Chapel Hill, NC, 1935), 630).

[73] *George Chapman: The Comedies*, ed. Parrott, 840.

and structural rigidity of a Morality play.[74] At the beginning, Touch-stone, the patriarch of the play, spells out the pattern: 'I have two prentices, the one of a boundless prodigality, the other of a most hopeful industry, so have I only two daughters, the eldest of a proud ambition and nice wantonness, the other of a modest humility and comely soberness' (I. i. 95–9). The authors clearly expect us to see the development of this symmetry in terms of that Morality favourite, the prodigal-son story.[75] The prodigal daughter and prentice behave just as the tradition requires them to, reject the careful father and assume they can impose their romantic self-assurance on the external world (this time the world of rapacious capitalism). The daughter, abetted by her mother, believes that once she is married to a knight she will be able to travel to a castle in the country where fairies and paladins will protect her from economic reality. The prentice and the bankrupt knight believe that they can escape to a Virginia where chamber pots are made of gold (as in More's *Utopia*) and rubies can be picked up on the beach. Both prodigals are shipwrecked, the daughter on land when her hired coach runs out of destinations, the prentice and knight quite literally, when they are washed overboard at Cuckold's Haven, Eastward ho, a few miles down the Thames.

In the Morality play proper the goodness of the father and the propriety of his judgement are unquestioned. In the modern world of *Eastward Ho*, however, the theatrical appeal of Parrott's 'honesty, industry and sobriety' cannot be taken for granted. The favoured daughter is a nullity; the good apprentice is prosy, canting, and complacent. When Touchstone proposes a wedding feast to match the spendthrift celebration of the prodigals, his answer replays Hamlet in the idiom of Uriah Heep,

Let me beseech you, no, sir; the superfluity and cold meat left at their nuptials will with bounty furnish ours. The grossest prodigality is superfluous cost of the belly; nor would I wish any invitement of states or

[74] The 'ethical clarity' obviously came too close to King James's activities to escape punishment: Jonson and Chapman were imprisoned, and Marston had to escape into the country. This scandal, following one about Daniel's *Philotas* (see below), may be the cause why the company (at this point called 'The Queen's Revels') had to give up the Queen's name and become simply 'the Children of the Revels'. Two years later there was another scandal, about Day's *The Isle of Gulls* (1606), and yet another in 1608, about Chapman's *Byron*. That seems finally to have led to the disappearance of the company from the Blackfriars.

[75] See I. i. 115–17; V. v. 223. 'Nice wantonness' is clearly meant to refer us to the Morality play *Nice Wanton* (1547×1553).

friends; only your reverent presence and witness shall sufficiently grace and confirm us. (II. i. 172-8)

The idle apprentice is called Quicksilver. The name refers us to fake gold, and in the moral pattern must be set against 'Touchstone' the father and 'Golding' the good apprentice. But 'Quicksilver' also describes the mercurial man. Quicksilver's extraordinary energy in self-recreation keeps him always ahead of mere moralism. Even when he is in prison on a capital felony charge, he takes control of his destiny once again and makes a final grand metamorphosis into John Bunyan, with a torrential eloquence in self-condemnation that sets the whole prison singing psalms.

Anthony Trollope objected to 'the old tradesman [Touchstone] being taken in by the mock repentance of the idle one'.[76] But are we meant to be sure that Quicksilver's repentance is a fake? Although the authors treat the idea of repentance as part of the fun, does that mean that we should think it not a serious idea? We are being given the structure of a Morality play, but not its unitary outlook. Hogarth's response to the 1744 edition[77] shows how easy it is to reinstate the story and ignore the telling. But the play ends with the theatre, not the world, as the determining framework. Quicksilver, in the last spasm of his Bunyan persona, makes it his punning 'suit' that he might walk home from prison still wearing his prisoner's rags. Touchstone spells out the moral for 'London', but Quicksilver[78] points to a more immediate audience:

Stay, sir, I perceive the multitude are gathered together to view our coming out at the Counter. See if the streets and the fronts of the houses be not stuck with people, and the windows filled with ladies, as on the solemn day of the pageant. (Epilogue, ll. 1-6)

These 'streets and houses' are of course the structures of the playhouse. In Hogarth's version only the good apprentice gets 'the pageant' or the Lord Mayor's show—the bad apprentice gets

---

[76] Cited in Van Fossen's edition of the play (Manchester, 1979), 22.

[77] The 'Industry and Idleness' series of 1747 (R. Paulson, *Hogarth's Graphic Works* (New Haven, 1970), plates 180-91). The Hogarth series seems to have led to the production of Charlotte Lennox's version (*Old City Manners*) in 1751, where the play is moved slightly closer to Hogarthian moralism (and to Lillo's *The London Merchant* of 1731). In Lennox's version the epilogue ends not with Quicksilver's triumph but with 'See the two ways which lead to shame or state | Choose ruin or fair fame—*work upon that*'.

[78] The Quarto only says 'Epilogue', but the 'sir' seems to show that Dodsley's assigning of the speech to Quicksilver is justified.

Tyburn —but in *Eastward Ho* the victory of morality is balanced by a celebration of imaginative energy as a theatrical form of the good. *Eastward Ho* does not simply condemn the romantic evasions of *Westward Ho* but redefines them as a form of play that should be enjoyed, yet understood as opposite to reality. In *Northward Ho*, which was performed at the Paul's theatre shortly afterwards (1605), Dekker and Webster seem to have accepted some of this redefinition. The audience is reminded of the continuity with *Westward Ho*: Ware has become the refuge for 'those poor wenches that before Christmas fled Westward with bag and baggage [and] come now sailing alongst the lee shore with a Northerly wind' (I. ii. 71–4). But we never meet the wenches. The denouement takes place in the 'fatal house of Brainford Northward' where (as previously) the whole cast assembles and sorts out the issues of cuckoldry and non-cuckoldry. But this is a version more conscious of moral pressures. It begins with a witty piece of italianate intrigue:[79] the solid citizen Mayberry is persuaded that he has been cuckolded by two gallants who presume that he will act cruelly and leave his wife in need of 'protection'. It looks as if the situation of *Westward Ho* is to be recapitulated. But this time the marriage bond is sustained not by equality in wrongdoing but through fidelity: the wife is able to show her husband that she has been slandered. The remainder of the play is therefore focused on the revenge that Mayberry takes against the gallants, ably abetted by his companion, the poet Bellamont. *Northward Ho* is better held together than its predecessor by taking a much darker view of the sexual disruption: the gallants are entirely fit objects for disgrace and punishment. But one must not push too far the idea of Dekker and Webster as reformed sinners. A great variety of minor and sub-plot characters supply a realistic image of a bustling metropolis in which Chaucerian fulness of experience softens the self-seeking of commercial and personal relations.

It is usually accepted that Bellamont is a picture of George Chapman. If this is a revenge against him for his part in *Eastward Ho*, then it is a very amiable revenge. Stoll has remarked that it 'is hardly satire; it is jolly raillery and the horseplay of raillery, but it does not hit'.[80] We see Bellamont entangled with a prostitute; he is detained in Bedlam as a lunatic. But his main function, to devise a

---

[79] Similar to Malespini, *Ducento Novelle*, pt. 1, novel 2. The earliest known edition of this book is dated 1609, so that we still do not know the immediate source.
[80] E. E. Stoll, *John Webster* (Boston, 1905), 69.

scenario of punishment for the gallants, still shows an inventive genius that does him credit.[81]

The modern critics who decry *Westward Ho* as immoral often explain how the 'wholesome' Dekker of *The Shoemakers' Holiday* came to be the decadent author of the later play by pointing to his unfortunate association with Middleton. Middleton, Parrott tells us, was probably 'the first deviser' of 'realistic comedy of London life . . . marked by a satiric note, a partiality for questionable scenes and characters and a general moral laxness . . . his attitude toward the life and manners of London citizens is characterized by a superior and somewhat cynical contempt'.[82] The chronology here is, as usual, quite unhelpful; if *The Phoenix* is the only Middleton play to precede *Westward Ho*, then it seems likely that Middleton followed Dekker and Webster into the sewage farm of London citizen comedy; but it is possible that *The Family of Love* is earlier and in that case Middleton can be blamed.[83]

The Family of Love (*c*.1602×1607) offers us a bourgeois family intrigue in the Chapmanesque mode of Roman and Italian New Comedy, but with an emphasis on local manners and on money as the key to human action. Gerardine, initially a romantic young lover (supplied with a rhetoric of love resembling Romeo's), cannot persuade Maria's uncle and guardian, Glister, to release the dowry Glister holds in trust. The hero is without a witty and resourceful servant, but, as in other English versions of the genre, he himself is plentifully supplied with the required ingenuity. He runs through a gamut of disguises that use the city's natural competitiveness to

---

[81] Dekker and Webster may be making a hit against Chapman's involvement with real-life drama in the lost scandal-play, *The Old Joiner of Aldgate* of 1603. Agnes Howe was an heiress of 17 whose fortune was fished for by both her father (the old 'joiner' or marriage broker of the title) and her mother, each with suitors in tow and arrangements to split the profits when the marriage was concluded. The printer Flaskett, who was the mother's client, says in one deposition in the court case that ensued that he gave a plot of the events to 'one George Chapman' who made a play of it and then sold the same to Thomas Woodford and Edward Pierce (manager and Master of the Paul's Boys) for 20 marks. The aim, it is said, was so to shame the girl that 'she might shut up and conclude a match with . . . Flaskett rather than suffer her name to be traduced in every playhouse as it was like to be'. Chapman, however, denied that he was in cahoots with Flaskett; he said that 'he made the same [play] of his own invention', sold it, and then forgot it; 'he never saw the same acted and played upon a stage'. The relation of real-life plots and dramatic plots could thus have been a sensitive point for Chapman. The full and juicy details of the Howe case can be found in C. J. Sisson, *The Lost Plays of Shakespeare's Age* (Cambridge, 1936).

[82] *George Chapman: Comedies*, ed. Parrott, 839.

[83] Unless we believe (as many do) that Dekker was co-author of this play.

forward his project. His tricks, however, come from the lexicon of Italian intrigue. He contrives to have himself carried into his beloved's bedroom in a chest supposed to contain his will and his fortune. Once there he can consummate his love, and that breeds his next and most bizarre trick. Maria has become pregnant; Gerardine vanishes again; Glister is now the obvious person to be blamed; he can be charged with incest and so is driven to accept Gerardine as his son-in-law saviour, and be happy to offer both dowry and reward.

This is a London that has taken over the characteristics of Ferrara or Siena as found in the *commedia erudita*—centred on young men's unfocused hopes to win the prize while wittily evading the full price. But the impediments here belong much more to the community than to the families, and it is by understanding communal assumptions that the hero can wind his way through the bizarre alternatives in front of him, with uncommitted amusement and the witty freedom of action that that allows and that the boys can so well represent. But he is given no moral superiority. Unlike the New Comedy of Chapman the play is entirely without controlling commentary; the satire (if that is the word) is entirely dissolved in the intrigue.

Middleton's *A Mad World My Masters* (1604×1607) repeats the basic pattern but generalizes it further. There is now no talk about love. The gallant needs money simply to keep up his status, and the search for money is no longer confined to the city; the blocking figure is not here a merchant but a jolly squire, Sir Bounteous Progress, whose bounty, however, does not extend to his nephew[84] and heir (Follywit). The succession of tricks or 'frolics' set up by this gallant creates a typical boys' plot. Falling into poverty he has become 'captain' of a gang of criminals (who seem at another time to be unfairly discharged soldiers) and with their aid he tries to anticipate his legacy by relieving his uncle of surplus wealth. But the fall into criminal life is given neither moral nor economic reality; the whole affair is treated with comic insouciance:

I was as well given till I fell to be wicked, my grandsire had hope of me, I went all in black, swore but o' Sundays, never came home drunk but upon fasting days to cleanse my stomach; 'slid, now I am quite altered,

[84] He is called *nephew* in the character list in the second quarto (1640) but is referred to everywhere in the text as the grandson. The Latin *nepos* (Italian *nipote*) covers both cases.

blown into light colours, let out oaths by th'minute, sit up late till it be
early, drink drunk till I am sober, sink down dead in a tavern and rise in
a tobacco shop. Here's a transformation.   (I. i. 12–19)

The insouciance leads to gross inefficiency in the intrigue; but
Follywit recovers after each disaster with extraordinary resilience
(and can claim that it was all a piece of wit). His grossest error is
to marry a 'rich virgin' who turns out to be his grandfather's cast
mistress—but this is also his most fortunate escape, since Sir Bounteous is happy to pension off the mistress with a substantial dowry.
    The capacity of this world of 'frolics' to undermine traditional
distinctions and make opposites run into one another[85] collapses the
ethical separation of exploiter and exploited. The intriguer cannot
control any outcomes, but his youthful exuberance is eventually
rewarded, not for moral reasons but as a tribute to qualities that in
real life (as in the theatre) do in fact spell success. In this sense the
play can be thought of as an anticipation of Restoration Comedy.
    Hillebrand has conjectured that when Edward Kirkham, the
theatrical manager, left the Blackfriars for the Paul's playhouse in
1605–6 (following the trouble over *Eastward Ho*), he took with him
some play-texts;[86] two printed texts have title-pages that he aligns
with this event: Marston's *The Fawn*, 'as it hath been divers times
presented at the black friars by the children of the Queen's Majesty's Revels and since at Paul's', and Middleton's *A Trick to Catch
the Old One* (1604×1607) 'as it hath been often in action both at
Paul's and the Black Friars'. If Hillebrand's view is to be accepted,
A Trick to Catch the Old One must be an early Middleton comedy.[87] But in artistic terms it seems to be the culmination of his
comedy for the boys. It shows no sign of immaturity; indeed the
play is an assured masterpiece.[88]

[85]   This is what city life was seen to be encouraging. See the quotations on pp. 313–21.
[86]   Hillebrand, 195–6.
[87]   The title-page can, however, be read as implying a move in the opposite direction: in
that case the play was written for Paul's and was acquired by the Blackfriars company when
the Paul's enterprise collapsed in 1606.
[88]   If one is looking for Middleton's 'immaturity', *Your Five Gallants* (1604×1607) is an
obvious choice, given its rather mechanical division of the London 'gallants' according to
their criminal specialisms: the bawd gallant, the whore gallant, the [pick]pocket gallant, the
cheating gallant, the [pawn]broker gallant. The play uncovers realistic rogueries rather in
the manner of Greene's pamphlets, but their interrelation is perfunctory and the denouement is presented in a dehumanizing formal ritual, harking back to Wilson's *The Three
Ladies of London*. I must emphasize, of course, that words like 'mechanical' and 'sophisticated' cannot be relied on as terms of chronology.

A Trick to Catch the Old One returns us to the grimmer world of the city, where 'frolics' are without effect and tricks need to be pursued with a ferocity appropriate to the usurious world involved. The main trick is very close to the one that Doll the harlot plays in *Northward Ho*: when Bellamont's roistering nephew, who has been her protector, is carried to prison for debt, Doll decides to survive by setting herself up as a wealthy country lady newly arrived in town. Drawn by this bait, various foolish suitors lavish money on her in the hope of persuading her into matrimony. Middleton combines this story (wherever he got it) with the Prodigal Son situation we have looked at in *Eastward Ho*. Witgood, the protagonist, is already, when the play begins, in the second stage of prodigality, a penniless outcast. He has, however, learnt a serious lesson, and it is not one of repentance; he now knows that he needs to be cleverer than the con-artists of the city who have robbed him of his estate. He must be able to manipulate others as they have manipulated his naïve notion of himself as a gentleman among gentlemen. And so he devises a plot so well adapted to the city outlook, in which human exchange is based on financial exchange— what we tend to call Reality—that it can run under the momentum of the city's pre-programmed responses. His mistress will present herself to the London scene as a rich country widow who is about to marry him and make him master of her considerable fortune. He himself must appear as naïve as ever, so that Lucre his usurer uncle, who has foreclosed his mortgage and bankrupted him, will expect new pickings from the new fortune. The matrimonial futures market thus set up is a brilliant success: money and equipage that will make Witgood more attractive to the widow pour in from every side. And greedy expectation is not the only financial technique that Witgood's plan exploits: raising the price by competitive bidding is even more effective. Lucre's great rival, Hoard, aims to outwit both Witgood and his uncle by marrying the widow himself. His 'cleverness' leads him on from folly to folly. He is carried away by the imagination of riding down to his newly acquired estates, stopping his carriage outside Lucre's house and so driving him to suicide. He entertains new servants, a huntsman, a falconer, a barber. Disdaining all caution he rushes the widow into matrimony so that, when the truth inevitably emerges, she can properly claim that

You . . . forced me; had I friends would follow it,
Less than your action has been proved a rape.

(v. ii. 122–3)

When all is out in the open and all that can be gained is got,
Witgood and the Courtesan drop on their knees and declaim a
palinode (as do the courtlings at the end of *Cynthia's Revels*). The
manipulators 'repent', and rejoice in married respectability; but is
respectability more than money? There is no Cynthia to hold this
world together, not even a Touchstone. Witgood is said to be in
love with Hoard's niece, and indeed they have exchanged two
letters. At the end of the play we are told that they are now
married. But the point is purely formal, has no erotic resonance. It
could hardly be otherwise with boy actors; the cut-throat Wall
Street ethos of the play, so well suited to the witty boys, leaves no
space for romantic emphases. This is just what moral critics object
to. But it is just where Middleton's appeal to the present can be
found: in the evocation of a financial system which we still recognize and fear (many fewer now fear the social disgrace of cuckoldry
that provides motive force in so many comedies). It gives us pleasure to see that the exploited individual's financial misfortunes are
recoverable and that the 'experts' are too pre-programmed to cope
with wit and imagination.

Michaelmas Term (1604×1606) again shows trickery as the en-
gine of plot; but the history of prodigality is now being depicted in
its downward phase: the tricks now belong to the city itself and are
less part of the victim's revenge. Master Richard Easy is another
naïve gentleman who supposes he can raise money in a gentlemanly way. But he finds himself in London in Michaelmas term,
in a six-week world where those who come to law lose their pasts
and find their futures detached from the natural processes of family and community. He meets up with a usurer called Quomodo
(the name perhaps intended to remind the audience of a real cheater
called Howe),[89] who leads him step by step down into the legal
labyrinth. We must marvel at the skill of the chess-like moves by
which Easy is entrapped, with every possibility of escape foreseen
and foreclosed. By the middle of the play he is as outcast and
desperate as Witgood in *A Trick to Catch the Old One*. But in

---

[89] See *Michaelmas Term*, ed. Richard Levin (Lincoln, Nebr., 1966), p. xii.

Michaelmas Term Middleton is concerned less with the individual than with the system that encloses him. Witgood's past life as a squire was concealed from us, but this play is built on a strong contrast between a value-free city, held together only by legal enforcements, and a country life where the land and those that live on it are bound by custom rather than law, where action and obligation belong inside a traditional nexus of relations. For all the characters who move from the country to the city, the 'Country Wench', the 'Father', Mother Gruel, Rearage, Salewood,[90] and Easy himself, the journey is one from continuity of meaning to an arbitrary freedom to discover value in whatever is saleable (see IV. i. 49–50) or is legally protected. This large-scale contrast gives Middleton the basis for a Morality structure which places financial realism in the role of antagonist. But (unlike Jonson) Middleton keeps the moral point merely implicit.

In this sense *Michaelmas Term* can be seen as a kind of negative festive comedy, in which characters are not redeemed in a 'green world' but rather transformed in a dark wood of bonds and recognisances from which only a witty eye for the main chance can extricate them. The impersonality of the system makes it easy for characters to rename and reinvent themselves. But the old selves haunt them like inescapable ghosts. The social climber Andrew Lethe's aim is to forget where he has come from (he has changed his name; he cannot remember his own mother). But he is easily recognized as one of the Scottish imports who seemed to the dramatists of this period to typify the loss of continuity at the end of the native Tudor dynasty.

The play can still be a comedy (though a dark one) because, though the gallant's natural machismo (the need to define himself by wenching, gambling, fighting) has been the cause of his downfall, it also serves as the basis of his rescue. When the usurer, activated by an appropriate distrust of everyone around him, decides to play dead (like Jonson's Volpone), so as to estimate how much continuity his family can sustain, his wife, who has watched Easy's duping with helpless sympathy, takes this opportunity to arrange for a more attentive bedfellow. Throughout the play it has been suggested that credit and sexual power are not only equivalent

---

[90] That is 'someone in arrears' and 'someone who has sold his forest lands for ready cash'.

but carry opposite charges. As 'Michaelmas Term' tells us in the Induction:

Where bags are fruitful'st, there the womb's most barren,
The poor has all our children, we their wealth.[91]

(ll. 22–3)

Having learnt his lesson and recovered his mortgage, Master Easy can escape from the law and the supposed widow and return to the hebetude of Essex; Quomodo must start from scratch again. There is no suggestion that the contradiction between the city and the country has any larger solution than in the highly stylized fiction we have been watching.

Citizen comedy, as we have pursued it through these pages, has seemed to culminate in the plays which give the most realistic account of city pressures on traditional values: *A Trick to Catch the Old One* and *Michaelmas Term*. The methods of manipulation we hear about in these plays are, like the topography of London used, painstakingly accurate. But the boy actors could not have given realistic performances of the characters. Obviously they must have emphasized the high spirits of the disguisings, tricks, and deceptions by which the plots progress. Middleton's greatest triumph in this genre, *A Chaste Maid in Cheapside* (1611×1613),[92] was performed, however, not by the boys but by the Lady [Princess] Elizabeth's Men, and one must wonder how far the change of actors[93] is responsible for the increased complexity of the characters.

A Chaste Maid in Cheapside changes Middleton's standard equation of sex and money by putting sex in the middle and making money its satellite. It sets up a society in which all the characters are grouped round the dilemmas that this relationship creates. Touchwood Senior is penniless because he cannot touch a woman without getting her pregnant; Touchwood Junior cannot marry

---

[91] For the antithesis between money growth and natural fertility see also: I. i. 107; III. iv. 135 ff., 150 ff.; IV. i. 34; IV. iv. 55.

[92] For the problems of dating, see *A Chaste Maid in Cheapside*, ed. R. B. Parker (London, 1969), pp. xxviii ff.

[93] For the relationship of the Lady Elizabeth's Men and the Children of the Revels, see p. 291. Chambers remarks (ii. 251) that in 1613 the Lady Elizabeth's Men were 'very much the Queen's Revels [boys] over again'. But this is true only in part. The amalgamation must have produced a company of mixed ages. Moreover, many of the former Queen's Revels boys were no longer boys. Nathan Field had been with that company since he was 13 (in 1600); he was now 26.

Moll Yellowhammer because his family is penniless. The Kixes are wealthy but cannot have children. The Yellowhammers' ambition is to sell Moll's chastity to Sir Walter Whorehound. Sir Walter pays Allwit for the use of his wife. Allwit rejoices in the profit he derives from Sir Walter's pleasure in paternity. The most powerful expression of the moral chaos that ensues appears in the great soliloquy where Allwit praises his choice to be a eunuch for the money's sake:

> I thank him, h'as maintained my house this ten years,
> Not only keeps my wife, but a keeps me
> And all my family: I am at his table;
> He gets me all my children and pays the nurse
> Monthly or weekly: puts me to nothing,
> Rent, nor church-dues, not so much as the scavenger:
> The happiest state that ever man was born to.
>
> (I. ii. 15–21)

The power of this speech depends largely on the specificity with which Allwit can gloat over the advantages that take the place of sexual independence. Allwit is not only a *wittol* (a contented cuckold) but also a man who has used his *wit* (like Quomodo and Lucre) to escape the ethical constraints that normally limit the acquisitive instinct. His satisfaction in his arrangements (he does not need to 'dye [his] conscience in the blood of prodigal heirs'; he can 'feed the plump wife for another's veins' without a twinge of jealousy—while his 'victim', Sir Walter, is tormented by it); and so he is unimpeded by any sense that men of discernment could think otherwise. And indeed Sir Walter *is* his victim. For all the subservience he finds around him, the Cheapside twitter over his presence, culminating in the bourgeois sentimentality that accompanies his bastard's christening, Whorehound has only to think of repentance when he is wounded in a duel and the Allwits know exactly what steps to take: they ditch their 'benefactor' immediately, take an inventory of his goods (pausing appreciatively over 'a close-stool of tawny velvet'), and make plans to furnish a high-class house (presumably a brothel) in the newly fashionable Strand.

  In a society in which all the parts are so closely tied together, where dowry, marriage, inheritance, adultery, fertility, and profit are held in a web of mutual dependencies, insufficiency being bonded to excess, fatherhood to whoredom, gain to loss, the power of intrigue to advance any one cause is bound to inflict disadvantage on every other cause, and so to be rendered suspect. Such plots as do produce results do so by accident rather than design. The happy ending for the young lovers, Moll Yellowhammer and Touchwood Junior, occurs only because the rapacity of Moll's parents becomes a scandal in the street. Denied community support, parental power collapses.[94]

A Chaste Maid in Cheapside marks the end as well as the apogee of Middleton's citizen comedy. But though fashion changed, the tensions these plays set up did not cease to appeal, and two later exercises played by the men may be mentioned here as examples of the changes time imposed upon the pattern.

Massinger's *A New Way to Pay Old Debts* (1621×1625), played by Prince Charles's Men, reworks the plot of *A Trick to Catch the Old One* in ways which show some hardening of the social arteries as Middleton's theatrical poise is nudged towards melodrama and sentimentality. The dialectic between sex and money which allowed Witgood's courtesan to become the object of city fantasies is replaced by a dialectic between money and honour. The courtesan has disappeared; it is now more important that Wellborn (the new Witgood) has lost his honour than that he has lost his fortune. The pretence of engagement to a wealthy widow is now less a trick than an example of class solidarity, the means by which old families (supported by a phalanx of loyal servants) can be protected from the depradations of money-grubbers. Unlike Hoard and Lucre, the usurer Sir Giles Overreach (perhaps based on the real Sir Giles Mompesson) is not simply a city trickster out-tricked, but the devil of insatiable capitalism incarnate. The projective power of such a figure is, of course, a power that a children's theatre could not hope to muster. And it is through this power that Massinger's play has maintained a theatrical presence such as no other city comedy has enjoyed. The star actor's capacity to project Sir Giles's demonic energy, his contempt for limits, his violent rages, his final lapse into madness, turn economics into psychology; and this means that every age can respond to the melodrama of threat without having to understand its immediate implications.

---

[94] The trick of presentation in a coffin to secure an escape from oppression can be found also in Beaumont's *Knight of the Burning Pestle*, IV. 190 ff. An even closer analogue can be found in Marston's *Antonio and Mellida* (V. ii. 209). But there the wish that the corpse could rise up and resume life is spoken by the Duke. Here it is given to *All*.

Massinger's other city comedy, *The City Madam*, (1632), played by the King's Men, reworks *Eastward Ho* in similar but less predictable terms. The Touchstone figure has now fulfilled his wife's ambitions and been knighted as Sir John Frugal, but London womenfolk's ambitions are still insatiable. He has apprentices still anxious to 'fly out', to drink and whore on the master's money. But the big change comes in the moralizing and sanctimonious part formerly taken by Golding, handled here by Sir John's brother Luke, a recovered spendthrift (like Witgood and Wellborn) now living on charity and menial services to his nieces. But Massinger's play does not treat this suspect sanctimony with the comic restraint of *Eastward Ho*. The power of *The City Madam*, like that of *A New Way to Pay Old Debts*, depends chiefly on the histrionic energy of the villain's part, as civil hypocrisy is tricked into displaying itself as melodramatic evil. Schelling praises *The City Madam* as superior to earlier citizen comedies in its 'underlying gravity and moral consciousness'.[95] These qualities are, however, bought at the cost of irony, wit, and the sharp separation of theatrical reality from life that the boys' theatre (necessarily) created, and, at its peak, made into a clear-eyed picture of the world.

It seems appropriate to end this section with a glance at two interesting comedies for the children that seem to be retrospective in their sense of the boys' theatre as in itself a metaphor for the society it had served. Beaumont's *The Knight of the Burning Pestle* (1607×*c*.1610) is a play *about* the performance of drama at the private theatre, and about the social tension that éliteness implies, together with the dramaturgic consequences of its expression. The seat that was most characteristic (as most expensive) of the private theatres was the stool on the stage. Here the gentleman (or quasi-gentleman) could demand attention for himself rather than the play.[96] But what, Beaumont's play asks, if the show-off on the stage is not the expected 'wit' or 'gallant' but a London grocer, if the coterie situation is invaded by someone who 'does not know his place', climbs onto the stage, pays for a stool, and joins the coterie?

This means, in literary terms, a collision of the sceptical and anti-idealist Inns of Court taste against the romantic taste for

---

[95] *Elizabethan Drama*, ii. 254.
[96] Dekker's *The Gull's Hornbook* (1609) provides the classic description of such behaviour.

swashbuckling heroics and idealizing sentimental love,[97] seen here as characterizing the naïve citizenry. As several critics have pointed out, the distinction worked out in the action is not, however, as simple as this.[98] The play that the boys intend to put on, *The London Merchant*, is rejected by the Grocer as anti-citizen, but it appears to be more like a standard romance than a Middletonian anti-capitalist drama. Jasper, the apprentice, loves his master's daughter, and is in consequence turned out of the house. He wanders into Waltham forest, where the course of true love can be seen in alternations of reunion and separation. Finally, Jasper achieves his end by dressing as his own ghost and forcing the guilt-stricken merchant not only to accept the match but to finance old Merrythought, Jasper's father, who drinks, eats, and sings ballads all day, assuming that tomorrow will look after itself. And so it does.

The grocer and his wife are not pleased by Merrythought's dereliction of his domestic responsibilities or by the spectacle of young lovers outwitting a provident master merchant. Their taste for romance points towards foreign aggression rather than domestic reconciliation. And so they demand the interpolation of a series of episodes in which their apprentice Rafe can act out chivalric fantasies à la Don Quixote.

Beaumont's first independent play, like Fletcher's *The Faithful Shepherdess*, was a theatrical failure (one sees why they were well advised to collaborate). Walter Burre, the publisher of the quarto, indicates that one reason was 'not understanding the privy marks of irony about it'. He does not note that the irony cuts both ways: the grocer and his wife think they are imposing a glorification of the city on top of an anti-citizen play; the children object to the distortion of the play they have prepared. But in fact Beaumont's subtle composition allows the convergence of the two plots to override the antithesis that is supposed to separate them. The

---

[97] The Inns of Court taste can be seen in paradigmatic form in Day's *The Isle of Gulls* (1606), where the mutually supportive politicial and erotic idealisms of Sidney's *Arcadia* are turned into sex farce. Basilius is no longer a misguided sovereign, but a father anxious only to satisfy his daughters. The princesses Pamela and Philoclea are presented as desperate to lose their maidenheads, and the interlopers Julio and Amintor, with more wit and opportunism than Sidney's heroes, seem to offer the quicker relief. The satire on King James that landed the sponsors of the play in Bridewell seems not to have survived into print.

[98] See Lee Bliss, *Francis Beaumont* (Boston, 1987); Philip Finkelpearl, *Court and Country Politics in the Plays of Beaumont and Fletcher* (Princeton, 1990).

action absorbs Rafe's chivalric interludes into a single story of two apprentices who overcome the restrictive reality of their environment by imaginative resource (Jasper drawing on *Macbeth*, Rafe on *The Spanish Tragedy*) and end by achieving everything they desire. Merrythought ends the play with

> Let each other that hath been,
> Troubled with the gall or spleen,
> Learn of us to keep his brow
> Smooth and plain as ours are now.
> .   .   .   .   .   .
> Hey, ho, 'tis not but mirth
> That keeps the body from the earth.
>
> (v. 336–43)

The grocer's wife picks up the challenge by inviting the 'gentlemen' sitting around them to visit them at home and partake of 'a pottle of wine and a pipe of tobacco' (Epilogue, l. 6).

The Knight of the Burning Pestle enacts the issue of the social status of dramatic performances. Jonson's *Epicoene: or The Silent Woman* (1609) shows us a cast of children discussing and enacting an even more fundamental problem, that of gender roles, in a sophisticated 'West End' setting. The boys are, of course, equally pretenders whether they act men or women, but their verbal capacities allow them to create a world in which reality is what they create. It is appropriate then that Jonson makes them create a world of leisured urban intercourse, where free cultural choice (especially gender choice) promises a release from natural limitations.[99] Clerimont's page and 'ingle' is admitted to Madam Haughty's chamber; she kisses him, puts her peruke on him, and offers him a gown. But Madam Haughty's challenges to nature go beyond this. She is also president of a college of ladies who 'cry down or up what they like or dislike in a brain or a fashion with most masculine or rather hermaphroditical authority' (i. i. 74–6). The principal neophytes in the college, Sir Amorous La Foole and Sir Jack Daw, are markedly less capable of 'masculine authority' than the ladies; their powers are purely verbal, and so in this leisured

---

[99] See Edward Partridge, *The Broken Compass* (London, 1958), ch. 7. R. G. Noyes (*Ben Jonson on the English Stage, 1660–1776* (Cambridge, Mass., 1935)) points out that eighteenth-century attempts to use a female actor to play the part of Epicoene resulted in dismal failure.

world of chattering boys they can pass for men until the requirement to fight shows them to be as unmasculine as the epicene Viola in *Twelfth Night* (whose dilemma is being imitated). At the beginning of the play Truewit tells Clerimont that fashion demands appearance rather than reality as the basis for human relations, and appearance seems to define the situation we are given here.

The basic story of *Epicoene* belongs to a type we have seen already in several Middleton plays: a young gallant has to secure his inheritance (or his wife's dowry) by a set of tricks that will reduce his skinflint uncle (or potential father-in-law) to compliance. Here the world of sophisticated culture and pretence is deployed to impose on uncle Morose's 'masculine authority' the discovery that the modern world makes old-fashioned assumptions about clear gender roles impossible to sustain. The 'silent woman' Morose has taken to be the ideal wife, who will bear him children to disinherit his tiresome nephew, turns out to be a loud-mouthed termagant, a probationer Fellow of the ladies' college, well acquainted with the means to prevent conception, a patron of the talking half-men who are the college associates. Can old-fashioned distinctions be restored? The clamour of the divorce lawyers invoked creates only a further dissolution of rigid things into malleable words, in a babel of dog-Latin propositions, from which even Morose's confession that he is 'no man . . . utterly unabled in nature by reason of frigidity to perform the . . . least office of a husband' (v. iv. 44–7) cannot extricate him. Rescue can come only when, in exchange for the inheritance, his nephew 'takes off Epicene's peruke' and reveals (as in Aretino's *Il marescalco*) that the bride is really a boy. But is a boy actor really to be trusted to be a boy, any more than an uncle? We are left with the anamorphic puzzle that the boys always raise. *Epicoene* only makes more obvious than usual the role of theatre to stage the process by which stabilities in culture are created artificially out of our inherent capacities for play-making.

TRAGEDY

I have argued that the qualities the boys could project in comedy —self-conscious role-playing, pleasure in deception, burlesque of romantic entanglement—pushed their repertory in the direction of elaborate intrigue, social satire, cynical realism. The question here is how these qualities operated in the tragedies that formed a minor yet significant part of their activity. How far did their tragic repertory point in a different direction from that of the men? What was the effect of boys' performance in *The Spanish Tragedy*;[100] and how did that change the play produced by Alleyn and the Admiral's Men? Did the boys offer innovations that could be taken over by the men, in tragedy as in comedy? R. A. Foakes, who has written an acute essay on the boys' tragic repertory,[101] sees a process of development leading from the extremism and satire of *Antonio's Revenge* of 1599×1601 to the epic ritualism of Chapman's *Bussy D'Ambois* of 1600×1604 and Marston's *Sophonisba* of 1605×1606 and then turning back towards tragicomedy in *The Insatiate Countess* (c.1610×1613) and *Cupid's Revenge* of c.1607×1612. This corresponds in general outline to the process I have described for comedy; but Foakes does not deal with the questions I have raised above, and says nothing about the particular strains that tragedy (as against comedy) imposed on the general pattern. And it is this issue that I wish to address here.

Clearly the case of tragedy is different from that of comedy. Tragedy had a social and intellectual status that made the writing of it a special kind of project. It was understood to be a form concerned with people 'greater than us', exciting the more harrowing emotions. To aim at the highest degree of emotional power (or *pathos*) would seem to be particularly inappropriate to the talents of the boys. Yet there was at least one aspect of contemporary understanding of tragedy that gave the boys a specific advantage. We should remember that the Renaissance theorists added *admiratio* or wonder (a distancing rather than involving emotion) to the two ends proposed by Aristotle.[102] Classical models of tragedy told

---

[100] See above, n. 65. Chambers (iv. 23)—followed by Philip Edwards in his edition of *The Spanish Tragedy* (London, 1959), and others—has argued that the *Jeronimo* the boys performed could not have been *The Spanish Tragedy* (usually called *Jeronimo* in the period), which belonged to the Admiral's/Prince Henry's Men, but must have been the anonymous *First Part of Jeronimo*, which, in Chambers's terms of 'it may' and 'if so', *could* have belonged to the Chamberlain's Men and so have provided an exact exchange for *The Malcontent*. But the words used in the *Malcontent* Induction only require an equivalence of *theft*. If the boys provided an example by stealing *The Spanish Tragedy* (from whomever), then the King's Men can provide 'One [theft] for another' by stealing one of their plays. The great popularity of *The Spanish Tragedy* made it a property well worth stealing. It does not seem probable that *The First Part of Jeronimo* was considered to have any such drawing power.

[101] 'Tragedy in Children's Theatre after 1600', *Elizabethan Theatre*, ii. (1970), 37–59.

[102] See Bernard Weinberg, *History of Literary Criticism in the Italian Renaissance* (2 vols.; Chicago, 1961).

stories of violence and horror, but told them in ways that were particularly formalized, ritualized, distanced, raising wonder at the fortitude as well as the pain of the protagonists. Furthermore, the classical restrictions on the extension of place and time involved, on the number of actors, on what might be properly delineated on the stage, predicated a form heavy on description and light on action, relying on a grave and sonorous poetry to create a lofty atmosphere of 'removed mysteries'.[103] Not all these restraints could be indulged on a real Elizabethan or Jacobean stage, even a coterie one; but the boys' talent for representation rather than enactment matches easily with the idea of a gravely decorous and controlled classicism that evoked the underlying meaning of life rather than its surface appearances, showing men as the preordained victims of passion rather than the projectors of their own destinies.

For many of the intellectual élite the neoclassical idea of tragedy indicated a form that could not be acted under Elizabethan conditions, for no contemporary audience could be expected to sustain the gravity of attention that 'authentic' tragedy required. Ben Jonson, writing for the popular stage his (theatrically unsuccessful) tragedy of *Sejanus*, regrets that it could not be a 'true poem'. It is not, he says in his preface, 'possible in these our times, and to such auditors as commonly things are presented, to observe the old state and splendour of dramatic poems with preservation of any popular delight'. Problems with 'popular delight' did not, of course, affect those like Fulke Greville, who says of his own 'closet' drama: 'I have made these tragedies no plays for the stage. Be it known it was no part of my purpose to write for them [that is, audiences] against whom so many good and great people have already written.'[104] The form as envisaged by Greville. or by Mary *Herbert (née Sidney), the Countess of Pembroke, or William *Alexander, the Earl of Stirling, is one whose rewards (such as they are) derive not from action but from the space opened up for discussion of morals and politics; an opportunity is created to express a sophisticated

---

[103] This may point to the best connection that can be forged between the boys and *The Spanish Tragedy*. Kyd's great work relies on poetry and ritual to make its specific effects. No doubt it can benefit from the projective powers of a great actor, but even in reading, its poetry controls the effects. A boy speaking well could make it as powerful as an oratorio in performance. And there is nothing inherently comic about a boy playing an old man (such as 'Old Hieronimo'). Jonson's epitaph on the boy player Salomon Pavy says that he played old men so well that the fates mistook him for one.

[104] *Life of Sir Philip Sidney*, ed. Nowell Smith (Oxford, 1907), 224.

disenchantment with the world of power, shown as a violent and unrelenting struggle for position, but held by the form in a safely generalized focus. Greville's two tragedies of the Turkish court, *Mustapha* (*c*.1594×*c*.1596) and *Alaham* (*c*.1598×*c*.1600), are probably the best of these deliberately undramatic dramas, tissues of long deliberative and descriptive speeches, sharp intellectual debates in stichomythia, moralizing choruses, all loaded with sententious comment, but sustained (for readers at least) in Greville's case by the tough sequaciousness of his moral thought, his realistic rejection of comforting conclusions.

Samuel Daniel's two tragedies, *Cleopatra* (of 1593) and *Philotas* (1604), are the products of a sweeter and weaker talent. Daniel was a follower of the Countess of Pembroke, a professional writer seeking to please his patroness, not a tormented Calvinist nobleman thinking aloud. *Cleopatra* was probably never performed. *Philotas* was, to Daniel's peril, and came to the notice of the Privy Council as possibly a public discussion of the Earl of Essex's revolt against the Queen in 1601 and a criticism of Robert Cecil for his part in the Essex trial. Daniel's various defences against the charges made open up for us in a most interesting way the presuppositions that lay behind this kind of tragedy. He began, he says in the 'Apology' he attached to the published text of his play, 'purposing to have it presented in Bath by certain gentlemen's sons, as private recreation for the Christmas' (p. 156). A private recreation, he assumes, is not subject to the same rules as an open exhibition, and he candidly admits to the impropriety of public performance. In his letter to the Earl of Devonshire he says that he was 'not resolved to have had it acted, nor should it have been, had not my necessities overmastered me' (p. 38).[105] His letter to Robert Cecil repeats the financial defence: 'my necesssity I confess hath driven me to do a thing unworthy of me and much gainst my heart, in making the stage the speaker of my lines, which never heretofore had any other theatre than the universal dominions of England' (p. 37). What is more interesting from our point of view than these bids for sympathy is the third (aesthetic) argument that follows in the Cecil

---

[105] We can probably link the idea of performance as a solution to his financial necessities with the fact that on 4 Feb. 1604 Daniel had been appointed licenser to the Children of the Queen's Revels. (See R. E. Brettle, 'Samuel Daniel and the children of the Queen's Revels', *RES* 3 (1927), 162–8). He thus had a company in some sense made available to help him pay his debts.

letter. The form of his play, he claims, gives an ethical generality to the content—one that avoids the particularity of performance— so that it must not be construed in narrow political terms. In *Philotas*, he says,

I sought to reduce the stage from idleness to those grave presentments of antiquity used by the wisest nations. I protest that I have taken no other form in personating the actors [that is, the real historical figures] that performed it than the very Idea of those times as they appeared to me both by the cast of the story and the universal notions of the affairs of men, which in all ages bear the same resemblances and are measured by one and the same foot of understanding. No time but brought forth the like concurrences, the like interstriving for place and dignity, the like supplantations, risings and overthrows, so that there is nothing new under the sun, nothing in these times that is not in books nor in the books that is not in these times.   (pp. 37–8)

Daniel argues that classical art requires any serious writer to admit that the world of power is a world of corruption. And it is true that the closet drama of the English aristocracy and its clients was inevitably driven, by the seriousness of its philosophic scrutiny of power, towards a dangerously political scrutiny of kingship. Fulke Greville burnt his *Antony and Cleopatra* in case it was held to have reference to Essex. Daniel, prominent because of literary skill but far from the centre of power, obviously hoped to finesse his way out of the dilemma by the usual methods of literary criticism, reinterpreting the ambiguities that were part of his (as of all) literary creation.

   Philotas tells the story of Alexander the Great's execution of his favourite general, a story of indiscreet pride, false security, court cabals passed off as loyalty, conflicting counsels, and confused evidence. It does not attempt to resolve the question whether Philotas' actions really threatened Alexander's life or whether they simply proved too useful to the competing favourites (those 'interstriving for place and dignity') to be passed up. The fourth 'Chorus of the Vulgar', as they are called (l. 399), has no doubts:

> See how these great men clothe their private hate
> In those fair colours of the public good;
> And to effect their ends, pretend the state,
> As if the state by their affections stood;
> And armed with power and prince's jealousies

Will put the least conceit of discontent
Into the greatest rank of treacheries,
That no one action shall seem innocent.

(ll. 1110–18)

Daniel could well deny that he was endorsing the views of 'the
Vulgar'; but the fact that the words were spoken at all was enough
to trouble the Privy Council. In a reading text it might well be that
his classically controlled quatrains could push all the competing
views into a unified and unthreatening middle distance; but spoken
on the stage it seems probable that the versification could no longer
regulate the topical meaning, aided by whatever visual signals the
company may have thought (and Daniel allowed) to be appropriate.

The children's theatre could not hope to secure dangerous political ideas behind the screen of unactability that was supposed
to protect closet plays. The vision of a corrupt world that drew
its satiric comedy into political danger operated equally to draw its
tragic repertory towards the same whirlpool. The history of boys'
tragedy can be seen as a series of attempts to place personal virtue
inside a world of political corruption and yet avoid the charge that
it advocated political change. The protective shield most usefully
to hand was the idea that virtue was a quality that belonged to the
inner economy of the individual (as appears in both Stoic and
Christian doctrine) and was therefore quite separable from politics.
Expectation of change could thus be deflected from politics to conscience; and properly, for (as Daniel told Cecil) all regimes must
have the same configuration.

This point could be made most easily when the virtue invoked
was that of a woman, a woman whose constancy and loyalty allowed
her to triumph over betrayal and temptation, not by assuming
power or executing justice but by high-minded martyrdom. Thus
in the interesting early children's play of The Wars of Cyrus (1587×
1594)[106] we are told of the captive wife Panthea, caught in the
mutations and violences of war and making her escape from male
harassment by choosing to rejoin her husband in death. The Prologue defends its 'sad and tragic terms' and sets these against the
'toys | Or needless antics, imitations, | Or shows, or new devices
sprung a late' (ll. 13–15). The mode is defended by classical example:

---

[106] It may have been written by Farrant, Master of the Children of Windsor, 1564–80.
See Wilson, The English Drama 1485–1585 (Oxford, 1968), 147–50.

Instead of mournful plaints, our Chorus sings;
Although it be against the upstart guise,
Yet, warranted by grave antiquity,
We will revive the which hath long been done.

(ll. 19–21)

Panthea is only one of a galaxy of virtuous heroines—Virginia, Lucrece, Mary Magdalen, Griselda—celebrated in Humanist and popular drama across Europe. Dido, for example, appears in plays by Dolce, Cinthio, Jodelle, and La Grange, and in two Latin plays by Englishmen, Halliwell and Gager. These were, by and large, written for the *cognoscenti*. *The Tragedy of Dido, Queen of Carthage* by Marlowe and Nashe (*c*.1587×1593) gives an early example of what happens when, in the children's theatre, Humanist tragedy meets the pressures of vernacular expectations. Set against Marlowe's plays for the public stage, *The Tragedy of Dido* looks like a model of restrained action and distanced observation. The clear outline of the well-known Virgilian story denies narrative suspense; our interest is attached rather to the methods by which the anticipated elements are handled. Speeches tend to be retrospective, fulfilling the emotions that belong to the part, rather than prospective of new action (more as in a Bach *Passion* than in a play).

What Marlowe and Nashe have done is to take classical restriction and give it emotional force as the expression of a failure to achieve selfhood—an expression particularly appropriate to the life experience of the boys.[107] The situation presented is one in which individuals are bound to a confused passivity, held inside the roles that Virgil and the gods have allotted. What gives the work its power is the sense of desperation that this passivity imposes on human nature. All the characters are victims; but only in Dido, transformed by the juice on Cupid's arrow from queenly control to self-destroying passion, do we find the emotions of the victimized in full flow. The rhetoric of aspiration towards self-fulfilment (Marlowe's hallmark) is here turned into an expression of despair, giving Dido arias of an insatiable desire that demands everything and promises nothing, her raw passion being framed in scorn by

---

[107] H. J. Oliver's edition (London, 1963) tells us he discovered, when he saw the play in 1964, that 'when a drama such as *Dido* is acted by boys, it is the parts of the *women* that "come over" realistically. A schoolboy has no difficulty in portraying the distress of Dido; but a schoolboy Aeneas . . . cannot be more than a puppet figure' (p. xxxiii).

the comic episodes of Jupiter's infatuation with Ganymede and the farce of the old nurse's desperate desire for a man (any man). *The Tragedy of Dido* offers a picture of passion held in stasis because mortals are powerless. Marston's *The Wonder of Women: or The Tragedy of Sophonisba* (1605×1606) takes the helplessness that history imposes on human beings, particularly on women, and shows how, by stoical acceptance, it can be turned into a mode of triumph. Marston obviously saw himself in this play as creating a new form. In the Preface to the second edition of *Parasitaster: or The Fawn* (1604×1606) he announced that his forthcoming tragedy would be one 'which shall boldly abide the most curious perusal'. In the Preface to *Sophonisba* itself, the qualities which will justify this judgement are made clear, even if only by indirection: 'know that I have not laboured in this poem to tie myself to relate anything as a historian but to enlarge everything as a poet.' The Aristotelian distinction being made seems to be aimed at Jonson's *Sejanus* (1603) (published in 1605 with a battery of historical references). *Sejanus* is seen by Marston as a work whose aim is 'to transcribe authors, quote authorities and translate Latin prose orations into English blank verse'. In these terms, it is history, not poetry. Jonson in his Preface had defended his tragedy first of all by its 'truth of argument': his Rome is a scene of political degeneracy, in which virtue is impotent, and that (he says) is how it actually was. Marston 'enlarges' his story of Rome by celebrating what cannot be contained by history, idealized personal integrity. His Carthage is no less degenerate than Jonson's Rome and indeed, as Peter Ure has remarked, his neo-Stoic heroes, Sophonisba no less than Massinissa, Gelosso, and above all Scipio, can hardly be understood apart from the 'environment of sin and moral chaos which really supplies the tragic rationale, and is the background from which the Stoicism derives its justification'.[108]

This is a story of the violent transitions that history imposes on female lives, as bride-bed switches to battlefield, rape to respect, happiness to suicide. But the focus of the presentation, ritualized in elaborate tableaux and dumbshows, tells us that these events can be held at arm's length: the individual always has the choice to cooperate or reject. The politicians of the play react with panic and desperate innovation to every change of fortune; the noble characters, knowing the soul's freedom from change, disdain passions,

---

[108] *Elizabethan and Jacobean Drama* (Liverpool, 1974), 91.

'loud and full of player's eloquence', (IV. i. 26) and move through the chaos of history with measured calm. Their pace is deliberately slowed, their verse lapidary and abstracted, weighed down with sententiae. The historical Sophonisba is expanded into 'the wonder of women'; *pathos* is rewritten as *admiratio*. As performers, the boys are given little opportunity to move outside the constraints imposed by music[109] and ritual (the play can be seen as halfway to opera seria). As in *Dido*, their roles merely fulfil the predeterminations of fate;[110] but in this case the expressionistic centre is not passionate complaint but the weight of self-conscious virtue in 'subject grave, | Noble true story' (Epilogus, ll. 6–7).

Chapman's *Bussy D'Ambois* (1600×1604) is probably the best known of the tragedies written for the boys; and certainly it is the only one with a prolonged afterlife among the men. It replays the pattern of female disengagement from the compromises of history in the startlingly paradoxical history of a contemporary swordsman (and in so doing it provided a model for the Heroic Tragedies of the next age).[111] Bussy stands in the line of Tamburlaine more obviously than that of Dido. Like Tamburlaine's, his obsession is with himself. Like Tamburlaine, he begins as an outsider (the first stage direction reads 'Enter Bussy D'Ambois poor').[112] But, unlike Tamburlaine, Bussy cannot dominate his world. In a realistically observed sixteenth-century French court he can only orate, display *virtù*, deny dependence. His claims are magnificent but patently unreal. He is the victim of social niceties the Scythian conqueror could not deign to notice. Like Dido, he needs other people, and most particularly he needs what he finds in the adulterous Tamyra, a shared commitment to the tragic world of pure passion outside social norms, sustained by the glory of its own transcendence. But

---

[109] In the note to the reader set after the *Epilogus* Marston excuses himself for the breach of classical decorum in the printing of his text (by including 'the entrances and music of this tragedy'); for 'it is printed only as it was presented by youths and after the fashion of the private stage'.

[110] What T. S. Eliot in his defence of *Sophonisba* as the best of Marston's plays ('the most nearly adequate expression of his distorted and obstructed genius') calls 'a pattern behind the pattern into which the characters deliberately involve themselves' (*Selected Essays* (London, 1932), 232).

[111] In spite of Dryden's violent rejection of *Bussy* in his dedication of *The Spanish Friar* (1681)—see *Essays*, ed. W. P. Ker (2 vols.; Oxford, 1926), i. 246—his most successful 'heroic tragedy', *The Conquest of Granada*, has much in common with Chapman's play. See Waith, *Ideas of Greatness*, 216 ff.

[112] Chapman obviously meant to make a point of this, since he changed his sources to procure the effect.

that in turn needs non-transcendent bodies. The relation between body and soul is the central subject of Chapman's play.

The body is treated here, however, as is fitting in a boys' play, in a curiously abstracted way, as if it was only a metonymy for the soul. And so it is the threat of its physical frailty that produces the most extreme response. It is Tamyra's letter written in her blood that 'Commands the life confined in all my veins . . . And makes me apt t'encounter death and hell' (v. ii. 94–6) and it is the sight of Tamyra's bloodstained body that finally breaks Bussy's heart:

> Fate, nor these murderers, Monsieur, nor the Guise,
> Have any glory in my death, but this:
> This killing spectacle: this prodigy.
>
> (v. iii. 179–81)

The story of revenge for adultery[113] appears indeed as if merely a shadow cast not only by the political plot but by another and vaguer idea, as if it is not the adultery but the body itself that must be atoned for. Bussy must find he is made of 'penetrable flesh': Tamyra must endure torture, Montsurry, her husband, must live in mournful deprivation; but at the same time, on a separate but parallel plane, Bussy is being stellified, Montsurry swears his love, and the Friar–Pander–Conjurer finds his way to heaven.

The Prologue printed in the 1641 edition of the play tells us that

> Field is gone
> Whose action first did give it name . . .
> to show the height and pride
> Of D'Ambois' youth and bravery.
>
> (ll. 15–19)

If Nathan Field was indeed the Bussy of the original performance in 1604,[114] then we have to think of the 'height and pride of D'Ambois' youth and bravery' as played by a 17-year-old,[115] who must have

---

[113]   The assimilation of the play to this stereotype in its later history is made clear by the subtitle Thomas D'Urfey gave it in his rewrite of 1691—*The Husband's Revenge*.

[114]   The play, as printed in 1607, is said to have been 'presented at Paul's'; Field belonged to the Chapel Children/Queen's Revels Company (and it was for the Chapel Children that Chapman wrote the rest of his plays). Perhaps the play started with the Chapel Children before 1607 and was transferred to Paul's (Parrott suggests it was one of the plays Kirkham took with him when he moved from Chapel to Paul's (see above, p. 329)). *Bussy* was in Field's repertory by 1610 and moved with him to the King's Men in 1617 (when he was approaching 30).

[115]   If not Field, then another of much the same age. We should note that puberty came much later then than now.

given the part a quality of heroic exaggeration. Field was cited as the principal actor in *Cynthia's Revels* and *Poetaster*. It is almost inevitable that in these plays he performed exaggerated and affected characters such as Amorphus, the self-inflating traveller,[116] or Crispinus, the Marston-type poetaster. Here were opportunities to show 'height and pride' as falsifications. But a competent actor could easily tune his flamboyant performance to modulate from absurd exaggeration to heroic 'bravery'.[117] Both Bussy and Crispinus are in flight from reality (as are the sophisticated gentlemen Field played in *Epicoene*). Both the comic and the tragic roles are sustained by an inner vision of self that defies social contempt. Bussy's greatness is 'theatrical' in a way that both accepts the limitation of the epithet and transcends it, offering poetic validation to an invisible inner power but conveying the impossibility of living by it in the real world. No one would call *Bussy D'Ambois* a play marked by classical restraint, yet the qualities described point to a separation of inner and outer worlds not dissimilar to that found in *Sophonisba*.[118] In that play the 'fury and the mire of human veins' mark a point of moral discrimination; in *Bussy* they appear as inevitable factors in corporeal existence, while man's 'native noblesse' soars free into a theoretical heaven.

The tensions that make *Bussy D'Ambois* so difficult to describe presumably made it difficult for Chapman to hold onto the energy that could sustain them. His sequel, *The Revenge of Bussy D'Ambois* (1610×1611), shows a world much more easily separated into good and bad, and to that extent it is less powerful. A brother Bussy never mentioned, Clermont D'Ambois, undertakes to revenge his murder, not against the Guise who did the deed (Clermont's patron and ideal), but against Montsurry, with whom the dying Bussy had exchanged forgiveness. Clermont, unlike Bussy, is all of a piece: he is the calmly detached Stoic, like Sophonisba;[119] but, unlike Sophonisba, the requirement imposed on him is not simply

---

[116] Robert Wren, in his unpublished Princeton dissertation (1965), argues for Amorphus (p. 165).

[117] We should remember that 'bravery' in this period carried the sense of 'display, show, ostentation'.

[118] On the separation of inner and outer worlds in Chapman, see Miller MacLure, *George Chapman* (Toronto, 1966), 112.

[119] Chapman, in his dedication, defends his 'poem', in the same terms as Marston in *Sophonisba*, preferring ethical meaning to factual truth: 'material instruction, elegant and sententious excitation to virtue and deflection from her contrary being the soul, limbs and limits of an authentical tragedy'.

to reject ills but to right wrongs. Chapman exhibits the usual private theatre understanding of court politics as a scene of political intrigue, favouritism, and perjury. In this context Clermont's quality of steadfast inner calm cannot be displayed as suffering the struggle to bring his inner being into touch with the outer world— the struggle that sparks so much brilliance in *Bussy*; his final suicide is simply the logical response to a world in which he cannot accept contact.

Chapman's concentration on contemporary French history for the matter of his two Bussy plays and for his two-part Byron play, *The Conspiracy and Tragedy of Charles, Duke of Byron* (1608),[120] separates him from his fellow dramatists.[121] But his handling of the milieu leads back, almost inevitably, to shared concerns. He picks up the dangerous problems of courtly emulation that we have noticed in Greville and Daniel and handles them (even more dangerously) in a contemporary setting that allows the case of France to serve as a mirror for contemporary England. He offers a flattering mirror, of course: in *Byron* England appears as the country France ought to be like, a country not racked by religious war, but held safe in the powerful but benevolent grip of its queen, and showing spasms of the French disease only at random moments, as in the revolt of Essex in 1601. But Chapman's history is focused more realistically than Greville and Daniel can allow. His concerns take him back to the central issue in Shakespeare's history plays, the unavoidable tension between a centralizing monarchy and a still powerful feudal aristocracy, claiming rights of prowess and honour in competition with the head of the ruling family. This is a drama which sets two kinds of good together inside the irony of history and details their tragic incompatibility.

The mode of the history play put all that (Hotspur and Hal, for example) into a safely completed past. But contemporary France, unlike the England of the histories, offered the playwright the dangerous point of view of the new historians, Machiavelli and Guicciardini, where prudence replaces Providence as the explanation

---

[120] Also the later *Tragedy of Chabot, Admiral of France* (1611×1613), played by the Lady Elizabeth's Men, discussed in Ch. 9 n. 31.

[121] We should note, however, that in 1597 Dekker and Drayton wrote for Henslowe a trilogy, *The Civil Wars of France* (now lost), and in 1599 Henslowe paid Dekker for a further *First Introduction of the Civil Wars in France*. But it does not seem likely that the focus of these plays was sceptical and politique, in the boys' mode.

of success and failure, so that virtue (in men as in women) may be understood as a private glory but is explicitly denied a decisive political role. *Bussy* shows us the assertion of individual *virtù* failing to achieve the freedom it demands. The two-part Byron play shows the tragedy, not of failure but of real achievement. As the greatest of the peers of France and Henry IV's companion in arms, Byron has all the power that Bussy lacked, with the limiting effect that his inner glory must inevitably appear in a political light and be understood not in the acutely personal terms of the earlier play but as a series of political manœuvres. Henry is a 'good' king with care for his subjects; but he operates with the virtues that the prudential world of contingency requires, and must judge Byron, like others, by *raison d'état*: by the terms in which Philip II's virtue is proved not by his devotion to the absolutes of religion (as Byron argues) but by his willingness to kill his son in order to preserve his empire (*Tragedy*, IV. ii. 160). Byron is seen, for all the power of the self-justifying rhetoric passed on from Bussy, as wilfully self-deceived in supposing that he can avoid such modernisms.[122] When faced by a statement of predestination, he asserts his existential freedom with characteristic brilliance:

> I'll wear those golden spurs upon my heels,
> And kick at fate; be free, all worthy spirits,
> And stretch yourselves for greatness and for height;
> Untruss your slaveries, you have height enough
> Beneath this steep heaven to use all your reaches.
>
> . . . .
>
> There is no danger to a man that knows
> What life and death is; there's not any law
> Exceeds his knowledge, neither is it lawful
> That he should stoop to any other law.
> He goes before them and commands them all
> That to himself is a law rational.
>
> (*Conspiracy*, III. iii. 129–45)

But of course the great duke cannot be anything 'to himself'; every private impulse is somebody else's public opportunity, and every

---

[122] He is made to refer to them specifically as the destroyers of true kingship: 'There are schools | Now broken ope in all parts of the world, | First founded in ingenious Italy, | Where some conclusions of estate are held | That for a day preserve a prince, and ever | Destroy him after; from thence men are taught | To glide into degrees of height by craft | And then to lock in themselves by villainy' (*Tragedy of Byron*, III. i. 2–9).

conversation has the potential for treason. By supposing that he is above prudence, that it is impossible that he could be considered a traitor (since his treason could only be treason against himself), he becomes merely the instrument of those who understand the world better than he does.

The boys' tragedies we have been looking at mainly lay their stress on the ambiguities of the corrupt world rather than on the direct villainies of public-theatre tragedy. Three tragedies played by the boys stand, however, outside this tradition. The basic text is Marston's *Antonio's Revenge* (1599×1601), the tragic half of the two-part *Antonio and Mellida*, where the 'comic crosses of true love' in Part One are replaced by what Marston calls in the Prologue to Part Two an 'unused peise of style and sense | That might weigh massy in judicious scale'. What we find here is the standard revenge pattern of a virtuous prince (Antonio) driven by supernatural solicitings to match a usurper (Piero) in deeds of treachery and horror, deeds seen as necessary if the state is to be cleansed of tyranny and handed back to rational government. At the same time as he shows us this, Marston uses the boys to undercut the tragedy by offering a running commentary on what is happening, pointing to the limitations of stage presentation and raising questions about the psychology and ethics of a revenge action. This is tragedy with one foot in the ambiguous soil of tragicomedy.

Life is depicted in the play as a desperate game of self-misrepresentation as the unhinged opposites continually shift position. The modes of civil discourse are always being outflanked by those of barbaric ritual, and so need continual reformulation. The action, like the style, is violently deconstructive. The ending, in which the revengers retreat into a monastery, is less an end than a confession of the endlessness of the condition represented.

John Mason's *The Turk* (1607×1608) is the second of my two aberrant tragedies. It appears, like Sharpham's *The Fleer* (discussed above (pp. 312–13)), to be another tribute to Marston's influence over young gentlemen amateurs. Mason, a Cambridge MA, was (like Lording Barry) one of the sharers in the Whitefriars theatre that was set up when the Children of the Revels lost their Blackfriars venue. It may be guessed that he used his investment to secure himself a place in the pantheon; but he did not buy a very prominent niche. If *Antonio's Revenge* is the model for *The Turk*, it must be

said that the imitation picks up only the superficies of the original.
At the height of his ambitions Marston's Piero imagines his success:

> Young Galeatzo![123] Ay, a proper man;
> Florence, a goodly city; it shall be so.
> I'll marry her[124] to him instantly.
> Then Genoa mine by my Maria's[125] match,
> Which I'll solemnize ere next setting sun;
> Thus Venice, Florence, Genoa, strongly leagued—
> Excellent, excellent!—I'll conquer Rome,
> Pop out the light of bright religion;
> And then, helter-skelter, all cocksure!

(IV. i. 260–8)

The energy of the speech shows us Piero imagining himself as the
stock tyrant. The play places such dreams of simple self-fulfilment
somewhere between intention and performance; action seldom
catches up with imagination. But Mason follows through his action
in objective detail. The title-page of the second Quarto (1632) calls
it a work 'full of interchangeable variety, beyond expectation', and
for once the publisher is accurate. *The Turk* is an extraordinary
confection of all the most lurid elements supposed to exist in
Renaissance Italy. Borgias, the governor of Florence, and Muleasses,
his Turkish companion/rival in crime, aim to secure the throne of
Italy by fraud, marriage, fake deaths, murder, and the help of the
Sultan, who will secure Borgias's gains in return for unimpeded
passage through the Mediterranean. A sub-plot of courtly lechery
shows a cast of eunuch, catamite, friar, bawd, and ghosts ('inferior
trivial persons' Mason calls them in the Epilogue) passing and
repassing through the labyrinth of the intrigue. Mason is a fluent
poet in the style of Greene and Peele: the mythology of Greece and
Rome is everywhere in use to decorate the speeches. And one can
imagine that the children spoke them well. But the interplay that
Marston set up between the taste for rhetoric and the functional
irrelevance of rhetoric is nowhere apparent; it was a mixture that
was not easy to imitate.

The pleasures of deception (or excitements of self-creation) that
the boys can convey to us in Marston's highly wrought arias of
self-congratulation are lost here in the speed of the actions the

---

[123] The Prince of Florence.   [124] Mellida, his daughter.
[125] The dowager Duchess of Genoa.

deceptions allow. In this obfuscation of the talents that gave the boys their special appeal, we can see (here as in the tragicomedies discussed elsewhere) the last stages of a dramaturgy that no longer could bring into focus the defining imagination of its audience.

The Insatiate Countess (*c*.1610×1613) is another play that indicates this impasse. It is said on the original title-page to be 'written by John Marston', but in a cancel to be 'written by Lewis Machin and William Bacster'. The second quarto (1616) avoids the issue by not mentioning authors at all; the third quarto (1631) says 'written by William *Barksteed'. Most critics allow that Marston had a hand in the play, and the vulgate opinion is that he began writing it, but abandoned the work when he was imprisoned in 1608. Machin and Barksteed/Bacster then finished the writing and the play was 'Acted at the Whitefriars by the Children of the Revels'. This story matches well our sense of what was happening in the children's theatre in these years. The closing of the Paul's playhouse, the eviction of the boys from the Blackfriars, Marston's turn from the theatre to the Church, all point to a *fin de siècle*.

The text of *The Insatiate Countess* shows the dramaturgy of Marston moving, or being moved, towards the norms of Beaumont and Fletcher (along with the rest of the repertory). The action avoids political implications and lacks any sense of ethical complexity. Giorgio Melchiori points in his edition to the loss of the 'deliberate irony or self-parody' in Marston's poetry, which was 'very imperfectly understood by the revisers of the play' who 'take far too seriously the rhetoric of the tragic speeches, obliterating the ironic counterpoint'.[126] In the main plot the Countess moves from man to man: as soon as she is married to one, she fancies another. And so, by the supposed logic of deviance, lust leads directly to murder. By the end of the action the bride price for her latest *innamorato* is the silencing of all his predecessors. The authors avoid the social explanations offered in the previous tellings (she did not belong to the nobility—her father was a usurer): they accept her as she is—as phenomenon rather than exemplum.

With high-handed assurance that her will is free, the Countess uses her social and sexual power to bypass accepted moral standards. In the second plot the same issues are played in the opposite direction. The insane rivalry of two bourgeois husbands demands that they scorn all limits. But their wives can reconstruct the social

---

[126] *The Insatiate Countess*, ed. Giorgio Melchiori (Manchester, 1984), 38–9.

bonds by turning their husbands' murderous contest into harmless channels, organizing a double bed trick so that each man sleeps with his own wife in the other's house. The assurance that he has been cuckolded by his enemy and that reputation has been irredeemably lost drives both men into ecstasies of despair. Rather than admit the shame, they confess to a murder they did not commit. But their execution, unlike the Countess's, was never seriously intended. An uneasy truce is set up between the sexes; and that, it is implied, is as much stability as we are likely to get:

> Since man's best of life is fame,
> He had need preserve the same.
> When 'tis in a woman's keeping,
> Let no Argos' eyes be sleeping.
> · · · · · ·
> Therefore, should'st thou Diana wed,
> Yet be jealous of her bed.
>
> (v. ii. 225–37)

It is hard to tell whether *The Insatiate Countess* should be called a tragedy or a tragicomedy (in this it is like *Cupid's Revenge*, see Chapter 10): the emotions, if not the consequences, of the bourgeois sub-plot can hardly be differentiated from those of the tragic main plot. Clearly the tension that gives an edge to the tragedies of Marston and Chapman, the ironic relationship between the telling and the told, between the confident articulation of the poetry and the violent uncertainty of the world it describes, has begun to lose its generalizing relevance. Social and personal ideals, honour and love, are still opposites, but no longer sharply incompatible. Indeed, it is not until we come to the Heroic Tragedies of the Restoration that this basic disjunction is again spotlit as a central dramatic issue, one that can best be represented by a totalizing rhetorical commitment that challenges our capacity to believe. But by that time, of course, the meanings of words like 'social', 'ideal', even 'love' have moved into a completely different focus.

Appendix. Shakespeare's *Troilus and Cressida*

The advertisement that the printer set before the 1609 Quarto of *Troilus and Cressida* (second state) is on many accounts a most revealing document:

A Never Writer to an Ever Reader. News.

Eternal reader, you have here a new play, never staled with the stage, never clapper-clawed with the palms of the vulgar, and yet passing full of the palm comical; for it is a birth of your brain that never undertook anything comical vainly. And were but the vain names of comedies changed for the titles of commodities or of plays for pleas you should see all those grand censors that now style them such vanities flock to them for the main grace of their gravities, especially this author's comedies, that are so framed to the life that they serve for the most common commentaries of all the actions of our lives, showing such a dexterity and power of wit that the most displeased with plays are pleased with his comedies. . . . And believe this, that when he is gone and his comedies out of sale, you will scramble for them and set up a new English Inquisition. Take this for a warning and, at the peril of your pleasure's loss and judgment's, refuse not, nor like this the less for not being sullied with the smoky breath of the multitude, but thank Fortune for the scape it hath made amongst you. Since, by the grand possessors' wills, I believe you should have prayed for them rather than been prayed. And so I leave all such to be prayed for (for the states of their wit's healths) that will not praise it. *Vale.*

What we have here is an explicit defence of booksellers' piracy of plays that the 'grand possessors', the theatrical shareholders, wished to retain as part of their portfolio, only to be cashed in when their acting value had depreciated. The present case is not only unusually explicit, however, but also rather peculiar; for it appears that this play had never been 'staled with the stage, never clapperclawed with the palms of the vulgar', nor 'sullied with the smoky breath of the multitude'. The point seems to be not that the play was unperformed but that it had never been performed on the *public* stage. Since Peter Alexander wrote his article on the play,[127] it has been generally agreed that *Troilus and Cressida* (1601×1603) must have been designed for performance at one of the Inns of Court. It is full of scabrous legalisms and bawdy jokes that would be entirely appropriate to a self-consciously sophisticated student audience. From this angle *Troilus and Cressida* looks as if it belongs alongside those written for the boys.

This alignment does little, however, to define the genre, for this

[127] 'Troilus and Cressida, 1609', *Library*, 9 (1928–9). Cf. R. Kimbrough, *Shakespeare's 'Troilus and Cressida' and its Setting* (Cambridge, Mass., 1964), 21.

is a play unlike the others that have come down to us.[128] The Prologue appears 'armed, but not in confidence | Of author's pen or actor's voice, but suited | In like conditions as our argument'. This sounds like a comment on the war between poet and players in the poetomachia, but if there is any specific reference to the personalities or issues ventilated in *Poetaster* (with its 'Prologue armed') and *Satiromastix*, it seems to be buried at a depth inaccessible to modern explanation. Certainly no such references are necessary for an appreciation of the power of Shakespeare's play.

The 'advertisement' to *Troilus and Cressida* describes it as a comedy, but if it is so it is an exceptionally bitter comedy. Its parodic or satiric treatment of heroic militarism and romantic passion draws on the uneasy mixture of rhetorical parody and ethical seriousness we find recurrently in the children's theatre. But it differs from most of the plays of that repertory in the intensity of its commitment to both idealism and disgust. It is probably closest of all to Marston's *Antonio and Mellida* diptych.[129] But whereas Marston's play presents characters whose switch from attitude to attitude is explicable in terms of an intrigue world where shift of identity is the precondition of survival, and therefore rational though factitious, in Shakespeare the contradictions are shown as elements of human nature. The various verisimilitudes supplied to the play by Homer and Chaucer are exposed as preconditioning fictions, and so undermine our belief in the freedom of choice the characters assert. The tissue of contradictions[130] in fact reveals only the absurdity of human nature under the condition of freedom. In *Antonio and Mellida*

---

[128] That the play puzzled its contemporaries seems to be shown by the fact that the Quarto advertisement tries to sell it as a comedy, while Heminge and Condell intended to place it in the Folio among the tragedies. The usual modern attempt to categorize it as a 'problem play' and link it with the very different *All's Well* and *Measure for Measure* seems to describe only the problem that categorizing critics have to face.

[129] In 'Marston's "Antonio" Plays and Shakespeare's "Troilus and Cressida"', in *Essays and Studies by Members of the English Association, 1980*, Jonathan Dollimore has linked the two plays together as exemplifying 'the birth of a radical drama'. Both show us alienated characters who achieve 'reintegration of self and self with society' by the 'creation of a subculture dedicated to revenge' against the world around them (p. 48). There seems to be a confusion here between the psycho-history of a conspiracy and the perceived trauma of a culture. The effort of Antonio and Troilus is not to establish a new sense of self but to face down a social aberration and so recover a former stability.

[130] Cressida as faithful and unfaithful, Troilus as naïve idealist and savage realist, Ulysses as severe moralist and political contriver, Ajax and Achilles as ideal warriors and 'great-sized bullies', Cassandra as never believed truth-teller, Thersites as condemner and enjoyer of corruption, Hector as deep-thinking philosopher and carefree warrior.

we are always aware of a Marstonian outlook controlling the tone of the fiction. In *Troilus and Cressida* the author has no presence: we move from dilemma to dilemma as one character after another is allowed the freedom to reach ends proposed by one part of his nature only to meet there the frustration required by another but equally integral part, as if the very organs of perception 'had deceptious functions | Created only to calumniate' (v. ii. 123–4), and 'where reason can revolt | Without perdition and loss assume all reason | Without revolt' (v. ii. 144–6). Shakespeare may have been an outsider in terms of Inns of Court Society, but no one ever anatomized its taste with equal force and virtuosity.

8. Later Comedy

The Companies and their Repertories

THE years 1593–4 mark an institutional divide in the theatrical enterprise of the English capital. Cessation of playing in time of plague had been written into the licence to perform since 1574.[1] In such periods (notably 1581–2, 1592–3, 1603–4, 1608–9, 1609–10, 1625, 1630) the always fragile economy of the profession was strained to breaking-point.[2] In 1604 and 1625 even the King's Men, the best established of all the companies, had to be bailed out by gifts from their patron.[3] In the catch-as-catch-can world of 1593 no such help could be imagined. Travelling into the plague-free provinces (with a reduced company) was an obvious resource, but even that descent into the unrewarding world of heavy wagons, muddy roads, hostile magistrates, unsuitable halls, unsophisticated audiences, could do no more than postpone the forced sale of such assets as costumes and playbooks, essential to a recovery of London status.[4] The 1592–3 outbreak seems to have caught a situation already in turmoil. In 1583 the profession had been granted a limited stability by the creation of a body of 'Queen's Players', selected from the best actors from the extant troupes and provided with a courtly status (as grooms of the chamber). But such attempts to secure control of an essentially fissiparous situation had only a temporary effect. The Queen's Men could not, any more than the other companies, hold together. By the early 1590s (after Tarlton's death) it seems to have lost its predominance and thus opened space for competing alternatives.[5] Out of the chaos created

---

[1] See Chambers, ii. 88. Also Leeds Barroll, *Politics, Plague and Shakespeare's Theater* (Ithaca, NY, 1991); F. P. Wilson, *The Plague in Shakespeare's London* (Oxford, 1962).

[2] By the end of 1625 four of the London companies had disappeared. In 1637 'most London acting troupes, except the King's Men, disbanded or had to be reorganized', *The Revels History of Drama in English*, iv. *1613–1660*, ed. Lois Potter (London, 1981), 95, 111.

[3] See MSC vi. 39 and Bentley, *JCS* i. 20.

[4] See the articles by Sally-Beth Maclean, Peter Greenfield, and J. A. B. Somerset in *The Elizabethan Theatre*, x (1988) for evidence that provincial touring was not necessarily the ruinous activity that has generally been supposed.

[5] The turmoil can be looked at from a literary as well as an organizational viewpoint: it may be that the talents of such famous Queen's Men as Tarlton and Robert Wilson were not

by the 1593 plague, however, a new stability emerged. In 1594 (at a time, we should remember, when competition from the boys was removed) the two most continuously successful companies on the Elizabethan stage were established—the Admiral's (later Prince Henry's) Men and (most successful of all) the Chamberlain's/ King's Men (Shakespeare's Company in our anachronistic terminology). This diarchy[6] provided a pattern entirely to the taste of the Privy Council, since it established control and yet gave access to a wide range of alternatives for court entertainment. Caught between the preachers' and the city fathers' desire to see all playing abolished and the Queen's intention to have professional players at command without having to pay for them, the Council's enactments show how much easier it was to temporize than to establish a coherent system. Throughout the 1590s the Council was bombarded by warnings from the city authorities that the toleration of plays would demoralize the whole population. On 8 July 1597, for example, it heard from the Lord Mayor and aldermen that

neither in polity nor in religion [should plays] be suffered in a Christian commonwealth, specially being of that frame and matter as usually they are, containing nothing but profane fables, lascivious matters, cozening devices and scurrilous behaviours, which are so set forth as that they move wholly to imitation and not to the avoiding of those faults and vices which they represent. Among other inconveniences it is not the least that they give opportunity to the refuse sort of evil disposed and ungodly people that are within and about this city to assemble themselves and to make their matches for all their lewd and ungodly practices; being, as heretofore we have found by the examination of divers apprentices and other servants, who have confessed to us that the said stage plays were the very places of their rendevous appointed by them to meet with such other as were to join with them in their designs and mutinous attempts, being also the ordinary places for masterless men to come together and recreate themselves.[7]

appropriate to the new drama of the University Wits. Certainly, as Andrew Gurr has pointed out, 'the turnover of company membership was faster between 1588 and 1594 than it ever was before or after' (*The Shakespearean Stage, 1574-1642* (2nd edn., Cambridge, 1980), 34).

[6] Andrew Gurr, 'Three Reluctant Patrons', *Sh. Q.* 44 (1993), 159-74, suggests that the councillors responsible were the Lord Admiral (Nottingham) and Lord Chamberlain (Hunsden). In the period 1583-94 they seem to have cooperated to sustain the primacy of the Queen's Men by limiting access to London and the court and so avoiding disruptive competition between the peers. The diarchy of the years following 1594 looks like an extension of that same policy. [7] See Chambers, iv. 321.

On the same day as it received this, the Council responded by ordering that 'not only no plays shall be used within London or about the city . . . but that also those playhouses that are erected and built only for such purposes shall be plucked down, namely the Curtain and the Theatre near to Shoreditch or any other within that county'. But seven months later they decreed that the Admiral's and Chamberlain's companies be allowed 'to use and practise stage plays whereby they might be the better enabled and prepared to show such plays before her majesty as they shall be required at times meet and accustomed, to which end they have been chiefly licensed and tolerated'.[8] In 1600 Edward Alleyn's proposal to build the Fortune Playhouse in Golden Lane produced an extension of the diarchy to buildings as well as companies.[9] The permission to build given to Alleyn was, however, made contingent on the Curtain being 'ruined or plucked down or put to some other good use'; the permission to the Chamberlain's Men states that they shall have only *one* playhouse on the Bankside no more. And the companies are to play no more than twice a week (and never on Sundays).[10]

These enactments describe only the idea of the companies as officially instituted. To enquire about what matters most to us, the plays, is to move into a field with completely different coordinates. It would be convenient to be able to describe a division of the repertory of 1594–1604 (the richest decade in Elizabethan drama) that corresponds to an institutional division between the Admiral's

---

[8] Ibid. 322–3; cf. 325. See also the Privy Council order of June 1600 (ibid. 330): 'her Majesty being pleased at some time to take delight and recreation in the sight and hearing of them [plays], some order is fit to be taken for the allowance and maintenance of such persons as are thought meetest in that kind to yield her Majesty recreation and delight, and consequently of the houses that must serve for public playing to keep them in this exercise.'

[9] 'There shall be about the City two houses and no more, allowed to serve for the use of the common stage plays, of which houses one shall be in Surrey in that place which is commonly called the Bankside or thereabouts and the other in Middlesex' (Chambers, iv. 330).

[10] The draconian language of these regulations should not be taken literally. In December 1601 the order was repeated; but in March 1602 Worcester's/Oxford's Men were allowed to play at the Boar's Head (and a little later at the Curtain). The Curtain continued to be used as a playhouse until at least 1622 (Chambers, ii. 404). As far as the restriction on the number of performances per week is concerned, there is little evidence. But one may note that in 1597 Henslowe was recording daily income at an average rate of twenty-one performances per month. In the post-1598 period he no longer gives a daily accounting, but his profits do not suggest that he had reduced his performances to eight days per month. See Bradbrook, *The Rise of the Common Player* (Cambridge, 1962), 111 ff., for pertinent comments on the powerlessness of the forces of law and order.

and the Chamberlain's Men,[11] but to attempt to do so is to stumble
into a jungle with only an imaginary map.[12] Our understanding
must be conditioned by the evidence available to us, and this is too
ambiguous and haphazard to yield a clear outline. The theatrical
papers of Philip Henslowe—the greatest body of evidence we possess—begin in 1592 with payments to companies that couple and
decouple in bewildering fashion. From 1594 until 1602, however,
he concei trates on the Admiral's Men, and the records for these
years provide us with the titles of some 230 plays paid for and
(usually) performed—of which about twenty-nine survive[13]—
together with details of payments to some sixteen authors, notes on
properties acquired, and accounts of income and outgoings. For
the Chamberlain's Men in the same period we have approximately
twenty-two Shakespeare plays, one perished court morality (*Cloth
Breeches and Velvet Hose*),[14] and seven other plays (*Every Man in
his Humour, Every Man out of his Humour, A Warning for Fair
Women, Thomas, Lord Cromwell, Satiromastix, A Larum for London,
The Merry Devil of Edmonton*). On the one hand, that is, we have
detailed knowledge of a whole theatrical enterprise; on the other
side, we have to deal with a repertory apparently dominated by a
single author whose theatrical presence can now be seen only in
the shadow of his literary power.

   To set up a comparison of the multifarious activities of the
Henslowe companies with the apparently Shakespeare-dominated
repertory of the Chamberlain's Men cannot, it would seem, be
accepted as a full description of what was actually going on. Allowing
that the Admiral's and the Chamberlain's were in competition for
the same population of customers, it makes no commercial sense to

---

[11] The minor companies that spent much of their time touring the provinces have not left
enough evidence to complicate the general picture.
[12] The danger of looking for simple distinctions is well documented in R. B. Sharpe, *The
Real War of the Theatres* (Boston, 1935). Sharpe's view that the Admiral's and Chamberlain's repertories were designed to serve the interests of anti- and pro-Essex factions and
that family names used in plays regularly point to extant families requires too much exclusion to be acceptable. Sharpe assumes that the Admiral's repertory was proletarian and
romantic where the Chamberlain's was aristocratic and patriotic (pp. 21–40), and in these
very general terms there is some truth in the distinction.
[13] The numbers are uncertain because of Henslowe's carelessness with titles. Some of his
plays are commonly supposed to have survived under different names. I rely here on the
conservative figures given in N. Carson, *A Companion to Henslowe's Diary* (Cambridge,
1988), table 1.
[14] Presumably based on Greene's *Quip for an Upstart Courtier*.

suppose that the Burbage management of the Chamberlain's would introduce only two to three new plays a year when the competitors down the road were offering something like twenty (see Chambers, ii. 165–71).[15] One may conjecture, I believe, that as many plays have been lost from the repertory of the Chamberlain's Men as we know to have been lost from the Admiral's (leaving the Chamberlain's Men with a repertory of 289 plays paid for, of which 259 are lost). The non-Shakespeare, non-Jonson Chamberlain's plays that survive also suggest that, if we possessed the whole list, then the two repertories would look more alike than a judgement in terms of only Jonson and Shakespeare suggests. Looking back from the end of the era (1642), it appears that the Chamberlain's/King's Men had relied on a succession of major writers (Shakespeare, Jonson, Fletcher, Massinger, Shirley) for their repertory; but this situation could hardly have pertained in the 1590s, if it was ever true. Shakespeare's writings should probably be seen as fitting into a repertory of plays not unlike the ones performed by the other company.

Can we, in spite of all these limitations, say anything that will make linkage between company and repertory more than a historian's pipedream? Occasionally (and what else is possible?) we can glimpse a relationship (like that between *Henry IV* and *Sir John Oldcastle* discussed above (pp. 240–5)) where the competitive impulse is clear. But there is not enough evidence to support a general assumption. Romantic adventure plays discussed below do not appear among the known Chamberlain's titles, and perhaps the older popular tradition of chivalric adventure, found in such plays as *Clyomon and Clamydes*, was more continuously present in the Admiral's repertory than in the Chamberlain's. On the other hand, prodigal-son and topographical genres seem to have been shared. It would make sense to suppose that no general principles were involved, that the competition was an *ad hoc* business, as both companies responded to new opportunities and new pressures.

---

[15] Cf. Edmond Malone's comment: 'It appears from Sir Henry Herbert's Office-Book that the King's Company between the years 1622 and 1642 produced either at Blackfriars or the Globe at least four new plays a year' (*1821 Variorum Shakespeare*, iii. 166); Bentley argues that the numbers should be even smaller. The contrast between these figures and Henslowe's records is usually held to be due to the gradual build-up of a stock of plays from the earlier period. Of eighty-eight plays performed at Charles I's court, sixty-four were old plays (Gurr, *The Shakespearean Stage*, 21).

Romantic Adventure Plays

To define the comedy of the popular stage by strict generic rules
looks like another hopeless task. These 'comedies' are so continuously concerned with dangers and threats of disaster that in generic language we have to call them tragicomedies. But that is too
precise. What we need is a word whose vagueness more properly
mirrors the uncertainty of the balance between laughter and violence. The appropriate word is Romance. But Romance is a house
with many mansions, and it is necessary in an analytic survey to
look for smaller units that define output in narrower terms. To
read through Henslowe's Diary for the period 1594–1605 is to
recognize one such subset. The new comedies being written in this
period for the Admiral's Men were not only romantic but particularly focused on what I may call romantic adventure.[16] This was a
focus especially popular, it would seem, with Henslowe authors in
the years around the turn of the century, and clearly it hit the
public taste, for plays of this kind remained part of the popular
repertory until 1642. Not all of them are set in a vaguely historical
past, but the majority find that the most appropriate background.[17]
These are, in the main, stories of enforced adventure imposed on
virtuous noblemen, conspired against and forced into exile by un-
scrupulous enemies. They lose their social status and are separated
from their families; they are obliged to live with boors, devious
foreigners, and cynical (though loyal) clowns; but they bear all this
with Christian cheerfulness, and eventually change of circumstances
uncovers the plot against them; the hero can then recover (usually
by military means) the status he lost. The king or other ruler,
who has been misled by villains, now confirms (though he cannot
create) the return of justice to the deserving individual.[18]

---

[16] The obvious precedents are to be found in the comedies attributed to Robert Greene
(see Ch. 4). There we find the same sprawling romance plots, the same quasi-historical
background. What seems to have disappeared is the emphasis on romantic love.

[17] Several plays of this kind are treated in Ribner, *The English History Play in the Age of
Shakespeare* (Princeton, 1957), as examples of 'The history play in decline'; and some very
similar ones I have included in Ch. 6. It is difficult to draw a clear line. Ribner thinks that
the 'didactic purposes' he assigns to history plays makes the difference. I would prefer to
argue that the line separates those that give historical events a central function from those
that use history to set up personal adventure.

[18] Heywood and Rowley's *Fortune by Land and Sea* (?1609) played by Queen Anne's
company (the old Worcester's Men), probably at the Red Bull, is a good example of the
variety the form could encompass. In the main it is a story of a usurious father disinheriting

As in the romantic comedies of the earlier generation, these plays drew on the widely disseminated plots of the Italian *novelle* and their English derivatives, such as Greene's *James IV*.[19] But *James IV* has a comparatively simple historical action; the patiently recuperative function of the queen in that play is certainly one that survived in the tradition (see below on prodigal-son plays), but more central to the Admiral's repertory of the decade spanning the new century is a male Griselda figure who can combine patience and loyalty in misfortune with military prowess when the opportunity to assert himself arises.[20]

The First (and only extant) *Part of The Blind Beggar of Bednall Green, with the Merry Humour of Tom Strowd the Norfolk Yeoman* (1600; printed 1659) may be taken as a representative specimen of this kind of play. To pay for it Henslowe laid out £5 10s. for Chettle and Day in May 1600; and that seems to have been a profitable investment, for he paid £3 10s. and £2 10s. for a second part in January–February 1601, and yet another 10 shillings for a third part in May 1601. But only Part One has survived, and that leaves no clues how the story could have been developed. The action is set in the period of Shakespeare's *2 Henry VI*. The Regent Bedford opens the play with comments on the dissensions between Gloucester and Winchester (here sparked by competition for the hand of Elinor Cobham) which are undermining the military victories in France. These issues are mainly scene-setting, providing a background of disorder that helps to explain the actual subject of the play. This concerns the good Lord Momford, accused by enemies of selling the town of Guines to the French. The charge is 'proved' by faked evidence and Momford is banished. Under this pressure he displays his sterling virtues. He bankrupts

a virtuous son, who must then work as servant to his sneering relatives; but his rescue is effected by daring deeds at sea in which his brother-in-law captures notorious pirates and so achieves wealth and knighthood.

[19] The source story in Cinthio's *novella* places the political conflict between two romantically unrealistic countries, Ibernia and Scozia. Greene gives the action extra resonance by attaching it to some real history, so that the defeat of Scotland at Flodden Field becomes a punishment for marital unfaithfulness and the restorer of marital order can be understood to be Henry VII.

[20] The Duke of Bullen in *The Weakest Goeth to the Wall*, Lord Momford in *The First Part of The Blind Beggar of Bednall Green*, Earl Marshall in *The Royal King and the Loyal Subject*, the Earl of Gloucester in *Look About You*, the Princes of France and Navarre in *The Trial of Chivalry*, Crispin and Crispianus in *A Shoemaker a Gentleman*, Elidure in *Nobody and Somebody*.

himself to pay off all his debts, dismisses his servants with a blessing, and will return to England, not as an exiled lord but in the guise of a sturdy and self-respecting 'blind beggar'.

Not only is Momford ruined financially and socially but his daughter Bess, who comes to look after him in his cottage on Bethnal Green (not knowing who he is), is made the victim of subsequent plots by the same villains, which Momford can frustrate but is powerless to avoid. Her misfortunes, however, attract fair-minded defenders, the upright military man Captain Westford, and the blunt Norfolk yeoman Old Strowd, whose clownish son Tom, a thick-headed yokel trying to cope with city slickers, seems to have provided one of the great attractions of the play (he is mentioned on the title-page). The villains overreach themselves; their malice becomes apparent and the issue has to be decided (on the orders of Henry VI) through trial by combat. And that, predictably enough, decides in favour of virtue. At the same time, on the national scene, Elinor finally escapes from the clutches of the cardinal and marries Humphrey of Gloucester; the nation settles down to an (unhistorical) concord. Will Bess marry Tom Strowd, who has saved her life? Hierarchy demands otherwise. By a clever trick (celebrated in a ballad collected by Bishop Percy), Momford disqualifies the crudely moneyed Strowds and finds her a more suitable mate in Captain Westford. Both Westford and Momford are given high offices by the King, and with 'each member seated in his proper seat' the play comes to an end.

The Blind Beggar of Bednall Green uses its action to establish a set of values that link it with such earlier folk comedies as George a Green. It validates the patiently poor against the grasping rich (the beggar against his enemies), the countryside at the expense of the city (the Strowds against Sir Robert Westford), the old against the new (Old Playney in preference to Young Playney), the aristocracy against the mercantile middle classes and the military against the legalistic (Captain Westford versus Sir Robert and Young Playney). And these values are attached, in a rather vague way, to a history of national strength and potential weakness. It is a breakdown in national hierarchy, it is implied, that allows fraud and exploitation to occur. The good man endures all until national harmony reappears, when the good king (never mind that he is Henry VI) will take charge again; only then can private virtue show itself and be rewarded.

The world of such plays is clearly polarized between good and evil. The audience is invited to identify with the powerless individual and to accept that the battle against powerful evil can succeed only when Providence provides the correct historical–political circumstances. Recovery of status by counter-intrigue is no part of the ethos. Political chaos (Roman–Christian conflict in William *Rowley's A Shoemaker a Gentleman* (1607×1609), the tension between Henry II and Henry III in *Look About You* (c.1598×1600), the departure for the Crusades of a Louis IX kind of king in *The Weakest Goeth to the Wall* (c.1599×1600), the Norman Conquest in Heywood's *The Four Prentices of London* (1592×c.1600) allows evil individuals a space in which they can subvert the social balance. History is seen, plausibly enough, as a scenario dominated not by the labyrinthine intrigue we find in classically derived comedy but by fortune, and the plot structures are obviously in pursuit of variousness, even randomness, rather than structured complexity. The casts are large and the action episodic as one trial after another is imposed on the patience and indomitability of the heroic characters. Thus in *The Weakest Goeth to the Wall* the loss of Bullen's son, his betrayal and exile, the control of his wife and daughter by the lecherous Dutchman, Jacob van Smelt, his escape from starvation by falling in with the Folk as sexton to an illiterate village parson, the hue and cry against his son's elopement, the claim on his wife by a Rochelle merchant, all these (and more—I have left out the political events) are handled by a linear, stop-and-start method, new characters continually appearing and creating unexpected situations right up to the end of the play.

To understand the history of this form it is desirable to consider the way in which it grew out of its antecedents. The extent of its social survey, as the roller-coaster of history carries us through the wickednesses of the world, inevitably reminds one of the Estates Morality drama of the previous generation. But, where the Estates Moralities show us non-chronological episodes of social ill analysed by a moralizing commentator who stands above the turmoil and sums it up in terms of abstract ideals, the historical romances offer us the chronology of a particular individual's struggle not only to see the wickedness around him but to escape from the hold it has on his life. This transition from Estates Morality to Romance formulae is nicely illustrated by putting side by side the popular *A Knack to Know a Knave* (still playing at the Rose in 1592) and its sequel, the moralized romance of *A Knack to Know an Honest Man*, performed by the Admiral's Men in 1594, no doubt hoping, as in most sequels, to cash in on the reputation of the earlier play. The protagonist of *A Knack to Know a Knave* is a morality figure called Honesty. Under the protection of St Dunstan, he offers to show Edgar (King of England from 958 to 975) the corruptions that infest his realm. He is given a roving commission, and, as the action proceeds, we watch his systematic exposure of the coneycatcher, the courtier, the farmer, and the priest, whose activities undermine the whole structure of the state—the farmer is a skinflint, despises traditional charity, exports the grain that the country needs; the coneycatcher gets rich by cheating the poor and ignorant; the courtier flatters the king, stirs up envy among the peers, curries favour with the commons, misuses the royal seal; the priest is a usurer, and brings the word of God into disrepute.

The King, however (and here we register the pressure of romance), allows his emotions to overrule his duty. He is unwilling to face the omnipresence of corruption. He would like to save the courtier; like Prince Edward in *Friar Bacon and Friar Bungay*, he sends his noble companion to persuade Alfrida to yield her virtue to her king, and like Edward he is murderously enraged when the friend marries the girl.[21] It takes all the moral authority of Honesty and Dunstan to return Edgar to the path of virtue. But such plays must end 'happily'—that is, virtuously. Honesty must be allowed to be both judge and jury for the four sinners (not the King, of course) and proposes savage punishments for their social deviance. He ends by warning the audience to act in such a way that they can avoid the same fate.

The Admiral's sequel, *A Knack to Know an Honest Man* (1594), seems to have been another good Henslowe investment. The accounts show it given repeated performances from October 1594 until November 1596. In terms of what we know, it may in fact be the earliest of these stories of a good man made vulnerable to social disgrace by false accusation.[22] The setting is a modern mercantile state (Venice). We see the good man's wealth seized by those he trusted, his supporters victimized by community leaders who are

---

[21] The tradition of the Edgar–Alfrida story is traced by J. M. Stochholm in her edition of Massinger's *The Great Duke of Florence* (Baltimore, Md., 1933), pp. xxv–lxvii.

[22] Of course, the story of Robin Hood provided an archetype which long preceded all the examples given.

more interested in profit than justice, the ruler caught up in 'vain ceremonies' and 'customs of the world', his son, the prince, a debauchee. When we compare it with its predecessor, it becomes obvious that the history of misfortune must now provide a narrative which will justify the detachment that Honesty is given by fiat.[23]

The play begins with a duel which leaves one man supposed dead, the other in flight as a supposed murderer. Both find themselves driven from comfortable acceptance or ignorance (what a theological age called 'security') into awareness of general corruption, for they are no longer inside Venetian society, looking out, but outside, trying to get back in. The morality strain is kept covered, but has not disappeared: the man left for dead is rescued by a hermit, nursed back to health, and becomes a changed character, now called 'Penitent Experience'; his new role is to move through society observing ills, though incapable of changing them and forbidden to reveal his identity. It is in this anonymous role that he can instruct others in 'a knack to know an honest man'. Money is still the root of all evil, as in A Knack to Know a Knave, but inside a sophisticated courtly and mercantile society the profit principle now appears as a normal mode of social intercourse. It provides the means by which all social activity (including envy, flattery, lust, hypocrisy, royal sloth) is justified and conducted.

An interestingly similar shift of morality form towards romantic adventure can be seen by laying side by side the Dekker, Chettle, and *Haughton comedy of Patient Grissil (which Henslowe paid for between 16 October and 1 November 1600)[24] and John *Phillip's The Comedy of the Patient and Meek Grissil: wherein is declared the good example of her patience towards her husband and likewise the due obedience of children towards their parents (1558×1561). Once again an original structure, handled in terms of abstractions (it is the Vice, Politic Persuasion, who moves the Marquis to judge Grissil's fitness to be his wife by political expediency rather than moral propriety) is repackaged as part of a more complex social system.

---

[23] Changes in taste do not turn around everything in their path. A curious play of 1603×1606, Nobody and Somebody; with the True Chronicle History of Elidure who was three several times crowned King of England, shows the Estates Morality (after some cross-breeding with Locrine) alive and well a decade later than A Knack to Know an Honest Man (and later still if we include its German imitations).

[24] The play's money-making potential can be gauged from the fact that Henslowe was willing to pay 40 shillings to 'stay' publication.

The rustic passivity of 'embracing the cross' is now given a defining opposite in courtly affectation and opportunism. The arbitrariness of court authority is spelt out in clear political terms by Grissil's hitherto undiscovered brother (a discontented university drop-out), though the issue is not pursued in these terms. Once again redemption through wifely obedience provides the final focus on human behaviour, and moral stability resolves political anxiety. Yet the reduction of patience from a saintly attribute to a social virtue[25] opens up the issue to a degree not found in Phillip. The sub-plot of the Marquis's sixteenth-century Welsh cousin shows us that marriage can be thought of as a spectrum of personal compromises as well as a model of Christian life.

Dekker's *The Shoemakers' Holiday* (1599; printed 1600, 1610, 1618, 1624, 1657) is probably the best loved of all the surviving comedies in the Admiral's repertory, in part at least because of the success with which it creates a rich overlap of its frames of reference. It manages (and without the disconnectedness of different levels in *Patient Grissil*) to be both historical, set in the period of the French wars of Henry V (or possibly Henry VI), and at the same time a convincing picture of artisan life in Elizabethan London. It offers us the usual story of disgrace and exile, resourcefulness under difficulty and eventual recovery of status, thus doubling the transgressive action that appears in the source, Deloney's *The Gentle Craft*. But Lacy's disgraceful retreat from military and social prominence and reappearance as Hans the Dutch shoemaker is the result not of a plot by his enemies but of a choice for love rather than honour. The play thus requires us to assimilate two contradictory value systems. The story of Lacy's success in avoiding war and achieving love is counterpointed against the real shoemaker Rafe's inability to avoid war, so that he returns a cripple, only to find his wife accepting (however unwillingly) a well-moneyed husband. Dekker's juxtaposition of the two weddings opens up very clearly the moral of 'it's the rich that gets the pleasure and the poor that gets the blame'; but the complex geometry of the play does not allow the moral to cancel its romance; the contrapuntal vitality enriches rather than obliterates the melody.

---

[25] Cf. the vulgarized version in the 1619 chapbook: *The Ancient, True and Admirable History of Patient Grissil, a Poor Man's Daughter in France; showing how maids by her example in their good behaviour may marry rich husbands and likewise wives by their patience and obedience may gain much glory*, ed. H. B. Wheatley (London, 1885).

At the centre of the action, embodying as well as mediating its contradictions, is the larger-than-life figure of Simon Eyre, whose trajectory from shoemaker to Lord Mayor of London and boon companion to the king is offered as a realistic myth and true romance of the success that is available to everyone. This does not mean that Eyre is a figure of patient virtue. The commercial success which makes it possible for him to start his social climb is shown to be half-luck and half-sharp practice. There is some justice in Harry Levin's characterization of him as 'Shylock masquerading as Falstaff'.[26] But the economic realism that underpins Eyre's romantic rise to power is handled as if financial success was a natural consequence of personal ebullience. His rise emerges from his verbal energy rather than his planned actions (things happen to him as if by accident); and this allows dominance to be construed as fun, for in verbal if not in practical terms his wife and his workmen can match violence with violence and yet endorse communion as well as subordination. Just as in the rough and tumble of the workshop the abrasiveness of hierarchy must coexist with its acted-out resistance,[27] so Eyre's economic advance is complemented (and to some extent defused) by the acted buffoonery that allows even the king to join him in playing the joker; and both aspects are held together by a patriotism which expands the conditional camaraderie of the shopfloor into the spirit of a nation at war.

Topographical Nostalgia

The power of all these plays about rich men becoming poor men becoming rich men again depends on their capacity to offer both an endorsement of social hierarchy and simultaneously a critique of the values by which it operates. Nostalgia no doubt is a contributory element in the endorsement: assumptions about the shared values of the nation are most easily celebrated when it is continuity from the tradition-forming past that is being evoked (as in the building of the Leadenhall and the establishment of the apprentices' Shrove Tuesday holiday at the end of *The Shoemakers' Holiday*). The sense of a shared past throws a mediating glow of distance

---

[26] Quoted by Jonas Barish, *Ben Jonson and the Language of Prose Comedy* (Cambridge, Mass., 1960), 282.

[27] On this topic, see James C. Scott, *Domination and the Arts of Resistance* (New Haven, 1990).

over the conflicts of the present, softening their outlines, making comic reconciliation seem possible, and turning history itself into another version of pastoral. The same effect can be obtained by measuring distance in space rather than time: nostalgia can be handled in topographical as in chronological terms, when simple, rural, unsophisticated lives are used to represent our own past, the good place we came from. Jonson's *A Tale of a Tub*[28] promises in its prologue to show 'no state affairs . . . But acts of clowns and constables . . . And all the neighbourhood from old records . . . With country precedents and old wives' tales'. What is evoked here is the sense of a timeless rural world in which 'the wise men of Finsbury hundred' can exemplify and live inside ancient traditions without ever knowing what they are. This is essentially a view designed for Londoners looking over the wall and imagining with some condescension but more delight the innocent lives of people who take the villages of St Pancras, Kilburn, and Paddington as their metropolises, 'people', as Anne Barton has put it, 'complexly enmeshed within a continuum'.[29] The idea of innocence has no doubt a particular appeal when set against courtly behaviour. 'We bring you now [this play]', says Jonson in the Prologue, 'to show what different things | The cotes of clowns are from the courts of kings'; the difference can be construed as not entirely in the court's favour, and certainly we learn from Sir Henry Herbert that the play was 'not liked' when performed at court on 14 January 1634.[30]

One of the great strengths of this delightful play (and it is a typically Jonsonian strength) comes from the classical limitation

---

[28] The play is dated 1596 in Harbage–Schoenbaum, with the caveat 'substantially new when licensed 7 May 1633'. The satire of Inigo Jones as In-and-In Medley must belong to the later date, but there is no evidence what else does. Modern critics (Anne Barton, David Riggs, Martin Butler) have pointed out that the nostalgia for a simpler time would fit in with Jonson's neo-Elizabethan mood in the 1630s; but it is hard to distinguish neo-Elizabethanism from the real thing, and difficult to think of the play ever existing free of nostalgia.

[29] *Ben Jonson, Dramatist* (Cambridge, 1984), 328. An interesting parallel to Jonson's play can be found in the sub-plot of *Grim the Collier of Croydon* (1600; printed 1662), probably written by William Haughton (see below, n. 59). This is the story of a demon sent from hell to test the virtue of earthly women. Gentlewomen prove to be worse than even Hell had imagined. The demon-servant, Akercock, cannot stand it any more, runs away to rural Croydon, and there finds an idyll of simple affection between a fellow blackface, the collier, and his true love Jug. He can then report back to hell (and the audience) that *some* women are capable of virtue.

[30] J. Q. Adams (ed.), *The Dramatic Records of Sir Henry Herbert* (New Haven, 1917), 54.

of scope that gives a sense of completeness to its structure.[31] For these nostalgia plays, unlike the romantic adventures, tend to be held together by neatness of plot and counter-plot. The timescale of *A Tale of a Tub* stretches from breakfast to supper on St Valentine's Day; and it is St Valentine who provides the whole occasion for the action. Audrey Turf has drawn John Clay, tile-maker of Kilburn, as her husband in a St Valentine's Day lottery, as her mother had drawn her father thirty years before. Her parents will have her married on this very day. The substance of the action then derives from the plots and counter-plots of Squire Tub of Totten Hall and various officers of the law and the Church to prevent the marriage and acquire Audrey for themselves. The action gets more and more complicated as it passes into the hands of intermediaries (Squire Tubs's 'governor' Baskethilts is a marvellous re-creation of the classical *servus*); and eventually it is one of these who acquires the girl. The fracas subsides, the enmities are forgotten; the natural order of society is reconstituted at a feast, and they all watch a wedding masque which deciphers the events of the day in a series of dumbshows.

Henry Porter's *The Pleasant Comedy of the Two Angry Women of Abingdon, with the Humorous Mirth of Dick Coomes and Nicholas Proverbs, Two Serving Men* (c.1585×1589; printed 1599),[32] is another comedy of rural life in which the search for traditional consensus provides the primary drive. It follows very closely the neoclassical requirements of limitation on space, time, cast list, and development of plot. And again the model in view seems to be the early Tudor classicism represented by *Gammer Gurton's Needle*, seen as a carefully crafted drama of rural simplicities and much ado about nothing. The characters are not now village bumpkins, however,

---

[31] In this respect the play that comes closest to *A Tale of a Tub* is *Gammer Gurton's Needle* of (c.1552×1563). Both authors apply classical structure to village life and intend their sophisticated audience to relish the ironies as well as the continuities in that juncture.

[32] I have given the Harbage–Schoenbaum date in the text, but it is hard to believe that the play was written as early as this. Porter was killed in a duel with John Day in 1599. His name appears in Henslowe's Diary from 1596 to 1599; the last entries for him concern the second part of *The Two Angry Women*. The normal relation between first and second parts of plays in the diary suggests that the surviving first part would have been written in 1598. The only evidence against this date is a reference in Richard Harvey's *Plain Percival* (1589–90) to a proverb spoken by 'the serving man of Abington', and indeed the proverb does appear in the play spoken by the serving man Nicholas Proverbs. The dilemma does not permit of any clear solution. See Marianne B. Evett's edition (1980) for a survey of the evidence.

but country gentlemen, free-choosing individuals seeking above all
to preserve the even tenor of a thoroughly comfortable existence.
The play therefore does not offer any contrast between classic
order and the endemic disorder of vulgar life and indeed very little
real threat of any kind. It is one of the few Elizabethan comedies
to show a real Terentian lucidity. Porter gives a different twist to
the standard New Comedy plot, however, by showing patriarchal
comfort threatened not by the younger generation but by 'angry'
wives. The play concerns two neighbouring families resident in
the country by Abingdon (near Oxford), the Barneses and the
Gourseys. Its actions are entirely domestic, arising from an inter-
ruption in the idyllic amity of the two husbands and the two sons,
Frank Goursey and Philip Barnes—an amity which leads to the
betrothal of Mal Barnes and Frank Goursey. The two wives
are, however, determined to quarrel, Mrs Barnes deciding to
suspect her husband of having a love-affair with Mrs Goursey.
The servants of both households are easily caught up in the quarrel, especially when drunk. The complex movement of the play
derives from the double plotting of the husbands and children to
forward the match while the wives, sporadically abetted by their
servants, try to prevent it. The second half of the action consists
of a prolonged chase through the woods after nightfall, a chase
in which the whole cast is deployed, organized and disorganized by
a repertory of different meetings and misunderstandings, falling
into ponds, hiding in ditches. The ingenious denouement occurs
when the husbands are infected by the jealousy of the wives (or
only 'feign anger' as Evett's edition suggests). It seems as if the
quarrel might become serious; but before that can happen the
wives, now thoroughly frightened by what has happened, start to
think about compromise. The sons then stage-manage a general
reconciliation.

Porter's comedy, like *A Tale of a Tub*, is a play about betrothal
and marriage, but not about romantic love. Mal and Philip are
happy to get married when fathers and brothers propose it. Marriage and procreation are a natural part of the wholly conventional
life depicted; relations between boy and girl are conducted in terms
of a spirited mutual attraction. The highlighted 'humours' of the
servants, with their addiction to proverbs, are part of the same
accepting attitude to social organization as it stands, marked by an
unwillingness to think about the escapist perils of romance. For

the London audience, of course, escapism is one of the pleasures of the play.

The Merry Wives of Windsor (1597×1602) seems to show Shakespeare fitting in with the topographical fashion, and producing a comedy which is quite different from any other he wrote, set in England, mostly in prose, domestic (and yet also romantic). Once again we have the invocation of a specific locality, a small country town centred on inn and church, surrounded by fields and close to the mysterious forest with the romantic castle beyond it. The cast is again a closed community of town worthies who seem to have known and allowed for one another from time immemorial. We see the even tenor of these lives disrupted by threats to the stability of marriage, coming this time, however, from outside the enclosed life of the community, more specifically from the alternative life represented by the court and the castle (Falstaff and Fenton). And once again an unspecific historical past is invoked. The presence of the character called Falstaff and the news that Fenton has 'kept company with the wild Prince and Poins' (III. ii. 72–3) tell us that the action is set in the reign of Henry IV. For all that, the life of Windsor is not a medieval life but an Elizabethan one (as references to the book of Songs and Sonnets (1557) and Lily's grammar (1540) tell us). Time here, as in other plays of the type, is becalmed in the shallows of an innocent society resistant to change and to the interference of those outsiders who seek to upset the achieved balance between aggression and vulnerability, between husbands and wives, parents and children, French doctors and Welsh parsons. The strength of Windsor does not lie in any individual but in the community itself, which closes ranks as soon as threat appears, but when the threat is defeated regains its poise by absorbing the aggressor, as the end of the play reminds us: 'let us every one go home | And laugh this sport o'er by a country fire, | Sir John and all.'

Shakespeare seems, however, to be less committed to nostalgia than his colleagues. His consensus is achieved only by 'sport' with a strong punitive edge; he does not operate as a reassuringly visible puppeteer like Jonson but passes control to his surrogates, the merry wives, who sketch out the plot and extemporize wonderful additions when the situation allows it (concealing Falstaff in the buck basket and so on). The two authors are closest in their reliance on templates of pre-formed comedy: Jonson imposes a classic

plot on his peasant imbroglio; Shakespeare finds the character list
of the *commedia dell'arte* alive and well in Windsor.[33] In both cases
the effect is reassurance, as if the comic end is already in place,
reducing the 'danger' to a question about which of the standard
answers will be supplied. The threat that Falstaff offers exists in
fact only in his imagination. In the reality of the town he is doomed
as soon as he makes his first move. Once the wives have read his
form letter, the only issue is the nature of his punishment. The
same is true for the passions of Master Ford, for these are quickly
absorbed as extempore additions to the scenario the wives have
constructed, and which they can bring to its denouement at any
moment they fancy. Ford, though he has no inkling of it, has the
standard part of the *cocu imaginaire* laid out for him, and we
applaud rather than suffer when he plays it to the top of his bent.

  The Merry Devil of Edmonton (1599×1604), like other anonymous plays of the Chamberlain's Men—*Mucedorus, The London
Prodigal, Thomas, Lord Cromwell, A Yorkshire Tragedy*—has been
assigned to the rag-bag of 'The Shakespeare Apocrypha', for no
better reason, it would seem, than the theatrical affiliation. It is an
eloquent and well-articulated play,[34] held within strict limitations
of time, but not in the least like Shakespeare. Of course it shares a
number of generic features with *The Merry Wives of Windsor* (one
innkeeper's verbal style is close to the other's—and both may be
indebted to Dekker's Simon Eyre), but the two plays use their
common generic inheritance to different ends. The period of the
action is again in a vaguely conceived past when Waltham Abbey
and Cheshunt Nunnery were thriving communities, but the place
(once again the rural outskirts of London) is precisely located. The
Prologue advises us that, if we doubt the existence of Peter Fabel
(the 'merry devil'), we should consult 'his monument . . . fixed in
the wall of that old ancient church [of Edmonton]'. The milieu,
like that of *A Tale of a Tub*, is one of small villages (focused on
church and inn) separated by open or waste land (here Waltham
Forest and Enfield Chase). The impediment to marriage in this

---

[33] See O. J. Campbell, *The Italianate Background of 'The Merry Wives of Windsor'* (Essays
and Studies in English and Comparative Literature by Members of the University of
Michigan, 7; 1932).
[34] It was obviously much appreciated in its own time—reprinted five times in the seventeenth century, in 1612, 1617, 1626, 1631, 1655. Jonson, in the Prologue to *The Devil is an
Ass*, desires that his audience will 'show this but the same face you have done | Your dear
delight, *The Devil of Edmonton*'.

case, however, is closer to that of city comedy: the arranged wedding between two families of minor gentry is cancelled when one father comes to believe the other insufficiently moneyed. It is a threat the community itself cannot contain; fortunately for nostalgia the young lover's Cambridge tutor is a magician. His powers, together with the misrecognitions in the forest at night (reminiscent of those in *The Two Angry Women of Abingdon*), smooth the path to happiness. And once in the forest, the emotional seriousness of the wedding plot begins to merge with the rustic humours of Banks, the miller of Waltham, Smug, the smith of Edmonton, Blague, the host of the George at Waltham, and Sir John the local priest, who have come to the forest hoping to steal some of the royal venison. The gamekeeper pursues them, but finds only the angry fathers, the runaway lovers, and various well-wishers. The confusion is not sorted out until all the parties turn up at the George, to find the problems resolved in a wedding breakfast of poached venison.

Unlike *The Merry Wives of Windsor*, *The Merry Devil of Edmonton* does not have a unified enough community to support an intrigue plot. The forest confusions are the result of chance rather than plan, and the merry devil himself is too easily in control to allow any counter-plot to develop. But his magic power does not disrupt the rural simplicities. Indeed the magic could all be handled by a little rustic sleight of hand: two inn signs are interchanged to delay the avenging fathers, the lover's identity is turned temporarily into that of a novice monk. But magic as threat is still part of the scene. The Prologue tells us that we must wait for 'the comic end of our sad tragic show', and the opening of the play is indeed a 'tragic show'. What we are shown is a replay of the last scene of *Doctor Faustus*: the servant fiend has come to carry to Hell the soul of the magician whose lease of power has ended. The memory of Marlowe is used to powerful effect:

> FABEL. Hah, what is thy due?
> [FIEND]   Fabel, thy self.
> FABEL. O let not darkness hear thee speak that word,
>   Lest that with force it hurry hence amain,
>   And leave the world to look upon my woe.
>   Yet overwhelm me with this globe of earth,
>   And let a little sparrow with her bill
>   Take but so much as she can bear away,

That, every day thus losing of my load,
I may again in time yet hope to rise.
                                    (Induction, ll. 18–26)

But suddenly all these grandeurs and miseries are thrown away. Fabel traps the devil in a trick chair, and demands a further lease of life before he will release him. Magic returns to the level of the folk superstition which allows that a Cambridge don might use his books of spells to help a former pupil gain the girl of his choice.

Prodigal Lives

In romantic adventure plays the individual's patience preserves, even when community collapses, the values that sustained him while he was a member; and so he can bring these back when he returns to the group. In the topographical romances the stable community absorbs the thrust of romantic individualism and finds a classical language of tradition and compromise that defuses conflict. Figures like Simon Eyre, Mrs Ford, Mrs Page, Grim the Collier of Croydon, the low-life characters of *The Merry Devil of Edmonton*, and all the characters in *A Tale of a Tub* find their justification by being members of a stable community; they do not seek definition by standing out against it, though they may have tested the edges of acceptability. Even those like Falstaff, or Master Harmon, the bourgeois would-be husband in *The Shoemakers' Holiday*, who seek to defy or exploit naïvety, can be contained. But communities can be thought oppressive as easily as supportive, and the action can be driven towards comic or tragic ends as the author chooses. In the early 1600s we have a set of comedies (produced by the Chamberlain's as well as the Admiral's Men) in which the balance between individual and community is no longer so easily achieved, plays which call on the audience's response not to patient virtue in misfortune but to the glamour of the nay-sayer, the dangerously romantic person who stands out and defies the oppressive consensual norm.

A tragic model for this kind of glamour can be found in *Doctor Faustus*, and indeed this is a kind of comedy where the action is always on the edge of tragedy. Dekker's *Old Fortunatus* (1599) is as diagrammatic as *Doctor Faustus*, but, written with less intensity, it stays closer to comedy. Like *Faustus*, Dekker's play is taken from a German *Volksbuch*; the popularity of both source stories derives from the episodic marvels that can be described once the 'fortunate' man has been liberated from the narrow bounds imposed by the norms of society.[35] But *Volksbücher* do not find it necessary to define such norms. In Marlowe they are represented momentarily by the scholars but centrally only by the ironies and conflicts inside the hero's own mind (the tragedy lies in the destruction of that mind by the freedom it seemed to need above everything else). Dekker's Fortunatus, however, is less an overreacher than an everyman whose career speaks to the spectators of their own impulses, their desire to escape (to win the lottery), as well as their fear of leaving the known. Yet it may seem merely wilful to include Fortunatus in a list of prodigals. He certainly does not fit the role completely. But his career (of desperate effort—and failure—to escape from restriction into the bright lights of achieved freedom) shows in outline the structure in which later (and more specifically defined) prodigal plays present everymen we can all recognize. First found 'meanly attired', Fortunatus is selected by Fortune to show the wholly arbitrary nature of her favours. He chooses unwisely from the menu of gifts she offers (wisdom, strength, riches, long life, health, beauty), but his choice of riches marks his common humanity rather than (like Faustus) his special nature.

The relationship of Fortunatus and his sons with the world around them is that of hunted and haunted men. They are exclusively concerned with (1) the hope to be able to enjoy the power over others their wealth ought to give them, countered by (2) the fear that someone will discover and steal the magic purse that is the source of their wealth. As with Faustus, their human capacity to change or grow has been cauterized by the curse that has made them 'fortunate'. Even Fortunatus' second son, who wants nothing to do with Fortune's gifts, and burns the magic hat, cannot escape the curse: 'He made no use of me', Fortune tells us, 'he muffled virtue in clouds; he did not make it shine'; his cloistered virtue cannot carry the burden that Fortune imposes. Only one outside society—like Queen Elizabeth, as Dekker points out in the last section probably added for the court performance[36]—one as active

---

[35] This is what C. H. Herford calls 'discursive romanticism'. See his *Studies in the Literary Relationship of England and Germany in the Sixteenth Century* (Cambridge, 1886), 214.

[36] In Henslowe's Diary for Dec. 1599 Dekker was paid £2 'for the end of Fortunatus for the court'.

as virtuous, can handle Fortune so that she offers a comedy free of tragedy.

As *Doctor Faustus* makes clear, the victim of a hunger for power can convey to his audience a charisma that contradicts the moralism of his story. But at the end of a moralizing play, charisma must wither, as the logic of the situation requires. When we move from the diagrammatic to the realistic, however, logic must yield to the ambiguity of desire. The comic structure then has to hold together both our excited admiration for the outsider and our sober understanding that to offer an exemplar he must consent to become an insider.

The splendidly dismissive figure of the soldier (later the *gallant*), a key figure in the culture of the time, provided a resolution to these opposites in realistic terms that the audience could respond to. The anonymous *Famous History of the Life and Death of Captain Thomas Stukeley, with his Marriage to Alderman Curteis' Daughter and Valiant Ending of his Life at the Battle of Alcazar* (1596—perhaps revised about 1599; printed 1605), provides an early example, still close to tragedy. It presents in an extreme form the glamour of military virtue (the word *virtue* itself carries the ambiguity), and the associated determination not to fit into the role of the tamed male that marriage and city require. As the ideal of the gentlemanly classes, soldierly bravado stands as a permanent reproach against civic calculation. But Stukeley can show prowess only if he can get hold of city money. Alderman Curteis's daughter is in love with him. His friend, Vernon, who is betrothed to the daughter, willingly gives up his claim; the alderman can only hope that marriage will tame Stukeley's 'wildness'. That, of course, does not happen. As soon as he has got hold of the dowry and his wife's jewels, he scatters the 'trash' (he will be 'frank as shall the emperor') among his horde of creditors and takes off for the wars in Ireland. His conscience is clear: his wife will be looked after by her father; but he himself must follow the path of honour and patriotism.

The rest of the play is a matter of drums and trumpets, fiery individualism, sexual magnetism, and incapacity to understand high policy—represented here as elsewhere by Philip II of Spain. With characteristic panache Stukeley escapes from imprisonment in Lisbon and persuades Philip to support his treasonable enterprises. What he cannot see is that Philip's support is only part of a larger plan to annex Portugal. These English, Philip tells his counsellors, are rash and simple-minded, 'using no precepts of art perspective', credulous and impolitic. It seems probable that the play's audience was meant to hear such sentiments with pride, honour being the opposite to policy, but also with a sense of disadvantage. The play is not simple-minded about this issue. The Chorus tells us that the interview with the Pope that Philip sets up is the climax of Stukeley's career. His 'comic history' ends here: 'now at the highest he declines.' The final episodes, dealing with the battle of Alcazar (already enacted in Peele's tragedy of 1589 (see Chapter 3)) lead Stukeley into a Tamburlainian world of high astounding deeds and terms. In political terms, of course, the battle is a romantic fiasco, and the play ends (as it must) with the death of Stukeley, once more being defended by Vernon, this time against his traitorous Italian mercenaries. Throughout the play we have seen Vernon's career cross Stukeley's, in London, in Ireland, in Portugal, and finally in Africa, playing Horatio to a military Hamlet, showing himself sober, responsible, right-thinking—everything Stukeley is not—yet transfixed by the glamour of his friend. As one moral centre to the play, Vernon offers the audience a counterweight to that glamour, gives it a sense of a golden dream that is bound to fail, yet one that still sustains the sober lives of sober men.

The play allows Stukeley's military charisma to override his political treason, but clearly his macho independence has carried him beyond the point where even Vernon's care and loyalty can ever restore him to social life. Most plays of prodigals in the period show the restlessness of the prodigal in a more local and domestic, and therefore more assuredly comic, context—yet still close to the domestic tragedies discussed below (Chapter 9). This allows a Griselda-type wife to reclaim her husband to domestic virtue at the end of the action, when his anti-social violence has brought him to dire extremity, yet, paradoxically, marked him as worthy of care and rescue. Three plays—the anonymous *A Pleasant Conceited Comedy Wherein is Shown How a Man may Choose a Good Wife from a Bad* (c.1601×1602), performed by Worcester's Men, *The Fair Maid of Bristowe* (1603×1604), performed by the Chamberlain's Men, and *The London Prodigal* (1603×1605), also belonging to the Chamberlain's/King's Men, may be cited to indicate the basic formula on which different dramatists work their variations. In the first of these we see a young husband chafing against the

restrictions that marrying and 'settling down' impose on his image
of himself as independent and dangerous. He abuses and degrades
his loving and patient wife. His need to 'fly out' is better served by
a prostitute, who is, of course (as a charter member of the outlaw
world he desires), quite unimpressed by his bravado but knows
how to play along until she has separated him from his money.
When that is gone, she can dispose of him by tempting him into
crime and then denouncing him to the law—the next customer is
already lined up. Branded with infamy, seared with guilt, the prodigal at last understands, as he prepares for death, just what he has
done. Once he has reached this state, it is time for the ill-treated,
ever-loving wife, the loyal friend, the grieving parents, to reveal
that they have in fact arranged that the 'crime' should prove harmless. So they are able to save him and welcome him back as a
redeemed member of bourgeois society. The final tableau marks
the self-knowledge that follows conversion. The prodigal is then
set on the stage between his wife and the prostitute and made to
spell out the moral his experience has proved:

> he that will choose
> A good wife from a bad, come learn of me
> That have tried both . . .
> Seek virtuous wives, all husbands will be blessed,
> Fair wives are good, but virtuous wives are best.
>
> (ll. 2720–40)

In *The Fair Maid of Bristowe* the mechanism is the same: the
prodigal must learn 'the difference twixt lust and chastity'[37] but
this time the point that such behaviour is really quite appropriate
for a young man of spirit is spelt out in the last words by the wife.
She, forgiving all, notes that a Griselda figure must suffer all: for
' 'tis incident for young men to offend | And wives must stay their
leisure to amend'. In *The London Prodigal* the wife insists on following her husband into prison. Her self-sacrifice ignites repentance: 'her chastity and virtue hath infused another soul in me.' All
present contribute cash to pay off his debts; the rite of passage into
the world of adult respectability has been completed. The audience

---

[37] Cf. the headnote attached to Marston's *The Dutch Courtesan* (disscussed in Ch. 7): 'the
difference betwixt the love of a courtesan and a wife is the full scope of the play.' Like the
other playwrights, Marston insists that the prodigal must be brought to the point of death
before he will truly repent.

has been allowed its dream of escape and allowed to convert it into a currency accepted in the real world. The title of Heywood's *The Wise Woman of Hogsdon* (?1604; printed 1638) suggests topographical comedy, and perhaps one can see some cross-breeding here, setting the fashionable excesses of the metropolis against the folk wisdom of the outlying villages. But in the main this is another story of violent and unstable youth having to be deceived and frightened into conformity with ordered society. The play opens with a powerful scene in which the four young gentlemen play macho games, dice, quarrel, challenge one another, and aim to steal one another's girl friends. Chartley is the most incorrigible of all, and therefore the central figure of the play. Boyser woos Luce 1,[38] but Chartley will steal her by pretending marriage. However, he is no match for the wise woman of Hogsdon, whose skills are honed by a lifetime of deceiving country folk. She so manipulates the marriage hopes of the gallants that they all lose their bearings—all but Chartley, whose energy cannot be so easily contained. Immediately after the 'wedding' she has organized, he spies a wealthy heiress and pursues her, swearing he is a bachelor; at the same time he aims to sleep with his new wife, swearing that he will poison the heiress as soon as he has possession of her dowry. The denouement, set up by the wise woman, is mainly concerned with the final containment of Chartley. His father comes in from the country (a standard device that provides a very amusing scene in *Stukeley*) and brings a weight of evidence against the prodigal. Like Bertram in *All's Well That Ends Well*, Chartley lies his way to the very end, and so by the end stands revealed to the whole company as a cheat and a betrayer. Luce 2, whom he abandoned in the country, will accept him as a 'penitent'.

In *The London Prodigal* the tearaway's father takes service with him (disguised by a scar), and encourages him to crime in hope that punishment will drive him to repentance. The positive role of the father, to supplement the negative forbearance of the wife, appears in very similar terms in Dekker's play for Prince Henry's Players (formerly the Admiral's Men), *The Second Part of the Honest Whore* (1604×c.1605; printed 1630), where Orlando Friscobaldo,

---

[38] The text creates confusion by giving the same name ('Luce') to two different characters. Luce 1 is the girl that Chartley persuades to marry him at Hogsdon. Luce 2 is the girl he debauched in the country, who has pursued him to London, and who is the substitute bride he actually marries at Hogsdon.

the father of Bellafront (the honest whore), comes disguised as a servant into the household of his daughter and her prodigal husband, Matheo. Once again the purpose is to play along with the wildness of the gallant, who must 'fly out' and encourage him to wade still deeper into prodigality. Finally Friscobaldo betrays him to the law, letting his folly 'hang him by the gills till I pull him on shore' (IV. ii. 13). Then, when he despairs of rescue, the father can throw off his disguise and clear the slate of crimes charged but never committed. What is remarkable here is that this rescuer's prime relationship is not with the prodigal but with his wife: he is activated by pity and protectiveness for her. It is a mark of Dekker's genius that he has found for this standard role a mode of speech that turns plot function into individual character, showing Orlando, both in and out of disguise, as crusty, self-consciously eccentric, at once grieving and fantastic, loyal and bitter, determined to help but determined to do so only in his own terms. Hazlitt's encomium is famous,[39] its romantic excess justified by the power of its rhetoric to mimic what Dekker has done—turn a dramatic function into a free-standing human being.

The amplitude of this two-part play allows everywhere a more complex, more multicentred interest than in other stories of prodigals. Bellafront appears as an early specimen of that typically Victorian figure 'the woman with a past'—the past being Part I (1604). There we see her converted from her trade by the eloquence and moral fervour of Hippolyto and 'rewarded' by the respectability of marriage to her prodigal deflowerer. In Part II (1605), her new Griselda role runs up against a difficulty that even Griselda did not have to face—the assumption of society, her husband and her father (even of her 'saviour', Hippolyto), that she is still a whore at heart. The complex history of Bellafront makes her the centre of a complex play; Griselda-virtue is no longer a given: it has to be struggled for through temptations, memories, the past, in order to achieve a convincing humanity.

[39] 'Dekkar's Signior Orlando Friscobaldo I shall never forget. . . . We sometimes regret that we had not sooner met with characters like these, that seem to raise, revive and give new zest to our being . . . The words and answers all along are so true and pertinent that we seem to see the gestures and to hear the tone with which they are accompanied . . . simplicity and comedy, homeliness and quaintness, tragedy and comedy, interchangeably set their hands and seals to this admirable production. We find the simplicity of prose with the graces of poetry' (*Complete Works of William Hazlitt*, ed. P. P. Howe (21 vols.; London, 1930), vi. 235–8).

As if in compensation for the loss of Griselda-like patience in the female lead, Dekker (who seems to have had Middleton's help in Part I[40]) supplements the Bellafront story with 'the humours of the patient man'.[41] Candido, a Milan (alias London) linen draper, is the victim of a series of *beffe* imposed on him by his 'longing wife', set up as a public spectacle for all the notables of the city, who are as intrigued by the oxymoron of a 'patient man' as much as that of an 'honest whore'.

It is in the company of these plays of prodigals in the first five years of the seventeenth century that Shakespeare's *All's Well That Ends Well* (1603×1604; printed 1623) shows most clearly its conformity to the interests of the time. Shakespeare found his story in Painter's *Palace of Pleasure* version of *Decameron*, III. ix, 'Giletta di Nerbona', but it was no doubt the contemporary theatrical scene that encouraged him to make a play of it. Bertram, the hero of the story, 'flies out' with the ambition of becoming a Stukeley, but no more than the other prodigals can he shake off the claims of the society he belongs to, the moral authority of wife and king and mother (not to mention his moralizing colleagues, Captains E and G). It is characteristic of Shakespeare that he places his prodigal in a foreign and aristocratic rather than London and citizen milieu and makes nothing of the money issues that bulk so large in the other plays. But the romance of high life does not liberate his hero from the family-oriented expectations of everyone around him. Boccaccio and Painter tell the story as a battle of wits: the haughty young Count Bertram has a wife of lower station foisted on him by the king; so, leaving her with a riddle to answer, he takes off immediately after the marriage, looking for self-fulfilment in the wars 'where noble fellows strike', eventually becoming a general in the conflict between Florence and Siena. His escape is frustrated, however, by his wife, who succeeds in answering the riddle and fulfilling conditions supposed impossible. Just when he is holding a great feast to celebrate his return to society, she appears and demands that he acknowledge her, the conditions having been fulfilled. The

---

[40] Somewhere between 1 Jan. and 14 Mar. 1604 Henslowe records a payment to Dekker and Middleton for 'the patient man and the honest whore'. Impressionistic studies differ in the estimate of how much Middleton contributed. There is agreement that Part II is entirely by Dekker.

[41] This is, in fact, the first title in the original entry in the Stationers' Register: 'A book called the humours of the patient man, the longing wife and the honest whore' (9 Nov. 1604).

Count, 'perceiving her constant mind and good wit . . . and to
please his subjects and the ladies who made suit unto him . . .
accept[ed] her from that time forth as his lawful wife' (*The Palace
of Pleasure*, i. 144). Social decency has triumphed, and the Count
has shown some maturity (at last) in acknowledging the propriety
of what has happened. The passions of shame, rejection, and bitterness that one might have expected are not allowed to modify
Boccaccio's understanding that cleverness wins all.

Shakespeare's alterations in the story pull the Count and his
wife closer to the contemporary stereotypes of the prodigal and
Griselda. Count Bertram is consumed by the idea that soldiership
will allow him to escape from women and old men into a masculine
world where he can forge a new identity; like Stukeley, his dowry
is his means to make his way abroad. The alternatives available are
set out for him in sexually explicit language:

> He wears his honour in a box unseen
> That hugs his kicky-wicky here at home,
> Spending his manly marrow in her arms,
> Which should sustain the bound and high curvet,
> Of Mars's fiery steed. . . .
>
> . . . .
>
> Wars is no strife
> To the dark house and the detested wife.
>
> (II. iii. 279–92)

However, this time we see the prodigal hold these views not by his
own choice but at second hand from the fake captain who is his
tutor in such affairs, the wordy Parolles, Shakespeare's addition to
the story. Bertram never acquires free-standing status: he runs from
his mother and his king, only to end up in the control of 'a most
notable coward, an infinite and endless liar, an hourly promise-
breaker' (III. vi. 9–10); and when disabused of that dependence, he
still shows the same second-hand quality in his own affairs. The unmasking of Parolles has to be repeated in the unmasking of Bertram,
as he tries to lie his way out of his disgrace, hoping to play one
accuser against another (like Chartley in *The Wise Woman of
Hogsdon*), and at last stands generally reviled, without clear understanding of what his problem is, and capable of redemption only
through the selfless love of a good woman. Why a good woman
should wish to redeem such a character has puzzled Shakespearian
critics, but it does not appear to have puzzled the audiences who

followed the careers of other prodigals of the period and who would in subsequent decades approve the careers of Fletcher's Theanor (in *The Queen of Corinth*) or Marcantonio (in *Love's Pilgrimage*).

In dramatizing the recuperative heroine, Shakespeare can be seen (once again) to have moved the character he inherited towards the contemporary stereotype. His Helena is no longer the omnicompetent go-getter who rescues Boccaccio's Rossillion from the confusions into which it had fallen while its count was absent, no longer the unambiguous problem-solving engineer of her own success. But neither is she a patient Griselda. Like Bertram, she is part of the society that both oppresses and empowers her; her attitudes come to her from outside as well as inside, from a world of intermediaries who understand and support her and share her emotional trauma. She returns to Rossillion not to take charge of its finances but to weep on the shoulder of the Countess, her mother-in-law. The sense of loss and lostness shared by the women in this great scene culminates in Helena's speech of renunciation:

> Poor lord, is't I
> That chase thee from thy country, and expose
> Those tender limbs of thine to the event
> Of the none-sparing war?
>
> . . . . . .
>
> No; come thou home, Rossillion,
> Whence honour but of danger wins a scar,
> As oft it loses all; I will be gone;
> My being here it is that holds thee hence.
> Shall I stay here to do't? No, no, although
> The air of paradise did fan the house,
> And angels officed all.
>
> (III. ii. 102–26)

The speech, like many others in Shakespeare, points us towards an emotional hesitancy, a play of shadows and nuances that allows the opposites it contains to remain poised between the top-lit shadowless world of the Italian original and the equally simplifying moralism of the prodigal and Griselda plots.

Shakespeare's Romantic Comedies

Comedies of prodigality differ from comedies of courtship in that the end-point of the former is not marriage as the fulfilment of desire but the reinstatement of marriage as the gateway to social integration. Marriage in these plays serves only as a springboard that the prodigal can kick and leap away from. The abandoned wife, however, continues to love, honour, and obey, and in this sense these plays tell love-stories. It is presumably significant of Shakespeare's taste that *his* prodigal comedy allows his heroine not only passive devotion but also an independent pursuit of love that links her more clearly to Rosalind and Viola than to Bellafront or the fair maid of Bristowe.

Shakespeare is the great dramatist of romantic love in this period; this is the emphasis that separates him from his colleagues in comedy most clearly. The sense of community that we have seen continually validated as the guarantor of value is in his plays made contingent on the capacity of his main characters (usually women) to find that value in their personal experience. This is what we see in that line of romantic comedies that runs from *Love's Labour's Lost* and *A Midsummer Night's Dream* of 1595 or so through *The Merchant of Venice*, *Much Ado about Nothing*, *As You Like It*, to *Twelfth Night* of something like 1600, the line that is usually taken to define the essence of Shakespearian comedy.

If one is looking for links between Shakespeare and his contemporaries, these are not the plays to draw on. Those I have discussed in this and the preceding chapter (*Measure for Measure*, *The Merry Wives of Windsor*, *All's Well That Ends Well*—perhaps one should add *Troilus and Cressida*[42]) form a collection that normal Shakespeare criticism prefers to place in a marginal category. The fact that the plays in which Shakespeare has the closest ties to his fellows are the ones which in later centuries seem to require most historical justification should tell us something about the nature of our assent to the plays in the other group. How is it that *As You Like It* and the other romantic comedies are so much easier to respond to nowadays? We can observe at least one quality that is involved: their value systems all depend less on reference to reality than on some degree of fantasy, whether in escapist forests (*Midsummer Night's Dream*, *As You Like It*), in Ruritanian fiefdoms (*Love's Labour's Lost*, *Twelfth Night*), in post-military recuperative furlough (*Much Ado about Nothing*), or in the company of heiresses

---

[42] The argument that *Troilus and Cressida* should be classified as a comedy can draw support from the description in the Quarto's advertisement (see Ch. 7). But the language of genre in this period cannot be trusted. No doubt its placing with the comedies in *The Riverside Shakespeare* gives the idea its widest exposure.

of international renown (*The Merchant of Venice*). Escapism is usually assumed to imply sentimentality. The sentiment in these plays is, however, always compromised (even if eventually supported) by surrounding and opposed realities (politics, shipwreck, court emulation, mercantile or legal rigidity) and commented on by 'realists' who stress its escapist quality rather than its magic (Touchstone, Feste, Jaques, Shylock, Costard, Don John, Puck, Launce). The emergence of love out of the polarized situations set up, and so the achievement of a comic structure, is thus dependent on Shakespeare's poetic capacity to present 'escapism' as no less profound and true than the realisms that oppose it. Shakespeare manages this by focusing on these fantastic situations less in social than psychological terms; they are experiences to react to rather than to live in. The space that is provided by a temporary freedom from the pressures of a real social world (the 'holiday' space of C. L. Barber[43]) allows characters to 'play' at solutions which could (we imagine) resolve the impediments that real life imposes on happiness. And we see the real world actually reconfiguring itself in response to the inventiveness, the irrepressible play of meanings in the languages of poetry, the vivacity, conviction, and eloquence of its idealists. And so the changes in the sense of possibility that holiday has allowed, do prevail—not completely, of course, that would alienate our assent; but enough to create a final space both real and fulfilling, even if fragile.

The balance that this process achieves allows us to believe in happiness without feeling cheated of probability. And the process itself is couched in terms generalized enough not to require a sympathy with Elizabethan manners, but only a capacity to imagine the ideals embodied in character with an intensity sufficient to make the world around them seem true. Only then can we accept idealism and the transformative power of love as a part of human nature as we understand it.

Shakespearian Techniques

Shakespeare's romantic comedies for the Chamberlain's Men are clearly differentiated from comedies produced by other companies at the same time (given the disappearance of the Chamberlain's

---

[43] *Shakespeare's Festive Comedy* (Princeton, 1959).

repertory, we cannot be sure if this reflects company or authorial choice). Shakespeare's own chronology is certainly part of the explanation. By date of birth he belongs to the generation of University Wits. He was already 20 when Lyly's first comedies were performed and 25 when Greene's *Friar Bacon and Friar Bungay* appeared on the stage. It is entirely proper that Ben Jonson, in the memorial verses he contributed to the First Folio, should name Lyly, 'sporting Kyd', and Marlowe as Shakespeare's competitors. But the University Wits had all disappeared from the scene by 1594, while the dramatists who were to take their place (Chapman, Chettle, Day, Dekker, Heywood, Jonson) were only on the threshold of their theatrical careers.[44] In these terms Shakespeare was a lone survivor, and brought to the last decade of the century a dramaturgy that had gone out of fashion. But not all the differences between Shakespeare's comedy and that of his contemporaries in the Admiral's company can be thus explained. If we accept the standard chronology, we find that the dates of *Love's Labour's Lost* and *A Midsummer Night's Dream* overlap with *A Knack to Know an Honest Man*, that *The Merchant of Venice* is the contemporary of *The Blind Beggar of Alexandria*, *Much Ado about Nothing* of *Robert, Earl of Huntingdon*, *As You Like It* of *Look About You*. The two repertories (authorial or company) seem to face one another across a clearly demarcated divide and suggest some degree of deliberate choice. On the one side, we have the rambling heroisms of romantic adventure; on the other, we have neatly plotted stories of coming-of-age in love, set in deliberately distanced locations, calling neither on patriotism nor on any nostalgic empathy with a golden age national past. One might say that, compared with his adult theatre contemporaries, Shakespeare's romantic comedies show him to be an unindulgent playwright, holding within severe limits the geographical and chronological spread of his stories and continually cutting off the romantic intensity of particular situations by introducing contrast and creating objective balance.[45] His fables of loss and recovery (*The Comedy of Errors*, *The Merchant of Venice*, *Twelfth Night*) do not involve us in extremes of deprivation such as we find, for example, in *The Weakest Goeth to the Wall* or

---

[44] We first hear of these men in Henslowe's account books for the second half of the decade: Chapman in 1596, Jonson in 1597, Day, Dekker, and Heywood in 1598.

[45] See J. R. Brown, 'The Presentation of Comedy: The First Ten Plays', in *Shakespearian Comedy* (Stratford-upon-Avon Studies 14; London, 1972).

A Knack to Know an Honest Man. The dukes who control Shakespeare's comedies provide a boundary that delimits the range of disorder that can occur. Even in the plays which involve banishment (*A Midsummer Night's Dream, As You Like It*), the new world of exile, as the antithesis of the intolerable place fled from, turns out to have positive (and indeed curative) qualities. These features are close to those found in the repertory of the boys; and one might guess that the closing of the boys' playhouses between 1590 and 1600 was one factor in determining a Shakespearian form of comedy that lay somewhere between that of the boys and that of the Admiral's company. On the whole (none of these distinctions can be made without thinking of exceptions) the boys performed comedies of witty verbal games and put-down intrigues, in which facility and cleverness carry all before them. The Henslowe comedies, on the other hand, are plays of romantic trauma in which the central characters are too deracinated, too much the victims of Fortune, to be effective as manipulators and where intrigue, if it has any prominence (as it does in *The Shoemakers' Holiday, The Wise Woman of Hogsdon, A Knack to Know an Honest Man*) is held in check by the pressure of strongly expressed social values (patriotism, militarism, nostalgia, family loyalties).

Of course, we cannot push Shakespeare too far towards the theatre of the children. Though acted by boys, the socially responsible trickery of Rosalind, Viola, or Portia is not like that of Lyly and very different from that of the later boys' plays. The tricksters of Chapman's or Middleton's comedies deceive in order to exploit weakness. Their power is coupled to a proper contempt for their victims. But the disguises of Shakespeare's romantic heroines create more resonance for imagination than for plot. They turn female disadvantage into strength by offering an unencumbered and liberating range of possibilities beyond what is available in real life, doubling not only the understanding of what is possible but also the self that projects the understanding, doubling the reticence of the woman with the would-be boldness of the boy, the restrictions of society with the free play of the game. And behind all these lies the doubleness of the boy actor who, as 'standing water between boy and man', as 'a squash is before 'tis a peascod' (*Twelfth Night*, I. v. 157–9), has not yet achieved full definition as either man or woman, and can slip comfortably out of one role into another.

It is obvious that the disguising of girls as boys is one of the

principal devices of Shakespeare's comic dramaturgy, allowing him
to use the doubleness of poetry to negotiate the space between self
and role, the indefinite and the specific, the romantic and the
classic. It is a device that very clearly differentiates his comedies
from those of his contemporaries. Disguise is, of course, a universal theatrical resource, from the *Bacchae* to *Charley's Aunt*. The
Henslowe plays are full of it, disguise being one of the obvious
means by which the virtuous man exiled or hunted can escape
from or intervene in the affairs of the hunters. But these are
essentially disguise roles for men. Indeed, out of the thirty-five
surviving adult comedies between 1594 and 1606 I find only two
non-Shakespearian page-boy disguises,[46] though there are fifteen
plays with male disguise (father as servant, lover as porter, gentleman as friar, and so on).

In these respects it seems that Shakespeare made his own way.
But we cannot forget what he learnt from Lyly and Greene. It was
probably from Greene's romances and plays (and their *novella*
sources) that Shakespeare (like other popular dramatists) learnt
how to mix comedy with anguished romance, female innocence
and royal inconstancy, poignant domestic emotions and a high
poetic eloquence. But Shakespeare was not content to express these
themes only in the form of sprawling Greenian romance, where
narrative supplies meaning. Lyly offered him an alternative (analytic) model of comedy in which the action is held together by a
formal antithetical structure so that the poignant and eloquent
Greenian moments can be perceived with ironic detachment as
parts of a self-conscious and neatly organized total pattern. By combining these two authors he thus created a form that was placed
between the boys and the men.

The creation of meaning by antithetical structuring is a technique found everywhere in Shakespeare's romantic comedies (twins,
good duke/bad duke, good brother/bad brother, good merchant/
bad merchant, realist lover/romantic lover, city/country, war/
peace, past/present, reason/imagination, love/learning, wit/folly)
and is used everywhere to give shape and continuity to the process
of perpetual change that a comic plot demands. Like Lyly, he
makes the self-conscious artfulness of such structures part of the

---

[46] In *The Four Prentices of London* the Princess of France follows Guy to Jerusalem disguised as a page. In *The Wise Woman of Hogsdon* Luce 2 visits the wise woman as a boy but
is then double-disguised as a girl. The device appears in passing in Sharpham's *The Fleer*.

effect; but he always leaves space for a complementary (Greenian) sense that it is the free drift of the story that creates the spontaneous eruption of feeling. Thus in *A Midsummer Night's Dream* the lovers run away from Theseus' power to enforce marriage, only to fall under the enforcement of the parallel power of Oberon. But Theseus and Oberon are not simply Lylian doubles, Tweedledum and Tweedledee (even when played by the same actor). They are differentiated enough for the symmetry to seem 'natural', dynamic not static. The uncontrolled mutability of the lovers' adolescent emotions proves inadequate to cope with real life; their problems are translated to another plane (into the mode of a dream or a play, we might say) so that the 'doubleness' of their vision[47] allows translation back from the highly organized system of the plot into the uncertainty of emotion, and so the discovery of a stable space somewhere between these two:

> DEMETRIUS. Do not you think
> The Duke was here and bid us follow him?
> HERMIA. Yea, and my father.
> HELENA. And Hippolyta.
> LYSANDER. And he did bid us follow to the temple.
> DEMETRIUS. Why then, we are awake.
>
> (IV. i. 194–8)

In *As You Like It* the place of exile is likewise a place of doubleness, simultaneous familiarity and strangeness, where the exiles find their new restrictions (disguise, bewilderment, low social status) translatable into the enabling devices by which they can achieve and take back into the 'real' world what was forbidden there. The shadowy dukedom of the Forest of Arden is not a simple antithesis to the formal dukedom of Frederick. It provides rather a new mode of articulation for the values of the past world, a language which allows both political and personal problems to be handled as metaphors rather than literals and so transformed. The 'translation' in *A Midsummer Night's Dream* is done by something external ('magic'); in *As You Like It* the magic is rather a quality of personal imagination, a power of extending the self into a double mode: reality becomes play so that play can become a redeemed reality.

---

[47] See IV. i. 189–92: *HERMIA.* Methinks I see these things with parted eye, | When every thing seems double. | *HELENA.* So methinks; | And I have found Demetrius like a jewel | Mine own and not mine own.

Classsic and Romantic Sources

Since the seventeenth century Shakespeare has been set against Ben Jonson in terms roughly equivalent to those set between 'romantic' and 'classic'. But these are not useful terms to describe Shakespeare's relation to the popular dramatists around him. More relevant is the opposition between realism (however defined) and fantasy—and that cannot be dealt with under the expectation that fantasy will always be romantic or realism always classic. 'Romantic' nostalgia for the simple life of other times and places is found in such plays as *The Shoemakers' Holiday* or *The Tale of a Tub* combined with realism. Even more pertinently, the plays of Lyly can be thought of as classic fantasies—fantastic in subject matter but classical in organization.

Exclusive concern with the classic–romantic axis also makes it difficult to deal with the body of European comedy that gave the mature Shakespeare the means to develop his Lylyan and Greenian inheritance. The Italian *commedia erudita* of the sixteenth century begins with close imitation of Plautus but soon exuberates into stories of love, with backgrounds from romantic adventure (pirates, Turks, shipwrecks) coupled to foregrounds of minutely observed urban realism, the whole carried by a romantic longing for emotional satisfaction, and completed by impeccably Plautine discoveries, recognitions, reconciliations of parents and children, brothers and sisters.[48]

Shakespeare's relation to this body of drama can only be sketched in outline here[49] by considering his response to one play—the anonymous *Gl'ingannati*, performed first in Siena in 1531, at the Academy of the Intronati (the thunderstruck). *Gl'ingannati* was one of the great successes of European dramaturgy, translated and adapted across the Continent and in various genres. To make connection with this play is to tap into a central current in Renaissance theatre, one acknowledged even in remote and backward

---

[48] It might be argued that Plautus' *Rudens* (for example) already possesses all these romantic–classic characteristics (it even has a shipwreck). But both the shipwreck and the union of the lover and the girl are primarily commercial issues in this play. What is central is the restoring of legal rights to the deprived characters: to the girl (whose freedom is already purchased), to the long-lost father, to Gripus his servant, and to the Temple of Venus, all of them equally violated by the improprieties of the *leno*.

[49] See Leo Salingar, *Shakespeare and the Traditions of Comedy* (Cambridge, 1974), for a full and lucid exploration of the relationship.

England. When *Twelfth Night* was performed in the Middle Temple on 2 February 1602, the lawyer John Manningham called it in his diary 'a play much like *The Comedy of Errors* or *Menaechmi* in Plautus, but most like and near to that in Italian called *Inganni*'. What is surprising in this comment is not that Manningham got the wrong one out of the collection of plays about *inganni* (deceptions) but that he knew enough to get it almost right.[50] Deceptions by disguise, deceptions by girls dressed as boys, abound in this repertory.[51] The turn of the screw that *Gl'ingannati* provides (the turn that caught the taste of Europe) is that not only does the disguised girl (Lelia), yearning to be close to her former lover (Flamineo), seek employment as his page, but that she is then sent to carry messages of love to his new mistress (Isabella), who then immediately falls in love with the 'page'. Shakespeare first drew on this situation in the Julia and Proteus plot of *Two Gentlemen of Verona*, where, like his immediate source (Montemayor's sprawling romance, the *Diana*), he emphasized narrative pathos. It is clear that one of the things that attracted him in both treatments of the story was the opportunity it gave for romantic exploration of female longing, frustration, hope—the material of Ovid's ever popular *Heroides*.[52] But *Twelfth Night* adds another dimension to this, a dimension found most obviously in the *commedia erudita*. In *Gl'ingannati* Lelia is a beleaguered and resourceful woman in the Boccaccian mode, little given to introspection. She keeps her gaze firmly fixed on her goal, the repossession of her lover. When Isabella (unlike Olivia) makes it clear that she is more interested in the page than the master, Lelia (unlike Viola) wastes no sympathy on a dilemma so like her own, but immediately grasps at the power this gives her. She promises to satisfy Isabella's desires, but not before Flamineo has been summarily dismissed. Then, she supposes, she herself will be able to catch him on the rebound.

Here, as in other Italian plays involving cross-dressing, the assumption of male dress seems to convert socially protected and conventionally demure girls into stereotypes of the sex they are

---

[50] *Gl'ingannati* had already appeared in England in the translation into Latin called *Laelia* and been performed in Cambridge in 1595 (and also perhaps in 1546).

[51] For Lodovico Castelvetro's assumption that *inganni* provide the basic substance of comedy, see *Castelvetro on the Art of Poetry*, ed. Andrew Bongiorno (Binghampton, NY, 1984), ch. 4.

[52] They seem to be remembered in *Two Gentlemen* in Julia's story of playing the abandoned Ariadne in a pageant (IV. iv. 167–8).

mimicking, into macho adventurers capable of imposing themselves on society and demanding satisfaction under threat. In
the highly popular *Alessandro* of Alessandro Piccolomini, Lucrezia
(disguised as Fortunio) falls passionately in love with Aloisio
(disguised as Lampridia) and become so much 'a real man' (as one
might say) that she breaks into her beloved's bedroom and aims to
seduce her. Her intention collapses only when she makes the not
unwelcome discovery that Lampridia is a man, and in fact Aloisio,
her old sweetheart.

Shakespeare's use of the disguised maiden topic uses these potentials to achieve different ends. His effects depend on the interpenetration of male role and female sensibility, so that 'a swashing
and a martial outside' (*As You Like It*, I. iii. 120) is managed with
ironic awareness that it cannot lead to a 'doublet and hose . . .
in disposition' (III. ii. 195–6). As in Italian comedy, the disguise
creates dramatic tension by the ever-present danger of discovery;
but in Shakespeare the most important developments are not in
the plot-twists to avoid this but rather in the opportunities provided for self-discovery, for a 'dialogue of one' between frustration
and desire,[53] as in Viola's

> she never told her love,
> But let concealment like a worm i' the bud
> Feed on her damask cheek; she pined in thought
> And with a green and yellow melancholy
> She sat like Patience on a monument
> Smiling at grief. Was not this love indeed?
>
> (II. iv. 110–15)

We, hearing this, understand what Orsino does not, so that we can
see round the whole situation and experience the range of contradictory and unspoken emotions that are present. The play between
knowledge and ignorance allows sympathy and comedy, involvement and detachment to coexist, especially between female characters—a quality already exploited with marvellous tact in Lyly's
Gallathea. In *Gl'ingannati* Lelia keeps reminding her master of the
faith in him that Lelia once displayed, with the clear intention of
turning Flamineo's mind away from Isabella. In *Two Gentlemen of*

---

[53] Some premonitions of this can be discovered in romance narrative. In Montemayor's
Diana the lovelorn heroine tells her hearers how she 'dissembled one emotion while showing another'. In Shakespeare, where we are shown not told, neither emotion is 'dissembled'.

Verona this is modulated into the dialogue in which Julia and Sylvia share the sadness of love's betrayal; the 'boy' achieves identification with the lovelorn lady both as differentiated witness and as identical participant. In Viola's case, even more specifically, we can watch her growth into definition both in terms of the empathy set up with Olivia and by her differentiation from Orsino's male love, supposedly identical. We watch the self-discovery of Rosalind in the playlets she organizes to parody and betray her real love, and in the unwitting self-revelation that appears in her 'objective' handling of the Sylvius–Phoebe affair. In all these devices, the crosscurrents of emotion ('between a sob and a giggle', as George Hibbard calls it[54]) fill the space at the centre of the comedy to a degree that could not be tolerated in Italian drama, where the complex web of circumstance leaves no space for contemplative stasis.

The capacity to 'answer back' in boys' disguise, however deviously, is a capacity that Shakespeare extends to the women in his comedies even when no disguise is involved. In *Love's Labour's Lost* (1594×1595) the Princess of France and her ladies are more than a match for their male suitors. The doubleness of their roles as political envoys and as objects of love allows them to manage their love-game comedy with an ambiguous power of play that permits the woman's imagination of possibilities to outstrip all male attempts to privilege 'real' expressions of feeling, sincerity, and faithfulness. The balance thus created can be beautifully sustained in such a highly artificial drama. But as soon as the situation comes into more realistic focus, the power of wit to control our response becomes more uncertain. Thus the deromanticized world of Kate the Shrew keeps us uneasily close to everyday ideas of shrewishness (so that many readers feel her acceptable only if she is understood to be 'playing' the shrew). Beatrice in *Much Ado about Nothing* (?1598) is kept more clearly on the weather side of any deviant mindset. Laughter, 'a merry soul', happy integration into a close-knit family group, all allow us to respond to her as one whose acerbity is merely witty, explicable in the social mode of a particular relationship, and therefore easy to reverse when society no longer approves. However, here too critics feel the need to supply a more romantic and personal explanation—that the 'merry

---

[54] 'Between a Sob and a Giggle', in Kenneth Muir, Jay Halio, and D. J. Palmer (eds.), *Shakespeare, Man of the Theatre* (Newark, Del., 1983), 122.

war' between Beatrice and Benedick is only the negative image of a declaration of love. But the model of Italian comedy suggests that this may be no more than an anachronistic indulgence in modern sentimentality.

It may indeed be the case that modern criticism creates many difficulties by concentrating attention on particular personal histories. Certainly the plays in which we meet Kate and Beatrice set their histories alongside alternative and opposite accounts of male–female relations. Shakespeare recurrently writes comedies which express the doubleness of the female position by showing us two heroines, one a passive and conventional maiden, the other a more active performer willing to break the conventions, to 'answer back', to take charge of her own scenario. Thus we have Hero coupled to Beatrice, Celia to Rosalind, Olivia to Viola, Bianca to Kate. Sometimes he makes the two heroines alternate between passivity and boldness (Jessica and Portia, Helena and Hermia, Silvia and Julia). If we take the double histories that these combinations provide as mutually dependent halves of a complex viewpoint, then we may sense that we are being offered a characteristically evasive commentary on the contradictions that ideal and real must set against one another, however the contrasts are managed. Neither half of the picture is privileged, yet some transcendence which would reconcile the opposites seemed to be implied. But what this transcendence would be like remains undescribed. In the plays of prodigals the problems of reconciling 'manly' men and 'womanly' women are made explicit in real-life situations. But Shakespeare breaks down and recombines the parts of this reality in playful patterns that disable prejudgement: he raises issues of morality but declines to be moralistic, thus fulfilling Bakhtin's criteria for polyphonic structure, where 'the plurality of independent and unmerged voices and consciousnesses and their worlds . . . are combined into the unity of a given event, while at the same time retaining their unmergedness'.[55]

In the two obvious shrew plays (*The Taming of the Shrew* and *Much Ado about Nothing*) Shakespeare deliberately manipulates his sources to give his double heroine plot an effect which straddles

[55] *Problems of Dostoevsky's Poetics*, trans. R. W. Rotsel (Ann Arbor, 1973), 4. It should be remembered, however, that Bakhtin thought that 'drama is by its nature alien to genuine polyphony . . . [it] cannot contain *multiple worlds*; it allows for only one, not several, systems of measurement' (ibid. 28).

the gap between realistic experience and literary understanding. In both plays he celebrates passive femininity by using a celebrated European story: in *Much Ado* the story of Ariodante and Ginevra from Ariosto's *Orlando Furioso*, repeated in at least seventeen contemporary versions (see Bullough, ii. 533); in *The Taming of the Shrew*, the plot of Ariosto's *I suppositi*, the model *commedia erudita*. He joins to these stories material which has no such renown, which lies outside the literary tradition and may indeed have been his own invention. Art and Nature are thus set against one another. The history of the plays' receptions tells us that readers and theatregoers have greatly preferred nature (and if they had not done so, Shakespeare's famous universality could hardly have been asserted). From at least 1613 *Much Ado about Nothing* has been thought of as the play of Beatrice and Benedick, and from 1611 the central interest of *The Taming of the Shrew* has been found in the story of Petruchio and Kate. It seems improbable that Shakespeare used these double plots to offer continental storytellers a lesson in popular entertainment. It is more likely that he aimed to offer the attractions of both folk art and high art, giving each its space and allowing their strange coexistence as versions of truth. The contrast of art against nature, romance against comedy, high life against low life, the economies of honour against those of survival is, of course, a constant feature of Elizabethan dramaturgy (as of Elizabethan life). The double-plot system of separate worlds, contrasting down-to-earth low life and the high-life emotional commitment, is one that dramatists from all the playhouses and across the whole span of time continued to rely on, so that we cannot set this aspect of Shakespearian comedy against the practice of his contemporaries, except in details of emphasis rather than generalities of form. In *The Merry Devil of Edmonton*, *The Blind Beggar of Bednall Green*, *Patient Grissil*, *The Witch of Edmonton*, *Grim the Collier of Croydon*, we see the local and contemporary set against the foreign or historical, the physical set against the spiritual, arbitrary and short-term aims against expectation of emotional constancy and long-view lives. And this is done in much the same way as appears in Shakespeare in his contrast of Touchstone and Audrey with Orlando and Rosalind, Bottom/Titania with Theseus/Hippolyta, or between Dogberry and Leonato, Launce and Proteus, Sly and Lucentio, Parolles and Bertram, Lucio and Angelo. But, as these examples will demonstrate, the contrasts are too various to be reduced to a formula.

The difference between Shakespeare's double-plot dramaturgy and that of his contemporaries appears most obviously in the range of roles he gives to women. The romantic women in his by-plots, Titania, Diana, Mariana, Phoebe, Jessica, are all disabled in one way or another from full romantic commitment. But each offers a different contrast to the central figure. The comedy of his contemporaries, however, shows little interest in this range of differentiation. Theirs is a comedy in which female characters are important as they support or undermine the fortunes of men, so that they move between the polarities of saint and harlot. Even a woman placed at the centre of the action, like Bellafront in Dekker's *The Honest Whore*, is positioned precisely so that she can contrast these two standard roles. Dekker and Middleton's *The Roaring Girl* (1604×1610) has been taken to provide a model of female life outside the standard range of options. Certainly the title-role of Moll Frith— a real woman of the time who dressed as a man—adds a new *frisson* to the usual options (believed to be a harlot, she shows herself in her care for the marriage of romantic hero and heroine to be something like a saint). But Moll's adventures in male attire do not raise the Shakespearian questions; the alternating roles of saint and harlot are not allowed to interrogate one another. They are presented simply as existing social facts, and at the end Moll walks out of the fiction like a put-it-right gun-fighter in a Western who rides off into the sunset, still enigmatic, separate and incapable of dramatized development.

Shakespeare and Jonson

Since the early seventeenth century Shakespeare and Jonson have been pointed to as the polarizing presences in late Elizabethan/ early Jacobean comedy (as romantic versus classic, natural versus artful, smooth versus laboured). The convenience of this half-truth is bought (as I have noted above) at the cost of distorting not only these dramatists' careers but also the larger dramatic scene to which they belonged. For Shakespeare and Jonson did not stand alone or above the rest of the age; they were competitors for the same public favour as was sought by the rest of their colleagues. Shakespeare is, of course, the poet of inwardness and love where Jonson is the poet of outwardness and power, and their energies push them into opposite interpretations of life. We may instance how, when he came in *Epicoene* to imitate the Viola–Aguecheek duel from *Twelfth Night*, Jonson dispensed with what is the central effect in Shakespeare—the self-consciousness of the double role that Viola must play—and showed effeminate pretention to masculinity as a mark of moral inadequacy. Yet the pursuit of power and the pursuit of love procure a similar theatrical excitement in both cases: we see the individual moved into the stratosphere of poetic fantasy and so able to bowl us over with the passionate eloquence that the situation creates.

Shakespeare's cornucopian gifts are spread before us with what appears to be careless ease. Jonson's riches are no less cornucopian, but they are presented inside a controlling intensity of judgement that hovers between delight and disgust, as between achieved order and proliferating fecundity. His classicism is not an art of repose (like that of Raphael or the Belvedere Apollo) but rather one of concentration and stress (like that of Michelangelo, the Laocoön, or the Pergamon altar): he uses the difficulty of control to express the turbulent energies of self-will and distortion. This is what he assumed the classical poets were telling him (as in Juvenal's *difficile est saturam non scribere* (Satire I, l. 30). The three great comedies of his middle years, *Volpone* (1606), *The Alchemist* (1610), and *Bartholomew Fair* (1614),[56] do not mark a radical departure from the standards of classicism I have already discussed in *The Case is Altered, Every Man in his Humour, Every Man out of his Humour*, and *Epicoene*. But now the cornucopia of local inventiveness is so heaped with realistic detail that it seems to defy organization, and yet turns out to belong to it. The marvellous thing about these plays is the extent to which they combine the dazzle of plenitude with the satisfaction of system. The gross scams that Volpone and Mosca, Quarlous and Winwife, Face, Subtle, and Doll concoct seem to survive only by spontaneous adaptation to their host societies, by their virus-like capacity to mutate into more and more irresistible forms. And yet by the end we understand that everything has been moving with preordained inevitability towards a necessary conclusion.

Consider some lines from the opening scene of *The Alchemist*:

---

[56] We should remember that the seventeenth century would have put *Epicoene* in place of *Bartholomew Fair* in this list.

FACE. Do but collect, sir, where I met you first
· · · · · · · ·
　　　　　　　　　　　　at Pie Corner,
Taking your meal of steam in from cooks' stalls,
Where, like the father of hunger, you did walk
Piteously costive, with your pinched-horn nose,
And your complexion of the Roman wash,
Stuck full of black and melancholic worms,
Like powder corns shot at th'artillery yard
· · · · · · · ·
When you went pinned up in the several rags
You had raked and picked from dunghills before day,
Your feet in mouldy slippers for your kibes,
A felt of rug and a thin threaden cloak
That scarce would cover your no-buttocks.

　　　　　　　　　　　　(I. i. 23–37)

Such effects are sometimes called realistic, but the reality the passage points to has been boiled down to a density greater than any
real world could sustain. If we cast our minds back to *Every Man
in his Humour* we can see that it is that play that marks the climax
of Jonson's attempt to represent 'Deeds and language such as men
do use' as the rational norm for reality. Already in *Every Man Out*
the pressure of moral concern has begun to squeeze the figures into
caricature; and *Volpone*, *The Alchemist*, and *Bartholomew Fair* are
essentially plays of compression and caricature, works of an all-
enfolding art of distortion, where moral concern is not forgotten
but is held in tension inside the pleasures of exaggeration. Here
there is no Cynthia, Crites, Horace, or even Justice Clement to
look down on vice from the commanding heights of virtue, for
there are no commanding heights. The word realism can be properly applied here only in the sense of a downgraded view of life, a
horrified acceptance of the fact that selfishness, energy, and street
smartness are necessary conditions of survival.[57]

Shakespeare's narrative procedures, like those of the Henslowe

---

[57] The Induction to *Bartholomew Fair* gives us the most cogent statement of this distinction between realism as a construct of art and reality as a collection of facts. The ignorant
stage-keeper laments that Jonson's play misses out things one would find at the real fair.
The book-holder denies the relevance of this. He describes the play as a promissory note to
provide entertainment within the stated condition that this 'Bartholomew Fair' will be a
recreation of the Fair's general effects, made out of true facts but given meaning by an order
that the author has devised.

team, use the interaction of different levels of the plot to indicate the entertaining variety of life. Jonson's interactions raise instead the question of who is exploiting whom; we are invited to admire the cleverness of the tricks and at the same time to abhor the villainy of the motives. In *The Merchant of Venice* the tricks belong to Portia and the villainy to Shylock, but in *Volpone* both reactions are concentrated on a single figure; there is no Belmont, no moonlight, no casket magic; enjoyment and judgement are pressed into one meaning. In these terms Jonson seems not so much the imitator of the classics as heir to the categorizing tradition of the morality play, where understanding is produced not by plot development but by an unfolding of parallel instances, so that a predetermined structure of meaning emerges. In *Volpone* the animal masks of fox, flesh-fly, crow, vulture, raven, hawk, and parrot replay in a modern scenario of money power the old moralized fable of the wily fox and the greedy birds. We understand the basic pattern of social interactions in Venice by reference to this controlling image, from which the episodes derive their moral order. In *The Alchemist* the gang of tricksters, Face, Doll, and Subtle, rephrase in a secularized modern idiom the morality functions of the World, the Flesh, and the Devil, tempting their victims not to commit sin but to allow credulity to blank out the common sense on which social functioning depends. Once again, as in *Volpone*, the diabolical energies of wickedness are sparked by the irrecoverable folly, the uncentred emptiness of a realistic society that hopes to give greed the face of normality ('everybody does it'). Deceiver and deceived are placed in a symbiotic relationship so that each new credulity is matched by a new scheme for its exploitation. In *Bartholomew Fair* the fair itself is a kind of hell, centred on the fire where Ursula roasts pigs, where control of fools by knaves has been given licence, the guardians of order (Overdo, Busy Waspe) being too close to folly to be able to see it.[58]

The Morality play proper exposed vice in order to bring it

---

[58] Jonson wrote this play, in contradiction to his usual practice, not for the King's Men acting at the Globe and the Blackfriars, but for the Lady Elizabeth's Men, currently performing at the Hope, the playhouse that doubled as a bear pit. He may well have done so as a favour to Nathan Field, his former student and now the leading actor with the Lady Elizabeth's Men. In any case, it is interesting to note the extent to which the specifics of *Bartholomew Fair* are matched to the atmosphere of the playhouse, with its attached bear-cages and kennels for the mastiffs, and the smell and noise of a circumambient world of sweat and blood, violence and despair (as wagers were won and lost).

eventually under the judgement of God or his deputies. And *Volpone* does indeed end with a judgement where the criminals are punished. But the court that condemns them is too much part of the system to be trusted. Venice remains as open to exploitation in the future as it has been in the past. In *The Alchemist* the conspiracy does indeed collapse before the victims have been squeezed completely dry. But the intervention of Lovewit, the owner of the house where everything has happened, does not mark a return of moral standards. In *Bartholomew Fair* the success of the gallants, Winwife and Quarlous, in securing the persons (and, more important, the fortunes) of Grace and Purecraft offers us only a more controlled form of the chicanery that characterizes the whole fair. What all these endings provide is less a restoration of virtue than a swing back of the pendulum from the extraordinary to the ordinary. The status quo is restored and society can continue on its heavily compromised but perfectly normal course. The self-satisfying 'normal' criminality of our actions is thus brought face-to-face with the image of a world in which such impulses have been given control. A moral judgement is forced on us which complements and contradicts the accepting mood that realism allows.

The great plays of Jonson's maturity achieve a remarkable balance between an economic realism of motives and a morality structure that turns all the episodes into evidence for moral judgement. His next comedy, *The Devil is an Ass* (1616; printed 1631) shows the same mixture, but with the opposites bound less closely together. The story of the devil who comes to earth expecting to find a kind of virtue that can be turned into vice draws obviously on a morality tradition.[59] But that tradition depends on its power to

[59] Jonson's remark about the play in his conversations with Drummond indicates that he thought of it as belonging to an English tradition of *Vetus Comoedia*—that is, to the morality play (see *Conversations* (Herford and Simpson's *Jonson*, 1. 143–4)). Earlier in the century two plays had told the same story: *Grim the Collier of Croydon: or the Devil and his Dame* (probably the play for which Henslowe paid Haughton on 6 May 1600 (printed 1662)) and Dekker's *If This be not a Good Play, the Devil is in it* (1611×1612). Both plays share with Jonson's the comic idea that the visiting demon finds himself outclassed by human wickedness, but both handle this as a matter of folk-tale diablerie (even though Haughton's comedy derives from Machiavelli's 'favola' *Belfagor; il Demonio che prese Moglie*, while Dekker's comes from the German folk-tale of Friar Rush). Haughton's gallimaufry of St Dunstan, Spenser's Malbecco, and low life in Croydon is focused (like *Belfagor*) on the wickedness of women. Dekker concentrates, like Jonson, on capitalism. But Barterville, Dekker's wicked merchant, is a generalized figure who can be disposed of only by a morality judgement—he cannot be dealt with on earth; he must be taken back to hell to be placed in a cabinet of extreme sins (along with Guy Fawkes, Ravilliac, and Moll Cutpurse).

show us the absolutes behind the contingents; the whole point of *The Devil is an Ass* is that hell comes to earth looking for antithetical absolutes, virtue and vice, and discovers that they cannot be told apart.[60] The demon expects to find himself in a Morality play and finds that he is instead in a realistically observed social scene where everything is contingent and open to revaluation. As salesman and con-artist, the 'projector' Meercraft is only doing what salesmen do; he is not an ornament to his society, but he is too integrated into it to be isolated in punishment. The same holds for his dupe Fitzdottrel; he is allowed to survive uncuckolded and unruined by the gallants who have exposed his folly. 'It is not manly to take joy or pride | In human errors', we are told—an unJonsonian sentiment we might read as a measure of the play's loss of moral energy rather than its conversion to humankindness.

Jonson had always shuttled between the polarities of cornucopian realism and abstracted moral judgement, and his career shows his difficulty in keeping these two in balance. The move from *Every Man In* to *Every Man Out* in 1599 or so shows the violent contradiction between these alternative viewpoints as human nature gives way to moral system. Free-standing individuals are abolished; characters are judged by their unified responses to the behavioural pressures of a defining area of life, town, or court. In the great comedies, liberating comic caricature and narrowing moral judgement are somehow held together. *The Devil is an Ass* shows an obvious weakening of this coordinating pressure: its realistic vignettes are not sustained by a pervading moral system.

Jonson's last plays (*The Staple of News* (1626), *The New Inn: or The Light Heart* (1629), *The Magnetic Lady or the Humours Reconciled* (1632; printed 1641)) take this dissipation a stage further. Dryden characterized them as 'dotages'[61]—plays marked by an inability to control their material. The metaphorical centres provided—the Staple of News (an exchange mart for gossip), 'the centre attractive' of the Magnetic Lady (whose function is to 'draw thither a diversity of guests, all persons of different humours'), and the Light Heart Inn at Barnet (with its Court of Love providing

---

[60] Iniquity tells Pug, the demon who seeks leave to visit earth: 'They have their vices there most like to virtues, | You cannot know them apart by any difference | They wear the same clothes, eat the same meat . . . As the best men and women' (ll. 121–6).

[61] 'Essay of Dramatic Poesy', in *The Essays of John Dryden*, ed. W. P. Ker (Oxford, 1926), i. 81.

quasi-legal 'proof' of true values)—now look like arbitrary inventions rather than (as with Venice or Bartholomew Fair) inevitable localizations of moral judgement. The central characters are not given a structure that allows them to dominate the mob of extras squeezed into the defining space, but must intrigue and struggle (like the audience) to grasp the uncoordinated activity all around them. The ending can no longer be a simple judgement delivered *ex cathedra* as in a true moral play. The complexity can be sorted out only by the theatrical legerdemain of romance: long-lost relatives, impenetrable disguises, babies exchanged at birth, recoveries from apparent death. These were methods that Jonson had spent his life decrying.[62] But clearly the romance framework is now seen as a means of subduing general indeterminacy, allowing the characters to live inside the appropriate labels of their moral significance. Hence, no doubt, the return to *Every Man out of his Humour*'s method of formal character descriptions (as in *The New Inn*), and to the habit of making one character introduce another with a defining speech (as in *The Magnetic Lady*). Hence, too, the presence of long arguments describing the values at issue and of choric interludes, supplied in both *The Staple of News* and *The Magnetic Lady*, defending the play by the rules of art, and damning those who disagree.

Jonson appears in these late plays as an embattled proponent of drama as a didactic art that can 'conceive, express, and steer the souls of men | As with a rudder' (Prologue to *The Staple of News*), even if he has brought himself to solve his ethical dilemmas by discovery scenes.[63] But not even this indulgence was enough to attract audiences; the harder he tried to create meaning (by all the techniques noted above), the less success he had. The wits of the time gathered round to defend him, but the stage had clearly passed him by. One title-page tells it all: *The New Inn: or The*

---

[62] It has been argued by Anne Barton (*Ben Jonson Dramatist* (Cambridge, 1984)) among others that these characteristics reveal the influence of Shakespeare's final plays. Romance is, however, a capacious enough concept to allow Jonson to employ it while remaining contemptuous of Shakespeare's efforts. For both it involves a loss of character autonomy, but in one case this creates a sense of guidance by providence; in the other it leads rather to merely individual resolutions of social disorder.

[63] Martin Butler speaks of these plays as the products of a 'beleaguered intellectual courageously rethinking his priorities' ('Late Jonson', in Gordon McMullan and Jonathan Hope (eds.), *The Politics of Tragicomedy* (London, 1991), 166). There is, of course, no necessary contradiction between artistic weakness and political correctness. Jonson's slacker dramaturgy is perfectly capable of carrying subversive political implications.

*Light Heart. A Comedy. As it was never acted, but most negligently
played by some, the King's servants, and more squeamishly beheld and
censured by others, the King's subjects. 1629. Now at last set at liberty
to the readers, his Majesty's servants and subjects, to be judged. 1631.*

A Mixed Inheritance

This disaster does not require us to say that there was no future
for a Jonsonian dramaturgy in which intrigue was used to illustrate
the stern realities of class–economic–moral judgement.[64] But the
new dramaturgy soon proved to be one in which moral distinctions
could not be placed as firmly as in Jonson, and where only verisimilitude in the social life of the town is strong enough to give plot
coherence. We can see this clearly in the comedies of Jonson's
sometime servant and pupil, Richard Brome. Brome's elaborate
intrigues of citizens, decayed knights, projectors, prostitutes, and
usurers are Jonsonian in the hard-headedness of their economic
relations, but compromise between manipulators and manipulated
is now more easily allowed as a social necessity. *The City Wit: or
The Woman Wears the Breeches* (1629×1637); printed 1653) draws
much of its strength from Jonson's practice. The supposedly bed-
ridden rich widow who draws suitors with gifts to listen to her
planned bequests is evidently modelled on Volpone. The three
conspirators actually refer us to *The Alchemist* when they make an
'indenture tripartite, like Subtle, Doll and Face' and codify their
roles as punk, pimp, and doctor. But *The City Wit* is not as sharply
focused as its Jonson originals. The chief manipulator, Crasy, is an
honest citizen whose trust in his courtier clients and failure to
pursue his debtors have bankrupted him. Only for the limited purpose of regaining his own does he undertake deception. Judgement
is given, but without Jonson's relish, rather with an apologetic

---

[64] A splendid and little-known example of the comedy of life lived along the economic
edge is Jo *Cooke's *Greene's Tu Quoque* (1611). Here the journeyman (Frank Spendall)
becomes the master when the owner is knighted and so has to give up trade. Success goes
to Frank's head: he becomes a gallant spendthrift and falls into debtor's prison (vividly
evoked). Only a rich widow can rescue him. In the second plot a foolish servant (Bubbles)
becomes master when his usurer uncle dies; he takes on his impecunious former master as
his servant (and tutor in gentlemanliness). But, when Bubbles courts the knight's daughters,
they make clear the difference between a *real* gentleman and a jumped-up chough; so the
servant returns to his proper status while the foolish master, who has frittered away his
wealth, is forced to return again to his servant role. This is a play that remained for long the
favourite of the apprentices as well as an esteemed entertainment at court.

sigh. Unjust relations are spelt out—between husbands and wives
(who wear the breeches), citizens and courtiers, creditors and debtors—but the realistic language of the play represents them as particular cases, not as models of human nature, so that the ending
can propose an easy and compromising acceptance.

Brome's comedy of city realities was praised by Alexander Brome
(no relation) as containing 'designs so probable that though | They
be not true, 'tis like enough they may be so' ('To the Stationer at
the Publishing of Mr Brome's comedies'). *The Damoiselle: or The
New Ordinary* (1637×1638); printed 1653) offers us indeed a survey of realistic characters held together by the bondage of economic necessity. We follow the fortunes of four families, two headed
by impoverished gentlemen, the decayed knight Dryground and
the ruined landowner Brookall, and two by rich citizens, the usurer
Vermine and the pawky citizen Bumpsey. The diagram looks set to
be the usual struggle between good and evil, but harsh moral
discriminations are avoided; the young gentleman's emotions are
now focused less on economic survival than on his success in love.
Prodigality and avarice are only elements in a generally benign
picture of human nature. Conscience uncovers the guilt of both
the knight and the usurer, and love of family at every level ensures
that more stable relationships can be developed. Cross-marriages
between the various families distribute assets across the whole cast.

The comedy of real economic life never deserted the English
theatre, but its Inns of Court cachet was soon overshadowed by a
cavalier taste for romance, promoted by an interfering and 'artistic'
court and eventually modulating (under the influence of Henrietta
Maria) into D'Urfé-esque confections about Platonic Love such as
*Davenant's *Love and Honour* (1634; printed 1649) or old Heywood's
operatic *Love's Mistress* (1634). The Prologue to Brome's *A Jovial
Crew: or The Merry Beggars* (1641; printed 1652), which may well
have been the last play performed on the London stage before
Parliament closed it down,[65] spells out the collusion as well as
tension between cultural forms that continued to define the London theatre as a site of struggle.[66] Brome looks back on the contrast
between his own kind of work and escapist comedies of romantic

---

[65] The dedication of the 1652 printing tells us that the play 'had the luck to tumble last
of all in the epidemical ruin of the scene'.
[66] Documented in some detail by the quarrel between Massinger and Davenant. See
Doris Adler, *Philip Massinger* (Boston, 1987), 73–80.

lovers protected by their own virtue from all the threats around them:

> Our comic writer, finding that romances
> Of lovers through much travail and distress,
> Till it be thought no power can redress
> Th'afflicted wanderers, though stout chivalry
> Lend all his aid for their delivery,
> Till lastly by some impossibility
> Concludes all strife and makes a comedy—
> Finding (he says) such stories bear a sway,
> Near as he could, he has composed a play.
>
> (Prologue, ll. 8–16)

What is omitted in such a description of the theatrical scene in terms of its antithetical forms is, of course, the capacity for compromise between romance and satire that the theatre had developed over the years. In fact, *A Jovial Crew* itself turns out to be less an attempt at escapist romance than a balanced critique of its characters' taste for escapist romance.

This indeterminate middle ground in the post-Shakespearian period is represented above all by the comedy of two 'attached' playwrights of the King's Men, Fletcher and Shirley,[67] who managed to allow the Shakespearian strain of love comedy to decline gently towards Restoration norms, in a repertory characterized by witty sexual intrigues among elegant members of society and also by the seamless theatrical fluency that comes from membership of a long tradition. Fletcher is not often thought of as a purely comic writer. But if we read (for example) *Wit without Money* (1614×1620; printed 1639), *Monsieur Thomas* (1615×c.1616; printed 1639), or *The Wild Goose Chase* (?1621; printed 1652), we find ourselves already comfortably ensconced in a 'town' world of witty competition between free-standing modern gentlemen and ladies. The mode is obviously derivative not only from Shakespeare but also from the later products of the children's stage, where Fletcher learnt his trade, such as Barry's *Ram Alley*, Jonson's *Epicoene*, Nathan Field's

---

[67] See Ch. 2, p. 17. Massinger has a just claim to be added here. But in comedy he seems to be a follower rather than an innovator; in his early collaboration with Fletcher his voice does not resonate against that of his senior partner.

Amends for Ladies and *A Woman is a Weathercock*, but handled
not with the satiric edge of those plays but rather with the cynical
gaiety of a cast of characters who must make their way in life
outside the moralizing pressures and formal rules of family and
social hierarchy.[68] Fletcher's women are not, like Shakespeare's,
given structured emotional freedom inside a limited range of social
possibilities, but rather in their typifying energy—'emotional absolutism' is Danby's phrase[69]—are allowed to constitute the social
situations in which they appear.

Love comedy in a situation of female self-sufficiency (where
patriarchalism is no longer an all-defining factor) tends to take the
form of a civil war between the sexes,[70] in which women, empow-
ered by wit,[71] can negotiate their own terms of agreement (not, like
Rosalind, in a never-never land, but in a world acceptably that of
the audience). Of course misunderstandings between lovers provide the basis of all modern comedy, but in most previous instances the impediments to love—love understood as social and
emotional fulfilment for both parties—have been the external and
circumstantial rules of society. In Shakespeare the freedoms as
well as the difficulties are often compounded by problems of self-
definition which delay or obscure the common purpose that links
Rosalind and Orlando, Viola and Orsino, Hero and Claudio, even
Beatrice and Benedick and Helena and Bertram. In Fletcher's comedies, however, the problems cannot be solved by the Shakespearian

---

[68] Lee Bliss (in A. R. Braunmuller and J. C. Bulman (eds.), *Comedy from Shakespeare
to Sheridan* (Newark, Del, 1986)) notes that for Beaumont and Fletcher 'the interaction
between generations holds no interest . . . Beaumont and Fletcher's young men have no
fathers, their world no past' (pp. 152–3).

[69] John Danby, *Poets on Fortune's Hill* (London, 1952), 152–3.

[70] One of the oddest manifestations of this interest is the play of *Swetnam the Woman
Hater, Arraigned by Women* (1615×1619). Swetnam, the author of *The Arraignment of Lewd,
Idle, Froward and Inconstant Women* (ten editions between 1615 and 1637), is incorporated
(under the name of Misogonos) into a romantic tale of misfortunes in a Sicilian royal family,
with lost heirs, imprisoned princesses, and so on. Enraged by the attack on women, the lost
heir (disguised as an amazon) beats Swetnam, threatens to export him to the infidels, and
forces him to endure torments from women and, finally, to abjure his writings.

[71] For Fletcher as a defender of women, see the Prologue written for some revival of *The
Woman's Prize*: 'Ladies, to you, in whose defence and right | Fletcher's brave muse pre-
pared herself to fight | A battle without blood; 'twas well fought too, | The victory yours,
though got with much ado'. The Second Prologue to *The Woman Hater* says that Fletcher,
'to the stars your sex did raise | For which full twenty years he wore the bays; | 'Twas he
reduced Evandra from her scorn, | And taught the sad Aspacia how to mourn; | Gave
Arethusa's love a glad relief, | And made Panthea elegant in grief'.

mode of self-discovery: men and women, when seen in independent social existence, show themselves to have fundamentally different attitudes to love. The end is often (as in Shakespeare) an acceptance of play or pretence as a natural part of life; but where in Shakespeare the pretence is seen as a key to release an otherwise obscure emotional reality, in Fletcher it appears rather as a social manœuvre, and that makes the discovery of agreement much more difficult to allow (at least for modern audiences).

The Woman Hater (1606), discussed below as part of the move to tragicomedy, gives us a first glimpse of a new kind of chaste heroine, seen as not only a desirable but also a free-standing figure, able to impose her own rules on relationships.[72] But the first full expression of Fletcher's interest in rewriting older stereotypes appears in *The Woman's Prize: or The Tamer Tamed* (1604×*c*.1617; printed 1647), which rehandles (and inverts) the story of *The Taming of the Shrew*. Petruchio (the tamer) has lost his first wife. The play opens with his second marriage, this time not to a shrew but to a 'tender soul'. But when Petruchio thinks to go to bed with the 'soft maid', he finds himself barred access. Efforts to break in only produce battle displays by legions of female auxiliaries—Fletcher may be recalling the *Lysistrata*. The siege is ended by Petruchio's assent to articles of female liberation. However, those agreed, he is then subjected to deprivation: no satisfaction in bed, and days spent in hearing his wife ordering expensive clothes, making plans to rebuild the property, and giving lectures on female equality. The rest of the play is a series of efforts by Petruchio to escape, each one countered by a 'careful' wife's response. He pretends to be sick: she declares quarantine, hires a nurse, packs up the household, will live by herself in the lodge. He makes arrangements to go abroad; she commends his educational purposes; after gathering wisdom he can return to her as Ulysses to an aged Penelope. He plays dead; when the coffin is carried in she rejoices that an early end has preserved his reputation from further follies. How happy she is that she denied him the opportunity to beget more fools. He starts up out of the coffin in understandable despair; he expresses total reliance on her ('I die indeed else') and misery for himself.

---

[72] Commanding women are everywhere in Fletcher: Lamira in *The Honest Man's Fortune*, the Duchess in *Women Pleased*, the Queen of Corinth, Quisara in *The Island Princess*, Hyppolita and Guiomar in *The Custom of the Country*, the princesses in *The Mad Lover* and *The Loyal Subject*.

And that is enough; she declares herself satisfied: 'I have done my worst and have my end . . . I have tamed ye.'[73]

Equally clear in its intention is the rewriting of Chaucer in *Women Pleased* (1619×1623; printed 1647). In main outline this play is a romantic narrative about a princess shut up in the citadel by her mother, but visited there by her socially unsuitable lover. When the liaison is discovered, the lover is sentenced to death; but the sentence will be cancelled if he can answer a riddle proposed by the mother—the same riddle as animates Chaucer's *The Wife of Bath's Tale*: what do women want most? The lover wanders through the world looking for help. Eventually he is given the answer by an ugly old hag, but only on condition that he will grant her one boon when she asks for it. The answer is that what women want most is 'maistrie'. That proves correct; and saves the lover's life; but his triumph is immediately followed by the hag's demand for her 'boon'—he must marry her. He is appalled; but then is offered a second riddle: would he rather have a young and unfaithful wife or an old and faithful one? He leaves the decision to the hag. She has achieved maistrie; so she can now reveal herself as the princess. The point is repeated in two other strands of the play, and the moral is summed up in the final lines:

> You young men that know not
> How to preserve a wife and keep her fair,
> Give 'em their sovereign wills and pleased they are.

> (v. iii. 111–13)

The power of woman as dominating controller of male appetite appears in a more purely comic context in *The Scornful Lady* (1613×1616), one of the great successes of this dramaturgy, perhaps written originally for the Children of the Revels but soon taken over (and replayed into the eighteenth century) by adult actors. The Scornful Lady (she has no other name) has sentenced her admirer, the elder Loveless, to a year of exile as punishment

---

[73] Fletcher plays on both sides of the sex power game with a commitment only to theatrical effect. In *Rule a Wife and Have a Wife* (1624) we have the story of a rich libertine wife who selects a simple-minded and complaisant husband as a 'cover' for her own liaisons. But simplicity and complaisance are also only a cover: as husband, he demands obedience, and discovers that his wife is happy to give it to him. This is balanced in the sub-plot (taken from Cervantes) where the aggrieved husband finds that his aggressive and deceitful wife is willing to co-opt him as a junior partner in her criminal enterprises. On that basis they have a happy marriage.

for kissing her in public. Like Fletcher's Petruchio he employs a series of tricks[74] to try to have the sentence commuted, but each one—reporting his own death, delivering diatribes against love, declaring himself cured of the affliction, rejecting her letters, appearing at church with another 'bride' (really his fellow suitor)— seems to be in vain until, stung to jealousy by the bride's leathery complexion, the lady decides to abate her scorn and claim the bride's place for herself.[75]

Sex-war comedy will, of course, fit easily into other generic patterns. *Monsieur Thomas* is mainly an intrigue plot of long-lost children in the neoclassical mode,[76] but Fletcher gives it comic energy by adding his standard situation of the rigid mistress and the scapegrace lover. As elsewhere, the lover tries to get round the lady's prohibitions by a series of tricks, sends her a 'hot' letter, serenades her, disguises himself as his sister (and ends up in bed with a blackamoor). With all these failures behind him he will travel abroad. But this evidence of defeat is enough to make the lady relent. In *Wit without Money* the situation is handled in terms of Middletonian city comedy. The brothers Valentine and Francisco have lost their family estates, but unlike Middleton's heroes they do not plan to return to status and the hebetude of the shires. The town is the place where wit and education will sustain a good life. But wit does not mean here (as in Middleton) the capacity to set up a campaign of deception. It rather represents the static power of virtue, standing above the sway of urban fashion and pretence. Powerful and independent women, besieged by fops, are looking for men they can esteem. A series of tests indicates that Valentine and Francisco are of this kind; they are loved and so redeemed from poverty.

The sex war can also be expressed in terms of a determined woman in pursuit of a reluctant man, as in the romantic *Love's*

---

[74] The skilful deployment of entertaining trickeries is characteristic of Fletcher's comic dramaturgy. The lightness of touch, the continual move from one focus to another, saves his action from the complexities of through-plotted intrigue and yet allows the interest of each moment to be attached to our concern with the ending.

[75] It should be noticed that the sub-plot treats wooing in a very different way. The rejected 'bride' is pitied by the scornful lady's sister, who will comfort her by taking her back home to bed. The male trick performed there short circuits the female tricks which would have kept him at bay for a 'twelve-month yet' (v. iv. 80); one sex's trick is seen as the complement of the other's in a situation that is essentially focused on equality of competitive aggression. [76] It is based on a story told in D'Urfé's *L'Astrée*.

Pilgrimage (?1616, revised 1635; printed 1647) and the more purely comic *The Wild Goose Chase*. This latter is a sparkling comedy of social manners, as close to Restoration comedy as Fletcher ever came, but still as removed from Etherege or Congreve, by lack of detail in the evocation of 'the manners of the town', as from Shakespeare's romantic emotionalism.[77] The scene is Paris; the cast is composed of the rich and idle. The 'wild goose' is Mirabel, 'a travelled monsieur and a great defier of all ladies in the way of marriage, otherwise their much loose servant'.[78] The determined woman is Oriana, 'the fair betrothed of Mirabel and witty follower of the chase'. All the characters belong to a nexus of sophisticated and self-confident families, well represented by the easy fluency that Fletcher brings to their conversation. It is a society in which women have a full say in social regulation, and wooing is conducted inside well-understood decorums.

The play begins with three 'travelled monsieurs' returning to Paris and an expectation that they will marry and settle down, but still buzzing with their admiration of Italy and (especially) of Italian women. Can they retain their libertine opinions inside the family circle? Mirabel thinks of himself as a Don Juan (he has a book of conquests and a trail of broken promises to marry) but in this company he is tied to the limitation on self-assertion that civil society requires and that female wit can impose. Here, as in Restoration comedy, women can have what they want if they can mask from their lovers the desire they reveal to us. To achieve equality they must recompense by wit what they lack in social power. The play is thus (like most of these Fletcher comedies) a series of tricks—in this case tricks by which the women disorient and defeat the men. Oriana deceives Mirabel with a string of pretences which hold his attention for a moment but then lose it again. Only when she appears as a 'great Italian lady' does she so impose on his

---

[77] Shakespeare had, of course, provided many examples of 'witty war' between the sexes, as in the dialogues of *Love's Labour's Lost* and *Two Gentlemen*, but the wit is too schematic and formal there to exert much influence. Only the exchanges of Beatrice and Benedick seem to have lingered in Fletcher's mind, as in the memory of Benedick's 'Well, I will have thee, but by this light, I take thee for pity' (v. iv. 92–3) that appears in *Wit without Money*, v. v. 16–17, and *The Wild Goose Chase*, v. vi. 86). But Oriana carries no traces of the shrew, as Beatrice does. She is a Hero *pretending* to be a Beatrice.

[78] The moral reprobation evident in this description is much stronger than appears in the play itself. All these character descriptions come from the prefatory matter of the first (Folio) printing (1652).

imagination her potential to be the woman of his dreams that he will marry her. But she must continue to wear her Italian garb. The balance between love and aggression which *The Wild Goose Chase* manages so skilfully is a rare achievement. Fletcher is commonly caught on the horn of his period's assumption that a gentleman's erotic vigour is inseparable from his soldierly violence, and could not be loved if it were not so. Jacomo, the hero of *The Captain* (1609×1612; printed 1647), must be admired by the heroine for his soldiership, for he is incapable of wit. He is one of Fletcher's standard military men, totally committed to competitive male company, drinking, quarrelling, and fighting. The tricks to catch him have to be as simple as his nature: empty a pisspot over his head and then run into the house; he is bound to follow, and there he can be held down while the lady announces her passion. It seems merciful for everyone that war is declared as soon as marriage is agreed. The situation of Stukeley (see pp. 380–1) is repeated, but without the economic realism of the earlier play. Even so, the tension between militarism and love is too wide to be managed by Fletcher's usual methods of distancing. The topic seems to be better suited to the complex divagations of tragicomedy, as in *The Mad Lover* of 1617 (see Chapter 10).

James Shirley illustrates very well the situation of the artist at the end of the tradition we have been following. He has great facility; he is a master of many techniques; his mind is obviously stocked with the formulae and devices of his predecessors.[79] He pleased Henrietta Maria enough to be made a valet of her chamber. King Charles himself gave him the plot for *The Gamester* (1633); and Sir Henry Herbert, the tiresomely self-important Master of the Revels, thought his *The Young Admiral* (1633) should 'serve as a pattern to other poets . . . for the bettering of manners and language'. But at the same time as he was drawing on the past Shirley was inventing the future. His historical importance is usually thought today to lie less in his capacity to improve others by his 'beneficial and cleanly way of poetry' than in the skill with which he carried Fletcher's comic methods forward through the bosky undergrowth of romance to the very threshold of Restoration comedy, particularly in two comedies, *Hyde Park* (1632) and *The Lady of Pleasure* (1635).

[79] See R. S. Forsythe, *The Relations of Shirley's Plays to the Elizabethan Drama* (New York, 1914).

Hyde Park is perhaps the less integrated of the two. The frame plot is a quasi-Boccaccian story of a long-lost husband turning up at the wedding feast of his supposed widow.[80] But this is placed and effaced inside a social whirl of wooing and refusing, realized in a brilliantly sharpened contemporary dialect. The opening lines show an extraordinary sophistication of theatrical technique:

> TRIER. And how, and how?
> LACY.   The cause depends——
> TRIER.   No
>   Mistress?
> LACY.   Yes, but no wife.
> TRIER.   For now she is a widow.
> LACY. But I resolve—
> TRIER.   What does she say to thee?
> LACY. She says—I know not what she says—but I
>   Must take another course; and yet she is—
> TRIER. A creature of much sweetness . . .
>
>   (p. 461)

The carefully managed hesitations and indirections of such speeches point to a quality that is new in English drama, a capacity to manage the light and shade of what is said or not said so as to reflect the velleities of self-conscious social manners.[81] Acts III and IV, at the races in Hyde Park, keep the three plots of the play continuously passing in front of one another. Couples and threesomes, and sometimes the whole cast, move in and out of sight, pursuing their private aims at the same time as they wager and chat, eat syllabub, and maintain a surface of elegant disengagement.[82]

The witty put-downs by which Mrs Carol keeps control of her three suitors have been given particular attention as anticipations of Congreve.[83] Shirley is drawing, of course, on Fletcher, whose spirited virgins, such as Celia in *The Humorous Lieutenant*, Mary in *Monsieur Thomas*, and above all the Scornful Lady, play the desire

---

[80] See also Marston's *What You Will* (1601), derived from Sforza D'Oddi.

[81] The central issues in *The Lady of Pleasure* (Aretina's adultery and her repentance) are airbrushed so delicately that readers can understand them only by inference.

[82] The scene should remind us of Act III, Scene iii, in Etherege's *The Man of Mode*, set in the Mall, in which the members of the whole group pass and repass, gossip and conspire. The comparison brings out the greater ease and transparency of the later play, even when the dramaturgy is the same.

[83] The contract scene between Carol and Fairfield in Act II, Scene iv, offers an obvious point of comparison with *The Way of the World*.

for control and the desire for surrender in continual witty counter-point. And behind Fletcher we can see Beatrice and Benedick.[84] In all these cases, self-preservation from the pressure of the plot demands a biting particularity in repartee that comedy cannot defang. It is only when we get to *The Lady of Pleasure* that witty self-protection becomes not only a particular but a general social mode. Abraham Wright, in his *Excerpta Quaedam* (probably written some time in the 1630s), thought *The Lady of Pleasure* 'the best play of Shirley's for the lines, but the plot is as much as none'.[85] The observation is acute: the disappearance of an overarching intrigue allows the action to concentrate on the flow of conversation in which society reveals itself as a network of visitings, gossip, backbitings, one-upmanships, all held within the bland proprieties of civil behaviour. The world of Tattle and Fashion is not far away. Wright notes in particular that 'the scene twixt Celestine and the lord is good for the humour of neat compliment'. The scene (Act IV, Scene iii) is indeed an extraordinary model of a refined society turned in upon itself, reminiscent of Shakespeare no less than Congreve. Changes in society alter the social mode, of course. Shakespearian manners have become more formalized; the group is more homogeneous and focused on a single model of style for which all must try and by which most must be disgraced. Failure in *Love's Labour's Lost* (for example in the Russian masque) can be an occasion for relaxed comedy, for if one ploy fails, others are still available; but in this tight grouping, in which every con-versation is a final exam, failure marks an irredeemable flaw. The language of impeccable idealism is used most skilfully, and with equal force, on both sides of the debate, leaving both contestants equally pleased with themselves. There is no overt cynicism (and in this we see an important difference from the Restoration stage), but ideals so manipulable must raise our suspicion. The penalty of a totalizing social mode is that everything inside it comes to look dependent on it, as everything outside it is excluded. Shirley's evasive dramaturgy is not quite prepared to acknowledge this im-plication; but it was a move that history was about to impose on his audience.

---

[84] Mrs Carol agrees to marry Fairfield 'only to save your life' (v. i. 252).

[85] For Wright's *Excerpta*, see J. G. MacManaway, *Excerpta Quaedam per A. W. Adolescentem*, in *Studies in Honor of deWitt T. Starnes* (Austin, Tex., 1967), 117–26, and Arthur Kirsch, 'A Caroline Commentary on the Drama', *MP* 66 (1968–9), 256–9.

9. Later Tragedy

TRAGEDY, I have suggested in Chapter 3, plots the urge of the individual to assert his freedom against the restrictions imposed by the community, against power as it is embodied in the existing social system. The hero's bid is to overwhelm the restrictions, and it is his tragic destiny to fail, but also to show, in the process of failing, the power of the individual to represent a daring, an untamability, an inventiveness, occasionally a capacity for love and self-sacrifice that idealizes our own effort to achieve such separate identity. In Greek and Roman tragedy the struggle runs against impersonal forces, as expressed in oracle, customary religion, family inheritance, the decrees of the gods; and so the heroes must be supermen ('greater than us', as Aristotle says), unintimidated by the metaphysical odds against them. But Elizabethan tragedy tends to construe 'greater' in set social terms, so that we are shown neither classical defiance of the gods nor modern concentration on one temperament exerting its power over others in a tightly knit grouping, without recourse to social conventions of honour or hierarchy. Elizabethan tragedy deals with the violent emotions of princes and generals, men who create political turmoil in the process of asserting self over other by the most melodramatic methods available. The anti-theatrical polemicist, John Greene, tells us in his *Refutation of the Apology for Actors* that

> The matter of tragedies is haughtiness, arrogancy, ambition, pride, injury, anger, wrath, envy, hatred, contention, war, murder, cruelty, rapine, incest, rovings, depredations, piracies, spoils, robberies, rebellions, treasons, killing, hewing, stabbing, dagger-drawing, fighting, butchery, treachery, villainy, &c. and all kinds of heroic evils whatsoever.[1]

It is not hard to document all these forms of 'heroic evils' in Elizabethan tragedy.

The seductive promises of power and the vulnerability of those who believe in them (thus condemned to *hubris*) provide the basic tragic situations in this period, whether the promise is that the

---

[1] (1615), Sig. H1–H1ᵛ.

individual can be guaranteed an indeterminate prolongation of power already possessed (as in tyrant tragedy) or that the individual can substitute his own destructive power for the one already embodied in society (as in revenge tragedy or villain tragedy) or that the individual can enforce social acceptance of a relationship or a self-image (as in love tragedy or heroic tragedy). These categories are, of course, of more value as critical scaffolding than as descriptions of actual Elizabethan plays, which, as they use the stereotypes, revise or combine them; they are street plans to follow, not life-sized houses to be explored. Elizabethan drama is characterized, here as elsewhere, by contaminations and border crossings. Yet generic descriptions still provide a useful grid by means of which one can see cross-generic choices being made, the recognitions and surprises that the audience is being called on to understand.

The basic structure of generic alternatives I have mentioned was well established before 1594. As I have noted in Chapter 3, *Tamburlaine* and *The Spanish Tragedy* (the most celebrated of the pre-1594 tragedies) bequeathed to authors in subsequent genera-tions a mixed legacy. They emphasized, on the one hand, the tra-gic capacity of the great individualist to soar beyond the limits of the moral life, and, on the other hand, showed the tragic necessity that the man who wishes to take control must join the corrupt society he seeks to redeem. The pre-1594 tragedies with the best survival rate (judging by Henslowe's Diary), *The Jew of Malta*, *Doctor Faustus*, *Tamburlaine*, and *The Spanish Tragedy*, can none of them be easily called 'political'. Tamburlaine transcends politics without noticing it; Hieronimo's career is only incidentally political. The Prologue to *The Jew of Malta* does indeed offer Machiavelli as a model of political success, but Barabas, in the play itself, refuses political power when it is offered him, preferring the satisfactions of personal betrayals and manipulations to involvement with the network of agents and consequences that real politics involves. As he says, 'Ego mihimet sum semper proximus' (I. i. 189).

These early model tragedies show political consequences, but only as the by-products of a personal drive. As the form devel-oped, the relations between these two became more complex, but the priority did not change. The presence of the English history play in the same theatres at the same time must also have helped to push tragic authors towards a form in which the values embodied in a society are made visible by the rise and fall of an individual.

Shakespeare's *Richard III* (called a tragedy on the title-page) presents a hero as energetic in his self-will as Tamburlaine, even though he never has the freedom to indulge in the pure self-assertion that can be imagined for a Scythian chieftain. He is entangled in a network of past family and clientage obligations, and as soon as old ones are disposed of, new ones appear. Public-theatre tragedy is continuously caught up in political action, but (even in as extreme an example as Jonson's *Sejanus*) concentrates less on the depersonalizing issues of real politics than on the individual's effort to transcend these limitations.[2] The tragic hero's story moves inevitably towards a point where the world is left emotionally drained by his disappearance; history asks its heroes to fade into the broader picture of the national life. And so historical tragedies (like *Richard II*) ask their heroes to play both roles.

The combination of a romantic extremism of action with a fascinated interest in the routines by which great men impose themselves on their environment—with an almost complete absence of a domestic focus which could give it a psychological explanation—posed a challenge to the understanding of those who first tried to understand Elizabethan tragedy outside Shakespeare. The nineteenth-century recovery of this theatrical repertory, not simply as a background for Shakespeare (as for the majority of eighteenth-century scholars), not simply as an occasion for poetic highlights (as for Lamb), but as a comment on life ('a mirror held up to nature'), obliged its critics to understand what they read in terms of nineteenth-century cultural values. These required it to be seen in comparison with and as inferior to that touchstone of good taste, the Athenian drama, inferior in ethical breadth, infected with the crudity and provincialism of Elizabethan culture in general. The surviving texts seemed to indicate an inability to rise above the decadent classicism of Seneca (aided and abetted by the decadent realism of the Italian *novelle*) into the purer air of Sophocles. The term 'tragedy of blood', which A. J. Symonds seems to have invented for his *Shakespeare's Predecessors in the English Drama*,[3] gave a usefully specific generic identity to what the nineteenth century saw: a tragic form appropriate to the robust tastes of the original audience and the violent tenor of their experience, with its subordination of

---

[2] In saying this I am differentiating acted tragedy from closet plays by such as Fulke Greville or Sir William Alexander.   [3] (London, 1884).

the private to the public sphere, its recurrent carnivals of execution and mutilation. For better or for worse, that mode of life had been overcome by Progress;[4] but its primitive vigour (as of 'warrior's harp, strung with twisted iron and bull's sinews', as Symonds puts it,[5] its unhesitating patriotism, its freedom from 'sick hurry and divided aims' still offered the fascination of Schiller's *Naïve* genre. And by a miracle it had been transcended and spiritualized in its own time by gentle Shakespeare. Yet even there, as the Victorian gentleman is supposed to have remarked of *Antony and Cleopatra*, 'how different from the home life of our own dear queen'.[6] This separation of Shakespeare from his contemporaries is obviously a historical absurdity. Shakespearian tragedy has clear connections with 'the tragedy of blood': if we wish to understand the range of his effects, we must know the variety of dramaturgies that allowed him to forge a medium intelligible to the sixteenth as to the twentieth century.

Revenge Tragedy

Most people, if asked to discuss Elizabethan tragedy outside Shakespeare, begin by talking about revenge tragedy. The phrase has a useful portmanteau quality and allows a fairly indeterminate number of 'representative' Elizabethan plays to be placed together. Fredson Bowers, in the standard monograph on the subject,[7] manages to deal with some sixty plays under this heading. But if one puts into a single package tragedies as different from one another as *The Jew of Malta* (in which a usurer murders everyone who stands in the way of his capital accumulation) and *The Duchess of Malfi* (in which a hired assassin repents of his crime and decides to kill his employers), then there is a danger that incidental connection will be turned into defining characteristic.

The revenge motive can be considered primary in tragedies in which an affront (real or imagined) imposes an obsessive duty to

---

[4] By concentrating on the *predecessors* of Shakespeare, Symonds suggests that the bloodlust of Elizabethan drama can be understood as a chronological factor, appropriate to its earliest phase. But the successors of Shakespeare show the same taste, quite unmitigated by the example of Master Will. Ravenscroft's rewrite of *Titus Andronicus* (1672×1686) did not reduce its horrors, but in fact increased them.   [5] *Shakespeare's Predecessors*, 387.

[6] The century of the horror movie and the gangster bloodbath shows that progress has not in fact done anything to modify the human taste for blood and guts.

[7] *Elizabethan Revenge Tragedy, 1587–1642* (Princeton, 1940).

wipe out the dishonour that is its consequence. The revenger then
has to undertake the exaction of a primitive justice. Elizabethan
society was, of course, one in which this duty was felt strongly:
centralized legality was only marginally able to control the sense
that an individual must respond in kind to violations of family
honour (male or female).[8] But the excitement that the duty of
revenge creates in the theatre operates far beyond Elizabethan confines. What is the *Oresteia* other than the story of Orestes' revenge
against the murderers of his father? Is not the *Bacchae* the story of
Dionysus' revenge against Pentheus? What of the many Western
films in which a good man returns to his homestead only to find
father, wife, daughter, son, murdered, kidnapped, raped, slaugh-
tered, by Indians, renegades, deserters, so that he is obliged to
shoulder the burden of individual revenge as the only honourable
course open to him, a course which imposes on him moral dilemmas that he cannot solve? The universality of the motif seems to
point us towards a human situation too basic to be confined to one
culture or outmoded by 'the progress of civilization'.

Not all these instances employ the same methods of embodying
the pattern. The classical exemplars impose on the human victims
the inexplicable malignity of the gods.[9] The Elizabethan and modern
ones, assuming a more optimistic theology, have to set up conditions of special deprivation, where normative assumptions about
human justice are abrogated. The protagonist can then be required
by his own ethos to enter into revenge's destructive element where
the only justice that can be achieved is one that destroys him along
with his enemies. The Western places its protagonist in a frontier
society where civil justice has broken down or has never been
established; yet it is a society contiguous to the audience's, though
separated from it, and committed to an ethos that the audience
accepts as an inevitable part of its own partly outgrown past. The
Elizabethan revenge dramatists place their action in times and
places more clearly divided from their own, in countries—Turkey,

---

[8] One of the fascinations of an 'Italian' world was that it provided, in imagination at least,
the image of a politically pluralistic and ethically individualist society in which religion
seemed not to forbid but rather to collaborate in the activities of the *condottiere*, the *bravo*,
the *stiletto*, the *vendetta*.

[9] Greville says ancient tragedies 'exemplify the disastrous miseries of man's life, where
Order, Laws, Doctrine and Authority are unable to protect Innocency from the exorbitant
wickedness of power, and so out of that melancholic vision stir horror or murmur against
Divine Providence' (*Life of Sir Philip Sidney*, ed. Nowell Smith (Oxford, 1907), 221).

Spain, Germany, and above all Italy[10]—seen to be in the grip of power establishments that lack the unified moral and legal system of England, and therefore lie wide open to what Bacon calls the 'wild justice' of revenge.

The Elizabethan revenger is often seen nowadays as no more than a homicidal maniac, and sometimes he is no more; but the revenger can be differentiated from the villain. The actions that a sense of justice imposes on the isolated individual revenger point to his divided duty. Opposite imperatives—to pursue individual justice and to avoid damnation (to kill and yet not to murder)— force on our attention the ethical paradox of the good man acting inside a bad society. Unlike the revenge scenario of the Western, where the hero is shown to be capable of rational, even if unethical, choices, the Elizabethan revenge play offers the alternatives of murder or submit to evil not simply as a social dilemma but as a religious and psychological one as well. The modern sentimentality of believing that the system of law can be strengthened by 'taking the law into one's own hands' could hardly be allowed in the sixteenth century, where the imperatives of the State seemed to reflect religious imperatives both awesomely remote and fully internalized. The contradictions of these inner and outer commands, when fully acknowledged, pointed towards madness.

Madness is, of course, a condition that appeared in classical tragedy. The madness of Ajax or of Agave, however, or of the Senecan victims of *Furor*, is an index of possession by powers alien to man but given unimpeded control of his mind. The Elizabethan madness of Hieronimo or Hamlet, on the other hand, or the lycanthropy of Ferdinand in *The Duchess of Malfi*, marks rather an unnatural fragmentation of consciousness, a liberation of integral aspects of the mind normally kept under control. The power exerted over us in the theatre derives less from the stark contrast between self and non-self (as when Hercules Furens, Agave, or Ajax suddenly see what they have done) than from the loss of boundaries between normal and abnormal, the extent to which hallucinations, dreams, or visions can come to seem natural extensions of everyday experience. Hence, of course, the interest of a stage madness that is balanced on the brink between intention and

---

[10] The anxious negotiation between legal responsibility and revenge in Chapman's *The Revenge of Bussy D'Ambois* presumably points to a perceived balance between these two in France.

helplessness, which may be a pretence, and may not be, as in the cases of Hieronimo and Hamlet, and Edgar in *King Lear* and Marston's Antonio. The power to 'tease us out of thought' in this way gives us an apprehension of madness not as the opposite of sanity but as an alternative mode of sanity, with its own acknowledged capacity to explain why the world is as it is, and why revenge is the suicidal action that seems alone to be capable of responding to it.

These incompatible but contiguous explanations of the sinful world are often presented as hoped-for present and abhorred past ('ere human statute purged the gentle weal'), reliance on blood revenge having been replaced by legal institutions. But human nature continued (and continues) to accept the force of both. In *The Spanish Tragedy* we are presented with two competing eschatologies: on one side the classical Hades which sends Andrea and Revenge back to earth to enjoy individual fulfilment, and on the other hand a biblical command, 'Vindicta mihi: ego retribuam', that forbids individual revenge. Which of these systems controls the social reality of the play? If the magistrates cannot do their duty (and Hieronimo is himself a magistrate), the patience commanded by the Bible is hard to find. Inevitably we travel in the same roller-coaster of hope and fear—a machine for evoking strong emotional response—as the protagonist; we see him forced into the wrong path (*hamartia*) but cannot see an ethical answer to his problem. An ending in which family honour is saved and the wicked are punished, in which the character who evokes the greatest sympathy outwits his enemies and accepts death as the proper price of triumph—this calms the mind, but leaves the ethical alternatives completely unsettled. Justice may be achieved, but only by undercutting the assumption that there is a natural moral process.

The pressure that Elizabethan assumptions imposed on the inherited revenge story is given clear expression in Thomas Goffe's *The Tragedy of Orestes* (*c*.1613×*c*.1618; printed 1633).[11] Goffe was an Oxford amateur who wrote plays to be 'acted by the students of Christ Church' (though his pastoral *The Careless Shepherdess*

---

[11] The matter seems to have been handled earlier not only at court in *Pickering's *Horestes* (see F. P. Wilson, *English Drama 1485–1585* (Oxford, 1968), 144–6) but on the public stage. In May 1599 Henslowe paid Chettle and Dekker for an *Agamemnon and Orestes Furious* and in June paid to have it licensed. It is not clear whether Henslowe's reference is to one play or two.

(1618×1629) was performed at the Salisbury Court playhouse by
Queen Henrietta's Men *c.*1638). But neither *Orestes* nor his two
Turkish tragedies (*The Courageous Turk* and *The Raging Turk*) can
be described as 'academic' or 'courtly' in any modern sense of these
words. What he has done in *Orestes* is to take the classical story
(derived from various sources but closest to Euripides' *Electra*) and
turn it into a tragedy of blood, a quasi-Senecan horror story with
fifteen characters, replete with witchcraft, ghosts, torture, infanticide, bowls of blood, madness, and adultery.

What is very relevant to the discussion here is the political
dimension Goffe adds to the story. After the murder of Agamemnon,
the main concern of the murderers, Aegisthus and Clytemnestra,
is to establish a new dynasty. Clytemnestra is soon pregnant, and
looks forward to the time when the inheritance is secured among
many heirs and the troublesome Orestes can be disposed of. But
Clytemnestra bears no more children. This allows Orestes to have
private access to the couple, posing as a physician who can assure
renewed fertility. His aim, of course, is just the opposite: to secure
the murder of their only son while the parents are forced to watch,
splashing their faces with the blood and so on. The fifth act shows
a further aspect of this political refocusing. After the revenge is
complete, Tyndareus, Clytemnestra's father, takes over the state
and, with the consent of 'the lords', exiles Orestes, Pylades, and
Electra. Orestes must be starved to death. But now room is found
for private virtue inside the political dispensation. Pylades cures
Orestes' madness and rescues his death from ignominy by arrang-
ing that the two friends should kill one another. And so the Epilogue can conclude that, in spite of 'vices contrived and murder's
punishment', there is 'no force so great, nor so disaster wrong | As
can unknit the bands which holdeth strong | United hearts' (sig.
I4). Only private virtue can rescue humanity out of the morass of
politics.

Orestes draws on both *Hamlet* and *Antonio's Revenge*, and perhaps Goffe could not see much difference between them. Like
Hamlet, Orestes is unhinged by the sight of his father's remains—
his skeleton in this case, as in Chettle's *Hoffman* (see pp. 435–6).
This is dug up for use in the necromantic spells which will allow
the dead Agamemnon to identify his murderers. And, like Hamlet,
Orestes talks wildly to his faithful companion of skulls and worms
and graves and epitaphs. As in *Hamlet*, the father returns to

whet his son's flagging purpose, but the occasion is as in *Antonio's Revenge*, III. iii, when the son proves reluctant to kill the pretty prattling child of the usurper.

The elder Hamlet would no doubt have preferred a son like Goffe's Orestes. His call for revenge (heard on stage before Shakespeare wrote his play (1600–1))[12] imposes the primitive duty of an eye for an eye and blood for blood; but his modernist son, though he begins with bloodthirsty enough threats, is soon caught in the same self-conscious double-bind of damned if you do and damned if you don't as is Hieronimo. Hamlet is not an officer of the law like Hieronimo, but his educated Humanist concern for civil proprieties commits him to the same duplicitous attitude to justice, though in terms which are psychological rather than biblical, raising less the issue of 'what can I do' and more that of 'How am I to understand what I have to do'. And again the denouement is one that satisfies without committing itself to a clear answer. The father's blunt demand and the son's refined ethical distress circle round one another in a process that is usually called 'delay'; but this delay is not simply, as in the sources, an interval in which we can enjoy the tricks and deceptions by which the revenger avoids detection, but rather a space in which the notion of revenge for honour is subjected to interrogations and transformations, until it finally fades into a Christian need to wait for God's prompting. In the scene of Claudius' prayer, Hamlet speaks with all the bloodthirsty commitment the primitive northern setting required. But he chooses not to kill the king, for reasons which eventually depend on Christian ideas of heaven and hell. The necessary action will be revealed to the protagonist when the time is ripe ('The readiness is all'), and the ripe time is when death is already known and accepted and the instrument put into his hand ('The point envenomed too! | Then, venom, to thy work' (v. ii. 321–2). It is only now that Hamlet can interpret his father's words in terms which are satisfactory to himself and to us (revenging a witnessed murder rather than revenging family dishonour), and not only kill Claudius but take command of the national ethic as the legitimate heir. But the heart of this final clarity of purpose remains a mystery—or, we might choose to say, an ambiguity that allows all the

---

[12] Lodge tells us in *Wit's Misery* of 1596 that he called out 'Hamlet revenge' . . . 'like an oyster-wife'.

frames of reference to be apposite. Hamlet instructs Horatio to
'tell my story', as if this would explain and justify what has happened. But Horatio explicitly denies continuity of purpose. He
speaks of 'accidental judgments, casual slaughters . . . purposes
mistook | Fall'n on th'inventors' heads' (v. ii. 382–5), as if the
whole action had been a chapter of accidents. And Fortinbras's
final judgement is equally askew. His praise of Hamlet as a soldier
tells us more about Fortinbras than about Hamlet.

   To discuss revenge tragedy in *The Spanish Tragedy* and *Hamlet*
is to present the genre in terms of its most profound explorations
—plays which might seem to have exhausted the potential of the
mode in its earliest years. To look forward, however, is to see deliberate transformation as well as decline, and to see also that *Hamlet*
differs from *The Spanish Tragedy* in ways which anticipate the shift
of fashion in the remaining years of the genre. Kyd's Spanish court
is a place of power, but without any particular ethical tone (the
failure to achieve justice is not to be blamed on any systematic
corruption in the palace). Ethical status is carried by individuals—
by Lorenzo, Balthazar, or Pedringano—not by the whole society in
which we find them, so that the final bloodbath looks arbitrary,
even meaningless. But Elsinore is given a characteristic tone that
pervades the lives of those who belong there: Osric, Polonius,
Rosencrantz and Guildenstern. It is 'an unweeded garden | That
grows to seed; things rank and gross in nature | Possess it merely'
(I. ii. 135–7). Hamlet, like Hieronimo, cannot find the justice that
will repair his loss of meaning. But where justice is a clear concept
for Hieronimo, requiring specific human actions, in *Hamlet* it is by
no means clear what actions can remove the smell of injustice that
is implicit in human nature, 'for virtue cannot so inoculate our old
stock but we shall relish of it' (III. i. 116–18), especially here, at
home, in the presence of aunt–mother and uncle–father, one of
whom must be killed and one restored to virtue. Hieronimo's
search is impeded by the manipulation of appearances; but in
Elsinore appearances are *naturally* deceptive. Here the revenger is
required to despise not only the villain but human nature in general, including his own. His mode of discourse becomes that of a
satirist.

   To bring *Hamlet* into relation to the tragedy closest to it in
structure and date (the children's *Antonio's Revenge* (see Chapter
7) is to find behind the complexities and intellectual sinuosities

of Shakespeare's play a basic structure, shared by the two plays, which provides a template for subsequent dramatists. They then could, without simply copying, change what was given by tradition into something new. I have spoken of Hamlet's disgust at the corruption of Elsinore. Yet the political evil of the state run by Claudius and Polonius is by no means established as an objective fact; we are left ambiguously poised between the private and public, between the 'sick' mind of Hamlet, who sees corruption everywhere, and the orderly efficiency of the Danish crown as enacted by Claudius in Act I, Scene ii.

There is none of this tantalizing ambiguity in *Antonio's Revenge*. Although Antonio reacts to his misfortunes in ways that are bizarre and unpredictable, there is no suggestion that he exaggerates the corruption he sees. The evil of this court is directly the consequence of the unbounded villainy of Piero, the tyrant who controls it. Claudius' sole ambition, as far as we can see, is to survive with his ill-gotten gains intact. If Hamlet could keep quiet, there would be no more murders. But Marston manages to combine the insatiable ambition of tyrant tragedy with a revenge action justified politically as tyrannicide. The mixture and the clarification of motive involved, with evil brought out of the shadow of personal guilt into the limelight of political ambition, provided imitators with a simpler model that could continue to generate theatrical success.

The Revenger's Tragedy (1606×1607)[13] is closer to the satirical plays of the boys' theatre (especially *Antonio's Revenge* and *The Malcontent*) than to most of the public-theatre plays considered here. Marston's plays are, however, too loose-jointed to bring the comparison close; their flashes of satirical brilliance are carried by a somewhat haphazard structure. Tourneur's structure, on the other hand, never loosens its grip. From the opening soliloquy, our vision is fixed on the objects of Vindice's revenge plot. Just how his intention will be fulfilled is not clear; we must wait for the members of the corrupt royal family to make the first moves and then rejoice in the cleverness by which Vindice can translate their desires into their destruction. Of course the range of the ducal family's possible moves is not large: lechery, hatred, and ambition sum up the motives available to them.

[13] The play is not assigned to any author in the first printing. In 1656 it is said to be by *'Tourneur' (later 'Cyril Tourneur'). Many now argue that it is the work of Middleton. It is, however, quite without the psychological realism of Middleton's tragedies.

The notional Italian dukedom where the action takes place is possessed by a Charles Addams-like family of moral grotesques: a duke who represents the 'parched juiceless luxur[y]' of sex-obsessed senility, a younger duchess, desperate both to find juicier flesh and to empower her own nasty brood (Supervacuo, the super-fluous man, Ambitioso, insanely 'desirous of honour',[14] Junior, the youngest, the wild boy of the family). Add to these Spurio, the duke's bastard, and Lussurioso, his lustful heir, each for his differ-ent reasons anxious to dispossess the others, and you have enough fissionable material to produce a final explosion when properly primed—not primarily aimed at politics, however, for there is no necessity that moral outrage point to political reformation.

Vindice, marginalized victim of this society (and so, as victim, a figure of virtue), carries a divided inheritance (like Hamlet and Hieronimo and Marston's Malcontent). He is both private moralist and public cynic. As an easy intimate of the language he finds around him (and so a 'right man . . . o'the time' (I. i. 94)) he is accepted as a natural agent in the ducal plots. His poetry of disgust serves not only to paint the scene but to paint himself into it as the enamoured relisher of its corruptions. In this we can see both the similarity and dissimilarity between Vindice and Hamlet.

Shakespeare gives the rhetoric of dispossession an appropriate place in a spectrum of alternatives. Hamlet's disgust with his mother and Ophelia is that of the categorizing scholar who seeks to impose meaning on the confused world around his individual system of simplifying contrasts. But in *The Revenger's Tragedy* Vindice's 'test-ing' of his mother and sister in Act II, Scene i imposes on them only the expectations of the whole society, 'for to be honest is not to be i'the world' (I. i. 95). His enthusiastic impersonation of a pander's rhetoric finds its both desired and feared consequence in his mother's agreement that it is sensible to press her daughter into well-paying prostitution—the combination of attitudes here offers us a preview of Webster's Flamineo and Bosola. And, as in Webster, the poetry here shows us a world of anti-human elements ferment-ing together to break down ethical distinctions. Human nature is seen as suffering continual transformation by the environment around it. There is continual exchange between the animate and inanimate: tempters 'open and unhusk' men; letters appear 'swelled

---

[14] The translations come from Florio's dictionary.

up with jewels', 'gold . . . will quickly enter into any man', 'stirring
meats' are 'ready to move out of the dishes', 'some stirring dish
was my first father', 'jewels [are] able to ravish [a woman] without
the help of man', 'daughters spring with the dew o'the court',
'woman [can be] changed into white money', and so on.

In such a world the notion of freedom is a romantic illusion.
The recurrent irony undercuts even the final gestures towards
moral stability. The revenge has destroyed the whole system and
the victims are now on top. But how could this have happened? The
news that virtue has been reinstated by treachery and murder is
greeted with horror by the politically correct. The virtuous do not
wish to know political facts. The dirty work done, the dirty workmen should die. Vindice and his brother accept the verdict with
cheerful cynicism, allowing that this moment is probably the best
that the world can offer ('our mother turned, our sister true; | We
die after a nest of dukes' (v. iii. 124–5)). We are left with a shrewd
suspicion that the virtuous will rule only until the next power-
hungry manipulator comes along.

Fletcher's *The Maid's Tragedy* (*c.*1608×1611; printed 1619), like
The Revenger's Tragedy, tells the story of a deprived lover's revenge against a lustful prince (this time a 'king' in some pseudo-
Lacedemonian state of indefinite date but modern manners). In
this case the king has destroyed the honour of the hero by requiring him to live as the titular husband of Evadne, the royal mistress,
and take responsibility for any bastards she may produce. The key
in which the narrative is set is, however, entirely different from
that of Tourneur's play. Here the poetry is used not to reflect
brilliantly on a world of teeming vice but to express the noble
suffering of individuals who are the victims of tyranny, yet see it as
embedded in a political system to which they give full assent, so
that they cannot (in honour) take action against it.[15] In *The Revenger's Tragedy* corruption finds its expression in sexual disorder. But
that, we are to understand, is only a synecdoche for a larger if
vaguer political malaise. In *The Maid's Tragedy* this implication is
avoided; disorder in the State is a political issue only because the

[15] Thomas Rymer's remark (*The Critical Works of Thomas Rymer*, ed. Curt Zimansky
(New Haven, 1956), 74) that only the quarrel between Amintor and Melantius saves the
play from mediocrity shows us (as does the widespread admiration for the quarrel scene in
Julius Caesar) the extent to which seventeenth-century audiences looked to tragedy for role
models of honour under stress (as in French and Spanish tragedies of the same period).

family vendetta is against the king; and that imposes a controversia-like paradox[16] of one kind of honour against another. The revengers, Amintor, the king's cuckold, and Melantius, brother to the king's mistress, are too self-consciously noble to condescend to the pranks and disguisings that allow Vindice and Hippolito (and the audience) to enjoy the transgressive cross-class ironies of their revenge action. Noble bewilderment and outrage (complemented by the lyrical sorrow of the cult figure[17] Aspatia—the *maid* of the title) are treated as individual emotional traumas which can only be escaped from by plot manipulation, as when Melantius uses his sword to persuade his sister that she is the appropriate revenger. Already tainted goods, she is a suitable scapegoat to carry the burden of regicide. Her death, following that of the king, is treated as if it presents a satisfactory balancing of the moral books. But the books are not really cleared until the honourable suicides of Melantius and Amintor complete the chain of challenges to the system.

Evadne is by far the most interestingly individualized figure in this ideologically confined tragedy, a complex woman of mature taste and experience set in a landscape of stock types and routine idealists. The great scene (to most modern tastes) is that in which she faces her adolescently eager husband with the dismissive contempt of one who already knows all the answers: 'A maidenhead, Amintor, | At my years?' (II. i. 93–4). Of course the play finds it necessary to punish her for such cynicism and to reduce her to a tearful penitent, hoping against hope that she can work her way back towards innocence. But the ethic does not allow that; only Aspatia is enabled to die blessed by remaining untouched, and can weep herself into sainthood. One is bound to wonder if the boy who played Evadne also played Cleopatra and Lady Macbeth, for the role has a similar, even if less well integrated, power. One waits for a modern actress of power and presence to create a sensation by giving the part the magnetism that it deserves.

On 31 October 1611 Sir George Buc (the Master of the Revels) gave his licence to a play which he called 'This second maiden's tragedy (for it hath no name inscribed)'. The play, now generally known as *The Second Maiden's Tragedy* (1611; MS) was thus seen

---

[16] See E. M. Waith (*The Pattern of Tragicomedy in Beaumont and Fletcher* (New Haven, 1952)) for the theatrical relevance of these rhetorical forms.

[17] See the repeated references to her in the poems set before the 1647 Beaumont and Fletcher Folio.

by the contemporary who was reading through the repertories of all the companies as a play parallel to Fletcher's *The Maid's Tragedy* (which had no doubt passed under Buc's eye in the preceding year). The elision of the two plays brings little credit to Buc's discrimination. The later play indeed contains a maid (called 'The Lady') who is lusted after by a tyrant (called 'The Tyrant'), a man who (like Fletcher's king) is given no interests other than his lust. But the smoothly managed complexity of Fletcher's play is nowhere in evidence. The author (sometimes thought to be Middleton—currently the favourite collecting box for unassigned plays) relies on melodrama to give colour to his episodic structure. The extremism of the situations—necrophily, ghostly prompting, 'quaint' methods of killing—come from the revenge tradition, but the motivations have little to do with revenge. The play is a celebration of the true love of the legitimate heir, who defends the lady against the usurping tyrant, and indeed agrees to kill her to preserve her honour. His passivity is broken only when her body is stolen from its tomb, and set up in the palace as a totem paramour. But by then the frenzy that promotes this arrangement has alienated the nobles, and they are happy to reinstate the legitimate prince.

The sideways slippage of the revenge motive, from *The Revenger's Tragedy* to *The Maid's Tragedy* to *The Second Maiden's Tragedy*, may serve as a model of the way in which traditions and conventions survive through change of priorities, moving centre to periphery (and vice versa). The idea of taking revenge does not hold together *The Maid's Tragedy* as it does *The Revenger's Tragedy*. The particularized role of the king in the former pushes the mood towards tyrant tragedy; the powerful role of the royal mistress anticipates those plays in which a commanding female figure imposes destructive realignment in the distribution of power (see pp. 466–78). One might say that *The Maid's Tragedy*, as it loses the intense continuity of its predecessors, compensates by a greater richness in competing frames of reference. *The Second Maiden's Tragedy* also deserves to be thought of as an eclectic work, but the traditions it handles do not catch fire as they touch one another. A 'revenge tradition' can be justified as an organizing principle for a large body of plays only if we are prepared to look for crosscuttings, overlaps, combinations, and allow that the power of the tradition lies in its incompleteness, its openness to reconstitution in different terms and from different angles.

The revenge plays I have dealt with here do, however, possess a common thematic interest that holds them together. Hieronimo must revenge a son killed for dynastic reasons; Orestes and Hamlet revenge the murders of the kings their fathers; Vindice must revenge the Duke's rape and murder of his betrothed; Amintor must take action against the king who has destroyed his manhood; Govianus, the hero of *The Second Maiden's Tragedy*, must kill the sex-crazed tyrant. In all these cases the action requires that an apparently stable political order be destroyed so that a quality of character be exposed and an individual crime be punished, a personal wrong be righted. Ethics is given an absolute priority. All these protagonists are young men whose need to destroy requires them to move from a marginal or detached position towards the centre which controls the political and moral ideology of their world. All have the idea of cleansing the State, but none of them operates in order to turn moral into political power; the anti-social route the revenger must take—backed by a solitary confidant (Pylades, Horatio, Hippolito, Melantius)—makes it impossible for him to look beyond the satisfactions of immediate personal action. To think of any of these men achieving stable compromise with the state apparatus would be to lose any sense of the total commitment that has given our emotions their focus.

Villain as Revenger

The need to take revenge to right a terrible wrong, and to do so with a broad sweep and with a passionate intensity that cannot stop to distinguish the innocent from the guilty—this easily slips into an ambition to destroy the political establishment even when no real personal wrong has been suffered, and so moves revenge tragedy towards villain tragedy. Tourneur's *The Atheist's Tragedy: or The Honest Man's Revenge* (1607×1611) is usually considered beside the other tragedy attributed to Tourneur—*The Revenger's Tragedy*— as yet another revenge play. And, of course, the subtitle supports this identification. Charlemont, 'the honest man', carries indeed the burden of revenging his father's murder; and, in keeping with the tradition, the fact of the murder is revealed to the son by the father's ghost. But, far from prompting revenge, the ghost forbids it:

Attend with patience the success of things
But leave revenge unto the King of Kings.

(II. vi. 21–2)

And the ghost does not even reveal the name of the murderer. The revenger is thus committed to passivity, to reaction rather than action, leaving the control of the play in the hands of D'Amville, the villain–atheist–murderer whose skilfully executed plots keep everyone under his control. In a balancing act between revenge tragedy and villain tragedy it is fairly clear that the weight of *The Atheist's Tragedy* falls on the villain side.

D'Amville, like Marlowe's Barabas, believes that gold is the only trustworthy source of felicity. Barabas is, however, mainly defined by his actions; D'Amville is more philosophically inclined (like a Chapman hero); his naturalist doctrine tells him that the here and now determines all and that the only future available derives from the children of one's body. So that, while Barabas in his counting house rejoices in his wealth for the power and pleasure it gives him, D'Amville in the same situation is more interested in confuting the standard positions, arguing that coins and not stars are the determinants that ensure family power. Charlemont, the honest revenger, is set up to be the opposite of all this: pious, honourable, and self-denying, leaving guidance entirely in the hands of God and perfectly prepared to leap onto the scaffold D'Amville has prepared for him, to embrace death as the gateway to heaven. The play is thus very clearly constructed as a *drame à thèse*. It is appropriate to this philosophic focus on the fate of individual souls that D'Amville should pursue his villainous courses not at a political but at a domestic level.

Most dramatists, however, leaving philosophy aside, found that politics provided a more tangible range of excitements. Chettle's *Hoffman*, and [Chapman's] *Alphonsus, Emperor of Germany*, deal with social worlds that differ little from those found in revenge plays proper; but these are not disoriented victims looking to recover the world as it 'ought' to be, but rather ambitious politicians seeking total power by fraud, deception, and murder. In both revenge and villain tragedies much of the excitement comes from the perpetual twists and turns of the plot as recognition is risked and evaded. And in this both forms come close to comedy. But the villain-hero is deprived of the close relationship to the victims that characterizes Hieronimo, Hamlet, Amintor, and Vindice. He is without the emotional volatility that comes from being placed between contradictory ethical demands; and so the weight of attention must be carried by the skill of his plot. The villain-hero must be endlessly inventive and resourceful, as smooth-tongued as ruthless. And these are exciting theatrical qualities on which Elizabethan playwrights could play endless variations.

Chettle's *The Tragedy of Hoffman: or Revenge for a Father* (which Henslowe paid for on 29 December 1602) shares obvious features with *Hamlet*. Once again a son is sunk in melancholy because of his failure to revenge his murdered father; the ingénue, like Ophelia, goes mad and comments on the events in mad songs; the potential heir, Jerome, has 'been at Wittenberg where wit grows'. But the play's devotion to villainy carries it in a very different direction. Hoffman's melancholy does not puzzle his will with moral conundrums, but rather allows him to 'plume up his will' by devising a string of ingenious deceptions and deletions, not simply of his father's enemies but of whole pages out of the Almanach de Gotha. And his father, it turns out, was no innocent victim, but a traitor to his country, executed after legal process. The obsession with revenge has produced here not a sorely troubled hero but a monster, not a revenger but a villain. The evil of the politics around Hoffman is the convenient fiction of a sick mind, incapable of interrogating, like Hamlet, the bases of its own beliefs. On the other hand, the Germany of this play offers little resistance to the insinuations and promptings to hatred that Hoffman employs. Marston's *Antonio's Revenge* had evoked an Italian anarchy of warring principalities, but these wars belong to the past or the future, and play no direct part in the drama set before us. In *Hamlet*, the wars between Denmark and Norway stand on the very edge of the play, almost as signs of a healthy exteriority. In *Hoffman*, however, the political chaos of the German states, tangled in dynastic calculations, incapable of coordination, now allied, now at enmity, provides a natural extension for the Gothic horrors of Hoffman's cave, set between the sea and

> the dismal'st grove
> That ever eye beheld. No wood-nymphs here
> Seek with their agile steps t'outstrip the roe:
> Nor does the sun suck from the queachy plot
> The rankness and the venom of the earth;

It seems frequentless for the use of men,
Some basilisk's or poisonous serpent's den.

(ll. 1999–2006)

The 'unweeded garden' of Hamlet's imagination has become a real place, home to the red-hot iron crown, the buried clothes, the hung-up skeletons of Hoffman's father and his first victim, and an external correlative for the protagonist himself.

In this use of German (or rather Imperial) politics as a natural seedbed for violent personal revenge, Chettle's play may be compared with *Alphonsus, Emperor of Germany*, said on the title-page to be by 'George Chapman, Gent.'[18]—a play of very uncertain date (printed 1654).[19] This offers a partly historical description of the interregnum in the Holy Roman Empire in 1251–73 when the Electors sold the crown to both Alphonso X of Castile and Richard of Cornwall (younger brother of Henry III of England). In the play the wicked Spaniard seeks to destroy the virtuous Englishman (and everyone else in the cast), on the basis of Machiavellian principles (set out at the beginning, as in the prologue to *The Jew of Malta*). With the aid of a tool villain (equivalent to Lorrique in *Hoffman*), Alphonso succeeds in building up a dizzying structure of betrayals and deceptions, playing the innocent and using the mutual suspicions of the Electors so that they perform like machines programmed to destroy one another. This is all handled with a sardonic pleasure in cleverness very different from the melancholy obsessiveness of Hoffman. But the plot is much the same: the tool villain betrays his master just when he is on the edge of total success. As it says in *The Malcontent*: 'two can keep counsel [only] when one is away.'

Lust's Dominion: or The Lascivious Queen (perhaps Henslowe's '*The Spanish Moor's Tragedy*', for which he paid Day, Dekker, and Haughton on 13 February 1600; printed 1657) shows most clearly the derivation of this kind of play from such earlier successes as *The Jew of Malta* and *Titus Andronicus*. Eleazer, the wicked Spanish Moor, stands, like Barabas and Aaron, on the margin of society

---

[18] The attribution has been ridiculed by all the editors. But the play is clearly not the work of a hack. It is full of detailed historical knowledge (about the Golden Bull, for example) and of accurate German dialect.
[19] The Epistle to the Reader tells us that the play was 'presented with all the elegance of life and action on the Blackfriar's stage'—a judgement hard to reconcile with the simplistic violence of the action.

because of the clearly marked fact of race. His motive, if he must be given one, derives from nothing as sympathetic as the loss of a loved relative but from the fact of marginalization itself. His route to the centre, like Aaron's, begins in the Queen Mother's bed. But the death of the King of Spain soon allows Eleazer's sexual authority to turn itself into political power. His skill in *Realpolitik* and his commanding energy allow him to outwit all his rivals. His success horrifies the establishment, but they cannot do anything about it. Like other heroes of this type, however, his pleasure in his own manipulative skill must carry him beyond his capacity. He wishes to play at the tortures of his next victims (as Jonson's Volpone and Middleton's Quomodo wish to play at being dead), but (as in their cases) the game turns out to be earnest. The self-dramatizing performer can escape from everything except the trap of his own plot.

Fletcher's *Thierry and Theodoret* (1613×1621) offers us another lascivious queen mother,[20] but with the variation that this time she is in control of her lovers, not their victim. Commanded to disband her court of letchers and panders, she retains independent power by playing her two royal sons one against the other, and in the space that this allows her she can take revenge on both sons and all others who seem to threaten her by their devotion to honour and justice. This is a version of the form that leaves little room for comic brio. Neither she nor her cowardly lover, who is the continual butt of soldierly derision (in typical Fletcherian scenes), is confident enough to enjoy the comedy of success. Disgust seems to be the appropriate emotion.

Revenge Motives and Heroic Loss

The great dramatic utility of a revenge motive is the strength it gives to denouement, when the purpose that has wound its way through the labyrinth of delays and reformulations emerges in clear statement, when Hieronimo reveals the murdered Horatio, when Hamlet kills Claudius, when the identity of Hoffman is revealed to the rest of the cast. A great many of the plays that are often called revenge tragedies have no more than this to justify the title. But

---

[20] Another example can be found in William *Heminges's *The Fatal Contract* (*c*.1638× ?1639; printed 1653).

there is a sophisticated version of the revenge plot proper (that is, where revenge fuels the action from the beginning) in which the fact that we are watching a revenge is hidden from us for most of the play. And in such cases our attention is focused not on the closing of the trap but on the intended victim, whose guilt cannot be exposed as the motive of the story and whose death must therefore be construed as a tragic loss.

Massinger's *The Duke of Milan* (1621×1623)[21] seems for most of the action to be a play of high-toned romance and courtesy. Lodovico Sforza, Duke of Milan, is devoted to love and honour, to an extreme degree. He worships his wife Marcelia and she responds with equal fervour. His clear-eyed sense of both his worth and his fragility converts the Emperor Charles V[22] from enmity to esteem. His trust in his favourite, Francisco, is equally absolute and unconditional, and when he leaves to make his surrender to Charles, he entrusts him with secret instructions to kill Marcelia and save her from rape, in the event that he is executed and the Spaniards sack Milan. But Francisco is in fact his dedicated enemy. Long before the play's opening Lodovico was betrothed to Francisco's sister, but abandoned her when Marcelia appeared. Francisco's presence in court, and his careful cultivation of persons of power, are all part of a probing investigation of the weaknesses that will allow him to destroy Lodovico and his wife. His plot is accurately designed to fit the temperament of his victim: once take away the source of idealism in love and his moral and political powers will wither. Like Othello, Lodovico kills his wife in a frenzy of frustrated love, but Massinger, unlike Shakespeare, relies on melodrama (taken out of the story of Herod and Mariamne) rather than consequences of character to explain the denouement. Lodovico, discovering what he has done, is now bent on self-destruction, and has to be brought under control by the pretence that Marcelia is not really dead. Now he dotes on her corpse and no one dares tell him the truth. It only remains for Francisco to paint Marcelia's face with poison (a device found also in *The Revenger's Tragedy*

---

[21] The plot device of the hidden revenge appears also in Massinger's *The Unnatural Combat* (1624×1625; printed 1639), but this time in a much darker handling. There the shadow of undefined criminal action in the past (incest in fact) hangs over the central character and finally erupts in long-pondered vengeance.

[22] Massinger has telescoped the historical Lodovico's defeat by the French with Francesco Sforza's much later defeat, surrender, and reinstatement by Charles V.

and *The Second Maiden's Tragedy*) and Lodovico's physical destruction will follow his moral collapse.

Massinger's moral is that 'There's no trust | In a foundation that is built on lust'—a view enlarged by Gifford's Johnsonian rhetoric into 'He who aims at intemperate gratifications disturbs the order of providence; and in the premature loss of the object he too fondly covets, is made to feel the just punishment of unreasonable wishes'.[23] This is certainly one side of the story being told.[24] But the intemperance of Lodovico that makes him open to disaster can also be called magnanimity. His final frenzy belongs to the same absoluteness of temperament as does his calm acceptance of death when he faces Charles.

To see *Othello* (*c*.1603×1604) beside *The Duke of Milan* is to recognize the extent to which both plays are tragedies of loss structured as revenges, and therefore lack the apparatus of external horror (ghosts, cries of *Vindicta*, torture, infanticide) that are often taken to be the hallmarks of the genre. The action of *Othello* is certainly motivated and controlled by the intention to take revenge, made clear to us in the opening lines of the play and carried forward unremittingly to the end. Of course the original insult (preferring Cassio to Iago) is only a starting-point in the trail of destruction. But it is a characteristic of the revenge play (as in *The Spanish Tragedy*, *Hamlet*, and *The Revenger's Tragedy*) that passion, once aroused, can hardly be stopped short of a massacre. Iago's bent to destruction has less external justification, of course, than we find in any of these other plays. He carries us back to the stereotype behind the revenger, to the Vice of the Moralities, whose impulse to evil is free of any moral or political self-justification.

This does not mean that Iago is dehumanized as a stage devil. 'I look down towards his feet', says Othello, but immediately corrects the fantasy that he is the devil: 'but that's a fable' (v. ii. 286). Iago's motivations belong clearly enough to a recognizable human type (like the arsonist evoked in the opening scene, finding power and

---

[23] *The Plays of Philip Massinger* (4 vols.; London, 1813), i. 347.

[24] Gifford's censure would be more appropriate if levelled at Davenant's first play, *The Tragedy of Albovine* (1626×1629)—perhaps never acted—and the difference between this play and Massinger's points to its limitation as a critique. Albovine is not only an enslaved lover but a brutal conqueror. When drunk he forces his adored wife to drink out of a cup made from her father's skull. This sets in train not only a refusal of conjugal rights (followed by extremes of penitence and self-abasement) but a general collapse of authority, multiple poisonings, and a plot to restore the state to its former rulers.

pleasure in seeing others suffer, especially those believed to be
superior or even invulnerable). These deeply embedded psychological traits allow Iago to operate (like Massinger's Francisco)
inside the immediate family of those he will destroy. But this time
we know what he is aiming at: we are complicit in the process by
which the structure of beauty is eaten away. This accounts for
much of the claustrophobic force of *Othello*.

Othello is a great general caught up in recent European history
(like the aptly comparable Lodovico il Moro); he is governor of
Cyprus and defender of Christendom, but his personal life is conducted without any of the external grandeur and distancing ceremoniousness of Massinger's Duke and Duchess (surrounded as
they are by the backbiting and sycophantic apparatus of an absolutist court). Shakespeare's emphasis thus exposes ethical qualities
uncontaminated by social explanations. Othello's grandeur depends
on an abolition of the distinction between public and private, a
complete transparency of nature that not only allows but expects
every aspect of behaviour to be known ('I must be known' is his
answer to Iago's advice that he should hide from the charges
Brabantio has brought against him). This unperturbed magnanimity, as it appears in his self-presentation before the Senate, inevitably reminds us of the magnanimity manifested in Lodovico's
appearance before Charles V. Othello is, however, a man without
secrets; he operates everywhere with openness and immediacy,
with a total giving of himself to the person and the situation. His
extraordinary romantic aura, manifested in the golden cadences of
his poetic utterance, derives from a simplicity of nature, a lack of
self-analysis that Rymer[25] (followed at some distance by Eliot and
Leavis) thinks appropriate to a 'booby'. It is indeed part of his
tragedy that the charge has so much to support it. His situation is
made to overlap with the reductive comedy of the imaginary cuckold, so that he becomes a caricature of himself, hiding and spy-
ing, rolling his eyes and groaning with false surmise, being 'led by
the nose | As asses are'. He must endure the idea that he has
become not only despicable, being old and black and ignorant, but
necessarily so. Yet, as he says, this is by no means the bottom of
the pit:

---

[25] *The Critical Works of Thomas Rymer*, ed. Curt Zimansky, 154.

Yet could I bear that too, well, very well;
But there, where I have garnered up my heart,
Where either I must live or bear no life;
. . . .
to be discarded thence!

(IV. ii. 56–60)

The bottom of the pit is the discovery that beneath the social
disgrace, the scorn of men, lies the loss of all meaning, a loss of
sustaining faith which, as Rymer pointed out, might well make us
'repine and grumble at Providence' and deny salvation ('if this be
our end, what boots it to be virtuous?'[26]). Iago achieves a revenge
like those in which the victim is forced to forswear belief in God
and then stabbed before he can recant, so falling immediately into
eternal damnation.[27] But in this case, even more terribly, the victim is persuaded to accept this as his proper end.

Lodovico's determination to take revenge on himself for the
murder of his wife is a public act made in the midst of his admiring
courtiers, while he is still the linchpin of the state. Their continuing hope for his recovery is cut short only by his assassination. But
Othello has no such supports. As an 'extravagant and wheeling
stranger' he has passed from country to country and has been
given identity not by attachment to a social network but by the
inner radiance of a self-sufficiency that was breached only when
he finally found his home, his spiritual reflection, in the love of
Desdemona. The wondrousness of that connection turns out to be
also the fatal point of his vulnerability.

In what we think of as the standard revenge plot, the relation
between revenger and victim is defined by preprogrammed opposition. Their actions are those of chess pieces, alternately attacking
and defending (or attacking in order to defend). Their moves are
conditioned by the need to destroy before being destroyed. And
this is the relationship between Hamlet and Claudius, Orestes and
Aegisthus, Vindice and Lussurioso, Hieronimo and Lorenzo. Iago's
aim, however, is not so much to destroy Othello as an enemy as to
take over his mind so that (like the vampire's victim) he is turned
into a replica, a duplicate revenger, jealous, obsessive, secretive,
cynical, the naturalized inhabitant of an underworld where heroic
love has assumed the lineaments of a sex comedy. One can imagine

[26] Ibid. 161.   [27] See e.g. Nashe, *The Unfortunate Traveller* (McKerrow, ii. 326).

that what would give Iago the greatest satisfaction would be to make Othello into a figure like Spenser's Malbecco, a self-lacerating cuckold, unable to live with himself but unable to put an end to his torment ('solamen miseris socios habuisse doloris', is Mephistopholis' explanation of the purposes of Hell). But this is beyond even Iago's powers. Othello does what his manipulator requires, but does it in terms that reflect his own standards, the standards of love and justice (in this reminding us of Hamlet's acceptance of the role of minister rather than scourge, relying finally on Providence rather than his father's instructions). And as in *Hamlet* and *The Spanish Tragedy* (and, with appropriate differences, in *The Revenger's Tragedy*), the catharsis comes about not so much because the evil one is unmasked and punished, but because his victim can discover again who *he* is, dedicated to death but standing above it in the clarity of his knowledge why it has to be thus.

The Heroism of Love

Othello can be called a villain tragedy given that the villain has most lines and controls the twists of the plot with the same dizzying skills as Eleazer or D'Amville. But our central attention is given here not to the victimizer but to the victim, for this play shows us the destruction not of a political establishment or an extended family but of a heroic figure whose power must be defined in ethical not political terms. It is the glamour of Othello's nobility that commands our identification, reinforced as it is throughout the action by the supportive nobility of those around him, the Duke of Venice, Desdemona, Cassio. It is the incapacity of the world to sustain nobility in the face of supposed facts that gives the sense of loss a central place in our response.

The Tragedy of Loss depends for its effect on the creation of figures of great appeal who need not, should not, die, but who are overcome, not so much by a 'tragic flaw' (that curious Victorian derivative from Aristotle's *hamartia*), as by the situation their very greatness has created. In *Othello* and (to a lesser extent) in *The Duke of Milan* the glamour of nobility reveals itself centrally in love, the most personal and therefore the most fragile of emotions, though in a great public figure the emotion must affect and be responded to by a large population of onlookers. Shakespeare is the prime dramatist of romantic love in this period, in tragedy no less than comedy. Outside Shakespeare the idea of love as an emotion able to define greatness and to defy the hunger for power and honour most often appears as a golden dream, an unsustainable illusion. The popular story of the beautiful Irene makes the point with brutal clarity: a powerful warrior king (usually Turkish) is so overcome by love that he forgets all the qualities that have given him his power; but faced by discontent in the army he arranges a ceremony in which he smites off the head of his beloved and so proves his undiminished magnanimity. The widespread diffusion of the story[28] indicates the extent to which it reflects a standard view of love as the solvent of nobility and at the same time indicates the extreme methods necessary to escape from it. Indeed, even in Shakespeare there is pressure everywhere to reveal love as a diversionary idealism in a real world driven by competition for power. In *Troilus and Cressida* passionate adolescent idealism proves incapable of facing absence or dishonour. *Othello* shows love capable of withstanding these tests, but not the destruction of the self that loves. *Antony and Cleopatra* does not show love and greatness to be incompatible, as in the Irene story, but as fatally compromising. Only *Romeo and Juliet* (1594×1596), not only in Shakespeare but throughout Elizabethan drama it would seem, offers love as a value that can triumph over all the oppositions society can raise against it. It is presumably no coincidence that this is a tragedy set against the standard background of romantic comedy, Italian civic life. *Romeo and Juliet* presents the innocence of adolescent desire as the discovery of selves that can exist without reference to the social world around them, a world that the Duke, the parents, the street gangs, all cooperate to maintain as an essentially stable balance of terror.

Shakespeare sets against this continuum the lovers' 'death-marked' spontaneity of response, designed not to challenge the power of the community but to transcend it. The structure of the play is very simple (as befits the emotions at its centre). Love is set against hate, youth against age, the personal against the social, the idealistic against the practical, the poetic against the prosaic, the

---

[28] It appears in the Bandello, Belleforest, and Painter collections of *novelle*. Its first appearance in Elizabethan drama is in Peele's lost play *The Turkish Mahomet and Hiren the Fair Greek* (1581×1594). It is also found in Goffe's *The Courageous Turk* of 1618, in Carlell's *Osmond, the Great Turk* (1622×c.1638), and, applied to Canute, in *Brewer's *The Lovesick King* (1607×?1617). Further dramatizations appeared in 1658, 1664, and 1708. The most celebrated version is Samuel Johnson's *Irene*, performed in 1749. In 1611 William Barksteed published a narrative poem on the topic.

innovative against the repetitive. What we watch is an increasingly desperate attempt to survive between these oppositions. The attempt has to be desperate, for both Romeo and Juliet are powerless youngsters, embedded in society, Juliet in her family, Romeo in the code of honour required by his manhood and his tribal identity. Comparison with the source text—Arthur Brooke's *Tragical History of Romeus and Juliet* (1562)—allows us to see how Shakespeare manages to secure the audience's assent to the absolute value of love. Brooke presents the story from the point of view of a narrator who (like other authors of the 'complaint' genre) knows (and tells) ahead of time what happens to high hopes and rash promises. Shakespeare, of course, does not deny the rashness of a commitment to love, but at the same time he expends his full poetic power to dazzle us with the rapture of its rewards. And he convinces us to go with the rapture by allowing us to participate in the discovery of new language for new selves at the very moment they are being discovered. Romeo and Juliet are caught up (as we are) into the pleasures of a poetry that lifts them out of the day-to-day contingencies of the plot, a poetry in which they (and we) discover that Petrarchan tropes can become real experiences.

The transcendent quality of such poetry, such love, together with the coincidences used to hold the plot together, are sometimes taken to show *Romeo and Juliet* as a 'weak' tragedy of chance[29] in which suffering and evil are not internal but external, and continually compromised by self-assurance that the choices made are not only inevitable but right; thus love screens the protagonists from the truth of human complicity in the evil done. The poetry here does indeed give those without social power a sustaining inner strength that allows them not only to defy their environment but eventually to impose their own values on it.

Romeo and Juliet suggests that a noble willingness to die for love can force the State to look at its practices by the light of individual experience, to see its closed routines from the tragically open perspective of individual life. Ford's *'Tis Pity she's a Whore* (1629×1633) repeats the *Romeo and Juliet* scenario of individual lovers refusing to be bound by the busy pettiness of Italian bourgeois life, where fathers are anxious to provide good husbands for their daughters, and the oppressed young people are caught between the antithetical

---

[29] See A. C. Bradley, *Shakespearean Tragedy* (London, 1904), 15.

advice of Nurse and Friar. Above all, Ford returns us to the child-like innocence and guilt-free sensuality of the lovers. But, if his Giovanni and Annabella are 'innocent', it is with the savage innocence of some pre-moral condition. Where *Romeo and Juliet* used the Italian setting to remind us of the ease with which the action could have been moved to a comic conclusion, Ford's Italy reminds us of the unconstrained ferocity of Italianate tragedy. The only intrusion of laughter in Ford's play comes from the harsh Middletonian handling of the simple-minded suitor, Bergetto, stabbed by mistake and allowed only comic death throes.

Intensity of erotic passion, making every other kind of loyalty insignificant, imposes an obvious claim on audience sympathy. By making the love incestuous, Ford has, however, created a counter-current equally violent, equally uncompromising, and raised a conflict of total commitments, not simply (as in *Romeo and Juliet*) between love and an already devalued system of family honour, but between whole belief systems that no kindly friar can hope to bring to compromise. Ford's Friar is given a powerful doctrinal presence and a well-focused rhetoric, not designed to comfort but to spell out the stark choice between fulfilling damnation and trivializing conformity—a choice more like that of Dr Faustus than of Juliet.

For all the circumscription of their contact, Romeo and Juliet can invite us to share in the relaxed sense of fulfilment given by their love. The poetry of Ford's Giovanni and Annabella is fierce, appetitive, haunted, always running pleasure against the grain. And that too, in its own way, frees them from fear by giving them a lurid superiority to all the striving and cross-plots with which the play is crammed. When Annabella's husband discovers that she is already pregnant, she is as contemptuous of his insane anger and physical violence as Juliet is of her Nurse's merely commonplace advice to marry again. It is only when the Friar has been able to reach into Annabella's soul that she begins to consider Hell and punishment, to 'grow up' we might say (Ford cannot be as sure as Shakespeare that innocence is a virtue). Giovanni, on the other hand, as the trap closes around him, becomes more confident in the oppositional identity he has chosen and in the love which confirms it. His famous last entry with Annabella's heart on his dagger comes like that of an infernal visitant who arrives to warn the feasters that Hell is in their midst. But of course Giovanni comes not from Hell but from the middle of this petty-minded

society, as an anti-self that belongs to it but which the onlookers
refuse to recognize as the shadow their own fumbling appetites
have created. Their blindness, set against his terrifying clarity of
vision, destabilizes the standard moral distinctions, so that the
terror of evil counterpoints but does not obliterate the pathos of
loss. The reward of seeing 'God's revenging aspect upon every
particular sin' (in Greville's phrase[30]) has to be set against the
sacrifice of the city's least compromised inhabitants.

Love, as a transforming and destructive power, is, in both
Romeo and Juliet and *'Tis Pity She's a Whore*, set against the careful
stability that social continuity requires. Ford's *The Broken Heart*
(1625×1633) shows us the same opposition between personal choice
and social requirements, but it does so without either the buoyant
optimism that gives Shakespeare's play its universal appeal or the
lurid melodrama of *'Tis Pity She's a Whore*. In this play the lovers
are not intent on defying the prevailing social norms, but on the
contrary are determined to fulfil them to the letter, even if that
means the destruction of self. The loss of love is regarded here as
simply the price that must be paid for the continuity of the state.
Ford's Sparta is a civilization sustained in power and independence by the iron self-control of its citizens. But self-control easily
destroys personal hope and so the wish to live: loss of love turns
into the loss of political will. The nobility of these characters is
shown not by their rhetorical power of self-expression (as in the
case of Othello) but by their denial of the usual continuities between inner feelings and their outer manifestation (Penthea's
'divorce betwixt my body and my heart' (II. iii. 57)). Ithocles has
required his sister Penthea to divorce her contracted husband
Orgilus and marry the mean-minded Bassanes. Penthea and Orgilus
cannot permit themselves to object to this by word or action; they
accept their original contract as totally binding: their feelings are
unchanged, but their lives are destroyed. Penthea can only look
forward to death by starvation, and Orgilus, contemplating that,
must condemn himself by taking revenge against Ithocles, who is,
in every respect but this, the man he most cherishes and admires.
And Ithocles must accept the revenge as a proper response to the
personal damage he has done. But the fulfilment of that propriety
means that Ithocles is no longer there to preserve the state.

---

[30] *Life of Sidney*, ed. Nowell Smith (Oxford, 1907), 221.

The famous scene in which Calantha, the princess of Sparta, continues her formal wedding dance as news of one disaster after another is brought to her ear—and only later, at the point of death, reveals that her heart has been broken since she heard the news of Ithocles' death—may be taken as a model of the whole play. Nobility demands loss, as what is noble in human nature must be accommodated to destiny and the oracle of the gods; the human puppets who are its instruments achieve their nobility by exercising their only freedom—the freedom to choose obedience, to restrain passion, to accept the mystery without repining.

Love tragedy makes an implicit claim that the lovers' golden dream of liberation gives them a hold on values that subsequent loss cannot obliterate. In *Romeo and Juliet*, society seems to accept this claim; in *'Tis Pity She's a Whore* the claim is flaunted, but society rejects it; in *The Broken Heart* the claim fades as soon as it is uttered: the good of the state has been incorporated into Spartan sensibilities so completely that self-denial becomes the immediate fulfilment of self-assertion. The result is that a state whose virtue depends entirely on individual ethics is unable to survive.

Massinger's *Believe As You List* (1631; MS) is not a love tragedy, but the glamour of Antiochus, the exiled king it deals with, depends on the evocation of a world of golden relationships, not unlike those of love (as if Antony had chosen not to die but to escape and live on with the memories of what he had lost—memories in which love and political greatness interpenetrate). Antiochus, however, is never given (like Antony) the rapturous assurance of a partner in glamour that death will validate his life's meaning. He is subjected to the judgement of history that defeat is not loss but failure, and we are made to understand that this is part of an inevitable historical process, as the grand individual is squeezed out by the Roman political machine.[31] Massinger's play was originally intended to be about Dom Sebastian, King of Portugal, defrauded of his inheritance by Philip II (that universal ogre) and therefore to the English a victimized hero. Sebastian was killed at

---

[31] A parallel pattern appears in Chapman's *The Tragedy of Chabot, Admiral of France* (1611–?1622; ? revised by Shirley 1635). More laborious, less glamorous than Antiochus, Chabot is the victim of a reckless devotion to justice, which he defends even in the face of the king's opposition. The king, presented as a good man, wishes to correct this extremism and allows enemies to prosecute Chabot. They succeed in twisting the evidence in his disfavour. The king immediately pardons him and punishes the twisters, but the shock of discovering that the social system does not endorse his political idealism kills the old man.

the Battle of Alcazar in 1578, but claims of pretenders who hawked their stories of survival across Europe were widely entertained, and Massinger no doubt relied on these to construct a plot likely to excite audience sympathy. But the censor thought the matter too 'dangerous' for the stage (that is, too close to current politics). Massinger was forced to rewrite it as a story about 'Antiochus' (based partly on the real Antiochus the Great (223–187 BC) and partly on Hannibal's career after his defeat at Zama in 202 BC— when he was the guest of Antiochus). The plot and most of the dialogue seem to have survived the change of historical reference without radical rewriting. We see the defeated monarch, recovered from his defeat, calling on the help of the clients and friends he favoured in his time of power, only to discover that magnanimity and probity are no match for political astuteness backed by an efficient military machine. The play is thus an elegiac treatment of a poetic past overtaken by a business present, in this like *Richard II*. But unlike Richard's, Antiochus' is a wholly personal tragedy. As in Ford's *Perkin Warbeck* (see Chapter 6), the claimant is given a sweeping rhetoric that convinces his hearers of his royal status. But where the history play's political focus allows us to wonder if we are dealing with anything more than rhetorical facility, in *Believe as You List* the remoteness of the historical consequences allows noble utterance to be understood as the natural outflow of a noble nature, and refusal to believe in him becomes a sign of narrow political self-interest.

Perkin Warbeck allows its pretender to die still comforted by loyalty and dignity (in this distorting the sources). Henry VII must ensure that this threat to his throne is removed, but Perkin is only one of his concerns. Titus Flaminius, the Roman general assigned to the task of hunting down Antiochus and destroying him, is an even more rigid automaton of duty, without a hint of feeling for the noble victim he has entrapped. Half the play is devoted to his unrelenting effort to force Antiochus—by bribery, by torture, by proffers of love, by starvation, by public ridicule, by years as a galley slave—to admit that he is an impostor. Only in the final scene, when the Roman aristocrats, Marcellus and Cornelia, recognize the man who was once their patron, is there any indication that the history of world conquest is compatible with a noble sense of loss. And even they can only protect Antiochus from shame, not from imprisonment and execution.

The Roman Scene

The Rome that we meet in *Believe as You List* is a Rome powered by an unwavering determination to force its suzerainty on the world. To Flaminius, Antiochus has no status other than that of an impediment in the way of manifest destiny. Republican virtue (here as in *Coriolanus* (1608)) finds justification for its narrow intensity in a vision of unquestionable superiority leading to inevitable conquest—a vision in which the glamour of personal relations can play no part. But, as even Coriolanus discovers, the demands of State must face the demand for love; the great man must lose, on one side or the other. The events of Rome's transition from Republic to Empire seem to have made their appeal to dramatists in part at least because they opened up so clearly these contradictions between heroic self-definition and political success, as found in the lives of Julius Caesar, Marcus Brutus, Octavius Caesar, Mark Antony, Marcus Cato, and Gnaeus Pompeius. In Shakespeare's career we can see his turn from English history to Roman tragedy as one which allowed the definition of 'the great man' to be understood in a wider frame of reference. Shakespeare's eight interconnected plays on English history had merely skirted tragedy because the continuity of history up to his own time ruled out any sense of irrecoverable loss. In these plays the system always tends to exceed its representatives: the king might die, but the State goes on. Roman history showed the individual mind facing a more open set of possibilities (senates, consuls, tribunes, dictators) that led back to individual choice and could not be so easily offloaded on to Fortune or other external cause. English history had to carry a burden of teleology; the past had to be seen in terms of what it led to. But Roman history was over; since it was not open to Elizabethan Englishmen to suppose that its legacy was fulfilled in the Papacy or the Holy Roman Empire, it had to be assumed that the end was not fulfilment but an understanding of the conditions within which the search for fulfilment was conducted. On the other hand, the open politics of Roman tragedy (especially in Shakespeare's handling) allows the action to stay close enough to history to screen out the melodrama of inexplicable evil.

Thus the tragedy of greatness in *Julius Caesar* (1598×1600) and *Antony and Cleopatra* (1606×1608) is focused not by the plotting of villains but by the endemic contradiction between personal loyalties and political power. Shakespeare, however, does not take the contradiction, but rather the free play of mind that acknowledges it, as his centre of interest. In these terms Brutus (as is often remarked) comes close to Hamlet: both are men caught in ethical dilemma, and must act for the State at the same time as they act for themselves. But, where Hamlet is driven by a perception of personal evil, Brutus, like other Roman heroes, responds primarily to political threat ('I know no personal cause to spurn at him | But for the general' (II. i. 11–12)). Can Brutus live up to his own standards if he does not enter into the political maelstrom that will destroy these standards? How can Antony succeed as both the great lover and the great general, yield himself to the 'infinite variety' of love and yet dominate the world by his dependability, imperturbability, consistency, and so 'hold this visible shape my knave'?[32]

In both cases tragic greatness comes from the determination not to evade the impossible contradiction that greatness has created. However, historians of Rome and dramatists responding to their perceptions were by the beginning of the seventeenth century becoming increasingly fascinated not so much by the ethical choices inside political turmoil as by the power of politics to abolish choice (and so the opportunity to show personal greatness). The *tacitismo* of seventeenth-century Europe can be seen as a response to the failure of Humanist political idealism, as an increased acceptance that morals and politics are separable spheres.[33] An earlier view had seen State power as the only possible guarantor of virtue. The Roman republic was defined in the title-page of William Fulbeck's *A Historical Collection of the Continual Factions of the Romans' Wars* (1600) as the scene of 'Continual Factions, Tumults and Massacres . . . during the space of 120 years next before the peaceable empire of Augustus Caesar'; and this yielded 'the evident demonstration that people's rule must give place and prince's power

---

[32] *Coriolanus* presents another moment of historical transition in which the status of the hero focuses the contradictions in the State. Is Coriolanus to be admired as a Roman warrior and hero, or feared and hated as an enemy to civilized society (thus returning us to questions present in *Titus Andronicus*)? This is not raised in *Coriolanus*, however, as a question to be debated by the hero but left as one that history will dispose of.

[33] See G. Toffanin, *Machiavelli e il Tacitismo* (Naples, 1921); Peter Burke, 'Tacitism in Tacitus', in T. A. Dorey (ed.), *Tacitus* (New York, 1969); J. G. A. Pocock, *The Machiavellian Moment* (Princeton, 1975), 350–7.

prevail' (as the title-page of W.B.'s translation of Appian (1578) declared). Tacitus had showed (in the strange event that experience failed to) that 'prince's power' does not always promote morality, and the notes of his commentators, particularly those of Justus Lipsius, brought the point up to date. Lipsius notes that the consequence of centralized power is more likely to be 'flattery, denunciations and other ills, not unknown in our age . . . you will find repeated charges of treason, the only crime that can be charged against those who are free of crime.'[34]

History offered to Renaissance writers a conspectus of the world in which long viewpoints allowed the reader to know the ambiguity of any story of political success. Should the period of the transition from the Republic to the Empire be described as one that moved from anarchy to order or from freedom to tyranny? The drama of the time allows us to see well the play of alternatives that the subject opened up. Two works of the 1590s, the academic *Caesar and Pompey: or Caesar's Revenge* (*c.*1592×*c.*1596); printed ?1607), 'privately acted by the students of Trinity College in Oxford', and Shakespeare's *Julius Caesar* make ambiguity the issue. The academic work, taken mostly from Appian's *Civil War*, is the more old-fashioned, presenting history inside the technique of *The Mirror for Magistrates*: Fortune rules all. Discord appears as a chorus (surrounded by 'flashes of fire') and gloats over the turn in Fortune's wheel: 'Let Rome, grown proud with her unconquered strength | Perish and conquered be with her own strength' (ll. 33–4). It appears that no one in particular is responsible for this. Caesar defeats Pompey; he grieves to do it but Pompey must die. The wheel turns again: now Caesar is at the top; but Brutus and Cassius are waiting for him. Brutus congratulates himself on his tyrannicide; Antony and Octavian, whetted on by the ghost of Caesar, prepare to do battle. Brutus and Cassius regret the measures they have had to take to raise their armies. But the unforgiving ghost of Caesar is waiting for them at Philippi. Discord rejoices in the slaughter. And we already know that Antony and Octavian are at odds. Soon there will be more corpses for Discord to gloat over. Though characters in this play consistently regret the actions taken, they are forced to act in accord with historical necessity:

[34] Invenies sub tyrannide adulationes, delationes, non ignota huic saecula mala . . . frequentatas acusationes maiestatis, unicum crimen eorum qui crimine vacabant (dedication of his 1574 edition of Tacitus' *Annals* to Maximilian II).

Caesar bewails the slaughter at Pharsalia, pardons Brutus, punishes Pompey's murderers, refuses to be king. Yet his career moves consistently forward to total power. Brutus wishes to retreat from action, and acts only to save liberty. At Philippi the conspirators die out o mistaken loyalty to one another. But virtue must yield to Forture, as Cato tells us; history reveals only the irrelevance of ethical judgement to the pattern of events.

By choosing Plutarch's lives of Caesar and Brutus as his principal sources for *Julius Caesar*, Shakespeare inevitably makes character, not Fortune, the determining factor in the choices of politicians. Contradictory impulses in the main characters of *Caesar's Revenge* revealed only their paradoxical relation to determinist history, but they now appear as free-standing qualities of temperament: Cassius is both a tempter and a genuine lover of liberty; Antony is loyal to Caesar and intent on using his death to improve his own position; Caesar sees himself as already a demigod and yet is unwilling to take on the trappings of kingship. Brutus is both self-sufficient in virtue and easily manipulable. And human nature being the medium in which history moves, the events that these men cause become equally indeterminate, only coherent in the terms their characters allow and that subsequent history confirms.

As a group, 'the conspirators' in *Julius Caesar* are more notable for their differences than their similarities. In the recurrent Shakespearian manner, the characters are exposed to one another at different angles and reflect off one another the different facets of being, change one another by their contiguity. Brutus with Cassius, Brutus with Portia, Brutus with the body of conspirators, Brutus in the market place, are all slightly different Brutuses; we can accept their unity, but the unity we see is one we construct out of contradictory elements. Seen in this context, the political issues no longer appear to be abstractions. If we want to know whether Caesar really intended to become a tyrant, we must seek answers in terms of personality, not historical parallels. For Caesar is not only a potential tyrant but also (in ethical terms) a 'great man'—great in his effortless superiority to everything around him and indeed so far above it all that he can hardly see its particulars. Can a society that respects itself bear to have such a person in its midst? Happy the country that does not need a hero. Everywhere we see people carving out a new world by their emotional reactions but at the same time trying to think about it in terms of impersonal generalities.

The theatrical advantage of making Caesar's tyranny potential rather than actual is that the status of the opposing sides remains open to interpretation. Ambiguity and interpretability undercut the simplistic antitheses of tyranny and liberty, order and anarchy, unity and faction. Given that, it must be judged no accident that Shakespeare, unlike other dramatists of the Roman scene, is prepared not only to mention but to dramatize the power of the mob to change the political equation. This allows him to stress the inconsequentiality of 'our slippery people' as Antony calls them (*Antony and Cleopatra*, I. ii. 185), not because history is ruled by Fortune (as in *Caesar's Revenge*) but because of human nature. The opening scene of *Julius Caesar* shows the 'mechanicals' as essential elements in the struggle for power, volatile in their loyalty but capable, when handled cleverly enough (as by Caesar when offered the crown, and by Antony in the market place), of subverting all the values of self-conscious evaluators.

We know that Ben Jonson was concerned about *Julius Caesar* (it is the only Shakespeare play named in the *Discoveries*)—no doubt because its classical subject matter seemed to infringe the patent of the learned. His first extant tragedy, *Sejanus, his Fall* (1603) (see pp. 456–8), treats Roman history of a very different phase from Shakespeare's, but his second, *Catiline, his Conspiracy* (1611), returns us to the subject matter if not the manner of *Julius Caesar*. It deals once again with that point in Roman history when the fate of the Republic lay still in the balance. But, unlike Shakespeare, Jonson (inevitably perhaps, given his concern to quote his sources) represents his contending characters as party men rather than individuals, and speech is now less a mirror of the mind than the medium of politics—but politics treated as cataclysmic. The rhetoric of his conspirators crackles with fire and swims in blood, but in fact we never see them strike a single blow. They despise Cicero as a 'talking fellow', but neither they nor their secret patrons, Julius Caesar and Marcus Crassus, can break through the net of political oratory. The air is heavy with the menace of future action, and we understand that the open Republican system of checks and balances is by now so corrupted by wealth and power that it cannot long resist the pressure of the discontented, whose stated aim is to

redeem ourselves to liberty
And break the iron yoke forged for our necks,
For what less can we call it, when we see
The commonwealth engrossed so by a few,
The giants of the state that do, by turns
Enjoy her and defile her . . .

.   .   .   .

People and nations pay them hourly stipends;
The riches of the world flows to their coffers
And not to Rome's. While, but those few, the rest,
However great we are, honest and valiant,
Are herded with the vulgar, and so kept
As we were only bred to consume corn.

(I. 344–56)

One does not need to be a historian to recognize the accent.
As far as the tight chronological sequence of the play is concerned, the Republic is saved from the consequences of this supremacist rhetoric; the revolt of the discontented noblemen is derailed by the selfless civil servant Cicero. But at the beginning and the end we are shown a larger meaning: behind the particular plot we see the systemic weakness of the State, evoked in the memory of Marius and Sulla (whose ghost arises from Hell to promote the disorder) and in the anticipation of the first triumvirate, which will soon overwhelm constitutional government (for the next millennium and a half, as it turns out). Cicero's necessary compromise, whereby Caesar and Crassus have to be absolved so that the Catilinarians can be killed, is a triumph in the short term, but (as Jonson no doubt expects us to remember) it paves the way to disaster in the long term. What *Catiline* can be seen to lack when compared to *Sejanus* is the sharpness of satire that grows out of a situation beyond anything but anger. We are at a point where the bad still assume that the personal flamboyance of their threats measures the effectiveness of their action, so that there are many ways to counter-check their moves. In these terms *Catiline* is more relevant to English politics of the period than *Sejanus*, and this may account for the respect in which it was held throughout the seventeenth century.[35]

[35] See G. E. Bentley, *Shakespeare and Jonson; Their Reputations in the Seventeenth Century* (2 vols.; Chicago, 1945), i. 109–12.

Tyrant Tragedy

The free-flowing action of *Catiline*, of *Caesar's Revenge* and *Julius Caesar* (indeed of all Shakespeare's Roman plays), in which tyranny is a threat but not yet an established system, allows that personal action may not make better but at least allows the heroic individual to defend his cause. The drama of established tyranny presents situations in which that possibility has been foreseen and stifled at birth. This returns us to *tacitismo* once again, to the view of history as a record of enslavement, not so much enslavement of the body as of the mind, by manipulation of the media, and by a general subversion of the traditional institutions. To some extent we are back with villain tragedy, but in institutional rather than personal terms, where revenge can be no more than self-indulgence, where society is too corrupt to respond to the opportunity created, and the individual is too caught in social toils to succeed by individual effort. We seem to be witnessing here a change of attitude parallel to that manifested in Fletcherian tragicomedy:[36] the active man cannot separate his motives and his actions from the prevailing social mode: only the passive man who lives inside the system can achieve as much good as is available.

The history of the Roman emperors, seen not in the open perspective of Plutarch but in the closed one of Tacitus and Suetonius, provides ample illustration of these points. The attitude that a reading of Tacitus inculcated is, of course, a learned one and the dramatic art that derives from it comes from learned sources, marginally from Seneca (Atreus, Nero), from neo-Latin drama, and from Italian tragedy (*Ecerinis, Orbecche, Il re torrismondo*). Jonson's *Sejanus, his Fall* is presumably the first full dramatization of the Taciteanism vision in English, but, once established, the image of corrupted imperial politics holds sway, in Fletcher's *Valentinian*,

---

[36] Fletcher's *Rollo, Duke of Normandy: or The Bloody Brother* (1616×1624; ? revised by Massinger, 1627×1630), performed at court, 1630, 1630/1, 1637, repr. 1640, 1679, 1686, 1718—'one of the most frequently performed pieces in the seventeenth century', Bentley tells us (*JCS* iii. 407)—gives us a valuable insight into both the continuity and the change of the form. The plot comes, like that of *Titus Andronicus*, from Herodian's account of the rivalry between the two sons of Septimius Severus (with echoes of the *Phoenissae* of Euripides and Seneca). But this time the emphasis is not on revenge against the tyrannical survivor, but rather on the effort to save what can be saved inside the prevailing corruption.

Massinger's *The Roman Actor*, May's *Julia Agrippina*, Richards's *Messalina*, Markham and Sampson's *Herod and Antipater*.[37]

Sejanus is deliberately a tragedy not of drums and trumpets but of great events secured by minimal means—and that may be one of the reasons for its failure in the first performance.[38] Tacitus himself apologises for the undisturbed surface of his history:

None must compare these my annals with the writings of those who . . . had for their subject mighty wars, cities sacked, kings taken captive. . . . The matter on which I am occupied is circumscribed . . . a state of undisturbed peace . . . the sad condition of affairs in the city and a prince indifferent about extending the bounds of the empire . . . matters which, though unimportant in a superficial view, frequently give the first impulse to events of magnitude. [It is] good to record these matters since few can by their own foresight distinguish between honesty and knavery.[39]

Jonson, quoting extensively from Tacitus, documents tyranny as a closed system in which the only politically significant actions are to

> Flatter and swear, forswear, deprave, inform,
> Smile and betray; make guilty men; then beg
> The forfeit lives to get the livings; cut
> Men's throats with whisperings . . .
>
> . . . .
>
> Laugh when their patron laughs; sweat when he sweats

(I. 28–33)

and in which, therefore, opposition is neutered, reduced to whispered generalities, spied on, denounced, and so destroyed in apparent conformity with the laws of the land.

Like everything else in this bureaucratic state, the spontaneity of violent rejection has already been taken care of. Arruntius, the boldest speaker of the political opposition, is allowed to use the old-fashioned rhetoric of: 'My sword should cleave him down

---

[37] See W. D. Briggs, 'The Influence of Jonson's Tragedy in the Seventeenth Century', *Anglia*, 35 (1912), 287–91.

[38] This in spite of the fact that the play may have been more diversified in the theatre. Jonson tells us that it was performed in a version 'wherein a second pen had a good share'— Chapman is often thought to have wielded the second pen.

[39] *Annals*, bk. iv, chs. 32–3; quoted from the Bohn translation (1903). The evocation of a world of superficial normality in which, however, good and evil are impossible to tell apart, a world of secrecy and oblique relationship, of constant fear of betrayal, must remind modern readers of Cold War spy stories written in the mode of John le Carré's *The Spy Who Came in from the Cold*.

from head to heart . . . and with my hand | I'd hurl his panting brains about the air' (I. 254–6). But such rhetoric has no political significance.[40] In fact it is tolerated only because such tolerance makes the regime look liberal, without endangering it. Arruntius has been co-opted into the system before he even opens his mouth.

Tiberius is a tyrant at the opposite end of the spectrum from the ranting tyrants of the older tradition. His intentions can be known only by their effects, but these effects are produced with such obliquity (through intermediaries, calculated ambiguities, misleading reports) that the connection between motive and event can hardly be guessed at. To be elevated in such a court is to stand on the edge of the abyss. Sejanus, as first minister, is at once the most powerful and the most insecure; his role is close to that of the tool villain in a revenge play, but this time there is no overt collusion, and the chance to betray is blocked; for responsibility for deeds done lies always with him, while the manipulative Emperor plays the innocent manipulated. He cannot secure his position, for the means available (to set up his own cabal) must expose his self-interest and so the reason he must be destroyed. And the destruction, when it comes, is achieved with clinical efficiency; transition is secured without disturbance of the overall system. No space for hope or freedom is created; Macro, the new executive, is simply a Sejanus revamped. The physical facts of the death of Sejanus are horrifying enough; but the real tragedy is not the death of the minister but the survival of the emperor.

Jonson presents all this as a particular picture of a particular period: the quarto of 1605 is dense with citations that justify the truth of his story. But, of course, the image of absolutist court culture presented would have no poetic power if it could not also suggest a general truth. We know from the *Conversations* that Jonson was called before the Privy Council and questioned about the play—presumably about its relevance to the English court— and it has been conjectured that the text we know has been doctored to remove any such reference. To say so is, of course, to imply that Jonson did not possess enough art to comprehend the specific without referring to it; certainly the art of the play that we have does not support any such assumption. The tightly controlled

---

[40] Cf. what Sejanus himself says: 'wrath, covered, carries fate: | Revenge is lost, if I profess my hate' (I. 578–9).

classical structure mirrors exactly a world in which reverberation from every move is registered at every other point. The poetry, dense with physical detail and powered with satiric energy, never allows us to escape from the pressure of the plot, to understand speech as simple self-expression—except perhaps (and typically) when Sejanus, at the beginning of Act V, believes himself to be at last free from the plots against him. Of course, he believes this because he is being lulled into the sense of security that will make his destruction all the easier.

The power of restriction and concentration in *Sejanus* is perhaps most easily seen by a comparison with the first surviving play that shows awareness of it: the anonymous *Tragedy of Claudius Tiberius Nero, Rome's Greatest Tyrant: Truly Represented out of the Purest Records of these Times* (?; printed 1607). The author (or 'father' of the play) is said by the printer to be an 'academician' because he is so 'well seen in antiquities, but most especially inward with Cornelius Tacitus, our best historian'. So far, so like *Sejanus*; the period covered is only slightly enlarged from that of *Sejanus*, beginning with the death of Augustus and ending with the murder of Tiberius by Caligula. But the progress of events is not seen by this author as the backward and forward calculation of a political chess game, but in the older terms of direct emotional commitment. Here the action is not refracted through the commentaries of observers but in top-lit statements by the principals. We meet Germanicus and hear of his contempt for Tiberius; Caligula, Sejanus, Tiberius, and the Germanici tell us directly of hopes and fears. In *Sejanus*, the wooing of Livia is conducted through the agency of the corrupt beautician Eudemus, so that the false face of the society lady and the false face of the corrupt politician reflect off one another; but here the wooing is a seduction scene directly imitated from that of Richard and Lady Anne in Shakespeare's *Richard III*.

Unlike *Sejanus*, *Claudius Tiberius Nero* is a play of incessant action. We *see* Piso poisoning Germanicus, the soldiers tearing Piso to pieces, Tiberius forcing his son Drusus to drink the poisoned wine, Sejanus' coronation with a red-hot crown. *Sejanus* gives us a shadow-play of commentary and report where, as with all shadows, the uncertainty magnifies the terror. *Claudius Tiberius Nero* bludgeons our attention with reckless *amplificatio*, long historical descriptions, and brings the action to an end by mere coincidence (Sejanus' letter to Livia is discovered among other papers), where Jonson makes the catastrophe depend on the one step Sejanus *must* reveal to Tiberius—his desire to marry into the imperial house. The tyranny of Tiberius in both *Sejanus* and *Claudius Tiberius Nero* is given its fullest political dimension by noting what we have already noted in *Catiline*—the place of these particular events inside the larger story of Roman liberty turned into the tyranny of empire. These are plays aimed at a public predisposed to think that the major patterns of political possibility are already set out in the Roman story, equally able to teach as to move and delight.

The *Tragedy of Herod and Antipater* by Gervase *Markham and William *Sampson (*c.*1619×1622) is not a play about Rome but still one that lives in the shadow of Rome. Herod (the Great), the tyrant of Judaea, is the client of Mark Antony and then of Augustus, anxious to measure his success by these models. His colourful career is well documented in the histories of Flavius Josephus, and the episode of his love for Mariamne became one of the great love-stories of the West.[41] It provides the major source of Massinger's *The Duke of Milan* (probably mediated by Markham and Sampson's play) and of Lady Elizabeth *Cary's closet drama, *The Tragedy of Mariam, the Fair Queen of Jewry* (1602×1605; printed 1613). Markham and Sampson are less interested, however, in the love-story than in the contest for power between Herod and his bastard son Antipater. Herod is the tyrant, wary, jealous, violent; Antipater is the tool villain who acts as Herod's security agent but with motivation less prompted by loyalty than by ambition. Like Jonson's Sejanus (the obvious model), Antipater must act to clear the path for his own succession and yet seem to do this only to safeguard the king his father. And so, like Sejanus, he must play on the tyrant's fears and jealousies with the hope that he can be saddled with responsibility for deeds that weaken him and strengthen his son. The pattern is that provided by Jonson, but the action is too devoted to the excitements of villain tragedy to fit inside the tightly controlled system of Jonson's Rome. The plot is a series of ups and downs, of coincidences and manœuvres that reflect well enough the instabilities of Levantine politics but leave the reader with little sense of dramatic shape, and none of Jonson's hold on significance for the future.

---

[41] M. J. Valency, *The Tragedies of Herod and Mariamne* (New York, 1940) lists thirty-seven dramatizations of the story.

Tyrant tragedy is inevitably a form in which personal life is narrowly restricted by political circumstances. The tyrant's obsessiveness—his reduction of relationship to threat, of all circumstances to dangers—imposes on himself and everyone else a mode of life in which a flexible sense of self is an impossibility. But history can offer patterns that transcend individual fates; and no doubt in a period when the trajectory of the Roman state seemed exemplary for modern existence (and when authors and audience probably knew Roman better than English history) the historical connections Jonson offers could give general meaning to particular stories. But the modern reader (lacking this background) inevitably misses the sense of individual lives completing their own significance within their own timescale.

Two plays of the early years of King James's reign, Barnabe *Barnes's *The Devil's Charter: a tragedy containing the life and death of Pope Alexander the sixth* (1607) and Shakespeare's *Macbeth* (1606; printed 1623), shift the balance of historical tragedy by making the tyrant's success depend less on a control of a political route into the future and more on intervention by supernatural forces. We watch his temporary advantage, noting that the price is to be paid by the individual rather than history. The King's Men brought *Macbeth* to court in July 1606, and they performed *The Devil's Charter* there in February 1607. Both plays may have been designed to catch James's well-known interest in kingship and the supernatural. But what a comparison throws up is less continuity than contrast. Rodrigo Borgia, Pope Alexander VI, seeks his 'charter' from the devil to secure family interests, aiming to turn political position into family possession. But the individual Borgias offer only separate illustrations of what exemption from limits means (as in *Old Fortunatus*). The play thus falls apart into a series of separate episodes: Alexander poisons his catamites, Lucrezia arranges her husband's 'suicide', Cesare, finding his brother Gandia too moralistic, throws him into the Tiber. When Cesare and his father finally combine, planning to poison the whole College of Cardinals, the devil changes the bottles and both are killed.

As if to complement this demon-driven family saga, Barnes adds to it the story of the destruction of Italian independence by invading French and Spanish forces. Guicciardini appears as chorus and commentator and rehearses what he tells more fully in his *Storia d'Italia*. Pope Alexander was certainly one cause of the collapse of

Italy. But Barnes shows little ambition to link the demonic individualism of the Borgia story with Guicciardini's abstracted political understanding. We see one looking to the future as the measure of what is happening, while the other, brief and violent, explodes action into magic and leaves no more remainder than does Doctor Faustus.

In *Macbeth*, on the other hand, the demonic is never separated from the historical–political. It must work through that mode, allow us to see the process of ambition as intelligible only in such terms, yet able to be short-circuited by forces that respond only to the imagination. The power of the supernatural appears in fact as a promise to abolish the contradiction between these two, between Macbeth's desire for innocence and his desire for power, his hope to control the future and his need for continuity with the past, his secret guilt and his approved external function. We meet the weird women[42] before we meet their victim; we hear that Macbeth is their target. He hears their prompting with instinctive recognition and dismay; yet something inside himself, which he fears and does not understand, seems to be echoing their words; the phantasmal, the 'is not', the internal, seems to be taking over from the real, the 'is', the external. But having swallowed the idea, having found the shape of the future inside himself, he has been conditioned, as if by a virus or a drug, and is ready for the ministrations of his next control, his wife. We are offered a conundrum: is he no longer capable of independent judgement? Where is the borderline between thinking and hallucinating? We know from Banquo's presence on the heath that the weird women were really there but had no absolute authority; yet even Banquo has to pray that 'merciful powers' will 'Restrain in me the cursed thoughts that nature | Gives way to in repose' (II. i. 7–9). He knows that, like Macbeth, he is never free of the 'natural' forces that will take him over if he relaxes his guard. For the demonic finds little institutional or customary impediment in the organization of this transitional society, where the past seems to be preserved in the weird women even while its explicit culture is intent on denying it. It is a society still reverberating with the memory of a time 'Ere human statute purged the gentle weal' (III. iv. 75), a time when, if 'the brains were out, the

---

[42] This is how Shakespeare, following Holinshed, names them in the text ('witches' in the stage directions). The usual modern assumption that 'witch' provides us with a simple and sufficient description is not justified. Simon Forman the astrologer, who saw *Macbeth* at the Globe on 20 April 1611, calls them 'fairies or nymphs'.

man would die | And there an end' (III. v. 78–9), when murder, in
other words, was the natural solution to a political problem, and
tyranny the natural consequence.

We are not given any idea how Shakespeare's Claudius or Jonson's
Tiberius came to possess the secretive and melancholy characteristics of the tyrant type. Macbeth, however, can be seen growing
into the space between the primitive and the modern, between the
fearless actor and the frightened thinker whose guilt and despair
define the role he must play. When we first hear of him, it is as a
man bathed in blood, but protected from moral uncertainty by the
sanctions of king and country. But king and country may be anachronistic sanctions in a pre-feudal society, where the relation of
peers and relatives to the sovereign is a matter always in negotiation, so that a defence of the king from his factious nobles has strict
limits. Primogeniture is only one of the options.

As loyal soldier and defender of the State, Macbeth has destroyed the 'multiplying villainies' of the merciless Macdonwald.
But when he comes home across the desolate heath these same
multiplying villainies now swarm around him with temptations
that are not so easy to conquer, that can be dealt with only by a
moral decisiveness he does not possess and that his situation hardly
allows. The weird women tell him of the rewards that victorious
generals can expect but cannot be assured of. And they make no
mention of a price. Perhaps there isn't one: 'If chance will have me
king, why chance may crown me | Without my stir'—he may be
the beneficiary of supernatural aid without having to notice whence
it comes (I. iii. 143–4). But whatever the happenstance of pre-
feudal politics in *Macbeth*, the play also invokes a contrary spiritual
realm not at all constructed to give space to random chances. In
this sphere every thought, even every reluctance to have a thought,
offers 'bloody instructions which, being taught, return | To plague
th' inventor' (I. vii. 9–10). An ineluctable process carries Macbeth
from the murder of Duncan, which he cannot bear to face, to the
murder of Banquo, in which he requires no prompting and which
he plans with great technical expertise. But again the contemplation of it 'unmans' him and destroys the pretence of a coherent
society which the great banquet is intended to reinforce. Finally, in
the assault on Lady Macduff and her children, we see political
murder as a thing of course. The inner impulses have conquered
the external impediments. All the elements of tyranny are now in

place: spies have been hired to report discontent, the husband has
to fly before he is trapped, the friends dare not stay lest they are
implicated, the victims pose no threat. This is an action with no
purpose; but, having accepted the meaninglessness of experience,
Macbeth is now tied to a logic that belongs to the role chosen but
not to the man who chose it.

And so by the end of the play Macbeth has acquired all the
stigmata of the tyrant. He has become, like Claudius and Tiberius,
fearful, devious, melancholy; he is isolated even from his wife and
co-conspirator, unable to justify his usurpation to himself, and
haunted by the knowledge of what his actions have made of him.
The central revenge here is not, in fact, the political one of Malcolm
and the invading forces but the moral one imposed by Macbeth's
own nature. Inevitably therefore the political conclusion, the rescue
of the nation from the tyrant (the type name increasingly taking
over from the personal one in *Macbeth*), is a fairly perfunctory
matter. For the fate of the nation cannot command the same poetic
assent as the fate of the hero, where we understand the tyranny
from the point of view of the tyrant and so share the horror of
living with acts that cannot be accepted and yet cannot be denied,[43]
and so must be repeated again and again (like Lady Macbeth's
hand-washing). The desolation of the country that Macduff describes in Act IV reads, therefore, as a mere copy of Macbeth's
desolate inner world. Malcolm may offer to dispel the mists ('the
time is free') with the sunshine of English civilization, turn thanes
into earls, but he cannot remove from the spectator's mind the
shadow of human nature caught in the grip of forces that turn
politics from choice to necessity, that have the power to make the
recuperations offered by history seem shallow and insubstantial.

Of the three characteristics of the tyrant set out by Otanes in
Herodotus' discussion of government[44]—he subverts law, he rav-
ishes free women, he puts men to death before judgement is
passed—the plays so far considered concentrate on the first (with
some consequences for the third) but show less interest in the
second. Tiberius' sexual peculiarities are noted, but only as a minor

---

[43] There is a preview of this division, in which the self as subject has to face and judge
the self as object, in Richard's soliloquy in Act V, Scene iii, of *Richard III*. But Richard does
not have to live with the condition, and Shakespeare does not there explore the psychological consequences of having to live with it.   [44] *Histories*, iii. 80.

aspect of his degeneracy. But the tyrant tragedy of the seventeenth century increasingly gives private morals a more central position than politics and so sexual misconduct becomes a key issue. Valentinian, Domitian, Tarquin[45] (like the eponymous 'tyrant' of *The Second Maiden's Tragedy*) are all characterized by lust for a virtuous woman who cannot be bought by promises of wealth and position, and so must be forced.

Fletcher's *Valentinian* (1610×1614; printed 1647) and Massinger's *The Roman Actor* (1626) are probably the later Roman tragedies most clearly in the tradition of *Sejanus*, and show the development of that tradition. In *Valentinian* the commentator roles of Jonson's republican senators are given to the two generals, Maximus and Aecius. But they (being soldiers) are not at all concerned with the extinction of liberty, but only with the question of loyalty to an established monarch who has proved degenerate. Jonson's play assumes, though he does not argue, the identity of public virtue and private morality; those who possess one are likely to possess the other. Fletcher, on the other hand, treats the relationship between the two as a dramatic issue. Aecius' loyalty leads him to think Valentinian able to submerge private vice in public duty. He sees the rape of Maximus' wife as giving the generals an opportunity to 'fright his follies | And once more bend him right again' (III. i. 215–16). It is their function to provide role models:

> Our honest actions, and the light that breaks
> Like morning from our service, chaste and blushing,
> Is that that pulls a prince back.
>
> (I. iii. 94–6)

Maximus cannot regard the rape and suicide of his chaste wife in these terms. He supposes that sexual degeneracy has poisoned all; it is no longer a question of what Valentinian *does* but only of what he *is*, so that revenge is the only possible response. And so, as revenger, Maximus becomes the central figure in the play. But the play condemns him: to take political revenge for private wrongs is unjust. And so we understand the logic that requires Maximus to be driven into his own version of tyranny, forgetting the cause in whose name he acts, sacrificing Aecius and, as usurper of the empire, making himself the proper victim of the next conspiracy.

---

[45] In Heywood's *The Rape of Lucrece* (1606×1608).

Massinger's *The Roman Actor* is, like *Sejanus* and *Claudius Tiberius Nero*, a tragedy based on Tacitus, and like them it is heavily influenced by seventeenth-century *tacitismo*—offering its spectators the melancholy pleasure of a history that teaches no providential lessons and reveals only the accidental quality of tyrannicide. This time it is Domitian who is the corrupt emperor, guilty not only of incest and rape but (perhaps worse) of allowing his sexual appetite to obliterate his imperial function. Tiberius planned his betrayals, but Domitian enacts his without noticing. Assuming himself to be a god, there can be no limitation on the passions of the moment. But then, of course, the passion is the master and he is the slave. Once he has snatched Domitia from her husband, he becomes not simply her lover but her worshipper, her footstool, and she becomes his tyrant, his contemner, and finally his executioner. Absolute power and absolute abasement meet in a world of extremes from which past and future have been removed, with the result that identity is destroyed. There is, however, one world in which the exclusion of compromise need not be fatal—the world of the theatre. The players of Rome are highly favoured by the emperor. The fictional existence that they present can be moulded to his wishes, and so fulfils his notion of his will as not simply controlling the world but creating it.

Like Jonson in *Sejanus*, Massinger has supplied a group of senators (Rusticus, Sura, Lamia) who stand for republican virtue, but, even by the standards of *Sejanus*, these are powerless men, members of an even more sycophantic senate; their real significance in the play is as Stoic adepts, alienated from the hopes and fears of the world, and therefore as free of physical needs as Domitian is enslaved by them. The problems of government have, indeed, become almost completely irrelevant to this reign. Hence, no doubt, the interest in acting as the one mode of representing reality that retains some interpretative coherence. The play begins with an attack on acting by the senate oligarchs, who find it intolerable that actors 'traduce | Persons of rank . . . Make even the senators ridiculous | To the plebeians' (I. iii. 38–43). The profession is defended by Paris in a speech which remained famous even when the rest of the play was forgotten. But the effective defence comes from Domitian, whose interest in the players is protective, though equally intrusive. If the senators wish to stop playing because it comes too close to the truth, the court wishes to promote acting because it gives real focus to the fictional values the courtiers live by. Domitia, having seen Paris act a romantic lover in *Iphis and Anaxarete*, must have him as a real lover. In the same vein, Domitian, having found Domitia kissing Paris, can bring himself to kill him only by acting out his revenge in the play of *The False Servant*. Thus fiction enables power-sated reality to believe in a balance of desire and impediment that life itself cannot supply.

Imperial Rome provides in these plays a situation in which the whole world is the tyrant's plaything. But, lacking resistance, power is without savour. Hence the drive to invent more and more outrageous behaviour. Hence also the attraction to the role of creative artist, the maker of new worlds and so new possibilities of conduct. In the anonymous *Tragedy of Nero* (?; printed 1624) the emperor wishes to be known as the supreme actor, musician, poet, and chariot-racer, and the population is required not only to bear but to applaud his performances. Here, as in *The Roman Actor*, the prince's aestheticism gives his cruelty a further *frisson*: the whole world is required to populate the stage on which he acts out his fantasies of omnipotence. As there the playlets are performed so that Domitian and his favourites can have the privilege of turning them into reality whenever they choose, so here Nero sets Rome on fire so that he can act out Pyrrhus singing over the flames of Troy. The screams of the victims are appreciated as aesthetic objects, as heaven-sent opportunities for the exercise of his rhetoric.

The Roman Scene: Women in Power

The tyrant's fear of competitors, and his need to forget the hatred with which he is regarded, drives him into the company of flatterers and women, whose role it is to persuade him that he is 'loved for himself'. But, of course, the delegated power thus achieved is no less dangerous to the State than that of the tyrant himself, for it comes from sources deprived of independent status. English Renaissance dramatists are liable to present women in power, whatever the circumstances, as symptoms of a degenerate culture; their mode of achieving power must rule out any grasp on impersonal truth; their rule is hopelessly contaminated by their personal lives. In these terms the presence of powerful women in the imperial families of Rome can be represented as another sign of political collapse. In this, as in other matters, Jonson's picture gave a lead to the rest. In both *Sejanus* and *Catiline* female susceptibility to flattery and light-minded concern with cosmetics and fashion quickly betray them into State matters whose long-term purpose they cannot perceive. In both plays they are, however, only the instruments of men; they exercise no independent power. Massinger's *The Roman Actor* moves female power one notch higher. Domitia's hold over Domitian is such that she can scorn him and cuckold him with apparent immunity. But this is still power by proxy, not as a main actor. It is only when we get to Thomas *May's *Julia Agrippina, Empress of Rome* (1628; printed 1639) and Nathaniel *Richards's *Messalina: the Roman Empress* (1634×1636) that we are given a picture of real and direct female power.

Julia Agrippina was well placed, as daughter to Germanicus, wife to Claudius, and Nero's mother, to exercise 'independent, absolute and free' control over the State. The historical action of the play ignores Agrippina's earlier history and concentrates on her plot to ensure that Nero becomes emperor as soon as the elimination of Claudius and his son Britannicus has been achieved. Her lover, the freedman Pallas, is her partner in this scheme, but in this case the man is very much the junior partner. It is she who understands the need for immediate action and ruthlessly carries it through. Her ambition to be co-emperor fails only because Nero is ungrateful enough to recognize that he will achieve independence only when she is dead. May is generally faithful to his copious sources but abandons them at the end so that he can make Poppaea the executioner. Obviously he wants to stress the moral that in such a society the decline of one ambitious woman naturally leads to the emergence of another (as earlier we saw Macro succeed Sejanus).

Messalina deals with Claudius' first wife, Juvenal's insatiable sexual athlete, who exhausts the efforts of twenty-five men in one night. Messalina exercises undisputed power over Rome, but her interests are entirely personal. What she aims to achieve in Claudius' absence is the total abrogation of moral standards. She sets up a festival in which the chaste are to be debauched and the Vestal Virgins ravished. The timid Claudius is willing that the festival should culminate in Messalina's 'marriage' to Silius, but his freedmen recognize political danger. Like Domitian in *The Roman Actor*, Claudius cannot bring himself to condemn his wife; it is up to the freedmen to redirect his attention and save Rome.

Fletcher's *The Tragedy of Bonduca* (1611×1614) plays an effective variation on this theme of Roman masculine ideals undermined by the power of women to corrupt its politico-military culture. The scene is Britain under Roman rule—the Romans being seen both as foreign invaders and as bringers of a code of military honour, the Britons as both noble barbarians defending their native soil and as a people ready to absorb the superior ideals of their enemies.[46] The barbarism is represented in a convenient shorthand by a strident female ruler, Bonduca, Queen of the Iceni (better known today as Boadicea). We meet her in the opening dialogue exulting in savage triumph over the defeated Romans:

> Dare they send these to seek us,
> These Roman girls . . .
>
> .   .   .   .
>
> Made themes for songs to shame 'em, and a woman,
> A woman beat 'em, Nennius, a weak woman,
> A woman beat these Romans.
>
> (I. i. 10–17)

Caratach, her cousin, spells out the dishonour of such 'unmanly' sentiments. He returns that last line with a dash of acid:

> So it seems,
> A man would shame to talk so.
>
> (I. i. 17–18)

His position is that 'Discretion | And hardy valour are the twins of honour, | And nursed together make a conqueror: | Divided, but a talker' (ll. 21–4). Conquering and conquered soldiers share a 'discretion' that binds them together in a bond of honour closer than that of nationality or sexual partnership. This does not mean that there can be political compromise between British and Roman armies. But victory or defeat must show the self-control that integrates individual honour and national loyalty, a self-control Bonduca cannot achieve and that only Rome can teach.

[46] These polarities are equally central in Shakespeare's *Cymbeline*, another play about Romans and Ancient Britons, written for the same company about the same time. There too it is the queen who (abetted by her boorish son) disrupts the terms of honour between Britain and Rome. There too the Roman general is presented as a paragon of gentlemanly soldiership, and conflict is handled in terms of mutual military esteem. But Shakespeare is writing a romance and not a tragedy: he can keep the exact nature of Britain's relationship to Rome in the shadow cast by the glow of personal reconciliations.

The chance of independence is blown away when Bonduca rashly leads her chariot charge into her own army; but she can restore her personal honour by suicide. Caratach must also face defeat, however honourable. He surrenders to secure the burial of his nephew, the heir to the throne. He is welcomed into the Roman ranks with every possible esteem (Suetonius, the general, thinks of him as already a Roman (I. ii. 260)); nevertheless he must travel to Rome as a captive.[47] Legend has it that he was welcomed there with respect and dignity; but the political fact that the Romans had gained control of Britain was in no way altered by any personal esteem.

Cleopatra is the most famous, the most written about, of these powerful female figures.[48] No less than Roman empresses or British queens, she is required both to fulfil and to vary the stereotype, and we see the challenge this posed not only in Shakespeare's *Antony and Cleopatra* but also in Fletcher's *The False One*, May's *Cleopatra*, and the anonymous *Caesar and Pompey: or Caesar's Revenge*. Like the other queens, she illustrates the danger (or at least the unsettling mixture) of sexual allure and heroic political ambition in a world already unsettled by war and faction. In *Caesar and Pompey* she has only a walk-on part. We meet her when Caesar pursues Pompey to Egypt. Both Caesar and Antony are enchanted. Memories of Tamburlaine's idealizing descriptions of Zenocrate suggest she is a prize for whom kings must compete. But larger issues suppress this romance. Antony is rebuked by his *bonus genius* as Virgil's Aeneas is by Mercury; the generals must first secure the Empire. The play ends as they do so, but the audience is not meant, I assume, to forget that Cleopatra is waiting in the wings for the next phase of history.

---

[47] Caratach (or Caradoc) appears also in R.A.'s *The Valiant Welshman* (1610×1615), where, having continued his war against the Romans for nine years, he is eventually betrayed by his protector's wife. But the Romans despise the betrayal and honour the captive (as before). A companion play, J.W.'s *The Valiant Scot* (? printed 1637), repeats the pattern, with the English invaders (in the reign of Edward I) standing in for the civilizing Romans and William Wallace appearing as a Scottish Caradoc. The great success of *The Valiant Scot* on the stage (running for five days consecutively) seems to have been due to the coincidence of the Bishops' War and the sympathy of the London audience for the Covenanters.

[48] One might add to those discussed in this section the closet plays, Daniel's *Cleopatra* (1593), and the Countess of Pembroke's *Antonius* (1590)—translated from Garnier. Fulke Greville also wrote an *Antony and Cleopatra*, but burnt it when he thought it might be taken as a reference to Elizabeth and Essex (as noted above, p. 343).

Fletcher's *The False One* (1619×1623; printed 1647)[49] seems to have been designed to avoid the obvious romantic highlights of the Antony–Cleopatra story: as the Prologue tells us: 'We treat not of what boldness she did die | Nor of her fatal love to Antony. | What we present and offer to your view | (Upon their faiths) the stage yet never knew' (ll. 15–18). The subject is 'Young Cleopatra . . . and her great mind | Expressed to the height, with us a maid and free'. It tells, in fact, the directly political story of Cleopatra's struggle to wrest the crown of Egypt from her brother Ptolemy, and of her seduction of Caesar in order to achieve this end. But the methods she uses do not detract from her heroic stature; indeed they are part of it. Caesar's infatuation is demeaning (he writes sonnets) and his lust for Egypt's gold invites her scorn; it is only when he shows his prowess in defeating the conspirators around him that she accepts his love. This shows her worthy to be made Queen of Egypt.

Unlike Fletcher, Thomas May in *The Tragedy of Cleopatra, Queen of Egypt* (1626; printed 1639) did not choose to avoid the most celebrated segment of Cleopatra's life and the comparison with Shakespeare. His faithfulness to the inevitable sources means that he has little alternative. Even so, there is space for May, for his central emphasis is different from what we find elsewhere: what he is centrally concerned with is the politics of decline. He begins (like Shakespeare) with soldierly disdain for Antony's infatuation, but unlike Shakespeare he does not allow the hyperbolic rhetoric of love to make the objections seem petty (just as well; his poetic power would hardly have sustained the ambition). His interest is in the love-story as a part of the larger decadence of Roman values, matching the breakdown of republican forms. We hear of consuls 'put to silence'; senators come to Alexandria hoping to find Antony a friend to the Senate. He promises much, but the soldiers tell us that he will not keep his promises. Soothsayers forecast the loss of liberty; one by one his captains fall away. After the defeat at Actium he isolates himself, imitates Timon, condemns mankind. Cleopatra, much more practical, considers what accommodations are possible, offers gold to Caesar, tests poisons for herself. Accommodations are in vain, but love remains as the

---

[49] The 'false one' of the title refers not to Cleopatra but to Septimius, the turncoat Roman who murders Pompey and offers 'politic' solutions to Caesar and other heroic soldiers around him.

final resource that allows heroic temperaments to find in its poetic expansiveness a sense of inner worth that nothing else will sustain. It is in this area, of course, that Shakespeare exercises a power that other dramatists cannot match. It is centrally a poetic power, but saying this should not allow us to suppose that poetry of this order can be readily distinguished from the dramaturgy that projects it. To make the poetry resonate one needs to be given a sense of characters to whom speaking such verse is entirely appropriate, in situations that justify the emotional pressure it puts on us. *Antony and Cleopatra* (*c.*1606×1608; printed 1623) is clearly designed to bring the heroisms of empire and sexual passion not only into tension against one another (as in many of the tragedies discussed here) but also into a mutually supportive grandeur of world-contemning, death-defying experience. Antony is now no longer the opportunist politician of *Julius Caesar*, able to produce emotional rhetoric for his public appearances and then retire to the smoke-filled corridor where deals are struck and lives are traded like business cards. Set in opposition to the politician Octavius, he now appears as a romantic grizzled warrior, of a type that Fletcher was to make one of his hallmarks. But where Fletcher (in *The Mad Lover*, for example) stereotypes the great warrior as dignified by loyalty and rendered absurd by love, Shakespeare (though he allows others to hold this view) provides a poetic exaltation capable of carrying us beyond such stereotypes, 'when such a mutual pair | And such a twain can do't' (I. i. 37–8).

As Antony offers us both the stereotype and the refusal to be bound by it, so Cleopatra not only fulfils the suspicion about women in power so plentifully illustrated, but also justifies her role as the proper object of exaltation. She is recognizably the *fatale monstrum* that both Horace and Virgil describe,[50] like Bonduca an enemy to Roman decency and order. Her political role is that of the other empresses: she is arbitrary and inconsistent; she imposes her private lusts on the public world; she wheedles her way into a battle she is bound to confuse, first assuming that 'as the president of my kingdom, [I] will | Appear there for a man' (III. vii. 17–18), and then taking flight like a startled nymph. But Shakespeare allows the lighting to shine on her from more than one angle. Her 'inconsistency' is also her 'infinite variety', her quicksilver and

---

[50] Horace, *Carmina*, I. xxxvii; Virgil, *Aeneid*, VII. 688.

creative superiority to reductive judgements made in terms of truth and falsehood; and this is a quality that not only captivates Antony but allows audiences the pleasure of sharing his captivity. Cleopatra is, like Hamlet and Falstaff, a character who achieves total freedom by representing action as play-acting. As Hamlet blurs the distinction between being mad and acting mad, and Falstaff the distinction between being a coward and acting a coward, so Cleopatra does not allow us to distinguish between loving and playing at loving. Like the other two she gives us pleasure through the pleasure she herself takes in the virtuosity of her own performance. Certainly her 'desolation does begin to make | A better life' (v. ii. 1–2) only when she discovers a script that will allow her a star role. 'Show me, my women, like a queen', she says, 'I am again for Cydnus, | to meet Mark Antony' (v. ii. 227–9). This is not simply nostalgia for the past, but a reanimation of the power of the past by being willing to die for it (as in Antony's determination to retain his identity as 'Antony . . . The greatest prince o'th'world', by killing himself).[51] Cleopatra's is, inevitably, the more complicated process. She plays out a series of roles with Proculeius, Octavius, Dolabella, and the clown, all the time preparing us for the big final scene. She has no intention of letting that be a scene in a Roman farce in which 'some squeaking Cleopatra [will] boy my greatness | I'th' posture of a whore' (v. ii. 220–1)—one must assume that the virtuoso boy who played Cleopatra did not squeak. She carefully organizes the final tableau; she holds dialogue with the phantom of Antony, addresses the asp, and leaves Charmian to complete the effect: 'Your crown's awry, | I'll mend it and then play' (v. ii. 319). Even at the point of death, what Cleopatra longs for are the notices, 'that I might hear great Caesar [called] ass unpolicied'. She need not have worried.

Looking at *Antony and Cleopatra* in the context of the other Roman tragedies discussed here, we can see that the Roman values whose loss Jonson, Massinger, Richards, and May record and deplore—restraint, realism, order, control, foresight—have been given by Shakespeare to characters who do not command our central interest or identification, while those who are at the centre, Antony and Cleopatra, share characteristics with imperial monsters like Nero and Domitian. Like them they take a dionysiac delight in

---

[51] So also in Othello's final speech.

transgressing the boundaries that convention sets between male and female, drunk and sober, human and divine, tragic and comic, serious and playful, spiritual and physical, royal and vulgar.[52] What then separates them from these decadents? In part it is that Shakespeare backs their grand pretension with poetic grandeur of temperament (and the temperamental grandeur of poetry). Nero and Domitian are, behind their tantrums, merely frightened children. Antony and Cleopatra carry off their extravagances with a panache and a playfulness that shows them standing above their status —as '[Antony's] delights | Were dolphin-like, they showed his back above | The element they lived in' (v. ii. 88–90). Glamour, and especially aging glamour, is a suspect commodity, and easily collapses into a *Sunset Boulevard* mode of sentimental self-protection. What redeems Antony and Cleopatra from this is that decline and failure lead them not to hide but to discover selves they can die with. Dryden rewrites the play as *All for Love: or The World Well Lost* (1678) and preserves this choice of fates, but sentimentalizes it. It is not 'love' in any ordinary sense that sustains Shakespeare's characters at the end, but rather the freedom to believe in one's self. This is not to say that love, the confirmation of identity from outside, does not also help.

The Italian Scene: Women in Power

The movement of these Roman tragedies from the military–political to the political–erotic is, I have noted, only part of a larger trend in the drama of the time, carrying concentration from public to private concerns, from revenge for a murdered father or son to revenge for a ravished wife, from power expressed, vindicated, and lost in political terms to power expressed, vindicated, and lost in sexual terms. In the comparatively crude treatment accorded the theme in *Lust's Dominion* (see pp. 436–7) the sexual infatuation of the sovereign is disastrous not as a breach of honour but because it subjects the State to one who can subvert all the coherent national values (legitimacy, primogeniture, orderly succession). In Rowley's *All's Lost by Lust* (*c.*1619×1620; printed 1633) the king's lust not only breaks the bond between the ruler and his army (as in

---

[52] Octavius reports with disgust the impropriety of Antony's willingness 'to reel the streets at noon and stand the buffet | With knaves that smell of sweat' (I. iv 20–1).

Valentinian) but forces the general (father to the lady involved) to revenge the dishonour by making common cause with the Moors he has just defeated, so destroying himself, his daughter, and the Christian state in Spain. The innocent victim of lust leaves the men in her family to revenge the private wrong at whatever public cost. A woman's exercise of sexual power outside the limitations imposed by family honour imposes a different kind of negotiation with the society around her. Two tragedies by Webster, *The White Devil* (1609×1612) and *The Duchess of Malfi* (1612×1614; printed 1623), and two by Middleton, *Women Beware Women* (c.1620×1627; printed 1657) and *The Changeling* (1622; printed 1653)—the latter with the assistance of Rowley—all deal with modern women, placed in societies unstable enough both to allow outsiders to gain a toehold in power and to be horrified when they do so. Middleton's handling of the situation is the more introverted: his heroines come to their sad ends by self-incrimination and self-destruction. Webster destroys them by revenge for family honour. But all must die to expiate sexual as well as class transgression; and sexual relations are, of course, the most obvious means by which traditional class boundaries can be transgressed.

Vittoria Corombona in *The White Devil* and Bianca Capello in *Women Beware Women* are both real-life figures from recent Italian history, whose success in marrying dukes shocked public opinion in their own day and made them natural subjects for sensational *novelle*. Both stories are bound to end unhappily, for the status quo cannot be expected to absorb this degree of displacement; but in neither case is the moral judgement a simple one. Webster requires of his audience a double response to Vittoria (the famous 'innocence resembling boldness'[53]); Middleton shows Bianca Capello as first the victim of the duke's lust and only thereafter the ruthless defender of the power she thus achieved but did not seek. Both operate from positions of gender disadvantage in which force of personality can create social space in the short term; but the longer strands of the plot show where the real power lies—with those long accustomed to the means and the intermediaries that control and forestall everything that is done.

[53] See *The Works of Charles and Mary Lamb*, ed. E. V. Lucas (7 vols.; London, 1903–5), iv. 190.

Both are tied to a court society where the interests of those in charge define right and wrong for the mass of flatterers, panders, spies, and social adventurers who surround them; and they are powerless to escape from the system. The pander who procures Vittoria for the Duke is her own brother. Bianca's husband, who has stolen her from her family in Venice, is a tremulous and possessive lover, but faced by the reality of power he quickly shows his mean-spiritedness; he can think of dealing with the disgrace only by repeating it, himself becoming the kept lover of a great court lady and striving to outface his wife with his own silks and satins. In both plays we see the Church making verbal defences of virtue, but the Cardinals and Princes are too closely integrated to permit one to make any serious challenge to the conduct of the other. In *Women Beware Women* the Cardinal warns his brother the Duke that his liaison with the still-married Bianca is a sin. But when this is answered by having the husband assassinated, the formal objection disappears. In *The White Devil* the Cardinal actually seeks to become a force for good. When he is elected Pope, he tries to undo what he has hitherto accepted. But his moralism is quickly circumvented. The assassin his brother has hired easily understands that this new goodness is only a piece of ecclesiastical window-dressing, behind which the basic interests of family honour and revenge against interlopers continue to control the world.

The Duchess of Malfi begins with what looks like a deliberate exposé of such a world. What we hear first of all is a description of an alternative kind of social organization, as found in the centralized monarchy of France (and no less in England). There,

> In seeking to reduce both state and people
> To a fixed order, their judicious king
> Begins at home, quits first his royal palace
> Of flattering sycophants, of dissolute
> And infamous persons.
>
> . . . .
>
> Considering duly that a prince's court
> Is like a common fountain whence should flow
> Pure silver drops in general. But if't chance
> Some cursed example poison't near the head
> Death and diseases through the whole land spread.

(I. i. 5–15)

Of course this ideal is presented only as a whispered conversation to one side of a court dominated by the very types the French king has displaced. But at the end of the scene the ideal reappears. The Duchess, sister to the vicious Duke and Cardinal, chooses to alienate herself from their corrupt ambitions by choosing a virtuous steward as her second husband. The Duchess, by social status and moral quality, has the best chance possible to prove that the independence of a great good woman can shed 'pure silver drops' across the landscape. But to suppose so would be to suppose that goodness has inherent power. A French king may be able to impose new standards on his society, but a widowed (and improperly remarried) duchess can be hunted down as an affront to the world around her. Greatness as personal integrity never deserts her, and in the end it is a rock against which her corrupt siblings dash themselves to pieces. But the world is not changed. Her heir, the young Duke, is innocent; but the action of the play has found little support for the idea that innocence is an effective political trait.[54]

The Duchess is a virtuous great lady and Vittoria Corombona is a clever harlot on the make, but they share the pathos of victims of the power games they must play and cannot hope to win. In both cases their disability as players has to be measured by the cynical commentary of their manipulators, Flamineo in *The White Devil* and Bosola in *The Duchess of Malfi*. These are socially disappointed 'superfluous men', like Vindice and Hippolyto in *The Revenger's Tragedy*, the children of landowners who turned their patrimony into cash and promptly spent it, graduates who were 'fain to heel [their] tutor's stockings | At least seven years' (*White Devil*, I. ii. 322–3) in order to survive, and who now relish with Montaignian detachment the immorality of the world in which they make their living. And it is in these terms that Webster can celebrate the failure of an individualism that sees into the vicious world of power, but cannot change it.

---

[54] Shirley's *The Cardinal* (1641; printed 1653), one of the last tragedies in the repertory, shows an interesting shift of focus on this topic of woman's strength and vulnerability. Like Webster's play, *The Cardinal* deals with the fate of a widowed duchess who chooses to marry a man of lower social station and so provokes revenge from a cardinal whose nephew had been earmarked for the honour. In both cases the plot is complex, full of reversals and surprises, but, in Shirley's rendering, the complexity is not driven by the intense family emotion (and its verbal manifestation, an intense poetry) that marks *The Duchess of Malfi*. There is little sense in Shirley of a society held together by its corruption; individuals whip up their own lines of advancement, and so (as in a soufflé) create large volume but less mass.

The Changeling is the tragedy in this group with the simplest moral structure, in part because it deals with people of lower status, and therefore with fewer lives depending on their whims.[55] Beatrice-Joanna, the 'great lady' of the action, is daughter to the governor of the fort in Alicante in Spain. But her 'greatness' comes more from her magisterial sense of herself than from social rank. She is about to marry when we first meet her; but seeing in church a man she fancies better, she becomes desperate to escape from the first choice and marry the second. A rough ex-soldier (given the premonitory name of Deflores[56]), her father's servant and hateful to her for his scarred face and lack of elegance, dogs her footsteps with dog-like devotion. His trade has been killing; why should she not draw on his devotion by getting him to kill the superfluous betrothed? The proposal fills him with ecstasy, and he quickly brings back her betrothal ring (with the finger attached to it, perhaps as a phallic hint) as a proof of service rendered and specifications fulfilled. She shudders at the sight though not at the advantage. He will need payment of course and she intends to be generous. But what he is after is not her money but her body. In the great recognition scene in the middle of the play (Act III, Scene iii), Beatrice-Joanna discovers that she is no longer the commander of action but its slave, as her assurance of superiority collapses into the requirement that she be 'the deed's creature' and the murderer's bedfellow-accomplice. As Deflores tells her,

> Look but into your conscience ...
>
>   .   .   .   .   .   .
>
>   ... you'll find me there your equal:
> Push, fly not to your birth, but settle you
> In what the act has made you, y'are no more now;
> You must forget your parentage to me:
> Y'are the deed's creature.

$$\text{(III. iv. 132-7)}$$

---

[55] William Archer's rewrite of *The Changeling* under the title of *Beatriz Juana* (printed in *Three Plays* (London, 1927)) shows that, in spite of his general attack on Elizabethan dramaturgy in *The Old Drama and the New* (London, 1923), he could find the structure of modern drama inside *this* play. Of course he remodels it after Strindberg's *Miss Julie* and so turns it into a study of a *femme fatale*. The intrigue becomes much more complicated, and, spread over a much longer period of time, loses the sense of the people in it as the puppets of a fate their poetry recognizes but which remains outside their control.

[56] This is the form of the name in the first edition.

Thereafter, in the hurried intrigues to conceal what has happened, she becomes more and more dependent on 'the wondrous necessary man' who can help her murder her way back into respectability. But the disruptive violence of their lust for one another cannot be held inside the roles that good society expects; all must come out. Beatrice-Joanna comes to see that she has indeed changed her parentage. As she tells her father:

> I am that of your blood was taken from you
> For your better health. Look no more upon't,
> But cast it to the ground regardlessly,
> Let the common sewer take it from distinction.
> Beneath the stars, upon yon meteor,
> Ever hung my fate, 'mongst things corruptible.
> I ne'er could pluck it from him, my loathing
> Was prophet to the rest, but ne'er believed,
> Mine honour fell with him, and now my life.
>
> (v. iii. 150–8)

She is a changeling, a child brought up as one of the family, but whose identity is suddenly revealed as coming from another source, from a fate that links her to Deflores.

The unity of this play, driven by the interaction of fate and passion has given it a hold on the modern imagination shared by few tragedies outside Shakespeare. It is a unity that is elaborated but not destroyed by the parodic sub-plot in which 'changeling' no longer refers to moral condition but to the change of status by which lovers try to gain access to an asylum-keeper's wife. Here, however, we meet the realism of a working woman who knows in advance that marital choice is for ever and that change invites ruin.[57] It is, of course, only in the higher-stakes world of the main plot that the metaphorical power of poetry gives us not only an outline story we can easily recognize (in such modern treatments as *The Postman Always Rings Twice* or *Double Indemnity*) but a density of discourse that reassembles the familiar inside a larger moral landscape.

---

[57] It is worth noting that it was the sub-plot that gave *The Changeling* its capacity to survive through the seventeenth century. Bentley notes (*JCS* iv. 863–4) that the famous actors who performed in it—Robbins, Reade, Sheppy—were all comedians.

Domestic Tragedy

To call *The Changeling* a 'domestic tragedy' would be to push the central emotional tangle too far out of the social situation that encloses it (as in all four of the tragedies just discussed) and determines its development. Yet its combination of strongly emphasized moral pattern with an accumulation of realistic details that make life seem to be safe from ultimate judgement connects it to a group of tragedies commonly called 'domestic' or 'homiletic'. I have discussed the first (and in many ways the best) of these plays, *Arden of Faversham*, in Chapter 3, and noted how the determinants of the plot—money and sexual passion—drive the characters out of their routines of bourgeois mediocrity by seeming to offer immediate profits they cannot refuse and whose moral consequence they cannot keep in focus. But *we* see them all the time inside the framework of God's laws and those of the English legal system, and see the characters' hope for escape as part of their enslavement.

Robert *Yarrington's *Two Lamentable Tragedies* (1594×*c.*1598)[58] seems to be making an effort to generalize in these terms the particulars of a local scandal by offering two murder stories together, one a 1594 event in London (celebrated in chronicle, ballad, and chapbook), the other a *novella*-like tale of an Italian orphan murdered by ruffians hired by his greedy uncle (much like the story of the babes in the wood). These are told in the play in alternating scenes and commented on by Homicide, Avarice, and Truth. What links the two stories is that in both cases Avarice leads to Homicide, and then Homicide is trumped by Truth, who calls on the London audience to verify the facts of the local case, and so (presumably) to notice that the same (true) pattern appears in the Italian one. Truth is able to end the story by assuring the audience that Homicide and Avarice cannot long enjoy their triumph

---

[58] The play is assigned to 'Rob. Yarrington' in the quarto, but is commonly thought to be the play called *Thomas Merry* (and on one occasion *Beech's Tragedy*) for which Henslowe paid Day and Haughton in November and December 1599. The only Yarrington known at this time was a member of the Scrivener's Company (who may therefore have been the scribe of the manuscript rather than the author). But these local scandals were sometimes given more than one airing and there may well have been two plays on the same crime.

Within the sea-embracing continent
Where fair Eliza, prince of piety,
Doth wear the peace-adorned diadem.

(sig. K3)

But when the play starts, Avarice seems to be in undisputed control. We begin with Merry, a London innkeeper overhearing one
of his customers (Beech) rejoicing in his contentment. Merry must
get Beech's money and then he too will have contentment. He
must kill him (Avarice leads to Homicide). But, as in *Arden of
Faversham*, ordinary people cannot handle murder cleanly; confusion and guilt immediately take over. Potential witnesses are everywhere. The first murder must be secured by a second. Merry's
sister and his hired man, Harry Williams, both see the body. Even
if they stay silent, how can the corpse be disposed of in a teeming
city of narrow spaces and prying eyes, closely controlled by the
authorities? And in the end the frenzied.effort to circumvent all
these difficulties proves pointless. Harry Williams finally decides
to confess what he has seen, driven by a burdened conscience and
hope for a reduced sentence. The clearing of conscience by confession and repentance is in fact the emotional driving force of the
whole denouement, restoring characters to their identities as members of the Christian community and enabling Christ's blood to
wash away their sin. Both Merry and his sister die assured of their
salvation, exhorting the public (both at the scaffold and in the
auditorium) to avoid the just punishment we see meted out.

I have discussed in Chapter 4 the induction to the anonymous
A Warning for Fair Women (*c.*1598×1599) as a pointer to prevailing
theoretical distinctions between tragedy and comedy. The actual
play, however, as I have noted there, gives no support to the
extreme generic oppositions set out in the induction. The plot is in
fact rather similar to the London story in *Two Lamentable Tragedies*, except that it is now lust rather than avarice that is the
motive of homicide. A 'captain' recently returned from the Irish
wars conceives an overmastering passion for a citizen's wife (Mrs
Sanders); he must murder her husband to gain access to her.
Friendly neighbours see the situation as one that can be milked for
profit, and cheer on the plot with hearty enthusiasm. As in *Arden
of Faversham*, the plans for murder meet so many setbacks (called
'accidents strange and miraculous') that the hand of God must be

assumed to be giving the sinner a second (and third) chance. But such merciful interventions only make the criminal more desperate; and in desperation he botches the deed carelessly and is quickly apprehended. All the principals are hanged, professing their repentance and looking to man's justice to liberate them into God's mercy. If it is the business of the chorus to suggest terror with its talk of 'whining ghosts' and 'ugly screech-owls', then we should note also that the actual life depicted, in which murder emerges imperceptibly out of the random processes of neighbourhood interaction, out of moves made on the assumption that nothing will come of them, asks rather for pity, a pity the audience owes to itself for the helpless way in which it is liable to see its relation with Last Things.

Interest in the homicidal actions of people like ourselves is a standard fact about human nature, and writers for the public have always been anxious to catch that interest while it is hot and turn it to immediate profit in chapbook, ballad, or play.[59] In 1605 the sensation of the moment was the wounding of wife and nurse and the murder of two of his children by Walter Calverley, a gentleman of Yorkshire. Ballad and pamphlet were quick to catch the story and two plays followed soon after: (1) *A Yorkshire Tragedy: not so new as lamentable and true* (1605×1608; printed 1608; reprinted 1619), said on the title-page to be written by Shakespeare, and (2) George *Wilkins's *The Miseries of Enforced Marriage* (1605× 1606; printed 1607; reprinted 1611, 1629, 1637). The relationship between these two plays has been much debated, but there being no safe evidence there is no trustworthy conclusion. The half-title of *A Yorkshire Tragedy* calls it *All in One; or one of the four plays in one called The Yorkshire Tragedy*. The text we have is only some 800 lines long and deals just with the end of the story, so it is

---

[59] The relationship between scandal-ballad and scandal-play is by no means clear. The best-documented instance is that of the lost 1624 play *The Late Murder in Whitechapel: or Keep the Widow Waking* (also called *The Late Murder of the Son upon the Mother*) written for the Red Bull by Dekker, Ford, Rowley, and Webster (see Sisson's *Lost Plays*). The play dealt with two recent scandals: Nathaniel Tindall's murder of his mother; and the forced marriage of a rich widow, kept drunk and sleepless for five days until she married a young fortune hunter. There were ballads on both these events. The more interestingly documented one deals with the marriage plot. This treats the widow's ordeal as a great joke and as a model for other fortune hunters, and was apparently sung outside the house of the victim. It ends with an invitation to visit the Red Bull and learn the whole story: 'And you who fain would hear the full | Discourse of this match-making | The play will teach you at the Bull | To keep the widow waking.'

entirely plausible that it is one part of a four-part play; but what the lost parts talked about cannot be known.

A Yorkshire Tragedy is a headlong account of a desperate man driven to suicidal violence by the perception that this is the only assertion of self that is open to him. Unlike the other domestic tragedies we have discussed, there is here no overt sense of guilt, until we get to the final scene, where we learn that this is a study in possession:

> Now glides the devil from me,
> Departs at every joint, heaves up my nails.
>
> . . . .
>
> Bind him . . . you blessed angels
> In that pit bottomless; let him not rise
> To make men act unnatural tragedies,
> To spread into a father, and in fury
> Make him his children's executioners,
> Murder his wife, his servants and who not.
>
> (x. 19–27)

A Yorkshire Tragedy has attracted a degree of attention quite out of proportion to the merits of the play because of the attribution to Shakespeare. The attribution may in fact have begun as a publisher's cheat,[60] but, once made, it assumed historical importance. In the eighteenth century, when the vogue for high romantic tragedy was waning, *A Yorkshire Tragedy* could be invoked as a play from the best of authors, offering an attractively novel perspective. In a rewrite of 1721 attributed to Joseph Mitchell (actually by Aaron Hill, it is said[61]) under the title of *The Fatal Extravagance*, first as a one-act then as a full-length play, it was not only an immediate success, but led to the landmark event of Lillo's *The London Merchant* (1731), which in turn led to Lessing's *Miss Sarah Sampson* (1755) and so to the whole vogue of the *bürgerliche Trauerspiel*. The opening to sentimentalism that was an essential part of this

---

[60] Pavier, the publisher, was involved later in an attempt to issue an unauthorized 'Works of Shakespeare' volume; the 1619 edition, published by Pavier and Jaggard, was part of this scheme; so perhaps the entry of *A Yorkshire Tragedy* under Shakespeare's name in 1608 was associated with it as well. See Chambers, iii. 479, and Greg 'On Certain False Dates in Shakespearian Quartos', *Library*, 9 (1908), 113–31.

[61] See Allardyce Nicoll, *History of English Drama 1660–1900* (5 vols.; Cambridge, 1923–46), ii. 119.

whole recovery of the domestic tragedy is often seen as if it was not a part of the original movement. And it is true that it is not essentially so: *Arden of Faversham* is totally unsentimental.[62] But if we look at the longer version of the Calverley story in *The Miseries of Enforced Marriage* we can see that Wilkins is making a deliberate effort to express what *A Yorkshire Tragedy* calls diabolical possession in terms of undeserved misfortune. When this play begins, Calverley (now called William Scarborow) is aged 18 and in ward to a guardian who has total control of his estate and his person. Scarborow falls in love and is betrothed to the daughter of a Yorkshire knight; but almost immediately he is recalled to London and forced into marriage with his patron's niece. Believing that his betrothal vows are registered in heaven, he must also believe that his marriage is adultery and his children bastards. His betrothed kills herself in despair and he himself embarks on a suicidal round of violent dissipation, aiming to destroy himself and (incidentally) all those around him.

By fleshing out the story with realistic details of tavern low life and the tricks of usury, Wilkins moves it closer to the mode of prodigal-son comedy, as described in Chapter 8. And so, in keeping with that mode (and in defiance of the historical events), the prodigal is reclaimed at the last minute. A faithful servant tricks the parasites and scroungers who have battened on the prodigality of despair, and eventually breaks through the guilt of his master to secure confession and repentance. Wife and children are saved. New sources of money suddenly spring up and ease the reconciliations.

The move from the terror of sin to pity for the sinner is more fully exemplified in Heywood's *A Woman Killed with Kindness* (1603) than in any other domestic tragedy. Perhaps this is part of the reason why it is the play with most appeal to a modern sensibility.[63] The social and personal assumptions it draws on are not

---

[62] But when Lillo rewrote it in 1759 there were a number of emollient changes: it now appears that Alice Arden had been betrothed to Mosbie in her youth, but was forcibly married to Arden. Even so, she cannot hold the dagger given her to stab him, and when Mosbie completes the deed she goes insane (see Ernest Bernbaum, *The Drama of Sensibility* (Boston, 1915), 35). It would be interesting to know how Dekker and Jonson handled such material in their lost play, *Page of Plymouth* (for which Henslowe paid them in 1599). As represented in ballad and pamphlet, this is another story of forced marriage leading to the murder of the unwanted husband.

[63] But it was not enough for the eighteenth century. Ben Victor's rewrite as *The Fatal Error* (1776) shows Mrs Frankford as even more deserving of pity than Heywood allowed (Bernbaum, *Drama of Sensibility*, 35–7).

different from those we have met elsewhere, but their doctrinal expression is more fully internalized. Like the others, this is a story (or rather two stories) of people caught up in actions they can hardly account for, where guilt as the natural accompaniment quickly follows transgression, and where pity is the predominant emotion. The play begins with wedding festivities, but these soon turn into violent competitiveness among the country gentlemen present, and competitiveness leads to murder, and murder to vendetta. Meanwhile the Frankfords (the newly married couple) settle down into an idyllic existence with the groom's dependent and best friend. But the best friend persuades the wife into adultery, and adultery is followed by immediate guilt and banishment from bed and board.

That the husband does not kill the adulterous couple marks a deliberately planned stroke against audience assumptions. The adulterers expect, and in some degree desire, death. As Mrs Frankford remarks: 'He cannot be so base as to forgive me | Nor I so shameless to accept his pardon' (Scene xiii, ll. 139–40). Death would give specific meaning to what has happened. But this is a play that exploits with great tact the mixed moralities and muddled apprehensions of a real world; the certainties that servants and onlookers seek to impose on the situation cannot be accepted by the central characters. In the vendetta story the merciless pursuer of the murderer turns into his secret benefactor, and the loving brother becomes the sacrificer of his sister. In the adultery story the adulterers are not found in lustful twines but 'lying | Close in each other's arms and fast asleep. | . . . two precious souls | Bought with my Saviour's blood' (Scene xiii, ll. 42–5), and the husband's prime emotion is not rage but regret:

> Oh God! Oh God! that it were possible
> To undo things done; to call back yesterday;
> That Time could turn his swift and sandy glass
> To untell the days and to redeem these hours.
>
> (Scene xiii, ll. 52–5)

Christian 'kindness' to the erring wife is not seen, however, as a cancelling of the sentence; she at once understands its significance and translates it into execution in death by starvation; the revenge that kills her is a Christian revenge enacted by the transgressor herself, in repentance, fasting, and prayer. Thus, having mortified her sinful body, she is justified at once in the eyes of God and of her husband; reacceptance into marriage and the Christian community become one and the same thing. In one sense we seem to have returned to the contradictions noted in *Two Lamentable Tragedies* and *A Warning for Fair Women*, between the clear-cut conventions used in the dramatic framework and the complex impulses of those whose actions are being portrayed.

Some fifteen to twenty years after the period of the domestic tragedies I have been discussing, Dekker, Ford, and Rowley wrote a play with obvious affinities to the domestic mode, but *The Witch of Edmonton* (1621; printed 1658) handles the material in very different terms. The Prologue invokes memory of *The Merry Devil of Edmonton* (see Chapter 8 on this as a nostalgic topographical play):

> The Town of Edmonton hath lent the stage
> A devil and a witch, both in an age.
> To make comparisons it were uncivil
> Between so even a pair, a Witch and Devil.
> . . . .
> In acts deserving name, the proverb says
> 'Once good, and ever'. Why not so in plays?
>
> (Prologue, ll. 1–10)

But the new play is not simply cashing in on a popular title. It raises the connection to make a comment on nostalgic comedy rather than to claim membership. It resembles the earlier mode by stressing the community that imposes meaning rather than the individuals who hope to hide from it. But the community is now no small-town idyll, but rather a trap for those without money, driving them towards desperate measures, and opening their minds to the Devil, who is present as an inevitable part of the common life. The three-part structure (perhaps reflecting the three authors who collaborated to produce it[64]) shows three different stories, all arising from the same narrowing and oppressive class structure. Winifrid, as a servant girl, is helpless to resist Sir Arthur Clarington's sexual exploitation until Frank Thorney, who believes she is his alone, marries her to save her child from the taint of bastardy. But he is helpless before his father's demand that he secure the dowry

---

[64] It is usually assumed that the Cuddy Banks part was written by Rowley, the Thorney story by Ford, and the Mother Sawyer episodes by Dekker.

of old Carter's daughter. Old Thorney is helpless in the face of bankruptcy if he cannot secure the dowry. Sir Arthur will give Winifrid a dowry, but only as a means to set up the safe and permanent liaison that her marriage will provide. And this, understandably, she refuses.

Caught in deprivation even more helplessly than these, Mother Sawyer is stuck at the bottom of the pile, and subjected to every slander and indignity; she cannot escape unless by cashing in the reputation the town imposes on her—that of a witch. On a particularly bad day she wishes aloud that she could have a familiar to give her the powers that the village charges her with. Enter the devil in the unthreatening form of a black dog. He will give her real power over her oppressors. Even more important, he can give her the same reassurance as a suckling child, one who tells her he loves her. The black dog also offers Frank Thorney an easy way out of his dilemma. He can escape from his bigamous marriage to Old Carter's daughter by murdering her. Inevitably, as in other domestic tragedies, the murder is bungled, and the culprit cannot conceal his guilt from the community; he is quickly arraigned and condemned. The black dog who prompted the murder will not help him; he is off now to join court life in the capital. This little town is not a separate world but only an outpost of big city corruption; and with these successes behind him, the dog can hope to move into higher spheres.

Frank Thorney and Mother Sawyer must face the legal penalties of their crimes. But here the emphasis is less on the need to secure God's forgiveness by confession than on the suspect nature of the justice system that claims to be His representative. At her trial Mother Sawyer offers a redefinition of witchcraft that indicts her oppressors no less than herself. These gentlemen-accusers think that their deployment of legal power is innocent (Sir Arthur is the most obviously self-deluded). She, being old and poor, must be supposed to be using forbidden means; but she has her own view of the high life of the court, the city, and the law:

> What are your painted things in princes' courts,
> Upon whose eyelids lust sits blowing fires
> To burn men's souls in sensual hot desires,
> Upon whose naked paps a lecher's thought
> Acts sin in fouler shape than can be wrought?
>   .   .   .   .

These, by enchantments can whole lordships change
To trunks of rich attire; turn ploughs and teams
To Flanders mares and coaches; and huge trains
Of servitors to a French butterfly.
. . . .
Are not these witches?

(IV. i. 103–17; cf. 125–36)

The rhetoric tells us that Mother Sawyer has been listening to the satiric court tragedies of Middleton and Webster.

The black dog, as an integrated part of village life, reflects what their relation to the community leads his victims to require. He devours only those whose social isolation makes them desperate. Fed by desperation, he becomes a monster. But his animal status allows him also to be a figure of comedy; we should remember that, however well acted, a talking dog will always have some pantomimic quality on the stage. Cuddy Banks in the third story shows us that the price of immunity is simple-mindedness. He is another frustrated lover, but he finds a talking dog only a comic wonder, not all that different from the hobby-horse that Cuddy plays in the local morris dance. The scene in which the dog plays the fiddle for the hobby-horse's dance returns the devil to his comic role as a rustic superstition. Cuddy is completely unfazed by the recital of the enormities the dog can commit; in his innocence and humility he can only wish him to be a good dog:

Were it not possible for thee to become an honest dog yet? 'tis a base life that you lead, Tom, to serve witches, to kill innocent children, to kill harmless cattle, to 'stroy corn and fruit &c[65] . . . Or, Tom, if you could give your mind to ducking, I know you can swim, fetch and carry, some shopkeeper in London would take great delight in you and be a tender master over you. (V. i. 152–9)

Real Politics

Domestic tragedy stands to one side of the staple commodity of the popular stage, the romantic melodrama in which kings and queens and princesses and generals impose their personal entanglements

[65] The '&c' that appears from time to time in dramatic texts seems to denote a licence for improvisation. If these lines were written by Rowley for his own performance, the appropriateness of the licence is obvious.

on the power structure of the State. Domestic tragedy has plenty of personal entanglements, but without effect on the constitution, being focused on the Protestant privacy of man with God. On the other side of the central body of Elizabethan tragedy stands a small number of plays in which politics in fact obliterates personal entanglement, allowing the documentary 'truth' about contemporary affairs to make a direct appeal to the political concerns of the audience.

The anonymous *A Larum for London: or The Siege of Antwerp, with the Ventrous Acts and Deeds of the Lame Soldier* (*c.*1598×1600) is a historical horror story, based on the eyewitness account by George Gascoigne (*The Spoil of Antwerp*), published in 1576, only one month after the events it describes. Gascoigne's interest is mostly factual. He does not conceal the extent of the rapes, mutilations, tortures ('like Michael Angelo [his] tables of doomsday'), but is short on explanations: it must have been 'God's just wrath', but he does not specify what could have provoked such wrath. He praises the military skill which allowed the Spaniards to brush aside the city defenders, standing 'every man armed in readiness before his door', as a technical matter quite independent of moral judgement.

The play, on the other hand, is totally obsessed by the moral issue. As in Greene and Lodge's *A Looking Glass for London and England* (see Chapter 3), the target aimed at is here and now: Antwerp is invoked only because what Antwerp was yesterday London may be tomorrow. The literary mode of both plays is that of Old Testament denunciation; in *A Looking Glass for London and England* this is quite specific: Hosea and Jonah are there in person to denounce Babylon and to turn the minds of the citizens towards repentance. And God's interest in the matter is made evident by a series of miraculous stage effects. But *A Larum for London* is painstakingly prosaic and relies on realistic detail, not poetic imagination, to convey the message.

Instead of the monarchical pomp of Nineveh, the sins of Antwerp are those of self-indulgent money-making. The citizens are 'swilling epicures', 'swollen-bellied burghers' whose 'degenerate minds' are incapable of understanding that self-interest will not protect them. Indeed the effeminacy of their flaunted and unprotected wealth is immediately understood as an invitation to rape: 'She must be courted; marry herself invites | And beckons us into her sportful bed' (ll. 83–4). The point once made, the plot is only one horror after another. The only resistance offered is led by the English.[66] The Spaniards pillage until there is no more to be squeezed out, and then Time as Epilogue draws the moral that all cities that 'in sin and pleasure take delight | Will suffer the same fate'.

The anti-capitalism of *A Larum for London* was certainly relevant to the situation of London; but the angle of attack was one which, in theory at least, everyone accepted. A political theatre which confined itself to arguing in general terms against economic values and on behalf of patriotism and military preparedness would have made censorship a superfluous activity. But consensus politics of this kind could not go on pleasing the more sophisticated audience of the seventeenth century, with results that kept the censor very busy.

The Tragedy of Sir John van Oldenbarnavelt (1619; MS) is usually assumed to be the work of Fletcher and Massinger. It offers us a remarkable example of the dramatist as foreign correspondent, working with all the promptitude that such a role requires; for the play was 'written, acted, censored, written again, within six weeks of [Barnavelt's] execution'.[67] The complexity of that list of activities points of course to the difficulty of being a foreign correspondent in this period. Clearly there was an appetite for a drama of contemporary politics, and the rewards of a successful production were presumably commensurate with the effort that had to be made to secure one. In the case of *Barnavelt*, negotiation seems to have produced the right result: a letter-writer of the time tells us that 'our players have found the means to go through with the play of Barnavelt, and it hath had many spectators and received applause'.[68] How many performances were allowed we do not know.

The play deals with the last (tragic) act of a long political career. Barnavelt was the 'advocate' of the States of Holland to the Netherlands Estates General. He was celebrated as a lawyer, orator, politician, and had made himself the dominant figure in the civil administration of the country, and so the obvious opponent to Prince Maurice of Nassau, the commander of the Dutch forces

---

[66] In Gascoigne, more plausibly, the main effort of the English merchants is to secure their own neutrality.
[67] *The Revels History of Drama in English*, iv. *1613–1660*, ed. Lois Potter (London, 1981), 170.   [68] Bentley, *JCS* iii. 415.

fighting Spain. Barnavelt's sense of the authority of the civil government, and of the need to keep princely and military power in subjection to it, raised obvious issues about the distribution of power in England; the censor's deletions in the manuscript are mainly designed to protect the Prince from the anti-monarchical sentiments that the play makes space for. But in fact politics is everywhere limited to the consequences of particular character, avoiding general issues. Barnavelt is presented as a man of tireless political resource, but fuelled by self-esteem rather than by any search for the good of his country. His Arminian religious position is likewise made to seem part of his hunger for power, stress being laid on the Arminian tendency to subordinate the theological to the political. The play offers no opinion on the propriety of the political judgements on either side of the questions at issue; indeed it hardly allows us to know what the basic issues are. Probably the most daring point made is that the Prince operates as a politician no less than Barnavelt, calculating the odds in terms of *realpolitik* though always presenting them in the rhetoric of idealism. It is a tribute to the openness (or inefficiency) of the censors of the drama that such a point could be represented on the stage.

If we can wonder at space for political comment in *Barnavelt*, what is left to say about the most remarkable example of free speech in the Elizabethan theatre, Middleton's *A Game at Chess* . . . *as it was acted nine days together at the Globe* (1624)?[69] This extraordinary event (perhaps more extraordinary as an event than as a play) broke all the rules for dramatic performance. It rode roughshod over the usual repertory mode of production; the playhouse was so crowded 'that by scores they came away for want of a place, though as yet little past one', 'old and young, rich and poor, masters and servants, papists and puritans, wise men etc., churchmen and statesmen',[70] so that the company earned between £1,000 and £1,500 over the week-and-a-half run.

That such an extraordinary event occurred at all implies that there were extraordinary circumstances behind the performance. Not only was the play not suppressed at once, but it was actually

---

[69] Ibid., i. 13 n. 2, undercuts the frequently assumed uniqueness of the 'nine days together' by pointing to other examples—*Rawlins's *The Rebellion* (9 days), *Marmion's *Holland's Leaguer* (6 days), J.W.'s *The Valiant Scot* (5 days), J.D.'s *The Knave in Grain* ('many days').

[70] See the 'Revels' edition by T. H. Howard-Hill (Manchester, 1993), 198, 205.

given a licence by the Master of the Revels. Suppression did indeed come, after nine days, and the players were forbidden ever to act it again; but it was printed without hindrance in 1625, and neither Middleton nor the actors were imprisoned. Most remarkably of all, on 27 August 1624, only some thirteen days after the last performance, the King allowed the company to resume acting. Letter-writers of the time[71] as well as modern scholars have suspected that some powerful faction at court protected the play and perhaps even set it up.

To look at *A Game at Chess* as a play rather than an event is to note not only the opportunity for political comment that an unusual situation[72] created, but also the limited range of things that could be said inside the norms of Jacobean dramaturgy. The story is told as a moral not a political allegory: Anglo-Spanish relations in 1623–4 are represented as a game of chess between the white house (England) and the black house (Spain and the Papacy), and this allows the antithetical and set structure of the game to absorb and conceal the manœuvring of the particular political history. It is no accident that the only two characters who escape out of their formalization as chess pieces—Gondomar, the Spanish ambassador, and De Dominis the turncoat Archbishop of Spalato—were long resident in England and already familiar targets of satire and pamphlet, and it is as caricatures of this kind that they make their mark rather than as agents of specific policies.

In its use of allegory to formalize the struggle between England and Spain, Protestantism and Catholicism, *A Game at Chess* is not unique. Most obviously it resembles Dekker's *The Whore of Babylon* (see Chapter 6). The comparison helps to define both what the two plays share and what the gap of time between 1606 and 1624 has set between them. *The Whore of Babylon* is an exercise in nostalgic hagiography, fed by emotions and images out of the Book of Revelation and *The Faerie Queene*, so that the politics is not flattened into game but exalted into apocalypse. Middleton's tone is more detached: as a chess game, politics has become a battle of wits,

---

[71] John Wooley's letter of 20 August ('Revels' edition, p. 203) says: 'The Master of the Revels . . . allowed of it, and it is thought not without leave from the higher powers (I mean the P[rince] and D[uke of Buckingham] if not from the K[ing], for they were all loth to have it forbidden'.

[72] The strongly anti-Spanish sentiment that swept the country when Charles and Buckingham returned from Madrid after the breakdown of the proposed 'Spanish marriage' united popular opinion with that of Parliament and of the court (led by Buckingham himself).

whether for good or bad ends. God's side wins (naturally); but only because His agents are clever enough to outwit their opponents. The difference between the two plays conforms closely to that noted above between the providential history of the chronicles and the pragmatic history of Bacon and Macchiavelli; one might guess that both instances point to a larger change in cultural sensibility.

Retrospect: 'King Leir' and 'King Lear'

King Lear (?1605) is one of the most difficult plays to place on a map of Elizabethan tragedy. A modern assumption that it can be grouped only 'with works like the *Prometheus Vinctus* and the *Divine Comedy*, and even with the greatest symphonies of Beethoven and the statues in the Medici Chapel'[73] might seem enough by itself to ensure that no other play could be like it. But it is not necessary to raise issues so grand to make the point that *King Lear* is not easy to describe in the usual terms of comparative study. Yet, when we look at it in the context of the standard types of tragedy discussed above, it becomes obvious that it draws constantly on the formulations that they employ. In this respect *King Lear* offers a searching glance at a whole range of tragedies around it.

In terms of subject matter the play harks back to an early phase of Elizabethan drama—to *Gorboduc*, to *The Misfortunes of Arthur*, to *Locrine*[74]—as a 'Complaint' tragedy concerned with the primitive history of the nation, seen as a saga of royal family discord, of sibling rivalry, of fatal discontinuities between fathers and children. And again, as in these earlier plays, the ability to achieve nationhood through compromise founders under the double burden of the father–king's weakness and his inflexibility. As a monarch, Lear is given the arbitrariness, the self-centredness, the inability to deal with opinions not his own that marks in other plays the attitude of the tyrant. But, as is characteristic of *King Lear*, attitude is not allowed to develop into action. Lear is obsessed by fantasies of his power to understand, to judge, to sentence, without

---

[73] Bradley, *Shakespearean Tragedy*, 244.

[74] *Locrine*, like *King Leir*, belongs to the group of 'Queen's Men plays' that came on the market in 1594 (see pp. 50–1). Henslowe reports a performance of *King Leir* at the Rose in April of that year by a (combined ?) company of Queen's and Sussex's Men.

reference to any evidence outside his own mind. But having given away his power in a supreme act of self-confidence, fantasy supplies the only world in which he can tyrannize. The weakness that leaves women in command then sets up the situation we have seen in *Bonduca* and *Julia Agrippina*; confusion between rule and sexual appetite turns domestic discord into national ruin.

The same pattern of action represented by fantasy can be discerned in the play's relation to revenge tragedy. 'No, you unnatural hags', says Lear, 'I will have such revenges on you both | That all the world shall—I will do such things— | What they are yet I know not; but they shall be | The terrors of the earth' (ii. iv. 279–82). But we all know that revenge operates by manipulative skills, by patience, cunning, secrecy—qualities completely opposite to any possessed by Lear. In *Titus Andronicus* and *The Spanish Tragedy* we have already seen old men (in *Titus*, a family tyrant like Lear) pushed aside by denizens of the new world, ingenious plotters who deprive them of power to revenge and leave them stranded on the shores of fantasy. But in these plays the felt need to revenge begets cunning, and cunning is fulfilled in a bloody outcome.[75] In *Lear* the fantasy of revenge is quickly absorbed into concern with a general injustice that revenge cannot cure and that indeed renders the individual history unimportant.

This movement from personal to generalizing moral concern points most obviously in the direction of *Henry VI* and to the history of Elidure in that curious play *Nobody and Somebody* (a near contemporary of *King Lear*). In both these plays a passive and virtuous king is the victim of factious nobles and wives whose quarrel for precedence produces national chaos. In this respect *Nobody and Somebody* clearly derives from the Estates play (of the type of *A Knack to Know a Knave*) in which the breakdown in central authority leads to corruption at all social levels. But again one must say that in *Lear* the symptoms of breakdown, the rascal beadle, the false justicer, the scurvy politician, are not presented in the action and appear only as part of the imaginative vision.

Many of these cross-currents in *King Lear* come from its source play, *The True Chronicle History of King Leir* (*c.*1588×1594; entered in the Stationers' Register, 14 May 1594; printed 1605). *King*

---

[75] In the play that Dover Wilson called 'Lear's still-born twin', *Timon of Athens* (*c.*1606×*c.*1608; printed 1623), the fantasy of revenge acquires power by the narrowness of the area on which it is focused, and so can be fulfilled by military means.

Leir (like *King Lear* after it) is a difficult play to place. Though intensely serious, it can hardly be called a tragedy, though it certainly handles tragic potentials: Cordella is reduced to rags and misery; Leir is brought near to death by starvation; Ragan hires the Oswald character to kill Leir and his faithful companion, Perillus. But nobody in fact dies. The invading French army is welcomed by the British population. Ragan and Gonorill are defeated and fly the country; Leir will spend the rest of his life under the 'kind nursery' of Cordella. In terms of plot structure probably we should call *King Leir* a romance; like the romantic adventure plays discussed in Chapter 8, it shows us malice, exile, and hardship leading back by chance to recovery of all that was lost. But unlike *The Weakest Goeth to the Wall* or *The Blind Beggar of Bednall Green* it makes the family, not the society, the centre of the struggle, and so develops a power of personal venom and a sense of despair not found in those plays. But, as if in compensation, it also shows, to a degree unparalleled in the analogues, an unshakeable trust in God's providence and belief in the power of passive goodness to disarm active evil.

The central and longest scene in the play shows us Leir and Perillus in a grove where Ragan has promised to meet them. But instead of coming herself, she sends a murderer to fulfil her purposes. For 340 lines the two old men practise what I suppose can be called passive resistance to murder. They assume that the assassin has come to kill them for their money; he can have (and gladly) everything they possess. They cannot believe he really means harm; or if he does he must be an agent sent by God to punish Leir for his unkindness to Cordella. That would be only just, and he should strike straight away. In any case, God's will must be accepted. Each offers to die if the other can be saved. Perillus should not die, says Leir; he has offended no one. To kill Leir by the order of his daughter, says Perillus, would be the damnable sin of parricide. As the scene develops, the murderer, who had intended to play with the two old men as a cat with a mouse, is forced into bewildered passivity. And then God speaks in thunder to confirm the arguments made; the murderer drops his daggers and runs away. The passive endurance of age, like that of innumerable wives in the drama of the time, is finally accepted and rewarded as a God-given strength.

Shakespeare takes this romantic story and turns it into what is unmistakably a tragedy. Lear may be too old to fight back in any literal sense, but he is never passive;[76] his emotional absolutism is unrelenting. In his own mind his power to curse, to exclude, to judge remains undiminished. What he lacks in soldiers, courts of law, furred robes, he can conjure out of imagination. When he misses human respondents, he can converse with the gods or the forces of nature. When royal clothes are inadequate to express the physical integrity of his power, he can rip them off and stride naked into the storm, still taking total responsibility for everything that happens. Such a force can only be given counterbalance by an equal absolutism in the daughters. In *King Leir*, Gonorill and Ragan work by evasion, uttering pious sentiments and sly innuendoes in public while conspiring in secret to kill their father. Shakespeare's more violent scenario demands more searing confrontations.

Lear's failure to become a 'real' revenger might be said to save him from the ethical short circuit of supposing revenge to be the answer to the mystery of evil. As in *Hamlet*, mental derangement opens up an unlimited range of possibilities, without commitment to any of them; so powerlessness enables Lear to understand power, as 'nothing almost sees miracles | But misery' (II. ii. 165–6). It is this transfer of focus from action to imagination that makes it impossible to confine *King Lear* inside any preconceived sequential structure of action, sustained as it is by poetry's essential capacity to metamorphose reality into imagination and imagination into a parallel universe of reality.[77] Edgar makes a rational decision to exchange his identity for that of a lunatic beggar; but almost immediately he suffers another metamorphosis as his voice has to be tuned to the chorus of madmen on the heath. Then he is 'a most poor man made tame to fortune's blows', then a sturdy rustic, beating down Oswald's rapier with his 'ballow', then a knight in armour, challenging his half-brother to chivalric combat. To take these literally as a chronological sequence of rational choices is to ignore what the poetry tells us—that they are parallel rather than sequential insights into a human nature which is shown to be

---

[76] Much of the source's passivity is passed on to Gloucester. We may notice the extent to which the whole sub-plot replays the main story as suffering in the body rather than the mental turmoil of Lear, 'cut to the brains'.

[77] It is no doubt this imaginative focus (or 'symbolic dimension') that has led critics from Lamb to Bradley to say that *King Lear* is too great for the stage, assuming that the stage is irremediably committed to real people performing real actions.

simultaneously sane and insane, revengeful and forgiving, spiritual and bestial, magnificent and pathetic.

The power of imagination to see into the interrelationship of things is continually invoked in *King Lear*, but also continually marked down as falsifying. Thus, after the battle, Lear can imagine that he and Cordelia can live a life of blessed deprivation in prison ('Upon such sacrifices, my Cordelia | The gods themselves throw incense' (v. iii. 20–1); and when the gods do nothing of the kind, with unflagging resource he can imagine that he sees her still breathing. The whole denouement is in fact set up to play against one another the human incapacity to conceive existence without imagining a future and the recognition that we are being offered not a future, but an end. The romance plot that Shakespeare inherited from *King Leir* (soon to be reinstated in Tate's version of the play) is rehandled here to show that the indomitable quality of the heroic will must be its own reward, since it finds no justification outside itself. The great antagonists of drama, the self and the world, imagination and reality, have fought to a standstill. We leave both of them drained of assertion, drained ourselves, and facing the basic paradox of tragedy: 'Is this the promised end | Or image of that horror?' (v. iii. 264–5).

10. Tragicomedy

PHILIP SIDNEY thought of tragicomedy as a 'mongrel' form, supposing that both social decorum and classical tradition (not easily distinguished) demanded a mutual accommodation of form and content such as comedy and tragedy separately provide. Battista Guarini, in the practice of *Il pastor fido* (1590) and the theory of the *Compendio della poesia tragicomica* (1603), looked rather for the tension of potential imbalance that an integrated form offering near-death but no-death provides, and argued that this was a more appropriate mode for a Christian civilization. Fletcher's *The Faithful Shepherdess* (1608) brought this baroque ideal to the attention of the London audience of the boys' theatre. But even this élite group was not much taken with such continental novelties. They were looking, Fletcher tells us in his Preface, for 'a play of country hired shepherds . . . sometimes laughing together, and sometimes killing one another' (as in Greenian pastoral romance). True pastoral tragicomedy, he declares, is not an alternation of kissing and killing, but is defined by the fact that 'it wants deaths, which is enough to make it no tragedy, yet brings some near it, which is enough to make it no comedy; which must be a representation of familiar people, with such kind of trouble as no life be questioned, so that a god is as lawful in this as in a tragedy, and mean people as in a comedy'.

It is no accident that these remarks relate to a play written for the boys' theatre. I have described their repertory as one of self-conscious innovation, in which static satire (which limits mobility of character) and dynamic comedy (that opens it up) struggled for union. In 1604 Marston defined the resultant form (as it appeared in *The Malcontent*) as *Tragiecomedia* in the Stationers' Register and as *aspera Thalia* in the dedication. In practice, of course, 'wanting deaths but bringing some near it' was already characteristic of both public and private theatre; the plays of prodigals (see Chapter 8) fulfil this requirement almost in excess, requiring their protagonists to stand under the gallows before the charges can be dropped and the hero returned to happiness. But Fletcher adds a dimension incompatible with this when he speaks of 'such kind of trouble as no life be questioned', which seems to imply that the 'bringing some near' to death cannot be handled too realistically. We must, presumably, be assured that we are watching a world in which the threats are too stylized (as in pastoral) to cause any actual anxiety. William Empson has pointed out with exemplary élan, in his *Some Versions of Pastoral*, that pastoral is basically concerned with imaginary solutions to class divisions. In the sixteenth century the only acceptable solution required that the division be preserved but that its political meaning become invisible. This is the mode of *The Faithful Shepherdess* (though not of Sidney's *Arcadia*) and we can see the Beaumont and Fletcher dramaturgy up to this point as a set of steps to turn the standard play forms towards that invisibility.

The Prologue to *The Woman Hater* (1606) illustrates the degree of self-consciousness involved, not only of fashion ('Gentlemen, Inductions are out of date, and a Prologue in verse is as stale as a black velvet cloak and a bay garland'[1]) but of the authors' own contribution to the change:

I dare not call it a comedy or tragedy; 'tis perfectly neither. . . . Some things in it you may meet with which are out of the common road: a duke there is, and the scene lies in Italy, as those two things lightly we never miss. But you shall not find in it the ordinary and overworn trade of jesting at lords and courtiers and citizens, without taxation of any particular or new vice by them found out but at the persons of them. Such he that made this thinks vile; and for his own part vows that he did never think but that a lord born might be a wise man and a courtier an honest man. (Prologue, ll. 12–26)

One thing is clear in this Prologue: the satiric impulse that lies behind the dramaturgy of Marston and Jonson (with its sharp antinomies in style and structure) is being disowned (as is, one might add, the whole tradition that descends from the Morality play). The author, we are told, 'means not to purchase [his audience] at the dear cost of his ears' (as the authors of *Eastward Ho* had been in danger of doing).[2] The loosely articulated plot is carried by a smooth and fluent verse that engages our admiration but distances it. This is an Italian dukedom, as the Prologue says,

---

[1] Cloak and garland provided the characteristic dress for Prologue actors.

[2] Of course such assertions of innocence are standard features of plays that are clearly uninnocent. *The Woman Hater* does contain elements that could be part of a political satire, but they are organized in a way that defuses such potential.

but the court's corruption is presented as a source of laughter not anger, and the duke's political function is mentioned only to be denied. We begin with the 'humorous' duke getting up at four in the morning. His courtiers guess that this is the beginning of a disguised duke play. Has he risen 'to cure some strange corruptions in the commonwealth' or 'to walk the public streets disguised | to see the street's disorders'? No. 'I break my sleeps thus soon to see a wench' (I. i. 11–29).

There is no evidence that *The Woman Hater*, in spite of its claim to novelty, raised much interest. The second Beaumont and Fletcher play, *Cupid's Revenge* (c.1607×1612), seems, however, to have been one of the most prized properties of the Queen's Revels company,[3] as that body passed through its various transformations.[4] It was played at court in 1612, 1613 (twice), 1624, and 1637. This time the authors start from the tragic end of the spectrum, picking up a melodramatic confrontation with evil from Sidney's *Arcadia*.[5] A tense political situation is offered, but politics is evaded. An infatuated old king is destroying the integrity of the State, but the noble prince cannot deal with what is happening except in terms of personal relationships. Cynical commentary by the courtiers is presented but is not given any political significance; their attitudes point to natures disengaged from any active interchange with the system. The 'humours' that drive the characters confine them to set roles, but these are not held up to scorn; they are shown merely as representations of social fact.

Beaumont and Fletcher's enormously popular play for the boys, *The Scornful Lady* (1613×1616), begins as if it was going to be a Middletonian city comedy. The young heir loses the mortgage on his estates to a city usurer. And, as usual, the usurer's next target, a rich city widow, is more affected by the young heir's sexual potential than by the old man's money bags. But no intrigue emerges from this situation. The prodigal heir recovers his fortune without

---

[3] See John H. Astington, 'The Popularity of *Cupid's Revenge*', *SEL* 19 (1979), 215–27.
[4] See below, n. 7.
[5] Technically speaking, *Cupid's Revenge* is a tragedy; but, as E. M. Waith remarks, 'if all the characters were saved from death and if the play ended in repentance and reconciliation, its total effect would be very little different' (*The Pattern of Tragicomedy in Beaumont and Fletcher* (New Haven, 1952), 14). Cf. Una Ellis-Fermor, *The Jacobean Drama* (London, 1936), 205: 'Something, then, in the mood . . . has disabled us from distinguishing, in the world we are now moving in, the characters, emotions and events that will lead to tragedy from those that will lead through romantic stress to escape'.

wit or reformation. Opposites are placed in relation to one another as psychological elements not as pressures in society and can be resolved without social consequence. The young man's erotic energy is separated from economic and political disruption; his desires can be fulfilled without bringing into play the contradictions of society. The usurer repents and gives away his money; the economic potential of the story is lost in the complexities of the struggle for personal 'maistrie' in the will-she-won't-she main plot.[6]

In these terms it does not appear that Fletcher's *The Faithful Shepherdess* is, as often thought, an extraordinary diversion from the main line of the Beaumont and Fletcher canon. One can recognize that, though it comes at the issue from a different direction, it centres on the same reduction of politics to erotics as has been noticed above. Chastity has become the controlling feature of social life in this never-never land of self-sufficient amours. Varieties of sexual arrangements are presented (as elsewhere in the *œuvre*) but all are subjected to a single standard, enforced in Clorin's re-education establishment. The liberation of the female voice, even inside the practical arrangements of Jacobean social life, is one of the triumphs of this new depoliticized drama; but the failure of *The Faithful Shepherdess* in the playhouse seems to show us that Italian avant-gardism had pushed the point beyond what London was prepared to tolerate.

This same time saw a number of institutional changes, however, that altered the balance of audience and dramaturgy in the capital and affected the fortunes of tragicomedy. In Chapter 7 I have already spoken about the collapse of the boys' theatres in this period.[7] The King's Men reacquired the boys' space in the Blackfriars in 1608, but seem not to have occupied it until 1610, when the plague abated. Some of this time was no doubt spent considering the dramaturgy that could marry the innovations of the children

---

[6] On this see further pp. 412–13.

[7] The transfer of the Queen's Revels boys to the Whitefriars playhouse in 1609 should probably be seen as part of their ghostly afterlife. By 1613 they had combined with the Lady Elizabeth's Men, the combined company alternating for a time between the private theatre and one or another of the public ones. The original boys' company was by then reaching adult status. In a lawsuit of 1635 the Burbages explain the takeover by the King's Men: 'the more to strengthen the service, the boys then wearing out, it was considered that that house [the Blackfriars] would be as fit for ourselves' (Chambers, ii. 509 n. 7). It must be supposed that 'the boys then wearing out' means they were already adults and showed that the playhouse was appropriate for a truly adult company.

to the ever-popular romantic adventures of the adult stage. And Shakespeare, as a shareholder, was no doubt part of this consideration. Did he respond by writing a new kind of comedy (now usually called 'romance')?[8] We cannot be sure whether *Pericles* was planned before the buyout of the Blackfriars, but the uncertainty should not prevent us from considering dramaturgical connections.

Perhaps even more important for the future of the company than Shakespeare's gear change was Beaumont and Fletcher's move from the boys to the men.[9] Though *The Faithful Shepherdess* had been a flop, the literary and social avant-garde rushed to its rescue, attaching their poetic testimonials to the quarto publication (probably in the same year). So there was some approval of Guarinian tragicomedy among the cognoscenti. The thirty-eight poems set before the 1647 Folio of the Beaumont and Fletcher *Comedies and Tragedies*,[10] written by all the most distinguished cavalier wits and poets of the time, tell us retrospectively that the King's Men had found a key to the taste of a newly self-conscious literary élite, so

---

[8] Edward Dowden, in his *Shakespere* (1876), seems to be the first person to use the word 'romance' for this purpose. He says that these plays 'have a grave beauty, a sweet serenity which seems to render the name "comedies" inappropriate . . . Let us then name this group . . . "Romances"' (p. 56). It is worth noting that the word appears in Dowden as part of an effort to construct an artistic chronology. My sometime pupil Chris Cobb has pointed out a startlingly prescient definition of romance in Hazlitt's notes on *Cymbeline* in his *The Characters of Shakespeare's Plays* (1817) (ed. Howe, iv. 179). Hazlitt calls the play 'a dramatic romance' and says that the reading of it 'is like going a journey with some uncertain object at the end of it . . . Though the events are scattered over such an extent of surface, and relate to such a variety of characters, yet the links which bind the different interests of the story together are never entirely broken . . . The ease and conscious unconcern with which this is effected only makes the skill more wonderful.' But Hazlitt never uses the word 'romance' in his discussions of the other plays in the group. Lacking the support of chronology, he cannot see the characteristics he describes so well as generic markers for a whole set of plays.

[9] John Danby (*Poets on Fortune's Hill* (London, 1952)) notes that Beaumont and Fletcher's plays 'could easily compete with the popular theatre in dramatic stir and skill; they had something to offer, too, to the aristocrat . . . whose connoisseurship was reserved for 'wit'' (p. 180).

[10] To avoid recurrent excursions on theories of authorship I follow the 1647 Folio's concept of a coherent canon of Beaumont and Fletcher plays, even though modern scholarship has anatomized the corpus into elements attributed to Beaumont, Fletcher, Massinger, Field, and Daborne. I attribute the authorship of all fifty or so plays to 'Fletcher' (meaning 'the school of Fletcher'). He seems to be the most recurrently present of all the collaborators, and to have provided the model dramaturgy that others followed. The 1647 poems recurrently speak of the volume as 'Master John Fletcher's Plays' (25 poems are addressed to Fletcher, 4 to Beaumont, 5 to the two of them (4 address the stationer, the edition, etc.)). On the other hand, it is now generally believed that Beaumont wrote the major part of plays in which he collaborated.

ensuring dominance in court and polite drama throughout the first half of the century.

Four interconnected aspects of the compromises in dramaturgy that the institutional change produced can be described here: Shakespearian Romance, collaboration and contrast between Shakespeare and Fletcher, a Fletcherian dramaturgy centred on tragicomedy, a more diffused taste for tragicomedy by Fletcher's contemporaries and imitators.[11] I treat these topics in that order.

Shakespeare and Romance

The standard chronology tells us that some time around 1607 Shakespeare wrote *Pericles*, as the first in a series of four plays— *Pericles* (1606×1608), *Cymbeline* (*c.*1608×1611), *The Winter's Tale* (*c.*1610×1611), and *The Tempest* (1611)—that are not only closely related to one another in structure but are different from all the comedies he had written before. *Pericles* seems to mark a decisive turn in Shakespeare's dramaturgy,[12] and perhaps for this reason (as well as the obvious corruption of the extant text) it looks a less finished product than the plays which followed.[13] Indeed it is only

---

[11] Lois Potter ('True Tragicomedies', in Nancy K. Maguire (ed.), *Renaissance Tragicomedy* (New York, 1987), 196–7) has noted that there is no consistent use of the word 'tragicomedy' in this period (the same is true of 'comedy', 'history', and 'tragedy'). But it can also be said that a majority of the Fletcher plays most esteemed in 1647 and now (for example, *Philaster*, *A King and no King*, *The Humorous Lieutenant*) appeal to a specific taste that is easy to call tragicomic, given their romantic excess, contradictory and violent emotions, happiness snatched at the last moment from despair, laughter (often contemptuous laughter) attached to corrupt characters.

[12] The shift can look logical if one pursues Shakespeare chronology looking for continuities. The romantic comedies show us heroines who know what they want and have a fairly good idea how to get it. The 'middle comedies' (*Measure for Measure* and *All's Well*— perhaps *Twelfth Night* belongs here as well) have heroines either puzzled about what is to be desired (*Measure for Measure*) or who face great difficulty in knowing how to secure it (*All's Well*). Helena has to learn that she is not in a romantic comedy but must embrace self-abnegation ('Come night, end day! | For with the dark, poor thief, I'll steal away') before she can have what she wants. She thus provides a preview of the later heroines, Marina, Imogen, Perdita, Miranda, who, though royal children, are given little or no power to impose themselves on the world and have to wait with passive endurance until fortune finally provides what effort could not achieve: time 'gives them what he will, not what they crave' (*Pericles*, II. iii. 47).

[13] If we allow that the plan of the play is of Shakespeare's devising—and many would not (it is not included in the First or Second Folios)—we must also allow that he could never have envisaged it as a tightly organized piece. Clearly the text we have does not represent Shakespeare's language with any accuracy and this no doubt adds to our sense of incoherence in the structure.

in the twentieth century (following the establishment of a consensus chronology) that critics have taken to arguing its genre; but the popularity of the play in its own age tells us that contemporaries did not find generic indeterminacy a bar to popular esteem; it was reprinted five times between 1609 and 1635 (giving it second place in the Shakespeare quick reprint stakes—*1 Henry IV* comes first). The source story, which Shakespeare had already used for the Aegeon plot in *The Comedy of Errors*, is drawn from the Latin (perhaps originally Greek) romance of *Apollonius of Tyre*. Two English versions of this are used in the play: Gower's, from the *Confessio amantis* of the late fourteenth century, and Lawrence Twine's *The Pattern of Painful Adventures: Containing the History of Prince Apollonius* (1594; 1607). Even if Shakespeare's attention was stimulated by the 1607 publication of Twine, none the less it was Gower he chose as his presenter, and the choice indicates something about the response he was aiming at. Gower begins by telling us that this is 'a song that old was sung', one which

> Hath been sung at festivals
> On ember eves and holidays,
> And lords and ladies in their lives
> Have read it for restoratives.
> (Act I, Chorus, ll. 5–8)

The story is presented to an audience with 'wits more ripe' as a distanced and naïve piece of ancient fiction. They are invited to construe it from the vantage point that allows sophisticated persons to enjoy fairy stories and folk-tales, narratives of marvels and surprises, flat characters, sudden conversions, long-drawn-out alternations of good and bad fortune. Tragic emotions are presented in terms of description rather than experience, and suffered across the many contrasting locations that exemplify, and to some extent predetermine, the alternations of sorrow and joy (and of the generic modes that convey them). But Shakespeare's concern is not only to flatter the audience's sophistication; he uses the story to focus for naïve as well as sophisticated the pattern of an individual's struggle to maintain identity in an essentially unstable world—the same pattern as in the Henslowe historical romances. In these terms *Pericles* seems well designed to appeal to the mixed audience of the Globe and the Blackfriars.

Ben Jonson thought *Pericles* 'a mouldy tale',[14] and by neoclassical standards almost everything is wrong with it. But public approval clearly encouraged Shakespeare and company to build on its success. Sophisticated nostalgia for older modes may be seen as a key to open up a new dramaturgy at once artful and emotional, distanced and immediate, romantic and comic.[15]

In writing in this way, Shakespeare was not flaunting innovation. He was, in fact, returning to the mainline taste of the Elizabethan theatre. E. C. Pettet in his *Shakespeare and the Romance Tradition* notes that the new Shakespearian mode aimed 'deliberately at the far-fetched, the astounding and the incredible . . . quite unhampered by any considerations of verisimilitude . . . With realism jettisoned, extravagance becomes a virtue' (p. 163).[16] It would be hard to find a better description of such paradigms of the Henslowe repertory as *The Four Prentices of London* (1592×c.1600), *Look About You* (c.1598×1600), *The Blind Beggar of Alexandria* (1596). The revised version of *Mucedorus*, played at court by the King's Men in 1610, is sometimes cited as evidence of a resuscitated taste for romance, but a look at the overall repertory detects no need for resuscitation. The deservedly obscure play, *The Thracian Wonder*, attributed to Webster and Rowley in the first and only edition of 1661 and dated 1599–c.1600 in Harbage–Schoenbaum shows us how closely Shakespeare's romances can be anticipated (or reproduced—the dates are impossible to fix) in the popular repertory.[17] But there is no need to suppose direct contact. The

---

[14] Jonson, 'Ode to Himself', published with *The New Inn*.

[15] The record seems to show that the impressiveness of the theatrical past weighed heavily on Jacobean taste. In 1615 John Chamberlain remarked of court performances that 'our poets' brains and inventions are grown very dry insomuch that of five new plays there is not one pleases, and therefore they are driven to furbish over the old, which stands them in best stead and brings them most profit' (*The Letters of John Chamberlain*, ed. N. E. McClure (2 vols.; Philadelphia, 1939), i. 567).

[16] (London, 1949), 163.

[17] The play tells the story (commented on by Time) of a daughter cast adrift at sea for marrying (and conceiving a child by) the Prince of Sicily, a man unacceptable to her father, the King of Thrace. A plague is then visited on the kingdom; a mission is sent to Delphos to find the cause; the message comes back that the King is guilty and will not be cleared till a 'Thracian wonder' appears as a shepherd. At first defiant, the King eventually repents and undertakes a pilgrimage to search for his daughter and son-in-law. They are now living among Thracian shepherds, unaware of one another's existence. At a shepherds' feast the princess is abducted. The pursuit gets absorbed into a general war between Thrace and Sicily, in which all the characters participate and, recognizing one another, achieve a happy ending. The relevance of this story to both *Cymbeline* and *The Winter's Tale* needs no elaboration.

plot of *The Thracian Wonder* comes from Greene's *Menaphon* (of 1589, 1599, 1605, 1616), while the plot of *The Winter's Tale* comes from Greene's *Pandosto* (reprinted twenty times before 1700). The continuity of these romantic confections across (and far beyond) the lifespan of Elizabethan drama points to their centrality in the taste of the time, whatever Jonson or Marston had to say about 'unpossible dry fictions' (see p. 262). The basic mechanisms of the mode (loss of status and identity, exile, incoherent travel punctuated by idyllic resting places, plots straggling across large tracts of time, marvellous coincidences, violent but inconclusive passions) not only persist inside the historical romances; they lurk behind the realism of the Prodigal Son plays and now they re-emerge in Shakespeare's repertory in their full Greenian form.

We see him now, at the end of his career, no longer controlling romance by what I have called 'unindulgent' structures (p. 390), but accepting romantic premises without seeking to balance them, either by the commentary of cynical clowns[18] or by the trickery of competent women. The central characters are now left open to change of fortune without any compensating idea that fortune can be *made*. In consequence, the double-plot structure, as a formal expression of balance, now carries less burden. When these late plays break in two, the contrasting halves are laid end to end and measure social distinction less than the chronological gap between destruction and reparation. Yet for all the arbitrariness of the plots, one may argue that they still display the mixed-mode kind of unity that Guarini had recommended; they are held together by a unified poetic that demands a response somewhere between sad acceptance of evil and a vision of love.

It is *The Winter's Tale* that confirms, beyond the other 'romances', the continuity[19] of these plays with the romantic taste of the 1590s. The political issues evident in *Pericles* and *Cymbeline* are attenuated here, and dominated by purely personal emotions. These

[18] Such figures as Autolycus, Trinculo–Stephano, the Jailor in *Cymbeline*, Boult in *Pericles* are mere shadows of the clown figures of earlier comedies. They are not oppositional figures, given the power of deconstructive commentary, but are absorbed as mere extras into the main story.

[19] The often-remarked stretching of time and place in these last plays is used, however, in a different way from that found in the earlier romances. Here the narrative energy is less; the recapitulation of the past in the final moments of presence gives time something of the effect of space (hence, no doubt, G. Wilson Knight's notion of 'spatial form'), as if all the events could finally be seen as a process and yet as simultaneously present.

bring into clearest view the primacy of an idea that in *Pericles* and *Cymbeline* only shares the limelight—the idea of power vested in the innocent girl whose self-sufficiency enables her to penetrate behind the political evil that controls the world. And so she can play a queen and reinvent the ideal world that the 'real' authority of the king her father could only destroy.[20] In *The Tempest* the pattern is seen largely in retrospect. The play begins at the point that *The Winter's Tale* reaches only in Act IV. The generating evil is now in 'the dark backward and abysm of time' and a continent apart. But once again the heritage of shared political corruption has to be relived in personal anguish before it can be converted into reparation, once again less by action than by a change in moral vision. Prospero is both victim and (as he intends) victimizer; and so the turning of evil into good, revenge into forgiveness, tragedy into comedy, has to be achieved inside the father's mind; the recuperative innocence of the daughter[21] is an adjunct but not a cause. The key exchange that points us to the transformation is handled in the more abstract and impersonal terms of Ariel's commentary on the sorrow and bewilderment of the imprisoned evildoers: 'if you now beheld them, your affections | Would become tender' and Prospero's response: 'Hast thou, which art but air, a touch, a feeling | Of their afflictions, and shall not myself, | One of their kind, that relish all as sharply | Passion as they, be kindlier moved than thou art? . . . The rarer action is | In virtue than in vengeance' (v. i. 18–28). The distanced calm of *The Tempest* reveals it as more a commentary on Shakespeare's Romance dramaturgy than an enactment of it.

Shakespeare and Fletcher

Shakespeare's romances can be linked not only to his own comedies but to the whole tradition of popular romance that spans the period. The tragicomedies of Beaumont and Fletcher, on the other hand, exemplify the new dramaturgical ideals that were to dominate

---

[20] The pattern is clearest here because, where Pericles is only the victim of evil, Cymbeline only its accidental cause, Leontes is the active destroyer of his family and himself.
[21] I have chosen to talk about *The Tempest* in terms of the relation between Prospero and Miranda, not (as commonly in the 1980s) between Prospero and Caliban. The former is more central to the dramatic structure and is the element that links this play to those around it.

the London theatre until 1642. Shakespeare uses the romantic evocation of wonder to suggest the capacity for redemption in human nature, set against larger patterns of selfishness and love, loss and recovery, manipulation and innocence; Beaumont and Fletcher use very similar patterns to suggest rather the indeterminacy of human experience in what Herbert Blau has called 'a repertoire of intense emotions achieved ... without any essential continuity or metaphysical ground.'[22] Yet the two modes share a great deal, and there is one play which ought to show what happens when shared authorship brings the two dramaturgies together.

The Two Noble Kinsmen (1613×1614) is described on its title-page as 'written by the memorable worthies of their time, Master John Fletcher and Master William Shakespeare, Gentlemen'. The plot's derivation from Chaucer's The Knight's Tale places it in the same region as the first half of Pericles, the region of chivalric love and honour, with the winning of noble ladies by deeds of prowess. But in Pericles, disillusioning experience leads the knightly hero into a humanized world we can respond to more directly. In Two Noble Kinsmen we are never allowed to be this close to the rituals of Palamon and Arcite, Theseus and Emilia. The bourgeois sub-plot in which a rustic lover has to take the name of Palamon in order to secure the attention of his beloved, remains too remote from the actions it parodies to provide any kind of bridge.[23] This regularly disappoints those who come to The Two Noble Kinsmen looking for Shakespeare's internalizing dramaturgy. But we should notice not only that ritual appears recurrently in Shakespeare's Romances (the oracle in The Winter's Tale, the 'banquet' in The Tempest), but that Fletcher also seems to have given up something of his characteristic quality—his typical complexity of plot and switches of focus. In its stately and muted mode of action perhaps we should see Two Noble Kinsmen as a work of two authors trying not to tread on one another's toes.

To get a purchase on the similarities and differences between Shakespearian romance and Fletcherian tragicomedy it is probably better to look at plays, written close in time, in which the separate authors are committed to their separate modes. The dates

---

[22] 'The Absolved Riddle', NLH 17 (1986), 552.
[23] The usual discrimination between Shakespeare's and Fletcher's stints gives Fletcher the dominant role in the sub-plot, but also indicates that Fletcher wrote some of the main-plot scenes.

of *Philaster: or Love Lies a-Bleeding* (1608×1610) and *Cymbeline* (*c*.1608× 1611) do not supply answers to the standard question, 'who learned what from whom'. Yet the two plays can surely be called contemporaries; we can see them responding (in similarity and difference) to the same pressures and fashions. And so we can understand both what was available and what was chosen.

Andrew Gurr, in the introduction to his edition of *Philaster*,[24] has suggested that the authors draw on their romance sources— Sidney's *Arcadia* (as in *Cupid's Revenge*) and Montemayor's *Diana*— less for the sake of the stories than for the conventions of character (or rather, ethos) that the stories exemplify,[25] particularly the conventions of idealized love set in confrontation with cynical lust, and of honourable self-sacrifice in the face of a corrupt world, found in both men and women. These are conventions, we should notice, that define individuals rather than societies; their relevance to action in the public sphere remains oblique.

Philaster begins with a description of a political situation: Sicily is ruled by a usurper, though the rightful heir (Philaster) still lives in freedom, protected by the knowledge that any harm done to him will result in a popular uprising. We hear of the king's plan to strengthen his hold on the country by marrying his daughter and heir to a Spanish prince. A situation in delicate balance between political possibilities is thus set up; but the play is not interested in advancing along political lines. It immediately moves its focus to the sex lives of the persons involved; and the central issues of the play will recurrently show us political ends as only reachable by sexual means. The Spanish prince hopes to be given immediate access to the bed of his betrothed, but, repulsed by the chaste princess as a gross boor, he quickly satisfies his needs elsewhere; the political plot can now be frustrated by a revelation of his unsuitability as a husband (or so we might think). The princess and the true heir are chaste and ideal lovers, but slander from the Spaniard's mistress—that the princess has sexual relations with Philaster's page Bellario (actually a girl in love with Philaster)—is

---

[24] (London, 1969), pp. xxix–xxx.
[25] Lee Bliss ('Pastiche, Burlesque, Tragicomedy' in *The Cambridge Companion to English Renaissance Drama*, ed. A. R. Braunmuller and Michael Hattaway (Cambridge, 1990)) notes how Beaumont and Fletcher develop Sidney's 'timeless thematic structure, allowing for sharp contrasts between kinds of scenes', that 'replaces plot as the primary organizing principle' and so provides 'a shifting configuration of lovers rather than a true narrative sequence' (p. 249).

easily believed in this cynical society, even by Philaster himself. The ideal characters are rendered politically impotent by the waves of grief and anger, condemnation and self-reproach, that sweep them from side to side. Aiming at generosity and nobility they are unable to turn their ideals into actions. The moral anarchy of a society unable to separate private from public can be ended only when political necessity breaks into the magic circle of personal distress. The king arrests the prince, and the populace rises in revolt. National stability can be restored only by the marriage of prince and princess—a stability now based on personal qualities of chaste and selfless virtue; innocent love and political correctness become joint enabling powers, so that misrepresentations can be cleared up and all can end happily.

An analysis of *Cymbeline* yields a very similar pattern: chaste love in Posthumus and Imogen, forbidden by the king, spotted by evil lust in Iachimo and Cloten, leads to female self-sacrifice, guilt and agony over loss of identity, all caught up in the political issues of a remote time which can achieve peace only when purity of motive is revealed as the ethical basis of the state. But ethics is not buried under cynicism in *Cymbeline* as in *Philaster*, so that redemption can be more easily believed. Shakespeare's good characters have a sustaining continuity in their sense of self and world which enables them to take responsibility for their reactions. We can easily understand the movement of their lives even while the changing world is forcing them to change position. Likewise with the evil characters: Iachimo, the Queen, Cloten show qualities which are individual rather than representative. And so we understand their changes of role as aspects of character rather than justifications for the theatrical *frisson* of surprise. The Queen, who is in part a fairy-tale witch like that in *Snow White*, and Cloten, the traditional uncouth witch's son (like the 'losel' in *The Faerie Queene*, III. vii), lead the nation in its patriotic defiance of Rome, and they are 'sorely missed' when the Romans attack; but we are invited less to gasp at the shift of focus than to register how a person who seems vicious in one context can be virtuous in another. Posthumus first exalts and then curses the sexuality of Imogen, and so finds himself, like Philaster, caught between opposed emotions. But these personal issues do not become mirrors of state policy; we see them cross-cut and counterchecked by other personal business. The heroine herself can show us, in typical Shakespearian fashion, a more direct way of drawing on resources of character to overcome misfortune.

A glance at the denouements of the two plays shows some of the ways in which these distinctions shape the meanings we attach to the action. The denouement of *Philaster* works as a series of increasingly desperate reversals as characters are required to deal with situations they cannot understand and actions they cannot justify. The fourth act in the woods has shown us Philaster dragged into meaninglessness, stabbing the Princess (although not wishing to), being wounded by an intervening 'country gentleman'—who seems incapable of understanding the protocol of courtly stabbing —crawling away into the forest (while not wishing to), finding his page Bellario asleep, wounding him to deceive the pursuers (and immediately regretting it), being hidden by Bellario, who would rather die than betray his master, allowing the pursuers to drag Bellario away, and then crawling out of the brush to demand that they recognize that he himself is the guilty party. The fifth act finds Philaster, the Princess, and Bellario all in prison. Each one wishes to die for the others. But the populace revolts, captures and tortures the Spaniard. Philaster must take charge, and can save the day and the Spaniard by marrying the Princess. But even at this point there is a last twist to the tale. The accusation of unchastity between the Princess and Bellario resurfaces. Bellario must be stripped and tortured. The melodrama of this occasion produces the surprising discovery that the page is a girl; and so the Princess *must* be innocent, and all is well—but only for the moment, we must feel, in a world so composed (like a Matisse painting) of brilliant juxtapositions on a flat surface.

The concentration in this process is on states of mind (rather in the mode of *nouvelle vague* films), not on the alternative lines of action available to a unified moral purpose.[26] In *Cymbeline*, however, the denouement is not expressed by an alternating current between emotional polarities, but must be discovered in the destiny the gods have laid up for the family and the state. The Act V

---

[26] Cf. Dryden, *Preface to 'Troilus and Cressida, Containing the Grounds of Criticism in Tragedy'*: ''Tis one of the excellencies of Shakespeare that the manners [*mores, ethos*] of his persons are generally apparent, and you see their bent and inclination. Fletcher comes far short of him in this ... there are but glimmerings of manners in most of his comedies, which run upon adventures ... you know not whether they resemble virtue or vice, and they are either good or bad or indifferent as the present scene requires it' (*Essays of John Dryden*, ed. W. P. Ker (2 vols.; Oxford, 1926), i. 217.

changes of Posthumus from Roman to Briton and back to Roman again represent not only an emotional switchback but an effort—controlled by the need to achieve a single and well-understood end—to die in expiation for his sin against Imogen. The major change in him is achieved by the vision of Jupiter and his parents, where he learns that 'the strength of the Leonati' he thought he needed to face guilt is in fact a strength needed for life. This gives him (and us) an assurance that *Philaster* does not search for—that the apparent psychological instabilities are only the troubled surface of a stable universe. The extraordinary series of recognitions in the last scene is not only a theatrical *tour de force* but also an enactment of the interconnected strength of this world, as each revelation inevitably triggers the next one (as Iachimo's confession leads to Posthumus', Posthumus' to Imogen's, Imogen's to Pisanio's, Pisanio's to the tale of Cloten's mission, the tale of Cloten to Guiderius' confession, Guiderius' to Bellarius'), so that the whole tangled skein is reduced to a straight thread, as predicted in the tablet that Jupiter handed down. The stability of the British state is not underwritten by the forced conversion of the king's character as in *Philaster* ('Let princes learn | By this to rule the passions of their blood' (v. v. 216–17)), but by a conjoint acceptance of the supernatural order that stands above kings:

> Laud we the gods,
> And let our crooked smokes climb to their nostrils
> From our blest altars.
>
> (v. v. 476–8)

As the camera draws back for the final take, what is revealed in these late Shakespeare plays is that the whole scene corresponds to a pattern laid up on high, now miraculously reassembled out of all the jarring elements that have seemed to compose it. The dead are returned to life, not merely in the discovery of their lost social identities, but as recreated out of emptiness, from the despair and helplessness that has imprisoned them in their pasts, making them no longer able to imagine renewal. The catatonic Pericles, who has seen his wife's coffin and daughter's tomb, Imogen, who has seen her husband's dead body, the guilt obsessed Leontes, the revenge obsessed Prospero, are all rewarded for an underlying continuity of purpose they did not know they possessed. The excitement of a Beaumont and Fletcher tragicomedy, on the other hand, depends

on final truths emerging with a shock of surprise. Only thus can
the brilliance of its alternations be secured.

Fletcherian Tragicomedy

The poems in the 1647 folio hold up for particular admiration two
aspects of Fletcher's dramaturgy: first, his portrayals of soldierly
honour (Mardonius, Arbaces, Melantius) and of female pathos
(Aspatia, Bellario, Lucina, Arcas)—the two polarities of his tragicomic mode—and, secondly, his 'wit', his artful poise, seen as a
middle point between the smoothness of Shakespeare and the
weightiness of Jonson, so that he can draw on the qualities of both.
The description has remained extraordinarily constant through
time, though the values encoded have been reversed. This is not
surprising, for we must allow that the 1647 praise itself encodes
a particular historical moment. The volume is clearly a royalist
manifesto; the authors are being co-opted into a celebration of
the (now-closed) theatre as a royalist institution: and, as that political and ethical connection raised their esteem in 1647, so in later
centuries it has damaged it, Fletcherian tragicomedy coming to be
seen as 'decadent', reflecting in its 'evasiveness' (between tragedy
and comedy) courtly society's flight from responsible action, and
so the conditions that led to the Civil War.[27]

These 'historical' judgements are neither focused enough to
describe the actual characteristics of Fletcherian tragicomedy nor
comprehensive enough to allow for the overlap between Fletcher's
tragicomedy and his comedy (discussed above, pp. 409–15).
Fletcher, like other prolific playwrights of the period (Middleton,
Dekker, Heywood, Shakespeare), was a dramatist before he was an
ideologue, and moved his ethical assumptions to suit his dramatic
focus.[28] Moreover, the 'Fletcherian' combination of passionately
individual and socially farcical manifests itself in a great variety of

---

[27] The 'modernist' position, to be seen in the criticism of (for example) L. C. Knights,
M. C. Bradbrook, T. B. Tomlinson seems to be giving way to a 'postmodernist' one. Two
recent anthologies, Nancy K. Maguire's *Renaissance Tragicomedy* (New York, 1987) and
Gordon McMullan's *The Politics of Tragicomedy* (London, 1991), show the post-modernist
taste for indecidability operating to the advantage of Fletcher and the whole tragicomic
genre.
[28] And indeed Philip Finkelpearl has been able to mount an argument that Beaumont and
Fletcher, far from being royalists, can be counted as dramatists of the opposition. See his
Court and Country Politics in the Plays of Beaumont and Fletcher (Princeton, 1990).

forms, many of which are tragicomic only in the traditional sense that they mix comic and tragic impulses, subject characters to life-threatening violence and then restore them to happiness. One may instance the disguised maiden's flight from patriarchy and her wanderings in forests full of outlaws in *The Pilgrim* (1621); printed 1647); the haphazard criminality of deracinated gentlemen and their disguised sisters in *The Night Walker or the Little Thief* (1611; printed 1640); the disguised maidens' pursuit of their philandering seducer in *Love's Pilgrimage* (?1616; printed 1647); the pseudo-historical labyrinth of usurpation in *Beggar's Bush* (c.1615×1622; printed 1647), with its lost heirs, disguise among gypsies, fortunes lost at sea; or the Spanish cloak-and-dagger imbroglio of *The Chances* (1613×1625); printed 1647), where random passers-by find themselves caught up with royal babies passed out of doorways, distressed beauties demanding protection, and duels in which the fighters cannot guess what is going on. In terms of the Guarinian ideal of a mixed genre sustained in coherent continuity by the balance of opposite points of view, these are very rough and ready approximations, where Guarini's interlacing of different levels of the plot is sacrificed to the standard excitements of a quick moving narrative. In Fletcher's handling of such plots, there is very little that would surprise Henslowe or Alleyn or that requires us to change our nomenclature from romance to tragicomedy.

There are, of course, clear distinctions to be made. Characters placed in worlds of indeterminate ethos are given little chance to impose themselves on the action.[29] The Fletcherian handling of these romantic stories concentrates less on heroic patience and active response than on emotional confusion, often of military men stranded in an unstable and corrupt society (as in *The Loyal Subject*). The hero has still, of course, to be a potential man of action, but he hardly ever needs to fight on stage; militarism has become a quality of character rather than performance, so that 'honour' appears as an ethical issue to be investigated rather than a duty to be fulfilled.[30]

[29] See Dryden, *Essays*, i. 217: 'for the manners can never be evident where the surprise of fortune takes up all the business of the stage; and where the poet is more in pain to tell you what happened to such a man than what he was.'
[30] In *The Nice Valour or the Passionate Madman* (c.1615–25) Fletcher sets the extreme (indeed absurd) 'niceness' of a man who cannot bear to live in a world where his honour might be touched against the madness of a man who constantly changes his mind about the standards which require him to fight. Cf. Middleton and Rowley's *A Fair Quarrel* (see pp. 521–2).

Constancy in love, rather than in war, is recurrently invoked as the true test of honour (as also, outside Fletcher, in Heywood's *The English Traveller* (*c*.1627), Ford's *Love's Sacrifice* (?1632), Shirley's *Love's Cruelty* (1631; printed 1640)). The usurer is still a characteristic blocking figure but is no longer a central source of dismay.[31] Intrigue is more tightly organized, but with a greater variety of interlocking mechanisms; double plots remain common (very often in the standard mode of romantic main plot, comic subplot),[32] but tend to be held together as contrasting aspects of a single world judged by a single social standard, so that they seldom offer antithetical visions of life. Thus there is no sense in which the parasite Bessus in *A King and No King* can break out into a different dimension, as does the parasite Parolles in *All's Well that Ends Well* with his 'simply the thing I am | Shall make me live' (IV. iii. 333–4). Bessus can offer only a debased version of the ethos ruling elsewhere in the play, and so with Syphax in *The Mad Lover* or Perez in *Rule a Wife*. Instead of socially contrasted plots, Fletcher generally prefers cognate actions where brothers or sisters or companions work out the same attitudes in different adventures.[33] Though the *liaison des scènes* is not yet a shibboleth, we can feel the stress on continuity getting closer as playwrights learn to avoid the unmediated transitions of the Elizabethan stage that carry us without preparation from one matter to another, related only by analogy—what Harbage calls 'plot ellipses'.[34]

The central suppositions of Fletcherian tragicomedy have been masterfully analysed in Eugene Waith's *The Pattern of Tragicomedy in Beaumont and Fletcher*. These, Waith finds, derive from the co-presence of two impulses inside a single situation, one involving

---

[31] In the Beaumont and Fletcher canon we see Middletonian figures like Sir Perfidious Oldcraft in *Wit at Several Weapons*, Justice Allgripe in *The Night Walker*, Moorecraft in *The Scornful Lady*, Cacafogo in *Rule a Wife*, all easily converted to comic virtue. Even Dryden complains of the ease with which the usurer in this last case is turned into a boon companion for the prodigal. See the *Essay of Dramatic Poesy* (*Essays*, i. 66).

[32] Orie Hatcher (*John Fletcher: A Study in Dramatic Method* (Chicago, 1905)) makes a relevant remark about Fletcher's use of Italian sources for plot and sub-plot. 'As a rule, Fletcher draws upon Bandello for the more serious interest of the main story and upon Boccaccio for the episodes of the comic sub-plot . . . [the settings of the *novelle*] were easily adaptable to the romantic coloring at which Fletcher aimed, while the intense passions which they portrayed fascinated the theatric side of his imagination' (p. 43). The emotionally neutral trickery of *The Decameron* then provides a low intensity contrast.

[33] As in *Wit Without Money*, *Love's Pilgrimage*, *The Nice Valour*, *The Wild Goose-Chase*, *The Custom of the Country*, *The Scornful Lady*.

[34] *Cavalier Drama* (New York, 1936), 83.

distance, the other requiring immediacy, one pointing to romance and idealism, the other to satire and reductive realism: 'operating together they produce the theoretical, the factitious, the hypothetical'.[35] If we set this formula against that which sustained the romances of the Henslowe dramatists, we can see the change as a shift in the relation of character to context. Heywood's *The Royal King and the Loyal Subject* (1602×1618; printed 1637) creates reality for its characters by making their beliefs reflections of the system they live in. The warrior monarch and his Earl Marshal display the esteem of great comrades-in-arms for one another's magnanimity, daring, outspokenness. But in peacetime they are faced by an equally clear assumption that they are now sovereign and subject. This is a clash of characteristics that exemplifies the basic structure of feudal society, where the political is always having to be renegotiated as a form of the personal.[36] So there is ample space for villainy to subvert the negotiation. But so many values are shared here that a return to a stable understanding appears, inevitably, as a confirmation of the agreed value system underlying the whole play.

One can see why this plot appealed to Fletcher. His *The Loyal Subject* (1618 (revised ?1633); printed 1647) offers a much more complex political diagram, in which the loyal subject can no longer cling to a standard morality and so appears much more an isolated 'humour', finding no consensus outside himself; his theatrical force becomes that of paradox. His loyal emotions have to focus on a duke who is without royal qualities. And they must do so without support from his natural constituency, those military purists (his son and his captains) who wish to destroy the political hierarchy (the only thing he can be loyal to) in the name of military ethics. The contradiction that Fletcher has set up between personal beliefs and a corrupt social scene stresses the theoretical status of both: no resolution can be imagined except by a *coup de théâtre*.

What is perhaps the most brilliant tragicomedy in the Beaumont and Fletcher canon, *A King and No King* (1611; printed 1619), tells a story of puzzling incompatibility between values that stands somewhere between *The Two Noble Kinsmen* and *The Loyal Subject*. It is a more accessible play than either, because Arbaces, the hero, manages to contain laughter and wonder inside a single believable

---

[35] *The Pattern of Tragicomedy*, 85.
[36] Sidney Painter (*William Marshall* (Baltimore, 1933)) documents the historical circumstances that support the fiction.

character. This quality transforms the contradictions in which he is involved from the remote and the ritualized into a brilliantly tragicomic immediacy of theatrical presence. Arbaces begins as a sharply foregrounded comic figure, a successful general, like the loyal subject, enamoured of his own (genuine) virtues, and possessed of a gay determination to impose equal happiness and virtue on all men around him. When tragedy strikes him, in the form of an incestuous passion for his supposed sister, Panthea, his comic self-assurance, and his determination to take every problem by the shoulders and shake it into conformity create a simultaneously comic and tragic effect, characteristically Fletcherian in its use of personal, domestic, and potentially comic means to cope with political issues and tragic dilemmas. The use of incest to create the tragic potential has been objected to (most categorically by Thomas Rymer[37]) but in fact the dramaturgy ensures that it is never more than a hypothetical topic upon which Fletcher can compose arias of passion and despair. We can appreciate these for their rhetorical power without being convinced that reality will justify their force.[38] Indeed, our distance allows us to suspect that the incest theme exists only as a further reflection of Arbaces' emotional excess; and it is one of the play's pleasures to discover that we are right.

The indeterminacy of a psychology that seems realistic in separate moments but wildly improbable in its alternations enables Fletcher to generate an exciting drama of surfaces (like a Fauve painting); a series of unprepared reversals of attitude keep us continually on the edges of our seats. *The Mad Lover* (1617; printed 1647) offers us again the paradox of a great and successful general, somewhat given to talking about his exploits, whose happiness in himself is destroyed by love. When Memnon meets the princess he is stunned into silence; he no longer knows who he is and can think only to impress her by a deed of suicidal courage, to give her as a gift the heart cut out of his body. The collision between grandeur and absurdity thus set up is never resolved (as it is in the case

---

[37] *The Critical Works of Thomas Rymer*, ed. Curt Zimansky (New Haven, 1956), 48: 'If the design be wicked, as here the making approaches an incestuous enjoyment, the audience will naturally loathe and detest it, rather than favour and accompany it with their good wishes.'

[38] We might compare the double effect to that, for example, of such an aria as *Come scoglio* in Mozart's *Cosi fan Tutte* where (once again) we wonder how the brilliant emotionalism of the expression can be justified by the farcical 'reality' of the situation.

of Arbaces); clearly the effect that Fletcher is after, the sense of paradox and indeterminacy in experience, does not require it to be. The often remarked rhetorical fluency of the Beaumont and Fletcher verse—its projection of strong emotions that define situations but stand apart from character—is an important part of the tragicomic effect. If we compare it to the distorted syntax of Shakespeare's last plays[39] we can see how far the psychological extremism of one stands from the other's careful orchestration of pathos and potential violence—in a scene of naturalistic dialogue like the following. Young Archas, the general's grandson, disguised as Alinda, is the Princess Olympia's beloved companion. But 'she' has also attracted the attentions of the corrupt duke, and it is supposed he has seduced her:

> ALINDA. Madam, the Duke has sent for the two ladies.
> OLYMPIA. I prithee go: I know thy thoughts are with him.
> Go, go, Alinda, do not mock me more.
> I have found thy heart, wench, do not wrong thy mistress,
> Thy too much loving mistress: do not abuse her.
> .   .   .   .
> ALINDA. Oh, who has wronged me? who has ruined me?
> Poor wretched girl, what poison is flung on thee?
> Excellent virtue, from whence flowes this anger?
> OLYMPIA. Go ask my brother, ask the faith thou gav'st me,
> Ask all my favours to thee, ask my love,
> Last, thy forgetfulness of good: then fly me.
> For we must part, Alinda.
> ALINDA.   You are weary of me.
> I must confess I was never worth your service,
> Your bounteous favours less; but that my duty,
> My ready will and all I had to serve ye—
> O heaven, thou know'st my honesty.
> OLYMPIA.   No more.
> Take heed, Heaven has a justice. Take this ring with ye,
> This doting spell you gave me; too well, Alinda,

[39] See Lamb's famous explication: 'His [Fletcher's] ideas moved slow; his versification, though sweet, is tedious, it stops every moment; he lays line upon line . . . adding image to image so deliberately that we see where they join. Shakespeare mingles everything, runs line into line, embarrasses sentences and metaphors; before one idea has burst its shell, another is hatched and clamorous for disclosure (*The Works of Charles and Mary Lamb*, ed. E. V. Lucas (7 vols.; London, 1903–5), iv. 341).

Thou knew'st the virtue in't; too well I feel it:
Nay keep that too, it may sometimes remember ye,
When you are willing to forget who gave it,
And to what virtuous end.
ALINDA.   Must I go from ye?
Of all the sorrows sorrow has—must I part with ye?
Part with my noble mistress?
OLYMPIA.   Or I with thee, wench.
ALINDA. And part stain'd with opinion? Farewell lady,
Happy and blessed lady, goodness keep ye:
Thus your poor servant full of grief turns from ye,
For ever full of grief, for ever from ye.
I have no being now, no friends, no country,
　　·　　·　　·　　·　　·　　·　　·　　·　　·

OLYMPIA.   How she wounds me!
Either I am undone or she must go: take these with ye,
Some toys may do ye service, and this money;
And when ye want, I love ye not so poorly,
Not yet, Alinda, that I would see ye perish.
Prithee be good, and let me hear; look on me,
I love those eyes yet dearly; I have kiss'd thee,
And now I'll do't again: farewell Alinda,
I am too full to speak more, and too wretched.   *Exit*
ALINDA. You have my faith, and all the world my fortune.
                                                   Exit
(*The Loyal Subject*, IV. i. 1–57)

It will be noted how effectively the rhetoric here conveys realistic emotions, but with a force of expression that has no basis in fact (for we know that Alinda has not been seduced). The emotions are thus cut off from any external consequence in action;[40] they are turned in on themselves as specimens of a poetic management which undermines the truth of the situation at the same time as it magnifies its emotional power,[41] and so substitutes connoisseurship for identification. Or take the more violently passionate dialogue (now usually attributed to Beaumont) between Philaster and his page, Bellario:

---

[40] This is what Shakespeare, in the scene of Guiderius' and Arviragus' mourning for the supposed death of Imogen (*Cymbeline*, IV. ii)—the nearest he comes to this mode of rhetoric—calls 'in wench-like words . . . protract[ing] with admiration'.
[41] We admire the excesses of Arcite refusing to leave prison (*Two Noble Kinsmen*, II. ii–iii), but we do not believe them.

PHILASTER. She kisses thee?
BELLARIO.   Never, my Lord, by heaven.
PHILASTER. That's strange; I know she does.
BELLARIO.   No, by my life.
PHILASTER. Why then she does not love me. Come, she does.
   I bade her do it; I charged her by all charms
   Of love between us, by the hope of peace
   We should enjoy, to yield thee all delights
   Naked as to her bed. I took her oath
   Thou shouldst enjoy her. Tell me, gentle boy,
   Is she not parallelless? Is not her breath
   Sweet as Arabian winds when fruits are ripe?
   Are not her breasts two liquid ivory balls?
   Is she not all a lasting mine of joy?
     .   .   .   .

   Thou think'st I will be angry with thee. Come,
   Thou shalt know all my drift; I hate her more
   Than I love happiness, and placed thee there
   To pry with narrow eyes into her deeds.
   Hast thou discovered? Is she fall'n into lust,
   As I would wish her? Speak some comfort to me.
BELLARIO. My Lord, you did mistake the boy you sent.
   Had she the lust of sparrows or of goats,
   Had she a sin that way, hid from the world,
   Beyond the name of lust, I would not aid
   Her base desires; but what I came to know
   As servant to her I would not reveal
   To make my life last ages.

                                      (III. i. 193–224)

    What we see here is Philaster and Bellario aiming at one another their powerfully realized and fluent theatrical emotions. As the power struggle swings to and fro, we see each contestant being made to take up the position that will best undercut the other, pushing into extremity both the obsessive imagination of total disloyalty and the assertion of total loyalty (Bellario bids Philaster to 'hew me asunder, and whilst I can think, | I'll love those pieces you have cut away | Better than those that grow' (III. i. 245–7). One line of assertion in the dialogue is known to be true, the other false, and it may be assumed that the true will triumph in the end; but this distinction matters little; it is the power of the rhetorical strokes that marks our pleasure in the game. It is not a case of the art pointing to the suffering but of the suffering pointing to the art. We find the prefatory material for the 1647 Folio making the same point. Shirley's Epistle speaks of 'passions raised to that excellent pitch and by such insinuating degrees that you shall not choose but consent and go along with them . . . and then stand admiring the subtle tracks of your engagement'. Just so!⁴²

Other Tragicomedies

Describing Fletcherian tragicomedy, I have spoken of the instability of the situations set up and of the hypothetical responses therefore imposed on the characters. The tragicomedies of Massinger, Middleton, and Webster, while not to be described simply as products of 'the school of Fletcher', show the extent to which these techniques continued to offer different writers opportunities each could exploit in his characteristic way, usually in terms of more slow-burning and so less brilliantly illuminated emotions than Fletcher uses.

It is not surprising that Philip Massinger, Fletcher's recurrent collaborator, should stay closest to Fletcher's model. *The Maid of Honour* (*c.*1621×1632) sets up the contradictory structure of tragicomedy by using (like Fletcher) a corrupt court as the context for noble aspirations. Bertoldo is a warrior purified in battle, presented in strong contrast to his cowardly and time-serving brother, the King. Camiola, the 'Maid of Honour', is a great lady, scornful of the courtlings who come to woo her, carrying recommendations from the king. The mutual esteem of these two figures of virtuous opposition cannot be resolved, given the world they live in, by tragic loss or comic fulfilment. When Bertoldo is captured in battle in his quixotic attack on Siena, the King refuses to ransom him. Camiola will sell her estate to right this wrong. But Bertoldo cannot secure his release without permission from the Duchess of Siena; and she will grant it only in return for a promise of marriage. Prospect of the power his brother has denied him makes Bertoldo accept the proposition. But Camiola's dignity persuades the Duchess that Bertoldo cannot be the man of integrity she took

---

⁴² Cf. William Cartwright's poem in the 1647 Folio: 'all stand wondering how | The thing will be, until it is.' (sig. d2.)

him for. Camiola sends for a priest, not to marry her, but to secure a monastic refuge from the twists and turns of the tragicomic world. Bertoldo must restore his honour in the Christian warfare of the Knights of Malta. The tragicomic form thus validates a middle space between acceptance of the status quo (comedy) and transcendence of its limits (tragedy), in which noble natures are too mired in the world to achieve more than half lives dedicated to selflessness.

Middleton's *More Dissemblers Besides Women* (?1615; printed 1657) tells a very similar story of a great lady's renunciation of the shifts and subterfuges that are needed to succeed in love. When we first meet the Duchess she is an icon of chastity, dedicated to the memory of her late husband. But, when she sees Andrugio, her heart melts, and she becomes an expert player in the game of deceptions and disguises she finds all around her. However, understanding the steps she would have to take to secure her desires, she prefers nobility to success and retreats from involvement.

Middleton and Rowley's *A Fair Quarrel: with the new additions of Mr Chough's and Trimtram's roaring, and the bawd's song* (*c*.1615×1617) handles a similar mismatch between the impulse to honour and a real world in which intention must twist before it can reach action; but the process is seen this time from a masculine point of view and in an uncourtly (English) setting. Captain Agar and the Colonel return from warfare and immediately find themselves embroiled in family quarrels about money. Tempers rise. The colonel calls Agar 'the son of a whore'; they must fight to clear their consciences. But what must Agar do when his mother tells him (to ensure his safety) that the charge is not a slander but a truth? Agar's honour tells him that he must not fight on this theme, and so he is disgraced. But when he is called a coward he is freed from the inhibition, and he gravely wounds the Colonel. Now it is the Colonel's turn to show exemplary honour; he must recompense Agar for the insult: he will bequeath his estate to his sister and his sister to Agar.[43] She objects, of course, but allows that this is the only way family honour can be cleared. Meanwhile, on the non-military side of the story, love and money are secured by trickery and military decorum is parodied in a school of 'roaring boys'. The

---

[43] In these moves Middleton is following the lead of Heywood in the second plot of *A Woman Killed with Kindness*.

choice of honour appears in this context as a purely hypothetical virtue, not validated by anything outside itself, but still demanding the allegiance of good men.

Middleton's *The Witch* (*c.*1609×*c.*1616) handles the discontinuities of the tragicomic plot from an opposite direction. Here we do not meet characters of honour trying to live inside a world governed by alternative assumptions. Instead, we find a cast of characters intent on tragic violence, but required to pursue their aims not in a world of real action but in a hall of mirrors, so that no move ever leads in the direction intended. We begin with a grand tragic gesture in which the duke (as in Davenant's *Albovine*) requires the duchess to pledge him in a cup made from her father's skull. The duchess plans revenge. But everything thereafter goes awry. The duchess seduces Almachildes, so that she can require him to kill the duke. Faced by the alternative of execution for attempted rape, he does the deed (as it seems) and now he must be killed in his turn. But it was not the duchess he was in bed with, and neither duke nor assassin dies. In a second plot a jealous husband kills his wife and her supposed lover, and then himself falls into a vault and dies. But again no one dies in fact.[44] This is to push the Guarinian definition of tragicomedy, as wanting deaths but bringing some near it, to such a degree of absurdity that one wonders if Middleton is not simply playing games with the tragicomic convention of evil turned into good. The local witches (whose songs somehow got into the printed text of *Macbeth*) offer all the characters the possibility of short cuts that will lead intention directly into effect. But the offer exceeds the result; even the witches are hobbled by discontinuity: they too are simultaneously threatening and comic, as pleased with a marzipan toad as with 'the privy gristle of a man that hangs'. Their charms quickly lose their efficacy or are overtaken by natural causes. The complex world cannot be simplified by their interventions.

Webster's *The Devil's Law-Case; or when women go to law the devil is full of business* (1610×1619) is more like Webster's two great

---

[44] The same device of tragic action suddenly cancelled by the discovery it did not happen appears in the Middleton–Rowley–Massinger *The Old Law* (*c.*1615×1618; printed 1656) where the law that fathers and mothers over age must face euthanasia is used as a hypothesis to reveal the consequences of youth liberation; but then we learn that the law was never carried out. See also Middleton, *Anything for a Quiet Life* (*c.*1620×*c.*1621; printed 1662) where the imperious and spendthrift wife suddenly reveals that she has only been teaching her husband a moral lesson.

tragedies than it is like the other tragicomedies considered here. Yet one can see that it resembles them in its use of labyrinthine plotting to turn evil intentions into improbable agreement and so fulfil the central issue of its form (it is called *Tragecomedy* on the title-page). In Webster's tragedies society exists only to serve the lusts and ambitions of the princes in power; the individual who tries to break free is quickly eliminated. In *The Devil's Law-Case*, however, we meet a bourgeois society in which power (and so the capacity to resist and achieve success) is made available in many forms to many people. Romelio, the protagonist, resembles Flamineo and Bosola, the tool villains in the tragedies, in his relish for corruption, his opportunism and wry self-awareness; but as a wealthy merchant he is his own master, constantly able to redefine his aims as one check after another requires him to trim his course, always in motion, always enjoying himself, like Marlowe's Barabas whom he so closely resembles. But, unlike Barabas, Romelio is subject to a power above himself: not that of the duel-fighting aristocrats, who are quite démodé here, but the power of the law to disentangle point by point the lies, deceptions, and inventions that have snared everyone in the complex society of the play. And so the law becomes the instrument by which tragedy is turned into tragicomedy, as the murderous intentions that bring many 'near death' are turned into legal debates, where lost identities become evidence in court, pieced together to create a denouement. And so, having discovered their actual relationships, the pregnant nun, the two supposedly dead aristocrats (the Palamon and Arcite of the story), and the Romelio family can survive, not only to enjoy happiness with one another but to use the money that has been the cause of so much complex plotting to achieve the most virtuous things imaginable—build nunneries and equip galleys to fight the Turks.

Fletcherian tragicomedy is probably the last substantial generic innovation to take possession of the Elizabethan stage—'substantial' because, as noted above, it proved capable of absorbing many different kinds of emphasis. In its late development it looks symptomatic of the direction in which the whole process of Elizabethan drama was moving, from poetry to plot manipulation, from emotions described to emotions enacted, from passion to prudence, from imagination to reality, from a form designed primarily for a poetic response to one that thrives on theatrical discoveries. The

first heirs of the tradition (the Restoration critics and comic dramatists) assumed that the movement could be called progress—progress
towards their own aesthetic, of course. It had liberated the theatre,
they supposed, from the predetermining judgements imposed by
fixed genres and allowed it to hold up a genuinely reflecting mirror
to the accidental quality of real life. From a modern literary standpoint, however, the development of Elizabethan drama is the story
not of progress towards rational representation, but a process
of decline, not to say betrayal[45]—a betrayal of poetic truth and of
the shared moral meanings that genre strictly applied gives to the
image of society.

The critic as historian, looking at these alternative judgements,
must recognize that they raise a specific question about his enterprise. He can allow that both points of view are justified, for hypotheses to 'prove' each view exist; but the contradiction between them
can be resolved only by constructing an infinite regress of further
hypotheses. In this book I have sought to avoid the too-easy unification that comes from either sentimentalizing the past (by assuming that its values are our own) or from demonizing it (for its
failure to be politically correct). I assume that the first impact of
Elizabethan drama on readers and spectators in the present is likely
to be one of recognition—a recognition of the present in the past;
I hope to complement that by a recognition of the past in the
present, as when we register the contradiction the detail of the past
imposes on the limiting certainties and unnoticed presuppositions
of the present. In this situation the critic must, like Desdemona,
confess to a 'divided duty'—a duty to compose an intelligible picture, faced by a contradictory duty to evoke the shadows that speak
to us in strange tongues from behind the particular structures that
can be described. The multiplicity of these semi-intelligible voices
cannot be reduced to any unison, let alone the unison of today, but
the duty to record their challenge to neat coherence must be (and
I hope has been) acknowledged.

---

[45] T. S. Eliot described Webster as 'a very great literary and dramatic genius directed
towards chaos' (*Selected Essays* (London, 1932), 117)—that is, as part of 'the movement of
progress or deterioration which has culminated in Sir Arthur Pinero and the present regime
in Europe'. Webster and Pinero are equally in thrall to 'the aim of realism' (p. 111) and
share the need to represent their characters as real people with whom the audience can
identify; so they step outside 'the conditions of art'.

Appendix: Entries, Masques, Jigs

IT seems only natural that the flourishing of a sophisticated drama (like that of the Elizabethans) should be embedded in a public culture where political relationships were regularly presented by what I may call para-theatrical action. The modern reader, embedded in a society that is largely suspicious of the public metaphors of power, cannot easily think of the-atrical entertainment as a just expression of state power. But the variant forms that a theatrical society has thrown up provide valuable aids (even today) to understanding the dramatic impulse, for they allow us to see what it is that allows regular drama to be its central manifestation.

The first two forms I have listed in the heading to this chapter illus-trate different ways of handling public theatricality. Entries and masques are courtly forms designed to celebrate the system in power and dazzle those outside it. Entries welcome important persons into cities and castles not only (as now) by presenting them with ornamental keys, but by enacting myths of necessary connection between person and place. The masque is differentiated from these by the fact that the important person (king, queen, or nobleman) is now in his own place. The show that celebrates him is part of the self-defining routine of tableaux, pageants, tilts, disguisings, processions, entertainments, banquets, triumphs, that filled, or even defined, the life of the court.

Plays at court can, of course, be absorbed into this routine, but drama in general should be differentiated from courtly shows by its power to survive outside the defining context. It is not dependent on the condi-tions of its first production, being based on narrative structures that turn our interest inwards to the fortunes of the characters, not outwards to the occasion of performance, and it holds our attention by the very openness of the possibilities made available, the uncertainty about what will happen and (even more tellingly) *how* it will happen. The linear process that carries its characters from desire frustrated to desire fulfilled or from hubris to death is intelligible in many different guises and so endlessly repeatable and rediscoverable.

It is this, of course, that gives drama its literary afterlife. The language which carries the events forward can retain, even in another age, suffi-cient charge from the original implications to allow for reconstruction or revival. For this is a language that expresses, however obliquely, the recurrent passions of human experience. But the words of a masque or entry, whether in dialogue or description, can offer us only a shadow of the original responses, the interplay implicit in the historical occasion, the wonder and delight of the audience involved. The unimportance of verbal sharpness to the masque is made clear by the ease with which the spoken word was taken over by *stilo recitativo*,[1] as (in longer perspective) masque drifted into opera.

Both drama and masque are depictions of change, but in the celebratory mode the change does not occur as a result of a sequence of events. The meaning of the new is not discovered there by attending to a process, but is revealed as something out of time, as the precondition on which the whole action depends. The forms of the celebratory mode are thus (as can be expected, given the sociology of the time) very close to those of religious ritual. The celebration of the Mass is, of course, the great model of non-linear discovery, of one truth (godhead) taking over and transforming another (humanity). In a deliberately similar way the Tudor–Stuart celebration of royalty discovers the spiritual body of the sovereign inside the carnal one, not by pursuing a process but by an epiphany.[2] When in the masque 'the scene changes' (to quote the ubiquitous stage direction), when 'the loud music' sounds and the curtain falls down, when the scenery turns on its axis and reveals the gods sitting on the clouds or the prince advancing in his chariot, we are meant to understand that the world of contingencies has been abolished and a realm of absolutes revealed, where the king is no longer a man but a meaning.

The case is the same in the processional entries into cities. In *The Magnificent Entertainment* of 1604, constructed by Dekker, Jonson, and Middleton to welcome James I into London, the king moves not into his commercial metropolis but into his own *camera regia*, the environment having been transformed by his presence. As he passes under one triumphal arch after another, at each point he is hailed not simply as the agent of virtue, fertility, peace, but as their embodiment. As he arrives, gardens burst into bloom, dormant fountains suddenly begin to spout. And these are parallel rather than sequential events. Each effort at hyperbole tackles the given fact of kingship from a different angle, but they all point to the same unchanging centre.

The annual Lord Mayor of London's show is, of necessity, a lower key event, but the technique of celebration remains the same. In Dekker's *Troia Nova Triumphans* (1612) the Lord Mayor is hailed, not simply as a

---

[1] Mentioned specifically in Jonson's *Vision of Delight*, and *Lovers Made Men* and in *Townshend's *Albion's Triumph*. Welsford (*The Court Masque* (Cambridge, 1927), 204) says that after 1610 *stilo recitativo* 'ousted all spoken monologue and dialogue from the French ballet de Cour'.

[2] In Daniel's *Vision of the Twelve Goddesses* (1604) we are told that the spectators have witnessed an actual incarnation. The 'divine powers . . . being otherwise no objects for mortal eyes' have descended and inhabited the bodies of the masquers. 'And no doubt but that, in respect of the persons under whose beautiful coverings they have thus presented themselves, these deities will be pleased' (*Samuel Daniel: The Complete Works in Verse and Prose*, ed. A. B. Grosart (5 vols.; London, 1885), iv. 204–5).

person charged with the administration of the city but as its statutory embodiment; in him the community finds its self-definition as the point at which virtue, justice, order are given their focusing reflection and where a triumphalist reading of history finds its confirmation.

The ceremonial presence of the person in command (in the only political system generally imaginable) thus 'sacralizes', we may say, the familiar hierarchical structure and brings justification to all the different degrees of the immutable order. In drama likewise, the fictional structure serves to give meaning to the standard social relationships. But the 'meanings' invoked in drama do not support a single social order but attach to the competing values of merely human behaviour, love, ambition, independence, loyalty, and so on—qualities with clear political implications but not usually presented in a political configuration.[3]

The standard form of regular drama depends on a process by which the strange challenges the familiar and is then absorbed inside it. In traditional comic form the son rebels against the father's idea of family continuity and falls in love with an unsuitable girl. The contest between the accepted and the unacceptable is resolved only by a narrative process that shows the girl to be suitable after all, and thus a welcome addition to the family group. The pattern owes its force and its survival through the millenium to the basic nature of the social situation depicted; most members of an audience will be able to bring common experience to complete the outline.

The masque and the entry show us the same basic pattern of the strange being made familiar, but show it from a different point of view. I have noted in *The Magnificent Entertainment* the sustaining fiction that the king enters London not as a visitor from Westminster but as a father entering his own home, his *camera regia*. His presence transforms difference into identity, makes the strange into the familiar without needing a plot to achieve this end. We see the same mode of presentation in entertainments put on to welcome sovereigns when they went on progress and quartered themselves in the houses of the nobility. Legally speaking, of course, the presence of the sovereign turned the house into the court. But the entertainments had to say more than this. When Elizabeth visits the Earl of Leicester at Kenilworth in 1575, she is first barred from the castle by an enraged Hercules figure, the porter. But then he sees that this is no intruder but the rightful owner of the property, and all is apology and welcome (similar fictional events occur in the entertainments at Cowdray and Elvetham).[4] Once she is inside, the whole landscape around the castle

---

[3] Even when a play (such as Middleton's *A Game at Chess*) describes a political process, it does so in terms of narrative sequences that draw their power from common human expectations.

[4] *The Complete Works of John Lyly*, ed. R. Warwick Bond (3 vols.; Oxford, 1902); i. 421–520.

is turned by her presence into an Arcadian fiction populated by gods and nymphs, questing knights and shepherdesses, who, every time the Queen ventures into the environs, appear out of hollow trees, beseech her mercy from bushes, or require her to break the spells that hold them imprisoned in lakes. The landscape is still earth and water but, by the Queen's presence, the film of mere objectivity is removed from it and the mystical truth of unity between the sovereign and the land she owns becomes visible.

The history of the court masque in these reigns allows us to see how such presuppositions are turned into a formal art. The masque seems to grow out of folk customs in which (at festive times) groups of neighbours visit houses in the village 'disguised' as strangers, recite their parts in a traditional play (the St George play, for example) and then, having revealed themselves as old friends, are paid money or welcomed with cakes and ale.[5] What *Hall's Chronicle* describes as the first English masque has precisely this form. In 1512, he tells us,

the king with eleven other were disguised, after the manner of Italy, called a masque, a thing not seen afore in England ... after the banquet done, these masquers came in ... and desired the ladies to dance, some were content and some that knew the fashion of it refused, because it was not a thing commonly seen. And after they danced and commoned together, as the fashion of masques is, they took their leave and departed.[6]

As so described, there is little that is formalized. The distinction between real king and disguised 'stranger' is present, but the disguises of this period are not part of a prearranged fiction. What we have is a 'game' played by the noble participants for their own amusement and not for the enlightenment of any spectators.

But the formality of court protocol in the succeeding reigns soon changed the relation of masquer and sovereign, and the masque moved closer to the entry and entertainment as a set form of compliment. The 'strangers' are then more like visitors from a foreign land (or from the gods), and the story of their travel to the English court turns into an occasion to express wonder at its magnificence and to praise the sovereign who sustains it. The masque thus becomes an occasion for national self-congratulation and the presence of the ambassadors of foreign states comes to be an important part of the scene.

The Masque of Proteus presented to Queen Elizabeth by the gentlemen of Gray's Inn in 1594 is usually seen as the first example of the form that governed the court masque for the rest of its life. It was a tradition of the

---

[5] For a more recent instance, see Hardy, *The Return of the Native*, bk. II, ch. 5.
[6] Edward Hall, *The Union of Lancaster and York* (1548), repr. as *Hall's Chronicle* (London, 1809), 526.

Inns of Court to elect each year a Christmas 'king' to preside over their holiday revels. On this occasion the revellers were invited to court at Shrovetide, when the 'king' had returned from his travel to 'Russia'. He returned, however, as a hostage, imprisoned inside an adamantine rock by Proteus, the god of the sea, who would release him and yield up his power over the ocean only if he was confronted by someone with more magnetism than himself. Elizabeth was, of course, the person with that power. When the rock had been trundled into her presence it flew open to reveal and release the Inns of Court masquers, who 'in a very stately masque, very richly attired and provided of all things meet for the performance of so gallant an enterprise . . . danced a new devised measure. After which they took unto themselves ladies and with them they danced their galliards, courants etc.'[7] And then, after gifts had been presented, they returned back into the rock, and were mere lawyers once again.

In *The Masque of Proteus* we can see a self-pleasing Christmas game turning into a complimentary device of elegant simplicity. It can give us no surprise to find Ben Jonson imitating the form in his earliest court masques (1605–8). The 'strangers' are now the Queen and her ladies, blacked up as the daughters of Niger. They have travelled the world in search of a cure for their blackness and now find that Britain is the place they seek, where King James's virtues 'are of force | To blanch an Ethiop'. Their pleasure in this discovery is expressed in dances with gentlemen of the court, and then they retire into the seashell in which they arrived. Magnificent clothes, elaborate scenes and machines, song, dance[8] and poetry, make of this material a composite form from which nothing can be extracted without loss. Ben Jonson, in his quarrel with the architect Inigo Jones, defended this unity in terms of the *idea* that controlled it all, which was the province of the poet, and therefore properly called the *soul* of the enterprise—everything else being mere body, merely instrumental. To the extent that it was the *idea* that linked the entertainment to the king and so sacralized it, Jonson was surely right. An answer to the question why any of this was happening at all depends on a series of cross-identifications that need a fable to support them.

---

[7] *Gesta Grayorum*, ed. Desmond Bland (Liverpool, 1968), 86.

[8] The attempt in the masque to use the physical to transcend the physical is nowhere more important than in the element most mysterious today—the dancing. The Pythagorean–Platonic tradition that harmony between man the microcosm and the heavenly macrocosm is shown most clearly in mathematics, allows that man comes nearest to heavenly purity in the mathematical control of his bodily movements. In Jonson's *Mercury Vindicated from the Alchemists at Court* (1616), the dancers are told to 'come forth, prove all the numbers then | That make perfection up, and may absolve you men' and subsequently, 'move, move again' for 'Nature is motion's mother . . . the spring whence order flows, | that all directs | And knits the causes with the effects' (Herford and Simpson, VII. 415–16, ll. 210–11, 239–44).

To secure this effect, however, the fable had to find a mode in which it could be accepted as in some sense true. Hence the pedantry that Jonson lavished on the tissue of mythological relationships he set up, arguing that 'antiquity and solid learnings . . . though their voice be taught to sound to present occasions, their sense or doth or should always lay hold on more removed mysteries'.[9] The 'more removed mysteries' are those that link appearance to a hidden reality, as effect to cause, as ordinary to ideal. Humanist learning can link pagan mythology to Christian belief, and so prove that the existing hierarchy is justified by poetry no less than by God. The theory also, it will be noticed, makes the poet part of the system; true representation cannot be effected unless 'the nobility of the invention be answerable to the dignity of their persons [who danced in the masque]' and unless 'the most royal persons [are] curious after the most high and hearty inventions to furnish the inward parts'.[10] This aesthetic marks the continuity between these forms and other Humanist tastes— for rebuses, emblems, and enigmata, for mythographies and the scutcheons that knights carried in celebratory jousts and barriers. In all these 'the inward parts' were deliberately made obscure, so that the pleasure of being on the 'inside' could be sustained as a gift of understanding derived from birth no less than learning.[11]

The court, however, was more willing to be defined by social difference than sustained by knowledge. The vulgar many may have been excluded from the Banqueting Hall (as Jonson was himself on one occasion), but they were there implicitly, as the differentiated 'other', the shadow that was needed if refinement was to be thrown into brilliant relief. If we are to believe Jonson, it was the Queen herself who made the first move to incorporate this understanding into the structure of the masque, feeling perhaps that the transformation from black to white or from strangeness to acceptability in her early masques was too lacking in dramatic energy; and so she commanded him to compose 'some dance or show that should precede hers and have the place of a foil or false masque'.[12] And so in *The Masque of Queens* (1609) Jonson brings onto the stage, before the appearance of the Queen and her ladies, an 'antimasque' of witches, named Ignorance, Credulity, Falsehood, Suspicion, and so on, whose aim is to prevent the queens from bringing back the Age of Gold. This they try to achieve by singing spells and by dancing 'preposterously' (that is, back to back, and moving anti-clockwise). But when 'the scene

---

[9] *Hymenaei*, ll. 16–19.   [10] Ibid., ll. 10–15
[11] Jonson's defence of his failure to explain the figures in the masque is that 'a writer should always trust somewhat to the spectator, especially at these spectacles'. He writes not for the sluggish ears 'of porters and mechanics that must be bored through at every act with narrations' (*Masque of Queens*, note on ll. 95–110). See also *Jonson*, VII. 91, for his comment on the arch at Fenchurch Street.   [12] *Masque of Queens*, ll. 11–12.

changes' and the loud music sounds, the witches vanish and the 'Temple of Fame' appears as a proper habitation for the twelve queens. They dance 'with singular variety' and in their figures spell out the name of Charles, Duke of York. This realization of the Queen's command seems to indicate that the keyword in it is *foil*. The witches (played by professionals, that is, commoners) exist only to highlight by contrast the natural virtues of the great ladies. The method is, once again, opposite to that of drama. There is no threat, for there is no interaction and no hint of a narrative to link the opposites. The wonder-making machinery that presents the Temple of Fame expresses the fiat of a divine system in which the beautiful inevitably replaces the grotesque, as epiphany replaces disorder, and strangeness gives way to the reassurance that the dancing bodies reveal the harmony in the souls of the great court ladies. And so, as antimasque gives way to main masque, Plutus must give way to Cupid, Comus must be defeated by Hercules, the Iron Age must be swept away by the Golden Age, and the paid actors must be replaced by those whose skills derive from innate grace and not from professional practice.

As is the way with epiphanies and apparitions, the masque offered a moment of total vision, of stunning beauty and magnificence, sharpened in its effect by the enigmatic quality of its meaning and the brevity of its appearance. The combination of splendour and ephemerality seems to have struck contemporaries with particular force: it has been thought to be referred to in Prospero's invocation of the 'cloud-capped towers, the gorgeous palaces' that 'dissolve' and 'leave not a rack behind'. The painted cloths, the lath and plaster, the sweating machine operators, were all that were left. And this sudden dissolution seems to have been part of the meaning intended. In his notes to *The Masque of Blackness* Jonson speaks of 'the rage of the people who (as part of greatness) are privileged by custom to deface [the masque's] carcases' Herford and Simpson (VII. 169–70). Hall retails an even more telling example. In 1511 Henry VIII and his queen held an entertainment at Whitehall, followed by dancing. But 'the rude people ran to the pageant and rent, tore and spoiled the pageant so that the lord steward . . . could not cause them to abstain, except they should have foughten and drawn blood'; they even

ran to the king and stripped him to his hosen and doublet and all his companions likewise. The ladies likewise were spoiled. . . . So the King with the Queen and the ladies returned into his chamber, where they had a great banquet, and all these hurts were turned to laughing, and thought *that all that was taken away was but for honour and largesse*; and so this triumph ended with mirth and gladness. (emphasis added)[13]

---

[13] Hall's Chronicle (1809 edn.), 519.

Clearly the nobility of the occasion, the vast expense, the specialized code of behaviour required, all belong self-consciously to a system in which the elements excluded are understood to be out there, waiting their turn. The antimasque in some degree incorporates this understanding into the game being played, especially in those later masques where the distinction is handled less in Jonson's metaphysical terms and more as a social contrast, so that midwives, pedants, roaring boys, courtesans, usurers, bawds, and so on can display cameo versions of the uncoordinated and ungracious life these same actors depicted in the public theatres. Jonson thought such characters 'heterogene', but James I (addicted equally to vulgarity and pedantry) preferred them to attenuated subtleties. The highest authority thus confirms the homogeneity of a culture in which the most exclusive form (the masque) is cousin to the most populist (the jig).

The Jig

The jig was a short dramatic routine by one, two, or three actors, dealing with personal relations, familiar follies, and betrayals and presented by actors singing, dancing, and playing on instruments (often all at once). Jigs seem to have been performed regularly as afterpieces in the public theatres (and such afterpieces continued to be part of a theatrical evening's entertainment until well into the nineteenth century), defining the 'legitimate' drama, once again, by the presence of an alternative form— one more interactive and responsive to the tastes of an undifferentiated audience. If, from the point of view of the court, the public play was a dangerously open form, in which opposite values are allowed to collide without reporting to a comprehensive higher truth, from the point of view of the jig the public play must have looked like a form overcommitted to 'higher truth' and therefore not speaking directly to its public.

The famous performers of jigs in the Elizabethan period were the great clowns: Tarlton of the Queen's Men, Kemp of the Chamberlain's Men, and Greene of Queen Anne's Men. This tells us something about the conditions of performance. Tarlton and Kemp were famous for their powers of extemporization, and it is easy to imagine that the public admired them for the degree of audience participation that their methods allowed. It follows that the surviving German and English texts[14] can give us little sense of what the performance of a jig was like. The repertory of the jig performer was close to that of the ballad singer, and indeed it is hard to maintain a hard-and-fast distinction between these two. Autolycus's ballad-selling in *The Winter's Tale* may be as near as we can come to the social dynamics of the occasion. The tunes seem to have been those

[14] See C. R. Baskervill, *The Elizabethan Jig* (Chicago, 1929).

currently popular and it is probable that different tunes could be produced and adapted as requested.

The characters we meet in the jigs are familiar to us from other popular forms and from city comedies—the cutpurse, the country bumpkin, the soldier, the lover, the prostitute, the eager wooer, the anxious husband, the prentice and his dame—but the situations in which these characters are presented are without complexity and too stereotyped to create surprise. Indeed, surprise would seem to be a quality little in demand; the virtuosity of the performers could not display itself to so great advantage if the audience could not anticipate the next move or note the variation newly introduced. There is evidence that local scandals were much appreciated (at least while the excitement lasted). The case of *Keep the Widow Waking* (see p. 481) suggests the continuity that was possible between the scandal jig or ballad and the scandal play on the same topic.

The jig was undoubtedly proletarian fare and as such was particularly subject to moral opprobrium. *This World's Folly* of 1615 speaks of 'obscene and light jigs, stuffed with loathsome and unheard of ribaldry sucked from the poisonous dugs of sin-swelled theatres' (quoted in Chambers, iv. 254). In line with such views the authorities sought to suppress them (see Chambers, iv. 340–1), but they were too close to the basics of human nature to be in any danger. And, indeed, the surviving examples show no threat to moral or political order. Like other proletarian art forms, they support all the family values that can be desired: constancy in love, patriotism, military prowess. Of course they do so in a generously accepting frame of mind and are little given to condemnation. That in itself no doubt appeared to be good reason for disapproval.

Brief Biographies

THE facts on which the following material is based are derived from Chambers; Bentley; *The Dictionary of National Biography*; Mark Eccles, *Brief Lives: Tudor and Stuart Authors* (Chapel Hill, NC, 1982), *SP* Supplement, vol. 79; *Elizabethan Dramatists*, ed. Fredson Bowers (Dictionary of Literary Biography, 62, Detroit, 1987); *Jacobean and Caroline Dramatists*, ed. Fredson Bowers (Dictionary of Literary Biography, 58, Detroit, 1987); C. J. Sisson, *Thomas Lodge and Other Elizabethans* (Cambridge, Mass., 1933); Samuel Schoenbaum, *Shakespeare: A Documentary Life* (Oxford, 1975).

ALEXANDER, SIR WILLIAM (*c*.1568–1640): educated at the Universities of Glasgow and Leyden, he was tutor to Prince Henry up to 1603. Knighted in 1609. Created Earl of Stirling, 1609 (later Viscount Canada). Secretary for Scotland, 1626. Author of (among many other works) four 'Monarchic Tragedies'—closet dramas concerned with political disasters in the ancient world.

BALE, JOHN (1495–1563): born in Suffolk, he attended Jesus College, Cambridge; BD 1528/9. He converted to Protestantism and broke his monastic vows. Under the protection of Cromwell he wrote plays attacking Catholic doctrines. When Cromwell fell, he fled to Germany, but returned in 1548. Appointed Bishop of Ossory (in Ireland) in 1552. Under Mary he fled again. Under Elizabeth he held a prebend in Canterbury and compiled surveys of English antiquities.

BARKSTEED, WILLIAM (b. ?1589) was a boy actor with the Children of the Queen's Revels up to 1616, when he moved with the rest of the company to the Lady Elizabeth's Men. He published two long narrative poems— on Hiren the Fair Greek and Myrrha the Mother of Adonis.

BARNES, BARNABE (*c*.1569–1609): his father was Bishop of Durham. He entered Brasenose College in 1593, but no degree is recorded. He accompanied Essex to France in 1591.

BARRY, LORDING (1580–1629): long supposed to be the son of David, Lord Barry. He now appears to be a London citizen, named Lording after his mother's family. Before 1609 he had become a shareholder in the Whitefriars playhouse, where his one play was produced. He became involved in various piratical ventures, after which he settled down to legal import–export business and achieved a respectable position.

BRIEF BIOGRAPHIES 535

BEAUMONT, FRANCIS ($c.$1584–1616): his father was a judge and an MP. He matriculated at Oxford in 1597. He married an heiress in 1613, and retired to the life of a gentleman on her estate.

BREWER, ANTHONY (fl. between 1607 and 1617): nothing definite is known about the life of this man. He may be the actor of the same name mentioned in the MS of *Two Noble Ladies* (1619×1623) designed for the Red Bull Company.

BROME, RICHARD ($c.$1590–1652) is mentioned in the Induction to *Bartholomew Fair* as Ben Jonson's 'man'. He wrote plays for the Salisbury Court and the Phoenix as their retained writer (some fifteen plays survive). After 1642 he published only occasional poems and seems to have died in poverty.

CARLELL, LODOWICK (1602–1675): at court by 1621. Between 1622 and 1638 he wrote nine plays for performance at court. Keeper of the Royal Deer Park at Richmond. He does not seem to have suffered confiscation under the Commonwealth. Granted a pension in 1660.

CARY, ELIZABETH (1585/6–1639): daughter of a wealthy lawyer (later ennobled). In 1602 she married Henry Cary, later Viscount Falkland. Her conversion to Catholicism dominated her later life and led to estrangement from husband and father. She was the author of many incidental works, and she evidently wrote two plays, of which only one, *The Tragedy of Mariam, the Fair Queen of Jewry*, has survived.

CHAPMAN, GEORGE (1560–1634): born in Hitchin, Herts. We have no record of his education, but he clearly became a man of learning. In the period 1596 to 1599 he wrote plays for Henslowe, but his later plays are designed for the boys. In 1603 he was appointed to the household of Prince Henry (to whom he dedicated his translation of the Iliad). After the death of Prince Henry he was patronized by Robert Carr, but when Carr was disgraced he was again without a powerful patron to protect his ambition to be the laureate of a heroic English culture.

CHETTLE, HENRY (d. between 1603 and 1607): apprenticed to a printer in 1577, he was free of the Stationers' Company in 1584. He 'edited' *Greene's Groatsworth of Wit* in 1592 and wrote pamphlets on his own account. By 1598 he is writing for the stage. Henslowe names forty-eight plays in which he had a hand.

COOKE, JO: [? Joshua or John] (fl. 1607): The only sure fact about this man is that he wrote *Greene's Tu Quoque*—one of the most popular plays in the period. Heywood, in the epistle to the Quarto (1622), speaks 'of my worthy friend the author' in the past tense.

DANIEL, SAMUEL (1563–1619): matriculated in Oxford, 1581. No record of a degree. On the Continent, 1585–90 (perhaps acting as an agent).

Patronized by Queen Anne and the Countess of Pembroke. In 1604 appointed licenser to the boys of the Queen's Revels. By 1607 he was Groom of the Queen's Privy Chamber, and in 1613 her 'Gentleman Extraordinary'. His plays are (like his poems and his masques) designed only for courtly and learned taste.

DAVENANT, SIR WILLIAM (1607–1668): son of a vintner in Oxford. Lincoln College, Oxford in 1620; left to become page to the Duchess of Richmond; later in service to Fulke Greville. Given charge of the Phoenix playhouse in 1640. Fought for the King in the Civil War. Captured 1650. Released 1652. At the Restoration he was given a royal patent to inaugurate theatrical performances.

DAVENPORT, ROBERT (fl. 1612–1640): in 1612 he is associated with the Fortune. He first appears in Sir Henry Herbert's day-book in 1624. The last mention is in the epistle to *King John and Matilda* (1655). We know titles of ten plays by him.

DAY, JOHN (c.1574–1640): admitted to Gonville and Caius college in 1592 (expelled 1593 for stealing a book). From 1598 to 1603 he appears in Henslowe's Diary, collaborating with Dekker. Chettle, and Haughton. Later he wrote for the boys. After the break-up of the Paul's and Revels companies he seems to have returned to collaboration with Dekker.

DEKKER, THOMAS (c.1572–1632): born in London. His name first appears in Henslowe's Diary in 1598. Thirty-six plays not published (mostly written in collaboration) are listed in Henslowe. In all, we know of forty-six books written by him. In prison for debt from 1612 to 1619. Wrote Lord Mayor's pageants, 1627–9. Died in debt.

DRAYTON, MICHAEL (1563–1631): born in Warwickshire. Grew up in the household of Sir Henry Goodyere. His fluent poetic skills, and his patriotic pride in the countryside and its history, secured him many noble patrons. In the years 1597–1602 he appears as a playwright for Henslowe, collaborating in some nineteen plays. In 1608 he was a member of the syndicate that controlled the boys' theatre in the Whitefriars.

DRUE, THOMAS (fl. 1623): perhaps the actor of that name, associated with the Queen Anne's and the Red Bull companies, 1613×1622. He wrote a play on the same subject as the Dekker, Webster, Rowley, and Ford *The Late Murder of the Son upon the Mother* of 1624 (see Chapter 9, n. 59), collaborated with Davenport.

EDWARDS, RICHARD (1524–1566): admitted to Corpus Christi College, Oxford. BA in 1544; MA and Lecturer in Logic in 1546. Ordained 1547/50. Gentleman of the Chapel Royal before 1557. In 1561 appointed Master of the Chapel Children, who performed plays under his direction.

FIELD, NATHAN (1587–1620): son of a Puritan preacher. Attended St Paul's School. Before 1601 was pressganged into the Children of the Chapel Royal. By 1614 he was the leader of the Lady Elizabeth's Men. In 1617 he joined the King's Men. His own plays seem to be written for the Queen's Revels–Lady Elizabeth's combine. As a King's Man he collaborated with Fletcher and Massinger.

FLETCHER, JOHN (1579–1625): his father became Bishop of London. Cambridge BA in 1595, MA in 1598. In 1600 he entered the Middle Temple. His collaboration with Beaumont began with plays for the Queen's Revels and then transferred to the King's Men. After Beaumont's retirement, Fletcher became principal dramatist for the King's Men, in succession to Shakespeare, both as individual author and as collaborator with Shakespeare, Massinger, and other dramatists. He set the tone for much of late Jacobean drama.

FORD JOHN (b. 1586): born in Devon, Ford came from a family of lawyers. He entered Oxford in 1601 and enrolled in the Middle Temple in 1602. Wrote plays for the King's Men and for Beeston at the Phoenix between 1621 and ?1638. Collaborated with Dekker, Rowley, and Webster.

FRAUNCE, ABRAHAM (c.1558–1633): scholar at Shrewsbury School at the same time as Sidney. St John's College, Cambridge, BA, 1580. Acted in Legge's *Richardus Tertius* in 1580. Fellow of St John's, 1581. MA, 1583. Wrote Latin plays for Cambridge performances. Entered Gray's Inn. Patronized by the Herbert and Sidney families, for whom he wrote works in both Latin and English. He seems to have given up literature in the 1590s.

GASCOIGNE, GEORGE (c.1535–1577): born in Bedfordshire, the son of Sir John Gascoigne. Educated at Trinity College, Cambridge, and Gray's Inn (for which he wrote plays). In 1573–4 he served in the Netherlands; prepared shows for the Princely Pleasures at Kenilworth, 1575.

GOFFE, THOMAS (c.1592–1628): born in Essex, and educated at Westminster School, he went to Christ Church, Oxford, in 1609, and took his MA in 1616 and his BD in 1623. As Fellow and Latin poet, he wrote his plays for student actors. His *The Careless Shepherdess* was acted before Charles I at the Salisbury Court playhouse. He was also famous as a preacher.

GOSSON, STEPHEN (1554–1624): born in Canterbury, he matriculated at Oxford in 1572; MA in 1576. In London, he became a playwright and perhaps a player, but by 1579 he had become a fervent enemy to the theatre. His dedication of one of his violent diatribes to Sir Philip Sidney is said to have prompted Sidney's *Apology for Poetry*. By 1584 Gosson had taken holy orders and thereafter he held several livings in the City of London.

538 BRIEF BIOGRAPHIES

GREENE, ROBERT (1558–1592): came from Norwich, son of a saddler. Cambridge BA in 1580, MA in 1583. Became a bohemian journalist in London. Published at least forty books (of which five are plays, written for the Queen's and the Admiral's Men).

GREVILLE, FULKE (1554–1628): at Shrewsbury School with Philip Sidney. Came to court and followed the fortunes of Essex. In 1598, Treasurer of the Navy. Disgraced during the ascendancy of the Cecil faction, after Robert Cecil's death he became Chancellor of the Exchequer and Privy Councillor. He was granted Warwick Castle by King James and in 1621 was made Lord Brooke.

HATH[A]WAY, RICHARD (fl. 1598–1603): he is praised (among the professional dramatists) in Meres's *Palladis Tamia* (1598). He collaborated in eighteen plays for Henslowe in the years 1598–1603.

HAUGHTON, WILLIAM (fl. 1597–1602): he wrote twenty-five plays for Henslowe, (of which two survive), mostly in collaboration with Chettle, Day, and Dekker.

HEMINGES, WILLIAM (1602–1653): son to John Heminge[s], actor–patentee of the King's Men and co-sponsor of the Shakespeare First Folio. He was educated at Westminster School and Christ Church, Oxford (MA 1628). He inherited his father's shares in the Globe and Blackfriars but does not seem to have been involved in theatre business. We have titles of three plays by him; two have survived.

HERBERT, MARY, Countess of Pembroke (1561–1621): sister to Philip Sidney, who wrote his *Arcadia* for her delectation. She completed her brother's translation of the Psalms and was a general patroness of poets. She translated Robert Garnier's closet play of *Antoine*, and encouraged Daniel and Kyd in their closet drama.

HEYWOOD, THOMAS (1573/4–1641): born in Lincolnshire, son of a clergyman. May have been in Cambridge, 1591–3. In 1596 Henslowe bound him to act only in his theatres. Became the regular dramatist for the Worcester's–Queen Anne's company. Wrote an *Apology for Actors* (c.1608). Said in 1633 that he had had 'an entire hand, or at least a main finger in 220 plays'. We have forty-six published works, of which twenty-five are plays.

JONSON, BENJAMIN (?1572–1637): born in London. His father, a minister, died early. Mother remarried a bricklayer. Alternated between Westminster School education and bricklaying. Appears in Henslowe's diary in 1597. Imprisoned in 1597 for writing *The Isle of Dogs* (acted by Pembroke's Men at the Swan). In 1598 killed Gabriel Spencer, a fellow actor. Branded as a felon. Converted to Catholicism in prison. In 1604 hired to write welcome pageants for James I. Commanded by the Queen to write court masques. Quarrels with Inigo Jones. Loses favour under Charles. In 1628 appointed Chronologer to the City.

KYD, THOMAS (1558–1594): his father was a scrivener in London. Educated at the Merchant Taylor's School. Arrested in 1593 for scandalous 'libels' and charged with atheism, he declared his room-mate Marlowe to be the guilty party, fearing he would lose his patron of six years' standing (?the Earl of Suffolk). His closet tragedy Cornelia (1594) seems to have been written to gain the favour of the Countess of Pembroke.

LEGGE, THOMAS (1535–1607): of Norwich origin, he matriculated in Corpus Christi College, Cambridge in 1552; MA, 1557; Master of Caius, 1573; LLD, 1575; Vice-Chancellor of the University, 1593. In addition to Richardus Tertius he wrote a long-lost (now recovered) play on the destruction of Jerusalem.

LODGE, THOMAS (c.1557–1625): son of Sir Thomas Lodge (Lord Mayor in 1562). He attended the Merchant Taylor's School and Trinity College, Oxford. In 1578 he entered Lincoln's Inn. In the early 1590s he sailed on a number of exploratory and privateering ventures. In 1597–8 he took a medical degree at Avignon. He was cited for recusancy in 1604 and 1605, and lived in the Spanish Netherlands, 1606–9. His friends enabled him to return and practise medicine in London.

LYLY, JOHN (1554–1606): from a learned and ecclesiastical family, Lyly matriculated at Magdalen College, Oxford, probably in 1569. BA, 1573; MA, 1575. Failing to secure Burghley's support for a university appointment, he turned to authorship. The spectacular success of his mannered moral romance, Euphues (1578), secured him the patronage of the Earl of Oxford and so an opportunity to write and direct plays for boys to act, both in public and at court. The idea that literature could serve as a means to court preferment proved as illusory for Lyly as for other men and he ended his life still complaining of hopes encouraged and never fulfilled.

MACHIN, LEWIS (fl c.1608): contributed poems to Barksteed's Mirrha (1607) and collaborated with Markham in 1607–8.

MARLOWE, CHRISTOPHER (1564–1593): he was born in Canterbury, his father a shoemaker. He is likely to have been educated at King's School, Canterbury, and proceeded to Corpus Christi College, Cambridge. BA in 1584; MA (by command of the Privy Council) in 1587. In 1592, probably still working as a secret agent, he was arrested in the Netherlands for coining. Under investigation by the Privy Council in 1593. Stabbed in Deptford in the company of other spies and agents.

MARKHAM, GERVASE (fl. 1621): now believed not to be the voluminous writer about horsemanship but another man associated in a lawsuit of

1623 with many of the principal actors in the Red Bull. A 'Marcum' is mentioned by Henslowe in 1596, but the context does not give us any hold on his identity.

MARMION, SHAKERLEY (1603–1639): born in Northamptonshire, his father a country gentleman; in 1617 in Wadham College, Oxford (MA 1624). Soldiering in the Netherlands in 1625. His plays pleased king and court and were performed at the Phoenix and the Salisbury Court.

MARSTON, JOHN (1575–1634): born in Oxfordshire. His father was a Bencher of the Middle Temple, his mother of an Italian family. BA Oxon., 1594, and living in the Middle Temple in the same year. His satires were burnt by order in 1599. Shareholder in the Queen's Revels in 1604–8. Imprisoned in 1608. Entered the Church: deacon in 1609. Succeeded to his father-in-law's parish in 1616.

MASON, JOHN (fl. 1608): perhaps he is the man educated at Bury St Edmunds School who matriculated in Cambridge, 1596 (BA, 1601; MA, 1606). He was a member of the syndicate that ran the Whitefriars playhouse.

MASSINGER, PHILIP (1583–1640): his father was a Fellow of Merton College, Member of Parliament, and agent for the Earl of Pembroke. Matriculated at Oxford in 1583, but no record of graduation. By 1613 he is associated with Henslowe. He appears in Sir Henry Herbert's office-book from 1626 to 1640. Collaborated with Fletcher in plays for the King's Men and after Fletcher's death became their principal poet. Asked to be buried by Fletcher's side.

MAY, THOMAS (1596–1650): born in Sussex. Matriculated in Cambridge in 1609. BA, 1613; entered Gray's Inn c.1615. His father dying intestate, he turned to literature in 1620–36, imitating Jonson's tragedies (perhaps only as reading texts) and translating Latin historical works. In 1640 he supported the parliamentary side and in 1645 was appointed Secretary to the Parliament.

MIDDLETON, THOMAS (1580–1627): born in London. Matriculated in Oxford in 1598; no record of a degree. He was deprived of his patrimony by his stepfather. From 1597 he published poetry and pamphlets. He first appears in Henslowe's Diary in 1602, as a collaborator with Dekker. From 1603 he writes city comedies for the Paul's Boys and thereafter collaborates in tragedies and tragicomedies for the King's Men and other adult companies. In 1613 he begins a series of Lord Mayor's Pageants. In 1620 he is appointed Chronologer to the city.

MONTAGU, WALTER (1603–1677): son of the Earl of Manchester; Cambridge, 1617/18. While in France he became a follower of the Duke of Buckingham. He lived in France as a secret agent for the crown, and converted there to Catholicism. Imprisoned and then exiled during the Commonwealth. He became abbott of the Monastery at Nanteuil.

MUNDAY, ANTHONY (1560–1633): apprenticed to a stationer, 1576. At the English College in Rome, 1579. Wrote an exposé of the experience. Is recorded as a writer of plays for Henslowe, 1597–1602. Worked as a City poet, devising pageants for the Lord Mayor's shows; completed and expanded Stowe's *Survey of London* (1633). Fifteen play titles known (six survive). Wrote nine city pageants, published twenty-seven original books and seventeen translations.

NASHE, THOMAS (1567–1601): born in Lowestoft, son of a clergyman, he matriculated in Cambridge in 1582. BA, 1586. He was a freelance writer from 1588. The bishops used his satiric talents in the anti-Martinist campaign. In 1597 he fled to Yarmouth to escape imprisonment for his part in the lost satirical play *The Isle of Dogs*. His pamphlet war with Gabriel Harvey was suppressed by the authorities in 1599.

PEELE, GEORGE (1556–1596): born in London, his father a schoolmaster. Oxford BA, 1577; MA, 1579. Well thought of in the academy; Oxford called on him to set forth university performances. As well as plays and poems, he wrote tilt pageants for the Earl of Essex and pageants for the Lord Mayor.

PHILLIP [or PHILLIPS], JOHN (fl. 1570–1591): the most plausible of the available John Phillips was educated at Queen's College, Cambridge, but took no degree. He published many pietistic works in the 1570s and 1580s, many of them lamenting the deaths of pious noblewomen.

PERCY, WILLIAM (1575–1648): younger son of the Earl of Northumberland. He dedicated his *Sonnets to the Fairest Coelia* (1594) to his close friend Barnabe Barnes. MSS of six plays intended for the Paul's Boys have survived, each one preceded by a list of properties required. He retired to Oxford, where he died 'having lived a melancholy and retired life many years'.

PICKERING, JOHN (fl. 1567): has been identified with Sir John Puckering (1544–96), admitted to Lincoln's Inn in 1559. He became Lord Keeper in 1592.

PORTER, HENRY (fl. 1596–1599): seven titles of plays by him appear in Henslowe's Diary, of which only one survives. He may have been killed in a duel with John Day (*q.v.*) in 1590.

RAWLINS, THOMAS (*c*.1617–1670): poet as well as playwright. His main profession was as an engraver of coins and medals (chief engraver to the Mint).

RICHARDS, NATHANIEL (fl. 1631–1641): he is probably the Kent man who published *The Celestian Publican* in 1630 (revised edition 1641). He is associated with men who belonged to the King's Revels company (at the Salisbury Court theatre).

ROWLEY, S. MUEL (*c*.1575–1624): actor and playwright, he was a sharer in the Admir il's–Prince's–Palsgrave's company, 1598–1613. He revised *Dr Faustus* for Henslowe. His name is not found after 1624.

ROWLEY, WILLIAM (*c*.1585–1625/6): probably brother to Samuel. Leading comic actor in Prince Charles's company. There are records of his collaboration with Dekker, Ford, Heywood, Massinger, Middleton, and Webster. Joined the King's Men in 1623. He is known to have had a hand in at least twenty-four plays.

SAMPSON, WILLIAM (*c*.1600–1656): he first appears in the household of Sir William Willoughby of Risley, in Derbyshire. He published a volume of verse in 1636.

SHAKESPEARE, WILLIAM (1564–1616): born in Stratford-upon-Avon. His father was a prosperous glover. Presumably he attended the town grammar school, but there is no record, and no suggestion that he went to university. By 1594 he was established as a dramatist, poet, and actor in London, and in that year he joined the newly reformed Chamberlain's Men. The rest of his life was associated with this company, in which he became a shareholder, and also an investor in their playhouses. In 1597 he bought an imposing residence in Stratford, and invested widely in the area. In his later years he seems to have curtailed his commitment to the London theatrical scene, and spent more and more of his time in his native town.

SHARPHAM, EDWARD (1576–1608): his father, a Devonshire gentleman, died while he was a minor. He entered the Middle Temple in 1594 but he does not seem to have been called to the bar.

SHIRLEY, JAMES (1596–1666): born in London, he attended Merchant Taylors' School, 1608–*c*.1612. He took his MA at Cambridge in 1620, and was ordained priest. In 1621 he was headmaster of St Albans School. By 1625 he was writing for the Lady Elizabeth's Men and then the Queen Henrietta's Men at the Phoenix. In 1636 he fled the London plague and wrote plays for the Dublin theatre. In 1640 he replaced Massinger as retained playwright for the King's Men. In the Civil War he followed his patron the Earl of Newcastle. He was chosen to write the prefatory epistle to the 1647 Beaumont and Fletcher Folio.

SKELTON, JOHN (?1460–1529): received the degree of poet laureate from Oxford, Louvain, and Cambridge. Ordained priest in 1498. Tutor to Prince Henry up to 1502. By 1504 he was rector of Diss in Norfolk. He lived in Westminster from 1512 as *orator regius*, and continued there in sanctuary to escape punishment for his satires on Wolsey. Several plays by him are mentioned, but only *Magnificence* survives.

TARLTON, RICHARD (d. 1588): the most famous Elizabethan clown. By 1583 he was a member of the Queen's Men and Groom of the Chamber. Stories of his wit circulated throughout the next century. Some of those printed in *Tarlton's Jests* (entered in the Stationers' Register in 1609) may be authentic, but most are merely traditional.

TOURNEUR, CYRIL (d. 1626): *c.*1590 he was secretary to Sir Francis Vere; in 1613 courier to Brussels. In 1613 Daborne mentions him to Henslowe. In 1625 he is secretary to Sir Edward Cecil during the second Cadiz expedition. Died in Kinsale after the failure of the exploit.

TOWNSHEND, AURELIAN (fl. 1601–1643): he was patronized by Robert Cecil. He was commanded to write masques by King Charles, *c.*1631.

WEBSTER, JOHN (?1580–?1634): son of a coachmaker. ?Merchant Taylors' School. ?Middle Temple, 1598. Mentioned in Henslowe's Diary, 1602. In 1604–5 he collaborates with Dekker in plays for the Paul's Boys. In 1624 he writes a Lord Mayor's pageant. In 1624, he collaborates with Dekker, Ford, and Rowley in *Keep the Widow Waking* for the Red Bull.

WHETSTONE, GEORGE (1544–?1587): he served in the Low Countries, 1572–4, and again in 1585–6. He went on the Newfoundland Voyage of 1578–9.

WILKINS, GEORGE (fl. 1607–1608): collaborated with Day and William Rowley on *The Travels of Three English Brothers* (1607). In the same year he published a jest book, a pamphlet, and *Three Miseries of Barbary*, and in 1608 *A True History of the Play of Pericles*.

WILSON, ROBERT: the name appears as that of a playwright in two different periods: first as a member of Leicester's Men in 1572–81 who was picked for the Queen's Men in 1583 (in 1585 he received payment from the company for five plays), and secondly as a Henslowe payee, who collaborated on fourteen plays between 1598 and 1600. We do not know if all the references attach to the same man.

YARRINGTON, ROBERT: his name appears at the end of the manuscript of *Two Lamentable Tragedies*. It may be placed there as the name of the author or (more probably) as the signature of the scribe. Robert Yarringon was apprenticed to the scrivener, Francis Kyd (father to Thomas Kyd) in 1578, and describes himself in a deposition of 1609 as 'citizen and court hand writer'.

Chronology

THE following list is designed to give a chronological perspective to the theatrical repertory discussed above. The information it contains (except where it comes from Henslowe's Diary (1592–1603) or from the office-book of Sir Henry Herbert, the Caroline Master of the Revels (1622–42)) is usually inferential. The dating (as can be seen) is often more general than particular. It relies on the sense of 'not before' and 'not after' that the usual authorities, Chambers, Bentley, and Harbage, provide (indicated here by a multiplication sign (×)). I have chosen to follow the Harbage–Schoenbaum 'limits' dates (in the second and (occasionally) the third editions), as providing an objective witness, even in cases where I disagree (and have recorded my disagreement in a footnote). Given these uncertainties, the chronology cannot be used to determine year-by-year questions of priority. It can indicate the drift of outlook or fashion, but nothing more. The names given to companies and playhouses in the documents of the time lack consistency; in the prefatory survey I have tried to disentangle the history and provide a consistent nomenclature (which may, of course, merely distort often haphazard relations between actors, companies, and playhouses). Asterisks mark those plays given performance(s) at court. Plays for which the range of accepted dates exceeds eight years have been excluded. The oblique (/) is used to indicate that different companies and/or playhouses seem to have been involved, either simultaneously or sequentially; used after a dash the oblique indicates that the information that follows refers to a date clearly later than that of the earliest production. The 'events' column has been restricted to those political and social happenings that can be judged to have had direct consequences in the theatre. Plays performed before 1585 are only sparsely represented. These are fully covered in F. P. Wilson's *English Drama 1485–1585* (Oxford, 1968).

COMPANIES

Admiral's   The Admiral's Men, of uncertain status till 1594 when, under Henslowe's management, they occupied the Rose. They moved to the Fortune in 1600. Renamed Prince [Henry]'s Men in 1603.

BB   Beeston's Boys (also known as the King and Queen's Young Company) performed at the Phoenix 1637–42.

Chamberlain's	The Chamberlain [Lord Hunsdon]'s Men emerge as a London company in 1594, and occupy (sequentially) the Cross Keys Inn, the Theatre, the Curtain, and the Globe. After 1603 they were called the King's Men and after 1608 they occupied both the Globe and the second Blackfriars.
Chapel Boys	The Children of the Chapel Royal, court entertainers under various choirmasters, performed in the first Blackfriars (BFR 1) from 1576 until 1584), and after 1600 in the second Blackfriars (BFR). For their career as the Children of the [Queen's] Revels, see below.
Derby's	Derby's Men, called Lord Strange's Men before Strange became 5th Earl in 1593. They are found in the Theatre, the Rose, and at Newington Butts in combination with the Admiral's Men. After 1594 a company patronized by the sixth Earl of Derby (not necessarily the same company as Strange's) performed in the provinces and occasionally in London.
King's	See Chamberlain's.
KR 1	This 'King's Revels' was a boy's company set up in 1607, playing at the Whitefriars 1608–1609.
KR 2	This 'King's Revels' was a mixed adult and children's company (sometimes called 'the Children of the Revels') playing at Salisbury Court, and perhaps at the Fortune, 1630–6.
Lady Eliz.	The Lady Elizabeth's Men, formed in 1611, under the patronage of King James's only daughter. They absorbed the Queen's Revels in ?1613, and amalgamated with Prince Charles's Men in 1615. Thereafter they appear only in provincial records until 1622, when they begin to play at the Phoenix.
Leicester's	Leicester's Men, mentioned in 1559, performed at court, 1560–3, 1572–83. James Burbage, a Leicester's Man, possibly built the Theatre for their use, and they probably performed there 1576–83.
Oxford's	Oxford's Men operated mostly in the provinces. In 1602 they were permitted to play in London in combination with Worcester's Men, at the Boar's Head. The Oxford name seems to disappear at this point.
Palsgrave's	The former Prince Henry's Men. After Prince Henry's death, they acquired the patronage of King James's son-in-law, the Palsgrave (Pfalzgraf) of the Palatinate on the Rhine. The company continued to play at the For-

tune until 1625, but fell apart during the plague of that year.

Paul's Boys The Children of St Paul's cathedral (nominally the cathedral choir) performed in their own playhouse 1575–90 and then again 1599–1606.

Pembroke's Pembroke's Men were active in the early 1590s when plague and administrative manœuvring was breaking and recombining groups of actors. They played at the Swan in 1597, and disappeared shortly after.

P. Henry's Prince's Henry's Men (formerly the Admiral's Men) occupied the Fortune playhouse from 1603 until 1612; after Henry's death they continued as the Palsgrave's Men.

P. Charles's Prince Charles's [Duke of York's, Prince's] Men were asociated with the Lady Elizabeth's and the Queen's Revels in the abortive Porter's Hall scheme of 1616. They played successively at the Hope, the Red Bull, the Phoenix, and the Curtain. They disintegrated when their patron became king in 1625.

Q. Anne's Queen Anne's Men were Worcester's Men before 1603. When Queen Anne died, they were called the Red Bull Company or the Company of the Revels; they were active 1603–1623.

QHM Queen Henrietta's Men, played at the Phoenix 1625–9 and at the Salisbury Court 1637–42.

Q. Eliz. Queen Elizabeth's Men, set up in 1583, dominated the London scene until 1588. They fell to pieces in the plague of 1593–4.

Revels The Children of the Queen's Revels, the former Children of the Chapel Royal—also described as the Children of the Revels, the Children of the Blackfriars or of the Whitefriars. Performed in the Second Blackfriars (BFR) from 1600 until 1608 and thereafter in the Whitefriars.

Strange's Strange's Men: see Derby's.

Sussex's Sussex's Men played at court 1573–83, while their patron (the third Earl) was Lord Chamberlain. Achieved two London seasons in 1593–4 under Henslowe's guidance and then disappeared from the records.

Worcester's Worcester's Men (after 1603 known as Queen Anne's) performed in the Boar's Head from 1599 to 1605, then retreated to the Rose and thence in 1606 moved to the Red Bull.

PLAYHOUSES

BFR 1   The first Blackfriars playhouse, a small 'private' playhouse built by Farrant in 1576 in the monastery building of the Black Friars as a showcase for his troupe of choirboy–actors from the Chapel Royal.

BFR   The second Blackfriars playhouse, a private playhouse converted by the Burbages in 1596–7, leased to the Children of the Queen's Revels in 1600, and recovered by the King's Men in 1608.

Boar's Head   The Boar's Head was a playhouse, converted in 1598–9 from an inn in Whitechapel, and occupied by a combined Oxford's and Worcester's company, then by Queen Anne's, and perhaps also by Prince Charles's.

Bull Inn   The Bull Inn in Bishopsgate Street was used for plays from the earliest days until at least 1594.

Cross Keys   The Cross Keys Inn in Gracechurch Street seems to have been used for playing 1579×1594 and to have been used by Queen Elizabeth's Men and the Chamberlain's Men.

Curtain   The Curtain was built c.1578, by Henry Lanman, on land a little south of the Theatre. Between 1585 and 1592 the profits of the two playhouses were shared. Queen Anne's Men used it as one of their playhouses in 1602–9. Prince Charles's Men occupied it in 1621–3.

Fortune   The Fortune was built in 1600 in Golden Lane (outside Cripplegate) by Alleyn and Henslowe. Burnt down in 1621, rebuilt 1623. Occupied by the Admiral's Men, Prince Henry's, the Palsgrave's, and the second King's Revels Company.

GB   The Globe and the second Blackfriars: in the period 1608–42 the King's Men (formerly the Chamberlain's Men) used both venues. Title-pages more frequently assign plays to the Blackfriars (for that was the more prestigious address), but that gives no general warrant to suppose that such plays were not also performed at the Globe.

Globe   The Globe was built by the Chamberlain's Men in 1599 on the South Bank. Burnt down 1613, rebuilt 1614. Occupied by the Chamberlain's Men—after 1603 called the King's Men.

Hope   The Hope was converted in 1614 from the old Bear Garden on the South Bank, to be used both for plays

and for bear-baiting; occupied for short periods by the
Lady Elizabeth's and then by Prince Charles's Men.

Paul's   The 'Playhouse in Paul's' was a small (possibly round)
theatre located somewhere in the precinct of St Paul's
Cathedral. Paul's choirboys had performed plays at court
from early in the sixteenth century, but it is not clear when
they acquired a specific playhouse building—perhaps it
was in the mastership of Sebastian Westcott (1552–82)—
or which part of the Cathedral complex provided space
for it.

Phoenix   The Phoenix or Cockpit in Drury Lane, converted to a
'private' playhouse by Christopher Beeston in 1617; occupied in series by Queen Anne's Men, Prince Charles's
Men, the Lady Elizabeth's Men, Queen Henrietta's Men,
and Beeston's Boys.

Porter's Hall   A space somewhere in the Blackfriars which the managers of the Queen's Revels–Lady Elizabeth's Men–Prince
Charles's Men combination thought to use as a replacement for the Whitefriars (whose lease expired in 1614).
The project was opposed by the residents and occupied
only under threat. It does not seem to have survived
beyond 1617.

Red Bull   The Red Bull, an inn in Clerkenwell, was converted to
a playhouse c.1605; it was used by Queen Anne's until
1617, and thereafter by Prince Charles's Men.

Rose   The Rose was built by Philip Henslowe on the South
Bank in 1587. From 1594 until 1600 it was home to the
Admiral's Company. It ceased to have any permanent
function when they moved to the Fortune.

Swan   The Swan was built 1595/6 on the South Bank by Francis
Langley. In 1597 he bound Pembroke's Men to play
there, but after the Isle of Dogs scandal in that year the
actors deserted to Henslowe and the Swan declined into
an occasional theatre.

Salisbury   The Salisbury Court theatre, built as a 'private' playhouse in 1630, was occupied by the second King's Rev-
els Company, Prince Charles's, Queen Henrietta's Men.

Theatre   The Theatre was built by James Burbage in Shoreditch
(outside the city wall at Bishopsgate) in 1576, perhaps
for use by Leicester's Men. In 1594 the Chamberlain's
Men established themselves there. In 1597, their lease
running into difficulty, they seem to have moved to the
Curtain. In 1598/9 they pulled down the timbers of the
Theatre and moved them to the Globe.

Whitefriars   The Whitefriars was a private playhouse occupying space in the former Whitefriars monastery; it was used by shadowy associations of the Revels Boys, the first King's Revels, and the Lady Elizabeth's c.1607–c.1613.

Earliest Date of Performance	Play Title	Author
1 1545×1552	*Ralph Roister Doister*	Udall
2 *c.*1547×1548	*King Johan*	Bale
3 *c.*1552×1563	*Gammer Gurton's*	Mr S. Master of
1558	*Needle*	Art
4 1558×1561	*The Comedy of Patient and Meek Grissil*	Philip
5 1559×1567	*Appius and Virginia*	R. B.
6 1562	*Gorboduc: or Ferrex and Porrex*	Sackville and Norton
7 ?1565	*Damon and Pythias*	Edwards
8 1566	*Supposes*	Gascoigne
9 1566	*Jocasta*	Gascoigne and Kinwelmershe
1567		
10 1570×1581	*The Conflict of Conscience*	Woodes
1575		
1576		
11 *c.*1576	*Common Conditions*	?
12 1579	*Hymenaeus*	Fraunce
13 1579	*Silvanus*	?

Company	Place of Performance	Events	
?	?		1
?	St Stephen's Canterbury		2
Cambridge Students	Christ's College Cambridge		3
		Accession of Elizabeth. Restoration of Protestantism.	
?	?		4
?	?		5
Gentlemen of the Inner Temple	Inner Temple		6
Chapel Boys	Court		7
Gentlemen of the Inns of Court	Gray's Inn		8
Gentlemen of the Inns of Court	Gray's Inn		9
		Brayne and Burbage build the Red Lion Playhouse.	
?	?		10
		Sebastian Westcott, Master of the choirboys of St Paul's, sets up a private playhouse in the Cathedral precinct.	
		Burbage builds the Theatre. Farrant sets up the first Black-friars playhouse for the boy actors of the Chapel Royal.	
?	?		11
Cambridge students	St John's College, Cambridge		12
Members of St John's College, Cambridge	St John's College, Cambridge		13

Earliest Date of Performance	Play Title	Author
14 1579×1584	*Fedele and Fortunio, Two Italian Gentlemen*	?Munday
15 1580	*Richardus Tertius*	Legge
16 1580×1583	*Victoria*	Fraunce
17 1580×1584	*Campaspe**	Lyly
18 c.1581	*The Three Ladies of London*	Wilson
19 1581	*Pedantius*	Forsett or Wingfield
20 c.1581×1584	*The Arraignment of Paris**	Peele
21 ?1582	*The Rare Triumphs of Love and Fortune**	?
22 1582×1584	*Sappho and Phao**	Lyly
1583		
23 1583×?1588	*The Famous Victories of Henry V*	?
24 1585	*2 Seven Deadly Sins*	?Tarlton
25 ?1585	*Gallathea*	Lyly
26 1585×1589	*The Spanish Tragedy*	Kyd
27 c.1585×1589	*The Pleasant Comedy of the Two Angry Women of Abingdon*	Porter
28 1585×1592 1587	*Arden of Faversham*	?
29 1587×1588	*Tamburlaine (1 and 2)*	Marlowe
30 1587×1588	*The Comical History of Alphonsus, King of Aragon*	Greene
31 1587×1590	*Mother Bombie*	Lyly
32 1587×1590	*John a Kent and John a Cumber*	Munday
33 c.1587×1591	*The Troublesome Reign of John, King of England (1 and 2)*	?
34 1587×1591	*A Looking Glass for London and England*	Greene, Lodge
35 1587×1592	*The Wounds of Civil War*	Lodge

Company	Place of Performance	Events	
?Chapel Boys	?BFR 1		14
Cambridge students	?Caius College, Cambridge		15
Members of St John's College, Cambridge	St John's College Cambridge		16
Chapel and Paul's Boys	BFR 1		17
Leicester's	?Theatre		18
Members of Trinity College, Cambridge	Trinity College		19
Chapel Boys	?BFR 1		20
Derby's	?		21
Chapel and Paul's Boys	BFR 1		22
		A company of the Queen's Players is formed.	
Q. Eliz.	Bull Inn		23
Q. Eliz.	?Theatre		24
Paul's Boys	Paul's		25
Strange's	?		26
Admiral's	Rose		27
?	?		28
		Mary, Queen of Scots executed. Henslowe builds 'the Rose'.	
Admiral's	Rose		29
?	?		30
Paul's Boys	Paul's		31
?	?		32
Q. Eliz.	?		33
Q. Eliz./Strange's	—/?Rose		34
Admiral's	Rose		35

Earliest Date of Performance	Play Title	Author
36 1587×1593	*George a Green, the Pinner of Wakefield*	?
37 *c*.1587×1593	*The Tragedy of Dido, Queen of Carthage*	Marlowe, Nashe
38 1587×1594	*The Wars of Cyrus*	?Farrant
1588		
39 1588	*Endymion*	Lyly
40 1588×1589	*The Battle of Alcazar*	Peele
41 *c*.1588×1590	*Love's Metamorphosis*	Lyly
42 1588×1592	*The History of Orlando Furioso**	Greene
43 1588×1592	*Doctor Faustus*	Marlowe
44 *c*.1588×1594	*The Old Wife's Tale*	Peele
45 *c*.1588×1594	*The True Chronicle History of King Leir*	?
46 *c*.1589×1590	*The Jew of Malta**	Marlowe
47 1589×1590	*Midas*	Lyly
48 *c*.1589×1591	*Fair Em, the Miller's Daughter of Manchester*	?
49 *c*.1589×1592	*Don Horatio: or The Spanish Comedy*	?
50 *c*.1589×1592	*Soliman and Perseda*	?
51 *c*.1589×1592	*The Honourable History of Friar Bacon and Friar Bungay*	Greene
52 *c*.1589×1593	*The Cobbler's Prophecy*	Wilson
53 1590	*Antonius*	Mary Herbert, Countess of Pembroke
54 1590	*1 Henry VI*	Shakespeare
55 *c*.1590	*2 Henry VI*	Shakespeare
56 *c*.1590×1591	*The Scottish History of James IV*	Greene
57 1590×1593	*The Comedy of Errors**	Shakespeare
58 1590×1593	*Jack Straw*	?
59 1590×1593	*Edward I*	Peele
60 1590×1594	*John of Bordeaux*	?
61 1590×1595	*Edward III*	?
62 1590×1595	*The Woman in the Moon**	Lyly
63 *c*.1591	*3 Henry VI*	Shakespeare
64 1591×1592	*Richard III*	Shakespeare
65 1591×1593	*Edward II*	Marlowe
66 ?1591×1594	*The True Tragedy of Richard III*	?

Company	Place of Performance	Events	
Sussex's	?		36
Chapel Boys	?		37
Chapel Boys	?	Spanish Armada defeated.	38
Paul's Boys	Paul's		39
Admiral's	Rose		40
Paul's Boys	Paul's		41
Q. Eliz./Admiral's	Rose		42
Strange's/Admiral's	Rose		43
Q. Eliz.	?		44
Q. Eliz./Sussex's	?		45
Strange's/Admiral's	?Theatre		46
Paul's Boys	Paul's		47
Strange's	?Rose		48
Admiral's	Rose		49
?	?		50
Q. Eliz./Sussex's/ ?Strange's	?Rose/?Theatre		51
?Q. Eliz.	?		52
Closet drama			53
Strange's/Admiral's	?Rose		54
Strange's/Admiral's	?Rose		55
?	?		56
?Strange's	?		57
?	?		58
?	?		59
Strange's	?Rose		60
?	?		61
?	?		62
Strange's/Pembroke's	?Rose/?Theatre		63
Pembroke's	?Theatre		64
?Pembroke's	?Theatre		65
Q. Eliz.	?Theatre		66

Earliest Date of Performance	Play Title	Author
67 1591×1594	*1 The Tragical Reign of Selimus, Emperor of the Turks*	?
68 1591×1595	*Woodstock*	?
69 1591×1595	*The Lamentable Tragedy of Locrine*	?
70 1591×1598	*The Life and Death of King John*	Shakespeare
71 1592	*A Knack to Know a Knave*	?
72 1592	*Summer's Last Will and Testament*	Nashe
73 1592×1594	*The Taming of a Shrew*	?
74 c.1592×1596	*Caesar and Pompey: or Caesar's Revenge*	?
75 1592×1599	*Edward IV (1 and 2)*	?Heywood
76 1592×c.1600	*The Four Prentices of London*	Heywood
1593		
1593–1594		
77 1593 (rev. 1607)	*Cleopatra*	Daniel
78 1593	*The Massacre at Paris*	Marlowe
79 c.1593 (rev. 1601)	*Sir Thomas More*	Munday
80 c.1593×1594	*Two Gentlemen of Verona*	Shakespeare
81 1593×1594	*David and Bethsabe*	Peele
1594		
82 1594	*Titus Andronicus*	Shakespeare
83 1594	*A Knack to Know an Honest Man*	?
84 1594×1595	*Love's Labour's Lost**	Shakespeare
85 1594×1595	*The Tragedy of Richard II*	Shakespeare

Company	Place of Performance	Events	
Q. Eliz.	?Theatre		67
?	?		68
Q. Eliz.	?Theatre		69
Chamberlain's	?Theatre		70
Strange's/Admiral's	Rose		71
?	Archbishop's Palace, Croydon		72
Pembroke's/Sussex's	?Theatre		73
Oxford students	Trinity College Oxford		74
Derby's	?		75
?Admiral's/Q. Anne's	?Rose/Red Bull		76
		Marlowe killed in a tavern brawl in Deptford.	
		A major plague closes all London playhouses from December 1593 to February 1594.	
Closet drama			77
Admiral's	Rose		78
Strange's	?Rose		79
?	?		80
?	?		81
		Reorganization of the London companies after the plague. Alleyn leads a new Admiral's Men. The Burbages form a new Chamberlain's Men.	
Sussex's/	?		82
Pembroke's/Derby's			
Admiral's	Rose		83
Chamberlain's	?Theatre		84
Chamberlain's	?Theatre		85

Earliest Date of Performance	Play Title	Author
86 1594×1596	*Romeo and Juliet**	Shakespeare
87 *c.*1594×*c.*1596	*Mustapha*	Greville
88 1594×*c.*1598	*Two Lamentable Tragedies*	?Yarrington
89 *c.*1594×*c.*1598	*The Taming of the Shrew*	Shakespeare
90 1595	*The Masque of Proteus*	Campion, Davison
1595		
91 ?1595	*A Midsummer Night's Dream**	Shakespeare
1596		
92 1596	*1 The Blind Beggar of Alexandria*	Chapman
93 1596	*Captain Thomas Stukeley*	?
94 1596	*The Merchant of Venice**	Shakespeare
95 1597	*The Isle of Dogs*	Nashe, Jonson
1597		
96 1597	*A Humorous Day's Mirth*	Chapman
97 1597×1598	*The Case is Altered*	Jonson
98 1597×1598	*Henry IV (1 and 2)*	Shakespeare
99 1597×1602	*The Merry Wives of Windsor**	Shakespeare
100 ?1598	*Much Ado about Nothing*	Shakespeare
101 1598	*Every Man in his Humour*	Jonson
102 1598	*Englishmen for my Money: or A Woman Will Have her Will*	Haughton
103 1598	*The Downfall and Death of Robert, Earl of Huntingdon (1 and 2)*	Chettle, Munday
104 1598×1599	*As You Like It*	Shakespeare
105 *c.*1598×1599	*A Warning for Fair Women*	?
106 *c.*1598×1600	*Look About You*	?
107 *c.*1598×*c.*1600	*Alaham*	Greville
108 *c.*1598×1600	*A Larum for London: or The Siege of Antwerp*	?

Company	Place of Performance	Events	
Chamberlain's	?Theatre		86
Closet drama			87
?	?		88
Chamberlain's	?Theatre/Curtain		89
Gentlemen of Gray's Inn	Court		90
		Langley builds the Swan.	
Chamberlain's	?Theatre		91
		Burbage purchases space in the Blackfriars and builds the second Blackfriars Playhouse.	
Admiral's	Rose		92
Admiral's	Rose		93
Chamberlain's	?Theatre		94
Pembroke's	Swan		95
		All playing in London is banned from July until October, following the performance of the scandalous *The Isle of Dogs*.	
Admiral's	Rose		96
—/Revels	—/BFR		97
Chamberlain's	Curtain		98
Chamberlain's	Curtain		99
Chamberlain's	?Curtain		100
Chamberlain's	?Curtain		101
Admiral's	Rose		102
Admiral's	Rose		103
Chamberlain's	Curtain/Globe		104
Chamberlain's	Curtain/Globe		105
Admiral's	Rose		106
Closet drama			107
Chamberlain's	Curtain/Globe		108

Earliest Date of Performance	Play Title	Author
109 1598×1600 1599	*Julius Caesar*	Shakespeare
110 1599	*Thomas Merry*	Day, Haughton
111 1599	*Old Fortunatus**	Dekker
112 1599	*Henry V**	Shakespeare
113 1599	*Every Man out of his Humour**	Jonson
114 1599	*Page of Plymouth*	Dekker, Jonson
115 1599	*1 Sir John Oldcastle*	Drayton, Hathway, Munday, Wilson
116 1599	*The Shoemaker's Holiday**	Dekker
117 1599×1600	*Antonio and Mellida*	Marston
118 1599×1600	*The Wisdom of Doctor Dodypoll*	?
119 c.1599×1600	*The Weakest Goeth to the Wall*	?
120 1599×1600	*The Maid's Metamorphosis*	?
121 1599×1601	*Antonio's Revenge*	Marston
122 1599×1602	*Thomas, Lord Cromwell*	?
123 1599×1603	*The Trial of Chivalry*	?
124 1599×1604	*The Merry Devil of Edmonton**	?
125 1599×1604 1600	*All Fools**	Chapman
126 1600	*Patient Grissil*	Dekker, Chettle
127 1600	*Grim the Collier of Croydon*	Haughton [? and I. T.]
128 1600	*Lust's Dominion?/ the Spanish Moor's Tragedy*	Day, Dekker, Haughton

Company	Place of Performance	Events	
Chamberlain's	Curtain/Globe		109
		The Chamberlain's Men dismantle the Theatre and build the Globe. The Boar's Head Inn is converted into a playhouse. Paul's Boys begin playing again.	
Admiral's	Rose		110
Admiral's	Rose		111
Chamberlain's	?Globe		112
Chamberlain's	Globe		113
Admiral's	Rose		114
Admiral's	Rose		115
Admiral's	Rose		116
Paul's Boys	Paul's		117
Paul's Boys	Paul's		118
Oxford's	?		119
Paul's Boys/Chapel Boys	Paul's/BFR		120
Paul's Boys	Paul's		121
Chamberlain's	Globe		122
Derby's	?		123
Chamberlain's	Globe		124
Revels	BFR		125
		Henslowe and Alleyn move from the Rose to the Fortune. The Chamberlain's Men lease the second Blackfriars playhouse to the Children of the Chapel.	
Admiral's	Rose		126
?Admiral's	?Rose		127
?Admiral's	?Fortune		128

Earliest Date of Performance	Play Title	Author
129 1600	*1 The Blind Beggar of Bednall Green*	Chettle, Day, Haughton?
130 1600	*Jack Drum's Entertainment*	Marston
131 1600×1601	*Cynthia's Revels: or The Fountain of Self-Love**	Jonson
132 1600×1601	*Hamlet*	Shakespeare
133 1600×1604	*The Malcontent*	Marston
134 1600×1604	*Bussy D'Ambois*	Chapman
135 1600×1605	*The First Part of Jeronimo, with the Wars in Portugal*	?
1601		
136 1601	*The Contention between Liberality and Prodigality*	?
137 1601	*Poetaster: or The Arraignment*	Jonson
138 1601	*What You Will*	Marston
139 1601	*Satiromastix: or The Untrussing of the Humorous Poet*	Dekker, Marston
140 1601×1602	*Blurt, Master Constable*	?Dekker
141 1601×1602	*How a Man May Choose a Good Wife*	?
142 1601×1602	*Twelfth Night*	Shakespeare
143 1601×1603	*Sir Giles Goosecap*	?Chapman
144 1601×1603	*Troilus and Cressida*	Shakespeare
145 1601×1609	*May-Day*	Chapman
146 1602	*The Tragedy of Hoffman: or Revenge for a Father*	Chettle
147 c.1602×1604	*The Gentleman Usher*	Chapman
148 1602×1605	*The Tragedy of Mariam, the Fair Queen of Jewry*	Lady Cary
149 1602×1607	*Sir Thomas Wyatt*	Dekker, Webster
150 c.1602×1607	*The Family of Love*	Middleton
1603		
151 1603	*The Second Part of The Return from Parnassus*	?
152 1603	*A Woman Killed with Kindness*	Heywood

Company	Place of Performance	Events	
Admiral's	?Fortune		129
Paul's Boys	Paul's		130
Chapel Boys	BFR		131
Chamberlain's	Globe		132
Revels/King's	BFR/Globe		133
Paul's Boys/Revels	Paul's/BFR		134
?Chamberlain's	?Globe		135
		Essex's revolt and execution.	
?Chapel Boys	?BFR		136
Chapel Boys	BFR		137
?Paul's Boys	?Paul's		138
Paul's Boys/ Chamberlain's	Paul's/Globe		139
Paul's Boys	Paul's		140
Worcester's	?Boar's Head		141
Chamberlain's	Globe		142
Chapel Boys	BFR		143
Chamberlain's	Globe		144
Chapel Boys	BFR		145
Admiral's	Fortune		146
?Chapel Boys	BFR		147
Closet drama			148
Worcester's/ Q. Anne's	Boars Head/Curtain		149
—/KR 1	—/Boars Head		150
		Elizabeth dies. James succeeds. Plague closes all the London playhouses from March 1603 to April 1604.	
Cambridge students	St John's College, Cambridge		151
Worcester's/ Q. Anne's	?Rose/?Boar's Head		152

Earliest Date of Performance	Play Title	Author
153 1603	*Sejanus, his Fall*	Jonson
154 1603	*The Old Joiner of Aldgate*	Chapman
155 1603×?1604	*All's Well that Ends Well*	Shakespeare
156 *c.*1603×1604	*Othello*	Shakespeare
157 1603×1604	*The Fair Maid of Bristowe**	?
158 1603×1604	*The Phoenix**	Middleton
159 *c.*1603×1604	*Measure for Measure*	Shakespeare
160 1603×1604	*The Dutch Courtesan*	Marston
161 1603×1605	*If You Know Not Me, You Know Nobody (1 and 2)*	Heywood
162 1603×1605	*The London Prodigal*	?
163 1603×1605	*When You See Me, You Know Me*	S. Rowley
164 1603×1606	*Nobody and Somebody*	?
165 1603×1609	*The Widow's Tears**	Chapman
166 1604	*Philotas*	Daniel
167 1604	*Monsieur D'Olive*	Chapman
168 1604	*The Magnificent Entertainment Given to King James*	Jonson, Dekker, Middleton
169 1604	*The Vision of the Twelve Goddesses*	Daniel
170 1604	*Westward Ho*	Dekker, Webster
171 ?1604	*Alphonsus, Emperor of Germany*	?Chapman
172 ?1604	*The Wise Woman of Hogsdon*	Heywood
173 1604×1605	*The Honest Whore (1 and 2)*	Dekker, Middleton
174 1604×1606	*Michaelmas Term*	Middleton
175 1604×1606	*Parasitaster: or The Fawn*	Marston
176 1604×1607	*A Trick to Catch the Old One**	Middleton
177 1604×1607	*Law Tricks: or Who Would Have Thought It*	Day
178 1604×1607	*Your Five Gallants*	Middleton
179 1604×1607	*A Mad World My Masters*	Middleton
180 1604×1610	*The Roaring Girl*	Middleton, Dekker
1605		
181 1605	*The Masque of Blackness**	Jonson
182 ?1605	*King Lear**	Shakespeare
183 1605	*Eastward Ho**	Jonson, Chapman, Marston
184 1605	*Northward Ho*	Dekker, Webster

Company	Place of Performance	Events
Chamberlain's/King's	Globe	153
Paul's Boys	Paul's	154
Chamberlain's/King's	Globe	155
Chamberlain's/King's	Globe	156
Chamberlain's/King's	Globe	157
Paul's Boys	Paul's	158
King's	Globe	159
Revels	BFR	160
Q. Anne's	Red Bull/Phoenix	161
King's	Globe	162
P. Henry's	Fortune	163
Q. Anne's	Boar's Head/Curtain	164
Revels	BFR/Whitefriars	165
Revels	BFR	166
Revels	BFR	167
Representatives of London	London Streets	168
Queen Anne and her Ladies	Hampton Court	169
Paul's Boys	Paul's	170
King's	Globe	171
Q. Anne's	?Curtain	172
P. Henry's	Fortune	173
Paul's Boys	Paul's	174
Revels	BFR	175
Paul's Boys/Revels	Paul's/BFR	176
Revels	BFR	177
Revels	BFR	178
Paul's Boys	Paul's	179
P. Henry's	Fortune	180
		'Gunpowder Plot' to blow up king and parliament.
Queen Anne and her Ladies	Court	181
King's	Globe	182
Revels	BFR	183
Paul's Boys	Paul's	184

Earliest Date of Performance	Play Title	Author
185 1605×1606	The Miseries of Enforced Marriage	Wilkins
186 1605×1606	The Wonder of Women: or The Tragedy of Sophonisba	Marston
187 1605×1608	A Yorkshire Tragedy: not so new as lamentable and true	?
188 1606	Macbeth*	Shakespeare
189 1606	The Isle of Gulls	Day
190 1606	The Puritan: or The Widow of Watling Street	?
191 1606	The Woman Hater	Fletcher
192 1606	Volpone	Jonson
193 1606	Hymenaei	Jonson
194 1606	The Fleer	Sharpham
195 c.1606×1607	The Whore of Babylon	Dekker
196 1606×1607	The Revenger's Tragedy	Tourneur
197 c.1606×1608	Antony and Cleopatra	Shakespeare
198 1606×1608	Pericles, Prince of Tyre	Shakespeare
199 1606×1608	The Rape of Lucrece*	Heywood
200 c.1606×c.1608	Timon of Athens	Shakespeare
201 1607	Cupid's Whirligig	Sharpham
202 1607	The Devil's Charter*	Barnes
203 1607×1608	The Turk	Mason
204 1607×1608	Humour out of Breath	Day
205 1607×1609	A Shoemaker a Gentleman	William Rowley
206 1607×c.1610	The Knight of the Burning Pestle	Beaumont
207 1607×1611	The Atheist's Tragedy: or The Honest Man's Revenge	Tourneur
208 c.1607×1612 1608	Cupid's Revenge	Fletcher
209 1608	Coriolanus	Shakespeare
210 1608	The Conspiracy of Charles, Duke of Byron	Chapman
211 1608	The Tragedy of Charles, Duke of Byron	Chapman
212 1608×1609	The Faithful Shepherdess	Fletcher
213 1608×1610	Ram Alley	Barry
214 1608×1610	Philaster: or Love Lies a Bleeding*	Fletcher
215 1608×1611	Cymbeline	Shakespeare
216 1608×1611	The Maid's Tragedy*	Fletcher

Company	Place of Performance	Events	
King's	Globe		185
Revels	BFR		186
King's	Globe		187
King's	Globe		188
Revels	BFR		189
Paul's Boys	Paul's		190
Paul's Boys	Paul's		191
King's	Globe		192
Ladies and Gentlemen of the Court	The Court		193
Revels	BFR		194
P. Henry's	Fortune		195
King's	Globe		196
King's	Globe		197
King's	Globe		198
Q. Anne's	Red Bull/Phoenix		199
King's	Globe		200
KR 1	BFR/?Whitefriars		201
King's	Globe		202
KR 1	Whitefriars		203
KR 1	?BFR		204
Q. Anne's	Red Bull		205
Revels	BFR/Whitefriars		206
?	?		207
Revels	BFR	King's Men recover Blackfriars lease.	208
King's	Globe		209
Revels	BFR		210
Revels	BFR		211
Revels	BFR		212
KR 1	?Whitefriars		213
Revels/King's	BFR/GB		214
King's	GB		215
King's	GB		216

Earliest Date of Performance	Play Title	Author
217 1609	*The Masque of Queens**	Jonson
1609		
218 1609	*Epicoene: or The Silent Woman*	Jonson
219 ?1609	*Fortune by Land and Sea*	Heywood, W. Rowley
220 1609×1610	*A Woman is a Weathercock*	Field
221 1609×1611	*The Golden Age*	Heywood
222 1609×1612	*The White Devil*	Webster
223 1609×1612	*The Captain**	Fletcher
224 *c.*1609×*c.*1616	*The Witch*	Middleton
225 1610	*The Alchemist**	Jonson
226 1610×1611	*The Revenge of Bussy D'Ambois*	Chapman
227 1610×1611	*Amends for Ladies*	Field
228 *c.*1610×1611	*The Winter's Tale**	Shakespeare
229 1610×1613	*The Insatiate Countess*	Marston/ Barksteed
230 1610×1614	*Valentinian*	Fletcher
231 1610×1615	*The Valiant Welshman*	R. A.
232 1610×*c.*1616	*Monsieur Thomas*	Fletcher
233 1611	*A King and No King**	Fletcher
234 1611	*The Night Walker or the Little Thief*	Fletcher
235 1611	*The Second Maiden's Tragedy*	?
236 1611	*Greene's Tu Quoque**	Cooke
237 1611	*Catiline, His Conspiracy*	Jonson
238 1611	*The Tempest**	Shakespeare
239 1611×1612	*If This be not a Good Play, the Devil is in It*	Dekker
240 1611×1613	*A Chaste Maid in Cheapside*	Middleton
241 1611×1613	*The Tragedy of Chabot, Admiral of France*	Chapman
242 1611×1614	*The Tragedy of Bonduca*	Fletcher
243 1612	*Troia Nova Triumphans*	Dekker
1612		
244 1612×1614	*The Duchess of Malfi*	Webster
245 1613	*The Honest Man's Fortune*	Fletcher
246 1613	*Henry VIII*	Shakespeare

Company	Place of Performance	Events	
Queen Anne and her Ladies	Court		217
		Beeston builds the Phoenix (Cockpit) in Drury Lane.	
Revels	Whitefriars		218
Q. Anne's	Red Bull		219
Revels	?		220
Q. Anne's	Red Bull		221
Q. Anne's	Red Bull		222
King's	GB		223
King's	GB		224
King's	GB		225
Revels	Whitefriars		226
Revels/Lady Eliz.	Whitefriars		227
King's	Globe		228
?Revels	Whitefriars		229
King's	GB		230
P. Henry's/ P. Charles's	?Fortune		231
Revels	?Whitefriars		232
King's	GB		233
Lady Eliz.	?Whitefriars		234
King's	GB		235
Q. Anne's	Red Bull		236
King's	GB		237
King's	GB		238
Q. Anne's	Red Bull		239
Lady Eliz.	Swan		240
?Lady Eliz./QHM	?Hope/Phoenix		241
King's	GB		242
Representatives of London	London Streets		243
		Death of Prince Henry.	
King's	GB		244
King's	GB		245
King's	GB		246

Earliest Date of Performance	Play Title	Author

1613

247 1613×1614	*The Two Noble Kinsmen*	Fletcher, Shakespeare
248 1613×1616	*The Scornful Lady*	Fletcher
249 *c*.1613×*c*.1618	*The Tragedy of Orestes*	Goffe
250 1613×1621	*Thierry and Theodoret*	Fletcher
251 1614	*Bartholomew Fair*	Jonson
1614		
252 1614×1620	*Wit without Money*	Fletcher
253 ?1615	*More Dissemblers Besides Women*	Middleton
254 *c*.1615×1617	*A Fair Quarrel*	Middleton, W. Rowley
255 *c*.1615×1618	*The Old Law*	Middleton, Massinger, W. Rowley
256 1615×1619	*Swetnam the Woman Hater*	?
257 *c*.1615×1622	*Beggar's Bush*	Fletcher
258 1616	*Mercury Vindicated from the Alchemists at Court**	Jonson
1616		
259 1616	*The Devil is an Ass*	Jonson
260 ?1616	*Love's Pilgrimage*	Fletcher
261 1616×1618	*The Queen of Corinth*	Fletcher
262 1617	*The Mad Lover**	Fletcher
263 *c*.1617	*The Chances*	Fletcher
264 *c*.1617	*Rollo, Duke of Normandy: or The Bloody Brother*	Fletcher
265 1618 (?rev. 1633)	*The Loyal Subject*	Fletcher
266 1618	*The Raging Turk: or Bajazet II*	Goffe
267 1618	*The Courageous Turk: or Amurath I*	Goffe
268 1619	*The Tragedy of Sir John van Oldenbarnavelt*	Massinger, Fletcher
269 ?1619	*The Humorous Lieutenant*	Fletcher
270 1619×1620	*All's Lost by Lust*	W. Rowley
271 1619×1621	*The Island Princess**	Fletcher

Company	Place of Performance	Events	
		Globe playhouse burns down. Princess Elizabeth marries the Elector Palatine.	
King's	GB		247
?Revels	Porter's Hall		248
Oxford students	Christ Church, Oxford		249
King's	GB		250
Lady Eliz.	Hope		251
		Second Globe playhouse built.	
Lady Eliz.	?Whitefriars		252
King's	GB		253
King's	GB		254
?	?		255
Q. Anne's	Red Bull		256
King's	GB		257
Courtiers	Court		258
		Ben Jonson first Folio published.	
King's	GB		259
King's	GB		260
King's	GB		261
King's	GB		262
King's	GB		263
King's	GB		264
King's	GB		265
Oxford students	Christ Church, Oxford		266
Oxford students	Christ Church, Oxford		267
King's	GB		268
King's	GB		269
P. Charles's/Lady Eliz.	Phoenix		270
King's	GB		271

Earliest Date of Performance	Play Title	Author
272 c.1619×1622	*The Tragedy of Herod and Antipater*	Sampson, Markham
273 1619×1623	*The False One*	Fletcher
274 1619×1623	*Women Pleased*	Fletcher
275 1619×1623	*The Custom of the Country*	Fletcher
276 1620	*The World Tossed at Tennis*	Middleton
277 c.1620×c.1621	*Anything for a Quiet Life*	Middleton
278 1620×1627	*Women Beware Women*	Middleton
279 c.1621	*The Witch of Edmonton*	Dekker, Ford, W. Rowley
280 1621	*The Pilgrim*	Fletcher
281 ?1621	*The Wild Goose Chase*	Fletcher
282 1621×1623	*The Duke of Milan*	Massinger
283 1621×1625	*A New Way to Pay Old Debts*	Massinger
284 1622	*The Changeling*	Middleton, Rowley
1623		
1624		
285 1624	*The Duchess of Suffolk*	Drue
286 1624	*A Game at Chess*	Middleton
287 1624	*The Late Murder of the Son upon the Mother: or Keep the Widow Waking*	Dekker, Ford, Rowley, Webster
288 1624	*Rule a Wife and Have a Wife*	Fletcher
289 1624×1625	*The Unnatural Combat*	Massinger
1625		

Company	Place of Performance	Events	
'Company of his Majesty's Revels' (the former Queen Anne's Men)	Red Bull		272
King's	GB		273
King's	GB		274
King's	GB		275
P. Charles's	Phoenix		276
King's	GB		277
?	?		278
P. Charles's	Phoenix		279
King's	GB		280
King's	GB		281
King's	GB		282
P. Charles's/QHM	Phoenix		283
?Lady Eliz./BB	Phoenix		284
		Shakespeare first Folio published.	
		Prince Charles and Buckingham return from Madrid with news that the proposed Spanish marriage has been abandoned.	
Palsgrave's	Fortune		285
King's	Globe		286
P. Charles's	Red Bull		287
King's	GB		288
King's	GB		289
		King James dies; Charles I succeeds; marries Henrietta Maria. A major plague closes all playhouses in London from April to November. John Fletcher dies.	

Earliest Date of Performance	Play Title	Author
290 1625×1633	*The Broken Heart*	Ford
291 1626	*The Staple of News*	Jonson
292 1626	*The Tragedy of Cleopatra, Queen of Egypt**	May
293 1626	*The Roman Actor*	Massinger
294 1626×1629	*The Tragedy of Albovine*	Davenant
295 1627	*The Great Duke of Florence*	Massinger
296 c.1627	*The English Traveller*	Heywood
297 c.1628×1634	*King John and Matilda*	Davenport
298 1628	*Julia Agrippina, Empress of Rome*	May
299 1629	*The New Inn: or The Light Heart*	Jonson
300 1629×1633	*'Tis Pity She's a Whore*	Ford
301 c.1629×1634	*The Chronicle History of Perkin Warbeck*	Ford
302 1629×1637	*The City Wit: or The Woman Wears the Breeches*	Brome
1630		
303 1631	*Love's Cruelty*	Shirley
304 1631	*Believe As You List*	Massinger
305 1631	*Holland's Leaguer*	Marmion
306 1632	*Hyde Park*	Shirley
307 1632	*The Magnetic Lady: or the Humours Reconciled*	Jonson
308 1632	*The City Madam*	Massinger
309 ?1632	*Love's Sacrifice*	Ford
310 1633	*The Gamester*	Shirley
311 1633	*The Young Admiral*	Shirley
1634		
312 1634	*Love and Honour**	Davenant
313 1634	*Love's Mistress**	Heywood
314 1634×1636	*Messalina: the Roman Empress*	Richards
315 1635	*The Lady of Pleasure*	Shirley
316 1635×1636	*Arviragus and Philicia**	Carlell

Company	Place of Performance	Events	
King's	GB		290
King's	GB		291
?	?		292
King's	GB		293
?	?		294
QHM	Phoenix		295
QHM	Phoenix		296
QHM	Phoenix		297
?	?		298
King's	GB		299
QHM	Phoenix		300
QHM	Phoenix		301
KR 2	?Salisbury		302
		The Salisbury Court playhouse built.	
QHM	Phoenix		303
King's	GB		304
P. Charles's	Salisbury		305
QHM	Phoenix		306
King's	GB		307
King's	GB		308
QHM	Phoenix		309
QHM	Phoenix		310
QHM	Phoenix		311
		William Prynne is pilloried and mutilated for attack on female actors.	
King's	GB		312
QHM	Phoenix		313
KR 2	Salisbury		314
QHM	Phoenix		315
King's	GB		316

Earliest Date of Performance	Play Title	Author
1636–7		
317 1637×1638	*The Damoiselle: or The New Ordinary*	Brome
318 *c.*1638×?1639	*The Fatal Contract*	Heminges
319 1638×1639	*The Rebellion*	Rawlins
320 *c.*1639	*The Knave in Grain New Vamped*	J.D.
321 1641	*A Jovial Crew: or The Merry Beggars*	Brome
322 1641 1642	*The Cardinal*	Shirley
1647		

Company	Place of Performance	Events	
		A major plague closes all play-houses from May 1636 until October 1637.	
QHM	Salisbury		317
QHM	Salisbury		318
KR 2	Red Bull		319
The Red Bull Company	Fortune		320
BB	Phoenix		321
King's	GB		322
		Parliament forbids all theatrical performances.	
		Beaumont and Fletcher first Folio published.	

Select Bibliography and List of Plays

THIS Select Bibliography is not designed to walk readers across the multitudinous and ever-changing sea of critical opinion, nor to enumerate all the accumulating comments on Elizabethan culture that might well be considered relevant to the plays discussed above. Some material in these categories has been addressed in the footnotes, but a full representation is out of the question, and has indeed been avoided in the later volumes in this series. What is selected here is designed only to point to the basic sources of our knowledge in this field, to indicate the range of technical discussions to which these give rise, and to list the works of reference that give access to further discussion. The list of plays should provide readers with an entrée not only to a range of little-read texts but also to a body of comment derived directly from the basic materials.

ORIGINAL DOCUMENTS

Arber, Edward (ed.), *A Transcript of the Registers of the Company of Stationers in London, 1554–1640* (5 vols.; London, 1875–77).

Bentley, Gerald Eades, *The Jacobean and Caroline Stage* (7 vols.; Oxford, 1941–68).

Carson, Neil, *A Companion to Henslowe's Diary* (Cambridge, 1988).

Chambers, E. K., *The Elizabethan Stage* (4 vols.; Oxford, 1923).

Greg, W. W. (ed.), *Dramatic Documents from the Elizabethan Playhouses* (2 vols.; Oxford, 1931).

—— *A Companion to Arber* (Oxford, 1967).

Henslowe's Diary, ed. R. A. Foakes, and R. T. Rickert (Cambridge, 1961).

Henslowe's Diary, ed. W. W. Greg (2 vols.; London, 1904–8).

Henslowe Papers, ed. W. W. Greg (London, 1907).

Herbert, Henry, *The Dramatic Records of Sir Henry Herbert*, ed. Joseph Q. Adams (New Haven, 1917).

Malone Society Collections (1901–). Archival material bearing on the history of the Elizabethan stage.

Records of Early English Drama, ed. Alexandra Johnson *et al.* (Toronto, 1979–). A county-by-county publication of all surviving records of English dramatic and quasi-dramatic activity.

White, Beatrice, *An Index to 'The Elizabethan Stage' and 'William Shakespeare' by Sir Edmund Chambers* (Oxford, 1934).

BIBLIOGRAPHIES

Adler, D. R., *Thomas Dekker: A Reference Guide* (Boston, 1983).

Allison, A. F., *Thomas Dekker: A Bibliographical Catalogue of the Early Editions* (Folkestone, 1972).

Bergeron, David M., *Twentieth-Century Criticism of English Masques, Pageants and Entertainments, 1558–1642* (San Antonio, Tex., 1972).

—— and de Sousa, G. U., *Shakespeare: A Study and Research Guide* (3rd edn., Lawrence, Kan., 1995).

Blackstone, Mary, *A Survey and Annotated Bibliography of Records Research and Performance History Relating to Early British Drama and Minstrelsy for 1984–1988* (Records of Early English Drama Newsletter, 15 and 16; 1990, 1992).

Bland, D. S., 'A Checklist of Drama at the Inns of Court', *RORD* 9 (1966), 47–61.

Champion, Larry S., *The Essential Shakespeare: An Annotated Bibliography of Major Modern Studies* (New York, 1993).

Corbin, Peter, and Sedge, Douglas, *An Annotated Critical Bibliography of Jacobean and Caroline Comedy (excluding Shakespeare)* (Hemel Hempstead, 1988).

Fordyce, Rachel, *Caroline Drama: A Bibliographic History of Criticism* (New York, 1992).

Greg, W. W., *A Bibliography of the English Printed Drama to the Restoration* (4 vols.; London, 1939–1959). A complete bibliographical description of all plays printed before 1660.

—— *A List of Masques, Pageants etc.* (London, 1902).

Harner, J. L., *Samuel Daniel and Michael Drayton: A Reference Guide to Daniel and Drayton* (Boston, 1980).

Kolin, Philip C., and Wyatt, R. O., 'A Bibliography of Scholarship on the Elizabethan Stage since Chambers', *RORD* 15, 16 (1972–3), 33–59.

Logan, T., and Smith, D. S. (gen. eds.), *A Survey and Bibliography of Recent Studies in English Renaissance Drama* (4 vols.; Lincoln, Nebr., 1973–8).

Mahaney, W. E., *John Webster: A Classified Bibliography* (Salzburg, 1973).

McGee, C. E., and Meagher, J. C., *Preliminary Checklist of Tudor and Stuart Entertainments* (*RORD* 24 (1981), 51–155; 25 (1982), 31–114; 27 (1984), 47–126; 30 (1988), 17–128).

Pennell, C. A., *Elizabethan Bibliographies Supplements* (18 vols.; London, 1967–70). Supplements to Tannenbaum's *Elizabethan Bibliographies*.

Pollard, A. W., and Redgrave, G. R., *A Short-Title Catalogue of Books Printed in England 1475–1640*, rev. W. A. Jackson, F. S. Ferguson, and K. F. Pantzer (3 vols.; London, 1976–91).

Ribner, I., and Huffman, C. C., *Tudor and Stuart Drama* (Goldentree Bibliographies in Language and Literature; Arlington Heights, Ill., 1978).

Saeger, J. P., and Fassler, Christopher, 'The London Professional Theater, 1575–1642: A Catalogue and Analysis of the Extant Printed Plays', *RORD* 34 (1995), 63–109.

Sarafinski, Dolores, *et al.*, *The Plays of Ben Jonson: A Reference Guide* (Boston, 1980).

Shakespeare Quarterly. Annual list of new works on Shakespearian topics.

Shakespeare Survey. Surveys works on Shakespeare and related material.

Sibley, Gertrude M., *The Lost Plays and Masques 1500–1642* (Ithaca, NY, 1933). An annotated checklist.

Smith, Gordon R., *A Classified Shakespeare Bibliography, 1936–1958* (University Park, Pa., 1963).

Steen, S. J., *Thomas Middleton: A Reference Guide* (Boston, 1984).

Studies in English Literature 1500–1900 (1961–). Each Spring issue contains an annual survey of the year's work in Elizabethan Drama.

Tannenbaum, S. A., and Tannenbaum, D. R., *Elizabethan Bibliographies* (41 vols.; New York, 1937–50; repr. in 10 vols, New York, 1967).

Tucker, Kenneth, *A Bibliography of Writings by and about John Ford and Cyril Tourneur* (Boston, 1977).

Wells, S. W. (ed.), *English Drama, Excluding Shakespeare: Select Bibliographical Guides* (London, 1975).

—— *Shakespeare: A Bibliographical Guide* (Oxford, 1990).

Woodward, G. L., and McManaway, J. G., *A Check List of English Plays, 1641–1700* (Chicago, 1945).

Zimmer, Ruth K., *James Shirley: A Reference Guide* (Boston, 1980).

INDEXES AND SURVEYS

Berger, T. L., and Bradford, W. C., *An Index of Characters in English Printed Drama to the Restoration* (Englewood, Colo., 1975).

The Cambridge Companion to English Renaissance Drama, ed. A. R. Braunmuller and Michael Hattaway (Cambridge, 1990).

The Cambridge Companion to Shakespeare Studies, ed. S. W. Wells (Cambridge, 1986).

Garrett, Martin, *Massinger: The Critical Heritage* (London, 1991).

Gerrard, Ernest A., *Elizabethan Drama and Dramatists 1583–1603* (Oxford, 1928).

Harbage, Alfred, *Annals of English Drama 975–1700* (1940), rev. S. Schoenbaum (London, 1964), rev. S. S. Wagonheim (London, 1989).

Holzknecht, K. J., *Outlines of Tudor and Stuart Plays 1497–1642* (New York, 1947).

Hunter, G. K., and Hunter, S. K., *John Webster* (Penguin Critical Anthologies; Harmondsworth, 1969).
Kawachi, Yoshiko, *Calendar of English Renaissance Drama 1558–1642* (New York, 1986).
Nungezer, Edwin, *A Dictionary of Actors* (New Haven, 1929).
The Revels History of Drama in English, iii. *1576–1613*, ed. Clifford Leech, and T. W. Craik (London, 1975).
The Revels History of Drama in English, iv. *1613–1660*, ed. Lois Potter (London, 1981).

TEXTUAL STUDIES

Bowers, Fredson, *On Editing Shakespeare and the Elizabethan Dramatists* (Philadelphia, Pa., 1955).
Gaskell, Philip, *A New Introduction to Bibliography* (Oxford, 1972).
Greg, W. W. (ed.), *Two Elizabethan Stage Abridgements: Alcazar and Orlando* (Malone Society, London, 1923).
Hinman, Charlton, *The Printing and Proof-reading of the First Folio of Shakespeare* (Oxford, 1963).
Honigmann, E. A. J., *The Stability of Shakespeare's Text* (London, 1965).
Shand, G. B., and Shady, R. C., *Play-Texts in Old Spelling* (New York, 1984).
Wells, S. W., and Taylor, G., *William Shakespeare: A Textual Companion* (Oxford, 1987).
Wilson F. P. (ed.), *Shakespeare and the New Bibliography*, rev. Helen Gardner (Oxford, 1970).

THEATRE BUILDINGS

Adams, Joseph Q., *Shakespearean Playhouses* (Boston, 1917; repr. Gloucester, Mass., 1960).
Armstrong, W. A., *The Elizabethan Private Theatres, Facts and Problems* (The Society for Theatre Research Pamphlet 6, 1957–8; London, 1958).
Beckerman, Bernard, *Shakespeare at the Globe, 1599–1609* (New York, 1962).
Berry, Herbert, *The Boar's Head Playhouse* (Washington, 1986).
—— *The First Public Playhouse* (Montreal, 1979). Essays on James Burbage's *Theatre*.
Bordinat, Philip, 'A Study of the Salisbury Court Theatre', Ph.D. thesis (Birmingham, 1952).
Foakes, R. A., *Illustrations of the English Stage, 1580–1642* (London, 1985).
Gurr, Andrew, *The Shakespearian Stage, 1574–1642* (2nd edn., Cambridge, 1980).

Harris, John, and Higgott, Gordon, *Inigo Jones: Complete Architectural Drawings* (New York, 1989). Disputes Orrell's views on the relation between the Worcester College drawings and *The Phoenix*.

Ingram, William, *A London Life in the Brazen Age: Francis Langley, 1548–1602* (Cambridge, Mass., 1978).

—— *The Business of Playing* (Ithaca, NY, 1992).

Loengard, Janet, 'An Elizabethan Lawsuit: John Brayne, his Carpenter, and the Building of the Red Lion Theatre', *Sh. Q.* 34 (1983), 298–310.

Orrell, John, 'Inigo Jones at the Cockpit', *Sh. S.* 30 (1977), 157–68.

—— *The Human Stage: English Theatre Design 1567–1640* (Cambridge, 1988).

Rutter, Carol C., *Documents of the Rose Playhouse* (Manchester, 1984).

The Site and Office of The Times: The History from 1276 to 1956 of the Site in Blackfriars Consisting of Printing House Square with Later Accretions (London, 1956).

Smith, Irwin, *Shakespeare's Blackfriars Playhouse* (New York, 1964).

Wickham, Glynne, *Early English Stages 1300–1660* (3 vols. in 4; New York, 1959–81).

THEATRICAL ORGANIZATION

Bald, R. C., 'Leicester's Men in the Low Countries', *RES* 19 (1943), 395–7.

Bradley, David, *From Text to Performance* (Cambridge, 1992).

Edmond, Mary, 'Pembroke's Men', *RES* NS 25 (1974), 129–36.

George, David, 'Shakespeare and Pembroke's Men', *Sh. Q.* 32 (1981), 305–23.

Gurr, Andrew, 'Three Reluctant Patrons and Early Shakespeare', *Sh. Q.* 44 (1993), 159–74.

King, T. J., 'The King's Men on Stage 1611–1632', *Elizabethan Theatre*, 9 (1981), 21–40.

Knutson, Roslyn, 'The Repertory of Shakespeare's Company' (Fayetteville, Ark., 1991).

McMillin, Scott, 'The Queen's Men and the London Theatre of 1583', *Elizabethan Theatre*, 10 (1983), 1–17.

—— 'Casting for Pembroke's Men: The *Henry VI* Quartos and *The Taming of a Shrew*', *Sh. Q.* 23 (1972), 141–59.

Murray, J. T., *English Dramatic Companies 1558–1642* (2 vols.; London, 1910).

Neill, Michael, 'Wits Most Accomplished Senate': The Audience of the Caroline Private Theatres', *SEL* 18 (1978), 341–60.

Pinciss, G. M., 'Thomas Creede and the Repertory of The Queen's Men 1583–1592', *MP* 67 (1969), 321–30.

—— 'Shakespeare, Her Majesty's Players and Pembroke's Men', *Sh. S.* 27 (1974), 129–36.

Riewald, J. G., 'The English Actors in the Low Countries 1585-*c.*1650: An Annotated Bibliography', in G. A. M. Janssens and F. G. A. M. Aarts (eds.), *Studies in Seventeenth Century English Literature, History, and Bibliography* (Amsterdam, 1984), 157–78.

Rosenfeld, Sibyl, *Strolling Players and Drama in the Provinces 1600–1765* (New York, 1970).

Schrickx, Willem, *Foreign Envoys and Travelling Players in the Age of Shakespeare and Jonson* (Wetteren, 1986). Especially Chapter vi, dealing with Marston, Dekker, and Tourneur.

Sturgess, Keith, *Jacobean Private Theatre* (London, 1987).

Wasson, John, 'Elizabethan and Jacobean Touring Companies', *Theatre Notebook*, 42 (1988), 51–7 (East and West Ridings of Yorkshire).

Wentersdorf, K. P., 'The Repertory and Size of Pembroke's Company', *Theatre Annual*, 33 (1977), 71–85.

CENSORSHIP AND CONTROL

Clare, Janet, *'Art Made Tongue-Tied by Authority': Elizabethan and Jacobean Dramatic Censorship* (Manchester, 1990).

Dutton, Richard, *Mastering the Revels: The Regulation and Censorship of Elizabethan Drama* (London, 1991).

Gildersleeve, Virginia, *Government Regulation of the Elizabethan Drama* (New York, 1908; repr. New York, 1961).

Hill, Christopher, 'Censorship and English Literature', *The Collected Essays of Christopher Hill*, i (Brighton, 1985), 32–71.

THEATRE AND SOCIETY

Bevington, David, *Tudor Drama and Politics* (Cambridge, Mass., 1968).

Bristol, Michael D., *Carnival and Theater: Plebeian Culture and the Structure of Authority in Renaissance England* (New York, 1985).

Butler, Martin, *Theatre and Crisis, 1632–1642* (Cambridge, 1984).

Heinemann, Margot, *Puritanism and Theatre* (Cambridge, 1980).

Knights, L. C., *Drama and Society in the Age of Jonson* (London, 1937).

Leinwand, T. B., *The City Staged: Jacobean Comedy, 1603–1613* (Madison, 1986).

Lever, J. W., *The Tragedy of State* (London, 1971).

Orgel, Stephen, *The Illusion of Power: Political Theater in the English Renaissance* (Berkeley and Los Angeles, 1975).

Sinfield, Alan, *Faultlines: Cultural Materialism and the Politics of Dissident Reading* (Berkeley and Los Angeles, 1992).

Smuts, R. Malcolm, *Court Culture and the Origins of a Royalist Tradition in Early Stuart England* (Philadelphia, Pa., 1987).

PLAY TEXTS

It should be said here that the list of editions given below draws on materials of very different kinds. 'Representative' collections of plays in one or two volumes, such as ADAMS, BASKERVILL, SPECIMENS, and BROOKS AND PARADISE, have had the aim of providing respectable modernized texts at prices affordable by students; they do not give much space to introductions or annotations. Their selections inevitably reflect the consensus tastes of the times when they were compiled. Modern single-author collections such as Fredson Bowers's Beaumont and Fletcher (BF), his MARLOWE and his DEKKER, Holaday's Chapman volumes (HOLADAY.COM., HOLADAY.TRAG.) are textually sophisticated but without explanatory matter (though the Dekker has a parallel series of commentary volumes, by Cyrus Hoy). Herford and Simpson's JONSON, Bond's LYLY, Edwards and Gibson's MASSINGER, Parrott's CHAPMAN (PARROT.COM., PARROTT.TRAG.), and Lucas's WEBSTER have elaborate annotation. Older single-author collections (Grosart's DANIEL, the Maidmant and Logan DAVENANT and MARMION, R. H. Shepherd's edition of HEYWOOD, the 'Pearson Reprint' of BROME, and the Gifford and Dyce SHIRLEY) must be taken in the terms in which they were produced, as models of pre-academic individual antiquarian scholarship. The editions not commented on here fall between at least two of these categories. The single-volume Shakespeare collections cited as alternatives to the basic RIVERSIDE text have, of course, only a token function. The Oxford volume is the most innovative of those named, but its innovations have not been universally welcomed. Its standard-format volume comes accompanied by a parallel one in old-spelling and a 'Textual Companion' containing elaborate arguments about authorship, text, and dating.

The single-play series cited are no less various. The ARDEN series of Shakespeare plays (with editions dated from the early 1950s to the early 1980s) has long been the most esteemed. The volumes are equipped with extensive introductions, textual commentaries, lexical and explanatory glosses. The OXFORD and New CAMBRIDGE single-play series (only the latest to carry such names) are still in progress. They are parallel in coverage to the ARDEN but more up to date and more theatrically self-conscious (ARDEN has responded by issuing the first volumes in a NEW ARDEN series). This is a field in which a bibliography is bound to be out of date before it is printed. The REVELS series is designed to provide for non-Shakespearian plays the same kind of coverage as ARDEN does for Shakespeare. The Regents' Renaissance Drama (RRD) and NEW MERMAID series supply a similar set of aids to understanding, but in briefer form.

Normally they provide accurate texts accompanied by sharply focused critical and historical commentary, at prices well below that of the REVELS. The MATERIALIEN series, and the MATERIALS, its post-war 1927 resurrection, provide models of laborious scholarship, accurate texts, with severe but thorough historical investigations, sometimes in German, sometimes in English. Malone Society texts (MSR) are type-facsimiles of original editions or manuscripts. The introductions describe the bibliographical make-up and scribal peculiarities of the original, but do not venture into non-textual matters. The GARLAND series prints typescript versions (sometimes corrected) of Ph.D. dissertations. The quality of the editions varies as much as might be expected from such sources. The same is true of the SALZBURG series. Tudor Facsimile Texts (TFT) provide photographic facsimiles of original editions. They are usually read as texts of last resort, for the quality of the photographs is not good; but the series contains several plays not available in any other reprint. Facsimilies of some texts have been issued by the Scolar Press and by the Da Capo press in Amsterdam. Microfilms of the original editions can be found in the University Microfilm series of Short Title Catalogue books up to 1642 and in Henry W. Wells (ed.), *Three Centuries of Drama* (1955–6).

In the list that follows, plays not reprinted are given the date of their first publication. Plays of unknown authorship are marked by (?). Asterisks indicate the editions used for line-counts and for the (modernized) quotations given in the main body of the book.

ABBREVIATIONS USED

Collections

ADAMS   *Chief Pre-Shakespearean Dramas*, ed. J. Q. Adams (Cambridge, Mass., 1924)

APOCRYPHA   *The Shakespeare Apocrypha*, ed. C. F. Tucker Brooke (Oxford, 1902)

BASKERVILL   *Elizabethan and Stuart Plays*, ed. C. R. Baskervill, V. B. Heltzel, and A. H. Nethercot (New York, 1934); repr. in 2 vols., 1971)

BF   *The Dramatic Works in the Beaumont and Fletcher Canon*, gen. ed. Fredson Bowers (Cambridge, 1966–)

BROME   *The Dramatic Works of Richard Brome* (3 vols.; London, 1873; repr. New York, 1966)

BROOKE AND PARADISE   *English Drama 1580–1642*, ed. C. F. Tucker Brooke and Nathaniel B. Paradise (Boston, 1933)

BULLOUGH   *Narrative and Dramatic Sources of Shakespeare*, ed. Geoffrey Bullough (8 vols.; London, 1957–75)

DANIEL	The Complete Works in Verse and Prose of Samuel Daniel, ed. A. B. Grosart (5 vols.; London, 1885–96)
DAVENANT	The Dramatic Works of Sir William D'Avenant, ed. James Maidment and W. H. Logan (5 vols.; Edinburgh, 1872–4; repr. in 2 vols., 1964)
DEKKER	The Dramatic Works of Thomas Dekker, ed. Fredson Bowers (4 vols.; Cambridge, 1953–61)
DODSLEY	A Select Collection of Old English Plays, now . . . Revised . . . by W. Carew Hazlitt (15 vols.; London, 1874–6)
EECT	Early English Classical Tragedies, ed. J. W. Cunliffe (Oxford, 1912)
FRASER AND RABKIN	Drama of the English Renaissance, ed. R. A. Fraser and Norman Rabkin (2 vols.; New York, 1976)
GASCOIGNE	The Complete Works of George Gascoigne, ed. J. W. Cunliffe (2 vols.; Cambridge, 1907–10; repr. New York, 1969)
GREENE	The Plays and Poems of Robert Greene, ed. J. Churton Collins (2 vols.; Oxford, 1905)
GREVILLE	Poems and Dramas of Fulke Greville, ed. Geoffrey Bullough (2 vols.; Edinburgh, 1939)
HEYWOOD	The Dramatic Works of Thomas Heywood, ed. R. H. Shepherd (6 vols.; London, 1874; repr. 1964)
HOLADAY COM.	The Plays of George Chapman: The Comedies, gen. ed. Allan Holaday (Urbana, Ill., 1970)
HOLADAY TRAG.	The Plays of George Chapman: The Tragedies, gen. ed. Allan Holaday (Urbana, Ill., 1987)
JONSON	Ben Jonson, ed. C. H. Herford and Percy and Evelyn Simpson (11 vols.; Oxford, 1925–52)
KYD	The Works of Thomas Kyd, ed. F. S. Boas (Oxford, 1901)
LYLY	The Complete Works of John Lyly, ed. R. Warwick Bond (3 vols.; Oxford, 1902; repr. 1967)
MARLOWE	The Complete Works of Christopher Marlowe, ed. Fredson Bowers (2 vols.; Cambridge, 1973; rev. edn., 1981)
MARMION	The Dramatic Works of Shackerley Marmion, ed. J. Maidment and W. H. Logan (Edinburgh, 1875)
MARSTON	The Plays of John Marston, ed. H. Harvey Wood (3 vols.; Edinburgh, 1934–9)
MASSINGER	The Plays and Poems of Philip Massinger, ed. Philip Edwards and Colin Gibson (5 vols.; Oxford, 1976)
MIDDLETON	The Works of Thomas Middleton, ed. A. H. Bullen (8 vols.; London, 1885–6; repr. New York, 1964)

NERO   *Nero and Other Plays*, gen. ed. Havelock Ellis (London, 1888)

OEP   *A Collection of Old English Plays*, ed. A. H. Bullen (4 vols.; London, 1882–5)

OEP (NS)   *Old English Plays*, ed. A. H. Bullen (3 vols.; London, 1887–90)

ORGEL   *Ben Jonson: The Complete Masques*, ed. Stephen Orgel (New Haven, 1969)

PARROTT COM.   *The Comedies of George Chapman*, ed. Thomas Marc Parrott (2 vols.; London, 1914; repr. New York, 1961)

PARROTT TRAG.   *The Tragedies of George Chapman*, ed. Thomas Marc Parrott (2 vols.; London, 1910; repr. New York, 1961)

PEELE   *The Life and Works of George Peele*, gen. ed. C. T. Prouty (3 vols.; New Haven, 1952–70)

SHAKESPEARE   *The Riverside Shakespeare*, ed. G. Blakemore Evans (Boston, 1974) (see also *The Complete Oxford Shakespeare*, ed. Stanley Wells and Gary Taylor (3 vols.; Oxford, 1987), and *The Complete Works of Shakespeare*, ed. Hardin Craig and David Bevington (Glenview, Ill., 1973))

SHIRLEY   *The Dramatic Works and Poems of James Shirley*, ed. William Gifford and Alexander Dyce (6 vols.; London, 1833; repr. 1966)

SIMPSON   *The School of Shakspere*, ed. R. Simpson (2 vols.; London, 1878)

SPECIMENS   *Specimens of the Pre-Shakesperean Drama*, ed. J. M. Manly (2 vols.; Boston, 1897; repr. New York, 1967)

TOWNSHEND   *Aurelian Townshend's Poems and Masks*, ed. E. K. Chambers (Oxford, 1912)

WEBSTER   *The Complete Works of John Webster*, ed. F. L. Lucas (4 vols.; London, 1927)

Series

ARDEN   The Arden Shakespeare, gen. eds. Una Ellis-Fermor, Harold Brooks, Brian Morris, and Harold Jenkins (38 vols.; London 1951–82)

ARDEN (NS)   A new series of Arden Shakespeare volumes, gen. ed. R. Proudfoot, A. Thompson, and D. S. Kasdan (four volumes have been issued (London, 1995))

BELLES   The Belles Lettres Series (series III: The English Drama), gen. ed. George Pierce Baker (Boston, 1903–30)

CAMBRIDGE	The New Cambridge Shakespeare, gen. eds. Philip Brockbank and Brian Gibbons, 1984–
GARLAND	Renaissance Drama: A Collection of Critical Editions/The Renaissance Imagination, gen. ed. Stephen Orgel (New York)
MATERIALIEN	Materialien zur Kunde des älteren englischen Dramas, gen. ed. W. Bang (44 vols.; Louvain, 1902–14)
MATERIALS	Materials for the Study of the Old English Drama, gen. ed. H. de Vocht (Louvain, 1927–58)
MSR	Malone Sociey Reprints, gen. eds. W. W. Greg, F. P. ˙ Wilson, Arthur Brown, Richard Proudfoot, and John Pitcher (London)
NEW MERMAID	The New Mermaids Series, gen. eds. Philip Brockbank and Brian Morris (London)
OXFORD	The Oxford Shakespeare, gen. eds. Stanley Wells and Gary Taylor (Oxford)
REVELS	The Revels Plays, gen. eds. Clifford Leech, F. D. Hoeniger, D. Bevington, E. A. J. Honigmann, J. R. Mulryne, and E. M. Waith (London; Manchester)
RRD	Regents Renaissance Drama Series, gen. ed. Cyrus Hoy (Lincoln, Nebr.)
SALZBURG	Salzburg Studies in English Literature, gen. ed. E. A. Stürzl (Salzburg)
TFT	Tudor Facsimile Texts, gen. ed. J. S. Farmer (160 vols.; London)
VAR.	*A New Variorum Edition of Shakespeare*, ed. H. H. Furness and H. H. Furness, Jr. (19 vols.; Philadelphia, 1908–19)
VAR. (SUP.)	Volumes in the New Variorum series supplementary to those produced by the Furnesses (Philadelphia)
VAR. (NS)	A new series of Variorum volumes of Shakespeare, printed in New York for the Modern Language Association of America

SINGLE PLAYS

Alaham (Greville)	GREVILLE ii
Albion's Triumph (Townsend)	TOWNSHEND
Albovine, The Tragedy of (Davenant)	DAVENANT i
The Alchemist (Jonson)	JONSON v (1937)*
	REVELS (F. H. Mares, 1967)
	A. B. Kernan (ed.) (New Haven, 1974)
	NEW MERMAID (D. Brown, 1966)

All Fools (Chapman)　　　　　　RRD (Frank Manley, 1968)
　　　　　　　　　　　　　　　PARROTT COM. (1914)
　　　　　　　　　　　　　　　HOLADAY COM. (G. B. Evans,
　　　　　　　　　　　　　　　1970)*
All's Well That Ends Well　　　ARDEN (G. K. Hunter, 1959)
(Shakespeare)　　　　　　　　CAMBRIDGE (Russell Fraser, 1985)
　　　　　　　　　　　　　　　OXFORD (Susan Snyder, 1993)
All's Lost by Lust (W. Rowley)　BELLES (Edgar C. Morris, 1908)
　　　　　　　　　　　　　　　C. W. Stork (ed.) (Philadelphia,
　　　　　　　　　　　　　　　1910)
Alphonsus, Emperor of Germany　PARROTT TRAG. (1910)
(?Chapman)　　　　　　　　　H. F. Schwarz (ed.) (New York,
　　　　　　　　　　　　　　　1913)
Alphonsus, King of Aragon,　　　GREENE i (J. Churton Collins, 1905)
The Comical History of (Greene)　MSR (W. W. Greg, 1926)*
Amends for Ladies (Field)　　　William Peery (ed.) *The Plays of*
　　　　　　　　　　　　　　　Nathan Field (Austin, Tex., 1950)
　　　　　　　　　　　　　　　NERO (A. W. Verity, 1888)
　　　　　　　　　　　　　　　DODSLEY xi (W. C. Hazlitt, 1875)
Antonio and Mellida (Marston)　RRD (G. K. Hunter, 1965)*
　　　　　　　　　　　　　　　REVELS (W. R. Gair 1991)
Antonio's Revenge (Marston)　　RRD (G. K. Hunter, 1965)*
　　　　　　　　　　　　　　　REVELS (W. R. Gair, 1978)
Antonie (Herbert)　　　　　　Alice Luce (ed.) (Weimar, 1897)
Antony and Cleopatra　　　　　ARDEN (M. R. Ridley, 1954)
(Shakespeare)　　　　　　　　CAMBRIDGE (David Bevington, 1990)
　　　　　　　　　　　　　　　OXFORD (Michael Neill, 1994)
　　　　　　　　　　　　　　　VAR. (1907)
　　　　　　　　　　　　　　　VAR. (NS) (M. Spevack, 1990)
Anything for a Quiet Life (?)　　WEBSTER iv (F. L. Lucas, 1927)
　　　　　　　　　　　　　　　MIDDLETON v (1885)
Appius and Virginia (R.B.)　　　MSR (R. B. McKerrow, 1911)
Arden of Faversham,　　　　　REVELS (M. L. Wine, 1973)*
The Lamentable and True　　　APOCRYPHA
Tragedy of Master (?)　　　　BASKERVILL
The Arraignment of Paris (Peele)　PEELE iii (R. M. Benbow, 1970)
　　　　　　　　　　　　　　　BROOKE AND PARADISE
Arviragus and Philicia (Carlell)　1639
As You Like It (Shakespeare)　　ARDEN (Agnes Latham, 1975)
　　　　　　　　　　　　　　　OXFORD (Alan Brissenden, 1993)
　　　　　　　　　　　　　　　VAR. (1890)
　　　　　　　　　　　　　　　VAR. (NS) (R. Knowles, 1977)
The Atheist's Tragedy:　　　　REVELS (Irving Ribner, 1964)*
or The Honest Man's　　　　　George Parfitt (ed.) (*The Plays of*
Revenge (Tourneur)　　　　　*Cyril Tourneur* (Cambridge, 1978))

Bartholomew Fair (Jonson)   JONSON vi (1938)*
                               REVELS (E. A. Horsman, 1960)
                               RRD (E. B. Partridge, 1964)
                               NEW MERMAID (M. Hussey, 1964)
                               E. M. WAITH (ed.) (New Haven,
                               1963)
The Battle of Alcazar (Peele)   PEELE ii (John Yoklavitch, 1961)
                               MSR (W. W. Greg and F.
                               Sidgwick, 1907)*
Beggar's Bush (Fletcher)   BF iii (Fredson Bowers, 1976)
                               BROOKE AND PARADISE
Believe As You List   MASSINGER iii
                               MSR (C. J. Sisson, 1927)
1 The Blind Beggar of Alexandria   PARROTT COM.
(Chapman)   HOLADAY COM. (L. E. Berry)
1 The Blind Beggar of Bednall   MATERIALIEN i (W. Bang, 1902)
Green (Chettle, Day)
The Bloody Brother   see *Rollo, Duke of Normandy*
Blurt, Master Constable   MIDDLETON i (1885)
                               SALZBURG (T. L. Berger, 1979)
Bonduca, The Tragedy of   BF iv (Cyrus Hoy, 1979)*
(Fletcher)   MSR (W. W. Greg and F. P.
                               Wilson, 1951)
The Broken Heart (Ford)   REVELS (T. J. B. Spencer, 1980)*
                               NEW MERMAID (Brian Morris, 1965)
                               RRD (D. K. Anderson, 1968)
Bussy D'Ambois (Chapman)   REVELS (Nicholas Brooke, 1964)*
                               PARROTT TRAG.
                               RRD (R. J. Lordi, 1965)
                               NEW MERMAID (M. Evans, 1965)
                               HOLADAY TRAG. (J. H. Smith)
Byron, The Conspiracy and   PARROTT TRAG.
Tragedy of Charles, Duke of REVELS (John Margeson, 1988)
(Chapman)   GARLAND (G. W. Ray, 2 vols.;
                               1979)
                               HOLADAY TRAG. (J. B. Gabel, 1987)*
Caesar and Pompey: or Caesar's   MSR (F. S. Boas and W. W. Greg,
Revenge   1911)*
Cambyses (Preston)   SPECIMENS
                               ADAMS
Campaspe (Lyly)   LYLY ii
                               REVELS (G. K. Hunter, 1991)*
                               ADAMS
The Captain (Fletcher)   BF i (L. A. Beaurline, 1966)

The Cardinal (Shirley) — REVELS (E. M. Yearling, 1986)
SHIRLEY V
BROOKE AND PARADISE
BASKERVILL

The Careless Shepherdess (Goffe) — 1656
The Case is Altered (Jonson) — JONSON iii (1927)*
Catiline, His Conspiracy (Jonson) — JONSON v (1937)*
RRD (W. F. Bolton & J. F. Gardner, 1972)

Chabot, Admiral of France, The Tragedy of (Chapman) — SHIRLEY vi
PARROTT TRAG.
HOLADAY TRAG. (G. B. Evans)

The Chances (Fletcher) — BF iv (G. W. Williams, 1979)
The Changeling (Middleton, W. Rowley) — REVELS (N. W. Bawcutt, 1958)*
NEW MERMAID (P. Thomson, 1964)
A Chaste Maid in Cheapside (Middleton) — REVELS (R. B. Parker, 1969)*
NEW MERMAID (Alan Brissenden, 1968)

The City Madam (Massinger) — MASSINGER iv
RRD (Cyrus Hoy, 1964)
Rudolf Kirk (ed.) (Princeton, 1934)

The City Wit: or The Woman Wears the Breeches (Brome) — BROME i
Claudius Tiberius Nero, The Tragedy of (?) — Uwe Baumann (ed.) (Frankfurt, 1990)
MSR (W. W. Greg, 1914)*
Cleopatra (Daniel) — MATERIALIEN xxxi (M. Lederer, 1911)
DANIEL iii (1885)
Cleopatra, Queen of Egypt, The Tragedy of (May) — MSR (W. W. Greg, 1913)*
Clyomon and Clamydes (?) — TFT (1913)
MSR (W. W. Greg, 1913)
Betty Littleton (ed.) (The Hague, 1968)

The Cobbler's Prophecy (Wilson) — MSR (A. C. Wood and W. W. Greg, 1914)
The Comedy of Errors (Shakespeare) — ARDEN (R. A. Foakes, 1962)
CAMBRIDGE (T. S. Dorsch, 1988)
Common Conditions (?) — C. F. Tucker Brooke (ed.) (New Haven, 1915)

The Conflict of Conscience (Woodes) — MSR (H. Davis and F. P. Wilson, 1952)*

The Contention between Liberality and Prodigality (?)   MSR (W. W. Greg, 1913)

Coriolanus (Shakespeare)   ARDEN (Philip Brockbank, 1976)
OXFORD (R. B. Parker, 1994)
VAR. (1928)

The Courageous Turk: or Amurath I (Goffe)   MSR (D. Carnegie and P. Davison, 1974)
GARLAND (S. G. O'Malley, 1979)

Cromwell, Thomas, Lord (W.S.)   APOCRYPHA*
Cupid's Revenge (Fletcher)   BF ii (Fredson Bowers, 1970)
Cupid's Whirligig (Sharpham)   GARLAND (C. G. Petter, 1986)
Allardyce Nicoll (ed.) (Waltham St Lawrence, 1926)

The Custom of the Country (Fletcher)   BF viii (Cyrus Hoy, 1992)

Cymbeline (Shakespeare)   ARDEN (J. M. Nosworthy, 1955)
Roger Warren (ed.) (Manchester, 1989)
VAR. (1913)

The Fountain of Self Love: or Cynthia's Revels (Jonson)   JONSON iv (1932)*

The Damoiselle: or The New Ordinary (Brome)   BROME i

Damon and Pythias (Edwards)   MSR (A. Brown and F. P. Wilson, 1957)
ADAMS
GARLAND (D. J. White, 1980)

David and Bethsabe, The Love of King (Peele)   PEELE iii (Elmer Blistein, 1970)*
MSR (W. W. Greg, 1913)
SPECIMENS ii (1897)
FRASER AND RABKIN i

The Devil is an Ass (Jonson)   JONSON vi (1938)*
REVELS (Peter Happé, 1994)

The Devil's Charter (Barnes)   MATERALIEN vi (R. B. McKerrow, 1904)

The Devil's Law-Case (Webster)   WEBSTER ii (F. L. Lucas, 1927)
NEW MERMAID (Elizabeth Brennan, 1975)
RRD (F. A. Shirley, 1972)

Dido, Queen of Carthage, The Tragedy of (Marlowe)   REVELS (H. J. Oliver, 1968)
MARLOWE i

Doctor Faustus (Marlowe)   MARLOWE ii*

	REVELS (J. D. Jump, 1962)
	W. W. Greg (ed.) (Oxford, 1950)
	NEW MERMAID (Roma Gill, 1965)
The Duchess of Malfi (Webster)	WEBSTER ii
	REVELS (J. R. Brown, 1964)*
	NEW MERMAID (Elizabeth Brennan, 1964)
The Duchess of Suffolk (Drue)	1624
The Duke of Milan (Massinger)	MASSINGER i*
	T. W. Baldwin (ed.) (Lancaster, Pa., 1918)
The Dutch Courtesan (Marston)	MARSTON ii (1938)
	RRD (M. L. Wine, 1965)*
	FRASER AND RABKIN ii
Eastward Ho (Jonson, Chapman,	JONSON iv (1932)*
Marston)	REVELS (R. W. Van Fossen, 1979)
	NEW MERMAID (C. G. Petter, 1973)
Edward I (Peele)	PEELE ii (Frank S. Hook, 1961)
	MSR (W. W. Greg, 1911)
Edward II (Marlowe)	MARLOWE ii*
	REVELS (C. R. Forker, 1994)
	NEW MERMAID (W. M. Merchant, 1967)
	Roma Gill (ed.) (London, 1967)
Edward III (?)	APOCRYPHA*
	W. A. Armstrong (ed.), *Elizabethan History Plays* (London, 1965)
Edward IV (*1* and *2*) (? Heywood)	HEYWOOD i*
Endymion (Lyly)	LYLY iii
	REVELS (David Bevington, 1996)
	BROOKE AND PARADISE
The English Traveller (Heywood)	HEYWOOD iv
Englishmen for my Money	MSR (W. W. Greg, 1912)
(Haughton)	A. C. Bough (Philadelphia, 1917)
Epicoene: or The Silent Woman	JONSON v (1937)*
(Jonson)	RRD (L. A. Beaurline, 1966)
	E. B. Partridge (ed.) (New Haven, 1971)
Every Man in his Humour	JONSON iii (1927)*
(Jonson)	RRD (J. W. Lever, 1971)
	NEW MERMAID (M. Seymour-Smith, 1966)
	G. B. Jackson (ed.) (New Haven, 1969)

Every Man out of his Humour JONSON iii (1927)*
(Jonson)   MSR (F. P. Wilson and W. W.
    Greg, 1920)
Fair Em, The Miller's Daughter   APOCRYPHA
of Manchester (?)   MSR (W. W. Greg, 1927)
    SIMPSON ii (London, 1878)
    GARLAND (Standish Henning,
    1980)
The Fair Maid of the Exchange (?)   HEYWOOD ii
    MSR (P. Davison and A. Brown,
    1963)
    GARLAND (K. E. Snyder, 1980)
The Fair Maid of Bristowe (?)   A. H. Quinn (ed.) (Philadelphia,
    Pa., 1902)
A Fair Quarrel (Middleton,   NEW MERMAID (R. V. Holdsworth,
W. Rowley)   1974)
    RRD (George R. Price, 1976)
The Faithful Shepherdess   BF iii (Cyrus Hoy, 1976)*
(Fletcher)   BASKERVILL
    GARLAND (F. A. Kirk, 1980)
The False One (Fletcher)   BF viii (R. K. Turner, 1992)*
The Family of Love (Middleton)   MIDDLETON iii (1885)
The Famous Victories of   BULLOUGH iv (1962)*
Henry V (?)   ADAMS
The Fatal Contract (Heminges)   MATERIALIEN (Otto Junge, 1912)
The Fawn   see *Parasitaster*
Fedele and Fortunio, Two Italian   GARLAND (R. Hosley, 1981)*
Gentlemen (? Munday)   MSR (P. Simpson and W. W. Greg,
    1909)
The Fleer (Sharpham)   MATERIALIEN xxxvi (H. Nibbe,
    1912)
    GARLAND (C. G. Petter, *The Works
    of Edward Sharpham*, 1986)*
Fortune by Land and Sea   HEYWOOD vi
(Heywood, W. Rowley)
The Four Prentices of London   HEYWOOD ii
(Heywood)   GARLAND (M. A. W. Gasior, 1980)
Friar Bacon and Friar Bungay,   RRD (Daniel Seltzer, 1963)
The Honourable History of   NEW MERMAID (J. A. Lavin, 1969)
(Greene)   BROOKE AND PARADISE
    FRASER AND RABKIN i
Gallathea (Lyly)   LYLY ii
    RRD (Anne Lancashire, 1969)

A Game at Chess (Middleton) REVELS (T. H. Howard-Hill, 1993)
R. C. Bald (ed.) (Cambridge, 1929)
NEW MERMAID (J. W. Harper, 1966)
MIDDLETON vii (1886)

The Gamester (Shirley) SHIRLEY iii
Gammer Gurton's Needle H. F. B. Brett-Smith (ed.) (Oxford,
(Mr S. Master of Art) 1920)
ADAMS
SPECIMENS ii

The Gentleman Usher (Chapman) PARROTT COM.
RRD (J. H. Smith, 1970)
HOLADAY COM. (R. Ornstein)

George a Green, the Pinner of GREENE ii
Wakefield (?) MSR (F. W. Clarke and W. W.
Greg, 1911)*
ADAMS

Gismond of Salerne (Wilmot, EECT
Stafford, Hatton, Noel)
The Golden Age (Heywood) HEYWOOD iii
Goosecap, Sir Giles (? Chapman) PARROTT COM. (1914)
HOLADAY TRAG. (J. F. Hennedy,
1987)
OEP iii (1884)
MATERIALIEN xxvi (W. Bang and
R. Brotanek, 1909)

Gorboduc: or Ferrex and Porrex RRD (Irby B. Cauthen, 1970)
(Sackville, Norton) EECT
ADAMS
SPECIMENS ii

The Great Duke of Florence J. M. Stochholm (ed.) (Baltimore,
(Massinger) 1933)
Greene's Tu Quoque (Cooke) GARLAND (A. J. Berman, 1984)
DODSLEY xi (1875)

Grim the Collier of Croydon TFT (1912)
(? Haughton) DODSLEY viii (1874)
Hamlet (Shakespeare) ARDEN (Harold Jenkins, 1982)
CAMBRIDGE (Philip Edwards, 1985)
VAR. (2 vols.; 1877)
OXFORD (Roma Gill, 1992)
1 Henry IV (Shakespeare) ARDEN (A. R. Humphreys, 1960)
OXFORD (David Bevington, 1987)
VAR. (SUP.) (S. B. Hemingway,
1936)

2 Henry IV (Shakespeare)	ARDEN (A. R. Humphreys, 1966) CAMBRIDGE (Giorgio Melchiori, 1989) VAR. (SUP.) (Matthias A. Shaaber, 1940)
Henry V (Shakespeare)	ARDEN (NS) (T. W. Craik, 1995) CAMBRIDGE (Andrew Gurr, 1992) OXFORD (Gary Taylor, 1982) VAR. (SUP.) (S. B. Hemingway, 1936)
1 Henry VI (Shakespeare)	ARDEN (A. S. Cairncross, 1962) CAMBRIDGE (Michael Hattaway, 1991)
2 Henry VI (Shakespeare)	ARDEN (A. S. Cairncross, 1957) CAMBRIDGE (Michael Hattaway, 1991)
3 Henry VI (Shakespeare)	ARDEN (A. S. Cairncross, 1964) CAMBRIDGE (Michael Hattaway, 1993)
Henry VIII (Shakespeare)	BF vii (Fredson Bowers, 1989) ARDEN (R. A. Foakes, 1957) CAMBRIDGE (John Margeson, 1990)
Herod and Antipater, The Tragedy of (Markham, Simpson)	GARLAND (G. N. Ross, 1979)
Histriomastix: or The Player Whipped (? Marston)	MARSTON iii SIMPSON ii
Hoffman, The Tragedy of: or Revenge for a Father (Chettle)	MSR (H. Jenkins and C. J. Sisson, 1951)*
Holland's Leaguer (Marmion)	MARMION
The Honest Man's Fortune (Fletcher)	J. Gerritsen (ed.) (Groningen, 1952)
The Honest Whore (*1* and *2*) (Dekker, Middleton)	DEKKER ii (Fredson Bowers, 1955)*
Horestes (Pickering)	MSR (D. Seltzer and G. E. Bentley, 1962)
How a Man May Choose a Good Wife (Heywood)	MATERIALIEN xxxv (A. E. H. Swaen, 1912)* DODSLEY ix (1874)
A Humorous Day's Mirth (Chapman)	HOLADAY COM. (Allan Holaday, 1970) PARROTT COM.
The Humorous Lieutenant (Fletcher)	GARLAND (P. Oxley, 1987) BF v (Cyrus Hoy, 1982)

Humour out of Breath (Day) NERO (Arthur Symons, ed., 1888)
Huntingdon, The Downfall and MSR (J. C. Meagher and A. Brown,
Death of Robert, Earl of 1965, 1967)*
(Chettle, Munday)
Hyde Park (Shirley) SHIRLEY ii
  FRASER AND RABKIN ii
Hymenaei (Jonson) JONSON vii (1941)*
  ORGEL
Hymenaeus (Fraunce) G. C. Moore Smith (ed.)
  (Cambridge, 1908)*
If This be not a Good Play, the DEKKER iii (1958)
Devil is in It (Dekker)
If You Know Not Me, You Know HEYWOOD i
Nobody (*1* and *2*) (Heywood) MSR (M. Doran and W. W. Greg,
  1935)*
The Insatiate Countess (Marston) REVELS (G. Melchiori, 1984)*
  MARSTON iii (1939)
The Island Princess (Fletcher) BF v (G. W. Williams, 1982)
  BROOKE AND PARADISE
The Isle of Gulls (Day) GARLAND (Raymond S. Burns, 1980)
  G. B. Harrison (ed.) (London,
  1936)
Jack Drum's Entertainment MARSTON iii (1939)
(Marston) SIMPSON ii
Jack Straw (?) MSR (Kenneth Muir and F. P.
  Wilson, 1957)
  DODSLEY v (1874)
James IV, The Scottish History GREENE ii
of (Greene) NEW MERMAID (J. A. Lavin, 1967)
  REVELS (Norman Sanders, 1970)*
  MSR (A. E. H. Swaen and W. W.
  Greg, 1921)
  SPECIMENS ii
Jeronimo, The First Part of, KYD
with the Wars in Portugal (?) RRD (A. S. Cairncross, 1967)
The Jew of Malta (Marlowe) RRD (R. W. Van Fossen, 1964)
  REVELS (N. W. Bawcutt, 1978)
  Irving Ribner (ed.) (New York,
  1970)
  NEW MERMAID (T. W. Craik, 1966)
  MARLOWE i*
Jocasta (Gascoigne, EECT
Kinwelmershe) GASCOIGNE i (1907)

John a Kent and John a Cumber (Munday)
MSR (Muriel St C. Byrne, 1923)
GARLAND (A. E. Pennell, 1980)

John of Bordeaux (?)
MSR (W. L. Renwick and W. W. Greg, 1936)

The Jovial Crew: or The Merry Beggars (Brome)
RRD (Ann Haaker, 1968)*
BROME iii

Julia Agrippina, Empress of Rome (May)
MATERIALIEN xliii (F. E. Schmid, 1914)

Julius Caesar (Shakespeare)
ARDEN (T. S. Dorsch, 1955)
OXFORD (A. R. Humphreys, 1984)
CAMBRIDGE (M. Spevack, 1988)
VAR. (1913)

A King and No King (Fletcher)
BF ii (G. W. Williams, 1970)
RRD (R. K. Turner, 1963)
FRASER AND RABKIN ii

King Johan (Bale)
MSR (Pafford and W. W. Greg, 1931)
SPECIMENS i

King John, The Life and Death of (Shakespeare)
ARDEN (E. A. J. Honigmann, 1954)
OXFORD (A. R. Braunmuller, 1989)
CAMBRIDGE (L. A. Beaurline, 1990)
VAR. (1919)

King John and Matilda (Davenport)
OEP (NS) 3 (1890)
GARLAND (J. O. Davis, 1980)

King Lear (Shakespeare)
ARDEN (Kenneth Muir, 1952)
CAMBRIDGE (Jay L. Halio, 1992)
VAR. (1880)
BULLOUGH vii (1973)

King Leir, The True Chronicle History of (?)
MSR (R. W. Bond and W. W. Greg, 1908)

A Knack to Know a Knave (?)
MSR (G. R. Proudfoot & A. W. Armstrong, 1964)

A Knack to Know an Honest Man (?)
MSR (H. De Vocht and W. W. Greg, 1910)

The Knave in Grain (J. D.)
MSR (R. C. Bald & Arthur Brown, 1961)

The Knight of the Burning Pestle (Beaumont)
BF i (Cyrus Hoy, 1966)*
NEW MERMAID (M. Hattaway, 1969)
RRD (J. Doebler, 1967)
REVELS (S. Zitner, 1984)

The Lady of Pleasure (Shirley)
REVELS (Ronald Huebert, 1986)
GARLAND (M. J. Thorssen, 1980)
BASKERVILL

A Larum for London: or The Siege of Antwerp (?)
MSR (W. W. Greg, 1913)*

Law Tricks: or Who Would Have Thought It (Day)
MSR (J. Crow and W. W. Greg, 1950)*

Liberality and Prodigality
See *Contention*

Locrine, The Lamentable Tragedy of (?)
APOCRYPHA
MSR (R. B. McKerrow, 1908)*
GARLAND (Jane L. Gooch, 1981)

The London Prodigal (?)
APOCRYPHA

Look About You (?)
MSR (W. W. Greg, 1913)
GARLAND (R. S. M. Hirsch, 1980)
DODSLEY vii

A Looking Glass for London and England (Greene, Lodge)
G. A. Clugston (ed.) (Ann Arbor, 1966)
GREENE i
MSR (W. W. Greg, 1932)*
FRASER AND RABKIN i

Love and Fortune, The Rare Triumphs of (?)
MSR (W. W. Greg, 1931)*
DODSLEY vi
Alan Holaday (ed.) (Urbana, Ill., 1950)
GARLAND (J. I. Owen, 1979)

Love and Honour (Davenant)
DAVENANT iii
BELLES (J. W. Tupper, 1909)

Lovers Made Men (Jonson)
JONSON vii (1941)*
ORGEL

Love's Cruelty (Shirley)
SHIRLEY ii
GARLAND (J. F. Nims, 1980)

*Love's Labour's Lost** (Shakespeare)
ARDEN (Richard David, 1951)
OXFORD (G. R. Hibbard, 1990)
VAR. (1904)

Love's Metamorphosis (Lyly)
LYLY iii*

The Love of King David and Fair Bethsabe
see *David and Bethsabe*

Love's Mistress, or the Queen's Masque (Heywood)
HEYWOOD V
SALZBURG (R. C. Shady, 1977)

Love's Pilgrimage (Fletcher)
BF ii (Fredson Bowers, 1970)

Love's Sacrifice (Ford)
MATERIALIEN xxiii (W. Bang, 1908)

The Lovesick King (Brewer)
MATERIALIEN xviii (A. E. H. Swaen, 1907)
GARLAND (R. Martin, 1991)

The Loyal Subject (Fletcher)
BF v (Fredson Bowers, 1982)*

Lust's Dominion: or The
DEKKER iv (1961)

Lascivious Queen (?)   MATERIALS v (J. Le G. Brereton, 1931)

Macbeth (Shakespeare)   ARDEN (Kenneth Muir, 1951)
OXFORD (Nicholas Brooke, 1990)
VAR. (2 vols.; 1873; rev. 1903)

A Mad World My Masters   RRD (Standish Henning, 1965)*
(Middleton)   MIDDLETON iii

The Mad Lover (Fletcher)   BF v (R. K. Turner, 1982)

The Magnetic Lady: or the   JONSON vi (1938)*
Humours Reconciled (Jonson)

The Magnificent Entertainment   DEKKER ii (1955)
given to King James
(Dekker, Jonson, Middleton)

The Maid of Honour (Massinger)   MASSINGER i
Eva A. W. Byrne (ed.) (London 1931)
BASKERVILL

The Maid's Metamorphosis (?)   LYLY iii
OEP i

The Maid's Tragedy (Fletcher)   BF ii (Robert K. Turner, 1970)*
REVELS (T. W. Craik, 1988)
RRD (H. B. Norland, 1968)

The Malcontent (Marston)   REVELS (G. K. Hunter, 1975)*
RRD (M. L. Wine, 1965)
NEW MERMAID (Bernard Harris, 1967)

Mariam, the Fair Queen of Jewry,   B. Weller and M. Ferguson (eds.)
The Tragedy of (Cary)   (Berkeley and Los Angeles, 1994)
MSR (A. C. Dunstan and W. W. Greg, 1914)
D. Purkis (ed.) (London, 1994)

The Masque of Blackness (Jonson)   ORGEL
JONSON vii (1941)

The Masque of Proteus (Gesta   MSR (W. W. Greg, 1915)
Grayorum) (Campion, Davison)   ed. Desmond Bland (Liverpool, 1968)*

The Masque of Queens (Jonson)   JONSON vii (1941)*
ORGEL

The Massacre at Paris (Marlowe)   REVELS (H. J. Oliver, 1968)
MSR (W. W. Greg, 1929)
MARLOWE ii

May-Day (Chapman)   PARROTT COM.
HOLADAY COM. (R. F. Welsh, 1970)

Measure for Measure (Shakespeare)	ARDEN (J. W. Lever, 1965) CAMBRIDGE (Brian Gibbons, 1991) OXFORD (N. W. Bawcutt, 1991) VAR (SUP.) (Mark Eccles, 1980)
The Merchant of Venice (Shakespeare)	ARDEN (J. R. Brown, 1955) CAMBRIDGE (M. M. Mahood, 1987) OXFORD (Jay L. Halio, 1993) VAR. (1888)
Mercury Vindicated from the Alchemists at Court (Jonson)	ORGEL JONSON vii (1941)
The Merry Devil of Edmonton (?)	APOCRYPHA*
The Merry Wives of Windsor (Shakespeare)	ARDEN (H. J. Oliver, 1971) OXFORD (T. W. Craik, 1989)
Messalina: The Roman Empress (Richards)	MATERIALIEN xxx (A. R. Skemp, 1910)
Michaelmas Term (Middleton)	RRD (Richard Levin, 1966)* MIDDLETON i
Midas (Lyly)	LYLY iii* RRD (A. B. Lancashire, 1969)
A Midsummer Night's Dream (Shakespeare)	ARDEN (Harold Brooks, 1979) CAMBRIDGE (R. A. Foakes, 1984) OXFORD (Peter Holland, 1994) VAR. (1895)
The Miseries of Enforced Marriage (Wilkins)	MSR (G. H. Blayney and Arthur Brown, 1964) DODSLEY ix (1874)
The Misfortunes of Arthur (Hughes, Bacon, *et al.*)	EECT
Monsieur D'Olive (Chapman)	PARROTT COM. HOLADAY COM. (Allan Holaday, 1970)*
Monsieur Thomas (Fletcher)	BF 4 (Hans W. Gabler, 1979) GARLAND (N. C. Clinch, 1987)
More, Sir Thomas, The Book of (Munday, *et al.*)	REVELS (V. Gabrieli and G. Melchiori, 1990)* APOCRYPHA MSR (W. W. Greg, 1911)
More Dissemblers Besides Women (Middleton)	OEP MIDDLETON vi (1886)
Mother Bombie (Lyly)	LYLY iii MSR (K. Lea and W. W. Greg, 1948)

Mucedorus, A Most Pleasant   APOCRYPHA*
Comedy of (?)   BASKERVILL
   J. Winny (ed.), *Three Elizabethan*
   Plays (London, 1972)
Much Ado about Nothing   ARDEN (A. R. Humphreys, 1981)
(Shakespeare)   CAMBRIDGE (F.H. Mares, 1988)
   OXFORD (Sheldon P. Zitner, 1993)
   VAR. (1899)
Mustapha (Greville)   GREVILLE ii
Nero, The Tragedy of (?)   NERO (H. P. Horne (ed.))
   OEP i (1882)
   GARLAND (E. M. Hill, 1979)
The New Inn: or The Light Heart   REVELS (Michael Hattaway, 1984)
(Jonson)   JONSON vi (1938)*
A New Way to Pay Old Debts   NEW MERMAID (T. W. Craik, 1964)
(Massinger)   MASSINGER ii (1976)
   BROOKE AND PARADISE
The Nice Valour: or the   BF vii (G. W. Williams, 1989)
Passionate Madman (Fletcher)
The Night Walker: or the Little   BF vii (Cyrus Hoy, 1989)
Thief (Fletcher)
Nobody and Somebody (?)   SIMPSON ii (1878)
   GARLAND (D. L. Hay, 1980)
Northward Ho (Dekker, Webster)   DEKKER ii (1955)*
Old Fortunatus (Dekker)   DEKKER i (1953)
The Old Law   GARLAND (Catherine M. Shaw, 1982)
The Old Wife's Tale (Peele)   PEELE iii (Frank. S. Hook, 1970)
   REVELS (Patricia Binnie, 1980)
   BROOKE AND PARADISE
Oldcastle, Sir John   APOCRYPHA*
(*Part I*) (Drayton, Hathway,   MSR (P. Simpson and W. W. Greg,
Munday, Wilson)   1908)
   GARLAND (J. Rittenhouse, 1984)
Oldenbarnavelt, The   BF viii (Fredson Bowers, 1992)
Tragedy of Sir John van   W. P. Frijlinck (ed.) (Amsterdam,
(Fletcher, Massinger)   1922)
   MSR (T. Howard-Hill and G. R.
   Proudfoot, 1980)
   OEP ii (1883)
Orestes, The Tragedy of (Goffe)   1633*
Orlando Furioso, The History of   GREENE i
(Greene)   MSR (W. W. Greg and R. B.
   McKerrow, 1907)*

Osmond, the Gréat Turk (Carlell)

Othello (Shakespeare)

Parasitaster: or The Fawn (Marston)

The Three Parnassus Plays (?)

Patient and Meek Grissil, The Comedy of (Philip)
Patient Grissil (Dekker, Chettle Haughton)
Pedautius (E. Forsett or A. Wingfield)
Pericles, Prince of Tyre (Shakespeare)
Perkin Warbeck, The Chronicle History of (Ford)
Philaster: or Love Lies a-Bleeding (Fletcher)

Philotas (Daniel)

The Phoenix (Middleton)

The Pilgrim (Fletcher)
Poetaster: or The Arraignment (Jonson)
The Princely Pleasures at Kenilworth (Gascoigne et al.)
Promos and Cassandra (Whetstone)
The Puritan: or The Widow of Watling Street (W.S.)
The Queen of Corinth (Fletcher)
The Raging Turk: or Bajazet II (Goffe)
Ralph Roister Doister (Udall)

Allardyce Nicoll (ed.) (Waltham St Lawrence, 1926)
ARDEN (M. R. Ridley, 1958)
CAMBRIDGE (Norman Sanders, 1984)
VAR. (1886)
MARSTON ii (1938)
RRD (Gerald A. Smith, 1965)
REVELS (David A. Blostein, 1978)*
J. B. Leishman (ed.) (London, 1949)*

MSR (R. B. McKerrow and W. W. Greg, 1909)
DEKKER i (1953)

MATERIALIEN viii (G. C. Moore Smith, 1905)
ARDEN (F. D. Hoeniger, 1963)

REVELS (Peter Ure, 1968)*
RRD (D. K. Anderson, 1966)
BF i (Robert K. Turner, 1966)*
REVELS (Andrew Gurr, 1969)
RRD (Dora J. Ashe, 1974)
Laurence Michel (ed.) (New Haven, 1949)*
DANIEL iii (1885)
MIDDLETON i (1885)*
GARLAND (J. B. Brooks, 1980)
BF vi (Cyrus Hoy, 1985)
REVELS (T. G. S. Cain, 1995)
JONSON iv (1938)
GASCOIGNE ii (1907)

BULLOUGH ii (1958)

APOCRYPHA

BF viii (R. K. Turner, 1992)
MSR (D. Carnegie and P. Davison, 1974)
MSR (W. W. Greg, 1935)
ADAMS
SPECIMENS ii (1897)

Ram Alley (Barry)

The Rape of Lucrece (Heywood)

The Rare Triumphs of Love and Fortune

The Rebellion (Rawlins)
The Revenge of Bussy D'Ambois (Chapman)
The Revenger's Tragedy (Tourneur)

Richard II, The Tragedy of (Shakespeare)

Richard III (Shakespeare)

Richard III, The True Tragedy of (?)
Richardus Tertius (Legge)

The Roaring Girl (Dekker, Middleton)

Rollo, Duke of Normandy: or The Bloody Brother (Fletcher)

The Roman Actor (Massinger)

Romeo and Juliet (Shakespeare)

MATERIALS xxiii (Claude E. Jones, 1952)
DODSLEY x (1875)
HEYWOOD v
Alan Holaday (ed.) (Urbana, Ill., 1950)
see *Love and Fortune*

DODSLEY xiv (1875)
HOLADAY TRAG. (R. J. Lordi, 1987)
PARROTT TRAG. (1910)
REVELS (R. A. Foakes, 1966)*
NEW MERMAID (Brian Gibbons, 1991)
George Parfitt (ed.) (*The Plays of Tourneur* (Cambridge, 1978))
RRD (L. J. Ross, 1966)
ARDEN (Peter Ure, 1956)
CAMBRIDGE (Andrew Gurr, 1984)
VAR. (SUP.) (Matthew W. Black, 1955)
ARDEN (Antony Hammond, 1981)
VAR. (1908)
MSR (W. W. Greg, 1929)*

Dana F. Sutton (ed.) (New York, 1993)
GARLAND (R. J. Lordi, 1979)
DEKKER iii (1966)*
REVELS (Paul A. Mulholland, 1987)
NEW MERMAID (A. H. Gomme, 1976)
FRASER AND RABKIN ii
John Jump (ed.) (Liverpool, 1948)
GARLAND Bertha Hensman (ed.), (New York, 1991)
MASSINGER iii (1976)*
W. L. Sandidge (ed.) (Princeton, 1929)
ARDEN (Brian Gibbons, 1980)
CAMBRIDGE (G. B. Evans, 1984)
VAR. (1871)

*The Royal King and
the Loyal Subject* (Heywood)

Rule a Wife and Have a Wife
(Fletcher)
Sappho and Phao (Lyly)
*Satiromastix: or The Untrussing
of the Humorous Poet* (Dekker,
Marston)
The Scornful Lady (Fletcher)
The Second Maiden's Tragedy (?)

Sejanus, his Fall (Jonson)

*I Selimus, Emperor of the Turks,
The Tragical Reign of* (?)
The Shepherd's Paradise
(Montague)
A Shoemaker a Gentleman
(W. Rowley)
The Shoemakers' Holiday
(Dekker)

Soliman and Perseda (?)

Sophonisba (Marston)
The Spanish Tragedy (Kyd)

The Staple of News (Jonson)

Stukeley, Captain Thomas (?)

HEYWOOD vi
K. W. Tibbals (ed.) (Philadelphia,
Pa., 1906)
BF vi (G. W. Williams, 1985)

REVELS (David Bevington, 1991)
DEKKER i (1953)

BF ii (Cyrus Hoy, 1970)
REVELS (Anne Lancashire, 1978)
MSR (W. W. Greg, 1909)
REVELS (Philip Ayres, 1990)
JONSON iv (1932)*
NEW MERMAID (W. F. Bolton, 1966)
Jonas Barish (ed.) (New Haven,
1965)
A. B. Grosart (ed.) (London, 1898)
MSR (W. W. Greg, 1909)*
1629

C. W. Stork (ed.) (Philadelphia, Pa.,
1910)
REVELS (S. W. Wells and R. L.
Smallwood, 1979)*
DEKKER i (1953)
J. B. Steane (ed.) (Cambridge, 1965)
NEW MERMAID (D. J. Palmer, 1975)
Anthony Parr (ed.) (New York,
1990)
KYD (1901)*
GARLAND (J. J. Murray, 1991)
see *The Wonder of Women*
REVELS (Philip Edwards, 1959)*
KYD
SPECIMENS ii
JONSON vi (1938)*
REVELS (Anthony Parr, 1988)
RRD (D. R. Kifer, 1975)
SIMPSON i
TFT
MSR (J. C. Levinson and G. R.
Proudfoot, 1975)*

Summer's Last Will and Testament
(Nashe)
Supposes (Gascoigne)

McKerrow, *Nashe* iii (1905)*
FRASER AND RABKIN I
BULLOUGH i (1957)*
BELLES (J. C. Cunliffe, 1906)
GASCOIGNE i (1907)
FRASER AND RABKIN i

Swetnam the Woman Hater,
Arraigned by Women (?)

C. Crandall (ed.) (Lafayette, Ind.
1969)
A. B. Grosart (ed.) (Manchester,
1880)

A Tale of a Tub (Jonson)

JONSON iii (1927)*
MATERIALIEN xxxix (Hans Scherer,
1913)

Tamburlaine (1 and 2) (Marlowe)

MARLOWE i, (1973)*
REVELS (J. S. Cunningham, 1981)
RRD (J. D. Jump, 1967)
NEW MERMAID (J. W. Harper, 1971)

The Taming of a Shrew (?)
The Taming of the Shrew
(Shakespeare)

BULLOUGH i (1957)
ARDEN (Brian Morris, 1981)
CAMBRIDGE (Ann Thompson, 1984)
OXFORD (H. J. Oliver, 1982)

The Tempest (Shakespeare)

ARDEN (Frank Kermode, 1954)
OXFORD (Stephen Orgel, 1987)
VAR. (1892)

Thierry and Theodoret (Fletcher)
The Thracian Wonder (?)

BF 3 (R. K. Turner, 1976)
W. C. Hazlitt (ed.) (Library of Old
Authors, London, 1857)

The Three Ladies of London
(Wilson)
Timon of Athens (Shakespeare)
'Tis Pity She's a Whore (Ford)

GARLAND (H. S. D. Mithal, 1988)*

ARDEN (H. J. Oliver, 1959)
REVELS (Derek Roper, 1975)
NEW MERMAID (Brian Morris, 1968)
REVELS (N. W. Bawcutt, 1966)

Titus Andronicus (Shakespeare)

ARDEN (J. C. Maxwell, 1953)
ARDEN (NS) (Jonathan Bate, 1995)
OXFORD (E. M. Waith, 1984)
CAMBRIDGE (Alan Hughes, 1994)

The Trial of Chivalry (?)

TFT (1912)
OEP iii (1884)

A Trick to Catch the Old One
(Middleton)

MIDDLETON ii (1885)
BASKERVILL
NEW MERMAID (G. J. Watson, 1968)*

Troia Nova Triumphans (Dekker)

DEKKER iii (1958)

Troilus and Cressida (Shakespeare)   ARDEN (Kenneth Palmer, 1982)
OXFORD (Kenneth Muir, 1982)
VAR. (SUP.) (H. N. Hillebrand, 1953)
The Troublesome Reign of John,   BULLOUGH iv (1962)*
King of England (1 and 2) (?)
The Turk (Mason)   SALZBURG (Fernand Lagarde, 1979)
MATERIALIEN xxxvii (J. Q. Adams,
1913)*
Twelfth Night (Shakespeare)   ARDEN (J. M. Lothian and T. W.
Craik, 1975)
CAMBRIDGE (E. S. Donno, 1985)
OXFORD (R. Warren and S. W.
Wells, 1994)
VAR. (1901)
The Two Angry Women of   GARLAND (M. B. Evett, 1980)
Abingdon, The Pleasant Comedy   NERO (Havelock Ellis, 1888)
of (Porter)   MSR (W. W. Greg, 1913)
Two Gentlemen of Verona   ARDEN (Clifford Leech, 1969)
(Shakespeare)   CAMBRIDGE (Kurt Schlueter, 1990)
Two Lamentable Tragedies   OEP iv (1884)
Two Italian Gentlemen   See *Fedele and Fortunio*
(? Yarrington)   TFT (1913)*
The Two Noble Kinsmen   BF vii (Fredson Bowers, 1989)
(Fletcher, Shakespeare)   RRD (G. R. Proudfoot, 1970)
OXFORD (E. M. Waith, 1989)
The Unnatural Combat   Robert S. Telfer (ed.) (Princeton,
(Massinger)   1932)
MASSINGER ii (1976)
Valentinian (Fletcher)   BF iv (R. K. Turner, 1979)*
The Valiant Scot (J.W.)   GARLAND (G. F. Byers, 1980)
The Valiant Welshman (R.A.)   V. Kreb ed. (Erlangen, 1902)
Victoria (Fraunce)   MATERIALIEN xiv (G. C. Moore
Smith, 1906)
The Vision of Delight (Jonson)   JONSON vii (1941)*
ORGEL
The Vision of the Twelve   DANIEL iii (1885)
Goddesses (Daniel)
Volpone (Jonson)   JONSON v (1937)*
REVELS (R. B. Parker, 1983)
John W. Creaser (ed.) (London,
1978)
A. B. Kernan (ed.) (New Haven,
1968)

A Warning for Fair Women (?)

The Wars of Cyrus (?)

The Weakest Goeth to the
Wall (?)
Westward Ho (Dekker, Webster)
What You Will (Marston)
When You See Me, You Know
Me (S. Rowley)
The White Devil (Webster)

The Whore of Babylon (Dekker)

The Widow's Tears (Chapman)

The Wild Goose Chase (Fletcher)

The Winter's Tale (Shakespeare)

The Wisdom of Doctor Dodypoll
(?)

The Wise Woman of Hogsdon
(Heywood)
Wit at Several Weapons (Fletcher)
Wit without Money (Fletcher)
The Witch of Edmonton
(Dekker, Ford, W. Rowley)
The Witch (Middleton)

NEW MERMAID (Philip Brockbank,
1968)
SIMPSON ii
C. D. Cannon (ed.) (The Hague,
1975)*
J. P. Brawner (ed.) (Urbana, Ill.,
1942)*
GARLAND (J. L. Levenson, 1980)
MSR (W. W. Greg, 1913)
DEKKER ii (1955)*
MARSTON ii (1938)
MSR (J. Crow and F. P. Wilson,
1952)*
REVELS (J. R. Brown, 1960)*
WEBSTER i (1927)
NEW MERMAID (Elizabeth Brennan,
1966)
RRD (J. R. Mulryne, 1969)
DEKKER ii (1955)*
GARLAND (M. G. Riely, 1980)
REVELS (Akihiro Yamada, 1975)
PARROTT COM.
RRD (E. M. Smeak, 1966)
HOLADAY COM. (R. Ornstein, 1970)
BF 6 (Fredson Bowers, 1985)*
GARLAND (R. H. Lister, 1980)
FRASER AND RABKIN ii
ARDEN (J. H. P. Pafford, 1963)
VAR. (1898)
OEP iv (1884)
MSR (M. N. Matson and A. Brown,
1965)
HEYWOOD v

BF vii (R. K. Turner, 1989)
BF vi (H. W. Gabler, 1985)
DEKKER iii (1966)*
BASKERVILL
MIDDLETON v (1885)
NEW MERMAID (Elizabeth Schafer,
1994)
MATERIALS xviii (L. Drees and
H. de Vocht, 1945)

MSR (W. W. Greg and F. P. Wilson, 1950)

The Woman Hater (Fletcher)   BF i (G. W. Williams, 1966)*

The Woman in the Moon (Lyly)   LYLY iii (1902)

A Woman is a Weathercock (Field)   William Peery (ed.), *The Plays of Nathan Field* (Austin, Tex., 1950)

NERO (A. W. Verity, 1888)

DODSLEY xi (1875)

A Woman Killed with Kindness (Heywood)   HEYWOOD ii

REVELS (R. W. Van Fossen, 1961)*

BROOKE AND PARADISE

FRASER AND RABKIN i

The Woman's Prize: or The Tamer Tamed (Fletcher)   G. B. Ferguson (ed.) (The Hague, 1966)

Women Beware Women (Middleton)   NEW MERMAID (W. C. Carroll, 1994)

NEW MERMAID (Roma Gill, 1968)

BF iv (Fredson Bowers, 1979)

Women Pleased (Fletcher)   BF v (Hans W. Gabler, 1982)*

The Wonder of Women: or The Tragedy of Sophonisba (Marston)   MARSTON ii (1938)

GARLAND (W. Kemp, 1979)*

Woodstock, Thomas of (?)   A. P. Rossiter (ed.) (London, 1946)*

MSR (W. Frijlinck and W. W. Greg, 1929)

The Wounds of Civil War (Lodge)   RRD (Joseph W. Houppert, 1969)*

MSR (J. Dover Wilson and W. W. Greg, 1910)

Wyatt, Sir Thomas (Dekker, Webster)   DEKKER i (1953)*

A Yorkshire Tragedy (?)   APOCRYPHA*

MSR (S. D. Feldman and G. R. Proudfoot, 1973)

The Young Admiral (Shirley)   SHIRLEY iii

Your Five Gallants (Middleton)   MIDDLETON i (1885)

GARLAND (C. L. Colegrove, 1979)

Index

Many incidental topics and names have had to be omitted from the index. No attempt has been made to record general references to Shakespeare, but references to him are included under a number of analytical headings. The main discussions of individual plays are printed in bold figures.

2. GENERAL INDEX